THE GOODNIGHT SYSTEM (1866 - 1885)

Because of the problems with settlers and quarantines on the Shawnee Trail, a young Texas cattleman by the name of Charles Goodnight decided to try another approach to trailing cattle north in 1866. He would go westward. In order to avoid possible confrontations with Plains Indians, he took a wide sweep south and west around the Texas Panhandle and trailed to Fort Sumner in New Mexico Territory. On this initial drive was a new partner by the name of Oliver Loving. The older and more experienced cattleman commanded the lead. Their new route was later referred to as the Goodnight-Loving Trail.

After the death of Loving, as a result of an Indian arrow, in 1867, Goodnight continued to drive cattle into New Mexico and Colorado Territories. Because of the reaction to the Texas Fever, he blazed a new route in 1868, one that was fifty and sixty miles east of Loving's Trail. In 1869, Goodnight moved his route further east again, to distance the herds even more from the ever encroaching settlements along the eastern slope of the Rocky Mountains.

With the continuing pressures from local ranchmen in Colorado Territory, Goodnight moved his northern outlet once again in 1875. It was referred to as the "new trail." In the following year, Goodnight established his Palo Duro Canyon Ranch in the Texas Panhandle. From this location, he blazed the Palo Duro-Dodge City Trail to Dodge City, Kansas, which was used until Dodge City was closed by quarantine. No other Texan established as many cattle trails as Charles Goodnight.

KILGORE MEMORIAL LIBRARY YORK, NE 68467

The Western Cattle Trail
1874-1897
ITS RISE, COLLAPSE, AND REVIVAL

by Gary and Margaret Kraisinger

Opposite page:

An unknown cowboy poses for a cameraman in one of the Fort Griffin, Texas, town stores in the 1870s. Fort Griffin was on the Western Cattle Trail and was a major stop for entertainment and supplies.

Courtesy of Lester W. Galbreath and the Fort Griffin State Historical Park.

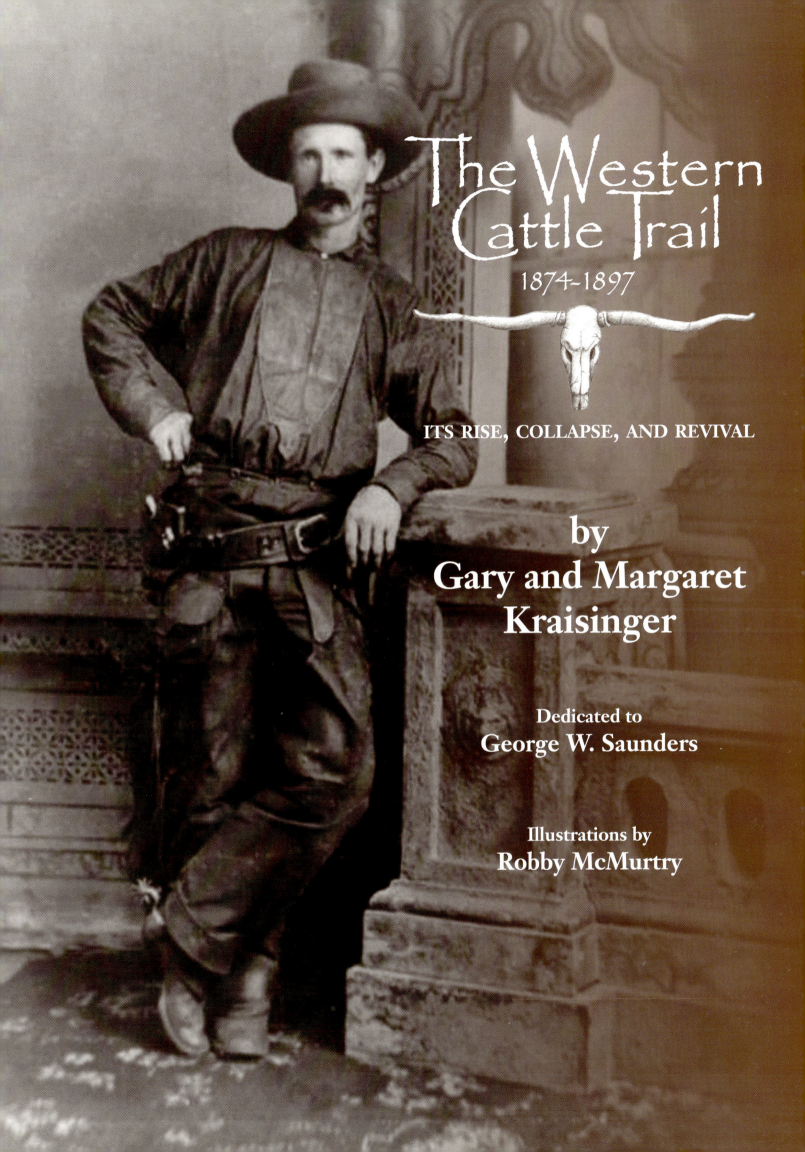

Other books published by Gary and Margaret Kraisinger:

Freedom in the Wilderness
Newton, Kansas: Mennonite Press, Inc. 1986

THE WESTERN, the Greatest Texas Cattle Trail, 1874-1886
Newton, Kansas: Mennonite Press, Inc. 2004

THE WESTERN CATTLE TRAIL
1874-1897
Its Rise, Collapse, and Revival

Copyright © 2014 by Gary and Margaret Kraisinger, Halstead, Kansas 67056. All rights Reserved. No part of this publication may be reproduced, stored in a retrieval system, or transmitted in any form or by any means, electronic, mechanical, photocopying, recording, or otherwise, except for brief passages to be used in a review, without the prior written permission of the copyright holder.

ISBN: 0-9754828-1-5

Library of Congress Control Number: 2014921992

Printed in the U.S.A. by Mennonite Press, Inc., Newton, Kansas 67114. www.MennonitePress.com

Design and layout by Jim L. Friesen

The quest of our research is to establish where the Western Cattle Trail and its feeder, splinter, and detour routes were located during the trail driving period of 1874 to 1897 and to record as accurately as possible, through text and maps, its history.

We also chose to examine the historical markers and monuments along the trail in the nine states and to discuss their accuracy in order to keep the record straight.

THE ILLUSTRATOR (1950–2012)

Robert Wayne (Robby) McMurtry was killed a few months before we submitted this book for printing. His sketches, penned especially for this book, were done from 2010 through 2012, but only a month before his death, he still had ideas about what he wanted to add to the project. When Robby drew the "Cowboy at Rest," he had no idea that it would ultimately be used as a tribute to himself. We miss his gentle soul and only hope that our work will do justice to his fine talent.

Robby was a talented artist, teacher, and American Indian historian. He was proud of his Irish, Cajun, and Commanche descent. At the time of his death, he was a teacher in the Morris Public Schools in Oklahoma and had just published his latest graphical novel, *The Road to Medicine Lodge, Jesse Chisholm in the Indian Nations*. Robby was an acclaimed gallery artist, winner of various art exhibitions, and the artist of the iconic mural for the Morris City Library. He leaves a wife and two daughters.

William Wallace Simpson (1880-1956) moved to Texas as a boy with his family and worked on numerous ranches. His love, however, was drawing pictures of ranch life and animals. Around 1914 he became an artist for the El Paso Times. *Four years later he became the "Cowboy Artist" for the* Fort Worth Star-Telegram. *Ten years later he moved to the* Dallas Morning News *where he worked as an artist and writer.*

In the home of the Saunders family today is this commissioned work by Simpson of George W. Saunders.
Thank you to the Tom B. Saunders IV family for sharing this artwork.

Opposite page:
George W. Saunders, whose first trip was to Abilene, Kansas at the age of 17, is pictured on the opposite page at the age of 21 in Dodge City, Kansas, on the Western Cattle Trail. The cowboy outfit and herd started south of San Antonio and trailed by Fort Mason, Texas, and on to Dodge City.

Courtesy of Tom B. Saunders, IV.

THIS BOOK DEDICATED TO GEORGE W. SAUNDERS CATTLEMAN, TRAIL DRIVER, AND TRAIL HISTORIAN

When trail driving ceased in 1897, it was the end of an era. Within three years, the Old West would fade away to a new century. The horse would soon share the streets of former cattle towns with the horseless carriage, and previously-driven cattle herds would be moved to faraway destinations by rail. Already, the world-wide famous showman Buffalo Bill was capturing the melancholy sentiment and was parading costumed cowboys, Indians, and sharpshooters in front of fascinated audiences in his Wild West road shows. Novelist Emerson Hough saw the end, too. In 1897 he wrote in his *The Story of a Cowboy* that after the ruts have disappeared, "the Long Trail of the cattle range will then be but a memory." Even the very first silent films (moving pictures) of the late 1890s depicted the reminiscences of the Old West.

True historical records of trail driving, however, was started by a trail driver himself, George W. Saunders, a Texas cattleman who had gone up the Eastern/Chisholm and Western trails. In 1915, Saunders realized that in the intervening twenty years, the tales of cowboys had been distorted, exaggerated, and fantasized. The location and names of the trails had been confused or forgotten altogether, and the memories of the remaining trail drivers were fading and dying. He, therefore, organized The Old Time Trail Drivers' Association, initiated the idea of a collection of narratives by its members, and for the rest of his life worked tirelessly "to keep the record straight." As part of that endeavor, Saunders was a technical advisor for the 1924 silent film "North of 36" by Paramount Pictures, based on Emerson Hough's book by the same name, and again in 1931 for the film "Fighting Caravans" by Paramount Pictures, based on a novel by Zane Grey. Without Saunders' foresight and effort, the history of trail driving would be sorely lacking.

THE WESTERN CATTLE TRAIL | 1874-1897

Members of the Old Time Trail Drivers Association gather around friend and entertainer Will Rogers at one of their annual meetings.

This photo is from the C. D. Cannon Collection, courtesy of the Witte Museum in San Antonio, Texas.

C. D. Cannon was the son-in-law to George W. Saunders and one of the organizers of the early Old Time Trail Drivers annual meetings. The authors believe this photo was taken on the afternoon of September 11, 1919 after the morning session of their annual meeting at the Gunter Hotel in San Antonio. According to the 1919 minutes, "members entered automobiles and were driven to the Saunders ranch, some twelve miles from the city, where, upon the banks of the beautiful Medina River, an old-time barbecue had been prepared for the "Old Trailers" and their friends. …after which the members and friends returned to the city for the closing session of the reunion."

Seated left to right are Col. Isacc (Ike) Pryer (1852-1937), board member of the association and president of the American Live Stock Association; John R. Blocker (1851-1927), past president of the asssociation; Will Rogers, entertainer; and George W. Saunders (1854-1933), president, host, and organizer. Standing behind the foursome is William B. Slaughter, an association member.

The saddled white horse could be Will Rogers' trick riding horse, Soapsuds.

On the left lapel of their coats, the old trail drivers are wearing the association's badge, designed by George W. Saunders.

Reference: Hunter's The Trail Drivers of Texas, *pages 5, 11, 18.*

THE WESTERN CATTLE TRAIL | 1874–1897

CONTENTS

Preface | xxi

Foreward by Tom B. Saunders, IV | xxiii

Appreciation | xxvi

Comment on Roadside Trail Markers & Monuments | xxviii

Chronology of Events: 1836 - 1897 | xxx

Terms the Reader Needs to Know | xxxix

PART I
One Brief Lifetime: The Four Texas Trail Systems and the Texas Fever

Chapter I **A Search for an Outlet** | 1
Against all odds, Indians, swollen rivers, and great distances, Texas cattlemen search for an outlet for their cattle.

Chapter II **The Shawnee Trail System, 1846 - 1875** | 9

The Shawnee was the earliest of the trail systems going north, used before and after the Civil War, into Missouri, eastern Kansas, and Nebraska. It was shut down because of western expansion and the Texas Fever.

Chapter III **The Goodnight Trail System, 1866 - 1885** | 23

Charles Goodnight and Oliver Loving decide to trail west into New Mexico and Colorado instead of using the Shawnee Trail. After the death of Loving, Goodnight continued to blaze three more trails in Colorado and one in the Texas Panhandle.

The Goodnight Trail of 1868	33
Goodnight Trail After 1868	35
The 1875 New Goodnight Trail	37
Another Goodnight Trail in the Texas Panhandle	37

Chapter IV **The Eastern/Chisholm Trail System, 1867 - 1889** | 41

Joseph McCoy opens up Abilene, Kansas as a new outlet for Texas cattle. As rails are built westward, other railheads are established along this trail system. Kansas shuts down its portion of the trail in 1875.

Chapter V **The Western Trail System, 1874 - 1897** | 57

The Western was the last and largest of the trail systems. Kansas shuts down its portion of the trail in 1885, but the system re-emerges, detours around Kansas, and continues another twelve seasons.

PART II
The Western Cattle Trail and its Feeder and Splinter Routes before the 1885 Kansas Quarantine

Chapter I **The Western Trail in Texas, The Staging Areas, and its Feeder Routes in Southwest and Central Texas** | 67

The Western Cattle Trail trunk line, its feeder routes, and staging areas in Texas are presented in chronological order from south to north, starting with the Matamoros Feeder Route at Brownsville, Texas.

The Matamoros Feeder Route, and Map #1-1 71
The Wilson County Feeder Route, and Map #1-2 76
The "Old Trail" Feeder Route, and Map #1-3 77
The Staging Areas--San Antonio, Bandera, and Kerrville 79
The Trunk Line of the Western Cattle Trail to Pegleg Crossing 85
Nueces River Feeder Route, and Map #1-4 90
The Trunk Line of the Western Cattle Trail from Pegleg Crossing to
  Dodge Crossing on Brady Creek, McCulloch County,
  and Map #1-5 93
The Fort McKavett Feeder Route, and Map #1-6 97
The Mason-Gillespie County Feeder Route, and Map #1-7 98
The Middle Colorado Feeder Route, and Map #1-8 99
The Trunk Line of the Western Cattle Trail from Cow Gap,
  McCulloch County, to Coleman, Coleman County, Texas 99
The Jinglebob (Trickham) Feeder Route, and Map #1-9 103
The Southern Tom Green County-Concho River Feeder Route,
  and Map #1-10 106
The Trunk Line of the Western Cattle Trail from Coleman and
  Jim Ned Creek to Albany in Shackelford County 106
The San Gabriel-Brownwood Feeder Route, and Map #1-11 109
The Potter-Bacon Trail-Splinter Route, and Map #1-12 110

Chapter II **Fort Griffin, Texas** | 117

Fort Griffin existed longer than many forts and played a vital role in the history of the Western Cattle Trail.

Fort Griffin on the Western Cattle Trail, and Maps #2-1 and #2-2 119
The Belton Feeder Route, and Map #2-3 129
The Northern Tom Green County - Buffalo Gap Feeder Route,
  and Map #2-4 130

Chapter III **North to Doan's Crossing and the Red River** | 135

After loading up with food stuffs and other necessary supplies at Fort Griffin or Albany, the outfits knew the next supply depot would be Doan's store on the Red River, one hundred and ten miles north from Fort Griffin.

The Western Cattle Trail through Throckmorton, Baylor,
  and Wilbarger Counties to Doan's Crossing, and Map #3-1 139

Doan's Crossing on the Red River 144
The Bosque County Feeder Route, and Map #3-2 146
The Quanah Detour Route or "Ghost Trail," and Map #3-3 153

Chapter IV Indian Territory: Military Forts, Feeder and Splinter Routes | 159

After the 1875 Kansas quarantine, trail herds in Indian Territory fed into the Western Cattle Trail from the former Chisholm Trail. In turn, when Caldwell, Kansas received rails in 1880, trail herds splintered from the Western Trail over to the old Chisholm Trail. The Western Cattle Trail trunk line and this network of trails is presented in this chapter.

The Fight Over Greer County, Texas, and Map #4-1 161
The Mobeetie Trail, and Maps #4-2 and #4-3 164
Frontier Forts and the Military Roads 169
The Trunk Line of the Western Cattle Trail, Greer
    County North to Comanche Springs, and Map #4-4 173
The Quanah Detour Route (Ghost Trail) through
    Greer County and Indian Territory (ref: Maps #3-3 and #4-2) 186
The Trunk Line of the Western Cattle Trail from
    Comanche Springs to Edward Rock Crossing, and Map #4-5 187
The Washita River Feeder Route, and Map #4-6 189
The Red Fork Ranch Splinter Route and Caldwell, Kansas,
    and Map #4-7 191
The Washita Splinter Route to Cantonment, and Map #4-8 195
"Cattle Trails Across Indian Reservation," 1881 Indian
    Affairs Map #4-9 199
The Trunk Line of the Western Cattle Trail to the South
    Canadian River 200
The Splinter Routes in Northern Indian Territory,
    and Maps #4-10 and #4-11:
        South Canadian River Crossing Splinter Route and the
        Persimmon Creek Splinter Route 203
Camp (Fort) Supply, and Map #4-12 207
The North Canadian River Feeder Route, and Map #4-13 210
The Cimarron (Cut-off) Feeder Route, and Map #4-14 212
The Yelton Store 214

Chapter V Kansas Homesteaders & Kansas Quarantines | 217

By the time the Western Cattle Trail extended into Kansas, the western movement of settlers was at its peak, and Kansas passed four more quarantines. The last quarantine was a major factor in causing the collapse to the entire trailing industry.

The Trunk Line of the Western Cattle Trail,
    South of Dodge City, and Maps #5-1 and #5-2 219
Feeder Routes from the Texas Panhandle, Across No Man's Land,
    to Join the Western Cattle Trail at Mulberry Creek,
    and Map #5-3 226
        The Adobe Walls Trail 227
        The Jones and Plummer Trail 228
        The Rath Trail 231
        The Tascosa Trail 233
        The Tuttle Trail 234

THE WESTERN CATTLE TRAIL | 1874-1897   XV

The Palo Duro-Dodge City Trail 234
Developing Ranches in the Texas Panhandle Change the
    Cattle-trailing Industry 235
The Trunk Line of the Western Cattle Trail into Dodge City,
    Kansas and Map #5-4 239
Kansas Homesteaders and State Quarantines........................ 242
North of Dodge: The Hays City-Ellis Trail, and Map #5-5
    Closed by the 1876 Kansas Quarantine........................... 243
North of Dodge: Route 1, to Ogallala, Nebraska and Beyond,
    and Map #5-6
    Closed by the 1877 Kansas Quarantine........................... 245
North of Dodge: Route 2, to Ogallala, Nebraska and Beyond,
    and Map #5-7
    Closed by the 1881 Kansas Quarantine........................... 246
North of Dodge: Route 3 and the Wallace Branch, to Ogallala,
    Nebraska and Beyond, and Map #5-9
    Closed by the 1885 Kansas Quarantine........................... 251
Cowboys and "Nesters" 257
The 1885 Kansas Quarantine Closes the Western Cattle Trail 258

Chapter VI Destination: Ogallala, Nebraska and Two Splinter Routes | 261

No other state, outside of Texas, had more cattle trails than Nebraska. The Shawnee Trial, the Chisholm Trail, the Ellsworth Trail, four routes of the Western Trail, and the National Trail extended into Nebraska. There were two major splinter routes, as well.

Early Cattle Towns in Nebraska... 263
Route 1 from Kansas to Section 5, T6n, R35w in Hayes County,
    (1874-1877), and Map #6-1...................................... 266
Route 2 from Kansas to Section 5, T6n, R35w in Hayes County,
    (1876-1882), and Map #6-1...................................... 269
Route 3 (1880-1884), and Map #6-1 271
The Trunk line of the Western Cattle Trail from Section 5, T6n,
    R35w to Ogallala 271
The Wallace Branch of the Western Cattle Trail in Nebraska
    to Ogallala (1883-1884), and Map #6-1 274
Destination--Ogallala 274
The Opening of Indian Lands to Settlers and Cattle Herds.......... 276
New Markets for Texas Cattle Herds 278
The Cheyenne, Wyoming Area and the Cheyenne Splinter Route to
    Cheyenne from Ogallala, and Map #6-2 279
The Missouri River Splinter Route, and Map #6-3 287

Chapter VII The Western Cattle Trail, From Ogallala to Canada and More Splinter Routes | 295

From 1876 to 1885, the Western Cattle Trail reached its peak in numbers of cattle on the trail. The Texas cattlemen's hope of establishing a lucrative northern market for their cattle and a dependable pathway to that market had been realized. In these years, the Western Cattle Trail expanded out from Ogallala into the Dakota, Wyoming, and Montana territories and even into Canada.

The Trail North of Ogallala 298

Sidney Bridge and Camp Clark, and Map #7-1 302

The Fort Buford Splinter Route North from Sidney Bridge, Nebraska
and Other Sub-routes, Map #7-1 302

   (1) The Niobrara River Route from the Fort Buford
     Splinter Route 307

   (2) To Red Cloud Indian Agency, the Spotted Tail Indian Agency,
     and the Pine Ridge Indian Agency, using the White River
     in Northeastern Nebraska and Southern Dakota Territory 311

   (3) The East Detour Route from the Fort Buford Splinter Route to
     deliver herds to the Cheyenne River Agency and the
     Standing Rock Agency 318

   (4) The Fort Buford Splinter Route to the Mining Camps in the
     Black Hills 322

   (5) The Fort Buford Splinter Route north to Fort Buford on the
     Missouri River 326

The Trunk Line of the Western Cattle Trail and Two More
Splinter Routes North of the Rawhide, and Map #7-2 329

The Judith Basin Splinter Route from the Western (Texas) Cattle Trail,
and Map #7-3 340

The Trunk line of the Western Cattle Trail Continues to the
Northern Ranges 346

The Little Missouri Splinter Route to Fort Buford from the Belle
Fourche River in Wyoming Territory to the Missouri River
in Dakota Territory, and Map #7-4 352

The Trunk Line of the Western Cattle Trail Continues from the
Belle Fourche River Crossing, Wyoming Territory to Miles City,
Fort Peck, MontanaTerritory and toward Canada 359

The Western Cattle Trail to the North West Territories, Canada 362

PART III
THE RE-EMERGENCE OF THE CATTLE TRAILING INDUSTRY
VIA THE NATIONAL TRAIL AND THE TEXAS-MONTANA FEEDER
ROUTE TO THE WESTERN CATTLE TRAIL, 1885 - 1897

Chapter I **Change and Turmoil Brews in the Cattle-Trailing Industry** | 371

Because of the 1885 Kansas quarantine and the 1886 Nebraska herd law, the cattle-trailing
industry collapsed. It was never the same after 1885. Trail drivers created another pathway around
Kansas and Nebraska in order to deliver their herds to the northern markets, but other factions also
stood in the way.

Chapter II **No Man's Land & the National Trail, 1885-1887** | 389

In order to reach the newly proposed National Trail in Colorado, Texas trail drivers knew that
they would have to trail through No Man's Land, seeminly the only open area left to reach the
northern markets.

   The Northern Feeder Route to the National Trail and
     the Jack Hardesty War, and Map #III, 2-1 388

   The 1886-1887 Seasons 392

   The Middle Feeder Route Across No Man's Land, and Map #III, 2-1 .. 397

   The Lower Feeder Route Across No Man's Land and Map #III, 2-2 398

The National Trail and Trail City, and Map #III, 2-3
    and Map #III, 2-4...401
The National Trail North of the Arkansas River and Trail City,
    and Map #III, 2-5 and Map #III, 2-6 408
Debate Over the Proposed National Trail Continues 413
The National Trail and Trail City, the 1886-1887 Seasons 418

Chapter III **The Texas-Montana Feeder Route (1884-1897) and the End of the Cattle-Trailing Industry** | 423

The Texas-Montana Route has been viewed for years as a separate pathway, the last one to carry Texas herds north. This route, more correctly, is part of the entire Western Cattle Trail System — it was a feeder route to the old established trunk line of the Western Trail that had been used since 1875-1876.

A Quick Review 425
The Texas-Montana Feeder Route becomes the last outlet from
    Texas to the north 427
The 1875 New Goodnight Trail (used again) Review,
    and Map #III, 3-1..429
The Potter-Bacon Trail of 1883-1884 (used again) Review,
    and Map #III, 3-1..429
The Potter-Bacon Trail in Colorado 430
The Jim E. May Route and the Texas-Montana Feeder Route to the
    Western Cattle Trail in Wyoming, and Map #III, 3-1 432
Further Development of the Texas-Montana Feeder Route to Wyoming
    and Maps #III, 3-2, 3-3, and 3-4.................................435
        The Yellow House-Colorado City route 437
Other Cowboy Journals Showing the Use of the Texas-Montana
    Feeder Route J. Ealy Moore, XIT trail driver, 1892 442
Perry Eugene Davis, trail driver/cook for the Hashknife, 1894............461
Main Ranches Using the Texas-Montana Feeder Route and the Number
    of Cattle Trailed North, 1885 to 1897, and Chart #III-1 470
Chapter Review..473

Chapter IV **"It ain't never goin' to be like it used to be"....** | 477

Annotated Bibliography | 485

Map Index (By Chapter) | 499

Index | 501

XX THE WESTERN CATTLE TRAIL | 1874–1897

PREFACE

In our first volume *The Western, the Greatest Texas Cattle Trail, 1874-1886*, the focus was on the trail's history, the trail drivers, and the longhorns. Our main mission was to tell our readers that the Western Trail "carried more longhorns a longer distance for more years than any other cattle trail." We presented a bird's eye view of the trail from its start in southern Texas to its tail in the provinces of Canada. We then concentrated on the middle section of this vast trail, from the Red River (Doan's Crossing) to Ogallala, Nebraska. Gary's maps showed detailed data on this portion including road houses, watering holes, forts, and towns across Indian Territory, western Kansas, and southwestern Nebraska. The book ends with the final cattle quarantine imposed by Kansas that closed down its borders to Texas cattle and altered the trail driving industry forever.

This second book gets down to the hide of the matter. Our mission is four part. (1) to present an overview of the four trailing systems that were used to drive herds north to market over a fifty year period. (2) to map the location of the entire Western Trail trunk line from south Texas to Canada — plus the feeder, splinter, and detour routes — from 1874 to 1897. (3) to examine the historical markers and monuments along the trail in the nine states, and (4) to explain what happened after the 1885 Kansas quarantine.

In our quest to present and preserve the history of the Western Cattle Trail, we have been faced with one large issue: many people don't realize the magnitude of this trail, its influence on history, or, most of all, understand where it was located. So many trails exist here on the High Plains such as military roads, freight paths, stage routes, mail paths, migration trails, and cattle trails. Then when one considers the feeder, splinter, and detour routes that are connected to the main trunk line of the cattle trails, it all becomes overwhelming to the student of history.

The four cattle systems also become tangled with one another, especially in Texas. The Chisholm Trail was not the only cattle trail, nor was it the first. The Western and Eastern/Chisholm trails started out in south Texas over the remains of the Shawnee. Then in Kansas, Abilene was not the first cattle town nor, after 1869, was it the end of the trail as has been believed for so many years. Herds continued on into Nebraska.

To sort out this understandable confusion, in Part I, we present the four cattle trailing systems. Each system is given its due respect showing its variations and branches, and how it differs from the others. In Part II, the pre-1885 Western Cattle Trail is mapped with emphasis on its many feeders, splinters, and detours and how, at times, other convenient pathways are used to deliver herds to the northern markets. The roadside monuments are introduced as well in this section in order to confirm or contradict facts that are written in stone about this trail.

Part III provides the discussion and mapping of the Western Cattle Trail after the 1885-86 collapse in the industry. When Kansas shut her borders to the Texas herds in 1885 and Nebraska followed with a herd law in 1886, an elaborate detour around Kansas and Nebraska had to be developed. The cattle-trailing industry was in its last decade, and blockades and irate ranchers and farmers were gradually fencing the open range, closing the pathway for the drovers who pushed herds north.

During this entire project, we have approached our research from a cartographer's point of view. Even though we include personalities, they are not our focus. Our mission remains the same — to record the location of this trail, using maps to present the path of the trunk line and its feeders, splinters, and detours.

George W. Saunders, to whom we dedicate this volume, was perhaps the first to realize that the history about the trails needed to be preserved. He wanted to keep "history accurate." However now, eighty years after his death, the history of these trails is still misunderstood and presented inaccurately by some groups. We just hope we have helped to untangle the confusion and have presented the trail systems, especially the Western Cattle Trail, in a clean, clear, and accurate manner.

Gary and Margaret Kraisinger
October, 2013

FOREWARD

It is my privilege and honor to have the opportunity to express my thoughts and feelings about this great book. It covers one of my most favorite topics because it follows closely the history of my family. This book is the best documentation of the cattle driving period that I have ever read. My early ancestors arrived in Texas in 1850 for the purpose of cattle ranching and were successful probably because T. B. Saunders I, his wife and seven sons were already well-experienced cattle people from Mississippi. This ready-made crew of cowboys, open free land, and all the free roaming longhorn cattle any outfit could handle, made a healthy environment that grew the Saunders family into a sizable operation. However, because of the great numbers of unmarked cattle in Texas before and after the Civil War, the problem was not having any local markets. In the 1830's, there had been a hide and tallow market in New Orleans via the Opelousas Trail out of Texas that serviced the Mexican and early Texas ranchers cattle trade, but only on a limited basis. In 1846 other trails opened up, like the Shawnee, which crossed the Red River near Preston Texas, and headed on in a northeasterly direction to Sedalia, Missouri and other points north. As drovers headed north, they encountered many new problems.

Just "surviving every day" on the trail was a problem--not only did the drovers have to contend with bad weather, heavy storms, high winds, hail and swollen river crossings, but also Indian attacks, rustlers, stampedes, long hours and days in the saddle. And if that was not enough, the trail drivers faced local cattlemen with strong feelings against the trailing of their herds through their country. All these local cattlemen knew when these Texas cattle came in contact with their domestic herds, their cattle got sick and died. These locals were so devastated from these losses that they went before their state legislatures (Missouri, Kansas, and Colorado) and got quarantine deadlines issued to keep the Texas cattle out.

Because "Necessity is the Mother of Invention" so it was with Texans and Texas cattle. Like all confederate states, Texas was broke after the Civil War. Its only assets were millions of grazeable acres, a multitude of free cattle, and, probably, the most important asset was a breed of men whose determination and will to survive was unsurpassed. They were men born and raised under God's open skies. They slept on the ground and drank from the same water holes as the cattle they sought. They raised good stout horses and were proficient with a lariat rope. They were cowboys and knew cattle as well as cattle knew themselves for they and their horses lived among their cattle every day.

Needless to say, these men were immune to hardships and diversity, and quarantines were no different. They found a way to keep driving their cattle north to market. From 1846 to 1897, it is estimated some 12 million head of cattle were trailed out of Texas and sold. They brought back over 250 million "cow dollars" to Texas. This put Texas back in business, and as Bertha Nance said in her poem, "Some states were carved or born, but Texas came from hide and horn."

The Opelousa, Shawnee, Goodnight-Loving, Eastern (Chisholm), and the Western trails were the major trails used. It was the Texas cattle and Texas cowboys that stocked the cattle ranges from Texas to Canada, creating what we enjoy today — "Good Beef" for our nation and the world.

This book documents many experiences as well as the technical history of this important part of America's history. Not only does it make for interesting reading, but it shows the grit and fortitude that form the basis of an American. The tales of these men's experiences and how they met their problems is a remarkable and important part of our history. Gary and Margaret Kraisinger should be proud of preserving the true history of the trail-driving period and recognizing those brave men who made it happen.

Tom B. Saunders, IV
5th Generation of Cow Folks in Texas

Tom B. Saunders IV and Gary Kraisinger stand outside of a cabin on the Saunders' ranch in Texas. For years, the two have discussed the importance of keeping trail-driving history accurate.

Photo courtesy of Paul Noack. 2013.

Tom B. Saunders IV inherited the love of Texas and its history of cowboy trails. He is a fifth generation Texas rancher. As he pointed out in the dedication of his 1997 book The Texas Cowboys, A Photographic Portrayal, *which he co-produced with photographer David R. Stoecklein, "my family, which started in Texas in 1850, has taken part in blazing the trails of the Texas cowboy for the past 150 years."*

Also being the great nephew of George W. Saunders, to whom we dedicate this book, Tom B. has a right to be proud of his family's accomplishments and has gained the respect of his fellow Texans. In 2006 Tom B. was inducted into the "Texas Trail of Fame" in Fort Worth which means there is a star in the sidewalk with his name in front of the stockyard office and coliseum in the old stockyard district of Fort Worth. Only the finest with credentials get this honor. George W. Saunders (1855-1933) was recognized with a star in 1998.

Therefore, when Gary and Margaret introduced themselves to Tom B. and his wife Ann in 2001 to share their idea of a project about the Western Cattle Trail from Texas to states north, Tom B. and Ann were, of course, cautious of these two from Kansas, of all places. What did they know about the great state of Texas and, especially, of the pride that goes along with being part of its heritage? But through the years, we have come to the common ground of the importance of preserving the history of the Texas cattle-driving trails.

It is with great pride, therefore, that we have been accepted and recognized by the Saunders as serious historians of the Texas heritage of trail driving. Tom B. endorsed our first book in 2004 and here, again, almost ten years later, he continues to support our research.

APPRECIATION

To present the Western Cattle Trail with its feeder, splinter, and detour routes through nine states, covering some 2,000 miles is a daunting task. The writer and map creator have been submerged for nine years with volumes of data, trying to present the material in its correct order and accuracy. In the process, assumptions were made by us and facts we knew sometimes failed to be clarified. Therefore, we are indebted to the following men who objectively read our manuscript, asked questions, and helped us to clear out the deadwood and underbrush so that you the reader would have a better journey up the trail.

Dr. Frank Norris of the National Parks Service in Santa Fe, New Mexico graciously agreed to read our manuscript. With his expertise and knowledge in national trails, geography, and an uncanny talent for detail, he helped us immensely to achieve a better manuscript.

Dr. Raymond Powers of Topeka, Kansas knows our mission. Co-author of *The Northern Cheyenne Exodus in History and Memory*, Dr. Powers edited our first book, *The Western, the Greatest Texas Cattle Trail, 1874-1886*, in 2004, and thus agreed to edit our second manuscript to verify that we had stayed true to our cause in content and style.

Jim Gray of Ellsworth, Kansas, editor of the *Kansas Cowboy* magazine and author of *Desperate Seed, Ellsworth, Kansas on the Violent Frontier*, is a fellow Kansan and historian of trail cowboys and cattle trails. He read our manuscript and visited with us at length about sticky points that have plagued trail historians for years.

William (Bill) Townsend of Oklahoma City, Oklahoma, a longtime friend, has traveled many parts of the Western Trail with Gary. He read the manuscript from a layman's point of view and gave us insight to where we could improve in clarity.

Tom B. Saunders IV of Weatherford, Texas, is a fifth-generation Texas cattleman and great nephew of George W. Saunders to whom this book is dedicated. He studied our manuscript and graciously agreed to again write the foreword and endorse our work.

We also wish to thank Paul Noack of Austin, Texas, a Texas historian and research expert who read the Texas portion of the manuscript for accurateness and sent us material from Texas libraries; to Lester W. Galbreath of Albany, Texas, park manager for Fort Griffin State Historical Park for helping us with the Fort Griffin chapter; to Jesse Bellard, executive secretary of the Baxter Springs Heritage Center and Museum for help with the Baxter Springs portion, to Harold Jobes, for reading and editing the Brady, Texas portion and sharing with us a valued family photo; to Charles Meade of Dodge City, Kansas and William Rector of Kerrville, Texas for personal photos; and to Myron Janzen who shared his research on Texas post offices.

Others who helped us greatly were:
- Peggy Ables, High Plains Western Heritage Center, Spearfish, South Dakota
- DeWayne Brown, Vici, Oklahoma
- Wayne Carlson, Brush, Colorado
- Bewlah Collins, Baca County Library, Springfield Colorado
- Debbie Colson, Director of No Man's Land Museum, and assistant Sue Weissinger
- Walter Couch, Kingsdown, Kansas
- Bill Mark Day, Brady, Texas
- Betty Deyle, Dundy County Historical Society, Benkelman, Nebraska
- Darrell Dorgan, North Dakota Cowboy Hall of Fame, Medora, North Dakota
- Peggy A. Ford, Research Curator of the Greeley Colorado Museum & Library
- Richard Gilfillan, The Chisholm Trail Museum, Welllington, Kansas
- Bob Klemme, Enid, Oklahoma
- Lida Mae Osteen, Springfield, Colorado
- Harold Potthoff, Trenton, Nebraska
- Phyllis Randolph, Cimarron Heritage Center Museum, Boise City, Oklahoma
- Jim Sherer, Dodge City, Kansas
- Debbie Lytle Smith, Development Assistant, National Cowboy & Western Heritage Museum, Oklahoma City, Oklahoma
- Ted Tietjen, Grant, Nebraska
- D. D. "Tex" Wright, Santa Anna, Texas
- Sharleen Wurm, Decatur County Last Indian Raid Museum, Oberlin, Kansas

We thank the other librarians, archivist, and local historians who allowed us to invade their space to acquire information. We especially recognize the Oklahoma State Historical Society Library in Oklahoma City, Oklahoma where Gary often helped turn off the lights at the end of the day. We appreciate the people who visited with us through the years about our passion to uncover facts about Texas trails. In short, as we turn this manuscript over to be finalized, we bow our heads in thanks to those mentioned and the many others who helped make our mission a possibility.

COMMENT ON ROADSIDE TRAIL MARKERS AND MONUMENTS

Many markers and monuments are scattered along the Western Cattle Trail, some dating back to the 1930s. State and local historical societies in all the involved states have, through the years, commemorated this trail's history. Some of the markers are very simple, made of metal or stone, not unlike a tomb stone with only a name and dates, while others are quite elaborate with full stories, maps, and pictures.

In 2004, Rotary International started to mark the Western Cattle Trail in its full length from the Matamoras, Texas, area to Val Marie, Canada. The marker selected was very similar to the one used by Chisholm Trail historians to mark that trail — a concrete post painted with lettering. The Rotarian post is white with red

lettering: "Great Western Tr." Their goal was to set a post at strategic locations in each of the nine states and Canada. At each post setting, a ceremony has been held with flags represented from every state that the Western touched.

As we prepare this book for print, the National Park Service is conducting a feasibility study on the Western and Chisholm trails to see if they merit national trail status. It is possible that after its study is complete, additional markers will be errected to pinpoint the location of both of these historic trails.

Our focus, however, has been on the older existing trail markers on the Western Trail. In our survey of these roadside markers, we have come across a wide diversity of facts and dates. The main reason for our research in the first place (to accurately locate, map, and date the Western Trail) has come to its fullest frustration at times when reading these markers. It became obvious to us that the dates of the trail in specific areas is a most mis-understood factor. Some of the markers are very accurate, some are close to being so, and others are flat-out wrong.

What started out to be a hobby or sideline to our major project — the searching out of these older monuments — has now become part of this study. Because of the confusion on dates, facts, and location of the trail in some of these locales, we decided to include these roadside markers and our evaluation of them. Our fullest respect goes to the societies and chambers that have marked this trail, its cow towns, and crossings, but we also sincerely hope that they understand that the several cattle routes coming out of Texas became mixed up and tangled in people's memories. Thus, since part of our quest is to untangle, straighten out, and separate fact from fiction, we have decided to include these markers and to analyse the information on them. We have also learned that not always do markers remain standing forever, but, in time, do disappear.

1940 Roadside marker *near Lusk, Wyoming, one of the oldest on the Western Cattle Trail System. It is also one of the very few to be accurate on the trailing dates. It is in remembrance of the cowboys who "drove their Texas herds across this spot" on the "Texas to Montana" Trail, 1876 - 1897. See Part III, Chapter III.*

CHRONOLOGY OF THE CATTLE-TRAILING INDUSTRY

1836 In March, Texans declare their independence from Mexico and become the Republic of Texas. Many settlers move to the new republic, and its population increases rapidly.

1845 In December, Texas joins the union and becomes its 28th state. Texas cattlemen trail small herds east over the Atascosita Trail to New Orleans.

1848 Charles Stillman purchases a large tract of land along the southern border of Texas and with partner, Samuel Belton, plats the town of Brownsville.

1853 A recorded herd of 3,000 cattle are driven north in June through the reservations of the Choctaws and Cherokees in Indian Territory to Missouri on what later would be called the Shawnee Trail.

1855 Missouri passes a law in December that bans diseased cattle from passing through their state. It is not strictly enforced.

1858 Herds are trailed up the far eastern border of Kansas Territory toward Kansas City.

1859 Because of a Texas Fever outbreak in 1858, the Kansas Territorial Legislature passes a quarantine law on February 1 stipulating that no person would be permitted to drive any infected cattle into the eastern territory.

1861 Kansas becomes a state and passes its first state quarantine law on May 1, making it illegal to drive Texas cattle into any part of Kansas between April 1 and November 1.

The Civil War stops the northern movement of cattle herds. A few herds are driven eastward across Lousiana to supply Confederate troops in the southern states.

1862 The Federal Government Homestead Act is passed in May. It provides that any person over the age of twenty-one, who is the head of a family, can obtain 160 acres of public land, and provided the individual lives on the land and improves it, after five years, will gain title to that land. The act opens up the West to thousands of homesteaders.

1866 In the spring, Texas cattlemen resume cattle trailing into the north on the Shawnee Trail, going to the farthest west rail teminal at Sedalia, Missouri.

Charles Goodnight and Oliver Loving make their first trail drive with 2,000 head from southwest of Fort Belknap, Texas, going west across the Staked Plains of Texas,[1] up the Pecos River, and into Fort Sumner, New Mexico. Loving delivers the balance of the herd into Colorado around the Denver vicinity.

Some 260,000 Texas longhorns are trailed north to be delivered to Sedalia, Missouri; Nebraska City, Nebraska, and Burlington, Iowa.

1867   Kansas repeals certain sections of the 1861 quarantine law on February 26, and draws its first deadline west of the 6th principal meridian and south of township 18. (sixty miles west of Abilene)

Joseph McCoy promotes the village of Abilene, Kansas, on the Union Pacific, Eastern Division as a cattle railhead. A few thousand head are driven into Abilene in this first season. Kansas Governor Crawford makes an exception to the Kansas quarantine law and allows Texas drovers to bring herds to Abilene.

The Nebraska Legislature in a special session in May passes a series of laws that state that no person is to drive any cattle "affected with any contagious or infectious disease through this state," and prohibits the running at large of stock in certain of the more populous communities.

Fort Griffin is established in Texas.

Oliver Loving, the partner of Charles Goodnight, dies on September 25 at Fort Sumner, New Mexico, as a result of injuries sustained from an Indian attack.

1868   Charles Goodnight creates another trail in Colorado, farther east than the original path, to deliver herds to Cheyenne, Wyoming.

Only around 75,000 Texas longhorns are sent up the trail.

1869   Nebraska Legislature enacts another law in February saying it is unlawful to bring Texas cattle into the state during the months of July and August. The law is met with indifference.

The Union Pacific, eastern division, Railroad completes its rails across Kansas in December. It is now referred to as the "Kansas Pacific."

Charles Goodnight again creates a trail farther east, away from the encroaching settlements along the east slope of the Rocky Mountains in Colorado.

Texas cattlemen are so relieved to finally have railheads in Kansas to receive their herds that 350,000 cattle are sent up the trail, four times as many as the year before. Rail

---

[1]The Staked Plains, also referred to as Llano Estacado, is one of the largest mesas or tablelands in North America. Early travelers staked their way across the mesa in order to signal to followers or to assure themselves they were still pointed toward their destination and not going in circles.

terminals are Junction City on the West Shawnee Trail, and Abilene on the Chisholm Trail.

1870 On May 2, the Missouri River-Fort Scott & Gulf Railroad connects Baxter Springs, Kansas, on the Shawnee Trail to the north.

Nebraska passes its first general herd law. (Everyone has to keep his stock from the crops of other people or pay damages.)

Colorado Territory prohibits the "introduction of Texas stock," but the law is ignored. In the fall, the quarantine law is voided by the territorial government.

In June, the Union Pacific Railroad arrives in Schulyer, Nebraska to build chutes and pens for Texas herds. Schulyer becomes an important Nebraska cattle town.

Some 300,000 cattle are sent up the trail to Kansas and Nebraska railheads.

1871 In the spring, the Atchinson, Topeka, and Santa Fe Railway arrives in Newton, Kansas. Newton becomes a cattle town on the Chisholm Trail.

Railroad investors convert thirteen acres of the West Bottoms in Kansas City into a stockyard operation. Within five years, the elaborate livestock exchange and its stockyard operation occupy fifty-five acres of ground.

The largest number of cattle in history are put on the trail. Kansas and Nebraska cattle towns and railheads receive 600,000 head.

A few herds are trailed to Ellsworth, Kansas--located farther west than Abilene on the Kansas Pacific.

In November a devastating winter snow storm hits Kansas and Nebraska. Thousands of animals die and many owners lose their ranches. It is called the "big die off."

1872 In the spring, the Atchinson, Topeka, and Santa Fe Railway arrives in Wichita, Kansas. Wichita becomes a cattle town on the Chisholm Trail.
The trail system moves west. Baxter Springs and Abilene, Kansas, and Schuyler, Nebraska cease to be cowtowns. Ellsworth replaces Abilene as a cattle town.

In the fall, the Burlington and Missouri Railroad connects with the Union Pacific at Kearney, Nebraska. New stock yards are built immediately.

350,000 head are trailed from Texas to Kansas and Nebraska.

1873 The Panic of 1873. An economic crash in New York reverberates across the nation. The cattle industry falters, affecting prices in Texas, Kansas, and Nebraska. Many of the 405,00 trailed cattle cannot be sold.

Texan L. B. Harris trails west of the cowtowns, moves his cattle from fort to fort, and blazes a pathway to Ellis, Kansas. Ellis and Hays City become railheads on the Kansas Pacific Railroad.

1874 Captain John T. Lytle faces the unknown and blazes a trail from Texas, across Indian Territory and western Kansas, to the Red Cloud Agency in Nebraska. The trail will become the Western Cattle Trail.

Dodge City, Kansas prepares to become the next cattle town of Kansas. The Union Pacific Railroad builds cattle pens at Ogallala and processes 50,000 head by the end of the season.

1875 Charles Goodnight blazes his fourth trail in Colorado known simply as the "new trail."

Fort Griffin on the Clear Fork of the Brazos River in Texas and its fort town at the bottom of the hill (the Flat), becomes a popular stop and supply depot on the new Western Trail.

Both the Chisholm Trail to Wichita, Kansas and the Western Trail to Dodge City are used in the 1875 season.

1876 The trail system moves west again. Wichita, Newton, and Ellsworth in Kansas, and Kearney in Nebraska cease to be railheads. The Chisholm Trail no longer goes to Kansas, and, for a short time, becomes a feeder route to the Western Trail.

Contractor Lewis W. Neatherlin oversees three herds up the new Route I through western Kansas to Ogallala, Nebraska. His journal becomes a classic in trail-driving history.

Charles Goodnight establishes a ranch in the Texas Panhandle in Palo Duro Canyon on the edge of the great Staked Plains. In the next year, he goes into partnership with John G. Adair, and the ranch becomes known as the JA Ranch.

Some 322,000 Texas longhorns are put on the trail.

Kansas passes another quarantine law, which moves the deadline close to Dodge City. Ellis and Hays City cease to be railheads.

1877 Kansas moves its quarantine deadline west again. Route 1 in Kansas ceases to be used.

1878 Corwin and Jonathan Doan establishes a store at the Red River Crossing, which becomes known as Doan's Crossing.

Charles Goodnight establishes his last cattle trail. This one is from the JA Ranch in the Texas Panhandle to Dodge City, Kansas. It becomes known as the Palo Duro-Dodge City Trail.

Approximately 265,600 Texas longhorns are put on the trail.

1880 Caldwell and Hunnewell, Kansas each receive railroads. Located on the Indian Territory and Kansas border, Caldwell receives the Atchinson, Topeka & Santa Fe Railway and Hunnewell, fourteen miles east of Caldwell, receives a spur of the Kansas City, Lawrence and Southern Railroad. Both border towns now become railhead options. The Chisholm Trail is revived for a short period.

Almost 400,000 Texas longhorns are on the trail.

1881   Kansas passes another quarantine law and the trail in western Kansas moves west. Route 2 is no longer used.

Texas Panhandle ranchers implement the Winchester Quarantine against herds coming up from south Texas.

1883   Col. Jack Potter under the employ of Alfred T. Bacon, manager of the New England Livestock Company, blazes a new trail splintering from the Western Cattle Trail at Albany, Texas to Cheyenne, Wyoming. It becomes known at the Potter-Bacon Trail.

Another route is established farther west of the Western Trail in Texas which crosses the Red River at Quanah (the Quanah Detour Route or "Ghost Trail").

Drovers trail 267,000 longhorns north.

1884   Kansas passes its final quarantine law and closes its borders to Texas cattle starting in 1885. Route 3 and the Wallace Branch of the Western Trail in Kansas are no longer used. Dodge City ceases as railhead after the 1884 season.

In April, New Mexico passes a similar quarantine law against Texas cattle. Colorado allows Texas cattle if they are certified by a veterinarian, and Nebraska and Wyoming Territory leave the matter up to "responsible executive officers." Gaps and loopholes exist, and Texas cattle continue to be trailed north.

The immense XIT Ranch in the Texas Panhandle is established.

Jim E. May from the LS Ranch in the Texas Panhandle blazes a route through Colorado to the LS's finishing ranges in Montana. It will later become known as the "Texas-Montana" route.

An estimated 300,000 head of Texas longhorns are put on the trail.

In the fall, a Texas Fever epidemic rages across Nebraska and Wyoming, killing thousands of local cattle.

1885   Texas drovers establish a route (the proposed National Trail) up the eastern Colorado border to Trail City on the Arkansas River and beyond.

Texas drovers and their herds face a blockade in No Man's Land (present-day Oklahoma Panhandle). Led by rancher Col. A. J. (Jack) Hardesty, the blockade and confrontation between the ranchers and the Texas cowboys becomes known as the "Jack Hardesty War."

An estimated 300,000 head of Texas longhorns are trailed north.

1886   In January, blizzards commence and severe winter weather presists until spring.

In April, the House of Representatives fails to pass the National Trail proposal because of the lack of a quorum. The trail-driving industry is on the verge of collapse.

Nebraska passes a herd law which makes a trail boss accountable for every animal. To avoid the risk of a Texas steer venturing onto homesteaders' property, Texas herds no longer are trailed across Nebraska.

The XIT Ranch starts to trail herds north to its finishing ranch in Montana, using the Texas-Montana Feeder Route.

A severe drought occurs in the summer. The trail-driving industry falters.

In December and the following January of 1887, winter blizzards and freezing temperatures hit the Plains from Montana to the Texas Panhandle. Thousands of cattle perish, and many ranchers are left financially broken, never to recover.

1887   Range 41W, the strip of land designated for the National Trail, is opened for homesteading. After the 1887 trail-driving season, the National Trail and Trail City, Colorado disappear.

The trail-driving industry revives. The Texas-Montana Feeder Route through Colorado which connects with the old Western Trail trunk line in Wyoming is now used.

1888   Texas longhorns on the trail come mostly from the Texas Panhandle.

Railing cattle by train becomes prevalent.

1896   Only a few herds, including 12,400 steers from the XIT Ranch, go over the trail.

1897   One herd, driven by "Scandlous John" McCanless, from the XIT Ranch is put on the trail. It is the last herd to be trailed north.

E. C. Abbott, aka "Teddy Blue," *left front, (1860-1939) went up the Western Cattle Trail from Texas three times and helped in various other trail drives of a shorter nature before settling down in Montana. At the age of seventy-eight in 1938, he narrated his life story to Helena Huntington Smith, telling of his younger days in Nebraska and of his career as a cowpuncher.* **The book was published in 1939 as** We Pointed Them North, **Recollections of a Cowpuncher.**

The authors believe that this photo was taken sometime between 1885 through 1889. In 1885, Teddy Blue started to work for Granville Stuart, an early-day stockman and Montana pioneer, on the DHS ranch near Ford's Creek, close to old Fort Maginnis in central Montana. Here he fell in love with Mary, one of Stuart's daughters. They were married in 1889.

Seated next to Teddy Blue is Bob Stuart, a brother-in-law. The two other cowboys are very likely also brothers to Mary. Granville Stuart's wife was Shoshone Indian, and the cowboy behind Bob looks very much like Stuart's wife and their daughter Mary.

Photo courtesy of the Montana Historical Society Research Center, Photograph Archives, Helena, Montana.

Reference: We Pointed Them North, *pages 130, 136, 207.*

HOW WIDE WAS THAT TRAIL?

The trail used to move Texas herds north was only about 200 to 400 yards wide. It was so prevalent after several herds had used the pathway, that, as Charles M. Harger wrote in 1892, it was like "a chocolate band amid the green prairies." The pathway became lower than the surrounding country…[1]

The impact of the cattle moving up the trail would be wider than that, however. Cattle were taken off of the trail to a bedding ground or for grazing and for watering, but were returned to the familiar trail in order to make the ten to fifteen miles per day and to reach the well-established creek and river crossings. Drovers knew the best locations for fording waterways, and those locations were used repeatedly by most of the herds going north.

Texas longhorns could go without water for several days, but "in order to maintain their flesh and staminia, they had to graze several hours a day. When good grass was available the drovers would slow the herd and let them fan out, but kept them grazing in the correct direction — perhaps for several days."[2] But when grass was poor or lacking, the herds were pushed harder on the trail in order to reach a destination. It was common to have two drives per day, in the morning after the herds were allowed to graze and again in late afternoon after another stop had been made for watering and grazing. Thus, the areas on either side of the trail were impacted by the Texas herds, BUT the trail itself was not very wide.

---

[1] Charles M. Harger, "Cattle Trails of the Prairies," *Scribner's Magazine*, Vol. XI, No. 6, Jan.-June, 1892, page 734. Harger had lived and worked in Kansas for thirteen years before writing this article.

[2] Correspondence from Tom B. Saunders, IV, Nov. 10, 2013.

TERMS THE READER NEEDS TO KNOW

The Trail: the main trunk of a path that led from Texas to a northern destination. It was approximately two to four hundred feet wide and, after much use, was worn deeply into the earth. Herds were taken off of the trail to graze or to be bedded down for the night, but were put back onto the trail to continue the journey.

Trail System: a major trail with its different branches as identified throughout the years. As cattle quarantines were imposed, the main trunk of a trail moved, but still was part of the system. There were four trail systems.

Feeder Route: a route that joined the main trail or "fed into" a major trail system going north. Most of the feeder routes were in Texas, Indian Territory (Oklahoma), and Kansas.

Splinter Route: a route that left the trunk line of the trail to go in another direction or diverged from a major trail system. Most of the splinter routes were in the north.

Detour Route or Trail: a pathway that left the main trunk of a trail but returned to the main trunk farther up the line. For example, the National Trail detoured Kansas, but its branches returned to the Western Cattle Trail in Kansas, Nebraska, and Wyoming.

Trail Branch: a pathway that is part of the main trunk line, but leaves the main stem for an alternate route. Some branches were for a short distance and rejoined the main trunk line while others re-defined the direction of the main trail. Each trail system had various branches.

Quarantine: refers to an area that is off limits to Texas herds and their outfits. A quarantine law stated that herds and their drovers had to stay in front of the quarantine line or be punished with fines, jail time for the trail boss, and the herd confiscated. The quarantine was imposed because of the cattle disease called, at the time, Texas Fever or Spanish Fever.

Texas Fever: a disease that was carried by Texas longhorns coming out of south Texas. The longhorns were immune to the fever, but other cattle that came in contact with the Texas longhorns, especially on the bedding grounds, soon became ill and died. Years later, the fever became known as "tick fever."

Deadline: the line that drovers knew should not be crossed, for it separated the quarantined area for cattle herds and the open range. This "line" was set down by state law.

Road Brand: a special brand used only during the driving of cattle north. The brand was burned lightly onto the animal and sometimes called a "hair brand." It was this brand that the drovers used — not the brand of the owner, when there were cattle from different owners in one herd.

Through-cattle: a term used by local cattlemen to distinguish the difference between the Texas herds passing through the area and herds from local ranches that were being moved from one range to another. Through-cattle were herds coming out of Texas and going north to a destination.

Remuda: a group of horses that were furnished by the cattle owners or purchased to be used on the trail. Each cowboy was assigned from five to ten horses. Therefore, a remuda could consist of fifty to over one hundred horses. The remuda was the responsibility of the wrangler, whose job was to be a constant care-taker for the horses.

THE WESTERN CATTLE TRAIL | 1874-1897

The trail-driving era began before and continued after the Civil War. For four years during the war, cattle drives to the north basically ceased, but after the war, driving herds to market became a necessity. The accounts of trail drives before the war seems to have faded in history, for most books and articles concentrate on telling of the driving of herds north after the war. Even the Old Time Trail Drivers, who in their old age, tried to preserve the history of trail driving, for the most part, only mention experiences after the Civil War. That was because of their age. They were born during the 1840s and 1850s and did not go up the trail until their teens or later. These cowboys outlived the trail-driving era. By the 1920s when they were reminiscing about their trail driving days, it was all over.

Those Texans who were born a decade earlier, in the 1830s, who may have experienced the War of Independence with Mexico, the Republic of Texas, its fight for statehood, and living among Indians, also could have outlived the trail-driving era from 1846 to 1897. It lasted only fifty years.

In one brief lifetime, the trailing of Texas longhorns north came into its glory and faded into history.

PART I
ONE BRIEF LIFETIME

The Four Texas Trail Systems and the Texas Fever

> *Other states were carved or born; Texas grew from hide and horn.*
> *Other states are long or wide; Texas is a shaggy hide.*
> *Dripping blood and crumpled hair, Some gory giant flung it there,*
> *Laid the head where valleys drain, Stretched its rump along the plain.*
> *Other soil is full of stone; Texans plow up cattle bones.*
> *Herds are buried on the trail, Underneath the powdered shale,*
> *Herds that stiffened like the snow; Where the icy northerns go.*
> *Other state have built their halls, Humming tunes along the walls;*
> *Texans watched the mortar stirred, While they kept the lowing herd.*
> *Stamped on Texas wall and roof, Gleams the sharp and crescent hoof.*
> *High above the hum and stir, Jingle bridle-rein and spur.*
> *Other states were made or born; Texas grew from hide and horn.*

Cattle, by Berta Hart Nance

CHAPTER I

A Search for an Outlet

THE WESTERN CATTLE TRAIL | 1874-1897

THE WESTERN CATTLE TRAIL | 1874–1897

Andy Adams in his 1905 historical novel, The Outlet, *expressed the foremost priority of drovers of his youth — in both the title of his book and in its contents — to find an outlet for Texas beeves. He lamented how the Civil War had "stopped almost all plans to market the range cattle" and that after the war, an outlet market "became imperative."[1]*

Most of the area we know today as Texas has for decades been abundantly stocked with cattle. While other areas of the United States were blessed with timber, waterways, vast grain fields or outcroppings of ore, Texas had cattle. The longhorn had been introduced to the open range of northern New Spain, an area that would later become southern California, Arizona, New Mexico, and Texas before white settlers ventured into the region. The ancestors of the trail-driven longhorns of the 1840s through the 1890s were the thousands of cattle that had stocked the ranches in Mexico in the late 1500s and 1600s, some tracing their bloodlines back to Cortes' Mexican hacienda.[2] Spanish cattle were driven north with Coronado in 1540 and were again brought north during the introduction of the Spanish mission system, the first near the Louisiana line in 1690. As the Spanish traveled, they brought their cattle and horses with them, many being lost or having escaped along the way. With the Pueblo Revolt in 1680, Spanish missions were abandoned, and their cattle were turned out to fend for themselves. Thus, the fierce and powerful longhorns survived and populated the open range before white settlers started entering that region of the country in the 1830s.[3]

The territory between the Nueces River and the Rio Grande became the primary nursery and stronghold for the Spanish cattle. Ranching had begun in the area about 1700, and it was estimated that "three million head of stock, including goats, sheep and horses as well as cattle, occupied the area in 1835."[4] By the time statehood had been granted in December of 1845, wild Spanish cattle were found, according to J. Frank Dobie, "from the Red River on the north to the Rio Grande on the south and from the Louisiana line on the east to the uppermost breaks of the Brazos on the west." Texas was developing as a cattle kingdom and within ten years would support over one million head. In another five years, the number would triple, and more than triple again over the following decade.[5] Dobie continues:

They [the longhorns] did not get out on the Great Plains. They did not run in the great herds sometimes reported, but kept in little

---

[1]Andy Adams, *The Outlet*, viii.

[2]According to J. Frank Dobie, in 1521 Gregorio de Villalobos was the first to bring cattle to New Spain (Mexico), and Cortes stocked his estate (named Cuernavaca or Cow Horn) with cattle. (Dobie, *The Longhorns*, 3)

[3]Dobie, Ibid., 4-10.

[4]Dobie, *The Longhorns*, 11. Because of Texas' climate conditions, it was an exceptional country for cattle breeding. In good years, a phenomenal figure of 95 calves to 100 cows could be reached. (Andy Adams, *The Outlet*, viii)

[5]In 1855, taxes were assessed on 1,363,688 head. Five years later the number had grown to 3,786,433, six times the number of people at the time. (Holden, *Alkali Trails or Social and Economic Movements of the Texas Frontier, 1846-1900*, 23)

bunches, staying in cover during the day and venturing out on the prairie only at night, grazing against the wind. A rider seldom saw one in daytime unless he happened upon it in a thicket. As watchful as wild turkeys, as alert in the nostrils as deer, they came, after being hunted, to flee the approach of any human being.[6]

The wild cattle population continued to be referred to as "Spanish cattle" or simply "wild cattle," but another term came into use as early ranchers added American bloodlines to the Mexican breed. The *Texas* longhorn evolved. Because of over 300 years of natural selection and survival of the fittest, its basic stature of long legs, long back, and a tail that dragged the ground, remained the same, but the "Texas" cousin to the Spanish stock became heavier and developed larger horns. By the mid 1850s, Texas claimed her own breed of cattle. The method of colonizing the area, starting in the 1830s, also had a hand in the future cattle industry of Texas. According to the Republic of Texas land grant system, if incoming settlers declared an intention to raise cattle, they could obtain a grant for a much larger area of land. So with the encouragement of ranching and a "hide and horn" product already in place, the destiny of Texas had been established.[7]

As with any state with a resource, the marketing of that product was vital. For years, Spanish cattle had been slaughtered for hides and tallow, but now, the heavier Texas longhorn was considered a beef animal that could be sold in outside markets to fill the meat shortages. The Republic of Mexico had thousands of its own cattle and, therefore, was not a consumer of Texas cattle. Thus, early ranchers, who were in business to sell cattle, looked in three directions for a market. To the west was a vast, unpopulated arid region. During the gold rush of 1849-1850, some cattle were trailed west to California, but the number of herds sent there was not significant and for the most part, the west coast markets were not pofitable. To the east, Arkansas and Loui-siana had offered an outlet since long before statehood, but the overland trip to New Orleans, for example, was challenging to reach because the terrain through which herds were trailed was heavily wooded, and those woods were infested with deadly snakes and mosquitos.[8] Cattle were driven east to supply the armies engaged in the Civil War in the 1860s, but the effort was short term. Therefore, cowmen looked for an alternative. They trailed small herds northeast into Missouri after which some stock went as far as Illinois and Iowa. Of that number, a few were taken all the way to Chicago where they were then shipped on to New York. Therefore, the most feasible

---

[6]Dobie, Ibid, 11.

[7]"The colonists found that by declaring an intention to raise cattle, they could procure a grant for ten times as much land as if they merely declared an intention to farm." (Dobie, Ibid, 29) The grants were controlled by the Republic of Texas and, later, by Texas state government which developed policies different than the federal homestead law in other states, like Kansas and Nebraska. A Texas land grant was for 4,400 acres, 4,220 designated for ranching and 200 acres for crops.

[8]From Texas statehood to the Civil War, thousands of cattle were driven from central Texas, the San Antonio and Nueces River area, and south Texas to Lousiana markets over the Atascocita and LaBania Trails. For further reading, refer to Jim Bob Jackson's 2008 book, *They Pointed Them East First*.

route to viable markets seemed to be to the northeast across the prairies of eastern Indian Territory to the farthest western points of the Pacific Railroad in Missouri.

Between the mid-1860s and the mid-1880s, changing settlement patterns in the mid-west and plains areas and markets in the east also altered the system of supplying cattle that prevailed up to the Civil War. Because of these changes, four Texas-based cattle trails — the Shawnee Trail System, the Goodnight Trail System, the Eastern/Chisholm Trail System, and The Western Trail System — were used to drive cattle north during the forty-year period between 1846 and 1886. Three of these trails originated in the lower Texas triangle.[9]

Three factors determined the longevity of each of these systems: the tolerance of farmers and local ranchers over whose ground the cattle were being trailed; the attitudes of state or territorial governments that imposed cattle quarantines or herd laws; and, the prevalence of the Texas Fever, the very reason why local farmers became difficult and state legislatures imposed quarantines. Texas Fever, a dreaded malady carried by south Texas longhorns, caused death to the domestic cattle belonging to ranchers and settlers located outside of Texas. These deaths, in turn, forced Texas drovers to drive their herds into areas west of most existing settlements. Because the disease became associated with the incoming Texas herds, it was called "Texas Fever."[10]

The history of the cattle-driving industry would have been written differently had it not been for the Texas Fever. Instead of four trails, Texas cattlemen probably would have established one or perhaps two cattle trails, one directed toward the eastern markets and one toward the northwestern territories. But as the result of the Texas Fever, each cattle trail had to face the consequences of the disease either by being forced to move — or by being quarantined out of existence altogether.

In the early years of trail driving, northern owners of cattle soon became aware of a cow disease that caused wide-spread deaths among their cattle allowed to mix with or bedded on the ground recently vacated by Texas longhorns. In 1853 the situation worsened when the Texas Fever occurred in Missouri and caused havoc.

The mystery was that the fatal disease was transmitted by apparently healthy animals. The Texas longhorn was not affected by the disease. Even the newly born calves were clean of the fever. The cause was unknown, but to farmers and ranchers, the reason for the disease was immaterial. What was known was that within days after a herd of Texas cattle passed through, local animals sickened and died.

The Texas Fever was very much apparent before the war in Missouri and eastern Kansas Territory, but after the war when larger herds were pushed to market, the Fever bacame a serious problem. The four-year war broke the cadence of trail driving only

---

[9]In the final ten years of cattle trailing, after 1886, the breeding ground was no longer in south Texas. Trail cattle were pulled from the Texas Panhandle. The Texas Fever was the main reason. This will be discussed in length later.

[10]The fever was also called "Spanish fever" or "splenic fever," from its characteristic lesions of the spleen. The disease also became known as hemoglobinuric fever and red-water fever and as dry murrain and bloody murrain. After the 1890s, it was referred to as "tick fever" because the south Texas tick caused the fever. The disease is still a problem today. ("Texas Fever," *The Handbook of Texas Online*, www.tshaonline.org [accessed July 24, 2009])

to start anew in 1866 with an avalanche of herds using the Shawnee Trail that had been established before the war. Because trail driving did not come to its full force until after the war, many authors concentrate on the years of trail driving after the Civil War. To see the whole picture, however, one needs to realize that Texas cattlemen were pushing herds to northern markets as early as 1846. These herds were smaller by comparison to later herds, less frequent, and less organized, but the purpose was the same — to walk the Texas longhorns to market, and trail drivers continued to do so until 1897.

  The geography of the cattle trails used by Texas cattlemen during the trail-driving era is not a simple matter to explore. There were four distinct trail systems used during the time period, but each one had feeder and splinter trails. The student of cattle trails can easily become confused by the numerous routes — some feeding into a trunk line, and in turn, others splintering off from the trunk line. The trunk line must always be kept in focus, and one must remember that each main stem was one of four separate trails. One needs to think of a single trail system like a tree. The roots in Texas feed into the tree trunk and then in the north, branched out to the various delivery locations. It is one of this book's primary purposes to show an aerial view, through maps, of the main path of each cattle trail and to explain its feeder and splinter routes.

  To complicate the picture even more, the time line for the four trail systems is not easily determined, and trail systems were not entirely separate entities of their own. In the beginning, one built on the other; next trails were overlapping; and for two seasons, 1874-1875, all four of the systems were operating at the same time. One would conclude, after looking at the four trail maps, that both the Eastern and Western trail systems traversed over the remnents of the Shawnee. It was the one that was first and, in south Texas, its path was used by its successors.

  All the trails usually followed an even earlier path, whether it be an old military road, an overland freight route, or an emigrant road. Those early pathways, in turn, had followed Indian or animal trails. A few drovers and their cattle herds did forge a virgin route, but it was much easier to use a pathway that had been established by a former transit.

THE WESTERN CATTLE TRAIL | 1874-1897

❝ *...the Shawnee Trail was the first of the three great cattle trails from Texas to Kansas. From 1850 until the Chisholm Trail was opened in 1867, it was the chief route by which Texas drovers took their cattle north, and it continued to carry some of the plodding herds, in diminishing numbers, for at least six more years.... in its heyday, it was the biggest outlet that Texas had for its surplus Longhorns.* ❞

Wayne Gard, "The Shawnee Trail,"
The Southwestern Historical Quarterly,
Vol. LVI, No. 5, Jan. 1953, pg. 359.

❝ *There was not over 150 miles of railroad in the state [Texas],....so the cattle driving to Kansas was the only hope at the time.* ❞

W. F. Crude, referring to 1866 in Hunter,
The Trail Drivers of Texas, 215.

CHAPTER II

The Shawnee Trail System, 1846-1875

R. A. Hibbard stands next to his oxen team in front of the Koontz Grocery store and other establishments in Baxter Spring, Kansas sometime in the 1870s. The Hibbards settled on Shoal Creek near Baxter Springs in 1870, the same year that Baxter Springs received the Missouri River, Fort Scott and Gulf Railroad. Over the next two years, Baxter Springs was a cattle town receiving thousands of Texas longhorns that were shipped from Baxter Springs' corrals or were trailed farther north on the Shawnee Trail.

This photo shows the east side of 11th and Military Avenue. R. A. Hibbard's wagon is loaded with corn to be hauled to the mill in Lowell, Kansas.

Courtesy of Jesse Bellard and the Baxter Springs Heritage Center and Museum

The Shawnee Trail System is the first of the major four systems used by trail drivers to deliver their herds to market. Because trail drivers used its original pathway so early, before the Civil War, much of the trail's history has been ignored, creating a belief, for many, that trail-driving from Texas did not start until after the war in 1866. Here, we present a brief overall history of this very important system. Refer to the Shawnee Trail System map inside the front cover.[1]

Early Texas cattlemen determined that the best market for their longhorns was in the northeast. To reach those markets, the herds would have to be trailed into Missouri toward St. Louis, Hannibal and other Mississippi river towns. After Texas statehood in 1845, cattlemen started to gather small herds of wild longhorns and prepare them for the long drive north. The first major cattle trail to become a repetitive route into Missouri followed what some called the Texas Road which had previously been used for immigration and trade. This old immigration route, in turn, followed an existing Indian trail that ran from Missouri through Indian Territory to the Trinity River (present-day Dallas) and on to Waco and Austin, Texas. The Texas portion of this trade route, south of the Red River, had been developed and laid out by the military under the direction of an 1839 Republic-of-Texas act of Congress to create a road to open up Northern Texas to further settlement and to stimulate trade. Preston Road, as it was called, was not completed until 1843, and started at Preston Bend, at the Washita Bend of the Red River, and continued to the Trinity River crossing.

A trading post had been established by Silas Cheek Colville and Holland Coffee at the Red River crossing in about 1837. The town of Preston Bend itself was not platted until two years after the trade route was completed. It was a boisterous frontier place, an important river crossing, the terminus of the Indian Nation's Texas Road, and the beginning of the Preston Road.

A few miles to the east was Colbert's Ferry, another crossing location. At the trail end of the trade road at the Trinity River crossing, the settlement of Dallas began in 1841. Numberous feeder routes in south Texas from the coastal plains, the Rio Grande, and the western ranges fed into this trade route to become a trunk line for a cattle trail and an outlet to the north.[2]

By the 1850s, the cattle trail had become known as the "Shawnee Trail," some say because of a Shawnee village on the Texas side of the Red River just below the trail crossing; or it was named after the Shawnee Hills which the route skirted on the eastern side before crossing the Canadian River.[3]

Trail drivers who began their trips in southern Texas headed north through Austin and Waco. They picked up the "Preston Road" at the Trinity River, crossed

---

[1] The Shawnee Trail's historical information has been buried in documents for years and has not been given full exposure. An extensive study and book needs to be devoted to this system.

[2] Wayne Gard, "The Chisholm Trail," *Along the Early Trails of the Southwest*, 66; Jean T. Hannaford, "Old Preston Road," *The Handbook of Texas Online*, [accessed February 10, 2008]; "The Shawnee Trail," state highway marker four files south of Lebanon, Texas; and Awbrey and Dooley, *Why Stop? a Guide to Texas Historical Roadside Markers*, 177.

[3] Wayne Gard, "Shawnee Trail," *Handbook of Texas Online*, www.tshaonline.org [accessed July 24, 2009]

THE WESTERN CATTLE TRAIL | 1874-1897   11

the Red River at Preston Bend or Colbert's Ferry, trailed northeasterly on the north side of the Shawnee Hills, crossed the Canadian and North Canadian near the Sac and Fox Agency, passed through the Creek Reservation and forded the Arkansas River west of forts Davis and Gibson.[4] The trail then crossed the extreme southeast corner of Kansas Territory, and trailed into Missouri. For a few years, this was the only route to the north.

The trail had its limitations. The timbered and mountainous landscape of eastern Indian Territory was not ideal for trailing semiwild cattle, and when a Texas Fever out-break occurred in Missouri in 1853, it made matters worse. As 3,000 cattle were being trailed into western Missouri in June of that year, local farmers blocked their passage and forced the drovers to turn back. Vigilante groups, who feared the mysterious disease that was killing their cattle, killed any cow or steer that entered their land. Some later Texas herds managed to avoid the blockades. In December of 1855, Missouri passed a law that banned diseased cattle from passing through their state, but the Texas longhorns were not diseased. They appeared healthy and strong, so the law was ineffective, and enforcement again fell into the hands of armed bands of farmers.[5]

In 1857, two separate outfits are recorded to have made the drive to Quincy, Illinois. Jesse Day and his son "Doc" from Hays County, Texas, and William McCutcheon with his son Willis of Bastrop, each drove a herd to Quincy. In 1858, Oliver Loving of Palo Pinto, and John Durkee of Parker County also used the Shawnee Trail route to Quincy.[6] In response, the border patrol increased on the Missouri border, and, to avoid a confrontation, drovers moved their route west into Kansas Territory. Herds were trailed up the far eastern border of Kansas toward Kansas City. Traveling close to the Fort Scott-Fort Leavenworth military road, trail bosses (owners) sold cattle to newly arrived immigrants, to Santa Fe traders or travelers, or to the U. S. Army at Fort Leavenworth and Fort Riley. The remainder of the herds were then driven on through Kansas to Nebraska, Iowa, Illinois, or Minnesota.[7]

The Texas Fever broke out in eastern Kansas Territory in 1858, causing the Kansas Territorial Legislature to pass an act on February 1, 1859 that stipulated that no person would be permitted to drive any cattle infected with the disease into the territory. An additional section of the law prohibited "Texas, Arkansas, and Indian stock from entering the counties of Bourbon, Linn, Lykins (Miami), and Johnson between June 1 and November 1." The act was disregarded by the incoming drovers, and many native cattle died in 1859 and 1860. Longhorns were shot by settlers, and Kansas Territorial farmers and Texas cowboys were poised for bloody encounters. On May 1, 1861, another law was passed by the new state's legislature which made it

---

[4]Charles M. Harger, "Cattle Trails of the Prairies," *Scribner's Magazine*, January-June, 1892, 735. The five Civilized Tribes occupied eastern Indian Territory, and Texas trail herds were allowed to trespass, usually for a fee or donation. West of there — Texas Panhandle, western Indian Territory, and western Kansas — was a different situation. Oklahoma Territory was not created until 1890.

[5]"Shawnee Trail," online, Ibid.

[6]T. U. Taylor, *The Chisholm Trail and Other Routes*, 76.

[7]This early diversion became a splinter route or branch off of the main East Shawnee Trail.

illegal to drive cattle into any part of Kansas between April 1 and November 1, but the Civil War broke out and cattle driving to Kansas diminished for the time being.[8]

Upon returning to their Texas ranches after the war, Confederate soldiers found their lands neglected and in ruins because Indians had raided, ransacked, and burnt the ranches. The womenfolk and children had exited to the eastern part of the state for protection, and the cattle had scattered, had returned to the wild, and multiplied. W. F. Cude, whose family lived in Montgomery County in the Texas Republic days and who later became a trail driver, wrote to the Old Time Trail Drivers Association that:

> In the year 1861 war broke out between the States and it lasted four years, and during all this time there was no market, so the country was beginning to be overrun with cattle so much that thousands died. Some people went out with a wagon and an ax and killed and skinned them for their hides, which sold for one dollar apiece...[9]

Millions of cattle, of little value, were in the thickets and brush of the poverty-stricken state. Andy Adams wrote in 1905:

> The civil war stopped almost all plans to market the range cattle, and the close of that war found the vast grazing lands of Texas fairly covered with millions of cattle which had no actual or determinate value. They were sorted and branded and herded after a fashion, but neither they nor their increase could be converted into anything but more cattle.[10]

However, the demand for beef after the war was huge. The war effort had exhausted the supply of cattle, horses, hogs, and chickens in the north, while Texas was over-supplied with cattle and bankrupt. Because of the huge population of longhorns and practically no local market for beef in Texas, the pressure for trailing cattle had become even stronger. The challenge was to round up the wild longhorns, some as old as eight years and weighing up to twelve hundred pounds, and trail them to market. Jimmy Skaggs, who studied the economics of cattle driving, wrote: "Landless cattlemen rounded up unbranded and unclaimed maverick cattle, hired drovers with merely the promise of wages after the animals had been sold, begged and borrowed the necessary supplies and equipment, the then set out toward some northern railhead-market."[11] J. Frank Dobie wrote: "Trail driving northward began early in 1866... They were not hunting grass to graze on; their world was full of

---

[8]Richmons, "Cowtowns and Cattle Trails," *Kansas, The First Century, Vol. I*, 255.

[9]W. F. Cude was born in 1844 and recalls his memories in an essay that he wrote around 1917-1923. He joined a Texas Ranger Company in 1861 (age 17), was involved in "a number of desperate engagements" during the War, hauled freight after the War (1866) and trailed his first cattle herd to Kansas in 1868. (W. F. Cude, "Gives Some Early Texas History," in Hunter, *The Trail Drivers of Texas*, 627-633)

[10]Andy Adams, *The Outlet*, viii.

[11]Jimmy Skaggs, *The Cattle-Trailing Industry*, 1.

grass, all free. They were hunting people with money to buy cattle. Looking back now, it seems as if they were hunting trouble."[12]

The old familiar Shawnee Trail was to be used again. To the traildrivers, the Missouri Pacific at Sedalia was the closest place to market their herds. Sedalia had been incorporated in 1860 along the Missouri Pacific Railroad, and by war's end was a railroad terminus for cattle drives. It was equipped with stockyards and loading pens. After leaving Baxter's Place in southeastern Kansas, drovers would trail approximately one hundred miles on to Sedalia. To some trail drivers, the route was referred to as the "Sedalia Trail."

Missourians, however, had not forgotten the Texas Fever, and the war had not diminished its impact. After Texas herds came through in 1866, local cattle in Missouri came down with a high fever, greatly enlarged spleens, deep red color urine, followed by rapid loss of strength, and then death. One Missouri citizen wrote:

> We are at a loss as to how the disease is communicated, as there is no apparent disease among the Texas cattle, but wherever they are herding any length of time, our cattle take some disease peculiar to dry murrain, and the actions of the animal, with the disease, are similar to a horse with the botts or colic....It does not look reasonable that the Texas cattle could communicate the disease themselves, but the general opinion is that the disease is communicated by the breath.

Another gentleman wrote, "...although it is very strange to me how an animal that is healthy itself can impart so dangerous a disease to other healthy cattle, I am nevertheless satisfied that it can be done, as I have lost about one hundred and fifty head by the disease."[13]

Thus, armed groups of farmers met the herds at the Kansas-Missouri border. They wanted nothing to do with Texas cattle. The post-war atmosphere had also created bands of white outlaws and ruffians who attacked, stampeded, and stole the herds. Guerrilla warfare during the war years had cast the border region between the two states into lawlessness. J. Frank Dobie wrote, "Desperadoes used the laws against Texas cattle as a disguise for robbery." and continued to note that some Missourians continued to try to prevent the herds from entering their state while Kansas had their 1861 quarantine law in place.[14] William Holden described the atmosphere in his book, *Alkali Trails*:

> Visions of great profits shimmered before the imagination of the owners as they nerved themselves for greater hardships. Their rosy

---

[12] J. Frank Dobie, *Up the Trail from Texas*, 37.

[13] "Many cattle herds were totally lost or had significant fatalities. There was a large lack of knowledge about the disease...." These are actual accounts among citizens of Missouri in 1868. ("Missouri Beef History, Texas Fever," Missouri State University Online)

[14] Dobie, Ibid, 39.

dreams were soon blasted by the unexpected reception given them in southeastern Kansas and southern Missouri by bands of organized, armed, and determined farmers. These fellows had a horror of "Texas Fever." It might play havoc among their milch cows. Besides, they did not relish the idea of having herds of reckless long-horn Texas cattle in the vicinity of their farms. The brutes would eat their grass, mangle their fences, and ravage their growing crops. There was "blood in the eyes" of the rustics.[15]

In the pivotal year of 1866, some trail drivers halted at Baxter's Place on Spring River at the Kansas-Indian Territory border to contemplate their fate. Baxter's Place had been a stopover for cattle drives since the mid 1850s. The land along and around the waters of the springs, that were thought to have medicinal properties, had originally been part of the land deeded by the United States government to the Cherokee Indians during the mid-1800s when the tribe was displaced from its native lands in southeastern United States. In the spring of 1849, "a charismatic, authoritative preacher with a booming voice and a massive six-foot seven-inch frame," along with his wife and eight children, arrived and established a trading post along the military road from Fort Scott, Kansas, to Fort Gibson in Indian Territory. Here, as before the war, herds were rested as trail hands visited Baxter's Place.[16]

In 1866, at the Kansas and Missouri border, a few outfits simply turned around and retraced their path to Texas. Others, to avoid a confrontation with the Missouri vigilantes, trailed west along, or south of the Kansas border to the vicinity of the Arkansas River. Here they turned north to the Santa Fe Trail near Lost Spring and continued, keeping west of the settlements and the Kansas quarantine. These herds were delivered into Kansas City or driven to Nebraska City and other river towns. J. N. Byler, who was a trail boss for Monroe Choate and James Borroum of Karnes County, Texas, in 1866, led a herd of "800 big steers" west of the Kansas settlements, turned north, and delivered the cattle into Iowa.[17] George C. Duffield, a Burlington, Iowa businessman along with his brother, traveled to Texas to purchase cattle in March of 1866. They speculated that the cheap cattle in Texas could be brought to Iowa and sold at a nice profit. Duffield started on April 5, west of Austin, Texas, with a herd, two wagons and seven hands to trail north. In his diary, Duffield noted on July 10th they were at Baxter Springs, Kansas and had camped on Spring River. By the 25th,

---

[15]William Holden, *Alkali Trails*, 25.

[16]"Baxter's Place" was incorporated in 1868 and renamed "Baxter Springs." It became a cattle town on the Shawnee Trail supporting numerous saloons and entertainment for the cowboys. Pastor Baxter, however, "who was well known in the area as a gun-toting preacher, was gunned down in a property dispute in 1859." ("First Cowtown in Kansas," unknown source, from the files of the Historical Museum and Heritage Center at Baxter Springs and "History of Baxter Springs," www.baxtersprings.us, [accessed Oct. 9, 2010], and "Baxter Springs — "First Kansas Cow Town" in *Kansas Legends* Online: http://www.legendsofamerica.com/OZ-BaxterSprings.html [accessed March 6, 2007])

[17]The herd crossed at Colbert's Ferry and continued through Fort Gibson before turning west of the Kansas settlements. (B. A. Borroum, "Pioneer Cattemen and Trail Drivers," *The Pioneer*, V, No. 12, 15. and J. N. Byler in Hunter, *The Trail Drivers of Texas*, 114)

THE WESTERN CATTLE TRAIL | 1874-1897

however, he noted: "We left the beefe road (Shawnee Trial) & started due west across the wide prairie in the Indian Nation to try to go around Kansas & strike Iowa. I have 499 beeves."[18]

Other trail drivers turned east through northern Arkansas and headed for the Mississippi River. Captain Eugene Millett, from Guadalupe County, drove a herd belonging to Alexander Ewing and Colonel J. J. Myers, and planned to deliver the 500-head to Westport, Missouri. Upon reaching the southern boundary of Missouri, however, he clashed with irate farmers and a sheriff who was armed with the 1861 Missouri statute that "forbade the importation of diseased livestock." Historian Jimmy Skaggs explained:

> As Millett could not prove conclusively that the herd under his supervision was fever-free, he was ordered to turn about. Seemingly stymied, the Texans retreated a few miles, turned eastward through northern Arkansas, and, once across the Mississippi River, proceeded northward to Cairo, Illinois, where most of the animals were sold...[19]

James Daugherty from Denton County, Texas, with five cow hands, drove a herd of 500 steers up the Shawnee Trail, crossed at Preston's Bend, stopped at Baxter's Place near the Kansas-Missouri line and planned to continue to Sedalia, where he "intended shipping the cattle by rail to St Louis." At Baxter's Place, however, Daugherty learned that "there had been several herds ahead of me and that [they] had been disturbed by what we called at that time Kansas Jayhawkers." One trail boss had been killed, the herd taken, and the cowboys ran off. Daugherty, thus, changed his mind and arranged to sell his herd at Fort Scott, Kansas. The six drovers pushed the herd along the Kansas-Missouri border (within quarantine lines), sometimes in Kansas and sometimes in Missouri. Twenty miles south of Fort Scott, "a bunch of fifteen or twenty Jayhawkers came upon us." They killed John Dobbins, one of Daugherty's cowboys, stampeded the herd, and tied Daugherty to a tree and severely beat him.[20]

A few trail outfits risked their herds and pushed their way through the chaos, ran the farmers' blockades, and continued through to Sedalia.

The 1866 season was a personally and economically harrowing experience for drovers. Many Texas drivers had no taste to ever try it again, especially after hearing about Daugherty's experience. Because of the quarantines, vigilantes, and marauding outlaws, the 1866, 1867 and 1868 seasons were discouraging on the Shawnee Trail. The numbers of cattle driven over the trail for those years reveals the response of

---

[18]Duffied's herd and crew crossed the Missouri River at Nebraska City the first week of September. "It was not until early November that the remaining cattle reached Burlington, Iowa, eight months after leaving Texas." (David Dary, *Cowboy Culture*, 177-181)

[19]Skaggs, ibid, 30-31.

[20]J. M. Daugherty, "Harrowing Experience with Jayhawkers," in Hunter, 696-699. Daugherty was released by another trail outfit, returned to his cowboys, and they eventually delivered the remaining herd, of about 350, by driving the herd at night to Fort Scott. "Uncle Jim" Daugherty continued to drive herds every year thereafter until 1887. He was nineteen in 1866.

cattle owners to the 1866 fiasco. According to Goins and Goble, and Joseph McCoy, the number of cattle herded north on the Shawnee Trail in that initial year after the Civil War was 260,000 head but the number dropped to a mere 35,000 in 1867, and improved only slightly in 1868 to 75,000 head.[21]

In 1867 and 1868, something had to happen. A new solution was needed to get Texas cattle to market. The numbers being herded north were only a fraction of the potential that Texas had to offer. The demand was still there, but the Texas Fever and the quarantine laws stood in the way.

As Missouri and eastern Kansas battled the Texas Fever, Kansas leaders assessed the situation. While they wanted to protect their constituents, they also wanted the Texas cattlemen's business. Therefore, on February 26, 1867, the state repealed certain sections of the 1861 law and drew its first deadline (quarantine line) west of the 6th principal meridian and south of township 18. This allowed Texas cattle to come into the state, but the deadline was still west of the settlements. Also Baxter Springs, located in the southeastern corner of Kansas, seven miles west of Missouri and two miles north of Indian Territory, tried to accommodate the cattlemen. Having incorporated in 1868, the town leaders organized an active Stockyards and Drovers Association for the purpose of buying and selling cattle. Corrals were constructed and grazing lands and fresh water were made available. The city government then issued bonds to entice the Missouri River, Fort Scott and Gulf Railroad to their town.

(Meanwhile, as will be discussed in Chapter IV, the Union Pacific Railroad, Eastern Division, which would become the Kansas Pacific in 1869, was building west through north central Kansas and had gone beyond the western limits of Kansas settlements in the spring of 1867, and an industrious Illinois cattle buyer and promoter by the name of Joseph McCoy had arrived in Kansas.)

Baxter Springs received the Missouri River, Fort Scott and Gulf Railroad on May 2, 1870. Even before the first engine arrived, the local newspaper bragged: "No City in Kansas, south of Leavenworth, can compare with us for size or compete with us for power. We will have all the trade of Texas, Arizona, southern Kansas, and the Indian Nation."[22] The rails had come by way of Leavenworth, Kansas City, Paola, Fort Scott and into Baxter Springs. The city fathers felt like their town was the terminus and future headquarters for Texas cattle being shipped east. But by this time, a small village by the name of Abilene on the Kansas Pacific in central Kansas had been actively receiving and shipping cattle for three years (see Chapter IV). There was competition. Baxter Springs, however, felt that its advantage was

---

[21]The 260,000 head (in that initial year of 1866 after the Civil War) used the Shawnee Trail only. The 1867 and 1868 figures includes the herds going into the newly established Abilene railhead as well. Another way to look at the dismal situation on the Shawnee Trail after the Civil War would be to break the numbers down into the number of herds. In 1866, when outfits were enthusiastic about heading north, 260,000 head would have represented from 260 to 371 herds, depending on the size of the herds, (700 to 1,000 per herd) while in the following year, 1867, only about 35 to 50 herds made the drive. (Lovett, John R. "Major Cattle Trails, 1866-1889," in Goins and Goble, *Historical Atlas of Oklahoma*, 117. Joseph McCoy also wrote in his 1874 book, *Historic Sketches of the Cattle Trade*, that 260,000 head "had crossed Red river during 1866." 20)

[22]"The Triumph of Baxter," *Cherokee Sentinel*, Baxter Springs, Kansas March 26, 1870.

location, and it continued to boast and point out their assets to the Texas customers. In June, when cattle started to arrive in the newly established railhead, the *Cherokee Sentinel* printed:

> The Texas cattle trade has now fully opened for the season, the receipts up to the present time have reached seven thousand head against three hundred this time last year….
>
> In the past, Baxter Springs has not been able to handle all of the cattle from Texas and some of the cattle drovers have hitherto been compelled to go to Abilene, a point on the Kansas Pacific Railroad, 163 miles west of Kansas City and 150 miles further from Northwest Texas than Baxter Springs.
>
> With a view to fully meeting the wants of drovers, large cattle yards and numberous side tracks have been established at Baxter Springs with sufficient capacity to handle speedy shipments of 3,000 per day or 21,000 head per week.

The newspaperman continued to point out that the advantage of Baxter Springs' location was that stockmen could "run their animals into market two to four weeks earlier than by any other route," and that they did not have the Indian trouble that "they have further west." With the connection at Baxter Springs, cattle could now be placed on Kansas City markets after a single night's train ride. The paper was confident that the town would see at least 100,000 head during the season.[23] Actually, their enthusiasm was not out of line, for an estimated 300,000 head were trailed from Texas that season.

The people of Baxter Springs were euphoric with the anticipation of being a major cattle-driving center. Town lots sold rapidly and at high prices. In 1871, twice as many cattle were driven north as the previous year, and Baxter Springs' rise to prominence as a cowtown occurred at the same time as the emergence of Abilene and Junction City to the far north and west. Charles Harger in his 1892 *Scribner's Magazine* article on "Cattle Trails of the Prairies" stated that "nearly a million cattle were driven north" in 1871. Six hundred thousand came to Abilene alone, while Baxter Springs and Junction City received half as many," he wrote.[24] Joseph Nimmo's report on Range and Ranch Cattle in 1885 is more realistic. His research indicated that some 600,000 were trailed north in 1871 — a more reasonable number.[25] It is

---

[23]*Cherokee Sentinel*, Baxter Springs, Kansas, June 4, 1870.
[24]Charles Harger, "Cattle Trails of the Prairies," *Scribner's Magazine*, 735.
[25]Joseph Nimmo, Ex. Doc. #267, from the Chief of the Bureau of Statistics to the House of Representatives, 48th Congress, 2nd Session., report on the range and ranch cattle traffic in the Western States and Territories, March 2, 1885. "The Texas Cattle Drive," chart, page 31.

clear by both reports, though, that Abilene, Baxter Springs, and Junction City shared the huge influx of cattle that year.[26]

Even though 1871 was a record year for numbers of cattle on the trail, many of those cattle were not sold. Numerous herds awaited on the prairies of central Kansas awaiting to be sold or shipped. Because the market was glutted, prices fell. Wet and cold weather weakened the herds, and the Texas Fever became rampant again.[27]

The prosperity Baxter Springs experienced from the cowboy culture and their herds was short lived. Because of Kansas quarantines, the trail moved farther west out in front of the deadlines leaving Baxter Springs stranded. The advantage of having a railroad also turned against it. Rail traffic pulled goods and people away from the developing community. The St. Louis & San Francisco Railroad built through the area and on west of Baxter Springs. The Missouri, Kansas & Texas Railway (KATY) laid its tracks just west of Baxter Springs, continued on to the Indian Territory line in 1870 and eventually extended on to Denison, Texas in 1872. The Atchison, Topeka & Santa Fe Railway built west from Topeka and arrived in Newton in July of 1871 and to Wichita in 1872 which gave those towns a direct connection with Chicago. If cattlemen wanted to ship their animals, they could do so now from other terminals beyond the quarantine line. Baxter Springs began to decline nearly as fast as it had grown.

There were three routes west of the original Old Shawnee Trail. Because of the border problems, mentioned above, the Sedalia route lasted for only one season (1866). In order to deliver herds that had been destined for Sedalia but could not get past the border guards, drovers established another route in 1866 to Fort Scott and Kansas City, flaunting the Kansas regulations which prohibited incoming southern cattle between April 1 and November 1. This was a branch of the Old (or East) Shawnee. (Refer to the map on inside cover.) A Middle Shawnee Trail was established in the following year, out in front of the quantine and settlements, in order to meet the demand in the northeast. These herds were delivered to Kansas City and St. Joseph, Missouri, and to Missouri river towns such as Brownville, Nebraska City, Plattsmouth, and Omaha. From each of the destinations, cattle were ferried across the Missouri River and sold to beef contractors and packing house agents, while others were driven into Iowa.

When the Kansas settlements continued to move west, the Middle Shawnee was abandoned. Another route was developed which became the West Shawnee Trail. Herds on this branch were trailed due north from Preston's Crossing on the Red River and splintered off of the old Shawnee trunk line at Boggy Depot on the Clear Boggy Creek, Indian Territory. From there the trail went to Stonewall in present-day Pontotoc County, and then north-northwest to the Old Sac and Fox Indian Agency at Stroud and on north to Cushing. The trail passed the Pawnee Indian Agency at

---

[26]At no other time in trail-driving history were there 600,000 Texas longhorns on the trail north. Neither Harger nor Nimmo mention that Ellsworth, which was in its first season as a cattle town, and Newton, which had received the Atchison, Topeka, and Santa Fe Railway in July, as well as Brookville and Salina, all shared in this influx of cattle herds.

[27]Harger, Ibid., 736.

Pawnee, continued on through Shidler, and crossed the Kansas state line. In Kansas the trail continued north-northwest through Burden and El Dorado, thence north to Diamond Springs. From Diamond Springs the trail continued north and east to White City and ended at Junction City, located on the Kansas Pacific Railroad.[28] If trail bosses preferred the old route to Fort Gibson on the Arkansas River, they could leave the East Shawnee Trail at that point and take an Arkansas River splinter route over to the new West Shawnee, joining it before entering Kansas. Some herds may have also been trailed from Junction City to Schuyler, Nebraska, another cow town and railhead.

Junction City, the terminus of the West Shawnee Trail, had been founded in 1858 and derived its name from the nearby junction of the Republican and Smoky Hill rivers. Three miles north at the rivers' junction sat Fort Riley. It had been established in 1853 as one of a string of forts to protect travelers using the Oregon-California and Santa Fe trails. The town received the Union Pacific Railroad, Eastern Division in 1866. It would not be until the following year that the rails would be completed to Abilene, twenty five miles to the west.

Therefore, in 1867, three railheads were receiving Texas cattle herds. Baxter Springs on the Old (East) Shawnee Trail received a few hundred, for the *Cherokee Sentinel* reported only 300 head arrived in June with even fewer the rest of the season. Junction City on the West Shawnee Trail, a route farther west, however, experienced more cattle. On July 20, 1867, the *Junction City Weekly* printed:

> There are some five thousand head of cattle within twenty miles of town, waiting for buyers from the east. The stock corrall [sic], five miles above town, we understand is being built for their shipment.... We heard a man say that the country is lined with them from this place south, and that there will be fully twenty thousand drovers [cattle] here this season.[29]

The rail yards at Abilene opened in September of 1867, and according to Joseph McCoy, that new railhead received in September and October approximately 20,000 head. Of the estimated 45,000 cattle that headed north in 1867,[30] Junction City on the West Shawnee Trail and Abilene on the new Chisholm Trail shared similiar numbers of cattle while a fewer number ended up at Baxter Springs.

The East Shawnee Trail route was revived when Baxter Springs' rails arrived in 1870, but its cattle trail business lasted only through 1872. The West Shawnee Trail to Junction City continued to be used alongside the Chisholm Trail to Abilene until

---

[28]Gaylynn Childs, "Historama," in the "Museum Musings," *Junction City Union*, July 8, 1996. "Cattle Trail That Ended Here Will Be Honorded With Oklahoma Marker," *Junction City Union*, Junction City, Kansas, June 19, 1970.

[29]Reprint of a July 20, 1867 article from *Junction City Weekly* Union in a June, 1961 Junction City Union issue.

[30]The estimated number of 45,000 head driven north in 1867 will be discussed in Chapter IV.

1872. Abilene had the bulk of the cattle trade between 1868 and 1871, (see Chapter IV), but Junction City continued to be used. When the Atchison, Topeka, & Santa Fe reached Newton in 1871 and Wichita in 1872, splinter routes from off of the West Shawnee Trail were established to these points. North of Fort Gibson, the Arkansas River Branch also connected to the West Shawnee and Chisholm trails. If cattle herds were driven to Baxter Springs in 1871 and 1872 and not sold or shipped, the drovers could then branch off to Newton or Wichita on the Santa Fe Railway. Even though these branches were lightly used compared to the newer Chisholm Trail, the West Shawnee Trail paralleled the Chisholm until the eastern Kansas railheads were quarantined out altogether in 1875.

> *As Texans strung out along these trails, the most superb of all the Great Plains Indians swarmed upon their flanks, and through the late sixties and seventies the toll that the Comanche levied was frightful. The greatest danger, as Goodnight observed, was the frontier itself. Once away from the settlements, the hazards were less, but for a few years — from 1865 until 1875 — every man who drove was in danger of losing his cattle and having his "hair lifted" besides. Nevertheless they drove, some recklessly, others cautiously, and month by month the Goodnight and Loving Trail broadened and deepened.*

J. Evetts Haley
Charles Goodnight, Cowman and Plainsman, pg. 186.

CHAPTER III

The Goodnight Trail System, 1866-1885

Charles Goodnight *(1836-1929) blazed more cattle trails than any other cattleman and became a foremost frontier breeder of livestock. Goodnight's biographer, J. Evetts Haley, who interviewed the cowboy in his old age, wrote: "For ninety years his iron will had ridden hard upon his sturdy frame. Nor would he quit. When his wide-bowed legs could no longer drive his body about the corrals from early day to late at night, he restlessly plaited rawhide ropes and bull-whips, while his mind flew faster than his hands as he outlined work, years in advance, which he felt sure there was still time to do."*

Photo courtesy of The Haley Memorial Library and History Center, Midland, Texas.

J. Evetts Haley, Charles Goodnight, page ix.

Charles Goodnight was not the first cowboy to trail a herd of cattle west into New Mexico Territory to Fort Sumner and on north into Colorado, but he and his partner, Oliver Loving, blazed a repetitive trail, which was to be followed by other trail drivers. History records this trail from Texas into Colorado simply as the "Goodnight and Loving Trail." The authors here, however, relate what happened after Oliver Loving was killed in 1867 and the expansion of the trail system by Charles Goodnight. The various branches of this trail system plus Goodnight's Palo Duro Trail in the Texas Panhandle represent Goodnight's trail activity up until 1885. Therefore, we choose to not use the term, "Goodnight and Loving Trail," but, instead, to label this entire system as the "Goodnight Trail System." In looking at the entire scope of the trail-driving industry and in particular the Western Cattle Trail System, one Goodnight route in Colorado also becomes important later on — in the last decade of trail-driving (Part III). Refer to the map on the inside cover.

Charles Goodnight and Oliver Loving are credited as being the first to blaze a trail from Texas to Fort Sumner in New Mexico Territory and on into Colorado in 1866. Instead of using the established Shawnee Trail into Sedalia, Missouri after the war, Goodnight decided to venture west and north to sell his cattle. In a recently published research essay, however, Morgan Nelson reveals the activities of James Patterson, gives the reader some pre-1866 background, and claims that Charles Goodnight and Oliver Loving were simply following the path, and success, of Patterson, who had been trailing cattle from Texas to Fort Sumner during the war.

Patterson's two brothers had settled on a cattle ranch in Palo Pinto County, Texas, the same county where Goodnight was living. James Patterson had gone to New Mexico Territory about 1859 or 1860 and worked in and around Fort Stanton and, later, Fort Sumner supplying them with wood, hay, and other needs. During the war, he became their beef contractor. He joined forces in 1864 with Thomas Roberts, a former captain of the California Volunteers, and they devised a plan to supply beef to the military in New Mexico Territory. To fulfill these contracts, Patterson, naturally, went to Texas to acquire the cattle. He formed a partnership with a rancher, William C. Franks, to drive cattle across the plains to New Mexico Territory. Patterson and Franks had an exclusive contract for Fort Sumner from September 1, 1865 to August 31, 1866. Therefore, in 1865 and 1866, the two made several drives to and from Texas. Also, according Morgan Nelson, John Chisum worked with Patterson in Texas in rounding up cattle for the contracts, and younger brother Pittser Chisum went to work for James and Tom Patterson, helping to drive and deliver beeves to Fort Sumner.[1]

---

[1]According to Morgan Nelson, "In September of 1864, there is evidence that James Patterson was in Confederate Texas buying cattle for the Union Forces in New Mexico…. John Chisum, a Confederate beef contractor, was in business contracting with James Patterson, a Union beef contractor."…"this was still wartime and there were good reasons why neither side would wish to publicize this trade: the South needed the money, if they even knew about it, and the North needed the cattle." (Morgan Nelson, "First Among the First," James Patterson, 1833-1892, *Wild West History Association Journal*, Vol. II, No. 5, Oct. 2009, 4)

At the same time, George T. Reynolds was also driving cattle to New Mexico Territory. Reynolds, S.I. Huff, and W. R. St. John started out on October 16, 1865, with about eighty beef steers. Reynolds had come to Palo Pinto County, Texas with his family in 1859, joined the Confederate Army at the age of seventeen, and was discharged in 1863 because of illness. By 1865, he called the Clear Fork valley of the Brazos River his home and was ready to "broaden his range," and decided to trail some Reynolds steers to Old Mexico. The three drovers discovered, however, upon reaching the Concho, that steers were not selling well in Old Mexico, so they changed course and headed for New Mexico Territory. They followed the Concho River to Horsehead Crossing on the Pecos and then trailed north to Fort Sumner. From there they drove west and sold their steers near the head of the Rio Pecos (present-day Santa Fe, New Mexico).[2]

Fort Sumner needed beef because it had been directed by Congress in 1862 to oversee the relocation of the Navajo and the Mescalero Apaches. In 1863, soon after the construction of the army post at the small trading village, approximately 9000 Navajo and Mescaleros were forced to relocate from their lands in Arizona and New Mexico. The reservation designated for the Indians was the Bosque Redondo Reservation, and it became the responsibility of the army to feed the thousands of dispossessed Indians.[3] Any cattle herds that could be driven to the fort were purchased by the agent. Thus, to aid their contractor, James Patterson, Captain William McCleave issued an order in July of 1865 to Company I, New Mexico Volunteer Cavalry and a detachment of privates to march to Emigrant Crossing[4] on the Pecos in Texas to meet a herd of cattle being driven to the fort. There at the crossing, the detail was to relieve a military escort coming from a Texas post.[5]

Texas did not surrender at the end of the Civil War until June of 1865. At war's end, Texas ranchers had few cattle under their control. The cattle were neglected and owners suffered great losses because the Confederate authorities had taken many of them; Indians had raided the herds; and cattle thieves had stolen many. As noted earlier, in the spring of 1866, just as soon as cattle could be gathered and branded, Texas cattlemen again looked to the familiar Shawnee Trail to deliver cattle into Missouri and Kansas and beyond. However, the young Texas cattleman, Charles Goodnight, was aware of the problems on the Shawnee Trail and the issues with the Missouri farmers. Also, because of the continued hassle with Indians, Goodnight wondered if another location for his cattle should be sought. He must have seen the

---

[2]Frances Mayhugh Holden, *Lambshead Before Interwoven, A Texas Range Chronicle, 1848-1878*, 95-96. The Reynolds Cattle Company (Long X) or the Reynolds brothers, George T., William D., and Ben continued to drive cattle into New Mexico and Colorado territories. In Texas, "the brothers bought land in Shackleford, Throckmorton and Haskell counties and before many years they had under control more than 100,000 acres, across which grazed 20,000 head of cattle." (C. L. Douglas, *Cattle Kings of Texas*, 189)
[3]Darla Sue Dollman, "History of Fort Sumner, New Mexico," http://www.suite101 [accessed Dec. 9, 2010]
[4]Emigrant Crossing was a fordable spot on the Pecos river and on the Butterfield Overland Mail Route. It was some fifty-five miles farther up stream from Horsehead Crossing.
[5]Morgan Nelson, Ibid.

success of Patterson and Franks and George T. Reynolds, who trailed cattle from his county during the war, so he reasoned that going west could be a profitable venture for him as well. Perhaps, Goodnight even knew that the exclusive military contract with Patterson was to end in August of 1866. (In an interview in 1909 with Emanuel Dubbs, Goodnight said that after the war his "affairs were in a worse shape than ever," and he was "determined to carry what cattle I had left elsewhere. I now turned my attention to New Mexico as a field offering fair advantages...").[6]

Goodnight had come to Texas from Illinois as a boy of ten with his family in 1846, just as Texas was becoming a state. By the time he was twenty he was working as a cowboy, served with the local militia, and had joined the Texas Rangers. During the war, he was a scout with the Rangers, assigned to protect the families and property in northwest Texas of those who had gone off to war. The ambitious thirty-year-old, who had begun outfitting for his first drive from his Elm Creek range,[7] knew that "the whole of Texas would start north for market" over the route that had been used before the war and decided that he should go west instead — for two reasons. First, "the mining region would have more or less money, and second, in that region there was good cattle country, so if I could not sell I could hold."[8] Gold had been discovered in the Pike's Peak area of western Kansas Territory almost a decade before, and the mining activities continued with the establishment of Colorado Territory in 1861. The Fifty-Niners were still hanging on, and Goodnight planned to head to the Colorado mining region.

The route west, however, was hazardous. Patterson had been a military contractor and had army excorts to help him to get his herds through. Goodnight would not have that advantage. Texans lived among Indians, and early settlers were in uncomfortable proximity to tribes that felt threatened with the presence of white settlers and the U.S. Army. The Comanches and Kiowas claimed the Staked Plains and held west Texas and the plains region that stretched into Kansas. For generations the area had been their hunting grounds which held vast herds of buffalo. These Indians objected to incoming cattle herds in contrast to the Five Civilized Tribes in eastern Indian Territory who permitted use of the Shawnee Trail through their lands. Also the miles and miles of migrating buffalo herds could be a hindrance to trailing cattle herds on the plains. In 1866, the encroachment of the white man into Indian civilization had become even more intrusive, and retaliation of the Native Tribes became routine.

To skirt around the Comanches grounds and to reach New Mexico Territory, Goodnight decided to take a wide trek southwest from Fort Belknap, cross the waterless semi-desert west from the Concho River to the Pecos River and then north

---

[6]Emanuel Dubbs, "Charles Goodnight," *Kansas Cowboy*, July-August, 2009, 23.

[7]Goodnight's Elm Creek ranch was located in Palo Pinto County, Texas, west of Fort Belknap.

[8]J. Evetts Haley, *Charles Goodnight, Cowman and Plainsman*, 121. Haley interviewed Goodnight in his old age at his ranch house numerous times; thus, records the old cowboy's own words. Haley's book, however, is not only about the life of the cattleman but about his personality, beliefs, and inner feelings. Goodnight died at the age of ninety-three in 1929. Haley's book was published in 1936.

up the Pecos to Fort Sumner. It was twice as long as a direct route, but safer. Just as drovers on the Shawnee Trail, in this early period, were shifting their route through eastern Indian Territory and going into Missouri and eastern Kansas, Charles Goodnight sought to avoid Indian hunting lands farther west.

Goodnight planned to use existing trails. He would use a portion of the old southern Butterfield Overland Mail route[9], which had run from Fort Belknap to the Horsehead Crossing on the Pecos. He would then traverse the well-used river route north to Fort Sumner. This route north up the Pecos had been used in the early days by Indians and the Spanish, and later by the Army and James Patterson. Goodnight originally planned to make the trip with a Mr. Mosely, but at the last minute, Mosely changed his plans because "the dangers of the trip proved too great." Even though the path had been used before, there were still many unknowns for the young cowboy, and he needed a seasoned trailsman. Therefore, nearing the end of his preparations, Goodnight hurried to Weatherford to buy more supplies and visited Oliver Loving's camp, where the older gentleman was working his cattle. Goodnight explained to the experienced cowhand his plans to go west with his cattle, and Loving decided to join him. Goodnight later commented in his memoirs that it was "the most desirable thing of my life." The two joined their herds twenty-five miles southwest of Fort Belknap and on June 6, 1866, started out with 2,000 head of longhorns and an outfit of fourteen men. Loving took charge of the drive while Goodnight scouted ahead, and they pointed westward.[10]

The herd was driven over the old Butterfield Overland Mail route, after which it passed Camp Cooper, thence to Fort Phantom Hill and then through Buffalo Gap. They passed Fort Chadbourne, drove south and west to cross the North Concho River which was about twenty miles upstream from where San Angelo would later be built. There they continued up the Middle Concho where they stopped to rest and prepare for crossing the Staked Plains, an arid expanse of land that stretched eighty or more miles. Loving had warned Goodnight about it during in their initial visit.

---

[9]The southern Butterfield Overland Mail route operated a biweekly stage service from September 15, 1858, until March 1, 1861. The entire route of 2,795 miles ran from Tipton, Missouri to San Francisco. The contract was awarded to John Butterfield who used a system of horse-drawn conveyances to transport mail and passengers. Stage stations were set up approximately every twenty to twenty-five miles. The portion that Goodnight and others used was from Fort Belknap to Horsehead Crossing on the Pecos River. (Rupert N. Richardson, "Butterfield Overland Mail," *Handbook of Texas Online*, www.tshaonline.org [accessed Nov. 26, 2010])

[10]Haley, Ibid, 127.
Oliver Loving was 54 years of age in 1866. Goodnight described him as "a man of religious instincts and one of the coolest and bravest men I have ever known, but devoid of caution." According the Goodnight, Oliver Loving drove the first herd out of northwest Texas in 1858, leaving Palo Pinto and Jack counties, crossing the Red River in the neighborhood of Red River Crossing, striking the Arkansas River near old Fort Zarah (Great Bend, Kansas) and then up the Arkansas to just above where Pueblo, Colorado now stands. Here he wintered and the following spring drove the herd to the Platte River near Denver where "he peddled them out." Loving delivered beef to the Confederacy during the War and also trailed cattle to the Mississippi River. Also: (Charles Goodnight, "The Killing of Oliver Loving," in Hunter, *The Trail Drivers of Texas*, 904. and Charles Goodnight, "More About the Chisholm Trail," in Hunter, 952.)

Goodnight later remarked that it was "the most severe drive on all the Texas trails."[11] An average day's drive was twelve to fifteen miles, but Goodnight knew they would have to push the longhorns hard and try to get across the Plains in three days. There would be no water. Following the old ruts of the mail route, the outfit pushed the cattle forward. After the first night, Goodnight and Loving agreed that to stop for camp was not working. The cattle milled all night and bawled for water, so for the next three days cowboys and cattle went without rest and continued to push day and night toward the Pecos. Evetts Haley described how the cattle suffered as told to him by Goodnight:

> Their ribs stood out like the bars of a grill, their flanks were drawn gaunt, their tongues lolled far from their mouths, sometimes sweeping in the alkali dust, and their eyes sunk in their sockets with approaching death.[12]

At two o'clock in the morning of the fourth day, they reached the Castle Mountains and passed through Castle Gap. Twelve miles beyond the mile-long opening in the mountains was Horsehead Crossing on the Pecos River.[13] When the cattle smelled water, there was no holding them back. Cattle poured over the Pecos' steep banks; some drowning while others became hopelessly mired in quicksand. Goodnight and Loving lost over 300 head to the desert and the river.

Goodnight and Loving crossed to the west side of the Pecos at Pope's Crossing, just below the New Mexico Territory line, and then crossed back to the east side of the river just above present-day Carlsbad in order to place the river between themselves and the Mescalero Apaches. The route up the Pecos River was treacherous. Goodnight hated the river. He called it the "the graveyard of the cowman's hopes." The natural wildlife seemed to have the same sentiment, for Goodnight noted that seldom did he see a living thing — no wolves or birds. There were rattlesnakes by the hundreds, however. Jack Potter, who was a veteran of eastern New Mexico Territory and a trail driver, later declared that:

---

[11]Haley, Ibid, 129. Also known as Llano Estacado, the Staked Plains is one of the largest mesas or tablelands on the North American continent.

[12]Haley, Ibid, 131.

[13]The Pecos River was a vicious narrow and meandering river whose waters flowed from the mountains of northern New Mexico and continued, twisting and turning, into the canyons of southern Texas. Horsehead Crossing was one of the few fordable points on the Pecos River and the most noted for hundreds of miles. The crossing sat on a main Indian trail and supposedly got its name from the Indian horses who drank too much of the Pecos' briney water and died. Also because of its steep, muddy banks and quicksand, many animals became mired and died. The crossing became "littered with horse, cattle, and mule skeletons." In the 1850s a stage station had been established about a quarter mile above the crossing. The trail that led north from the crossing was called "The Horsehead Trail." (Glenn Justice, "Horsehead Crossing," *Handbook of Texas* Online. www.tshaonline [accessed Nov. 22, 2010] (Haley, Ibid., 129-134)

this trail up the river the worst driven by Texas cowmen. [I] never saw a herd come up the Goodnight Trail but that its men were afoot. Steep, narrow trails led to the water, down which cattle slid and drank while standing on their heads. If they stepped in a little too far, the quicksands pulled them under, and after drinking they often had to back up the trail.[14]

The herd trailed by Comanche Springs, Bosque Grande, and into Fort Sumner. Goodnight and Loving arrived at Fort Sumner in late June of 1866, and sold the majority of their cattle to "the general contractor, named Roberts, and the sub-contractors, Jim and Tom Patterson."

The contractor wanted only the two-year olds, three-year olds and up, and paid eight cents a pound on foot. Goodnight and Loving were elated at the good price they received for their steers but were left with seven to eight hundred head of cows and calves. After resting for a few days on Las Carretas Creek, the two decided that Loving should continue north into Colorado with the outfit and remaining herd while Goodnight returned to Texas to bring in another herd before winter.[15]

Oliver Loving and his outfit drove by Las Vegas, crossed the Raton Range, skirted the base of the Rockies, crossing the Arkansas River near Pueblo, and arrived in the Denver vicinity, where he sold the remaining stock cattle to John W. Iliff, a well-known rancher.[16] This portion of the trail from Fort Sumner to Denver became known as the Loving Trail.

Goodnight, along with three cowboy companions and as many pack mules and with some twelve thousand dollars in gold, headed back to Texas, a 700-mile saddle trip.[17] They rode by night and lay up out of sight during the day in order to avoid Indians in the area. After seventeen days, Goodnight was back in Weatherford starting to prepare for his return trip.

---

[14]In a letter to J. Evetts Haley on August 26, 1932, in Haley, Ibid., 135. Note that in later years, Potter referred to the trail as the "Goodnight Trail," not the Goodnight-Loving Trail.

[15]Nelson, Ibid, 5 and Haley, Ibid, 137-138.

[16]John Iliff was the king of Colorado cattlemen, according to the *Rocky Mountain News* in Denver. He arrived in Colorado Territory from Ohio during the gold rush days of 1859 at the age of 28. Seeing that gold mining was a long shot, Iliff went into the general store business exchanging goods for beef that he fattened on the open range. In 1868, he contracted to supply beef to the Union Pacific Railroad construction crews and bought 800 longhorns from Charles Goodnight. By 1870s he owned as many as 35,000 head and was supplying other railroad crews and Indian reservations. By 1878, Iliff owned a ranching empire of more than 15,000 acres and controlled 150 miles of water frontage that gave him control of range land estimated at 650,000 acres. Every season he bought thousands of Texas cattle. He died in 1878 at the age of 47. (Tom Noel, "Iliff crafted kingdom from cattle, Ohioan struck gold by buying up land, selling livestock," *Rocky Mountain News*, March 1, 2008, online: www.rockymountainnews.com [accessed June 14, 2009])

[17]Different sources site a different amount of money carried back to Texas by Goodnight. C. L. Douglas (*Cattle Kings of Texas*) says "about $10,000, in gold and silver coins" p. 136; Haley wrote, "some twelve thousand dollars in gold," p. 140, and Emanuel Dubbs, (in *Kansas Cowboy*) wrote, "a mule bearing six thousand dollars in gold."

Loving and Goodnight came together again in late 1866 at a camp at Bosque Grande, approximately forty miles south of Fort Sumner. They fashioned dugouts into the bluffs on the east side of the Pecos River and settled in for the winter. Here they made a pact between them to form a partnership for any future dealings with the herds. From their camp, they made monthly deliveries to Fort Sumner.[18]

By the spring of 1867, news of Goodnight and Loving's success had spread and other cattlemen were willing to face the hazards of driving a herd to New Mexico Territory. New beef contracts had been let at Fort Sumner, and a man by the name of Andy Adams (not the writer) had outbid the Pattersons. To fulfill his agreement at two and a half cents a pound on foot, Adams went to Texas and contracted for several thousand head from J. D. Hoy. Hoy gathered three herds, sending out two ahead of him, bossed by Lew Soyer and George Fowler, with plans that he would follow with the third herd.

By this time, however, the Comanches had also discovered the route that had been used by Patterson, Franks, Loving, and Goodnight. The Indians waylaid the Soyer and Fowler herds, stealing the cattle and causing the cowboys to run for cover in a nearby pecan grove. When the third herd reached Castle Gap, under the guidance of Hoy, it was also attacked by Indians who captured the herd and shot and wounded three of Hoy's cowboys. The outfit took refuge in an abandoned ruins of a Butterfield stage station.[19]

Because of this mishap, Adams was not able to fulfill his contract to the government agent at Fort Sumner. However, it turned out to be an opportunity for Loving and Goodnight. Knowing that their cattle could be sold to a fort contractor, they again gathered a herd for the trail in the spring of 1867. Loving acquired cattle in Palo Pinto Country, and Goodnight purchased cattle from the area surrounding his ranch.[20]

Like Hoy, Loving and Goodnight also had problems on the drive. Just beyond the settlements on the Clear Fork and near Camp Cooper, Indians attacked the combined herd during the night and stampeded the cattle.[21] After gathering the herd, they moved out into the valley where they expected and prepared for another attack. The Indians attacked again the following day. While Goodnight was attempting to protect the horse herd, the cattle herd was scattered and stampeded again. After a day of rounding up the herd, the drivers drove the cattle through the night, hoping to move out of reach of the Indians. It rained and stormed, with lightning and thunder, and the herd again stampeded.

---

[18]Haley, Ibid, 138-148.

[19]Mexican bandits were also a threat to cattlemen. Early in 1867, Goodnight with the help of Fort Sumner soldiers had to recover six mules and saddle horses that were rustled from him. For complete stories and Goodnight's recollections, read Haley's *Charles Goodnight*, 148-155.

[20]Haley, Ibid, 162.

[21]Camp Cooper on the Clear Fork in Shackelford County was ten miles above Camp Wilson (Fort Griffin) that would be established in a few months on July 31, 1867. Goodnight was shot at while sleeping on a buffalo hide. The arrow, however, was deflected by the hide and saved the life of Goodnight. (Dubbs interview, ibid.)

The next morning, it was estimated that over 300 longhorns had been lost or stolen. The owners knew that they and their drovers could not recapture the cattle held by the Indians. They continued on for another one hundred miles.

Oliver Loving became anxious and insisted on going ahead to Santa Fe to secure the beef contract. It was late July, and the contracts were to be let early in August. Since there were other herds on the trail that might beat them to a profitable contract, he suggested to Goodnight that he be present at the bidding and close a deal while Goodnight and the outfit moved up the Pecos. Goodnight protested about his partner striking out on his own because of the danger, but Loving would not be dissuaded and left with a one-armed man named J. M. Wilson, promising to travel only at night and to keep out of sight. About three days out, the Comanches found the pair, surrounded them, and held them in a ravine. Loving was shot, the bullet shattering his wrist and penetrating his side. He convinced Wilson to try to escape and to go back to the herd for help. The one-armed cowboy heroically sneaked past the Indian lookouts and worked his way back to Goodnight, taking over three days. Goodnight, with five other cowboys, immediately set out to find Loving. They were unsuccessful. He assumed Loving had been taken and killed or had taken his own life.

Loving, however, was eventually found alive. He had swum down the Pecos during a dark night to the trail junction in hopes of being found. He was discovered by some Mexicans and taken to Fort Sumner where he seemed to be recovering. Then gangrene set in, and his arm had to be amputated. Complications followed. Oliver Loving asked his partner to promise to continue the partnership until his share of the debt was paid and regreted "to have to be laid away in a foreign country." Loving died on September 25, 1867. Several months later Charles Goodnight exhumed his partner's body at Fort Sumner, had it encased in a tin casket, loaded it onto a wagon, and returned his partner to his home in Weatherford, Texas. W. D. Reynolds, the younger brother of George T., who had taken a herd out to Fort Sumner in 1865, worked with Goodnight and was in the funeral cavalcade formed to go back to Texas.[22]

Another cattleman, who followed closely behind Loving and Goodnight's lead was John Chisum. Wanting to move farther west where there was more elbow room and fewer neighbors, Chisum followed his brother's suggestion and moved to the Pecos in New Mexico Territory. Pittser Chisum had praised the range country along the Pecos, and so John trailed nine hundred steers to New Mexico Territory in the spring of 1867. He liked what he saw and knew that there was a ready market nearby at Fort Sumner. Chisum established his herd at Bosque Grande and over the next few months made arrangements to furnish cattle to James Patterson. A year later, in 1868, Patterson moved farther south and sold his squatter's rights to Chisum at Bosque Grande.

---

[22]Haley relates the story directly from his interviews with Charles Goodnight in Chapter X, "The Pecos — 'Graveyard of the Cowman's Hopes,' in *Charles Goodnight*, 162-184. A like incident is fictionalized in the novel and movie "Lonesome Dove" by Larry McMurtry when Captain W. F. Call returns the body of his long-time friend and partner, Augustus, traveling from Miles City, Montana to Lonesome Dove, Texas.

Patterson moved farther south because the plan to relocate the Navajos and Mescalero Apache and create the Fort Sumner post had been a failure. The government agents at Bosque Redondo had envisioned a new Indian reservation west of Indian Territory where the Navajos and Mescaleros could be farmers, go to school, and learn Christianity. But the Navajos and Mescalero Apaches were bitter enemies, and the reservation site contained poor water and minimal firewood. Shortly after the establishment of the fort and reservation, many of the Apache eluded the military guards and left the compound. Finally, the government admitted that the plan was not working and in June of 1868 allowed the remaining Indians to return home.[23]

THE GOODNIGHT TRAIL OF 1868:

The Fort Sumner Indian contracts ceased because, in a treaty of 1868, the Navajos were returned to their old country in northwestern New Mexico Territory and northeast Arizona Territory, and the fort was no longer obligated to provide for them.[24] Goodnight was now turning his attention to other markets — the delivery of cattle to ranchmen and other contractors on the Colorado Plains and farther north into Wyoming around Cheyenne.

Goodnight had also discovered a canyon in southern Colorado that he considered "beautiful cow country" during his late fall drive of 1867. The Apishapa Canyon was one of the many that had been formed by the streams that flowed from the Raton Mountain Range through the plateaus to the Arkansas River valley. It was forty miles northeast of Trinidad and seemed to Goodnight to be ideal for a cattle ranch. The canyon was twenty miles long, not very deep, lined with box elders, and hosted a stream called Apishapa. Its name, from the Ute, meant "stinking water" because of the stench of the decaying leaves. To the Texan Goodnight, it was to be his swing station (ranch)[25] on the Goodnight Trail. A handful of cowboys, including John Rumans, a spunky independent cowhand, were directed to build a cabin, and, in the future, they would tend the herds brought up the trail.

Goodnight had in the back of his mind to change the trail route. The earlier trail, that Loving and Goodnight used, had gone through Las Vegas, up the Santa Fe Trail to Raton Pass, and then around the base of the Rockies by Trinidad and Pueblo to Denver. It was a long roundabout way to reach Denver, and besides, Uncle Dick Wootton had irritated Goodnight during his 1867 drive through Raton Pass. Wootton had applied for permission to build a toll road from New Mexico Territory and Colorado Territory through the pass in the mountains that divided the two

---

[23] "Fort Sumner — Pride of the Pecos," Legends of America Online, http://www.legendsofamerica.com [accessed Dec. 10, 2010]

[24] The fort was closed in the fall of 1868. On June 13, 1870, the building, stables, and fifty sections of the Fort Sumner reservation were sold at auction. (Haley, ibid, 205)

[25] A swing station (ranch) is one where herds on the trail could be dropped off to be watered and rested, a fresh remuda acquired, repairs made, sore-footed cattle left, and additional animals added to the herd before continuing north.

the western cattle trail | 1874-1897

territories. His request was granted, and in the spring of 1866, he moved from Pueblo, built a twenty-seven mile long road and proceeded to charge a toll to all who used the passage. He also maintained a thriving roadhouse at the station. Wootton's price was ten cents per animal, whether one cow or a herd of three thousand. Goodnight protested the unfair rate and swore to Wootton that "if the toll was not reduced, he would find another pass and blaze another trail." Wootton had laughed at him.[26] Settlements along the eastern slope of the Rocky Mountains were also spreading out and putting pressure on the cattle drives. Also fear of the Texas Fever caused settlers to express opposition to the drives.

In 1868, Goodnight had his and Loving's cattle located in three locations: on his Texas ranch southwest of Fort Belknap; on the partnership ranch at Bosque Grande in New Mexico Territory; and on the newly established ranch in Apishapa Canyon in Colorado Territory. As the result of the 1867 drives, Goodnight was in debt, not only did he have his own losses, but also the debts of his late partner that he was obligated to pay. A new market in the north had to be established. During 1868, Goodnight blazed a new route, one that was fifty to sixty miles east of the earlier trail. He asked Jim Loving, son of Oliver Loving, to prepare the remaining herd in Weatherford, Texas and drive it to Bosque Grande. Goodnight made a contract with John Wesley Iliff to deliver his Apishapa Ranch cattle to both Cheyenne and even farther north up to the Chugwater. Goodnight had been buying cattle from John Chisum, whose cow camp was downriver from Fort Sumner; Chisum was willing to sell his imported cattle from Texas on a fifty-fifty basis, allowing Goodnight a dollar extra per animal for his risks on the trail.

During the next two seasons, as soon as Goodnight had one herd on the trail, his cowboys had another prepared for trailing north. Starting from the partnership ranch at Bosque Grande, Goodnight cut out the original detours and blazed the new trail toward Cheyenne as straight north as terrain, water, and grass would allow. He left the river north of Fort Sumner and pointed to Alamogordo Creek, then drove across the plains by the Juan Dios and Cuervito creeks. The herd followed the Cuervito to Cuervo and then crossed the Canadian about twenty miles west of Fort Bascom.[27] From the fort, Goodnight's herds passed just west of Capulin, dropped down to the Cimarron Seco, and then turned up the South Trinchera to cross the mountains through Trinchera Pass. This pass, a full two days east of Wootton's toll road, had easier grades and was shorter. When Wootton realized that the Texas and New Mexico Territory cattle herds were following Goodnight's lead, he offered

---

[26]Haley, Ibid, 199-200.

[27]Fort Bascom was on the south bank of the Canadian River slightly west of the Texas border. It had been built in 1863 as one of a series of forts to control the Comanches and Kiowas who frequented the Red and Canadian River region. The troops were also there to protect the Goodnight-Loving Trail and the Santa Fe Trail. It was short lived. In 1870, the poorly constructed post was abandoned before it was finished, and its troops were transferred to Fort Union. (National Park Service Online: "Soldier and Brave" Survey of Historic Sites and Buildings, Fort Bascom, New Mexico, www.nps.gov. [accessed Dec. 18, 2010])

Trinchera Pass marker
Thousands of Texas Longhorns were trailed thorugh this area in 1868-1875 over the Trinchera Pass Route pioneered by Charles Goodnight to avoid Raton Pass toll fees.

Location: Between the Trinchera turn-off and San Isidro Creek on the north side of Highway 160, Las Animas County, Colorado coordinates are 37 degrees 11.094' - 104 degrees 8.727'

Authors' commentary
This stone monument was erected in 1976 by Richard and Willard Loudon, Larry Gilstrap, and Eldridge and John Hudson. The picture was taken after vandals broke the stone. Today only the base of the monument remains. The engraved marker is gone.

Information obtained from John Hudson, La Veta Colorado, and Brad Doherty, Branson, Colorado

Goodnight free passage if he would turn back to the original trail. It was too late, however, and Goodnight had the last laugh.[28]

From Trinchera Pass, the new trail continued north out of the mountains, turned northwest to Picketwire Creek, past the Apishapa Canyon, and then headed straight north to Cheyenne.

GOODNIGHT TRAIL AFTER 1868:

In 1869, after passing through Trinchera Pass, Goodnight again moved his route farther east. This route distanced the herds even more from the ever encroaching settlements along the east slope of the Rocky Mountains. The trail crossed the Purgatoire River and continued as straight north as the terrain would allow to the Iliff Ranch on the South Platte River.

Opposition to Texas herds because of the Fever persisted in eastern Colorado. Experience revealed that cattle over-wintered in an area where the temperatures fell below freezing were free of the dreaded fever, and many of the Texans (like Goodnight and Chisum) drove cattle into the Fort Sumner area and wintered them there before trailing them north the following spring. In Colorado Territory, the issue became which herds had been over-wintered and which ones were not? It was impossible to establish a procedure to make that determination.

---

[28]Haley, Ibid., 210

Another complaint by local ranchers was the impact of Texas cattle on the price of cattle in the region. These ranchers considered the longhorn as a cheaper grade of cattle, and Texans were flooding the market with them. Ranchers with their "American" cattle could not compete and according to a local paper, "It caused many of our ranchmen to dispose of their American cattle and invest in the Texas [cattle] in order to compete with the prices of Texas stock."[29]

Colorado Territory prohibited the "introduction of Texas stock," but the impossibility of proving which herds had been wintered created a confusing law. Complicating the situation, merchants, bankers, and livestock dealers benefited from the incoming cattle herds, consequently, the law was not enforced. When cattle herds were driven through settled districts in Colorado Territory, local ranchmen (as in Missouri) on occasion took the law into their own hands to divert or drive the herds away. Some local owners met Texas drovers with armed force. One of Goodnight's hands, John Rumans, related that fifteen or twenty men stopped them at one drive at the Arkansas River and tried to prevent them from crossing the river. At another time, on the divide east of Denver, settlers shot into one of Goodnight's herds, stampeding it. The Colorado Cattle Association, organized in Boulder, Arapahoe, El Paso, and Fremont counties, tried to keep Texas stock away from settlements in order to protect the American cattle. The association demanded that cattlemen drive their herds outside of the line of settlements or, as one news article stated:

> ...they will encounter serious difficulties; because there are at least fifteen hundred men who have pledged themselves that no herds of Texas cattle shall pass over the main thoroughfare between the Arkansas and Platte Rivers, unless they have been at least one year within the limits of the Territory.[30]

The association, in addition, quoted the Colorado quarantine law as their legal defense. It forbade the importation of "any Texas cattle, for any purpose whatever." In the fall of 1870, however, the federal judge of the Second District ruled that the quarantine law was unconstitutional and void. Local newspapers made fun of the decision because the law in question had never been enforced in the Territory to begin with and had already been repealed by the last state legislature.[31]

Goodnight had carried his late partner's debt and partnership for two years after Oliver's death. He paid Loving's family half of his earnings for that two year period. His promise to his old partner was fulfilled, and from then on Goodnight was on his own.[32]

By 1870, this Goodnight Trail — the third trail he had created — was well

---

[29]"When stockmen had a better grade of cattle, [they] distinguished from the Texas breed by the term 'American.'" (Haley, Ibid, 226)

[30]*The Colorado Chieftain*, April 15, 22, and 29, 1869 (Haley, Ibid, 228)

[31]*The Colorado Chieftain*, Oct. 27, Nov. 3, 1870; *Dallas Herald*, Dec. 3, 1870. (Haley, op cit)

[32]According to Haley, Goodnight paid the family one half of seventy-two thousand dollars. (Haley, Ibid, 216)

established and had become dominant. Cattlemen who drove herds northward along the eastern edge of the Rockies followed Goodnight's path to a cattle kingdom that was developing on the northern plains at the upper end of the trail.

THE 1875 NEW GOODNIGHT TRAIL:

Because of continuing pressures from farmers and local ranchmen in Colorado Territory, Goodnight moved his northern outlet once again. The "new trail," as it became known, was the fourth trail Goodnight blazed. It left Alamogordo Creek, north of the old Fort Sumner, and followed the Goodnight Trail of 1868 to Cuervo Creek, turned to the east by Laguna and then crossed the Canadian River about ten miles below Fort Bascom. The trail continued up Ute Creek, passed on the east side of Rabbit Ears Mountain near present-day Clayton, New Mexico, and on to the Cimarron Seco near Robbers' Roost.[33] It then turned up Carrizo Creek, which went slightly northwest to Freeze Out Creek and to Two Butte Creek and on to the town of Granada on the Santa Fe railroad.[34] The route from the Freeze Out Creek to Two Butte Creek and on to Granada was the recently abandoned Granada- Fort Union Military Road which was a branch of the Santa Fe Trail. The upper portion of his new 1875 trail would later be used by drovers on the Texas-Montana Feeder Route in the last decade of trail driving.

ANOTHER GOODNIGHT TRAIL IN THE TEXAS PANHANDLE:

In 1876 Goodnight established a new ranch — his fourth — in the Texas Panhandle. He chose to locate in Palo Duro Canyon on the edge of the great Staked Plains. The canyon's features, he felt, furnished shelter for the cattle in the winter and there was sufficient water and grass in the deep valleys even though the plains above were a vast desert. He was over two hundred miles from any settlement in New Mexico, Kansas or Colorado, and the nearest military forts were Fort Elliott, some one hundred miles to the east, and Fort Griffin, over a hundred miles to the southeast. The ranch provided him with plenty of room for his cattle operation. His first living quarters was a dugout, but he eventually built a three-room ranch house from timber in a wide spot on the canyon floor. He dubbed it the "Home Ranch."

In the following year, Goodnight went into partnership with John G. Adair, a financier from Denver. The ranch then became known as the JA Ranch, and for the next eleven years, Goodnight expanded the ranch and its herd. When Adair died in 1885, the JA covered 1,325,000 acres upon which 100,000 head grazed.[35]

---

[33]Robbers' Roost was located on a mesa four miles northeast of Kenton in No Man's Land (present-day Panhandle of Oklahoma). It overlooked the junction of the Cimarron River and Carrizo Creek.
[34]Haley, Ibid, 229.
[35]Haley, Ibid., 284.

From his Panhandle ranch location, Goodnight blazed another trail in the summer of 1878. It was the Palo Duro-Dodge City Trail over which he trailed JA cattle to market, led by a steer he called "Old Blue." Panhandle ranchers used this path for several years. In December of 1887, Goodnight and his wife moved into a two-story ranch house that he built near present-day Goodnight, Texas, just north of the JA Ranch in Armstrong County.

No other cattleman established as many trails as Charles Goodnight. Pauline Robertson and R. L. Robertson said it best:

> No driver so branded the West with the stamp of his character and the power of his personality. With an indomitable courage, a constitution of rawhide and a will of iron, he drove himself night and day to live up to the standards he set for himself.
>
> Colonel Goodnight always said that his trail-driving days were the happiest of his life, notwithstanding the dangers and hardships involved. He and his cowboys had been solitary adventurers in a great land, fresh and new, and they were free and full of the zest of darers. "When all went well, there was no other life so pleasant."[36]

---

[36] Robertson, Pauline and R. L. Robertson. *Cowman's Country*, 22.

THE WESTERN CATTLE TRAIL | 1874-1897

"But my pap done told me that since Texas taken most of the earth away from Mayheeco, Uncle Sam, he's had about six government surveys made a-trying and a-trying to find whereat is the one hundredth meridian, and likewise how far north is 36-30, so's they can tell where Texas stops at. They can't not one of them people agree even with hisself where either of them places is at. Them surveyor don't know no more'n that claybank steer. Trail? There ain't no trail. We're lost from the first jump, unless'n that steer knows. There wasn't never no Chisholm Trail nowheres, and I can whip any man say there was. I don't read of no such thing in the blue-black speller. But I allow, give me a good North Star and a dun steer, I kin find Aberlene ef there is ary such place."

"Oh, we'll find a trail," replied the younger man. I'm telling you, there is a trace called the Chisholm Trail north of the Red River. You can get to Baxter Springs that way, or to Little Rock, and I recken to Wichita; and Aberlene's north of Wichita somewheres. There's grass and water all the way through."

"There's a road up from Santone to San Marcos and Austin, so I recken we'll head up Plum Creek and strike in north over Cedar and Onion. Ef there is a trail we'll find it. Ef there ain't we'll make one. Foller that dun steer — he knows where Aberlene is at."

Emerson Hough
North of 36, printed in 1923, pgs. 88-89.
time period: 1867

CHAPTER IV

The Eastern/Chisholm Trail System 1867-1889

In 1866, Joseph G. McCoy was a young cattle dealer, along with his father and brother, in Springfield, Illinois. When he heard of the difficulties Texas cattlemen were having getting their herds to market, he came to Kansas in the spring of 1867 and devised a plan to establish a market in the north where the southern drover could drive his longhorns to a railhead without being molested or harassed along the way. The place was Abilene, Kansas on the Union Pacific Railroad, Eastern Division. By September, 1867, cattle herds reached Abilene. Because of McCoy's efforts, what later became known as the Chisholm Trail was started. More than four million longhorns were trailed north over this trail.

Sketch taken from the front of McCoy's book, Historic Sketches of the Cattle Trade, published in 1874.

The term "Eastern/Chisholm" was chosen to identify this trail system because of the controversy among historians about the accurate name of the trail. As was discussed in length in our first book, The Western, the Greatest Texas Cattle Trail, *there is a division of opinion, especially in Texas, over the term to describe this trail system. For years, the term "Chisholm" has been used to identify the trail from South Texas to Abilene, Kansas, but after years of in-depth study of the cattle trail systems, we use the language found in the documented history. In the early days, the trail was called simply "the trail," the "Abilene Trail," or the "Kansas Trail." We also found names such as the "Texas Trail," or the "Northern Trail."[1] The cattle route to Waco, Texas, up through 1866 was the old Shawnee Trail which carried the bulk of trail traffic before the Civil War.[2]*

Drovers did not follow Jessie Chisholm's Trail, or more accurately the Fort Arbuckle Trail to Fort Arbuckle, until they were in Indian Territory (present-day Oklahoma), and the term "Chisholm Trail" was not used in writing until 1871, five years after Abilene was a cattle town. After the Western Trail started to be used in 1874, the Texas trail through Fort Worth was described, not as the Chisholm, but as the "Eastern."[3] Thus, to be accurate, in Texas, after 1874, the trail is the Eastern,[4] while in Indian Territory and Kansas, the trail was referred to as the Chisholm. Furthermore, this trail system continued beyond Abilene, Kansas, into the cattle towns of Schuyler and Kearney on the North Platte River in Nebraska. (These towns will be discussed later in the book.) Therefore, on our maps and in text, this historically important trail system is referred to as the Eastern/Chisholm. Refer to the map on the inside back cover.

As Charles Goodnight and Oliver Loving were risking their cattle and their lives trailing herds through the Texas Panhandle and New Mexico Territory in 1866 and 1867, six states enacted laws — specifically in the early months of 1867 — to prevent the trailing of Texas cattle across their borders. Fear of the Texas Fever had created road blocks all along the western line of settlements. Nebraska, Kansas, Colorado, Missouri, Illinois, and Kentucky all were determined to bar importation of Texas herds. The Illinois law carried a fine of $1,000 to any drover who brought Texas cattle into the state. Missouri authorized the county cattle inspectors to inspect, impound, and condemn cattle coming into the state and "to order the condemned stock to be removed or killed."[5]

---

[1]Wayne Gard, *The Chisholm Trail*, 75.
George W. Saunders, in "Origin and Close of the Old-Time Northern Trail," address to the assembly of the Reunion of the Old Time Trail Drivers' Association in 1917, used the term "Northern trail." Hunter, *The Trail Drivers of Texas*, 25.

[2]In Texas, the trail followed the old Shawnee Trail to Waco where it split. From there, trail drivers turned off of the Shawnee Trail, went through Fort Worth, and continued north to Abilene, Kansas. Recall that in 1866, 260,000 head were trailed over the Shawnee Trail. (Wayne Gard, "The Shawnee Trail," *The Southwestern Historical Quarterly*, 370.

[3]Wayne Gard wrote that "Years later, after a new trail [Western] was opened farther west, some called the older route the Eastern Trail." Ibid., 75.

[4]George W. Saunders, "Official Trail Names Adopted, Old Trail Drivers' Association Decides 'Eastern' and 'Western' Proper Title, Fort Worth Newspaper between Oct. 21, and Dec 31, 1931. Saunders said, "All the boys said we were on the Chisholm trail after crossing Red River."

[5]Wayne Gard, *The Chisholm Trail*, 55.

As noted in Chapter II, Texas cattlemen were in limbo on their ranches in early 1867. They were seeking a profitable outlet for their stock, but the future looked bleak. The West Shawnee route to Junction City on the Union Pacific, Eastern Division, which had arrived there in 1866, was being used, but the drovers faced a backlash against the Fever from area farmers, and possible confrontations with post-war ruffians who raided herds.

A dramatic change was needed, and it came in the form of a promoter by the name of Joseph McCoy. He realized, he later wrote, that, "The close of the year 1866, left the business of driving Texan cattle prostrate, and the entire drive fraternity both North and South, in an utterly discouraged condition." Thus, the Illinois cattle shipper saw the need to establish "a market whereat the Southern drover and Northern buyer would meet upon an equal footing, and both be undisturbed by mobs or swindling thieves."[6]

McCoy was encouraged by the fact that in February of 1867, Kansas had repealed parts of her 1861 cattle quarantine law (see Chapter II) allowing a window of opportunity. The arrival of thousands of head of cattle and the cowboys who accompanied them meant big business to merchants and businessmen in the railhead towns. While the State of Kansas wanted to protect its citizens, it also wanted the Texans' money and their cattle at the loading docks on the Union Pacific, Eastern Division. The law still quarantined the eastern settled areas, but the southwestern area of Kansas approximately west of present-day McPherson was left open to cattle drives. The revised law allowed drovers to take their herds north from this open region, under certain conditions, to the railheads, if they gave a bond of $10,000 to guarantee payment for damage that might occur to local stock. Also, it was to be understood that all longhorns loaded onto rail cars had to be shipped to some location outside of the state.[7]

At the time, the Union Pacific's Eastern Division (later Kansas Pacific) was completed and operating as far west as Salina. McCoy journeyed to Kansas and headed westward in search for a location to establish a railhead for Texas cattle herds. He first went to Junction City and offered to purchase a tract of land to build a stock yard and cattle shipping facilities, but because, as he later wrote "an exorbitant price was asked, in fact a flat refusal to sell at any price was the final answer," McCoy left the town and looked farther west.[8]

The citizens of Junction City did not want the Texas cattle because of the Texas Fever. Editor George W. Martin wrote in the *Junction City Union*, in January of 1867, a couple of months before McCoy arrived, that

> During the past season, the people of Humboldt, McDowell, Clark's Creek in this county, have lost over six thousand dollars worth of cattle due to Spanish fever. It is rumored that when the grass starts again in the Spring that large herds will again be driven this way. It is

---

[6]Joseph McCoy, *Historic Sketches of the Cattle Trade of the West and Southwest*, 39-40.

[7]Gard, Ibid, 55.

[8]McCoy, Ibid., 41.

proposed that if legal steps are of no avail in stopping such cattle beyond the state line, the farmers turn out and drive them back. The people of these neighborhoods have suffered greatly, Enough is enough![9]

When the Kansas Legislature revised the quarantine law in February, Junction City was within its limits, but Joseph McCoy was not going to let that stop him from getting his stockyard for Texas cattle. Following the railway tracks westward, inspecting various points "with regard to their adaptability to a cattle business" he arrived in Solomon City. Upon finding a "fine site for stock yards," McCoy discovered that the citizens also "regarded such a thing as a cattle trade with stupid horror, and from all that could be learned upon thorough inquiry, the citizens of Salina were much in the same mood." The fear of the Texas Fever was thwarting McCoy's efforts to find a suitable location for his enterprise. He retraced his steps up the line and selected "a very small, dead place, consisting of about one dozen log huts, low, small, rude affairs, four-fifths of which were covered with dirt for roofing." The cluster of shacks, which conducted business from two small rooms in a hut that was also a saloon, was called Abilene.[10] McCoy noted that the country around Abilene was entirely unsettled, well watered, and had excellent grass in an area suitable for holding cattle. He then bargained with the railroad executives of the Union Pacific, Eastern Division to provide facilities near Abilene's array of cabins in exchange for a percentage of the revenues. McCoy's part of the bargain was to build cattle pens and to solicit and advertise the location to the Texas cattlemen. He then persuaded Kansas officials to not enforce the state's quarantine law for that area because Abilene sat within the quarantine. The newly drawn deadline was sixty miles west of Abilene, but the country was so thinly populated at the time.[11] He convinced Governor Samuel J. Crawford that herds entering the area would not harm any of the settlers and received an endorsement from him to create his cattle market. McCoy also successfully lobbied the Illinois legislature to revise its restrictions against the entry of Texas cattle into the state with a provision that herds coming from the Kansas location would have documentation showing that these cattle had been wintered in Kansas and were clean of the Texas Fever.[12]

McCoy followed up on his part of the bargain with the railroad and sent runners to Texas to promote his new venture, advertised his newly built rail-side cattle pens, mailed out handbills to Texas ranchers and cattle buyers in Illinois, and sent a rider, W. W. Sugg, to intercept herds coming north to tell the drovers of the new shipping point. The rider, according to McCoy, was "sent into Southern Kansas and the Indian Territory with instructions to hunt up every straggling drove possible, and tell them

---

[9]George W. Martin, "Texas Cattle," *Junction City Union*, Jan. 1867, reprinted in the *Junction City Union*, Junction City, Kansas on September 8, 1991.

[10]McCoy, Ibid., 44.

[11]Richmond, "Cowtowns and Cattle Trails," Chapter XI in *Kansas, the First Century, Vol I.*, 258.

[12]William Holden in his book, *Alkali Trails*, says this was a real joke. "A cattleman could arrive with a herds fresh from Texas in the afternoon, visit a disreputable notary public in the evening, and the next morning send out a shipment of 'wintered' cattle." 27

THE WESTERN CATTLE TRAIL | 1874-1897

of Abilene….a good, safe place to drive to, where he could sell or ship his cattle unmolested to other markets." McCoy later wrote: "This was joyous news to the drover, for the fear of trouble and violence hung like an incubus over his waking thoughts alike with his sleeping moments."[13] Soon word of mouth spread that Abilene was the place to trail Texas cattle.[14]

This new trail followed the old Shawnee Trail from as far south as the Rio Grande, through the brush country straight north using the Shawnee's beaten path to Beeville, Gonzales, Lockhart and to Austin. From Austin the herds passed Round Rock, Georgetown, Belton, and Comanche Springs. At Waco, the drovers split from the Shawnee Trail and branched off in a northwesterly direction toward Fort Worth. This community had become a more convenient outfitting station than Dallas on the old Shawnee Trail route, thirty-three and a half miles east. Fort Worth furnished needed items such as saddles, six-shooters, ropes, and groceries. At Fort Worth the trail crossed the West Fork of the Trinity River and continued due north to the Red River.

When Abilene opened up as a railhead in 1867 and for

Abilene—The Cattle Market

Another spring has opened upon Texas with unusual promise and luxurience. The crop of grass, is even better than last year, and the increase of the herds of cattle of our grazing country, between the San Antonio and the Rio Grande, will be larger and better than any previous year. During the past season thousands of hides have been brought to this market from the frontier because of the necessities of the stock raisers to realize something from their herds. This killing of cattle for their hides is a terrible waste to our State, and a shameful loss to our stock raisers. Until beef packing establishments are put up on the frontier, the question of a market for our increasing herds of cattle is one of great importance. The only way seems to drive them to market. New Orleans furnishes a very meagre market, which is under the control of a few monopolists, and we must look to another quarter. In consequence of the unjust prejudice of the people of Missouri, our cattle drovers have been cut off from the privilege of driving through to St. Louis and Chicago. But through the enterprise of the McCoy Brothers, a new market has been established at Abilene, Kansas. Although this cattle mart has only been estalbished about one year, it has grown to proportions that begin to overshadow even the old marts of St. Louis and Chicago.

The route to Abilene, is perfectly free from hindrance and through a fine grass region. The proper route to drive is via Bolen's Crossing on Red River; thence to Fort Arbuckle; thence to Chisms ranch; thence to Abilene. Total distance from Northern Texas about 350 miles. Abilene is accessible by rail to all the markets of the country. In making up a drive for the Abilene market, our cattle men should select the largest and best.

Instead of killing cattle for their hides, let our stock raisers drive to Abilene during this favorable year, and we feel confident of a great addition of our prosperity.

San Antonio Express, April 29, 1868, page 2

---

[13] McCoy, Ibid., 51, 66.

[14] One component of the 1948 classic movie, *Red River*, (filmed by Howard Hawks) is the conflict between the two main actors, John Wayne and Montgomery Clift. On a cattle drive right after the war, the old timer (Wayne) is following the old (Shawnee) trail to Missouri, but the younger man (Clift), just returned from the war, insists that he has heard of a better route — to a place called Abilene, Kansas. (Walter C. Clapham, *Western Movies, The Movie Treasury*, 42-44)

the next four seasons, cowboys chose to use the Arbuckle Trail[18] in Indian Territory to reach the new depot. The trail was a few miles farther west of the route used by John Chisum the year before. According to an 1866 war department map, the pathway was an old Indian route that crossed the Red River and pointed directly to Fort Arbuckle on the Washita River.[19] Also, according to Jim Cloud, there was a pathway from Fort Arbuckle to the Cloud Ranch which was located just above Saddler's Bend on the Red River, south of present-day Leon, Oklahoma. The ranch was a main stopping point for travelers coming from Montague and Head of Elm, Texas, and was located above the crossing of the Red River on a pathway to Fort Arbuckle. Ike Cloud, as early as the mid 1850s, was supplying beef to the Army garrison at Fort Arbuckle. This is quite possibly the same route. Either way, old Indian route or the Cloud Trail, as it was called, it is known that in 1867 there was already an established pathway to Fort Arbuckle for the trail drivers to follow north of the Red River.[20]

According to Joseph McCoy, who started his stockyards in Abilene, Kansas on July 1, 1867, the first herd to come to Abilene over the new "Abilene Trail," as he called it, was owned by Col. Oliver W. Wheeler, Wilson and Hicks. McCoy wrote in 1874 that the partnership

...visited the Lone Star State early in the year, and purchased a

---

An Earlier John S. Chisum Route in Indian Territory:

There was activity in this area in Indian Territory with cattle herds before 1867. A route between the later-used Red River Station Crossing and the Fort Arbuckle Trail was used by cattleman John S. Chisum. Two obscure sources mention this route. Skipper Steely in an unpublished manuscript at the Texas A & M Libraries, describes John S. Chisum using this route in Indian Territory in 1866. Even though "CowJohn" [John Chisum] did not use the pathway to go to Abilene, Steely wrote, "he personally moved cattle from Bolivar [Denton County, Texas], crossing the Red [River] at Fish Creek northwest of Gainesville. He took a northwestward trip from here across Indian Territory, selling the cattle on the Smokey River."[15] Charles Moreau Harger, editor of the Abilene Daily Reflector, in Kansas, relayed this same information in an 1892 Scribner's Magazine article. Even though Harger confused the spelling of the Chisum sur-name, he wrote:

He forded the Red River near the mouth of Mud Creek, followed that stream to its head, kept northwest to Wild Horse Creek, to the west of Signal Mountains, and crossed the Washita at Elm [later Erin] Spring. Due north took him to the Canadian River,...[16]

A map of 1866 Indian Territory, located at Oklahoma State University, shows the Red River above Gainesville, Mud Creek running north, Wild Horse Creek, and Signal Mountains. The John Chisum route was west of Fort Arbuckle.[17]

---

[15]Skipper Steely, unpublished manuscript, "Forty Seven Years," 1988, Commerce, TX: Texas A & M University, Special Collections, 671.
[16]Charles Moreau Harger, "Cattle Trails of the Prairies," *Scribner's Magazine*, Vol. XI, No. 6, Jan-June, 1892, pages 732-742.
[17]Engineer Bureau, War Department map: "Indian Territory with part of the adjoining State of Kansas," 1866, located at the Oklahoma State Universtity Library in Stillwater, Oklahoma.

---

[18]"Indian Territory " map of 1889 by the United States Indian Bureau shows this route as the "Jesse Chisholm Cattle Trail." The 1867 Arbuckle Trail connected with the Jesse Chisholm Trail farther north; thus in 1889 after Fort Arbuckle had been abandoned, the Bureau labeled the route as the "Jesse Chisholm Cattle Trail." Map is located in the Western Collection at Oklahoma University at Norman.
[19]Engineer Bureau, War Department map: "Indian Territory with part of the adjoining State of Kansas," 1866, located at the Oklahoma State Universtity Library in Stillwater, Oklahoma. The map shows the route from Gainsville, Texas to Fort Arbuckle as an "Indian Trail." Fort Arbuckle had been built in April of 1851 to keep order among the Plains Indians and to protect immigrant wagon trains on their way to the California gold fields. In late 1859, however, Fort Cobb had been built farther northwest on the Washita River, causing Fort Arbuckle to be less important. Fort Arbuckle was abandoned in 1870. ("Fort Arbuckle," http://digital.library.okstate.edu)
[20]Jim Cloud, "Cloud Road: The Way From Texas," *War Chief of Oklahoma Westerners*, Vol. 13, No. 3, (Dec. 1979), pages 6-8. Cloud Ranche was located in Sec. 17, 18, 19, and 20 of Township 8S, Range 2W. According to surveyors, Cloud Road crossed the Red River into Section 20 in Indian Territory.

select herd of twenty-four hundred head of cattle, and over one hundred head of good cow ponies, and employed fifty-four sturdy men, all of which they armed in the best manner, with superior rifles. No more complete outfit, or better herd of stock ever left Texas.[21]

The cowboy outfit and herd "was the first to pass through the Indian Nation and broke the trail over which the drive of 1867 came," according to McCoy.

After crossing the Red River above Gainesville, the Wheeler, Wilson and Hicks herd followed the Fort Arbuckle Trail north. They reached the fort in July of 1867. When the outfit arrived at the fort, William (Buffalo Bill) Mathewson was there with a wagon train on its way to establish a new Indian agency at Eureka Valley on the Washita. Mathewson "directed the cowman over the new trail" and guided the Wheeler, Wilson and Hicks' herd as far as the South Canadian River where the cowboys and herd picked up the tracks of Jesse Chisholm's trade route.[22] From there the outfit and herd trailed across Indian Territory and crossed the Kansas line near where Caldwell would later be established. The Wheeler partnership's intention was to turn west upon nearing Abilene and to continue on to California, where Colonel Oliver Wheeler's business for the past several years had been to supply beef to California miners, but the trip from Texas had been tiresome. The drive had faced constant rain and flooding, and the Asiatic cholera had broken out on the western plains, with soldiers, homesteaders, and drovers dying from the disease. Therefore, the partners changed their plans and sold the herd in Abilene.[23]

Another outfit to use the Fort Arbuckle Trail to connect with Jesse Chisholm's trade route was Randolph Paine from Denton County, Texas, who drove 3,000 four and five-year old steers north in 1869. He crossed the Red River above Gainesville and forded the Washita River above Fort Arbuckle. At Abilene, he sold the steers for thirty dollars a head, receiving a nice profit over his original investment of twelve dollars a head. The Rev. George Webb Slaughter and his outfit also used the Fort Arbuckle Trail in 1869. The outfit started from the Slaughter ranch in Palo Pinto County, Texas, on September 2 with about 2,250 longhorns. Two weeks later they crossed the Red River and Muddy Creek into Indian Territory and arrived at Fort Arbuckle on the seventeenth day of their drive.[24]

C. H. Rust, in his essay for the Old Time Trail Drivers Association, wrote that "this right-hand trail crossed the Red River below [near] Gainesville, thence to Oil Springs, on to Fort Arbuckle, crossing Wild Horse Creek, and intersecting the main trail [Jesse Chisholm's trade route] at the south fork of the Canadian River."[25] J. F. Ellison, Jr. mentioned the route two different times in his essays. He said that his first

---

[21]Joseph G. McCoy, *Historic Sketches of the Cattle Trade*, (1874), 261.

[22]Wayne Gard, *The Chisholm Trail*, 74.

[23]Joseph G. McCoy, Ibid, 261.

[24]Wayne Gard, Ibid, 97, 101-102.

[25]C. H. Rust, "The Location of the Old Chisholm Trail," in Hunter, *The Trail Drivers of Texas*, 40, 210.

trip up the trail was with his father, Col. J. F. Ellison, in 1868 (or 1869) and that they went "over the old Fort Arbuckle trail to Abilene, Kansas."[26]

Cowboy J. H. Baker wrote in his lengthly unpublished diary that he went up "the trail" three times, in 1869, 1870, and 1871, and used the Fort Arbuckle Trail.[27]

Around 1870, trail drivers chose to cross the Red River farther west at Red River Station[28] and continue their journey to the Washita River by way of Addington, Tucker, Duncan, and Marrow. Perhaps the reason was that Fort Arbuckle was abandoned in 1870, and, thus, the cattle trail to Abilene moved west.[29] Very few maps show both the Fort Arbuckle Trail and the Indian Territory Chisholm Trail. The United States Indian Bureau map of 1889 shows both pathways, the "Jesse Chisholm Cattle Trail" (or the afore mentioned Fort Arbuckle Trail) going by way of Healdton, Hennepin, and Fort Arbuckle, while farther west was the "Abilene Cattle Trail." Halfway between the two marked routes is Erin (Elm) Springs, where John Chisum had crossed in 1866.[30]

The pathway of the Abilene Cattle Trail extended north from the Red River to camp on Beaver Creek, past Monument Rocks, to Rush Creek, to the Little Washita, and on to Rock Crossing on the Washita River. A day's drive placed the herds on the Walnut Creek, which, after camping, the outfit followed upstream. The next camp was on the South Canadian, and thirteen miles farther on was the North Canadian. At the South Canadian, drovers started to follow a trade route used by Jesse Chisholm. They called it Chisholm's Trail.[31] The trail continued over the prairies, crossing Deer Creek, Kingfisher Creek, and the Cimarron River. Six miles farther placed the herds at Turkey Creek and another nine miles found them at Shawnee (Skeleton) Creek. The outfits trailed across the treeless plains along Nine Mile Creek to the Salt Fork

---

[26]J. F. Ellison, Jr. "Traveling the Trail with Good Men was a Pleasure," in Hunter, 538, and J. F. Ellison, Jr., "Seven Trips Up the Trail," in Hunter, 92, and "Sketch of Col. J. F. Ellison," in Hunter, 477.

[27]J. H. Baker manuscript, University of Texas Library, Austin, Texas.

[28]By the mid-1870s Red River Station had a post office by the name of Salt Creek, and a ferry boat crossed at the site. In 1884 the post office's name was changed to Red River Station and existed until 1887, when the town also apparently ceased to exist. (Brian Hart, "Red River Station, TX," *Handbook of Texas Online*, www.tshaonline.org [accessed Jan. 1, 2011]

[29]In 1868 Fort Arbuckle was used to store supplies for Gen. Phillip H. Sheridan's 1868 winter campaign. When those supplies were depleated in 1870, the fort was abandoned. By then the threat by the Plains Indians had diminished. Troops and operations were transferred to Fort Sill. ("Fort Arbuckle," http://digital.library.okstate.edu)

[30]"Indian Territory," From a United States Indian Bureau map of 1889, located in the Western Collection, Oklahoma University at Norman.

[31]Kansas State Historical Marker "Caldwell & the Chisholm Trail," south of Caldwell on US-81. — "Jesse Chisholm, Indian trader, whose route lay between the North Canadian river and present Wichita." According to the renowned historian, J. Evetts Haley in his 1926 thesis, Chisholm went as far south as the Washita valley. He wrote, the "trader among Indians" Jesse Chisholm who "was living near the mouth of the Little Arkansas River, at about the present site of Wichita, Kansas," set out on a trading trip in the spring of 1865 and followed the tracks that had been made by the retreating Federal troops four years earlier, and made "his way to the valleys of the Canadian and Washita Rivers." (In 1861, because the Confederates cut off supplies and the advancement of a Texas force, the Army retreated from Forts Washita, Arbuckle, and Cobb in Indian Territory, leaving a path made by their heavy military wagons to Fort Leavenworth, Kansas.) J. Evetts Haley, "A Survey of Texas Cattle Drives to the North, 1866-1895," a thesis presented to the University of Texas, Midland, Texas, June, 1926, page 247.

Number of Trailed Cattle in 1867:

According to Robert Goins and Danney Goble and other sources, only a total of 35,000 head were driven up the trail from Texas in 1867.[33] Wayne Gard, however, wrote that "between thirty and forty-five thousand Texas and Indian cattle were walked into Kansas in 1867, most of them to Abilene."[34] We agree with Gard on the 45,000. As pointed out in Chapter II, Baxter Springs on the Shawnee Trail received some three hundred or so head in 1867, and Junction City on the West Shawnee bragged of receiving 20,000 head. Herds on the Abilene Trail did not reach Abilene until September of 1867. Thus, the 45,000 number was divided among the three cattle towns. Of the cattle that reached Abilene, most were shipped to Chicago and some were put out to pasture. Also according to Joseph McCoy, a packing house had been quickly erected in Junction City and a "large number were packed" there, but it is not known exactly how many thousands were packed or shipped out at Junction City.[35] McCoy, we feel, over estimated the cattle coming into Abilene in 1867. Gard felt that Abilene received the majority of the herds in 1867. However, from the numbers soundly reported by the Junction City *Cherokee Sentinel*, it is likely that both Abilene and Junction City in 1867 shipped a similar amount of cattle.

---

[33]Goins and Goble, *Historical Atlas of Oklahoma*, 117.

[34]Wayne Gard, *The Chisholm Trail*, 83. Indian cattle were herds coming out of Indian Territory.

[35]According to Joseph McCoy, the packing plant lasted only two seasons. "The cattle were not as good or fat as both parties had anticipated (packers and drovers), and it proved a disastrous loss to all concerned... the establishment [packing plant] was soon abandoned, and finally torn down." (McCoy, Ibid., 106)

---

of the Arkansas River. Just north of the crossing was Pond Creek. There was a pond east of the trail where large Indian campgrounds were located. To enter Kansas the drovers and their herds crossed Polecat Creek and came into the state below Bluff Creek and Fall Creek. The drive across Indian Territory could take thirty days or more.

To reach Abilene the outfits trailed across the open prairies of Kansas, crossing the Chikaska River, Slate Creek, the Ninnescah River, Cow Skin Creek and the Arkansas River.

McCoy had been right in that this trail across Kansas seemed to be easier on the stock than the old Shawnee Trail. The crossings were less troublesome, and because they were farther west, Kansas farmers were less bothersome. The new trail paralleled the West Shawnee which still led into Junction City.[32]

McCoy later wrote in his book that he and others estimated that by September of 1867, 35,000 head of cattle had been driven to Abilene. When people saw the McCoy pens, which could hold 1,000 head of cattle, and The Drover's Cottage, a $15,000 hotel, built by McCoy, any objection to Texas cattle was silenced. After all, even the governor had endorsed the possible cattle market boom. The season had begun late, but the following seasons would hopefully fulfill McCoy's expectations.

It appeared that in the fall of 1867 McCoy had broken open the stalemate for Texas drovers. According to McCoy, nearly one thousand railroad cars had been loaded, thus, it would seem that he had created a shipping point for Texas cattle, but, in fact, the whole enterprise that year was considered a failure.[36] The cattle were thin in flesh and were considered lower grade beef. The summer had been extremely sultry with heavy rainfall which produced grass not as beneficial for grazing animals. Because it was thought that Texas cattle could not withstand the northern winters, animals not shipped were sold cheaply instead of going into winter quarters. Also, the cost of shipping the cattle outweighed the receipts of selling the animals at the

---

[32]Gard, Ibid., 79-82, and Oklahoma Historical Society, 1936 map, "Map of a Portion of Oklahoma Showing the Location of the Chisholm Trail," reprinted from *The Chronicles of Oklahoma*, Vol. XIV, No. 1 (March, 1936) from H. S. Tennant, article "The Two Cattle Trails," 84-122.

[36]A thousand cars of cattle at approximately 22 to 24 head per car would be over 20,000 head.

end of the line. As a consequence, the prices received for the cattle were low, and owners lost heavily. Local parties, wrote McCoy, "expressed [the view] that no cattle would be driven there the next year," and others told him, "I told you so." Even Kansas Pacific officials in the St. Louis office "jested at the whole project, regarding it as the 'big joke' of the season."[37]

McCoy eventually prevailed. He continued to advertise his rail-side facilities and send riders south. The town, where he constructed the facilities, grew, adding more houses, businesses, and saloons. The 1868 season brought seventy-five thousand cattle, and the market prices had increased significantly, netting some drovers a "snug fortune." But the excitement did not last through the whole season. In late July, the Texas Fever struck with force. A Chicago firm went to Texas and contracted for a delivery of forty thousand head of cattle to be shipped by water, using the Mississippi River. The cattle were crowded onto unventilated decks of large steamboats without room to lay down or drink. When the cattle were unloaded at Cairo, Illinois, some twelve days later, they were exhausted and in poor shape. These forty thousand head were scattered throughout Illinois, and some were sold into Indiana. The Texas cattle were mixed with local cattle on the pastures of farmers and small ranchers. Local cattle began to sicken and die at an alarming rate. Some lost entire herds, and in one township in Illinois every milk cow died except one. In Champaign County, losses were estimated at $150,000. Vigilance committees were formed by enraged farmers to keep out Texas cattle. Waves of the Texas Fever epidemic reached the New York market and prices plummeted. Throughout the East, buyers refused to buy Texas cattle.

Losses were also suffered in and around Abilene. According to Wayne Gard, "Drovers at Abilene contributed $1,200 to stockmen whose animals had died, and McCoy paid several thousand dollars to claimants near Abilene."[38] As for the rebellion in the East, Joseph McCoy quickly came to Abilene's defense: "It appeared in a much less fatal and less malignant form in other portion of Illinois, among domestic cattle which had been grazed with Texan cattle that had been introduced via Abilene, Kas." he said. He added that only "a few cases of disease actually occurred after exposure to Texan cattle coming via Western Kansas, and those [cases] that did occur were of a milder type…." Cattle coming directly out of South Texas were the primary carriers of the disease.[39]

McCoy related the excitement caused by the Texas Fever epidemic of 1868:

It was the subject of gossip by everybody and formed the topic of innumerable newspaper articles, as well as associated press dispatches. A panic seized upon owners of domestic herds everywhere and many rushed their cattle off to market only to meet panic-stricken operators

---

[37]McCoy, Ibid., 107-108.
[38]Gard, Ibid., 96.
[39]McCoy, Ibid., 149.

from other sections and ruinously low prices for their stock. The butchers, venders [vendors] and consumers were alike alarmed and afraid to buy, sell or consume beef of any kind.[40]

The governor of Illinois, in response, quickly became pro-active. He soothed the anger of the governor of New York who was threatening to quarantine all cattle from the west or northwest into his state, and he called for a convention in Chicago of experts to get to the bottom of the problem. Many state governors sent representatives to the convention — mainly to relieve the anger back home over the Fever. The convention's purpose was to determine a way to protect domestic cattle from the disease and to recommend a practical basis of legislation against the introduction of Texas cattle. The convention only gave the attendees an avenue to vent their anger. The cause of the disease was not determined, and the members recommended that individual states form their own legislation in the ensuing months. Eventually the excitement died down, and Texas cattle were again trailed to Kansas railheads.

The season of 1869 stopped the doubts of the naysayers. The atmosphere in Abilene was as if the previous two season's obstacles had not happened. Some 150,000 head were trailed to the town of a few hundred residents. An outlet to a dependable Kansas railhead had been established, and Texas cattlemen responded. According to McCoy, the cattle commerce in Abilene amounted to more than three million dollars annually. The surrounding farmers were also emerging from their "hovels of dirt built in the bank of some ravine — into substantial frame houses with other outdoor improvements."[41]

McCoy's role of bringing cattle and dollars into Abilene in 1869 tells only a portion of the story. Texas cattlemen were so relieved that finally there were railheads in Kansas to receive their herds. They sent up 350,000 cattle that year, more than four times as many as arrived the year before. Abilene continued to share the wealth with the other cow towns of Baxter Springs on the Old Shawnee Trail and Junction City on the West Shawnee Trail. In the following years of 1870 to 1873, the Chisholm Trail was used to funnel into the state and beyond one herd after another during the long summer seasons. It was not unusual to have herds numbering more than three thousand each, and the total numbers of cattle coming into the eastern Kansas railheads reached approximately 300,000 in 1870, 600,000 in 1871, 350,000 in 1872 and 405,000 in 1873.

The complexion of the trail itself changed during these banner years. Because of the millions of dollars at stake, fierce competition occurred in 1870 within the railroad companies in the East over the carrying of livestock. This drove up the price of cattle. Thus, in 1871, when the number of cattle coming north doubled, each owner assumed he was going to be a wealthy man at the end of the season. But it was a stormy season. It was rainy; the cattle stampeded often; the grass was spongy; the cattle were poor in flesh; and there were fewer buyers at the end of the trail. Also, the

---

[40]McCoy, Ibid, 150-151.
[41]McCoy, Ibid, 204-206.

railroads adjusted their rates, imposing a higher freight tariff on livestock, and at the end of the line, cattle prices fell. As mentioned earlier, over half of the herds driven north in 1871 went unsold and had to be pastured. In July of 1871, the *Salina County Journal* reported:

> The entire country east, west, and south of Salina and down to the Arkansas River is filled with Texas cattle....There are not only cattle 'on a thousand hills' but a thousand cattle on one hill and every hill. The bottoms are overflowing with them, and the water courses with this great article of traffic. Perhaps not fewer than 200,000 head are in the state, 60,000 of which are within a day's ride of Salina. And the cry is, 'Still they come!'"[42]

Over the next two seasons, thousands of cattle continued to be driven to Kansas. Only now, other cattle towns had emerged. Almost any town with a rail switch and stock pens tried to get in on the boom. Cattle were shipped from Junction City, Solomon City, Salina, Brookville, and Ellsworth in 1871. Also the Atchinson, Topeka, and Santa Fe Railway reached Newton in the spring of 1871, which was on the path of the Chisholm Trail and sixty-five miles closer than Abilene. Within weeks, under the guidance of Joseph McCoy, Newton was ready to ship cattle. The year was also the last one for Abilene as a railhead for cattle shipments. The town fathers or "circle" decided to exclude the cattle drovers from their community, so the drovers moved their herds sixty miles west to Ellsworth.[43] Even though the herds of 1871 overwhelmed the market, a record of 350,000 more head were trailed north in 1872. Historian Wayne Gard contends that this number is low, for "someone kept a record of the Texas herds passing that town [Ellsworth] between May 1 and November 1. He listed 292 herds, totaling 349,275 head." However, the gentleman did not include the herds going up the Shawnee Trail or the herds that went north to Newton and Wichita.[44]

In 1872, Wichita was connected to the Atchinson, Topeka, and Santa Fe and drovers could diverge from the Chisholm Trail at Pond Creek in Indian Territory, cross Bluff Creek at Cox's Crossing and use this cut-off to go directly to Ellsworth. Because drovers used Cox's Crossing, this cut-off route to Ellsworth was also called Cox's Trail.[45] The new cut-off not only diverted herds from Wichita, it allowed drovers to avoid the increasing numbers of settlers in Sumner, Sedgwick, and Reno counties. The 1872 season was a prosperous one for those involved in the

---

[42] *Salina County Journal*, July 20, 1871 and Gard, Ibid., 157.

[43] As the area around Abilene became crowded with settlers and homesteaders, and as town folk complained about the cowboys and their activities, the city fathers of Abilene enforced laws against the brothels and dance halls. The laws were referred to as the "sin laws." In response, drovers diverted their cattle drives to Ellsworth starting in 1871, where it was less crowded and town folk were accommodating.

[44] Gard, Ibid., 190.

[45] The crossing and trail were named after William Cox, the Kansas Pacific Railroad livestock agent at Ellsworth.

trail-driving business. Prices increased, the grass was good; there were no severe storms; and Texans were mixing their herds — no longer did they put all beef steer-cattle in the herd but added young she-stock cattle into the mix to be sold to ranchers for building herds.

The years of 1869 to 1873 had brought over two million cattle to the new Kansas railheads — they were years of ups and downs as well as a shifting of locations of railhead terminals. Baxter Springs and Abilene had ceased to be destinations for Texas cattle by 1872, and Newton, Coffeyville, and Ellsworth started receiving cattle in 1871. Ellsworth had taken over Abilene's cattle business, including McCoy's Drover's Cottage Hotel, in 1872. In the same year Wichita, Hutchinson, and Great Bend on the Santa Fe became railroad towns capable of shipping cattle to eastern markets. These Kansas cattle towns were running full throttle by 1873, but the boom would not last into the next season. On September 18 a financial crash hit the East. The Panic of 1873 syphoned credit out of the region, causing a dramatic contraction of the cattle business.[46] Because of the following depression and the blizzard of 1873, the numbers of cattle being trailed north for the next two seasons dropped to less than half of the 1872 numbers.

And, then there was the Texas Fever. As unsold Texas cattle populated the plains of Kansas, reports of domestic animals dying of the Fever began to appear. In the Kansas Legislature's March, 1876 session, a quarantine for the eastern part of the state was enacted. The law's deadline was about thirty miles west of Great Bend. If Texas cattlemen had not already done so, in the 1876 season, they rerouted their herds farther west. There was, however, an allowance made for some herds to enter at the west edge of Sedgwich County, west of Wichita, follow a designated corridor, and drive to Wichita's stock yards. 12,380 head of cattle were driven to and shipped from Wichita in 1876.[47]

The whole exciting enterprise of trail driving to Kansas railheads started by an Illinois cattle shipper, with its highs and lows, lasted ten seasons. Texas herds had been coming into Kansas since 1866 via the Shawnee Trail and its branches and the Chisholm Trail and its branches. Both systems in Kansas were shut down by Kansas law because of the close approximately of the Texas longhorns to Kansas settlements. It was time for the Texas cowboys to again move west to create another cattle trail system.

---

[46]The Panic of 1873 was similar to ones experienced by some of us in the next century. Because of rapid expansion and wild speculation in business after the Civil War, several large eastern firms failed, especially the banking and securities firm of Jay Cooke and Company. There was a Black Friday; the New York Stock Exchange closed for ten days; many banks went broke, and many men were put out of work. The Panic affected the whole country including cattle prices.

[47]Interview: Jim Gray, August 8, 2013 and Gard, Ibid., 232.
State of Kansas: Session Laws of 1876 and Memorials, Passed at the Sixteenth Annual Session of the Legislature, Commenced at the State Capital, January 11, 1876. Topeka, KS: George W. Martin, Kansas Publishing House, 1876, pages 316-317.

> *From two hundred to four hundred yards wide, beaten into the bare earth, it reached over hill and through valley…a chocolate band amid the green prairies, uniting the North and South. As the marching hoofs wore it down and the wind blew and the waters washed the earth away it became lower than the surrounding country and was flanked by little banks of sand, drifted there by the wind. Bleaching skulls and skeletons of weary brutes who had perished on the journey gleamed along its borders, and here and there was a low mound showing where some cow-boy had literally "died with his boots on." Occasionally a dilapidated wagon frame told of a break-down, and spotting the emerald reaches on either side were the barren circle-like "bedding grounds," each a record that a great herd had there spent a night.*
>
> *The wealth of an empire passed over the trail, leaving its mark for decades to come. The traveller of to-day sees the wide trough-like course, with ridges being washed down by the rains, and with fences and farms of the settlers and the more civilized red-man intercepting its track, and forgets the wild and arduous life of which it was the exponent. It was a life now outgrown, and which will never again be possible.*

Charles Moreau Harger
"Cattle Trails of the Prairies,"
Scribner's Magazine, Vol. XI, 1892.

CHAPTER V

The Western Trail System 1874-1897

Captain John T. Lytle *(1844-1907), at the age of 30, left the Lytle Ranch in Medina County, Texas with his partner and cousin Tom M. McDaniel on March 16, 1874 to deliver 3,500 head of aged steers to the Red Cloud Indian Agency in unpopulated western Nebraska. Lytle had a government contract with the newly-established agency and needed to establish a new route. The route that Lytle blazed across Texas (via Fort Griffin), Indian Territory (via Camp Supply), and by way of Dodge City, Kansas was followed by other outfits and became known as the Western Trail. In Lytle's outfit was nineteen-year-old Frank Collinson who later wrote of the trail drive. It appears in the book,* Life in the Saddle.

Photo courtesy of the Dickinson Research Center, National Cowboy and Western Heritage Museum, Oklahoma City, Oklahoma.

The Western Cattle Trail System was the last of the four major trail systems to come out of Texas. This system, which lasted the longest and went farther and blazed into more states than any of the other three, is complex and, at times, perplexing. It has always been our mission to untangle the facts and to present this trail system in a way to create better understanding of it in its totality. The difference between this chapter and the balance of the book is that in this chapter we explain the Western Trail System (with reference to the map of the system) and how it compares to the other three systems in the whole scheme of a trail-driving industry, and the balance of the book presents the Western Trail in detail, state by state. For this chapter, refer to the map on the inside of the back cover.

The Kansas law makers issued another quarantine in 1875. Texas cattlemen knew it was coming. As homesteaders filled in the Kansas plains and the settlement line moved west, it was only a matter of time before another deadline would be drawn. The likely adjustment for cattlemen, of course, was to establish another cattle trail to the west, and the most reasonable railhead in western Kansas was on the Atchinson, Topeka, and Santa Fe Railway at Dodge City, which was located adjacent to Fort Dodge. It wasn't quite that simple, however. Even though rail lines reached Dodge back in 1872, western Kansas, at that time, was still wide open prairies with almost no settlement. While the Chisholm was being used to bring cattle to the railheads of eastern Kansas and Nebraska, changes were rapidly happening in the prairies west of the settlements. The Southern Indians Wars had been raging since the Sand Creek Massacre in Colorado ten years earlier.[1] The Plains Indians fought back ferociously in an attempt to stop white man's encroachment on their hunting grounds. As the Army sought to force the tribes into submission, rifle sharpsman were engaged to eliminate their food supply and staple — the buffalo. Dodge City was strategically located near a fort and on the Santa Fe Railway, and became a hide center. The town was a den of buffalo men who spread out across the southern plains and killed buffalo for the hides which were taken into Dodge for shipment back east. Because of the warring tribes, the surrounding area was not conducive to settlers or cattle drives.

By the winter of 1875, the Indian wars on the southern plains had largely ceased, and the tribes had been forced onto reservations — and given the new Kansas quarantine law, it was a time for cattlemen to establish a new, more western route. Still, it was a gradual process. Two years earlier, L. B. Harris, a cattleman from San Antonio, decided to try a westerly route. His herds had been among some of the early arrivals in 1872 to rangeland south of Wichita when that cattle town hosted its first

---

[1] At dawn of the cold morning of November 29, 1864, Colonel J. M. Chivington and his regiment of 800 attacked a village of Cheyenne on Sand Creek in eastern Colorado near Fort Lyon. The peaceful village had no more than 500 people of which the regiment killed between 150 to 200, most of them elderly men, women and children. The Chivington Massacre, as some preferred to call the incident, ignited a quick and violent rampage from the Cheyenne, Northern Arapaho, and Sioux. The confrontation between the army and the revenging Indians lasted for the next ten years. Historians have referred to this time as the Southern Indian Wars. ("The Indians," The Old West series by *Time-Life Books*, 183-187, and Stan Hoig, *The Sand Creek Massacre*.)

THE WESTERN CATTLE TRAIL | 1874-1897   59

season for cattlemen and drovers. He may have felt the tension or heard a rumor in the wind, for in the spring of 1873, he drove his herds from Uvalde in west Texas northward going from fort to fort, obviously for protection — in Texas he passed by Fort Terral, Fort McKavett, Fort Chadbourne, and Fort Belknap. North of the Red River in Indian Territory, they passed by Fort Sill, Fort Cobb, and Camp Supply. In Kansas, Harris stopped at Fort Dodge and Fort Hays. His destination was the loading pens at Ellis on the Kansas Pacific Railroad.[2] The *Ellsworth Reporter* on April 17, 1873 reported that "L. B. Harris of San Antonio opened the new trail to Ellis," and Joseph McCoy, who bragged about his friend in his book published the following year, wrote that Harris had sold 7,000 head to a single firm in 1873 for "the snug sum of $210,000."[3]

Also in 1873, another veteran trail driver looked to western Kansas for his upcoming spring drive. Captain John T. Lytle contracted in the late winter of 1873 to deliver a large herd to the Red Cloud Indian Agency near Camp Robinson on the White River in northwestern Nebraska. The reservation was established, and the government agent needed beef to feed the tribes that had been persuaded to forgo their nomadic lifestyle. The route that Lytle established from Medina County, Texas, across Indian Territory, and on to Dodge City is acredited by most historians as being the first drive over the route that became the Western Cattle Trail. Even Frank Collinson, a cowboy in Lytle's outfit, knew that they were blazing a new trail. He recalled later, "We beat out a trail over sections of the country that had not been traveled before, and over which thousands of cattle would later be driven…"[4]

Other trail drivers followed Lytle's lead. Even before the eastern terminals were shut down by the Kansas quarantine of 1875, Dodge City in Kansas and Ogallala in Nebraska were hastily building and preparing for the influx of herds that had begun to arrive in their towns. Dodge had to quickly convert from a buffalo hide center to a cattle town. Ogallala also received the wave of drovers and their herds from farther east in Nebraska and had to suddenly adjust to the fact that it was also going to be a cattle railhead. The cattle-trailing industry made a significant shift westward along in a line from Texas to Nebraska, and that new path became the Western Cattle Trail.[5]

Just because Kansas lawmakers closed down eastern Kansas depots does not mean that the Eastern/Chisholm was completely abandoned. When the quarantine became effective, herds and outfits, especially from ranches in south Texas and the eastern portion of the state, continued to use the familiar Eastern Trail, but because the trail no longer had rail destinations in Kansas or Nebraska, trail drivers created splinter routes to the Western. From 1875 to 1880, the Eastern/Chisholm was a

---

[2] A. W. Ziegalasch, map: "The Old Chisholm Cattle Trail and Subsidiary Trails in Texas, 1873." The map shows the "L.B. Harris New Trail to Ellis." Property of the Harvey County Historical Library and Museum, Newton, Kansas. Also printed in Kraisinger and Kraisinger, *The Western, the Greatest Texas Cattle Trail*, 29.

[3] Joseph McCoy, *Historic Sketches of the Cattle Trade of the West and Southwest*, 14-16, and Jim Gray, "Tracking Down an Old Trail-Driver — L. B. Harris," *Kansas Cowboy*, Sept/Oct., 2003, 5.

[4] Frank Collinson, *Life in the Saddle*, 31. Collinson was a nineteen-year-old cowboy in Lytle's outfit on this 1874 trail drive. His accout will be covered more fully later in this volume.

[5] L. B. Harris' trail was not followed by other Texas drovers to any recorded degree. The trail laid out by Captain Lytle, however, to Dodge City was followed and used for the next eleven seasons.

feeder route to the Western Trail. If trail drivers did not cross over to the newly established Western Trail in Texas, they crossed the Red River at Red River Station and fed into the Western Trail at various locations in Indian Territory. *(These splinter routes will be discussed in more detail later in the book.)*

The Eastern/Chisholm Trail was revived to a major trunk line again in 1880 when the Atchinson, Topeka, and Santa Fe Railway reached the border town of Caldwell which became a shipping point for Texas cattle. Even though the town had a Kansas address, cattle grazed in Indian Territory while waiting to be loaded onto freight cars. Caldwell had the advantage of being a closer railhead and being on a well-used, familiar route. In some cases, the tables were turned. Drovers from western Texas who crossed at Doan's Crossing on the Western Trail, splintered off of that trail at various locations and fed into the Chisholm Trail in Indian Territory in order to take their herds to the shipping pens at Caldwell.

Even though most historians agree that Captain John T. Lytle was the one who blazed the Western Cattle Trail from Texas, the *exact* route of the trail and its beginning in Texas seems to be up for debate. Early authorities don't seem to agree. Joseph Nimmo, perhaps the first to attempt to trace the early cattle trails, reported in his massive report to the House of Representatives in 1885 that the Western began near Bandera and extended in an irregular line northward through Clyde, Fort Griffin, and Doan's Crossing to Dodge City.[6] Edward Everett Dale, in his 1930 study, stated that the trail started "somewhere about Bandera, Texas, [and proceeded] north past Fort Griffin to the Red River crossing at Doan's Store...."[7] On his 1931 map of the trail, Walter Prescott Webb indicated that the trail started southwest of Bandera and went northward through Kerrville, then northwestward to San Angelo, extending on northeastward to Clyde, and on to Fort Griffin, and Doan's Crossing.[8] Helena Huntington-Smith, who wrote *We Pointed Them North* in 1939 based on her interviews with E. C. Abbott (Teddy Blue), an old trail cowboy, maintains the trail ran northeastward from San Antonio, using the Eastern's trunk line to Waco, then north of Waco using the Old Shawnee Trail, trailed by Dallas, forded the Red River at either Preston's Bend or Colbert's Ferry, ascended the Washita River in a northwesterly direction, and turned northward by way of Camp Supply to Dodge City.[9] William Curry Holden, an early respected authority on western Texas, claims that the trail extended from Bandera northward through the hill country, through Mason and Coleman counties, and then on to Fort Griffin, Doan's store, etc.[10]

---

[6]Joseph Nimmo was the Chief of the Bureau of Statistics who presented his extensive report to the House of Representatives in March of 1885. Part of its contents and impact will be discussed in Part III. The map that accompanies his report shows this route.

[7]Edward Everett Dale, *The Range Cattle Industry*, 64

[8]Walter Prescott Webb, *The Great Plains*, 225-226.

[9]Helena Huntington Smith and E. C. Abbott ("Teddy Blue"), *We Pointed Them North, Recollections of a Cowpuncher*, map on page vii. Abbott went from San Antonio, Texas to Montana in 1883. This route shows how drovers might use old trails in Texas before connecting to the Western, in this case south of Camp Supply. Jimmy Skaggs in his thesis (page 23) misread Abbott's map and said that the herd crossed the Red River at Red River Station (via Dallas) which is was not likely.

[10]William Curry Holden, *Alkali Trails, or Social and Economic Movements of the Texas Frontier*, 34. (published in 1930)

THE WESTERN CATTLE TRAIL | 1874-1897

Another source that trail scholars use is trail drivers' maps. These maps are not based on research and interviews like those sources listed above, but from first-hand experience. Jack Potter's map shows the Western starting at Brownsville (using the Matamoros Feeder Route) and going through San Antonio, Kerrville, Waldrip, Albany, Seymour and on to Doan's Crossing on the Red River.[11]

What is important here is that *the above historians and trail driver accounts are not wrong*. The slight differences among the accounts is the basis for this book. The variations in these routes derive from the fact that the varied accounts are of the feeder routes used in Texas.

In order to reach the main trunk of the Western Trail, many feeder routes were used, and over the years, those who wrote about the trails came to believe they were describing a section of the main trunk. When one includes the old Eastern route (like Huntington-Smith did in *We Pointed Them North*) more differences appear. For another example, the Clyde route as shown on the Nimmo map is a feeder route; the San Angelo/Clyde path on Webb's map is a feeder route; and the Mason and Coleman route that Holden mentions is a feeder route. All of these historians ended their description of the main trunk line at Fort Griffin (except for Huntington-Smith's account), thence on to Doan's Crossing on the Red River. The basic point is made by Ernest M. Fletcher, an old cowboy, in his memoirs: "Of course every herd didn't start at San Antonio. They hit the trail wherever it was convenient and left it the same way."[12] In Part II these various feeder routes will be discussed.

Historians do agree that the Western Trail started in and around the San Antonio, Bandera, Kerrville area, but again most maps of the trail (including ours) show the path starting at the southern tip of Texas at Brownsville. That section of Texas from Browsville to San Antonio contained countless feeder routes that came from various ranches in that cattle breeding area. Those feeder routes blended into a major artery which Jimmy Skaggs, in his trail research in the 1960s, indentified as the "Matamoros Feeder Route."[13] Through the years, this major feeder route has been identified as part of the main trunk line, and, in turn, has merited a place on trail maps as a section of the Western Cattle Trail. To scholars of this cattle trail, however, there is an understanding, that trail herds were not sorted, branded, assigned to trail bosses, and prepared for the long journey north until reaching the staging areas of San Antonio, Bandera, and Kerrville. The cattle were not pointed north to a certain destination, in fact, until after these staging preparations were complete. The Matamoros route was a feeder route and San Antonio, Bandera, and Kerrville can claim to be the origin of the Western Trail.

Another fact needs to be kept in mind. Not only did the Matamoros Feeder Route supply the Western Trail, but it was used as well to feed the Shawnee Trail, and later, the Eastern Trail. Southeast of San Antonio, the Shawnee and Eastern branches turned north, northeast from the feeder route and continued to Waco. Just

---

[11]*Fort Worth Star Telegram*, Oct. 30, 1949, page 2.

[12]Ernest M. Fletcher, *The Wayward Horseman*, 33.

[13]Jimmy M. Skaggs, "The Great Western Cattle Trail to Dodge City, Kansas," thesis presented to Texas Technological College, Lubbock, Texas, Aug. 1965, 25.

north of Waco, the Shawnee turned northeasterly and the Eastern, northwesterly. All three cattle trails had a common root — the Matamoros Feeder Route.

> *…the great Texas Trail…will not be forgotten in American history, for it was the greatest and most spectacular pastoral institution of all time.*

J. Evetts Haley, 1929
The XIT Ranch of Texas, page 143 (1967 edition).

PART II
THE WESTERN CATTLE TRAIL

AND ITS FEEDER AND SPLINTER ROUTES BEFORE THE 1885 KANSAS QUARANTINE

> *Later on the Southern herds quit the old trail...intersecting the Western trail in Kimble county…*

George W. Saunders
"A Log of the trails," in
Hunter, *The Trail Drivers of Texas*, 963

> *[We] entered the Western trail at Cow Gap.*

Jack Potter
"Coming up the Trail in 1882," in
Hunter, *The Trail Drivers of Texas*, 59

> *Near Brownwood we turned north, struck the Western Trail near Albany,…*

Richard (Dick) Withers
"The Experience of an Old Trail Driver,"
in Hunter, *The Trail Drivers of Texas*, 311

CHAPTER I

The Western Trail in Texas, The Staging Areas, and its Feeder Routes in Southwest and Central Texas

In order to present the Western Cattle Trail and its feeder routes in Texas, a chronological order has been developed — from south to north. Even though the staging areas were where the trunk line of the trail began, this chapter starts with the feeder routes south of that point. Each feeder route will be presented as you, the reader, moves up the trail.

By the time the Western Cattle Trail was conceived, the practice of trailing Texas longhorns had been tried, tested, and honed to perfection. For more than thirty years, cattle owners and the working cowboys had been developing a defined technique of gathering, trailing, and delivering longhorns to destinations in the north. From the days of the Shawnee Trail of the 1840s and 1850s to the Goodnight trails and Eastern/Chisholm Trail of the mid 1870s, thousands of longhorns were coaxed from their hiding places and formed into herds for the march north. During the Civil War, local longhorns had been ignored and allowed to forage on their own. The cattle had become wild and unmanageable. The first cattle drives after the war must have been challenging, to say the least.

As bi-annual round-ups became a norm,[1] trail-driving Texans became more sophisticated in their craft. After the initial trips north over the new trails, cattle owners no longer tried to accompany their herds north — for they could not afford to be away from their developing ranches for five or six months at a time — but instead hired professional trail drivers to deliver their cattle to the railheads and ranches of the north. These contractors were seasoned drivers who knew the waterways and sand traps of the trail, the temperament of cattle, and the desires of the buyers. They were the ones who made it a win-win situation for the cattle owners. A cattle owner could send a few hundred head up the trail or could contract for several thousand. The contractor did all the work. He was the one who determined how the herds were put together. He hired the trail boss, the outfit, and cook. He bought the supplies and furnished the remuda. For all his organization and time, the contractor received a cut of the final sale price of the herd.

The contractor and owner worked together in selling the herds. Some owners took the long journey north and met their herds at the railhead to negotiate a final sale price. Others depended on the contractor to get the best price for his cattle at the railhead. An animal in south Texas was worth about $4.00, or the value of hide and tallow,[2] but in Kansas or Nebraska, the same longhorn was worth $25 to $30. Because cattle on the open range grazed freely, there was no cost to the owner. Depending on the starting point in Texas, trailing cattle to Kansas cost only about fifty cents to one dollar per head which covered the expense of supplies, horses, and wages for the cowhands. The profit, therefore, was tremendous at the end of the trail. The owner and the contractor could both realize a tidy profit — that is, if the herds were sold. In 1873, an economic crash occurred in New York that reverberated across to the

---

[1]A spring roundup was for counting the cattle and branding the calves. Cattle were also selected at this time for trailing. Another roundup was done in the fall for the purpose of moving the herd to a winter location and for separating and sorting.

[2]Because there was no local market for cattle, longhorns were sold for hide and tallow. In the northern markets, longhorns were sold for beef consumption.

railheads of Kansas and Nebraska. Many cattlemen incurred financial losses that year. Again in 1886, the cattle market was depressed and both owners and contractors suffered with the downturn. As in any business, it was a gamble. There were fortunes made and fortunes lost.

For the most part, the years of cattle trailing changed the complexion of Texas. With millions of dollars acquired from the trailing of cattle, vast ranches were developed, and Texas recovered from a post-war depression. As the Nance poem states: "Texas grew from hide and horn."

Cattlemen using the Kansas Trail from 1867 to 1875 were primarily focused on getting their herds to Kansas and Nebraska railheads from which the cattle were shipped to the eastern markets. The northeast was demanding meat supplied by slaughter houses in Chicago, St. Louis, and other cities in the midwest. The Kansas City Stockyards was established in 1871 along the tracks of the Kansas Pacific and Missouri Pacific. Some cattle were sold to settlers or ranchers in Kansas and Nebraska, but most of the Texas longhorns were now destined to provide beef for the dinner tables in the northeast.

The years of 1874-1875 witnessed major changes, however, even though people at the time did not realize it. Because of the Kansas quarantine law of 1875, the Chisholm Trail was shut down in eastern and central Kansas in 1876, and the Indian wars on the southern plains were over. Tribes were forced onto reservations which left expansive grasslands open — free, for the most part, of Indian villages and buffalo herds; and in 1874, gold was discovered in the Black Hills. The door of opportunity swung wide open for land hungry homesteaders, ranchers, and miners, and at the same time, the Western Cattle Trail started its push northward to supply beef and stock cattle.

Because of the these events, the Western Cattle Trail had two additional markets not available to those who used the former cattle trails. The Indian Bureau needed beef for the Indians on the reservations in Indian Territory and Nebraska and especially, by 1877, on the Great Sioux Reservation in the Dakota Territory.[3] A government contract for a herd of cattle was a lucrative venture.

Secondly, after the buffalo were removed — nearly exterminated — ranchers exploited access to the open range. After it was discovered that the Texas longhorn could survive most northern winters,[4] they were in demand to stock the vast grasslands of Dakota, Montana, and Wyoming territories. The Western Cattle Trail became the major supplier of stock cattle to the north, especially one and two-year olds.

All the major cattle trails in Texas were fed by smaller intersecting routes. It is impossible to identify all of these paths. George W. Saunders said it best when he

---

[3]The Great Sioux Reservation was established in 1868. A great number of the northern Plains Indians were forced into its confines after the Battle of the Little Bighorn where General George Armstrong Custer and his regiment were annihilated on June 25, 1876.

[4]The hardy longhorn on open range could forage and survive winters that were not substantially severe. In December of 1886 and January of 1887, however, a killer blizzard with sub zero temperatures swept through the central plains from Canada to Oklahoma and killed thousands of cattle. After this, ranchers realized that they had to lay up hay for the winter months and provide some shelter to guard against such a disaster from happening again.

wrote: "herds starting from ranches in all parts of the state would intersect the nearest of these Northern trails, coming in from both sides and I doubt if there is a county in the state that did not have a herd traverse some part of it during trail days."[5] On the Western Trail, however, there were several feeder routes that are worth mentioning. These routes seem to have been used numerous times during the trail-driving period. The largest of them all started at Brownsville.

THE MATAMOROS FEEDER ROUTE:
(Map #1-1)

From the beginning of the trail-driving days on the Shawnee Trail, the majority of the longhorns came out of the lower triangle of

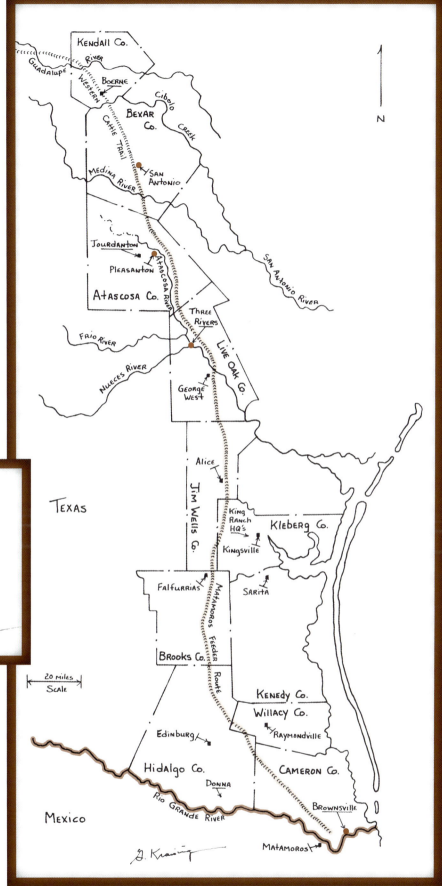

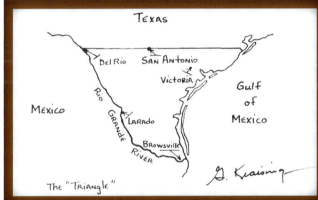

#1-1
The Matamoros Feeder Route:
The Matamoros Feeder Route started at the southern tip of Texas at Brownsville and went to the staging area of San Antonio, the start of the trunk line of the Western Cattle Trail. Many small feeder routes from various ranches in the lower triangle (shown above) fed into this main feeder artery. Even though this heavily used route fed the Shawee, Eastern, and Western cattle trails, it is not part of the trunk line.

---

[5] George W. Saunders, "A Log of the Trails," in Marvin J. Hunter's *The Trail Drivers of Texas*, 964.

THE WESTERN CATTLE TRAIL | 1874-1897

Jimmy Skaggs is the only historian we have found in all of our research who used the term "Great Westerern." It seems to be his exclusive term. Nowhere, before his research (pre-1965) does one find the trail identified with the adjective "great." Today, however, when one sees the term on the internet, in brochures, on roadside markers, and in research, it comes from Jimmy Skaggs' research. The "Great Westerern" term is used often in Texas — Skaggs' home state and where he did his research — but farther north the adjective is dropped. To those in Kansas and Nebraska, for instance, it is just the "Western Cattle Trail." When the Rotary Clubs that organized their trail identification project in Texas began to mark the Western Trail in 2004, they chose to use the term, "Great Western."

Texas. This triangle was the nursery and gathering area for the multiple herds that were trailed north. Here various routes were used to move cattle from one destination to another. When herds were destined to go north to be prepared (staged) for the trail, one feeder route used more than others, which smaller paths led into, was the Matamoros Feeder Route. It traversed the coastal plains area from the southern tip of Texas at Brownsville to San Antonio. Brownsville started as a small squatters' settlement and was in existence when Texas declared its independence from Mexico in 1836. Ten years later General Zachary Taylor's forces constructed, near the settlement, a defensive position against Mexico which lay on the other side of the Rio Grande River. The stronghold became Fort Brown. In 1848, Charles Stillman purchased a large tract of ground that lay along the southern border of Texas and with a partner, Samuel Beldon, laid out a town in the area near old Fort Brown and called their new town Brownsville. It became the county seat of the new Cameron County the following January.

The river town was prosperous during the Civil War and a strong Confederate supply point until Union forces marched on Brownsville. The last battle of the Civil War was just outside of Brownsville at Palmito Ranch.[6] After the Civil War, the town grew modestly and boasted of a population of nearly 5,000 in 1884.[7] The area north of Brownsville, however, was sparsely populated ranch land.

This Matamoros Feeder Route was first identified and named by Jimmy Skaggs in his 1960s research of the "Great Western." Brownsville is the southern terminus of present-day U.S. Highway 77 and 83 and is a major point of entry to Matamoros, Mexico, which is the city across the Rio Grande River from Brownsville. Since Mexican cattle were transported across the river, Skaggs took the name of the Mexican port-city for this feeder trail. He never considered the Matamoros Feeder Route a part of the trunk line but only one of many feeder routes to the Western Cattle Trail.

Using the *Map of the Trail Drivers*,[8] Jimmy Skaggs described the Matamoros route as going:

---

[6]The last land engagement of the Civil War was fought at Palmito Ranch on May 12-13, 1865, thirty-five days after Robert E. Lee surrendered at Appomattox. The battle pitted federal troops, which occupied Brazos Island, and Confederate troops which had occupied Fort Brown since capturing it the year before. The Federals attempted to recapture the fort, but were defeated. (Roadside monument, "Battle of Palmito Ranch," 12 miles east of Brownsville on State Highway 4. and Betty Dooley Awbrey and Claude Dooley, *Why Stop? A Guide to Texas Historical Roadside Markers*, 63)

[7]Alicia A. Garza and Christopher Long, "Brownsville, Texas," *Handbook of Texas Online*, [accessed Dec. 2, 2007]

[8]This *Map of the Trail Drivers* that Skaggs relied on heavily in his research appeared in the *Fort Worth Star Telegram* on Oct. 30, 1949. George W. Saunders also mentioned a "Texas map with those four trails marked, showing their correct route[s]" in a *San Antonio Express* article of Oct. 16, 1931. The map in the *Fort Worth Star Telegram* is actually Jack Potter's map. He was a member of the Old Time Trail Drivers Association. We have been unable to find the Texas map referred to by Saunders or "my 1932 calendar" that was suppose to have "the same kind of map." Both newspaper articles identify that the Western and the Eastern as two different trails and that the Chisholm Trail was north of the Red River — Saunders wrote this some thirty-four years before Skaggs' research.

through creosote brush country, from Brownsville to Escantade, thence turned north-northwestward to Santa Rosa where tall, blue-stem grasses began to replace the creosote bushes, and...continued through the mesquite grass region of Jim Wells and Live Oak counties to the ford of the Nueces River at George West.[9]

This route through Hidalgo and Brooks counties to Jim Wells and Live Oak counties passed west of the expansive King Ranch,[10] through Charles Stillman's old Santa Rosa Ranch,[11] and across the vast George West ranch in Live Oak County.[12] It was long-horn country, and the the Matamoros artery received thousands of cattle from numerous capillary routes throughout the lower triangle.

After crossing the Nueces River, the Matamoros Feeder Route headed upstream to present-day Three Rivers, and continued an almost straight course, going up the east bank of the Atascosa River to a point northeast of Pleasanton. This settlement has been at the confluence of Bonita Creek and the Atascosa River since 1858. It was a perfect location for the early settlers at a junction of two old Spanish roads on the banks of the river under big oak trees. The area had been used as a resting place for years. E. B. Thomas was the first to risk settlement there in 1858 with a home and a general store, and soon there was a church and school. Pleasanton post office was established in 1860. The small community survived Indian attacks and was a thriving settlement of over 200 residents when the cattle drives began in the area. Pleasanton was located among several large ranches and catered to local cowboys as well as trail cowboys.[13]

> Most map makers today show the Shawnee, the Eastern (or erroneously, the Chisholm), and the Western trails as starting at Brownsville, Texas. They are using this Matamoros Feeder Route as part of the trunk trail when they do so. We agree with Skaggs that it was not part of the trunk line. Cattle drivers on the trails did not actually "start up the trail" until after supplies, wagons, horses, etc. were gathered at San Antonio, Bandera, or Kerrville. Road branding took place at these staging areas if the herds had not been branded before leaving the ranch. Herds were trailed into these staging areas on numerous feeder routes including the Matamoros.

---

[9]Jimmy M. Skaggs thesis: "The Great Western Cattle Trail to Dodge City, Kansas," (1965), 25-26.

[10]Richard King and Gideon K. Lewis set up a cattle camp on Santa Gertrudis Creek in South Texas in 1852. They began purchasing Spanish land grants the following year. King bought out Lewis' interest upon the latter's death in 1855. The Running W — King Ranch eventually covered parts of Nueces, Kenedy, Kleberg, and Willacy counties or a total of 825,000 acres. (John Ashton and Edgar P. Sneed, "King Ranch," *Handbook of Texas Online*, [accessed January 10, 2007])

[11]Charles Stillman came to Matamoros, Mexico in 1828, and developed a network of mercantile and industrial enterprises. In 1848 he purchased a large tract of land north of the river on the Texas side. With his smart business sense, he was considered one of the richest men in America by the end of the Civil War. He later sold his enormous ranch to a partner, Mifflin Kenedy. He died in New York in 1875. (John Mason, "Charles Stillman," *Handbook of Texas Online*, [accessed Jan. 25, 2011])

[12]George West and his wife moved to Live Oak County in 1880 and purchased a 140,000-acre ranch and 26,000 head of cattle. The ranch extended from the Nueces River on the north and east to McMullen County on the west. The town of George West was established in 1913 when West donated the land and built a $75,000 courthouse. George West died in 1926. (Kurt House, "George Washington West," *Handbook of Texas Online*, [accessed December 2, 2007])

[13]The old Laredo Trail and the newer Laredo Road ran into the Pleasanton area. Pleasanton was the county seat of Atascosa County until October 1, 1910, when the seat was moved to Jourdanton. The city of North Pleasanton, located north of the old city, was founded in 1912 because of the coming of the Missouri Pacific (Antonio, Uvalde and Gulf) Railroad. In 1961, the two Pleasantons were joined as one city. (Jack Keller, "A History of Pleasanton, Texas," [accessed online July 8, 2005], and Robin Dutton, "Pleasanton, Texas," *The Handbook of Texas Online*, [accessed February 10, 2008])

Menger Hotel, San Antonio, Texas
Nineteen years after the historic battle at the Alamo, German immigrants William and Mary Menger in 1855, purchased the land next to the Alamo Mission in San Antonio and established the first Texas brewery. The success of the brewery led to the addition of a tavern and boarding house. In 1857, the Mengers hired local architect John M. Fries, and he designed and built a two-story limestone building with classical features. Upon its completion in February of 1859, it became the best known and finest hotel west of the Mississippi River. Cattle baron Richard King, who established the King Ranch in south Texas and sent thousands of longhorns up the trail, was a part-time resident of the hotel and died at the Menger in 1885. His funeral services were held in the Menger lobby.

Photo courtesy of the Texas State Library and Archives Commission, Austin, Texas.
www.mengerhotel.com

Texas herds on the Matamoros Feeder Route crossed the Medina River south of historic San Antonio. San Antonio had been founded in 1718 when Spaniards built the mission of San Antonio de Valero and a fort to protect themselves from Apache and Comanche Indian attacks. San Antonio came under Mexican rule when Mexico won its independence from Spain in 1821, and the mission became the location of a the famous Battle of the Alamo on March 6, 1836. Texans won their independence at the Battle of San Jacinto the following month. In 1837, San Antonio was incorporated as a city in the new Republic of Texas and the city grew rapidly.

Cowboys coming in off the feeder trails in the late 1870s would have observed the construction of Fort Sam Houston. By 1880, San Antonio had a population of over 20,000. The Galveston, Harrisburg and San Antonio Railway was built to the city in 1877, and the International-Great Northern railroad reached the city from the northeast in 1881.[14]

The Matamoros Route had been used in the days before statehood as a Mexican road and was later the feeder route for cattle herds to the Shawnee and the Eastern Trails.

At San Antonio, however, a new trail was established when drovers and their herds turned northwestward. No longer did they follow the old route of the Matamoros Feeder that had led into the Shawnee trail toward Austin and Waco, but veered off to create the Western Cattle Trail.[15]

The reason for this new direction was because the *Eastern no longer had an outlet*. If trail herds, starting in the 1876 season, were not turned northwestward at San Antonio, they had to do so farther up the line. The eastern terminals in Kansas were closed. The new railhead was Dodge City, Kansas, and it was west of the old trail systems. George W. Saunders explained in his 1931 address to the seventeenth Old Trail Drivers Reunion that after 1875, "all southern cattle left the Eastern Trail" and "intersected the Western Trail at the nearest point possible."[16]

Therefore, at San Antonio, where the herds turned northwestward, the Matamoros Feeder Route ceased, and the main route began. Outfits and their wagons were supplied at San Antonio, and the next major supply points would be Kerrville or Fort Griffin.

It was in this area — south of San Antonio — that John T. Lytle became a rancher- businessman. He had come to San Antonio as a teenager with his father's

---

[14]Because San Antonio was an economic and military center, most of the area's population was in the city or concentrated in the San Antonio River valley. The rest of the surrounding area was lightly settled and undeveloped. Bexar County (and San Antonio) was located at the "northern apex of the diamond-shaped area that was Texas cattle kingdom." It, therefore, became an important center for the ranching industry. Even though San Antonio had two railroads by 1881, cowboy labor was still cheaper than the cost of shipping by rail. ("San Antonio," *The World Book Encyclopedia*, Vol. 17 (1982), 81, and Christopher Long, "Bexar County," *The Handbook of Texas Online*, [accessed October 4, 2007])

[15]Skaggs, in his research, describes the Matamoros Feeder as going to Kerrville. We disagree with this assertion because the trail herds and their handlers had already prepared, for the most part, for the trail and had turned off of the old course, the Shawnee, to head northwest. Captain Lytle drove his herds to San Antonio in 1874 and turned northwest, a route that proved to be the forerunner of the Western Trail.

[16]"Official Trail Names Adopted," *San Antonio Express*, Oct. 16, 1931, page 7.

family. Four years after returning from the Civil War, where he served with the 32nd Texas Cavalry, he went into partnership with a cousin, Thomas M. McDaniel. They raised livestock and opened a cattle company in present-day Lytle, Texas, where they bought and sold animals on the local market. In 1872, when Captain Lytle was twenty-eight, he and McDaniel started driving herds north to Kansas. In 1874, Charles A. Schreiner of Kerrville[17] and John W. Light of Kimble County[18] joined the firm, which strengthened its prestige and wealth. When it became apparent that the eastern Kansas depots were soon to be shut down, Captain Lytle and his partners were in an ideal location to drive with their herds into San Antonio and blaze the new Western Cattle Trail to Dodge City.[19]

The Matamoros Feeder Route would continue to be used for several more years — only now, it would feed the new Western Cattle Trail.

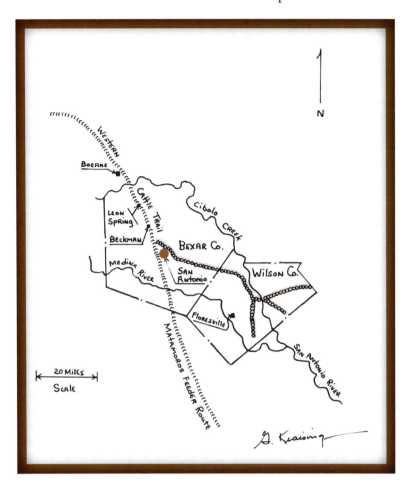

MAP #1-2
The Wilson County Feeder Route:
The Wilson County Feeder Route came out of Wilson County, Texas and cattle herds continued into Bexar County to the staging area of San Antonio, the start of the trunk line of the Western Cattle Trail.

THE WILSON COUNTY FEEDER ROUTE: (Map #1-2)

Another feeder cattle route lead into San Antonio — the Wilson County Feeder Route. It connected the area to the east and southeast of San Antonio to the new trunk line of the Western Cattle Trail. Several smaller feeder routes merged in Wilson County to feed into the Wilson

---

[17] Charles A. Schreiner was born in Alsace-Lorraine, France in 1838 and came to San Antonio in 1852 when "San Antonio was little more than a village." In 1859, he started ranching on Turtle Creek in Kerr County. In 1869, he established a bank and mercantile store in Kerrville. Eventually he became engaged in banking and mercantiles at Junction City and Rock Springs and was connected with the same type of institutions in San Antonio. Captain Schreiner was in the Ranger Service for five years and also served in the Confederate Army. ("Captain Charles Schreiner," in Hunter, 359-362)

[18] C. L. Douglas considered John Light as a "lesser and minor king, as cow royalty went," in his book on *Cattle Kings of Texas*, but Light was to be admired for having started with $8 in his pocket and building a herd of 5,000 by 1876. (Douglas, 200-201)

[19] Lytle was a trail driver who probably used the Western Trail more than any other cattleman. Lytle's company drove between 600,000 to 1,000,000 cattle to market over the Western Cattle Trail, "far more than any other transportation agency." Because of where his ranch was located, the company herds later on could be driven through San Antonio or could procede up the Medina Valley to Bandera and on to Kerrville. (Jimmy Skaggs, "Northward Across the Plains, The Western Cattle Trail," *Great Plains Journal*, Vol. 12, 1972, 55-56, and "Captain John T. Lytle," in Hunter, 322)

Route which followed closely present-day U.S. Highway 87 to San Antonio. The Matamoros Route and the Wilson Route merged into the Western Cattle Trail.

Wilson County had been on the direct path of the earlier Shawnee trail as drovers on that trail pushed their herds to the outfitting center of Austin, Texas. When the Eastern Trail was no longer a viable route to Kansas railheads, the Wilson County trails were redirected, headed northwest instead, and became feeder routes to the new Western Trail.

In 1931, long before Skaggs identified the Matamoros Feeder Route, George W. Saunders indicated that the Western Trail started in Wilson County and went to Wilbarger County (Doan's Crossing.)[20] However, because herds were outfitted in San Antonio, the Western Trail actually started in San Antonio — not in Wilson County.

THE OLD TRAIL FEEDER ROUTE: (Map #1-3)

When the Shawnee Trail was active, cattle were fed into its trunk line from the Matamoros Feeder Route and routes coming out of the Uvalde, Medina, and Frio country area through Bandera. When the later Eastern Trail became active in the late 1870s, these feeder routes fed the same trunk line (Eastern/Shawnee). When the Western Trail started replacing the Eastern Trail in 1874-75, only a part of the Uvalde, Medina, Frio-county area feeder routes continued to be used — the route on the west side of the Western Trail trunk line through Bandera, that fed into Kerrville. The northeastern portion of the old route, on the east side of the Western Trail trunk line, toward the Eastern/Shawnee Trail trunk line, was abandoned. Because this feeder route had been used since the earlier Eastern/Shawnee Trail days, the feeder route that joined the Western Trail trunk line at Kerrville became known as the "Old Trail."[21]

To reach Bandera, herds were trailed from the southwest through Uvalde and from the grasslands of the upper Nueces River valley west and southwest of Castroville.[22] Upon reaching Bandera, cowboys and their herds were only a two day's drive from the main trunk of the Western Cattle Trail at Kerrville. Bandera was in the right location to benefit from the cattle herds and their drovers that were on their way north.

---

[20]George W. Saunders, "A Log of the Trail," in Hunter, *The Trail Drivers of Texas*, 963, and Jimmy Skaggs, thesis, "The Great Western Cattle Trail to Dodge City, Kansas," 25-27.

[21]Jimmy Skaggs in his 1965 thesis referred to this feeder route on his map and in his text as extending into Bandera and labeled it the "Old Trail." He may have been the first to call this feeder by that name. As stated previously, he was the one who identified the feeder route out of Brownsville as the "Matamoros Feeder Route." (Skaggs' thesis, Ibid, 26-28)

[22]Castroville in Medina County was a very old community. It had been colonized by Henri Castro and his followers who were mostly Catholic Alsatian farmers. They chose to settle on the bend of the Medina River in 1844. Their houses were distinctly European, and they built St. Louis Catholic Church, the first church in Medina County in 1844. Castroville also had the county's first post office that opened in 1847. During the cattle driving era, the county seat of Castroville was a thriving community with a population of around 1,000. (Ruben E. Ochoa, "Castroville, Texas," *Handbook of Texas Online* [accessed Dec. 2, 2007])

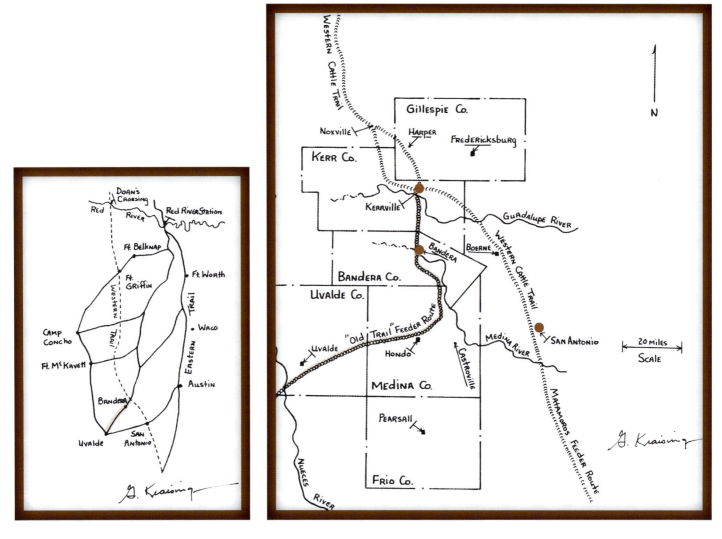

MAP #1-3
The "Old Trail" Feeder Route:
The "Old Trail" Feeder Route came out of the counties south of Bandera including Frio, Uvalde, and Medina, through the staging area of Bandera in Bandera County and on to Kerrville to connect with the Western Trail trunk line.

Before the Western Trail existed, various feeder routes fed into the Shawnee Trail. When the Western Trail replaced the Shawnee Trail, these feeder routes ceased going into the Shawnee, but still were used to feed into the Western. The insert shows the network of routes east of the Western Trail that were abandoned when the Western Trail was established. This old Shawnee Trail route was then referred to as the Eastern Trail.

The larger detailed map shows a portion of the old feeder route ("Old Trail") coming out of the Bandera area, only now it merged with the Western Cattle Trail and did not continue northeast to the older trail system.

THE STAGING AREAS —
SAN ANTONIO, BANDERA,
AND KERRVILLE:

In the area of San Antonio, Bandera, and Kerrville, cattlemen prepared, or staged their stock for the long trip to Kansas and beyond. It was in this area that the contractor, owner, or trail boss hired additional hands and prepared the herds and outfits. If there were several herds coming in from various ranches on the feeder routes under the arrangements of one contractor, here was where he would take over the operation of sorting and assigning the cattle to a trail boss or bosses. He hired cooks and cowboys to handle the task at hand, bought chuck wagons, supplies, and the needed horses (remuda), and saw to it that the trail bosses under him were doing their job. Road branding the cattle for the trail was started as soon as holding pens could be constructed.

One such contractor was Lewis W. Neatherlin. A Confederate veteran whose family had moved to Frio County, Texas, in 1850, Neatherlin was an experienced trail driver, and in 1876 his cousin John H. Slaughter[23] asked him to oversee the operation of trailing his cattle to the northern markets. Neatherlin had been up the Eastern/Chisholm as a trail boss in 1875, that trail's last year in Kansas. The state had quarantined its eastern railheads against the Texas Fever, and Neatherlin had experienced the repercussions of the law. He and his drovers had been arrested for crossing their herd over private property, but had managed to secure his release.

Thus, in 1876, when Slaughter planned to send his cattle north, he knew his herds would have to follow the lead of Captain Lytle and explore the newly established Western Trail toward Dodge City, Kansas. It was an unknown route to Neatherlin, as well as to many of the Texas trail drivers. Dodge City had been receiving cattle for only two seasons, and had been busily building pens and cattle chutes, not to mention saloons and mercantile stores. In 1876, with no eastern railhead open, Dodge was ready to receive an extra onslaught of cattle coming from Texas.

Aware of the circumstances of traveling on an uncertain route, Slaughter entrusted the older, experienced Neatherlin to

Jimmy Skaggs laid much of the groundwork of research on the Western Trail in Texas. In his 1965 thesis, however, he showed the Matamoros Feeder Route and the "Old Trail" Feeder Route as going into Kerrville, where he proposed that the Great Western Trail began. In his 1978 book, *Ranch and Range in Oklahoma*, he restated his direction and wrote: "the new cattle trail in Texas — called the Western or Dodge City Trail — merely absorbed the older route from Brownsville previously used by the Shawnee and [Eastern] Chisholm trails. Once at San Antonio, however, the Western Trail swung northwestward to Kerrville and then turned northward..." (page 13) Skaggs had eventually come to the same conclusion that we have here--the Western Trail started farther southeast, namely at the point where drovers turned northwest out of San Antonio. The Matamoros Feeder ceased at San Antonio, and the trunk line of the Western Cattle Trail began with the route from San Antonio to Kerrville.

Skaggs also emphasized in his 1978 work that "In Texas, the [Eastern] Chisholm Trail was merely the old Shawnee Trail northward from Brownsville to Fort Worth." (page 10) This is an error. The old Shawnee Trail actually went to Waco, not Fort Worth. From Waco, the trail turned northeast toward Dallas. Readers need to understand that the Eastern/Chisholm Trail — or more accurately the Abilene Trail during these early trail days — followed the "the old Shawnee Trail northward," and trail markings in that area of Texas should explain that the Shawnee Trail was there first.

---

[23]John Horton Slaughter was a cattle baron and a cousin to Lewis Neatherlin. The large ranching operation in Frio County involved Ben Slaughter, his father, and brothers: William James (Billie), Charley, and John H. This family should not be confused with the enormous Lazy S. Ranch in Palo Pinto County where another set of Slaughter brothers ran a ranching operation, Col. C. C. Slaughter, Peter E., John B., and William B. Slaughter. Their father was the Rev. George Webb Slaughter. (Hunter, *The Trail Drivers of Texas*, 607-611)

handle his cattle. He was to oversee the trailing of three herds of three thousand head each to Ogallala, Nebraska. Neatherlin met with two of the herds on Leon Creek, six miles west of San Antonio on the evening of March 12, and caught up with the third just below the Medina River three days later. They had been driven up from the south Texas Slaughter ranch, and each herd was lead by a trail boss. Over the next twenty-six days, the forty-three-year-old Neatherlin purchased supplies in San Antonio, hired men and cooks, acquired horses, and as he wrote in his journal of March 22, "Met Kellogg [a trail boss] in town. Bought leggins and overcoats for his men. J. W. Caie, who is in charge of now no. 3 [herd], come in this evening, and I bought him a wagon, 1 work horse, supplies and hired him a cook, and sent him out." On the following day he "Went to the bank with Slaughter where he made arrangements for me to draw money at Fort Griffin to buy supplies."[24]

During the month, Lewis Neatherlin rode among the three cow camps that were scattered several miles apart. He did so to determine the needs of each one or to drive horses or stray animals to the herds. He helped with round-up in camp no. 3

---

[24]Kerrville (about 65 miles farther northwest) was the next supply point for herds coming from the San Antonio area. Since Neatherlin had outfitted at San Antonio, his next planned supply point was Fort Griffin, 270 miles up the trail.

on March 24. More than twice, he recorded, "my pony give out," and he had to stay the night wherever he could.[25]

The outfits, meanwhile, were preparing the cattle for the trip. In the cow camps, a road brand was burned into the side of each animal so that all the cattle in one herd could be recognized as belonging to that herd. The brand was not as deep into the hide as the owner's brand on the rump of the cow. This "hair brand" was to be used only to identify stock for the duration of the trip. The chances of a stampede or the mingling of several herds at river crossings was inevitable, and the road brand helped the cowboys to find animals that belonged to their herd. The contractor was required to carry papers from each owner to show any inspectors that the cattle were under his jurisdiction. The Texas Legislature in 1870 had authorized the governor to appoint cattle inspectors to check herds moving north in order to prevent the practice of trailing lost or stolen cattle. In Slaughter and Neatherlin's situation, all the cattle belonged to Slaughter. Therefore, the cowboys had to be sure that all animals had a clear brand and that there were no stray animals. Every animal had to be checked for brands and quality of fitness to withstand the long trail ahead.

When finished with the branding in the cow camps and the acquiring of supplies in San Antonio, drovers pushed their herds northwestward to Beckman and then along the east bank of Leon Creek to Leon Springs, a popular watering hole. The route then crossed the "Balcones Creek, forded the Cibolo Creek at Boerne and the Guadalupe River at Comfort, and then followed the north bank of Cypress Creek to Kerrville."[26]

As the Slaughter herds started their trek north out of San Antonio, Lewis Neatherlin went to Boerne and acquired an inspector to look over the second herd that was passing through the area. On March 31, he wrote of the citizens of Boerne checking out the herd: "All the Dutch turned out in mass; men, women and children." he said. "Some on foot and some on horseback. We crossed the Cibolo without any trouble, or without them [the settlers] finding anything in the herd." Neatherlin then journeyed back eight miles to meet the third and last remaining herd.[27]

On the following day, April 1, the number one herd, according to Neatherlin, trailed through Boerne, passed inspection, and crossed the Cibolo River. Again, according to Neatherlin, there was a "Good turnout of Dutch, but not so many as yesterday. ...we had no strays."

On April 3, the three herds continued to ease their way north while Neatherlin bought horses and "swap[ed] a poor one for a fat one." On that day the first two herds

---

[25]A few days later, Neatherlin dismissed J. W. Caie as a trail boss and replaced him with his younger brother Jim Neatherlin. The problem he had with Caie was not explained in his journal, but Neatherlin purchased Caie a horse and sent him away. "Round-up" here refers to the process of cutting out, sorting, and branding the animals for the trail. (Kelly, ed. *Up the Trail in '76, the Journal of Lewis Warren Neatherlin*, 3-8)

[26]Skaggs, thesis, Ibid, 27.

[27]Neatherlin journal, March 31, 1876. Boerne was about half way between San Antonio and Kerrville. It sat on the north side of Cibolo Creek and had been a settlement since the organization of the county in 1859. A community of "free thinking" German immigrants, Boerne, along with her neighbor to the north, Comfort, were the first established post offices in Kendall County, both opened in the summer of 1859. Here Neatherlin is commenting about the local settlers turning out to check the herd for their own cattle that may have joined the passing herd.

THE WESTERN CATTLE TRAIL | 1874-1897

camped three miles "above Comfort." Neatherlin and the two camped herds waited for the third herd, led by Jim Neatherlin. On April 7, all three herds passed through Kerrville and camped three miles above town on Goat Creek.[28] The Neatherlin-lead herds were on the trunk line headed north.

Bandera was also a staging area and supply depot for trail cattle. Herds using the "Old Trail" Feeder Route through Medina County had followed the western bank of the Medina River and, south of Bandera, had passed the abandoned Mormon Camp.[29]

When arriving at Bandera, drovers discovered a community that had existed since 1856. Its residents, for the most part, earned their living from sheep and cattle ranching and were well equipped to be part of the cattle driving industry during the 1870s and 1880s. As thousands of cattle were funneled into the community starting in early spring, local farm boys hired out as cowboys; ranchers built holding pens and became trail bosses; and shopkeepers contracted as outfitters.[30] The community understood that large quantities of supplies were needed to outfit each herd. Chuck

---

[28] About ten years later (1886-87), Jasper Lauderdale, a veteran trail driver, also wrote that they watered herds "at Leon Springs, Cibolo, at Boerne, the Guadalupe at Comfort, Goat Creek, Devil's River, James River...." (Jasper (Bob) Lauderdale, "Reminiscences of the Trail," in Hunter, 409)

[29] Led by their elder Lyman Wight, the colony of Mormons in 1856 built a furniture factory and sold furnishings in nearby San Antonio. When their elder died in 1858, the colony of approximately 250 people scattered. Today the camp is covered by Medina Lake. (Christopher Long, "Bandera County," *The Handbook of Texas Online* [accessed October 9, 2007])

[30] Long, "Bandera County," in *Handbook of Texas* and Myron Janzen, "Bandera County Post Offices," in *Texas Post Offices*, unpublished manuscript.

wagons were filled with barrels, tins, and sacks of food items. If the cowboy outfit and herd were larger than average, a supply wagon, called a hooligan wagon, was sometimes added to carry the gear including tarps, bedrolls, rain slickers, tents, and horse tack.

Jasper Lauderdale and C. F. Carroll started to Kansas in the spring of 1880, and they used this route. Lauderdale later recalled: "at Bandera we threw our herds together because several of Carroll's hands quit him, and I drove the combined herds to Ogallala."[31]

Equipped with supplies and a remuda, the trail bosses pointed their herds north out of Bandera and traversed Bandera Pass as Indian, Spaniards, and various armies had for centuries before them. A long limestone ridge separated the Medina and Guadalupe river valleys. Three miles outside of the pass in Kerr County, the abandoned post of Camp Verde would have been visible. As early as 1846, whites had

Favorite Saloon, built in 1874, Kerrville, Texas
This saloon was located on Water Street in Kerrville across from the Schreiner store. Here cowboys could stop at the Favorite Saloon for a drink of whiskey before heading out on their long trail drive. The stone building was built in 1874 and was designed by Alfred Giles of San Antonio.
Photo courtesy of owner William Rector, Kerrville, Texas.

---

[31]Lauderdale, Ibid, 407.

THE WESTERN CATTLE TRAIL | 1874-1897

tried to settle the area of Kerrville and to colonize the Guadalupe River valley into the 1850s, but were faced with frequent Indian raids. In response, the United State Army established Camp Verde on July 8, 1855, on the northern bank of Verde Creek to provide protection. At this post, the Army experimented with the use of camels as a means for transport, communications, and travel. The camp was abandoned in 1869, only a few years before the Western Trail got underway.[32]

At Kerrville the "Old Trail" Feeder joined with the Western Cattle Trail. Kerrville was a center for outfitters, and what supplies not acquired at Bandera or San Antonio (by trail bosses and their herds coming from the south), were purchased in Kerrville — mostly at the Charles A. Schreiner Mercantile. Cowboys and trail bosses knew it would be a stretch before they would reach another supply point, Fort Griffin.

The Schreiner Department Store in Kerrville, Texas
Charles Armand Schreiner (1838-1927) moved to Kerrville with his family in 1869 and with the aid of August Faltin went into the general merchandising business. Their first store on Water Street consisted of a slab white-washed building heated with a box stove. As Schreiner prospered, he bought out his partner in 1879. The Charles Schreiner Company extended its activities to banking, ranching, and marketing wool and mohair. Schreiner purchased the YO Ranch in 1880 for his cattle operation which encompassed also the Live Oak Ranch for his sheep operations. Schreiner was part of the Schreiner, Lytle and Light partnership that trailed over 150,000 longhorns north over the trail. As the trunk line of the Western Trail moved west, Schreiner, being a shrewd businessman, also placed mercantiles in Rock Springs and Junction for the convenience of the trail drivers.

This photo shows the Schreiner Department Store and Bank in Kerrville around 1893. The building in the background is the Schreiner Wool Warehouse.

Photo from the Schreiner family collection, courtesy of William Rector, Kerrville, Texas.

---

[32] Secretary of War Jefferson Davis had arranged for forty camels to be used for a system of overland transportation of supplies from Camp Verde. As late as 1949, remains of camel corrals and buildings were still standing. ("Camp Verde." *The Handbook of Texas Online* [accessed December 9, 2007])

Like San Antonio and Bandera, Kerrville had been settled early and was a growing community during the cattle driving days. Its original settlement was as a shinglemakers' camp on the Guadalupe River in the early 1850s and was called Brownsborough, named after one of the colony's shinglemakers. Kerr County was created and organized in 1856, and Brownsborough became "Kerrsville" and the county seat. On June 9, 1858, Kerrville obtained the first post office for the county.[33] In 1869, Captain Schreiner started his mercantile business.

All three communities today claim to be the beginning of the Western Cattle Trail. Since the staging process was completed at all three locations, and since all three communities helped outfit and supply the drovers, it is understandable that each one would now view themselves as the start of the trail. In a sense, their claims are justified.

THE TRUNK LINE OF THE WESTERN CATTLE TRAIL TO PEGLEG CROSSING:

On the main trunk line of the Western Trail, there were rivers to cross and a vast open range ahead. There was no looking back, but only thoughts of their destination. For the local trail drivers, it would be four to seven months before they would return south. Cattle herds stretched out one behind the other. G. F. Boone, who was a trail driver for Buchanan and Beatty in the early 1880s, commented: "This was in the days when a herd a day went up the trail, each one following the other."[34] It was early spring, and several contractors and owners prepared herds and outfits. For several days, as each one was readied for the trail, a herd was placed in line for the journey north.

Upon leaving Kerrville, outfits followed one of two routes. Perhaps because of the congestion in linning up for the trail, or because of a preference of the Johnson Creek or the Town Creek routes, whichever creek had flowing water at the time, a split was created. The Johnson Creek route went west-northwest and the Town Creek route went straight north. For Lewis Neatherlin's three herds, the west-northwest route was chosen. He noted in his journal the delay in leaving the Kerrville area: "The citizens stopped all the herds and cut out strays, or their own cattle, as they term it. Did not get through till 2 o'clock, at which time we started up the mountain."[35] They started from Goat Creek and pushed along the Guadalupe River (in Kerr County)

---

[33]Camp Verde opened the second post office in the county on the following day, June 10, 1858. (Janzen, Myron. "Kerr County Post Offices," Texas Post Offices, unpublished manuscript)

[34]A "herd a day" was true only during the peak season, three or four months. Herds were not trailed all year long. An average of 100 to 150 herds a year went up the trail (G. F. Boone. written recollection for *American Life Histories: Manuscripts from the Federal Writers' Project, 1936-1940*. [accessed online December 9, 2007]

[35]Neatherlin Journal, April 8, 1876. Some historians say that Neatherlin was one of the first to blaze the new Western Trail in 1876. The Millett & Mabry and Ellison & Deewees outfits had trailed herds totaling 100,000 head the year before, but the trail was still new and unknown by many trailhands in 1876. By the 1880s, however, when the Western Trail was in full bloom, herds going through Kerrville stacked up one behind the other to enter the Western, as witnessed by G. F. Boone.

1

GREAT WESTERN CATTLE TRAIL

IN 1874, RANCHER JOHN T. LYTLE FOUNDED THE GREAT WESTERN CATTLE TRAIL WHICH BECAME THE PRIMARY ROUTE THROUGH WHICH CATTLE CAME TO NORTHERN U.S. MARKETS. THE ROUTE , ALSO KNOWN AS THE WESTERN TRAIL, THE DODGE CITY TRAIL, AND THE FORT GRIFFIN TRAIL, WAS OVER 2,000 MILES LONG, EXTENDING FROM TEXAS TO CANADA. DURING ITS EXISTENCE, HUNDREDS OF THOUSANDS OF HEADS OF CATTLE PASSED OVER THE TRAIL EACH YEAR. IT ENTERED KERR COUNTY AT BANDERA PASS FOLLOWED THE OLD ROAD (NOW STATE HIGHWAY 173) THROUGH CAMP VERDE AND VERDE PASS, CROSSING THE GUADALUPE RIVER AT KERRVILLE. KERRVILLE BECAME A CENTER FOR TRAIL OUTFITTING AND CONTRACTORS, MOSTLY AT THE CHARLES A. SCHREINER MERCANTILE, WHILE CATTLE PENS OPERATED NEAR McFARLAND STREET ABOVE TOWN CREEK. THE TRAIL THEN FOLLOWED TOWN CREEK ALONG WHAT IS NOW HARPER ROAD AND DEPARTED THE COUNTY NORTH OVER THE PERIL DIVIDE.

IN 1874, CHARLES A. SCHREINER OF KERRVILLE AND JOHN W. LIGHT JOINED LYTLE'S CATTLE BUSINESS; THEY OPERATED THEIR FIRM OUT OF LYTLE (ATASCOSA CO.) AND KERRVILLE. IN 1887, SCHREINER BOUGHT FULL CONTROL OF THE FIRM. SCHREINER WAS POLITICALLY AND FINANCIALLY INSTRUMENTAL TO KERRVILLE; HE INVESTED IN LOCAL BANKING AND MERCANTILE VENTURE, AND WAS A PHILANTHROPIST IN THE COMMUNITY.

BY 1886, THE ROUTE WAS NO LONGER USED AS A CATTLE TRAIL, THE OVERGRAZING OF GRASSLANDS, EXTENSION OF RAILROADS, FENCING IN OF THE OPEN RANGE AND OVERSUPPLY OF CATTLE WERE AMONG THE FACTORS THAT LED TO THE DEMISE OF CATTLE DRIVES. HOWEVER, THE GREAT WESTERN TRAIL CONTINUES TO BE REMEMBERED AS A SIGNIFICANT DEVELOPMENT THAT SHAPED THE CULTURE AND HISTORY OF KERR COUNTY, AND OF TEXAS AND THE NATION AT LARGE.

MARKER IS PROPERTY OF THE STATE OF TEXAS (2009)

Location: two miles north of Kerrville on Highway 783

Authors' commentary:
This recent road-side marker shows the careful research done by the Kerr County Historical Commission. It is very well done and accurate. However, the traveler should be aware that this is not the only route that entered and left Kerrville. This Town Creek route goes north out of Kerrville, but there was another route that went west and then north out of Kerrville.

The route that "entered Kerr County at Bandera Pass [and] followed the Old Road" was the Old Trail Feeder Route that we refer to, and it then fed into the main trunk of the Western Trail at Kerrville. This main trunk line entered Kerrville from the southeast from San Antonio.

for about three miles to the mouth of Johnson Creek. They followed Johnson Creek west fork, passed Mountain Home,[36] and crossed over to the headwaters of the Little Devil's River where they watered the cattle. They then proceeded to the James River in Kimble County and followed that river down its east side to a small settlement called Noxville.

Lewis Neatherlin noted almost daily the problems with water north of Kerrville.

On April 9: "No water for stock."
On April 10: "Grazed South Fork of James River. Several cows left in river. Could not get [them] out."
April 11: "Had to drive 6 miles to make a watering on James River. Very bad watering. Lost other cattle in the bog."

Neatherlin also faced problems with the horses.
April 8: "Two horses got down today and could not be got up, and was left on the road."
April 11: "The lame horse gave out late this evening."
April 14: "Lost five horses last night. I think they are stolen."

And on the next day, Neatherlin "Swapped a poor horse and cow & calf for a fat horse."

The Town Creek route out of Kerrville was straight north into Gillespie County. Herds were pushed from the cattle pens that were near McFarland Street above Town Creek They trailed north, following Town Creek, departed Kerr County, and then drove over the Peril and Nott divides in Gillespie County. They passed west of Harper[37], trailed to the head of the Pedernales River, crossed Little Devil's River to the James River, and eventually reached the Llano River at Beef Trail Crossing.[38] See Map #1-3.

One account of the Town Creek route was written by Ernest Schwethelm, who was a cowboy who followed this branch in 1885. Captain Schreiner of Kerrville decided to send up four herds late that year, and twenty-four-year-old Schwethelm hired on as the horse wrangler under trail boss Alex Crawford. There were eleven cowboys in the outfit, and they started "from the gathering pen on Town Creek in the month of August" trailing 2,000 head. "We drove up Town Creek, and into

---

[36] Between Goat Creek and Little Devil's River in Kerr County on Johnson Creek was Mountain Home, a small colony on the trail after 1879. Hiram Louis Nelson was granted a postmaster's position on December 1, 1879, in his residence. It may have been a stop for trail hands. (Janzen, Ibid)

[37] At the Harper location, Matthew Taylor and Eli McDonald settled with their families in 1863. In August of 1864, two members of the McDonald family were killed by Kiowa Indians and a young mother and four children were captured. In 1883, George Franklin Harper established a post office, and the settlement became known as "Harper." (www.realestate-harper.com/harpertexas)

[38] Mrs. Joe Felps, Chairwoman, "Old Beef Trail Crossing," *Recorded Landmarks of Kimble County*, Junction, TX: Kimble County Historical Survey Committee, 1971, 27. The route today is Harper Road or Highway 783. (State of Texas highway marker, two miles north of Kerrville on Highway 783) Confirmation of this route is found on a 1885 U. S. Department of Interior Geological Survey map, 1894 edition. Upon reaching Kimble County, the route is Highway 479 to Noxville. (email and interview: William R. Rector, MD, of Kerrville, May 26, 2010)

OLD BEEF TRAIL CROSSING MARKERS 1965 AND 1997

2
OLD BEEF TRAIL

300 YARDS DOWN THE MAIN LLANO IS CROSSING USED 1867-1900 BY CATTLE HERDS OF REAL, FRIO, KERR, KIMBLE, MEDINA, EDWARDS, UVALDE COUNTIES. CAPTS. CHAS. A. SCHREINER AND JOHN LYTLE PUT HALF A MILLION "SL" CATTLE OVER THIS END OF WESTERN TRAIL, UP TO MARKET IN DODGE CITY. ALSO THIS WAY WENT HERDS OF "7 O L," WESTERN UNION BEEF CO., SETH MABRY, TERRY, HODGES AND SCHMELTER RANCHES.

IN EARLY DAYS VEHICLES FROM LONDON AND JUNCTION FORDED HERE ON WAY TO FREDERICKSBURG, SAN ANTONIO, KERRVILLE. HERE ALSO IN OLD-TIME CAMP MEETINGS, SETTLERS CONVENED FOR WEEKS.   (1965)

2
OLD BEEF TRAIL CROSSING

ONCE USED FOR REVIVALS, THIS USED 1867-1900 BY CATTLE HERDS OF REAL, FRIO, MAIN LINE OF THE SPRING CATTLE DRIVES FROM 1867 TO THE 1880S. CAPT. C.A. SCHREINER AND HIS PARTNERS HERDED CATTLE ON THEIR WAY TO ABILENE AND DODGE CITY ON THE WESTERN TRAIL; MANY AREA COWBOYS RODE WITH THEM, PRECEDED BY A TRAIL BOSS AND CHUCKWAGON, AS MANY AS 2,000 CATTLE PER HERD TOOK HALF A DAY TO CROSS. WITH THE AIR FULL OF DUST, LOCAL RANCHERS SAT ON THEIR HORSES WATCHING THEIR OWN CATTLE CLOSELY TO ENSURE THAT NONE OF THEIR HERD JOINED THE TRAIL DRIVE. THIS SITE LATER BECAME A VEHICLE CROSSING.

Location: at Yates Crossing on Llano River on FM 385, 6.3 miles south of London, Kimble Co., Texas

Authors' commentary:
In describing this marker, Mrs. Joe Felphs wrote: *"It is one of several feeder trails that merges with the Western Trail."*[1]

A marker placed here in 1965 appears to have been replaced by the later one, perhaps because it specifically describes the Nueces River Feeder Route and not the Western Trail. It was an important marker for it gave the names and brands of the ranchers who used the trail.[2]

Note that this marker was pre-Jimmy Skaggs, so the trail is "the Western." The dates are incorrect. They should be 1874 to late 1880s.

Location: on FM 385 where it crosses the Llano River, just below where the Red Creek flows into the Llano. The marker is on the south side of the river and east side of the road near Yates, Texas, Kimble Co.

Authors' commentary:
This marker, placed in 1997, provides confusing information on the Eastern and Western trails and dates and cattle towns! The marker is about the Llano River Crossing on the Western, but the beginning date (1867) is of the Abilene Trail which did not use this crossing. This crossing was not used by the Western Trail until 1874 to go to Dodge City, Kansas. Abilene, Kansas should not have been mentioned on this marker for it is on a different trail system and ceased to be used after 1872.[3]

---

[1]Mrs. Joe Felps, "Old Beef Trail Crossing," opcit.
[2]Awbrey & Dooley, Why Stop? *A Guide to Texas Historical Roadside Markers*, 248.
[3]"Kimble Co. Historical Marker," www.forttours.com. [accessed Jan. 23, 2011] Abilene, Texas, was not a consideration here because it was not on the Trail.

Gillespie County by way of Harper and the James River ranch," he wrote. Because the herds were started late in the season, two of the herds were delivered to Hardeman County, Texas, in November and wintered out. Schwethelm and his companions returned to Kerrville "spending a good part of our wages coming home."[39]

The two routes out of Kerrville joined at the James River at Noxville. At first, the only resident at the river was Creed Taylor. He had come to the James River area sometime in 1868 or 1869 and had built a two-story native stone ranch house there in 1869-1871. Captain Taylor was a hero to many fellow Texans because of his part in the Texas War for Independence, especially at the Battle of San Jacinto. He joined the Texas Rangers in 1841, and had served in the Civil War. His ranch house on the James River, where he lived with his wife and several children, was considered one of the finest homes west of San Antonio.

Early in the 1870s, or perhaps about the time that Captain Lytle started trailing north with his cattle on the Western Trail, others came to the area and settled four and one half miles east of Captain Taylor's ranch house on the Little Devils River. Noah Nox opened a store, and it was designated as a post office in 1879, and his wife, Persis, was the postmistress. A year later the Noxville school, also made of native stone, was built.[40]

When the Slaughter herds camped on the James River in 1876, Neatherlin noted in his journal that they were "1 mile from Taylor's Ranch." On April 12, Lewis Neatherlin went to visit Captain Taylor and "asked his advice about leaving the trail. He thought it best to do so and went to show us the way, going about 4 miles with us and giving us the course."[41] Neatherlin was still working his way up an unfamiliar trail. Several herds were behind him, and Neatherlin stopped to ask advice.[42] Watering had been a problem and perhaps he was looking for a sure route with water. His journal notes that they traveled six miles that day "on some high prairie hills or mountains," but still there was "no water."

As one herd, like Neatherlin's led the way, others would follow, spreading out two or three miles on each side of the route for grazing opportunities. At first, the cattle were driven hard and kept in a fairly tight formation until they were out of the way of settlements and on the open range. As G. F. Boone recalled, "we'd just drift

---

[39]Ernest Schwethelm wrote this account in 1931 at the age of seventy. He wrote, referring to their herd, that "It was a bad winter and many of them died." (the blizzard of 1886.) The cattle, however, were later "driven into Indian Territory." Schreiner, "joined the herd on the way up, [and] infact, [sic] went back and forth between the herds, advising with the foremen." (J. J. Starkey, "Pioneer History," *Kerrville Times*, Nov. 19, 1931)

[40]Anthony B. Gaxiola, "Noxville, TX," *Handbook of Texas Online* [accessed Feb. 1, 2011] and "Texas Ghost Towns, Noxville, Texas," TexasEscapes.com [accessed Feb. 5, 2011]

[41]Neatherlin journal, April 12 entry. Dovie Tschirhart Hall, "Creed Taylor," *The Handbook of Texas Online* [accessed February 23, 2008] "Site of Creed Taylor Ranch Home," historical marker on FM 1534, 19 miles east of Junction and just west of the James River on FM 479, west of Noxville, Texas. Betty Dooley Awbrey & Claude Dooley, *Why Stop? A Guide to Texas Historical Roadside Markers*, 249. Captain Creed Taylor died on December 26, 1906, and was buried in the Old Noxville Cemetery.

[42]Remember that Jim Neatherlin, the younger brother of Lewis, was trail boss for herd number 3. He had been selected by an association of trail drivers to "perfect a route through the settlements north of San Antonio." The older brother, Lewis, was out in front of the three heards, scouting the way. (Jack Potter, *Cattle Trails of the Old West*, 17)

along and let the cattle grow fat on the place. We'd drive them five or six miles in a day, then drift three or four miles 'til they bedded down at nightfall."[43]

After heading northward through sprinkled groves of cedar and oak trees, the herds forded the Llano River at Beef Trail Crossing where the Red Creek dumps into the Llano. Here at the crossing, the Western Trail trunk line continued north toward Pegleg Crossing on the San Saba River and Waldrip's Bend on the Colorado River. Beef Trail Crossing, however, has a great significance in that another sizable cattle route made this its crossing. The 1965 historical crossing marker alluded to this route.

NUECES RIVER FEEDER ROUTE: (Map #1-4)

After the Western had been used for a number of years, another feeder route developed and followed the Nueces River. It joined the Western trunk at Beef Trail Crossing. As settlements crowded the main trunk and central Texas filled up with communities, trailing cattle herds moved farther west. George Saunders, in his "A Log of the Trails," explained this later route:

> Later on the Southern herds quit the old trail in San Patricio county and went through Live Oak, McMullen, LaSalle, Dimmit, Zavala, Uvalde, Edwards, and intersecting the Western Trail in Kimble county, from where all followed the well defined and much traveled Western trail to Doan's Crossing on Red River.[44]

When Saunders states that the route intersected the Western in Kimble County, he was referring to Beef Trail Crossing on the Llano River. Saunders, in a later article, added Real County to the route[45] and wrote that in Kimble County, "it joined the first Western Trail."[46]

Looking on the map, one can see that the Nueces route swung around the congested areas of developing Texas settlements. This route began to be used in about 1883 and followed the Nueces River Valley to the Nueces Canyon near its headwaters in Edwards County and then continued down the South Fork Llano River to its junction with the North Fork to the Old Beef Trail Crossing in Kimble County. It became the preferred route to use, and the "old trail" or the "first Western Trail," to Beef Trail Crossing, as Saunders called it, was used less.[47]

---

[43]Boone, Ibid.

[44]George W. Saunders, "A Log of the Trails," in Hunter, 963. Saunders' above article was included in the 1924 publishing of Hunter's *The Trail Drivers of Texas*.

[45]Texas map in the flat-map archieves at the Texas State Library in Austin, Texas, shows a military road through the Nueces Canyon in Real County. This road was probably used by the cattle herds.

[46]"Official Trail Names Adopted," *San Antonio Express*, Oct. 16, 1931.

[47]This Nueces River route also split off west of Juntion, Texas, went through Fort McKavett north to San Angelo. This "Ghost Trail" will be discussed later.

This later feeder route passed east of Rock Springs and through Junction. Captain Charles Schreiner, a shrewd business man, established mercantile and banking interests in those towns as well. He started in Kerrville, but as time passed, he could see that the movement of cattle was shifting farther west, so he placed mercantile stores on the new path.

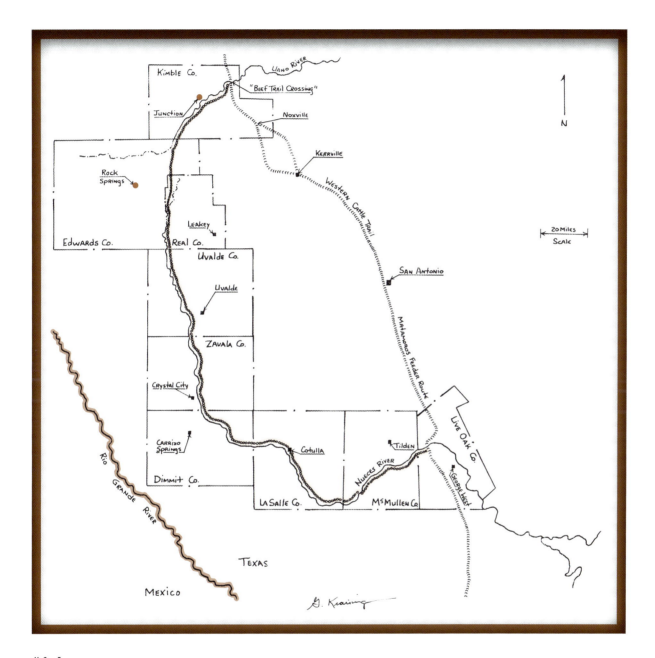

#1-4
The Nueces River Feeder Route:
The Nueces River Feeder Route followed the Nueces River from Three Rivers in Live Oak County, Texas, to its source in Edwards County, down the South Llano River in Kimble County and connected with the Western Trail trunk line at Beef Trail Crossing.

Even though this route was very rough, starting about 1883, this feeder route became the preferred route for cattle herds because settlements were crowding the main trunk line of the Western Trail.

3
PEG LEG CROSSING
ON THE SAN SABA: ABOUT 1 MI. NE

AN HOURGLASS-SHAPED PASS THROUGH THE HILLS WHERE MCDOUGAL CREEK JOINS SAN SABA RIVER, FOR YEARS A FAVORED INDIAN CAMPGROUND, IT ENTERED WRITTEN HISTORY, 1732, AS SITE OF SPANISH-APACHE BATTLE.

SAW PASSAGE OF ADVENTURERS, MUSTANG HUNTERS, INDIAN FIGHTERS, GERMAN SETTLERS, GOLD-SEEKERS.

PROBABLY NAMED BY LANDOWNER WILHELM HARLEN FOR ONE-LEGGED LAND COMMISSIONER T.W. WARD.

CROSSING BECAME STATION ON STAGE LINE. GAINED NOTORIETY FOR MANY HOLD-UPS THAT OCCURRED AT "ROBBERS' ROOST" (1 MI. W). PEGLEG SERVED IN LATER ERA AS CROSSING ON GREAT WESTERN CATTLE TRAIL.

(1970)

Location: in roadside park, State Highway 29, about 10 miles SE of Menard, Menard County, Texas

Authors' commentary:
Here the term, "Great Western," is used in 1970. This is a well-done marker.

Awbrey & Dooley, *Why Stop? A Guide to Texas Historical Roadside Markers*, 310. emails and interview: Paul G. Noack, Austin, Texas, Dec. 29, 2010.

Webster Witter, who went up the trail in 1884 for M. A. Withers, started in LaSalle County with an outfit trailing 4,300 "aged steers" destined for Ogallala, Nebraska. He recalled that when "we went out the Nueces Canyon we crossed the Nueces River twenty-eight times in forty miles, and our cattle became tender-footed from rocks and crossing the water so much."[48]

W. B. Hardeman also referred to this Nueces River route as a tough route. In 1886, he worked for Blocker, Driscoll, and Davis and was in an outfit driving one of their herds. That year the firm "drove forty thousand head of cattle, and had fourteen hundred horses," according to Hardeman. His comment about the route was: "We started for Uvalde, went up the East Fork of the Nueces River, the roughest trail I ever went. We could not see all of the cattle, only at bedding time."[49]

Regardless of whether the cattle came up the earlier Western Trail or used the later feeder route up the Nueces River, both crossed at Beef Trail Crossing and continued on a northerly route passing west of London, Texas. A small store was opened by three brothers, Ed, Tom, and Robert Stevenson on the London site in 1881. When a post office was established in the store in 1882, it was named London. By 1884, about thirty people lived in the town.[50] The cattle crossed the Big Saline Creek west of London and continued straight north to the west bank of the Little Saline Creek. The trail drivers followed the Little Saline to its headwaters, crossed over the ridge, and reached McDougal Creek in Menard County. Herds followed the McDougal until they arrived at the San Saba River where

---

[48] Webster Witter, "Would Like to Go Again," in Hunter, 884. The Nueces River Feeder Route through the Nueces Canyon was very rough country, but the lower end of the Western Trail around San Antonio was filling up with settlers.
[49] W. B. Hardeman, "Punching Cattle on the Trail to Kansas," in Hunter, 150. Hardeman does not state where these cattle were delivered, but by the title of the article, we can assume in 1886, that they may have been delivered to a Kansas border town with a railhead because Kansas proper was quarantined.
[50] John Leffler, "London, Texas," *The Handbook of Texas Online* [accessed December 12, 2007]

92   THE WESTERN CATTLE TRAIL | 1874-1897

the cattle crossed at Pegleg Crossing. The crossing had received its name from the Pegleg stage depot located a quarter of a mile down stream on the San Antonio-San Diego stage route.[51]

Menardville, the county seat since 1871, was twelve miles up stream and in the mid 1880s had a church, a school, several stores, and 150 residents. Its post office had been established on June 16, 1868, and was, therefore, in operation when Neatherlin went through in 1876: "We are crossing the San Saba at what is called Peg Leg." he wrote. "Fine grass and plenty of prairie dogs." Then, on the next day, April 18, he wrote: "I went to Manardville [sic] today after supplies."[52]

According to Neatherlin's journal, he and his brother were out in front of a large wave of herds coming up the trail. He scouted the country for the best watering opportunities, sought advice from people along the trail, and carefully recorded his path in a journal. The Lytle herds had blazed the trail in 1874, and numerous herds of the partnerships of Millett & Mabry and Ellison & Dewees had used the Western Trail in 1875, but the Western Trail had not been "perfected" and described until the 1876 season. Col. Jack Potter, in his reminisces in 1935, wrote that a "direct route" was perfected "early in 1876."[53] (He may have been referring to the work of the Neatherlin brothers.)

The assessment that the Western Trail had not been "perfected" (its route fully understood) is no doubt correct. In 1874, the Eastern/Chisholm Trail was still active. But when Kansas shut down its eastern railheads after the 1875 season, the Eastern/Chisholm Trail had to be abandoned or re-routed to feed into the Western Trail. Thus, according to Col. Jack Potter, the old trail was abandoned and this new trail to "Dodge City, Kansas, and on to the Ogallala and Red Cloud Indian Agencies in Nebraska" saved "20 to 30 days' drive, as it was not necessary to make a detour over the Eastern trail in Indian Territory which we had been making." Potter was asserting that by 1876, drovers did not need to go by way of the Eastern Trail and then cut over to the Western. The Western Trail was now perfected and "led out to the crossing of the San Saba River at Pegleg station in Menard county,…"[54]

THE TRUNK LINE OF THE WESTERN CATTLE CATTLE TRAIL FROM PEGLEG CROSSING TO DODGE CROSSING ON BRADY CREEK, McCULLOCH COUNTY: (Map #1-5)

From Peg Leg Crossing, the cattle and drovers pushed eastward along the north bank of the San Saba River for five or six miles and then turned northeastward into

---

[51]Skaggs, thesis, 29. According to the Pegleg Crossing roadside marker, the name came from the one-legged land commissioner, T. W. Ward.

[52]Janzen, "Menard County," *Texas Post Offices*, unpublished manuscript. Neatherlin journal, April 17 - 18. Neatherlin uses the early name for Manard.

[53]Laura R. Krehbiel and Jack Potter, *Cattle Trails of the Old West*, 17.

[54]Potter, *Cattle Trails of the Old West*, 17.

McCulloch County.[55] Continuing north, the trail crossed Calf Creek near the present-day Calf Creek community. From there, the herds were driven north northeast until they reached Brady Creek, six miles west of Brady, Texas. The cattle were watered here and cowboys could visit "Brady City." McCulloch County's early settlers had followed the lure of free range land and had established small ranches for their herds of cattle and sheep. When the county was organized in 1876, Brady City became the county seat and acquired a post office on August 8.[56] McCulloch County, the geographic center of the state, was an ideal location for feeder trails to join up with the trunk line.

Having the distinction of being a county seat and located along a major cattle trail, Brady grew rapidly. Within a year of establishment, the town had three hotels:

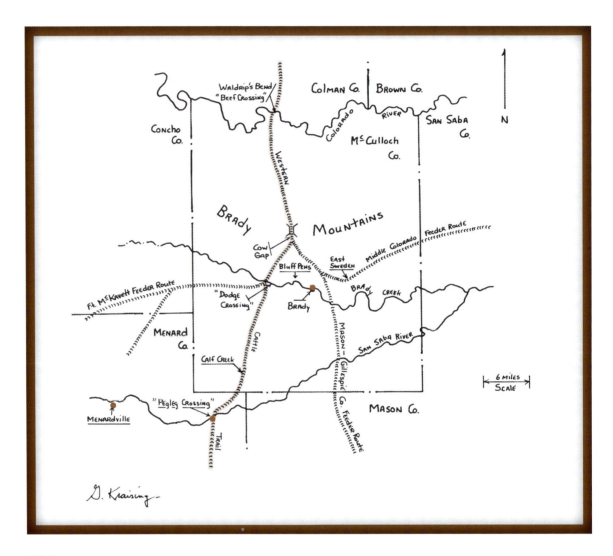

#1-5
McCulloch County, Texas:
This map shows a portion of the Western Cattle Trail trunk line in McCulloch County, Texas, and three different feeder routes merging into the trunk line south of Cow Gap in the Brady Mountains. The trunk line continued on to Waldrip's Bend on the Colorado River.

---

[55] The trail entered McCulloch County at approximately Farm Road 1311. (Skaggs, thesis, 30)
[56] The first postmaster was Rupert R. Claridge. The town name was from Peter Brady, one of the original surveyors of the county. ("McCulloch County," Janzen, Ibid.)

the McCulloch House, operated by G. W. Jones; the City Hotel, ran by W. H. Albritton; and the Brady Hotel, operated by a Mr. Brooks. There were also two mercantile stores, two saloons, a blacksmith shop, a wagon shop, and a school-church building. By 1880, there were 115 permanent residents.[57]

While cowboys visited Brady City's saloons with their billiard parlors, the cattle were held in a natural formation approximately two and a half miles west of town known as "Bluff Pens."

Here the "creek cut into the limestone in such a manner that there is a large U that contains about 100 to 150 acres." The bluffs rose from fifteen to thirty-five and forty feet enclosing an ideal grassed pasture area that gradually approached the creek.

Six cowboys on horseback in the late 1870s or early 1880s stop in Brady, Texas long enough to have their photo taken and to visit the town. This group from Kimble County, Texas, was driving a herd to Camp Supply in Indian Territory where they were to be sold to the government. They are from left to right: Joe Clements, Samuel Jobes, Claiborn Allen, John Allen, David Allen and A. J. Allen. The Allen family and son-in-law Sam Jobes worked for Charles Schreiner and also for Creed Taylor. The cattle likely belonged to one or both of these ranchers.

Here the outfit is pictured in front of a Brady hotel and the A.E. Ballou Groceries. Many of the herds coming through Brady on the Western Trail were corraled at the Brady Bluff Pens outside of town.

Thank you to Harold D. Jobes, Leander, Texas, great grandson to Samual Jobes, for sharing this prized family photo.

---

[57]Wayne Spiller, Comp. *Handbook of McCulloch County History*, Vol. I, 266, 269, and Galveston News, Sept. 18, 1877 and Sept. 29, 1877.

Herds were driven into this natural pocket and held overnight. At the open end of the U, on the west, the trail drivers camped and held their herd. At the spot where Brady Creek cuts back to the east toward town, the cowboys built rock walls to close the space between the bluff and the creek.[58]

The trail drivers and their herds crossed Brady Creek farther west of the Bluff Pens.[59] The crossing in that area was selected, no doubt, for its rocky bottom and for the ease with which herds could follow the terrain that funneled down to the creek on the south. After crossing the creek, some herds were driven in a north-northeast direction towards Cow Gap, while others were turned east and trailed down the creek to Bluff Pens for holding while drovers visited the town. There was a crossing on Brady Creek that was later called "Dodge Crossing," but locals believe that the cattle actually crossed the creek a quarter mile upstream to the west.[60]

A small community called Dodge later developed south of the creek and was named for I. A. Dodge, who settled on Brady Creek in 1883.[61]

In 1882, W. K. Shipman recalls that the outfit that he worked for "received 1,400 yearlings at Brady, and started up the trail." They delivered the herd to Ogallala, Nebraska.[62] In the same year, Andy Adams, with a Circle Dot herd that had been formed near Fort Brown at Brownsville, wrote that "two herds met on a branch of Brady Creek." This outfit was especially concerned about cattle rustlers who were very active in 1882. They had been told that "along the Colorado...those hills to the westward harbored a good many of the worst rustlers in the State."[63]

In 1883, cattle contracted to Schreiner and Lytle were finalized for the trail at Brady and assigned to be trailed to Dodge City. Tim Driscoll was the trail boss for one of the herds. J. L. Hill was a member of the outfit, and he later wrote in the book, *The End of the Cattle Trail*, that they started at the Lytle ranch and gathered the cattle "through Medina, Kerr, Llano, San Saba, and Brown counties." The ranchers had been notified of their coming by Lytle, and "Most of them had the cattle rounded up already to put the road brand, SL on them." When the herds and outfits reached Brady, "Mr. Lytle met us" and gave the trail boss Driscoll "instructions to pull for Dodge City." Hill was put in charge of the remuda, and they started off with twelve men. [64]

---

[58]Portions of this rock wall are still visible today. Judge V. Murray Jordan, landowner, Brady, Texas. email: Feb. 21, 2011.

[59]Bluff Pens was between the town of Brady and the crossing which was six miles west of Brady. Skaggs thesis, 30, and *The Baird Star*, Dec. 10, 1937, and V. Murray Jordan, Brady, Texas, email: Feb 21, 2011.

[60]William Mark Day, Brady, Texas: email: Feb. 22, 2011 and letter, March 28, 2011 and V. Murray Jordan, email: Feb 22, 2011.

[61]William Mark Day believes that the Dodge community was located close to the intersection of FM 2028 and County Road 118. Today Dodge Crossing is covered by Brady Lake. The old Dodge school house was located there. (Day letter, dated March 28, 2011)

[62]W. K. Shipman, "A Cowboy Undertaker," in Hunter, 881. W.K. was working for John Davidson, who in 1882 had a ranch on the Jim Ned, near Coleman City, Texas.

[63]The Circle Dot outfit was headed toward the Colorado River, north of Brady. The herd was eventually delivered to a Blackfoot Agency in Montana. (Andy Adams, *The Log of a Cowboy*, 87)

[64]The outfits were met at Dodge City by Captain Lytle. Two of the herds were sold to the Tower's and Gudgell outfit and were to be delivered to the Little Missouri River, near the mouth of the Little Beaver Creek, Montana. The boys who stayed with the herd received a raise in wages, and they continued on. (J. L. Hill, *The End of the Cattle Trail*, 54-57)

Hill amusedly wrote about the herd:

> Driscoll would never encourage crowding the cattle off the bed grounds. He would let them remain as long as they would on the grounds and get up and graze off at their will. The result was we had few sore-footed cattle. By the time we reached the Northern line of Kansas that was the best trained herd it has ever been my good fortune to see. We had about forty head of big two-year-olds and they led the herd from Texas to the end of the trail. They were as a trained mule in an eight-mule team under a jerk line. They would get up and graze off the bed grounds, the pointers seeing that they always started in the right direction and by the time the cook washed the tinware and was ready to pull out and would overtake them, they had their fill of grass and would hit the trail behind the wagon. I am like Old Mart, the nigger cook, who said, "I believe dem ar cattle would follow dis her chuck wagon to de Nor' Pole or Souf Pole, either."[65]

At Dodge Crossing near Brady, Texas, another feeder route connected with the Western Trail, and a few miles north of Brady, two more feeder routes came into the main trunk line of the Western.

THE FORT McKAVETT FEEDER ROUTE: (Map #1-6)

Fort McKavett was located in southwest Menard County and had been a military post known as Camp San Saba as early as the mid 1850s. Later the post was reactivated into Fort McKavett in 1868. Unlike many other military facilities, Fort McKavett continued to be active during the cattle-driving days. The nearby town had a school, a church, and a variety of shops.[66] The feeder route came across Menard County, a corner of Concho County, and into McCulloch County to connect with the Western Trail at Dodge Crossing.

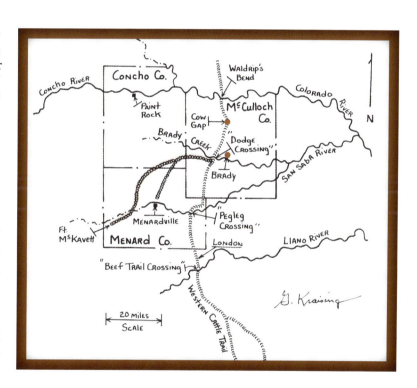

#1-6
The Fort McKavett Feeder Route:
The Fort McKavett Feeder Route came out of the Fort McKavett area in Menard County, Texas, and connected with the Western Trail trunk line at Dodge Crossing on Brady Creek in McCulloch County. Trail herds from the Menardville area also used this feeder route.

---

[65]Hill, 61.
[66]Vivian Elizabeth Smyrl, "Fort McKavett, TX," *Handbook of Texas Online*, [accessed Feb. 9, 2011), and "The Post on the San Saba," www.texasbeyondhistory.net [accessed Feb. 9, 2011]

THE WESTERN CATTLE TRAIL | 1874-1897

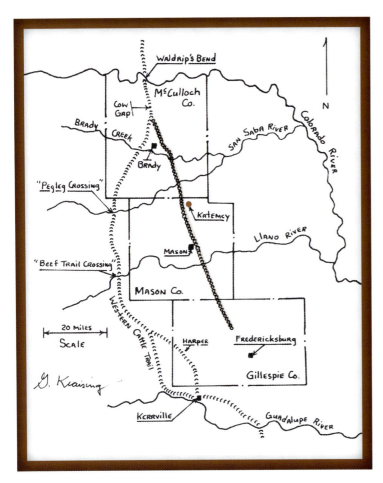

#1-7
The Mason-Gillespie County Feeder Route:
Trail herds in Gillespie, Mason, and southeast McCulloch counties used this feeder route to connect with the Western Trail trunk line at Cow Gap in McCulloch County.

Nine miles north of Brady were the Brady Mountains. After crossing Brady Creek, the Western Trail trunk line continued north until reaching Cow Creek. It followed the western bank of Cow Creek and wound its way through Cow Gap in the Brady Mountains.[67] The Hill Country was left behind at Cow Gap and the country beyond was rolling prairie. Two additional feeder trails converged with the Western Trail at Cow Gap.

THE MASON – GILLESPIE COUNTY FEEDER ROUTE: (Map #1-7)

The Mason-Gillespie County Feeder Route paralleled the Western Trail on the east side, in the Beef Trail and Pegleg crossing areas. Drovers pushed their cattle across the San Saba River northwest of Mason and joined the Western Trail at Cow Gap. Col. Jack Potter, who came into the Cow Gap area on the Mason County Feeder Route, mentioned this feeder route in his description of his 1882 trail drive when he wrote: "We went out by way of Fredericksburg, Mason and Brady City, and entered the Western trail at Cow Gap…."[68] Ernest Schwethelm, who was with one of the Schreiner herds in late 1885, also mentioned this feeder route, when he wrote: "We drove out of Gillespie into Mason County then into McCulloch County, passed by Brady and on through McCulloch…."[69]

According to Jimmy Skaggs' research, the town of Katemcy, located about ten miles north of Mason "was reportedly settled in 1880 to capitalize upon trail traffic from Mason and Gillespie counties to the Great Western at Cow Gap."[70] This feeder route must have carried a fair volume of cattle because it has been mistaken

---

[67] From east to west, the Brady Mountains form a ridge which has three breaks or gaps: Salt, Cow, and Onion. The Western Trail passed through Cow Gap. (Vivian Elizabeth Smyrl, "McCulloch County," *The Handbook of Texas Online*, [accessed October 9, 2007]

[68] Jack Potter, "Coming up the Trail in 1882," *The Trail Drivers of Texas*, 59.

[69] J. J. Starkey, *Kerrville Times*, Nov. 19, 1931.

[70] Skaggs, thesis, 37. West of Katemcy, near Highway 87-377, is an area today called Peter's Prairie. Here are the remains of a rock corral (pens) that are believed to have been used by cattle herds on this feeder route. (William Mark Day, Brady, Texas, interview: March 24, 2011)

as the main route of the Western Trail. When this feeder route ceased, and the Gulf, Colorado and Santa Fe Railroad arrived in Santa Anna, many of Katemcy's citizens moved away, and the town declined.

THE MIDDLE COLORADO FEEDER ROUTE: (Map #1-8)

Another feeder came from Lampasas and San Saba counties on the east. Jimmy Skaggs called this the "Middle Colorado Feeder Trail," because it crossed the Colorado River.[71]

The trail "may have followed an old military road, passing by East Sweden," says Bobbe Hurd. Two and one half miles east of East Sweden was "Soldiers' Watering Hole" on Onion Creek.[72]

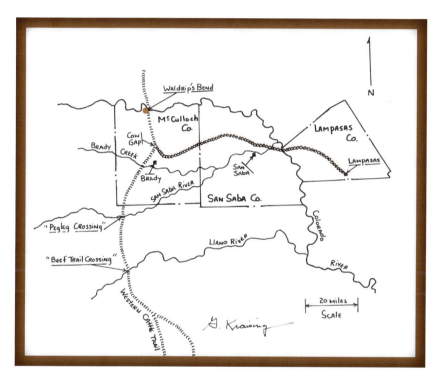

#1-8
The Middle Colorado Feeder Route:
Trail herds from the east out of Lampasas and San Saba counties used this feeder route to connect with the Western Trail trunk line at Cow Gap in McCulloch County.

THE TRUNK LINE OF THE WESTERN CATTLE TRAIL FROM COW GAP, McCULLOCH COUNTY, TO COLEMAN, COLEMAN COUNTY, TEXAS:

From Cow Gap, herds continued straight north, crossing the Colorado River at Waldrip's Bend, also called "Beef Crossing," near the mouth of Bull Creek.[73] A.M. Waldrip was the first rancher in McCulloch County, and part of his ranch became

---

[71] Skaggs, thesis, 37.
[72] Bobbye Hurd, interview, March 29, 2011. Hurd lives near East Sweden, one mile south of the cemetery, and has evidence that an east-west trail went through his property. He has been told that it was a cattle trail.
[73] The trail was about a mile west of the present-day Colorado River Bridge. (D.D. Tex Wright, Santa Anna, interview: March 15, 2011)

THE WESTERN CATTLE TRAIL | 1874-1897   99

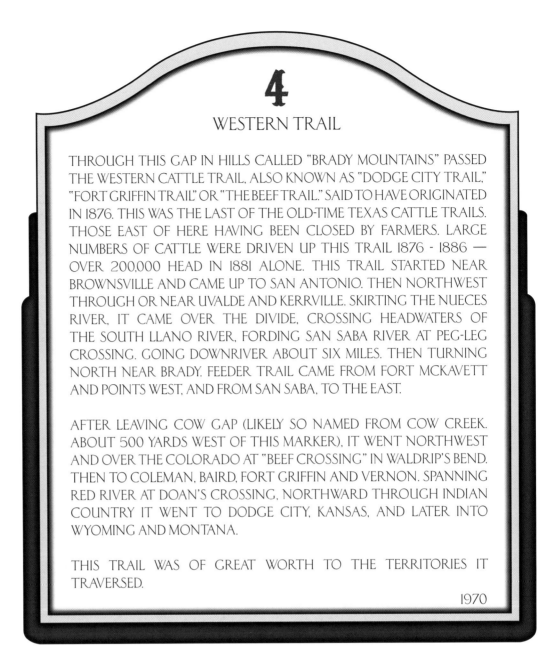

Location: On west side of U.S. Highway 283, near Cow Gap, ten miles north of Brady, Texas, in McCulloch County

Authors' commentary:
This marker covers a great deal of information. The one confusing statement, however, is reference to the trail going "northwest through or near Uvalde." If the trail had come up "to San Antonio" and then northwest, why is Uvalde mentioned, which is west of San Antonio and southwest of the trail? The marker may be referring to the "Old Trail" Feeder Route from Uvalde, Castroville, and Bandera. The confusion may also have arisen because of the later route, the Nueces River Feeder Route, that joined the Western Trail at Beef Trail Crossing south of here. It went up the Nueces River and passed near Uvalde. As discussed, that route replaced the San Antonio - Kerrville route in later years. (see Map #1-4)

It is significant that the marker recognizes the two feeder trails that joined the Western trunk line near Brady, the one from Fort McKavett and the one from the San Saba region (our Middle Colorado Feeder Route). It, however, does not mention the Mason - Gillespie County Feeder Route.

The trails "east of here having been closed by farmers," refers to the Shawnee and Eastern trails.

Note, also, a name is given here for the crossing at Waldrip's Bend.

the site of the town named for him that was organized in 1876, one mile south of the crossing. The post office opened on November 24, 1879. During the trail driving days, Waldrip had a school, a church, and a few residents. By 1884 there were thirty people living there. If there were any stops to be made by the cowboys at Waldrip, it would have been at the post office.[74]

North of the Colorado River, herds stretched out in a straight northerly path across Coleman County. Before cattle started to be trailed up the Western, a military road crossed Coleman County. It ran from Fort Mason, in Mason County, to Fort Belknap on the Brazos River in Young County, crossing the eastern portion of Coleman County. One of the posts on this military line was Camp Colorado on Jim Ned Creek. The post had been at this location since July of 1857. The Camp became the designated county seat in 1864 and acquired the first post office in the county in March of 1872.[75]

When Lewis Neatherlin brought three herds up the Western Trail in 1876, he specifically mentioned Camp Colorado in his journal. He did not visit Coleman which was in its first year as a recognized community. Because of its central location, Coleman had just received the honor of becoming the new county seat. By February, there was a post office, but in April, when the Neatherlin herds came through he probably was not aware of the county seat change nor of establishment of Coleman's post office. He went to Camp Colorado instead for his supplies:

April 28:
After dinner I saddled my horse and started to overtake the other 2 herds. Rode some 15 miles and overtaken them in 3 miles of Camp Colorado, where we camped for the night. Plenty of grass and water.

April 29:
Went to the store at Camp Colorado to get provisions for nos. 2 and 3. Plenty of flour but no bacon. None in the country. Crossed Jim Ned Creek.[76]

---

[74]Vivian Elizabeth Smyrl, "Waldrip, Texas," *The Handbook of Texas Online* [accessed December 16, 2007] Myron Janzen, "McCulloch County Texas Post Offices," unpublished manuscript.

[75]Camp Colorado was originally an army camp set up near the Colorado River to protect the area against the Indians. It was established in early 1856 by Major Earl Van Dorn. In August of 1856, it was moved to Mukewater Creek, about six miles north of the Colorado River, on a military trail between Fort Belknap and Fort Mason in Mason County. It was moved again in July of 1857, twenty miles north to Jim Ned Creek. The Army operated it until the outbreak of the Civil War. Texas Rangers were stationed at Camp Colorado from 1862 to 1864. It served as the county seat from 1864 to 1876. The site was sold in 1870 to H. H. Sackett, and he rebuilt the guardhouse into a combination store and residence. The post office operated until December 31, 1902. (Beatrice Grady Gay, "Camp Colorado," *The Handbook of Texas Online* [accessed March 2, 2008]; Rusty Tate, "Coleman County," *The Handbook of Texas Online* [accessed October 9, 2007]; and Janzen, Ibid, "Coleman County Post Offices.")

[76]Camp Colorado was approximately twelve miles northeast of Coleman. On the following day, Neatherlin wrote letters while waiting for the last herd to catch up. He camped "3 miles northwest of the post." (Neatherlin journal, 15)

It appears that Neatherlin guided his herds north across Coleman County east of the developing Coleman community, but did not use the old military road going directly into Camp Colorado.

The Western Trail passed west of present-day Santa Anna and trailed toward Coleman where watering holes awaited for both the cattle and the cowboys. Marion M. Callan had the post office in his home and made arrangements with area ranchers to get their mail from Camp Colorado on a weekly basis if they would buy their supplies from him.[77]

The small community of Coleman catered to the cowboys. In its first years there were three local saloons, but by 1880 the main street had been broadened to one-hundred feet wide to handle the cattle passing through on their way north to Hords Creek. Each store front along the street showed off its variety of wares and

Location: Coleman, Texas
Coleman County Court House Lawn

Authors' commentary:
This is one of our favorite markers. It is simple and yet one that should not be overlooked.

The dates used are for the entire cattle-trailing period after the Civil War for the different cattle trails systems. Only the Western Cattle Trail went through Coleman, Texas. Therefore, the dates should read: 1874-1889.

Photo courtesy of D.D. "Tex" Wright, Santa Anna, Texas.

---
[77]Jansen, Ibid.

entertainment as the cowboys passed by. The community had grown to at least a dozen saloons by 1880 and offered brothels and a race track outside of town. Promoters of the town's businesses even dispatched riders to head south every day, beginning the first of April, to meet and greet the trail bosses and cowboys and invite them to enjoy Coleman's entertainment.[78]

J. P. Morris came through Coleman in 1880 with two herds of steers bound for Ogallala, Nebraska. His herds left the San Antonio area and used the Mason County Feeder Route passing Fredericksburg, Mason, Brady, and passed through Cow Gap to cross the Colorado River at Waldrip's Bend. At Coleman the herds were trailed down Colorado Street through town and halted at Jim Ned Creek which was flooded. The Morris herds had to wait until the water receded. It was during this wait that Morris became fully aware of the lush grasses of the broad valley in which Coleman was located. He made a note that he especially liked this locale.

Morris left the cattle trailing business after the 1880 season, but remained active as a cattle buyer and trader. On a cattle-buying trip to Coleman County in the spring of 1884, he again discovered the well-watered valleys of the area. He became enchanted with the old Clay Mann Ranch located at the confluence of Indian and Jim Ned creeks about seven miles northeast of Coleman. He purchased the ranch on April 7, 1884 and moved in cattle the following year. His ranch and brand became the Rafter-3. In late 1888, Morris moved his family from DeWitt County to Coleman where he bought a house.[79]

Two more feeder routes joined the Western Trail trunk line in the Coleman area.

> The authors speculate that in this first active year of the Western Trail, Lewis Neatherlin and his younger brother were exploring the possibilities of a "perfected trail," as Jack Potter later wrote. In following seasons, the trail was probably straightened out and passed through Coleman, four to six miles to the west. Coleman's proactive marketing of its main street and town likely had a lot to do with this. The community offered many services to the cowboys.

JINGLEBOB (TRICKHAM) FEEDER ROUTE: (Map #1-9)

When the Western Trail became reality, the established Jinglebob (or Trick'em) route from the John Chisum Ranch[80] was extended and became a feeder route for other ranches to the new northbound trail to Kansas and beyond. Chisum's ranch headquarters was located on Home Creek in the southern part of Coleman County where he had moved in herds in the fall of 1863. From this ranch, starting in 1867, Chisum established a route to trail his cattle to Horsehead Crossing on the Pecos River in Texas and then on into New Mexico Territory (see Chapter III in Part I). On the route was a small settlement on Mukewater Creek that had been established around 1855-1856 and was the oldest town in the county. A brother-in-law of John Chisum's, by the name of Emory Peyers, decided to take advantage of the location

---

[78]Skaggs thesis, 90.

[79]John T. (Jack) Becker. "J.P. Morris and the Rafter-3 Ranch," a thesis in history, Texas Tech University, Lubbock, Texas, 2001. 36-44.

[80]John S. Chisum used an earmark on his cattle that was very distinct. It was a deep slit in the animal's ear that left the lower half of the ear flapping down or "bobbing. Thus, his cattle were called "jinglebobs."

THE WESTERN CATTLE TRAIL | 1874-1897

6
SANTA ANNA, C.S.A.

MOUNTAIN AND TOWN NAMED IN HONOR OF MAN IN POWER HERE IN 1840'S, A COMANCHE CHIEF FRIENDLY TO TEXANS. SANTA ANNA IN 1846 VISITED PRESIDENT POLK IN WASHINGTON DURING U.S. NEGOTIATIONS TO ANNEX TEXAS. ALSO SIGNED AND KEPT UNTIL HIS DEATH OF CHOLERA IN 1849 PEACE TREATIES THAT ALLOWED THE GERMAN EMIGRATION COMPANY TO SETTLE LANDS NORTH OF THE LLANO RIVER.

COMANCHES USED SANTA ANNA PEAKS AS SIGNAL POINTS. EARLY SURVEYORS, TRAVELERS, EXPLORERS AND SETTLERS TOOK THEM AS GUIDE POINTS. IN 1857, NEARBY UNITED STATES CAVALRY AT CAMP COLORADO KEPT LOOKOUTS HERE.

IN THE CIVIL WAR, 1861-65, FRONTIER RANGERS CAMPED AT FOOT OF MOUNTAIN, WITH SENTRIES ON HEIGHT WATCHING AT THE PASS THE MILITARY ROAD FROM SAN ANTONIO NORTHEASTWARD TO FORT BELKNAP, A STRATEGIC OUTPOST GUARDING TEXAS FROM INVASION BY INDIANS AND FEDERAL TROOPS. DURING THE 1870&S, THOUSANDS OF LONGHORNS WENT THROUGH THE GAP, OVER THE WESTERN CATTLE TRAIL.

IN 1879, "THE GAP" HAD A STORE AND POST OFFICE TO SUPPLY THE CATTLE DRIVES. WHEN GULF, COLORADO AND SANTA FE BUILT HERE IN 1886, SETTLERS MOVED FROM THE GAP TO THE RAILROAD, STARTING THE PRESENT TOWN.

(1965)

Location: This marker used to be located at the east end of Santa Anna on Highway 67-84. As of this writing, however, the marker is missing. It was taken down during repairs on the road and not replaced.

Authors' commentary:
The Gap was located one-half mile northeast of present-day Santa Anna. Thus, the longhorns that "went through the Gap" were on the Jinglebob (Trickham) Feeder Route and not on the Western Cattle Trail. The community of "the Gap" was located on the south side of the east peak, approximately one half to three-fourth mile from Santa Anna. The Gap post office (1879-1885) and stores were there during the zenith years of the Trail. By 1886, when the cattle herds no longer used this feeder route, residents of "The Gap" moved to the railroad site of Santa Anna. Research indicates that the Trickham Feeder Route actually went east of the Gap and around the east peak — closer to the military road that came from San Antonio, through Fort Mason, and "northeastward to Fort Belknap."[1] Cattle herds had used this pathway for some ten years, but after 1885, the trail shifted again. Santa Anna was established after the trail drives.[2]

---
[1] Drovers would have been aware of the old military road three miles east of The Gap. It had opened in the 1850s to carry supply trains along a line of U.S. forts from Belknap on the Brazos River to Fort Mason and to Fort Clark near the Rio Grande. (Awbrey & Dooley, Why Stop? A Guide to Texas Historical Roadside Markers, 436)
[2] D. D. "Tex" Wright, Santa Anna, Texas, interview: March 21, 2011.

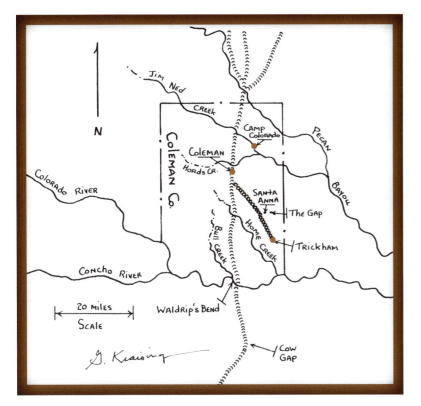

#1-9
The Jinglebob (Trickham) Feeder Route:
The Jinglebob Feeder Route came out of the Trickham, Texas, area on the Mukewater Creek, Coleman County, and connected with the Western Trail trunk line south of Coleman, Texas. Trickham was located on the Jinglebob Trail that had been established by John Chisum in 1867 from his home ranch on Home Creek in southern Coleman County. The Jinglebob Trail originally went to Horsehead Crossing on the Pecos River. When the Western Trail became reality, the Jinglebob Trail was redirected and became a feeder route to the Western Trail trunk line.

and opened a combination store and saloon at the settlement in order to sell refreshments to the cowboys on the trail.[81] The settlement's saloon keeper, Bill Franks, played tricks on so many thirsty drovers that the place became known as "Trick'em."

In April of 1879, when a post office was authorized, the name was misspelled by the post office department, and the post office and community became "Trickham." Within a couple of years, because the route sat on the pathway of herds heading for the trunk line of the Western, the community grew and had at least two saloons, a general store, a stone mason, and a commissioners' court.[82]

As herds and their drovers progressed northwesterly from Trickham, they passed through or around the Santa Anna Mountain. Neatherlin had led his herds east of the mountain in 1876, and others followed, but some herds may have passed through the gap after a community sprang up at the base of the east peak in 1879. "The Gap," as it was called, provided an opportunity for the drovers to stop over for refreshments or to post a letter. When the trail herds ceased to use the feeder route, and the railroad established Santa Anna, the residents of The Gap and its post office moved to the Santa Anna.

The Jinglebob Feeder Route merged with the Western Trail near Coleman.

> Jimmy Skaggs named and discribed this feeder route in his 1965 masters' thesis. On page 31, he says that the "Jinglebob Trail" from Trickham joined with the Western Trail "just to the south of town [Coleman]." His source was the West Texas Historical Year Book., of Oct. 1953, page 101.[83] On the other hand, D. D. "Tex" Wright from Santa Anna says that his grandfather, who grew up at Trickham, told him that the Feeder Route joined up with the Western Trail farther north—near or at Jim Ned Creek.[84]

---

[81] Skaggs, thesis, 104.
[82] Virgina H. Taylor, (State Archivist), "Notes on Coleman County History," West Texas Historical Assoc. Year Book, Vol. 34, (1958), 128-129; and Janzen., "Coleman County Post Offices," and Skaggs thesis, 104.
[83] Taylor, Ibid, Vol. 28, (Oct., 1953), 101.
[84] D.D. "Tex" Wright, Santa Anna, Texas, interview: March 15, 2011.

THE SOUTHERN TOM GREEN COUNTY — CONCHO RIVER FEEDER ROUTE: (Map #1-10)

Another feeder route to merge with the Western Trail around the Coleman area came from the Tom Green and Concho counties area to the southwest. Several small feeder routes were created in the region around San Angelo, but the Southern Tom Green County-Concho River Feeder Route that descended the left (north) bank of the Concho River to its confluence with the Colorado River is the one of interest for this study. After crossing the Colorado, trail drivers on this route pointed their herds in a northeasterly direction to join the Western Trail north of Coleman.[85]

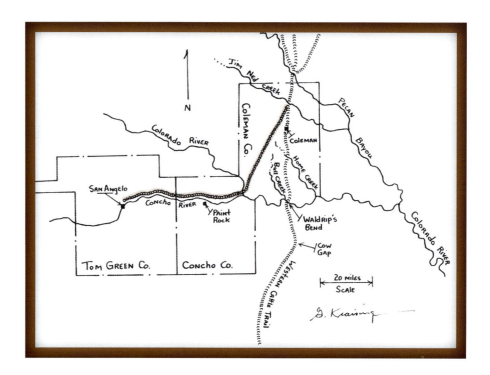

#1-10
The Southern Tom Green County-Concho River Feeder Route:
Trail herds from the west out of Tom Green County and Concho County, crossed the Colorado River, went through Coleman County, and connected with the Western Trail trunk line north of Coleman, Texas.

THE TRUNK LINE OF THE WESTERN CATTLE TRAIL FROM COLEMAN AND JIM NED CREEK TO ALBANY IN SHACKELFORD COUNTY:

Merging herds from the southwest feeder routes and herds on the Western Trail crossed Jim Ned Creek north of Coleman and continued on to Pecan Bayou in

---

[85] The Southern Tom Green County-Concho River Feeder Route was named and identified by Jimmy Skaggs in his 1965 thesis, 37.

Callahan County. On the Pecan Bayou, however, trail bosses had a choice as to which branch of the Western Trail they would follow to continue north. The three alternates fanned out east, north, and west but eventually all rejoined the main trunk of the trail at Albany in Shackelford County.[86]

One branch went northeastward through Callahan (Belle Plain) in Callahan County and on to Hulltown (Moran) in Shackelford County before reaching Albany. Callahan, an early settlement, sat at the juncture of several military roads and was Callahan County's first county seat from 1877 to 1880.[87]

The only other community on this right fork of the trail was Hulltown in Shackelford County — it was established after 1883. The Texas and Pacific Railroad built through the area in 1880, and three years later, Swoope Hull opened a grocery store at the rail crossing on Deep Creek. Hull was installed as postmaster on August 29, 1883 and was trying to start a "village" at the location. "He bought 160 acres between Post Oak and Deep Creek and platted a townsite in March 1884." The community was called "Hulltown."[88] Today's roadside marker at the intersection of SH 6 and FM 576 says: "a branch of the Western Cattle Trail passed nearby."[89]

Another alternate branch went north and westward through Clyde, which, like Hulltown, sat on the Texas and Pacific Railroad. It, too, was established after the

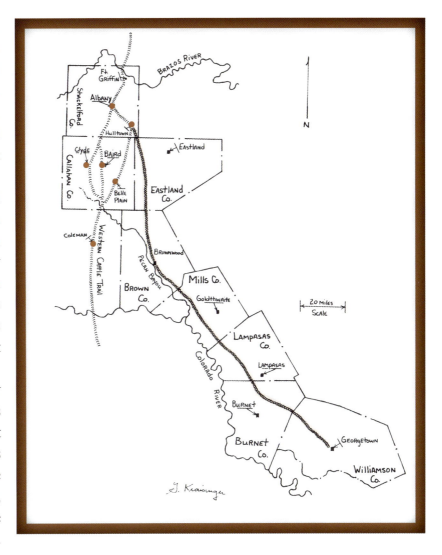

#1-11
The San Gabriel-Brownwood Feeder Route:
Trail herds as far southeast as Williamson County were trailed through Burnet, Lampasas, and Mills counties to Brownwood on Pecan Bayou River in Brown County, Herds from these counties on this feeder route continued north across Eastland County to Hulltown in Shackelford County and on to Albany to connect with the Western Trail trunk line.

---

[86] Skaggs, thesis, 31.
[87] Callahan was an established post office on February 26, 1877. The name was changed to "Belle Plain" on June 18, 1878, when the post office moved to a local store owned by appointed postmaster, William H. Parvin. Belle Plain lost the position of county seat when the seat of government was moved to the newly established railroad town of Baird, six miles to the north. Belle Plain ceased receiving mail in 1909 and today is a ghost town. (Janzen, Ibid.)
[88] Aubrey and Dooley, Ibid, 324. The town's name was changed in 1890 to "Hicks" and in 1892 to "Moran" after the Texas and Pacific Railroad president, John J. Moran.
[89] Roadside marker at the intersection of SH 6 and FM 576 in Shackelford County, erected in 1970.

THE WESTERN CATTLE TRAIL | 1874-1897   107

There are **two historical markers** in the Albany area that mention the Western Cattle Trail. The "Shackelford County" marker is located in the park west of the Albany city limits on the intersection of US Highway 180 and US Highway 283. In one line, it states: "Griffin, the lawless settlement that grew up around the fort, attracted buffalo hide hunters and cattlemen driving herds up the western cattle trail." This marker, erected in 1976, is referring to a settlement that appeared next to Fort Griffin in northern Shackelford County, some fifteen miles north of Albany. The marker is in the wrong location and should have been near the fort.

There is also a plaque on the Shackelford County Court House lawn in Albany that reads: "Texas Cattle Trail to Dodge City, Kansas and other northern points, 1875-1890." The beginning date should be 1874 because John T. Lytle used the trail in 1874, and the ending date should not be any later than 1889. Even though the trail lasted into the 1890s, this lower portion of the trail, through Albany, was essentially not used after 1889. Texas cattlemen and contract trailsmen changed their strategy after the Kansas quarantine of 1885. Large numbers of cattle were trailed through the area in 1885 and 1886, but the numbers declined steadly until 1889.

railroad came through. According to one account, a large railroad construction crew gathered at Robert Clyde's camp on the south side of the tracks. The place became known as "Cylde's." When the construction crew moved on, a few stayed behind, and within a year the new settlement was formed with a post office authorized in June, 1881. By 1883, several Irish families who had migrated from Pennsylvania appeared in the Clyde area, and a group of Portuguese who had come in by the railroad formed a colony.[90]

The most frequently used route, however, was the one that lay directly northward toward Baird. Baird, like Hulltown and Clyde, also began along the tracks of the Texas and Pacific Railroad in 1881. This settlement's post office was established on February 7, 1881, and there were about 150 people in the community at the time.[91]

Before 1881 and the arrival of the Texas and Pacific Railroad, Brady in McCulloch County and Coleman in Coleman County were the only communities to provide any entertainment to the trail drivers since they had left the San Antonio area. Clyde, Baird and Hulltown were not yet in existence, and Callahan was just a post office.

Regardless of which route the drovers and their herds followed, they ended up in Albany in Shackelford County. Albany had been platted to become the county seat on November 8, 1874. It was centrally located in the county and was selected to house the county government rather than to have it remain at Fort Griffin. Within months, T. E. Jackson built a general store and the town was on its way to becoming a cattle town and supply point for the Western Trail. A post office was established in Albany on August 1, 1876. The timing was ideal for the community. The Western Cattle Trail, with its hungry and thirsty drovers, was becoming a recognized source of income, and Albany lay in its pathway. In fact, the community could seize the opportunity to serve the drovers before they reached Fort Griffin, fifteen miles to the north.

---

[90]Clyde is on Highway 20 and Farm Road 604, five miles west of Baird and eight miles east of Abilene in Callahan County. The community sits on the Callahan Divide between the Brazos and Colorado rivers. ("History of Clyde, Texas," www.clyde.govoffice2.com [accessed Feb. 11, 2011], and "Clyde, Texas," http://texasescapes.com [accessed Feb. 11, 2011])

[91]According to Myron Janzen, in *Texas Post Offices*, Clyde and Baird in Coleman County both paid their respects to the Texas and Pacific Railroad in their town names. "Clyde," was named after Robert Clyde, boss of the Texas and Pacific Railroad, and Baird changed its name from "Vickery" to "Baird" after Matthew Baird, director of the Texas and Pacific Railroad. Thus, after 1881, Texas cattle on the trail crossed over the tracks at Clyde and Baird.

Five years later in December of 1881, the Texas and Pacific Railroad arrived in Albany which made the town a receiving point for supplies and a shipping point for sending out cattle. In 1883, a courthouse was constructed. Albany became the area's "mercantile center." During the trail-driving days, drovers watched Albany grow and prosper as Fort Griffin slowly declined.[92]

THE SAN GABRIEL — BROWNWOOD FEEDER ROUTE: (Map #1-11)

From as far south as Williamson County, herds were driven to the northwest and merged with the Western Trail at Albany. In turn, smaller pathways from various ranches funneled into this feeder route in order to connect with the Western farther up the line. Richard (Dick) Withers trailed a herd for James F. Ellison in 1879 and used this route. His instructions were to deliver the herd to the "Millett Brothers at their ranch on the Brazos River, north of Fort Griffin." Coming from the Ellison ranch on the San Marcos River in Caldwell County, Withers described his route:

> The herd was the first [that season] to cross the Colorado at Webberville. For about ten miles after crossing the river the country was bushy, but other herds followed us and soon made a good trail through there. We went by way of Georgetown, up the Gabriel and on toward Brownwood. Near Brownwood we turned north, struck the Western Trail near Albany, and on to Fort Griffin to the Millett ranch and delivered the herd.[93]

Withers had used the old Eastern/Shawnee Trail to Georgetown near the junction of the four branches of the San Gabriel River. More than likely, the outfit followed the north branch of the San Gabriel, moving upstream toward Brownwood on the Pecan Bayou. The route Withers desribed was a feeder route that used the Shawnee/Eastern in order to feed into the Western Trail. For four seasons the Eastern had had no Kansas railhead and lay in populated areas of Texas. Herds and their drovers now crossed over to the Western Trail.

After crossing Williamson, Burnet, Lampasas, Mills, and Brown counties, the route turned almost due north to finally join the Western Trail at Albany. After delivering the herd to the Millett Brothers, Withers received a telegram from Col. Ellison telling him to immediately take the stage "for Fort Worth and hasten home," for Ellison wanted Withers to pick up another herd and trail it to Ogallala, Nebraska.

---

[92]Marilynne Howsley Jacobs, "Albany, Texas." *The Handbook of Texas Online*. [accessed January 10, 2007], and Janzen, "Shackelford County" *Texas Post Offices*.

[93]Richard (Dick) Withers, "The Experience of an Old Trail Driver," in Hunter, *The Trail Drivers of Texas*, 312. Ellison and Sherrill were one of the largest trail contracting outfits operating out of Texas, owned by James F. Ellison and James H. Sherrill. Withers worked directly for Jim Ellison.

Upon arriving at the Ellison Ranch, there were two herds. William J. (Bill) Jackman was to be in charge of one herd, and it was to be delivered to the Millett Brothers ranch. "So we traveled together," wrote Withers.

Using the same course, the two herds reached the Millett Brothers Ranch on the Brazos. However, the Millett Brothers decided that they did not want the Ellison herd, "so we threw the two herds together and drove them to Ogallala. We had 5,500 head in this herd, and it was the largest herd ever seen on the trail." The outfit consisted of only nine drovers plus Withers, a cook, and a horse wrangler.[94]

THE POTTER-BACON TRAIL — SPLINTER ROUTE: (Map #1-12)

In 1883 a splinter route emerged from the Western Trail at Albany. The Potter-Bacon Trail, as it was called, was named after trail driver Col. Jack Myers Potter[95] and his employer, Alfred T. Bacon. Potter, who blazed the route, referred it as a "cut-off Trail" or a "collateral branch of the Western Trail."[96]

Potter was one of thirteen children of "Fightin' Parson" Andrew Jackson Potter who moved his family from Prairie Lea, Texas in 1869 to San Antonio where they located on a stage route from San Antonio to El Paso, near what would later become the Western Cattle Trail. While his Winchester-packing father preached and rode the circuit, young Jack would dream of striking out on his own when he was able to ride to town on the top of a stage.

Potter learned to ride herd, and in 1882 hired on with the New England Livestock Company to help drive a herd of short horns from "a point near San Antonio" to Greeley, Colorado. The company had put together four herds totaling 3,000 head, and the fourth herd was bossed by John Smith of San Antonio. The trailboss asked young Potter to join the outfit. According to Potter, in his account in *The Trail Drivers of Texas*, he was "a boy not yet seventeen years old, two thousand miles from home."[97] On this trip, the cowboy outfit left the Western Trail near Fort Griffin and trailed west using the "Double Mountain Fork of the Brazos, Wichita and Pease Rivers to the Charles Goodnight ranch on the Staked Plains."[98] The outfit then turned west through Tascosa to the foothills of the Rockies, and then drove north along the foothills until they arrived at the South Platte River near Greeley, Colorado, on August 10, 1882.

---

[94]Withers, Ibid, 312.

[95]The title of "Colonel" was not earned but added by Potter himself. In 1935, however, Texas Governor Clyde Tingley granted Potter an honorary commission of colonel on his staff. (Jean M. Burroughs, *On the Trail, The Life and Tales of "Lead Steer" Potter*, 3-7)

[96]Col. Jack Potter, Laura Krehbiel, ed., *Cattle Trails of the Old West*, 19. C. Robert Haywood, "Potter-Blocker Trail," *The Handbook of Texas Online*, [accessed April 17, 2007] Jimmy Skaggs in his thesis, "The Great Western Cattle Trail to Dodge City, Kansas," also called it a splinter route, 38.

[97]Jack Potter, "Coming up the Trail in 1882," in Hunter, *The Trail Drivers of Texas*, 59.

[98]The Staked Plains ranch that Potter referrs to is the Palo Duro Canyon ranch that Goodnight established in the Texas Panhandle in 1876.

In the following spring of 1883, Potter's boss, Alfred T. Bacon, manager of the New England Livestock Company, headquartered at Greeley, Colorado, purchased 3,000 head of Mexican cattle and directed Potter to pick them up at Pena Station, near Hebbronville, Texas, and deliver them to Cheyenne. Potter, now with some experience at trailing stock over a long distances, drove the herd from Hebbronville to Collins Station, near present-day Alice, Texas to connect with the Matamoros Feeder Route. There he would use the Western Trail to continue on to Albany. At Albany, however, Potter received word from Bacon that he wanted his trail driver to leave the Western Trail and try a cutoff that might save some twenty days' trailing time, "if I could break out the trail that way," he later commented. "It was a barren trail that crossed the Llano Estacado — a trail of arid sameness that promised nothing better until we neared the Goodnight Ranch."[99] A map for him to follow was enclosed in

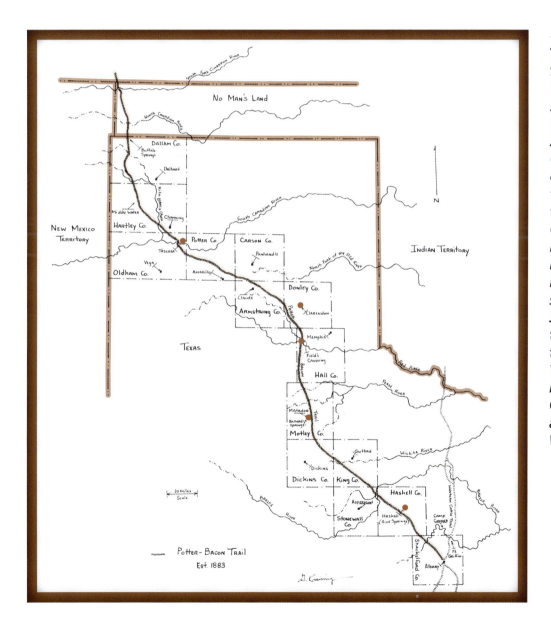

#1-12
The Potter-Bacon Trail - Splinter Route:
The Potter-Bacon Trail splintered from the Western Cattle Trail at Albany in Shackelford County, Texas, and continued northwest to Buffalo Springs at the head of Coldwater Creek in Dallam County in northern Texas Panhandle. Only the lower portion of this splinter route is shown. Jack Potter blazed this trail in 1883 when he trailed herds for Alfred T. Bacon, manager of the New England Livestock Company, into Colorado and on to Cheyenne, Wyoming.

---
[99]Burroughs, Ibid, 15.

his correspondence. So Potter headed northwest, passed Rice Springs[100] and crossed the Brazos River to reach the Matador Ranch.

The Matador Ranch had been established in 1878 when Alfred M. Britton and Henry H. Campbell brought a small herd of cattle into the area and acquired the land around Ballard Springs on Ballard Creek. The partners organized the Matador Cattle Company but sold out, in December of 1882, to a Scottish investor who renamed the company the Matador Land and Cattle Company of Dundee, Scotland. As Potter drove through their ranch land in 1883, the Matador owned approximately 300,000 acres of land in present-day Motley, Dickens, Cottle, and Floyd counties and 62,000 head of cattle.[101]

From Ballard Creek, Col. Potter continued north to Fields Crossing on the Red River. The crossing had been named after Jacob Fields, a former buffalo hunter, who had built a dugout nearby in 1872 in the river's south bank, where he lived with his family for several years.[102]

Jack Potter did not mention near-by Clarendon, nor did Jimmy Skaggs include the town in his description of the Potter-Bacon route. Clarendon, the county seat of Donley County, sits just east of the trail and was in existence in 1883. Perhaps it was because Clarendon, a Methodist colony, did not cater to the cowboy life. There were no saloons or dance halls in the town, and a trail drover probably did not feel welcomed at the "Saint's Roost," as it was called by other Panhandle inhabitants. Its original site was at the junction of Carroll Creek and the Salt Fork of the Red River. At this location, a Rev. Lewis Henry Carhart, a Methodist minister, and his brother-in-law, W. A. Allen, had platted a town site in October of 1878 and established a

---

[100]Today Rice Springs is known as Haskell Springs and is in the Haskell city park on the south side of town, in Haskell County. The springs was named "Rice Springs" after a cowboy by the name of Ryus Durrett who was an employee of the Reynolds and Matthews Cattle Company, established by George T. Reynolds and John A. Matthews in 1877, headquartered on California Creek. In the fall of 1882, W. R. Standefer, a former buffalo hunter, placed a hut at the springs and brought his flock of sheep to its Willow Pond. By the summer of 1884, L. M. Smith and W. F. Draper added shanty stores, selling a few groceries and whiskey to passer-bys. Within months other vendors built establishments around the square. They called their little town "Rice Springs." S. W. Scott, a cattleman from Granger, recalled that when he went to Rice Springs in 1884, "there were five houses there at the time." When the county was organized in 1885, the small community asked for a post office; it was renamed Haskell, after Charles Haskell, a soldier in the Texas Revolution who died at Goliad. In 1883, when Col. Jack Potter trailed by the Springs, there would have been only the Standefer hut. (Rex A. Felker, *Haskell County and Its Pioneers*, 1975, 74-75) (R. E. Sherrill, *Haskell County History*, Haskell Free Press, 1965, 55-56) (Gunnar Brune, Springs of Texas, Vol. I, Fort Worth: Branch-Smith, 1981, 218) ("Haskell, Texas," *The Handbook of Texas Online* [accessed April 29, 2009])

[101]The ranch had a post office in 1886, but the town of Matador did not exist until the county was organized in 1891. Henry H. Campbell, the Matador Ranch manager, quickly laid out a town site in 1891 in order to qualify to become the new county seat of Motley County. The Matador Land and Cattle Company continued to expand and eventually, by 1910, occupied 861,000 acres in Texas and had 650,000 acres under lease in South Dakota and Canada. The Motley County ranch was used as a breeding ground. Yearling steers were sent to the Texas ranch, and then shipped to the northern leases to be finished out. (William R. Hunt, "Matador, Texas," *The Handbook of Texas Online* [accessed April 30, 2009])

[102]Fields Crossing is approximately four miles northwest of present-day Parnell, Texas, on State Highway 86 in central Hall County. The town was platted in 1905 and received a post office in 1912 (H. Allen Anderson, "Parnell, Texas (Hall County)," *The Handbook of Texas Online* [accessed Sept. 5, 2007])

colony of followers. There was a post office, newspaper (the *Clarendon News*), a public school, and several shops and stores. Clarendon became the county seat when Donley County was organized in 1882.[103]

Since the Winchester quarantine was in force in 1883, (to be discussed in Part III, Chapter I) Potter detoured around the JA Ranch in Armstrong County. Charles Goodnight saw to it that a mile and a half of range on either side of the detour route was set aside for drovers coming up from south Texas. He also built a large tank for watering the herds on Running Water Draw and had the earth marked by a plow in order to keep the northbound drovers within bounds, but Jack Potter and his outfit were not headed for Dodge City along with other Texas herds. He was headed in a northwesterly direction toward Colorado, so Potter swung his herd around the Goodnight (JA) Ranch, crossed over the Palo Duro-Dodge City Trail, and headed toward Tascosa.[104]

According to trail historian Jimmy M. Skaggs, the Potter-Bacon Trail went westward up the Caprock through present-day Claude and north of present-day Amarillo.[105] When crossing the South Canadian, Potter's cowboy outfit visited Tascosa. Potter remembered the busy supply depot from the summer before, but this season, the town was abuzz about a cowboy strike. Local cowboys were upset with work conditions that had become prevalent on the Panhandle ranches such as the LIT, LX, the LS, the LE, and the T Anchor. In the previous decade, open-range ranching had dominated the area where cowboys who worked for the ranchers could take part of their pay in calves or mavericks and run their own small herds on the owner's open range. In the 1880s, new owners from the east and European investment companies had come into the Panhandle and changed the way the cattle business operated there. They fenced the range and concentrated on expanding their holdings so they could make big profits from stock farming. Ranch hands, who received an average of forty dollars a month, were now expected to work longer hours during the seasonal work, were terminated in the off-season, and received no benefits. All calves and mavericks were regarded as company property.

---

[103]When the Fort Worth and Denver City Railway came through in 1887, the town was moved six miles south to be located next to the tracks. Over the next decade it flourished and became a cultural center for the Panhandle. Clarendon College was opened in the fall of 1898. (H. Allen Anderson, "Clarendon, Texas," *The Handbook of Texas Online* [accessed May 3, 2009])

[104]The Potter-Bacon route passed approximately midway between present-day Ashtola and present-day Goodnight, on Highway 287. Ashtola was not established until 1906 as a section house on the Fort Worth and Denver City Railway. Goodnight, north of the Red River, was established as the Railway came through the country in 1887 and named after Charles Goodnight whose ranch was near by. Goodnight's ranch house, built in 1887, was the first building at the townsite. ("Ashtola" and "Goodnight, Texas," *The Handbook of Texas Online* [accessed May 3, 2009])

[105]Both Claude and Amarillo came into existence four years later when the Fort Worth and Denver City Railway built through. Claude became the county seat of Armstrong County in 1890 and a cattle-shipping point during the 1890s. Amarillo became the county seat of Potter County and, with its freight services, by 1890, "emerged as one of the world's busiest cattle-shipping points," with a population of over 1,400 residents. (Skaggs, thesis, 38, and "Claude, Texas," and "Amarillo, Texas," *The Handbook of Texas Online* [accessed May 3, 2009])

THE WESTERN CATTLE TRAIL | 1874-1897

In early March of 1883, Tom Harris of the LS along with outfits from the LIT, the LS, and the LX drew up an ultimatum. Expanding their support with other ranch hands from the LE and T Anchor, the group presented a written list of grievances to the five ranch owners including a demand for higher wages. Twenty-four men committed to the ultimatum and agreed to strike on March 31. Other cowboys joined the cause but over the next two and one half months the various ranch owners dealt with the strike in their own ways. Officials at the T Anchor and the LE fired striking cowboys on the spot. The LS and LIT owners offered a slight increase in wages and fired workers if they refused their offer. Spring roundup continued as planned, with managers hiring replacement workers at termporarily increased wages. By the end of May, the strike was no longer effective. Syndicates and large investment companies were taking over the cattle industry, and the cowboy became a low-wage employee.[106]

The Potter-Bacon Trail Splinter Route continued northwest going by present-day Channing and Middle Water both of which would later become part of the immense XIT Ranch. In 1883, however, there were no improvements in this area of the Panhandle, not even a cowboy camp. Potter and his outfit continued on to the headwaters of Coldwater Creek (Buffalo Springs) and into No Man's Land in present-day Oklahoma.

Even though the Potter-Bacon Trail Splinter Route was shorter and saved time, it was drier and traversed more barren land. As long as the majority of the herds were going to Dodge City, Kansas, the Potter-Bacon route was not used by very many herds, but in 1884 and 1885 when drovers were starting to use alternative routes to bypass Kansas, the upper portion of the Potter-Bacon Trail was used more. The northern portion of Potter's trail in No Man's Land and into Colorado will be discussed in later chapters.[107]

CHAPTER REVIEW:

The Western Cattle Trail trunk line received feeder trails from every direction. T. C. Richardson, in an article published in the *Texas Geographic Magazine* of November, 1937, wrote of the concept this way: "trails originated wherever a herd was shaped up and ended wherever a market was found. A thousand minor cattle trails fed the main routes..."[108] Feeder routes were actually quite complex activities in a vast trail system and not as simplistic as Richardson conceived. A feeder route is one used numerous times by various herds. What has been described in previous pages, by no means, is inclusive, but we have attempted to describe and map the *well-used* feeder routes in Texas.

---

[106]Robert E. Zeigler, "Cowboy Strike of 1883," *The Handbook of Texas Online*, [accessed Jan. 31, 2010]

[107]Potter worked for the New England Livestock Company for eleven years. After three trips on the trail, he took charge of their breeding ranch near Fort Sumner, New Mexico. Col. Potter preferred to call the route the Potter-Bacon Cut-off, even though after Abner Blocker used the trail for a short time, others called it the "Potter-Blocker Trail."

[108]Wayne Spiller, comp, *Handbook of McCulloch County History*, Vol. I, 267.

The Matamoros Feeder Route from Brownsville extended to San Antonio, where the Western Cattle Trail began. Here the Wilson County Feeder Route joined the Western from the east. At Kerrville, the "Old Trail" Feeder Route joined the Western trunk line. Above Kerrville in Kimble County at Beef Trail Crossing on the Llano River, the Nueces River Feeder Route connected with the Western Trail. Just west of the Dodge Crossing on Brady Creek near Brady, the Fort McKavett Feeder Route merged with the trunk trail, and approximately nine miles north at Cow Gap in McCulloch County, the Mason-Gillespie County Feeder Route came up from the southeast, and the Middle Colorado Feeder Route came in from the east. South of Coleman in Coleman County, the Jinglebob Trail (Trickham) Feeder Route joined the trunk line of the Western Trail. North of Coleman, the Southern Tom Green County-Concho River Feeder Route connected with the Western Trail trunk line. At Albany in Shackelford County, the San Gabriel-Brownwood Feeder Route came in from the southeast. Also at Albany, in 1883, the Potter-Bacon Trail Splinter Route left the Western Trail to go northwest through the Texas Panhandle to No Man's Land, through Colorado, and on to Cheyenne, Wyoming.

As the Western Cattle Trail became well established in Texas, the feeder routes changed. Pressure from settlers claiming land that had been part of the open range led to the fencing of the range with barbed wire. Congested routes caused some movement of the feeder trails. The Nueces River Feeder Route is an example of this shift.

From the staging areas of Bandera, San Antonio, and Kerrville to Albany was less than two hundred miles. In the earlier years of the trail, there was no major supply depot before reaching Fort Griffin. Later, however, Albany, fifteen miles to the south, became the supply center. Fort Griffin lay ahead on the trail where more feeder trails merged with the Western.

Fort Griffin, Texas
This Edgar Rye woodcut shows the Fort Griffin military post and the town of Flat in the late 1870s. The large compound in the right foreground is Frank Conrad's emproium.
Courtesy of Old Jail Art Center and Archieve, Albany, Texas.

CHAPTER II

Fort Griffin, Texas

> *All the old trail drivers will remember Fort Griffin in Shackelford county on the trail, and all herds had to be inspected at the crossing of the Clear Fork of the Brazos, near the mouth of Tecumpsee. The writer at one time had the honor of being inspector there, and the memory of many pleasant events come back over the fleeting years as I sit here and write.*

John C. Jacobs, San Antonio, Texas
in Hunter, *The Trail Drivers of Texas*,
pg. 665 written around 1918-1923

118 THE WESTERN CATTLE TRAIL | 1874-1897

During the years of trail driving, drovers witnessed constant changes. Cattle routes were abandoned, and new ones created. Towns sprang up along the creeks, river crossings, and beside the trail, but, in a few short years, vanished. Military forts that were, for the most part, built during the Indian wars were abandoned and left to be dismantled. Fort Griffin existed longer than many forts and played a vital role in the history of the Western Trail, but it too succumbed to changes.

When trader Corwin F. Doan, who catered to the cowboys at Doan's Crossing on the Red River, referred to the trail in the region, he called it the "Fort Griffin - Dodge City Trail." He knew that this trail lay west of the Eastern Trail that had earlier crossed the Red River approximately one hundred miles east of his store and stables at Doan's Crossing in Wilbarger County. Since 1878, he had counted cattle and conversed with the cowhands and trail bosses as they purchased needed supplies and rested their horses in the pens and stables he provided. To his thinking, the drovers who had herded thousands of cattle up the trail each year had last stopped for supplies at Fort Griffin some three counties south of his river crossing. He also knew that their next major destination was the railhead of Dodge City, Kansas, to the north — after crossing Greer County and Indian Territory. His establishment lay between the two, and it was logical to him to call the Western Trail in Texas, the Fort Griffin - Dodge City Trail.

Consequently, for many, the name stuck. In 1933 the Oklahoma Legislature enacted House Bill 149 which stipulated that the Western and Chisholm cattle routes be researched and mapped. The name that C. A. Doan used was referenced in the legislation. When the map was produced in 1936 by the Oklahoma Historical Society, using the research provided by the Engineering Department of the Oklahoma State Highway Commission, the Texas Cattle Trail through Oklahoma was known as the "Western Cattle Trail " and the "Ft. Griffin-Ft. Dodge Dodge City Trail."[1]

Fort Griffin, the namesake of this trail, was established as one of a string of border outposts to protect Texas settlers against hostile Indians and outlaws. It lay in the middle of a line of forts across northwestern Texas from Fort Concho at San Angelo to Fort Arbuckle in Indian Territory. Lt. Col. Samuel D. Sturgis chose the site for the fort on the Clear Fork of the Brazos River on July 31, 1867. It was constructed on a hill providing a commanding view of the countryside in all directions. A sawmill was built on a small creek nearby which became known as Mill Creek. The army originally intended to build the fort of stone as teamsters brought building materials from San Antonio to supplement the local oak, cottonwood, and elm timber. Years of intensive labor at stone construction soon gave away to the building of temporary, quick framed structures of the green, fresh cut local timber covered with canvas. Privates and non-commissioned officers were housed in small wooden

---

[1] Oklahoma Historical Society 1936 map. Obviously, the name of the trail was no longer referred to by this name north of Dodge. The complete discussion of the various names used for the "Western" trail is found in Kraisinger & Kraisinger, *The Western, the Greatest Texas Cattle Trail, 1874-1886*, 10-20.

THE WESTERN CATTLE TRAIL | 1874-1897

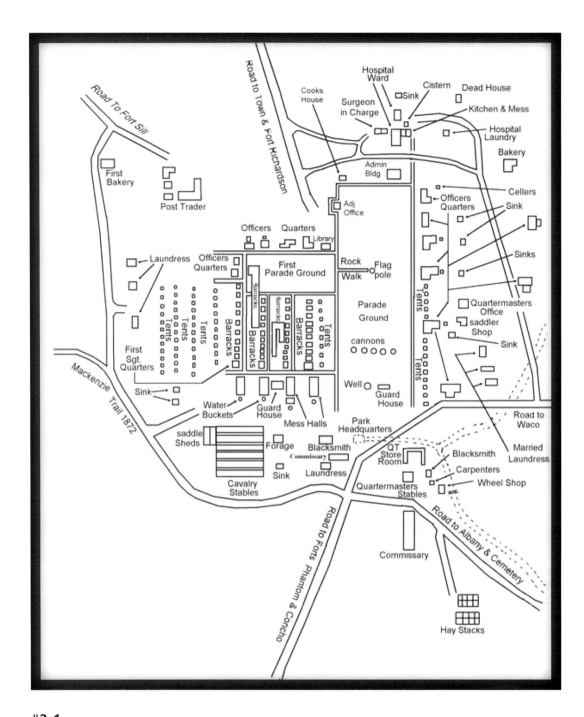

#2-1
Fort Griffin:
Looking at the layout of Fort Griffin, one can feel the chaos of the location. In the earlier years, during military action, the fort was closely connected to other area forts, Phantom, Concho, Sill, and Richardson. On the north, near the administration building and the adjutant's office, was the "road to town." The town was simply referred to by the soldiers and cowboys as "The Flat." When the town acquired a post office and was designated as the county seat, the more official name of "Ft. Griffin" of "Griffin" was used.

Map courtesy of Lester W. Galbreath, Albany, Texas.

buildings. Some of the soldiers' quarters were no more than huts made of salvaged materials gathered from abandoned near-by ranches. The hospital, commissary, and quartermaster's storeroom were made of logs, but were improved as better lumber became available. At first there were no stables, and horses suffered miserably, dying from exposure to the intense heat and cold.[2]

The first post office in the county was established at the fort on March 17, 1869. Four mail deliveries per week were received at the post, provided they were not delayed by floods, bad weather, or Indians.

Like a magnet, the fort drew ranchers and homesteaders to its location. Settlers soon built a string of houses along the Clear Fork reaching for a mile or more from the fort. The fort offered protection, schooling, and employment. Contracts were entered into for beef, hay, and wood. The army paid good money for commodities like eggs, milk, and butter and, in turn, it introduced imported canned goods to the locals.

Soldiers stationed at the fort had the arduous duties of escorting government mail and surveying parties, plus pursuing and punishing bands of threatening Indians. Most of the time the expeditions sent out to "discipline the Indians" were in vain, but there were a few successes. Many of the depredations against white settlers, however, were caused by white outlaws, not by the Indians, and the law-breaking desperadoes operated within the fort's shadow at a place called "the Flat."

While Fort Griffin was under construction, the level bottomland just below "Government Hill," the crest of the hill on which the fort was built, became a gathering area for gangs of lawless desperadoes, squatters, and Tonkaway Indians. Merchants quickly put up temporary stores with a saloon, knowing that off-duty soldiers and drifters wanted refreshments. By 1872, the Flat had grown from a few squatter houses to a boisterous village that extended from the foot of the hill to the Clear Fork. On both sides of the main street were gambling dives, eating places, and saloons.[3]

Joe S. McCombs, a lad of 18 years, rode into Fort Griffin in 1872 and later recalled seeing "a fort on top of the hill overlooking the Clear Fork of the Brazos River at which were stationed several hundred soldiers." The Flat at the foot of the hill was a "trading point for the few settlers in that region as well as for the soldiers. According to my recollection there were three saloons and three stores there then."[4]

The Flat was a "free town" in that any man could put a house or business anywhere he wanted. There was no plan or plat layout or permanency about the town. Buildings were crude and flimsy. By 1874, the lawlessness and intoxication became so extreme that the commander of Fort Griffin placed the town under government control and forced a number of undesirable residents to leave. Within months Shackelford County became organized and "the Flat" became known officially as the

---

[2]Lawrence Clayton, "Fort Griffin, Texas," The Handbook of Texas Online [accessed December 27, 2004]
[3]Carl Coke Rister, *Fort Griffin on the Texas Frontier*, 72-73.
[4]Ben O. Grant and J. R. Webb. "On The Cattle Trail and Buffalo Range, Joe S. McCombs." *West Texas Historical Association Year Book XI*, 1935, 94.

THE WESTERN CATTLE TRAIL | 1874-1897

town of "Fort Griffin," or referred to by locals as just "Griffin." It was also named the county seat.[5] It didn't last long, however. Within the year, the county seat was moved to Albany because, it was said, Albany was more centrally located. The truth was that in 1874, the nearby fort town was in a state of lawless upheaval, and the fort itself was starting to physically decline. The Commander of the Army's Department of Texas toured the line of defense in that year to review the conditions of the state's forts. His report was as follows:

> At most of the posts they [the soldiers] are comfortably quartered. Fort Griffin is an exception to this rule. It may be made to answer this coming winter, but no longer, and if troops are to be kept there another year, new barracks must be built for them. There is nothing there on which repairs can be made. The buildings are mostly huts…This post is a very important one, in my opinion, and should be retained. I respectfully recommend that $80,000 be asked for to build suitable quarters there for six companies, four companies of Cavalry and two of Infantry.[6]

Then to add to the population of the Flat in the early years, and to the activity of the fort, during the years of 1874 to 1876-77, the area became a haven for the buffalo hunters. They came to sell their hides and salted meats, and the fort and its surroundings became a headquarters for the hide industry. The presence of buffalo hunters usually meant trouble, but they were always welcomed because they spent money freely.[7]

To add to the challenge faced by Fort Griffin, the cattle drives on the Western Trail began flowing by the fort in 1874 and 1875. In 1874, Frank Collinson, who was working for John T. Lytle and Tom McDaniel, brother-in-law to Lytle, was with the first recognized herd on this trail that went by Fort Griffin. Collinson recalled that his outfit was delivering 3,500 "good, big, aged steers" to the Red Cloud Indian Agency at Fort Robinson on the Niobrara River in northwestern Nebraska, and he remembered Fort Griffin:

> We reached Fort Griffin in Shackelford County the last of April and rested up a few days on Collins Creek. We bought fresh supplies in

---

[5]Lawrence Clayton, "Fort Griffin, Texas." Ibid.

[6]Rister, Ibid, 12.

[7]Ben O. Grant. "Life in the Town of Fort Griffin." *Tracks Along the Clear Fork*, 110. Buffalo hunters killed millions of bison for their hides, which wiped out the Indians' main source of food and contributed to the Army's effort to force them onto reservations starting in 1875. When buffalo herds were depleated in Western Kansas, hunters moved south into the Texas Panhandle and operated out of Mobeetie near Fort Elliott and Fort Griffin. These forts replaced Dodge City as hide centers. Army officers and soldiers operated as middlemen and shippers of the skins east. "It has been estimated that in 1877 between one hundred thousand and two hundred thousand hides came through Fort Griffin alone." (Howard R. Lamar, *Charlie Siringo's West*, 71)

that thriving frontier town, alive with soldiers, teamsters, and the first of the buffalo hunters.

Since we planned to head across unknown country from Griffin to Camp Supply, Indian Territory, with the first herd of cattle to be pointed in that direction, the government furnished us a guide, Champ Means, who well knew the country, the watering places, etc. ...This was a great help to us and enabled us to reach Camp Supply without too much delay.[8]

Joe McCombs, a local buffalo hunter, recalled that the "Millet Outfit from South Texas" was one of the first herds to trail past Fort Griffin. He continued, "…from that time on [1874] cattle moved over this new trail in increasing numbers."[9]

In the 1876 season, when herds from the Eastern Trail started feeding into the Western Trail, the added business on the Flat that had become the town of Fort Griffin, created even more incentive for the merchants to build permanent business houses and to increase their wares. Charles Meyer and E. Frankel each built substantial saloons and boasted of their offerings. Meyer's saloon kept ice during the summer months, and Frankel offered fresh sea food.[10] Another saloon named the "Beehive" had painted a large beehive on its store front with this verse on it:

In this hive we are all alive,
Good whiskey makes us funny,
And if you are dry
Step in and try
The flavor of our honey.[11]

With the added activity of the cattle herds coming into Fort Griffin, the town began to boom and double in size.[12] Fort Griffin merchants, knowing their town was on a splinter route from the Eastern Trail, by way of Belton, for drovers destined for Dodge City, sent agents to Belton to intercept the trail drivers to persuade them to point their herds up the Leon River and on north to Fort Griffin rather than continuing on to Fort Worth, a supply depot on the Eastern Trail. The Griffin merchants delighted in the advantage they now had over Fort Worth merchants, who had for years enjoyed an exclusive trade with the cowboys. They —

spared no effort to welcome the dusty trail drivers and to show them every courtesy. A Griffin reporter for the Fort Worth Democrat,

---

[8]Frank Collinson, age 19, hired out to Lytle for $60 a month because he had with him "seven good horses" that he could ride well. Collinson did not mention Doan's Crossing because the Doans did not establish their trading post on the Red River until 1878. (Collinson, *Life in the Saddle*, 31, 35)

[9]Grant and Webb. Ibid. 94.

[10]Grant, ibid. 111.

[11]Sallie Reynolds Matthews. *Interwoven, A Pioneer Chronicle*, 45.

[12]By 1880, the Flat had about 1,000 people plus twice that many transients. (Rister, Ibid, 132)

THE WESTERN CATTLE TRAIL | 1874-1897

writing under the pseudonym "Lone Star," literally exuded his town's new spirit. In April, 1876, he informed envious Fort Worth readers that southern Texas cattle were coming in rapidly, and that the driving season's total over the Western Trail should reach 125,000 head. He stressed the fact that these cattle drives to Dodge City were moving from southern Texas via Griffin…[13]

The Griffin reporter's boastful estimate of cattle coming up the trail was probably on target. The *Jacksboro Frontier Echo* of July 21, 1876, reported that 73,000 cattle had already passed Fort Griffin, bound for Dodge City.

The cattle drives also attracted the "hangers on" who were desperadoes or outlaws who hung around Fort Griffin waiting to hire on with an outfit. Because cowboys for trail driving were scarce, especially with so many herds moving up the trail in one season, the "hangers on" followed the herds looking for short-term work. Many of them applied for a trail-drive job at Fort Griffin to help with the herds going to Dodge City, but then disappeared when the herds reached Dodge. These "hide outs" stayed away from the lawmen of Dodge, but felt safe in Fort Griffin.[14]

While thousands of cattle grazed on the Clear Fork of the Brazos River, trail bosses bought supplies for the chuck wagons from the fort store on "Government Hill," and cowboys were supplied with entertainment in the town Fort Griffin on the flat bottom ground. In 1876, contractor Lewis Neatherlin purchased supplies for Slaughter's three herds at Fort Griffin as they trailed through the area, and he wrote in his journal about an experience with his cowboys who visited the town:

> **May 4:**
> I left the herds this morning and went to Griffin. Found everything all right. Met Ellison there who said he would let me have all the supplies I needed. Returned to Field's camp, 6 miles from town on Foil Creek and stopped for the night.
>
> **May 5:**
> Went down the road and met the 2 foremost herds. Found them out of meat. Went back to town and carried some out on a horse to their camps, 4 miles. No. 1 not come up yet.
>
> **May 7:**
> Went to town. Swapped wagon after a great deal of trouble trying. Bought supplies and made camp, 3 miles west of Griffin, just at night.

According to his May 8 journal entry, he went to town to settle his bill for the last few day's of purchases and found one of his drovers in town "who had lost his

---

[13]Rister, Ibid, 145.
[14]Rister, Ibid, 146.

horse and wanted ten dollars." Neatherlin noted that the fellow: "Did not get it." Another cowboy had spent the night in town and "has not come out yet." Both lads seemed to have lost their horses. Neatherlin left town without the drovers. The next day's journal entry gave the results:

May 9:
The 2 men not come yet. I went back to hunt them, or rather, the horses. Met them coming. One asked me to go to town and redeem his pistol. He, having been a good hand, I did so. It took ten dollars to get it. I returned and overtaken the herds at 4 in the evening. Made 9 or 10 miles. Good grass but very rocky and hilly.[15]

Sallie Reynolds Matthews, whose family moved to the area in 1866 when she was five years old, remembered that by the late 1870s, the town of Fort Griffin was populated by the "scum of the earth," but at the same time "others were honorable and respected citizens." Buffalo hunters were still around and the Western Cattle Trail was trailing thousands of head through Fort Griffin. It was the "zenith of Griffin," she wrote. Matthews continued:

There were enterprising merchants who carried first class merchandise, and a very good hotel, clean and well kept by Jack Swartz and his wife, served as headquarters for cattlemen. There was a school building which was also used for church services, with a Masonic hall on the second floor.[16]

Cowboys, however, saw Griffin from a different perpective than a young lady from a local ranch. In 1878, cowhand John Young described Fort Griffin:

...the worst hole I have ever been in. The population at this time was perhaps five thousand people, most of them soldiers, murderers, wild women, buffalo hunters, altogether the most mongrel and the hardest-looking crew that it was possible to assemble. The fort proper and a big store were up on a hill. The "Flats" [sic] where every house was either a saloon, a gambling den, or a dance hall, generally all three combined. No man who valued his life would go here unarmed or step out alone into the darkness. If about daylight he walked down to the river he might see a man hanging from the cottonwood trees with a

---

[15]Perhaps the cowboy had his gun taken from him because in some Texas counties it was against the law to carry a firearm into town, or a saloon keeper was "holding" it for the cowboy, perhaps, to cover a gambling debt. In a wild frontier town like Fort Griffin, it was not uncommon for horses to be stolen. Neatherlin seemed to be as concerned about losing the horses as the cowhands. He knew that eventually the drovers would appear, but he was not so sure about the horses. (Kelley, *Up the Trail in '76, The journal of Lewis Warren Neatherlin*, 16-17)

[16]Sallie Reynolds Matthews, Ibid, 109.

placard on his back saying, "Horse Thief No. 8" — or whatever the latest number was."[17]

In May of 1879, James C. Shaw journeyed to Fort Griffin to catch up with a herd of cattle going north. He had in tow, besides his own mount, three horses and hoped to get work with the Ellison and Sherrill outfit. On his way, however, Shaw got the "flux" and was delayed in reaching Fort Griffin in time to meet up with the herd. He noted that Fort Griffin was a "good post with about 400 soldiers and a small town." Shortly after arrival, a local saloon owner, however, gave him the advice to "swim the river and catch the herd tonight" because "The men you see around here are one and two-time men killers and I would not go about with them." So Shaw bought

"a biscuit or two and a small piece of bacon" with his last 50 cents and swam the river with his horses. Shaw remembered:

> I was now in Throckmorton county and there was nothing in sight. There were no settlements from there to Indian Territory, 150 miles away, and many wild Indians. I poured the water out of my boots while the horses grazed and then took the trail where the herd had gone.[18]

The herd that James C. Shaw finally caught up with was the Jim Ellison herd bossed by Dick Withers. Shaw was hired for $40 a month taking into account the use of his three horses. He was put on night herd, from midnight until two o'clock.[19]

During the trailing season, herds were coming into Fort Griffin daily. G. F. Boone noticed this in the early 1880s when he was a drover for Buchanan and Beatty. They were driving 1,000 head of stock cattle into Indian Territory. Boone was from Coryell County and, to him, in his early twenties, he had not been "as far north as this one [trail drive]." In his recollection he told of his outfit's stop at Fort Griffin that was longer than expected due to high water on the Clear Fork:

> When we got to Fort Griffin, there were already two herds there before us. I can't recall the names of the owners,

---

[17]Five thousand people is likely an over exaggeration, but the reader sure gets the impression that the town was a very lively place. The "big store up on the hill" was where the trail bosses acquired most of their trail supplies. (J. Frank Dobie, *A Vaquero of the Brush County*, 133 and Lamar, *Charlie Siringo's West*, 71)

[18]Brayer, ed. and James C. Shaw, *North From Texas*, 31.

[19]Ellison and Sherrill were one of the largest trail contracting outfits operating out of Texas, owned by James F. Ellison and James H. Sherrill. Richard (Dick) Withers was their trail boss on this 1879 trip. This was the sixth herd that Ellison and Sherrill had put on the trail for Ogallala that year. More will be written of this trip in later chapters. (Brayer and Shaw, Ibid. 31 & 91)

because in the 10 days we were there five or six more herds came up. This was in the days when a herd a day went up the trail, each one following the other, it appeared.

Well, those herds began to stack up. That was bad enough; but for no reason a-tall, they'd run every night and mix up with other herds. What a time we had! A stampede every night! By the time that water started to going down, there wasn't a man in camp that wasn't suspicioned of starting a run; and that was grounds for gun trouble. Every man's gun hung loose in its holster, ready for instant use. It seemed like we were all on tip-toes, and ready to kill. After the water went down far enough to ford, all the herds were mixed up into one herd. The way out was to pick a referee, to see that every man got his own cattle. Then the cowpunchers started driving and cutting. Every herd was on its way in two days, and possible murder was side-tracked. After we crossed the herd at Doan's Crossing, we got plum out of sight of any other herd.[20]

> The circumstances around the different river crossings is not known. Perhaps over the approximately eleven seasons that the Western Trail was used in this area, the crossings were changed because of conjestion in the area, inspector stations, river crossing conditions, local politics, or the closing of the fort in 1881. It is also possible that all four were used at the same time.

Joe McCombs, a local Shackelford County resident of the day, recalled the "big rush" into Fort Griffin during the 1880s:

The big rush was at the beginning of the Eighties during which in the spring and summer drives cattle came through in small and large herds daily and by the thousands. The big drives continued until about 1886 and from that time on they came through in diminishing numbers until they played out completely in the early Nineties.[21]

The Western Cattle Trail outfits and their herds could cross the Clear Fork of the Brazos River at four different locations in the Fort Griffin area. (Map #2-2) The first opportunity was on the southeast side of the post at the present-day highway bridge crossing. Another possibility was near the former fort town of "the Flat," at the Fort Griffin-Fort Richardson Crossing. If the river was not forded at one of these two places, the drovers could continue into Throckmorton County and cross the Clear Fork at the Butterfield - Military Road Crossing. The next crossing was farther north at the Tecumseh Crossing where John C. Jacobs had been an inspector. There was also a crossing located on the Belton Feeder Route which came into the post area from the southeast.[22]

There were two feeder routes that joined the Western Cattle Trail in this area.

---

[20]G. F. Boone interview, *American Life Histories: Manuscripts from the Federal Writers' Project, 1936-1940*. [accessed online December 9, 2007]
[21]Grant and Webb, Ibid, 94.
[22]Lester W. Galbreath, *The Western Cattle Trail*, map.

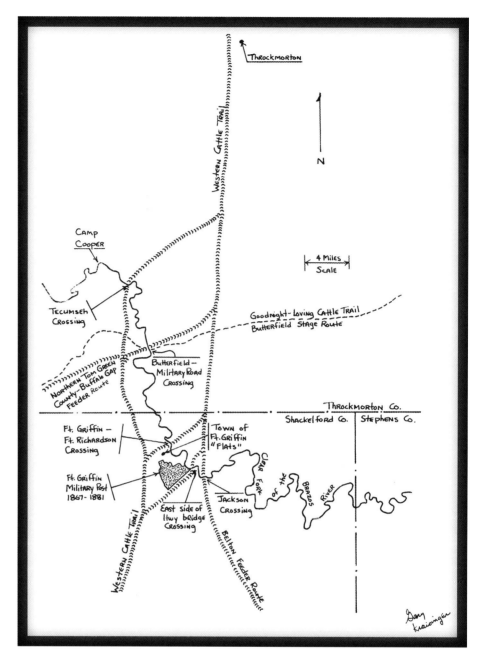

#2-2
The Fort Griffin Area, Showing Feeder Routes to the Western Trail and Clear Fork River Crossings:
Feeder routes coming into the Fort Griffin area to connect with the Western Trail were the Belton Feeder Route from the southeast, joining the Western Trail on the east side of the fort, and the Northern Tom Green County-Buffalo Gap Feeder Route connecting with the Western Trail north of Fort Griffin in Throckmorton County. The Western Cattle Trail continued north on the west or east side of Fort Griffin, depending on where the trail boss decided to cross the Clear Fork of the Brazos River. There were four possible river crossings.

BELTON FEEDER ROUTE: (Map #2-3)

This route came out of Bell County through Belton and passed by Fort Griffin on the east, crossing the Clear Fork of the Brazos River at Jackson Crossing. The route joined the Western Trail just north of the river. It was one of the routes that connected the old Eastern Trail to the Western. Maxwell and Morris took this route in the early years of the Western. H. S. Drago wrote about this trail drive in his *Great American Cattle Trails*:

> Maxwell and Morris, with a big herd of stock cattle from south Texas, bound for Ogallala, Nebraska, left the Chisholm Trail at Belton and, striking northwest, followed the Leon River through what are today Coryell, Hamilton, Comanche, Eastland and Stephens counties. They had no trail to follow, and as the old saying had it, they were just following their noses, with the North Star their only compass. Another forty miles brought them to Fort Griffin.[23]

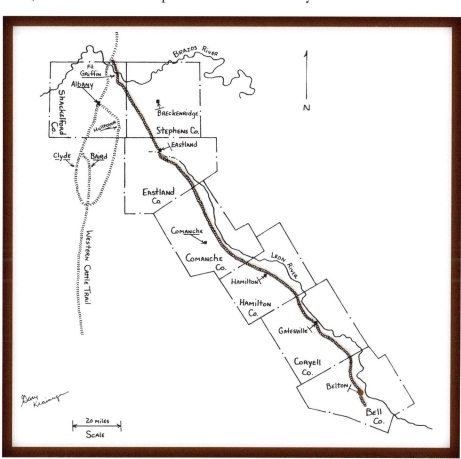

The Eastern Trail had ran along the eastern edge of Belton toward Fort Worth where a total of 51,923 head had been shipped out by rail in 1877. Traffic from the Eastern Trail into Fort Worth began to diminish because of the 1875 Kansas quarantine closed off its access to the railheads of Wichita, Newton, and Ellsworth in 1876 and created a need for the more direct Western Trail to Dodge City.

By the 1878 season, Fort Worth businessmen began to notice that trade was falling off drastically because of this shift in trails and realized that Fort

#2-3
Belton Feeder Route:
The Belton Feeder Route traversed several counties, starting from Belton, Texas, in Bell County. Following the west bank of the Leon River, outfits with their herds came from the southeast to eventually merge with the Western Cattle Trail north of the Clear Fork of the Brazos River in Shackelford County near Fort Griffin.

---

[23] Harry Sinclair Drago, *Great American Cattle Trails*, 172. Note that Drago mistakenly called the Eastern Trail in Texas — the "Chisholm."

THE WESTERN CATTLE TRAIL | 1874-1897   129

Griffin had become the new supply post for northbound cattle outfits. The editor of the *Fort Worth Democrat*, who remembered the jabs from the Griffin reporter two seasons before, now berated the merchants of his city for being lax and losing sight of the importance of the trail business and suggested that a representative be sent to Belton, the starting point of the splinter trail to Fort Griffin, to "offset the influence of Fort Griffin's enterprise." Fort Worth businessmen sent Dave Blair in the 1879 season to Belton to convince drovers to not use the splinter route toward the Western Trail but to remain on the Eastern Trail to Fort Worth. *The Fort Griffin Echo*, in its first year of publication, picked up the theme of the threat and wrote that one of its citizens, Frank E. Conrad, was ready to bet $500 to $1,000 that more cattle would be trailed by Fort Griffin than by Fort Worth that year! The *Fort Worth Democrat* responded that they had two cattlemen that would bet up to $2,500 that three fourths of the cattle drive in 1879 would stay on the old Eastern Trail and go into Fort Worth. Conrad sent a check for $500 to a Dallas bank to open the challenge, but there were no takers. As it turned out, Fort Worth would have lost the bet because of the estimated 250,927 cattle trailed that year, Fort Worth received 135,847, considerably short of the boasted three fourths. Fort Griffin had 101,010 cattle pass by its town.[24]

NORTHERN TOM GREEN COUNTY — BUFFALO GAP FEEDER ROUTE: (Map #2-4)

Coming in from the west side to join the Western Trail north of Fort Grffin was a route from Tom Green County. This route did not trail into Coleman, as did the South Tom Green County Route, but instead continued northeast, crossed the Colorado River at present-day Ballinger, left the Edwards Plateau through Buffalo Gap on the Callahan Divide, crossed Elm Creek at Abilene and joined the Western Trail trunk line north of the Clear Fork of the Brazos in Throckmorton County.[25]

Λ natural pass or gap in the Callahan Divide was an old worn buffalo trail that came out of Runnels, Coke, and southern Taylor counties. At this gap a small settlement developed and took the name of the pass, "Buffalo Gap." From all the surrounding area, cattlemen funneled their herds through the pass toward the Western Trail north of Fort Griffin. When Taylor County was organized in 1878, Buffalo Gap was the only settlement of any size in the county. Thus, it became the county seat.[26]

---

[24]Wayne Gard, *The Chisholm Trail*, 240-241. Charles R. Goins and Danney Goble in their book, *Historical Atlas of Oklahoma*, state that 257,927 cattle went up the trail in 1879 (page 117). The herds that did continue on the Eastern Trail to Fort Worth eventually crossed over to the Western Trail farther up the line.

[25]The Neuces River Feeder Route splintered off from its course west of Junction where it joined the South Tom Green County Feeder Route to San Angelo. At San Angelo, the trail drivers had three choices: they could trail east to Coleman to join the Western Trail; they could continue north-northeast on the Northern Tom Green County-Buffalo Gap Feeder Route; or they could pick up the Goodnight-Loving Trail to New Mexico Territory and beyond.

[26]Skagg thesis, 37, 104-105.

Two years later, when the Texas and Pacific Railway began to push its way across Texas, several ranchers and businessmen lobbied H. C. Whiters, the Texas and Pacific track and townsite locator, to have the rails run through ranch land in northern Taylor County, therefore bypassing Buffalo Gap. In the agreement, a new town was to be established between Cedar and Big Elm creeks east of Catclaw Creek. When the Texas and Pacific arrived on the site in January of 1881, railroad promoters advertised the spot as "Abilene," the "Future Great City of West Texas." Railroad officials platted the townsite and soon several hundred people arrived and settled before the sale of town lots, and businesses appeared practically overnight. On March 15, 1881, Abilene was officially established when town lots were auctioned and over 300 lots were sold in two days. In January of 1883

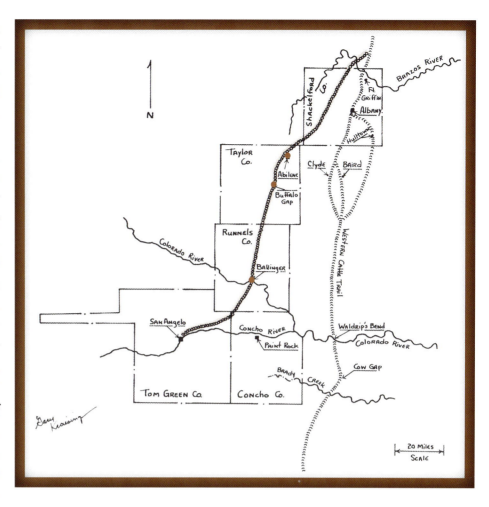

#2-4
Northern Tom Green County - Buffalo Gap Feeder Route:
This feeder route came from the southwest from Tom Green County, Texas, (around San Angelo), continued through Runnels County, passing through Buffalo Gap in Taylor County, crossed Shackelford County, and merged with the Western Cattle Trail north of Fort Griffin in Throckmorton County.

Abilene was incorporated, and by an election in October of the same year, the county seat was moved from Buffalo Gap to Abilene.[27]

A youth from Boston by the name of Godfrey Sykes "noted with interest, as the Texas-Pacific train with which I had become involved made its leisurely way westward...that the surroundings were to my liking." He made his train trip shortly after the opening of Abilene, and in his autobiography remembered:

---
[27] The name of "Abilene" was apparently suggested because of the cattle town in Kansas by that name. Abilene, Kansas, was the first major railhead in Kansas on the Abilene (Chisholm) Trail. The town had boomed with the cattle business starting in September of 1867. The promoters were hoping that Abilene, Kansas's reputation would fuel a similar enthusiasm in Texas and duplicate its success. It worked, for by 1890 Abilene had a population of over 3,000. ("Abilene, Texas," *The Handbook of Texas Online*, accessed Nov. 29, 2004)

THE WESTERN CATTLE TRAIL | 1874-1897

My ticket was good to a place called Abilene, and so to Abilene I went and made it my temporary headquarters. I could not have done better. It was at that period a real "cow-town," with horses, cattle in immense herds, troops of vociferous equestrians who I knew instinctively were "cow-boys," and all the other appurtenances and diversions of the period and region.

I made enquiry about the herds of cattle, the first of which I had seen from the train; and found that they were "trail herds," bound for some far off region for purposes I did not at first clearly understand, and that the men who had them in charge, and who were reported to have to convoy them safely through hundreds of miles of country infested by Indians, presumably hostile and blood-thirsty, were the *ne-plus-ultra* of the cow-boy profession.

This was undoubtedly the life for me, and so I determined off-hand to go along with some of them.[28]

The youthful Sykes, upon acquiring a gun and saddle in Abilene, continued to search for a "needed horse and a job." At an Abilene stable he agreed to drive a buckboard for a man, who had dislocated his shoulder, to meet his herd that had already passed through Abilene and was bound for Dodge City, Kansas. The cattle were being held fifteen or twenty miles outside of town waiting for the injured man's final trail instructions to the foreman, but he could not drive the buckboard. Sykes continued:

We reached the herd before night and he found that one of the men were sick and wanted to go back to town and so, as I had talked my wish to try a trip "up the trail" while we were driving out from town, he talked it over with the foreman and offered me the job. My saddle and a pair of blankets, which he offered to buy for me, were to be sent out on the "chuck-waggon" as soon as the sick man had driven him back to town, and as I was now a full-fledged "cow-puncher," although still without my saddle, I stood my first guard that night on the sick man's horse and saddle….The night was fine, the cattle bedded-down and quiet, and all in all I thought that the life of the cow-boy was pretty much an affair of "beer and skittles." I confess that I afterwards discovered that there were other phases in it which were not quite so attractive,….[29]

---

[28]Godfrey Sykes' "rambling autobiography" as he called it, was written "nearly sixty five years" after his "happy and irresponsible wanderings or temporary sojourns in that fascinating earlier West…" The English-born Sykes was in Boston in 1879; was a full-fledged cowboy by 1881; was a cattle ranch foreman in western Kansas in the mid 1880s; was a mining engineer in Japan in 1886-87; voyaged on a tramp steamer among the islands of the South Pacific in 1888-89, and was in Flagstaff, Arizona by 1895. This was only the beginning. Sykes continued to wander over six continents and seven seas. (Godfrey Sykes, *A Westerly Trend,…Being a Veracious Chronicle of More Than Sixty Years of Joyous Wanderings, Mainly in Search of Space and Sunshine*, 63-66.)

[29]Sykes, Ibid, 66.

Sykes, who was at first called "Red" because of his light English complexion, was later referred to as "Axolotl" which Sykes later learned was an amphibian salamander of Mexico and Texas or more commonly known as a "water dog." He earned this nickname from the fact that he chose to cross the rivers "on my own" rather than stay in the saddle of his horse or swing on the tail of his horse like the other cowhands.

Upon reaching Dodge City, the owner, the man with the dislocated shoulder, was there waiting for his herd. He informed his men that the herd and horses had been sold to a purchaser in Ogallala, another two hundred and fifty miles farther north. He then seemed to be very interested in Sykes' health and wondered if the lad had experienced any illness while on the trail. "Then he told us, and both he and the trail foremen seemed to think that it was rather a good joke, that the sick man whose place I had taken and whose blankets I had been sleeping in, had been in rather an advanced stage of small-pox when he left the outfit." They all attributed Sykes' ability to ward off infection to the "air of the plains, and the bean-pot and corn-bread of our cook."[30]

Herds from the Webb Ranch in Runnels County also used the Northern Tom Green County - Buffalo Gap Feeder Route. High Webb's ranch was on the Colorado River adjoining the John Blocker ranch. In 1885, Webb sent a herd of 2,300 head to the Frost Ranch in Colorado. In the outfit was a lad of seventeen years named Phil Wright. He later wrote that they gathered the cattle from the ranges "covering Runnels, Tom Green, Concho and adjoining counties" and started up the trail "from a point on the Colorado River where the city of Ballinger now stands." They went "by way of Abilene" and connected with the Western Trail above Fort Griffin.[31]

Within two years after Fort Worth had tried to hold on to the cattle trade for the Eastern Trail, settlements around Fort Griffin expanded, and the fort troopers found themselves unneeded as a protective force. The buffalo had been depleted, and the Indians had been moved to reservations in Indian Territory. Other sources of law and order had come to the communities of developing frontier Texas. Albany had been awarded the county seat in 1874, and in 1881 the Texas Central Railway arrived. The town replaced Fort Griffin as a supply center for the cattlemen. On May 31, 1881, Captain J. B. Irvin closed the fort and marched the single remaining army unit southward several hundred miles to Fort Clark at Bracketville, between the Uvalde and Del Rio. Without the soldiers and the fort, the buffalo hunters, and the cowboys, who now stopped at Albany for their supplies, the town of Fort Griffin or "the Flat" soon declined. *The Fort Griffin Echo* ceased publication in 1882.

---

[30]Sykes, Ibid, 69 & 73.
[31]Phil L. Wright eventually returned to San Antonio, Texas, where he went to work for the San Antonio Fire Department. By 1918, we became the fire and police commissioner of the city. ("Phil L. Wright," in Hunter, 423-425)

THE WESTERN CATTLE TRAIL | 1874-1897

> *Our foreman returned before noon and reported a favorable stage of water for the herd, and a new ferry that that had been established for wagons. With this good news, we were determined to put that river behind us in as few hours as possible, for it was a common occurrence that a river which was fordable at night was the reverse by daybreak.*
>
> *The cattle were strung out in trailing manner nearly a mile, and on reaching the river near the middle of the afternoon, we took the water without a halt or even a change of horses. This boundary river on the northern border of Texas was a terror to trail drovers, but on our reaching it, it had shallowed down, the flow of water following several small channels….the majestic grandeur of the river was apparent on every hand, — with its red, bluff banks, the sediment of its red waters marking the timber along its course while the driftwood, lodged in trees and high on the banks, indicated what might be expected when she became sportive or angry. That she was merciless was evident, for although this crossing had be in use only a year or two when we forded, yet five graves, one of which was less than ten days made, attested her disregard for human life. It can safely be asserted that at this and lower trail crossings on Red River, the lives of more trail men were lost by drowning than on all other rivers together.*

Andy Adams, *The Log of a Cowboy*, pgs. 120-121 about an 1882 trail drive to the Blackfoot Indian Agency in Montana

CHAPTER III

North to Doan's Crossing and The Red River

THE WESTERN CATTLE TRAIL | 1874-1897   135

136   THE WESTERN CATTLE TRAIL | 1874-1897

Each trail boss planned a drive based on river and creek crossings, camping spots, and supply depots. The experienced drover knew where the best spots were for crossing swollen rivers, how long it would take to ford the obstacles, and what time of day to do so. Along the way there were springs, watering holes, a rare shaded or sheltered area, or a friendly rancher who offered an area for a camp. Food and supplies were rationed to last from one supply depot to another. After loading up with food stuffs for the cook's wagon and other necessary supplies at Fort Griffin or Albany, the outfit knew the next supply depot would be Doan's store on the Red River, one hundred and ten miles north from Fort Griffin.

The gentle rolling hills and plains of bluegrass of Throckmorton County must have been calming to the cowboys on the trail after leaving the hustle and chaos of the Fort Griffin area. The county had fewer people, and most residents lived in and around the county seat of Throckmorton. Herds often bunched up at the Clear Fork crossing at Fort Griffin, and stampeding and mixing of the cattle was always a threat. After the crossing, drovers could spread out and move their herds away from other herds and make good time trailing across a serene area to the next fork of the Brazos River and on to Doan's Crossing. Lewis Neatherlin remarked in his journal of May 11, 1876: "Got fine grass and plenty of water in all the small creeks, which are plentiful in number."[1]

Even though some herds may have crossed over the Clear Fork at Fort Griffin to the east side of the creek, the main trunk of the Western Trail continued north on the west side of the fort and creek. One of the Clear Fork crossings in Thockmorton County would have to be used by the herds on the east side of the river to join the Western Trail.

Footprints of earlier events were soon evident to the observant cowboy. The old Butterfield - Military Road ran across the southern end of Throckmorton County that had been used heavily until the Civil War.[2] At its crossing of the Clear Fork, there was the Butterfield Stage stand or "Clear Fork Station." First Sergeant John G. Irwin and family had come to the Clear Fork from Fort Chadbourne and settled on the abandoned Comanche Reservation in September of 1859. After putting in a crop on his newly established ranch, he left to operate the stage stand at the Clear Fork Crossing. He dug a well and kept horses for the stage changes.[3]

After the War, in 1866, Charles Goodnight and his partner Oliver Loving started using the established route and the Clear Fork Crossing to trail their cattle to Horsehead Crossing on the Pecos River and on into New Mexico Territory. Now, a

---

[1]Leo Kelley, ed. *Up the Trail in '76, The Journal of Lewis Warren Neatherlin*, 17.

[2]The Butterfield Overland Mail route operated from September 15, 1858 to March 1, 1861. It provided semiweekly mail and passenger stage service from St. Louis, Missouri and Memphis, Tennessee, across northern Texas to San Franciso, California. This old route come from Fort Belknap to the Clear Fork Station on the Brazos and on to Fort Phantom Hill. This established route was also used as a military road between Fort Belknap, Fort Griffin, and Fort Phantom Hill--therefore, the name Butterfield - Military Road. (Rupert N. Richardson, "Butterfield Overland Mail," *The Handbook of Texas Online* [accessed Nov. 29, 2004])

[3]Frances Mayhugh Holden, *Lambshead Before Interwoven*, 89.

THE WESTERN CATTLE TRAIL | 1874-1897

portion of the road was used by trail drivers from Tom Green, Runnels, and Taylor counties to feed their herds into the Western Trail at the crossing.[4] The old stage and military crossing was still being used — except now by trail herds.

Just north of the Butterfield - Military Road, seven miles north of Fort Griffin, a Comanche Indian reservation, six miles by six miles in area, had been established by the Texas Legislature in January of 1856 in order to oversee some 450 Comanches who were there trying to adapt to an agricultural way of life. As early as 1851, a campsite for three companies of the Fifth Infantry was established there, and the location was known as "Camp Cooper," but when the reservation was placed there, the post became the headquarters for two squadrons of the Second United States Cavalry under the command of Lt. Col. Robert E. Lee, who arrived in April of 1856.[5] At forty-nine, this was Lee's first position as a post commander. It was infested with rattlesnakes and ranging wolves.

In July of 1857, Lee was reassigned to another regiment and was replaced by Lieutenant I. F. Minter. The Indians were relocated to Indian Territory in 1859, and the reservation land was returned to the State and opened for preemption in one hundred and sixty acre tracts.[6] When the land opened for settlement, John G. Irwin and family arrived and settled just downriver from the fort. Two years later, when Camp Cooper was closed down, Lieutenant I. F. Minter gave permission to Irwin to move into the agent's house.

Other early settlers were W. H. Ledbetter, the Joseph Beck Matthews, and Barber Watkins Reynolds and their families who arrived in 1858 and 1859. At first the Matthews and Reynolds settled near present-day Breckenridge, about thirty-five miles southeast of where the Irwin family located, but after the war, the families built rock houses along the banks of the Clear Fork.[7] It was these stone ranch houses that the trail-driving cowboys would have noticed in the mid-1870s. At the Clear Fork Corssing, there was Judge Striblings's ranch house, and at the Tecumseh Crossing area was the Matthews' stone Tecumseh Ranch house. In 1877, the oldest son of Joseph Matthews, George T., who had married Elizabeth (Sister Bettie) Reynolds in 1867, built a residence at the confluence of the Clear Fork and Tecumseh Creek. It "was the last of the family residences constructed of stone on the Clear Fork," and was called "Tecumseh Ranch." It sat on the public road from Albany, the county seat of Shackelford County, and Throckmorton, the county seat of Throckmorton County, and many travelers along the road stopped at the house, which became a landmark.[8] At

---

[4]One of the ranches to use this feeder route could have been the Hashknife Ranch operation that had choice grazing land along the forks of the Concho River in Tom Green County in 1883 and 1884.

[5]According to Carl Rister, "Texas had a frontier of more than 1,200 miles, with only 2,886 United States officers and enlisted men to defend it." On March 3, 1855, Congress had authorized more troops to help protect 8,000 miles of western frontier against an estimated 30,000 Indians "in widely dispersed raiding bands." There were some 11,000 troops in frontier posts. Lee was part of this increase in troops. (Carl Coke Rister, "Robert Edward Lee, "*Handbook of Texas Online* [accessed April 19, 2011])

[6]Lee commanded the post for fifteen months, and during that time, he led a 1,600-mile expedition to scout out the region. A post office operated at the camp from March 31, 1860 to October 1860. (Charles G. Davis, "Camp Cooper," *The Handbook of Texas Online*, [accessed April 19, 2011])

[7]Holden, Ibid, 88-89.

this crossing, the Clear Fork of the Brazos turns west abruptly, and Tecumseh Creek converges with the Clear Fork from the north. Trail herds continued north with the destination of Doan's Crossing in mind. Also, according to John C. Jacobs, there was an inspector station "at the crossing of the Clear Fork of the Brazos, near the mouth of Tecumpsee,[sic]" and he was an inspector.[9]

The drovers of the trail herds of 1875 - 1878 would not have known of Throckmorton, the county seat. The county was not organized until 1879, and the town was established the same year in the center of the county. After the town appeared, the Western Trail continued its path a short distance west of the town and forded Elm Creek at the mouth of Horse Creek[10] Herds crossed both the North and South forks of Boggy Creek, three or four miles west of their confluence, and within a few miles entered Baylor County where "the trail fanned out to take advantage of the tall blue-stem grasses."[11]

On the southern border of Baylor County sat the Miller Creek Ranch. Drives going to Dodge City and on north passed through the ranch, and the ranch was also the destination of some herds coming out of south Texas. The Millett

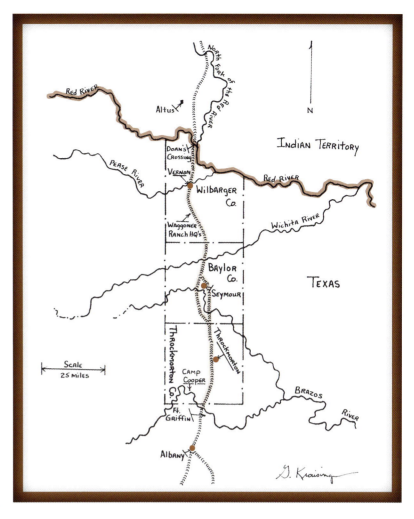

#3-1
The Western Cattle Trail Through Throckmorton, Baylor, and Wilbarger Counties:
From Fort Griffin, Texas, on the North Fork of the Brazos River, the Western Trail trunk line continued north across three counties to reach the Red River.

brothers had established the ranch along with their partner William C. Irvin in 1874. The ranch sat on Miller's Creek, a tributary of the Upper Brazos River, and extended approximately sixty miles southwest into Throckmorton and Haskell counties. The headquarters was within sight of the Western Cattle Trail, while the rest of the ranch was protected from the surrounding Indians and outlaws by a series of line camps situated about every six to eight miles. Each camp house was constructed of native stone and surrounded by a five-foot high stone wall. Line riders patrolled the ranch and were known to be a tough outfit. The Millett boys were hired for their skill with

---

[8] Sallie Reynolds Matthews, *Interwoven, A Pioneer Chronicle*, 141-149.
[9] John C. Jacobs, "Reminiscences of an Old Trail Driver," in Hunter, *The Trail Drivers of Texas*, 665.
[10] This roadway is present-day U.S. Highway 183.
[11] Jimmy M. Skaggs, 1965 thesis: "The Great Western Cattle Trail to Dodge City, Kansas," 33.

cattle, but more often, for their ways with the gun. The Millett brothers wanted able gunmen and cowboys who could handle any situation that might present itself. The armed cowhands intimidated local homesteaders who tried to fence or farm the open range. "It was said that even the Comanches steered clear of the tough Miller Creek outfit."[12]

Like Captain John T. Lytle, who had delivered a herd of beeves to the Red Cloud Agency in Nebraska in 1874, the Milletts, and business partner Major Seth Mabry, secured government contracts and arranged to deliver approximately 102,000 cattle to northern Indian reservations. The partners bought all the cattle they could possibly acquire for ten dollars a head in 1874 to try to fill the order. By the spring of 1875, they had amassed 52,000 head to be put on the Western Trail. Another partnership, Ellison and Dewees,[13] joined the venture with their 50,000 head to complete the contract. Millett & Mabry employed 275 trail hands, purchased 900 horses, and hired R. G. Head[14] to supervise their seventeen trail herds destined for Ogallala, Nebraska.[15] The herds that made up the 102,000 head were dispersed at Ogallala. Little Jim Ellison, Jr., who was one of the trail bosses for his father, Col. James F. Ellison, said that they "received our cattle southwest of San Antonio" and that the "cattle were strung out from San Antonio almost to Dodge City."[16]

The Millett-Mabry partnership incurred heavier expense than expected during the drive of their seventeen herds north. The contract was for twenty dollars per head for steers and twelve dollars for cows. It cost on an average of four dollars per head to deliver the cattle. Millett and Mabry split $100,000 in net profits in August of 1875 and dissolved their partnership.

While Millett & Mabry were delivering cattle to the northern Indian reservations, their Texas rangeland was being cleared of its native inhabitants. Because of the fierce determination of the Comanches to keep settlers out of their hunting grounds, settlement of the area was late in coming. The Comanches were defeated by the United States Army in 1874 in the Red River War, and bands were moved to

---

[12]The Millett boys had grown up in Seguin, Texas. Eugene, Leonidas, Alonzo, and Hiram all served in the Confederacy. Leonidas was killed fighting at Gaines Mill, Virginia. After the Civil War, in 1866, Capt. Eugene Millett attempted to drive a herd of 500 head to St. Louis, Missouri, on the Shawnee Trail, but, because of the fear of the Texas Fever, was turned away by Missouri border ruffians. He trailed cattle again in 1868, only this time on the newly established Arbuckle Trail to Abilene, Kansas. The Milletts continued to drive cattle for the next several years. (Jim Gray, "Those Wild Millett Cowboys!" *Kansas Cowboy*, Vol II, No. I, Nov - Dec, 2006, 4)

[13]John O. Dewees had served in the 32nd Texas Cavalry during the Civil War in Company B under the command of Cap. Eugene Millett. In the 1870s, Dewees formed a partnership with another veteran, Col. James F. Ellison. (Hunter, 941) Major Seth Mabry also had served in the Confederate Army. His large ranch was located in Mason and Kimble counties. Thus, all four of these cattlemen were veterans.

[14]R. G. (Dick) Head assumed the general management of the Ellison, Dewees & Bishop cattle business out of San Antonio in 1875. Head was a highly experienced cattleman who had worked for Col. John J. Meyers for seven years prior to his employment with the Ellison, Dewees & Bishop partnership. Head had driven Meyers cattle to Abilene when it was "a mere post containing but half a dozen habitations" and "camped a herd of cattle on the spot where the city of Wichita, Kansas, now stands, when not a white man resided there." ("R.G. (Dick) Head," in Hunter, *The Trail Drivers of Texas*, 734)

[15]Jim Grey, Kansas Cowboy, Ibid.

[16]J. F. Ellison, Jr. "Traveling the Trail with Good men was a Pleasure," in Hunter, 539.

reservations in Indian Territory. Baylor County, however. was not organized until June of 1879. By the next year, the county supported a population of 715. Settlers had trickled into the area starting in 1875, after the Indians were removed, but the Millett brothers did not welcome settlers and discouraged the intruders on the open range. Within months of the county's organization, in November of 1879, a post office contract was awarded the Millett operation with Alonzo Millett as its post master.[17]

The Miller Creek operation continued to send cattle up the trail until the Millett brothers sold out to the Continental Land and Cattle Company in 1881. The company developed out of the beginnings of the Hashknife Ranch in Taylor County. J. R. Couts and John N. Simpson established a cattle operation from an Elm Creek-bank dugout, near the present-day Abilene, in 1875. Couts had designed a brand he called the hashknife because it resembled a common kitchen tool of the time, and when he and Simpson formed their partnership, they chose it for the brand. In the next few years the Hashknife expanded into Nolan County and in 1880 acquired control additional free range land on the southwest bank of the Pecos River. According to historian Skaggs, "The range ran from the New Mexico line 100 miles downstream to Grand Falls and twenty-five to thirty miles out from that river. Charles W. Buster, another investor, was put in charge of this range, which branded 10,000 calves annually for the next five years."[18]

John N. Simpson, Charles W. Buster and his brother, and William E. Hughes, who had bought out J. R. Couts in 1881, formed the Continental Land and Cattle Company and purchased the Miller Creek outfit in Baylor County. This new Hashknife addition gave the company a total of 50,000 cattle. The company didn't stop there.

When the Texas and Pacific Railway began building into West Texas, Simpson arranged to meet with the railroad officials at the Hashknife headquarters and was influential in getting the line routed through Taylor County. As a result the town of Abilene developed just southwest of the headquarters. After the completion of the railroad in 1882, the former Millett spread in Baylor County became the center of the Hashknife Ranch operations.[19]

> Historians, rightfully so, assert that the Millett-Mabry - Ellison & Dewees drive of 102,000 head managed by Richard Head in 1875 was the largest in history. The Lytle, McDaniel, Schreiner, and Light partnership drove 91,000 head in 1884. There were also others, like the King Ranch, that sent herds up the Western Trail in one season in great numbers.

---

[17]H. Allen Anderson, "Hashknife Ranch," *The Handbook of Texas Online* [accessed Nov. 28, 2007] Myron Janzen, "Baylor County," *Texas Post Offices*, unpublished manuscript.

[18]Eugene Millett purchased another ranch in Kansas, near Ellsworth, along the Smoky Hill River in late 1876. The proceeds from the sale of his Texas ranch to the Continental Land and Cattle Company was used to improve the Kansas ranch. He left the operations to his brother Alonzo, however, for Eugene was living with his new bride in a Kansas City mansion. (Skaggs, Ibid, 38)

[19]Anderson, "Hashknife Ranch," Ibid. The Continental Land and Cattle Company disposed of the Hashknife Ranch in Baylor County in 1889. The site of the old Hashknife headquarters in Taylor County is now part of the campus of Abilene Christian University.

1

NEAR ROUTE OF THE WESTERN TRAIL

PRINCIPAL CATTLE TRAIL FROM TEXAS TO KANSAS AND BEYOND FROM 1876 TO 1887; SUPERSEDED THE CHISHOLM TRAIL AFTER DODGE CITY REPLACED ABILENE AS THE MAIN INTERMEDIATE NORTHERN BEEF MARKET.

AS ITS NAME IMPLIES, THE WESTERN TRAIL RAN WEST OF THE CHISHOLM TRAIL, BY ABOUT 100 MILES. MOST OF ITS FEEDER TRAILS STARTED IN SOUTH TEXAS, ALTHOUGH SOME MADE CONNECTIONS AT SAN ANTIONO AND FORT GRIFFIN.

HERE IN BAYLOR COUNTY THE TRAIL CROSSED THE BRAZOS RIVER PASSING HALF A MILE EAST OF SEYMOUR, A MAJOR SUPPLY CENTER. THE HERDS BEDDED NEAR SEYMOUR CREEK, AT THE SITE OF THE PRESENT FAIR GROUNDS. THE MILLETT RANCH (ESTABLISHED 1874) SERVED AS A WATERING SPOT, AND THE MILLETT BROTHERS — EUGENE, ALONZO, AND HIRAM — WERE AMONG THE FIRST USERS OF THE TRAIL.

FROM SEYMOUR THE ROUTE CONTINUED NORTH, LEAVING TEXAS AT DOAN&S STORE ON THE RED RIVER. IT THEN RAN THROUGH OKLAHOMA TO DODGE CITY, LESSER EXTENSION PROCEEDING TO NEBRASKA, WYOMING, AND MONTANA.

DURING ITS LIFE, THE WESTERN TRAIL MOVED HUNDREDS OF THOUSANDS OF CATTLE NORTH TO STOCK RANGES, INDIAN RESERVATIONS, AND MARKETS. BUT AFTER THE FENCING OF THE OPEN RANGE AND BUILDING OF THE TEXAS & PACIFIC RAILROAD, IT CEASED TO BE USED BY THE CATTLE INDUSTRY.

1972

Location: northeast of the city limits of Seymour; in a roadside park on US Highway 87 / 277

Authors' commentary:
The author of this text understood that there was a trail system and mentions feeder routes into the Western, which is correct. The explanation of the term "Western" is also appropriately stated.

The comment of Dodge City and its "lesser extensions proceeding to Nebraska, Wyoming, and Montana," however, under-states the fact that this Western Trail leaving Dodge handled some 80 to 85 percent of the volume of cattle going up that trail. These "extensions" were massive.

Seymour was established in January of 1879. It was a stop for the drovers, but probably not a "major supply center." The major bulk of the trail supplies were purchased at Albany or at Fort Griffin, and additional supplies would have been acquired at the Doans' shops in Vernon or at Doan's Crossing.

The dates of the trail should read: 1874 to 1889.

North of the Miller Creek Ranch, and later the Hashknife Ranch, cattle herds were pushed up the east and west banks of the Brazos River. Their destination for the next campsite, at the end of the day, was a watering hole at a town named "Oregon City," after a colony of settlers who moved to the site in 1876 from Oregon. To get to Oregon City, some herds followed the west bank of the Brazos River to the crossing at Oregon City while others forded the river at the mouth of Miller's Creek and ascended the east bank to the town.[20] The post office, the first to be established in the county, was opened in Oregon City on January 14, 1879, the same year that the county was organized. However, the post office name was changed to "Seymour" two and one half months later, using the name of a cowboy, Seymour Munday, who had a line camp just west of town.[21] The site had been used as a campsite for years by Indians and cowboys. Along the Salt Fork tributary of the Brazos River, cowboy outfits established their camps. The cattle were bedded on the high grounds on the east side of Seymour Creek.

William C. Irvin established a ranch in the Oregon City area in 1875. He had been up the trail seven times by 1875 and decided to locate a ranch to winter out herds in Baylor County. With his share in the Millett operation and the new ranch, Irvin was on his way to becoming one of the wealthiest stockmen in the state.[22]

After crossing through southern Baylor County and the Millett and Irvin ranches, trail herds had to cross the Wichita River in northern Baylor County. Lewis Neatherlin in his journal of his 1876 drive described the area north of the Oregon City settlement, later Seymour, and southern Wilbarger County.

May 14:
Crossed the Big Wichita River. After crossing had some 5 or 6 miles of hilly salt-land, which was very difficult to drive over [as] every animal [wanted] to stop and lick or eat the salty dirt and weeds. A little rain just at dark. A man taken sick this morning.

May 15:
Crossed what is called Beaver Creek. Had considerable trouble in getting the wagons over. Had to let them down the bank and across the run by hand. The water in said creek very red. In fact, everything has been red since we left the San Saba, but gets a little more red each day. The sick man no better.

---

[20] Skaggs, thesis, 33.
[21] Seymour, the first post office of Baylor county, is also the last and only operating post office today. Fifteen other post offices have come and gone, including the Millett's on the Miller Creek Ranch. (Janzen, "Baylor County," *Texas Post Offices*, Ibid)
[22] William C. Irvin returned to southwestern Texas five years later, establishing the Irvin Ranch in La Salle County, that encompassed 60,000 acres. He married Medina Dewees;. his sister Ann also married a Dewees. ("William C. Irvin," in Hunter, 620) L. B. Anderson (in Hunter, 203) said, "[we] drove to the Millett & Irvin ranch in the Panhandle, camping right where the town of Seymour is now located, and remained there several months helping to round up several thousand head of cattle. Among those who were with me there on the range were Tom Peeler,...." Thomas M. Peeler worked on the Irvin & Millet ranch in Baylor County until the ranch sold.

May 16:

…Crossed a large, sandy, brackish creek. Reached Pease River. One herd crossed but the other did not. We had a rain and hail storm at 4 o'clock and a very heavy rain at sunset.

May 17:

Still raining this morning. The other herd got over without any trouble. The sick man is better. The ground being very wet and heavy, we made a short drive, and camped in the valley of the Red River. The inspector overtaken us after we camped.[23]

In the early years of the Western Cattle Trail, this area of Texas was very sparsely settled. When Millett & Mabry and Ellison & Dewees were gathering herds for their 1875 drive, most settlements had not yet been established. When Lewis Neatherlin came through in 1876, with three herds, Oregon City's colony had just arrived, and what would become the historic Doan's Crossing on the Red River did not appear for another two years.

DOAN'S CROSSING ON THE RED RIVER:

The cattle drives indirectly brought one of the first Anglo settlements to the area when Jonathan and Corwin Doan and their families, who were friends to the Indians, set up a trading post at a well-used Indian camping area and cattle crossing on the Red River. The Doans were Quaker pacifist and had been operating a trading post on Cache Creek two miles from Fort Sill in Indian Territory. Jonathan's nephew, Corwin F. Doan, was a government agent in 1874-75 and traded with the Indians on the reservation. The Doans befriended some of the Comanches, learned their language and ways. As the cattle drives over the Western Trail became larger, the Indians suggested to their friends that they establish a store at the shallow water crossing of the Red River, a location that had been used for years by the Indians. There was no store on the trail in Indian Territory, and the Indians assured the Doans that they would continue to trade with them. There was also the trade with buffalo hunters, freighters, and, of course, the trail drivers. (Corwin's granddaughter later explained that the Indians were supportive because they could buy shot and powder at an establish trading post off the reservation--in Texas which they could not do at the reservation agent's store.)[24]

In the fall of 1877 Jonathan and Corwin, inspired by the commercial possibilities of a store on the Red River crossing, decided to open a trading post the

---

[23]Kelly, ed. *Up the Trail in '76, the Journal of Lewis Warren Neatherlin*, 17-18. It was not uncommon for cowboys to sicken. Exposure to the elements, poor and limited diets, and long hard hours of work could weaken even the strongest and youngest of the cow hands. The large, sandy, brackish creek that Neatherlin refers to was Paradise Creek. Neatherlin does not mention Vernon nor Doan's Crossing because he went through before either was established.

[24]H. S. Tennant, "The Two Cattle Trails," *Chronicles of Oklahoma*, Vol. 14, 1936, 99.

following spring and arranged to have supplies freighted to the location. Corwin, however, became seriously ill and returned to the family home in Wilmington, Ohio. Jonathan and two friends, however, arrived in Wilbarger County in the spring of 1878 and established the store in his absence. They constructed a 24-foot by 30-foot picket and mud building that would serve as a store and home. The roof was prairie grass and mud, and a buffalo robe covered the door. The store opened for business in April of 1878. A cattle drover, Jasper Lauderdale, was one of the first to see the newly opened trading post. He jokingly said that Doan's Store "consisted of three buffalo hides and a wagon sheet."[25]

By fall of 1878, Corwin Doan returned from Ohio with his wife, their one-year-old daughter, and Jonathan's brother, Calvin W. Doan. Corwin immediately set about making the drafty make-shift picket shelter that his uncle and friends had constructed into a more comfortable adobe living quarters for the large family. A huge fireplace was built, skins were hung for room dividers, and furniture was constructed. At first, the trade goods sold at the post consisted mainly of ammunition and a few groceries, and the family lived at one end of the picket building. Corwin Doan, who had taken over the family business, later wrote that his first experience with cattle herds was in the "spring and summer of 1879" and that "one hundred thousand cattle passed over the trail by the little store in 1879."[26]

Also in the spring of 1879, William B. Worsham established his R2 Ranch a few miles south of the crossing on the Pease River. As settlers trickled into the area, Doan's Store was awarded a post office late in the year, and Worsham's dugout became the second post office in June of 1880. His place was known as "Worsham Springs."[27] At this point, the drovers could post a letter at either post office. Cowboys gathered at Worsham's place and at Doan's Crossing. The crossing at the Red River was the last chance for drovers to write to their loved ones back home before "jumping off" into the vast unknown and perhaps hostile wilderness north of the Red River. Corwin Doan also held letters for the cowboys from their families and sweethearts. He noted that, "Many a cowboy asked self-consciously if there was any mail for him while his face turned a beet red when a dainty missive (letter) was handed him," wrote Doan.[28]

It was in the 1879 season that the Ellison & Sherrill herds came through the crossing. James C. Shaw, who rode the drags of the large herd, did not mention Doan's in his memoirs, but he commented that the Red River "looked to be a mile wide, but it was not swimming deep except for a short distance. There were three

---

[25]Harry S. Drago, *Great American Cattle Trails*, 194, and Jasper Lauderdale, "Reminiscences of the Trail," in Hunter, 409.

[26]For Corwin F. Doan's (1848-1929) full account see "Reminiscences of the Old Trails" in Hunter, 772-779. Corwin was 74 years old when he wrote his reminiscences. Hunter published his first edition of *The Trail Drivers of Texas* in 1924. Corwin lived in his adobe home until 1929. Today, it is the only original structure still standing at Doan's Crossing.

[27]Corwin F. Doan was the postmaster of the Doan's Crossing post office. It handled mail from November 13, 1879 to August 31, 1919. Worsham Springs' first postmaster was Robert D. Rector. That post office lasted only two years: June 21, 1880 to August 10, 1882. The mail service was diverted to the new town of Vernon. (Janzen, "Wilbarger County," Ibid)

[28]Doan in Hunter, 778.

channels that were swimming, but when I reached the river the cattle were going in nicely and the only trouble we had was when some of the cattle bogged and we had to pull them out."[29]

In September of 1880, a third post office was established at a small settlement of twenty-five people who referred to themselves as "Eagle Flat." The name was changed shortly afterward, however, to "Vernon." Vernon was designated as the county seat when Wilbarger County was finally organized in 1881.[30] According to S. H. Tittle, who helped trail cattle in 1879 into Indian Territory, "the trail went right through the town of Vernon, Texas, about a quarter of a mile west of the public square."[31]

The C. F. Doan & Company flourished, and over the next couple of years two log cabins were built for the families, and a 30 foot by 50-foot trading post was built which replaced the adobe store at Doan's Crossing. When the town of Vernon was established, the company started a branch store there. Supplies for the two stores were hauled in primarily from Gainesville. At the peak of the cattle trailing business and at the height of Doan's store business, there were not enough teams and wagons to be found to haul the goods needed to supply the various Doan stores.[32] Doan wrote that in 1881, "the trail reached the peak production and three hundred and one thousand were driven by...."

Doan described the crossing in 1881:

> Wichita Falls failing to provide suitable branding pens for the accommodation of the trail drivers, pens were provided at Doan's. Furnaces and corrals were built and here Charley Word and others fitted with cartridges, Winchesters by the case, sow bosom [sow belly or bacon] and flour, and even to Stetson hats, etc. This store did a thriving business and thought nothing of selling bacon and flour in carload lots, though getting our supplies from Denison, Sherman, Gainesville, and later, Wichita Falls.[33]

When Doan wrote this, he was referring to a feeder route that came into the crossing from the east.

BOSQUE COUNTY FEEDER ROUTE: (Map #3-2)

From as far south as Bosque County, Texas, cattle were trailed parallel to the Western Trail and then connected with the main route at Doan's Crossing. Herds

---

[29]James C. Shaw, *North From Texas*, 38.

[30]Wilbarger County had been created as early as 1858, but because of the lack of people, was not established until 1881. Even at that time, there were only fifty-six voters in the entire county. By late 1881, cattle drives had been going through the area for eight years. (John Leffler, "Wilbarger County," *Handbook of Texas Online*, [accessed Oct. 9, 2007 & April 24, 2011]) (Janzen, Op cit)

[31]Tennant, Ibid, 103.

[32]Keith R. Owen. "Doans: The Birth and Death of a Frontier Town," *West Texas Historical Association Year Book*, Vol. 71, 1995, 88.

[33]C. F. Doan in Hunter, Op cit.

146   THE WESTERN CATTLE TRAIL | 1874-1897

were trailed by Glen Rose in Somerwell County, Granbury in Hood County, Mineral Wells, in Palo Pinto County, Jacksboro in Jack County, Henrietta in Clay County, and Wichita Falls in Wichita County.

Calvin Doan mentions that Wichita Falls, the last stop on this feeder route for the cowboys before coming into Doan's, did not supply needed facilities for branding. Therefore, the Doans built the branding pens, furnaces, and corrals to provide this service. Herds were prepared at the onset of the drive at a staging area, but as more cattle were picked up enroute, there were always some without a brand. In order to claim these animals in the herd, they had to be branded before the inspectors checked the herd. This was done at Doan's Crossing. Herds were not allowed to cross the river until inspected.

Starting in 1883 the lower part of Texas that had used the Bosque County Feeder Route to the Western Trail, and other feeder routes, started to ship their cattle to Wichita Falls. The Fort Worth & Denver City Railway arrived in that city on September 26, 1882. According to the *Cheyenne Transporter*, out of the Darlington Agency at Fort Reno in Indian Territory, in May of 1883, "herds passing up the western trail since the drive commenced …are shipped [now]

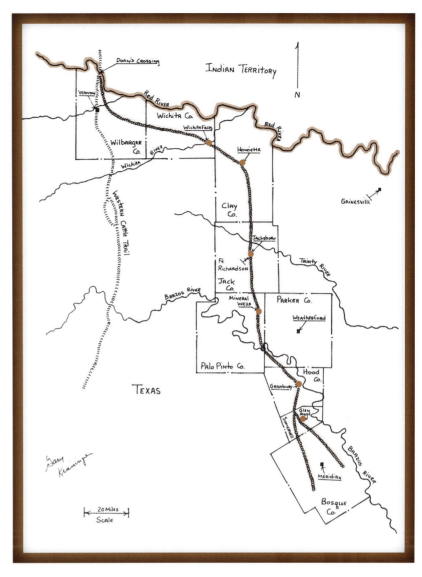

#3-2
Bosque County Feeder Route:
Trail herds from Bosque, Somervell, Hood, Parker, and Palo Pinto counties were trailed northwest by Fort Richardson in Jack County, through Henrietta in Clay County, through Wichita Falls in Wichita County to connect with the Western Trail trunk line at Doan's Crossing in Wilbarger County.

by rail from all parts of Texas to Wichita Falls, as it is no longer possible to bring a herd through the state on account of the fences. Thus the drive commences at Wichita Falls, Tex., where the herds take the trail."[34] George W. Saunders also stated that "Some of them [cattle] were shipped from different points in Texas by railroad all the way from Taylor [City] to Denison."[35]

---

[34]*Cheyenne Transporter*, printed at the Darlington Agency, May 18, 1883, as reprinted in H. S. Tennant, "The Two Cattle Trails," 107
[35]George W. Saunders, "Trail Historian Corrects Errors," *San Antonio Express*, October 17, 1931.

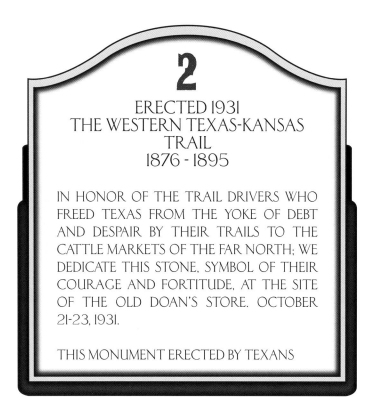

Location: At Doan's Crossing. The crossing is approximately two miles upstream where the North Fork of the Red River empties into the Red River. The actual cattle crossing is one and one half miles east of Doan's Store.

Authors' commentary:
This twelve-foot gray granite monument was erected in 1931 with the funds donated by an old trail driver by the name of Peter P. Ackley. "Daddy" Ackley, as he liked to be called, promoted the trail by marking it along its route, but instead of labeling it the "Western" or the "Dodge City Trail," he insisted upon using the words "The Longhorn Chisholm." This error stirred the ire of George W. Saunders, a former trail driver and, at the time the monument was erected, president of the Old Time Trail Drivers' Association. The monument was installed in spite of his vivid protest, and the last two lines on it read:

"The longhorn Chisholm and the Western Trail, 1876-1895.
This monument built of Texas Granite, by G. W. Backus."

Today this monument does not contain this statement. At some time, these two lines were deleted and the following words inserted: "This monument erected by Texans."[1]

The bronze plaque that is on the monument was commissioned by P. P. Ackley and depicts 19 head of cattle which we are informed represent the number of years of the trail — thus the dates: 1876 to 1895 (see page 174). However, Capt. John T. Lytle, who is accredited with blazing the Western Trail used this crossing in 1874. Therefore, we do not know where the "1876" date comes from. It is understandable that they used the ending date 1895. We use 1897 as explained later.

The Western Cattle Trail lasted longer than 19 years, but did not use the crossing for those inclusive dates. Doan's Store did not exist before 1878, but it is understood that many cattle herds were using the crossing before the Doan family came to the Red River, and because of the shift in the trail system, Doan's was rarely used for cattle herds after 1886. It is assumed, however, that the large monument is "in honor" of all trail drivers who "freed Texas from the yoke of debt and dispair," and, thus should have the dates 1874 - 1897.

Because this monument is a very early marker, 1931, and because of its ending date, other markers up the line into Oklahoma also used that date — even though the trail did not actually go through their locale in 1895. When historical societies and chambers erected their local markers, they were not aware that the inclusive dates (1874 [76] - 1895 [97]) represented the entire life of the Western Trail which included Doan's Crossing (1874-1889) AND the trail's later routes into Colorado and into the northern territories (1886-1897). For the most part, by 1886, cattle drives from South Texas ceased. The flow of southern cattle had stopped, and cattle were now coming out of the Texas Panhandle. Consequently markers to the north, in Oklahoma, Kansas, and Nebraska, should not show a date beyond 1889.

---

[1]Kraisinger & Kraisinger, *The Western, the Greatest Western Cattle Trail, 1874-1886*, "The Controversy," Chapter 1.

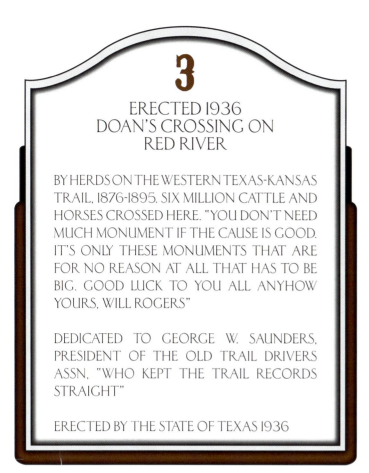

Location: next to the large 1931 monument at Doan's Crossing

Authors' commentary:
George W. Saunders died in 1933. The words quoted from Will Rogers were taken from a note written to the daughter of C. F. Doan, Bertha Doan Ross. Rogers, a friend of Saunders, is referring to the large 1931 monument with the trail-name error which caused Saunders so much anguish. The stone noted here was placed by the state of Texas at the request of Bertha Doan Ross.

Aubrey & Dooley in their book, "Why Stop?" says that a marker with that exact inscription was at the bridge twenty miles north of Vernon on US Highway 283. Some locals say it was at one time "closer to the river on the trail." Today it sits next to the larger monument. Because of the history behind the two markers, the larger Ackley marker must have been altered some time after 1936, and the smaller one moved to its current location. Again, we prefer the dates 1874-1889.

    The village of Doan's Crossing eventually grew to fourteen or more buildings. By 1885, Doan's Crossing, in addition to the store, had the Bat Cave Cafe, a restaurant in a dugout operated by George McTaylor; the Dave McBride Hotel; Louie Lowenthall's blacksmith shop; Hufstedler's wagon yard; Dr. F. C. St. John's Drug Store for any drover that might be ill; the Charles Cleveland Store, for any who did not want to buy goods from the Doan's store; Hufstedler's Cowboy Saloon, for liquid refreshments; a school; a non-denominational chapel; and several private homes including one owned by Judge Jonathan Doan. The headquarters and warehouse buildings of Ephraim Harrold's Bar X Ranch were located at Doans. In 1885, the community had nearly three hundred inhabitants. The third and final Doan's Store was constructed in 1887. It was a frame structure made of lumber freighted from Gainesville.[36] Since the Doans were Quakers, there were never any brothels at Doan's Crossing.

    Doan's Crossing was a major gateway to the Dodge City, Kansas market and beyond. It was the last supply center for the trail herds in Texas and a social spot and postal service for the trail hands before "jumping off" into unknown territory. Doan's was also the ideal spot to cross the Red River because the low water area had a sandy river bed rather than a muddy one, while farther to the west up river, high bluffs looked out over the river on both sides which

---
[36]Owen, Ibid, 88. Two years before Corwin Doan's death in 1929, Tom and Mrs. Hamilton became storekeepers. They ran the store until 1953. The building was demolished that year.

ERECTED 1993 | ERECTED 2004

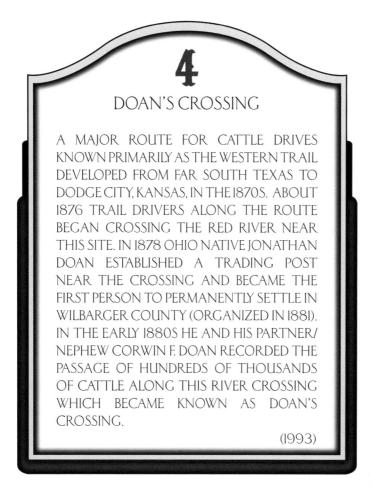

Location: next to the large granite monument and the Will Rogers' marker at Doan's Crossing

Authors' commentary:
This monument erected by the Texas Historical Commission in 1993 recognizes the Western Trail as extending only to Dodge City, Kansas. Dodge City was about the half-way mark for the entire trail, which stretched all the way into Canada.

The river crossing was used by cattle drives as early as 1874, not 1876. The actual trail was about a mile or mile and a half east of the Doan's store, and the community was not located on the Red River, but was about one and one half mile up the bank from the river.

Location: east of the historic C. A. Doan's adobe house

Authors' commentary:
This concrete post with black letters was dedicated in May of 2004 to the Western Cattle Trail. It was erected by the Rotarians International as the first in a series of markers to be placed along the entire trail.

Sketch done by Mary McCuistion, Vernon, Texas to represent the white concrete posts used to mark the Western Cattle Trail.

made crossing more difficult. Even though this crossing had been selected as the best spot to ford the river by the natives for centuries, the Red itself was capable of going on rampage and was sometimes difficult or impossible to traverse.

Sometime in the mid to late 1880s a straw bridge was provided by packing straw across the river bed making for a good road until a flood washed it out. Historian Edward Everett Dale recalled that when he was a boy in 1888, the two young men who created the bridge charged fifteen cents per wagon to use it.[37] Maurine Igou Keefe, Corwin's granddaughter, wrote that the straw bridge was operating in the early 1890s in order to stimulate trade with the settlers north of the river. Prairie grass was stacked in piles as deep as six feet and wide enough for two teams and wagons to pass. At that time, twenty-five cents was charged for using the straw bridge.[38]

Just as cattle bunched up at Fort Griffin on the Clear Fork while waiting for inspection or for the trail boss and cook to lay in a wagon full of supplies, the chances of a general mix up of herds or a dreaded stampede had to be guarded against. One of these situations did occur at Doan's Crossing in 1882. W. M. Nagiller wrote of the drover's nightmare. Hudson & Watson sent up three herds from their Burnet County ranch in May of 1882. Nagiller was with the first herd.[39] Upon reaching Doan's Crossing —

These accounts indicate the beginning of the closing of the trails in south Texas.

Settlements and ranches had taken over the area and "fences" were barring the way for herding cattle on trails to the north. The Eastern/Chisholm was also in this list of trails that was affected. Even though it had functioned as a feeder route to the Western from 1875 to 1880, the trail had re-opened when a new outlet at Caldwell, Kansas became a railhead and was now shipping Texas cattle. The Eastern/Chisholm revived. However, in 1883 the route north was being restricted by an invading population of settlers. Also at this same time, the Potter-Bacon Splinter Route was moving west out of Albany, which also diverted cattle away from Doan's Crossing. In only three more years, by 1886, the entire configuration of cattle driving would change. This will be covered in the later part of this book.

There we laid over two weeks for two more trail herds to overtake us which belonged to the same men, Hudson & Watson. When the two herds arrived we threw all three herds together, which made about 9,000 head of cattle….At sundown when we bedded the cattle down for the night there were eleven trail herds in sight. Along in the night a terrible storm came up. It was the worst that I ever experienced. The thunder, lightning and rain was awful. All the cattle were turned loose except small cuts we were holding. The following morning cattle were dotting the plains in every direction as far as the eye could see. All the trail herds were mixed up. After we had finished our breakfast we started to make the big roundup. There were about 120 cowboys. When we had the roundup made we had about 33,000 head in one bunch. We worked about ten days before we got the cattle shaped up to start on our way.[40]

---

[37]Owen, Ibid. 90.

[38]Maurine Igou Keefe, "Brief History of Doans," insert in the 1978 Doan's May Picnic Program.

[39]It is very likely that the Hudson & Watson herds followed the San Gabriel/Brownwood Feeder Route to Albany where it joined the Western Trail. See Map #3-2.

[40]W. M. Nagiller, "A Big Mixup," in Hunter, 669-670. One of the Hudson & Watson herds went to Caldwell, Kansas. The herd that Nagiller stayed with passed through Ogallala, Nebraska, by Fort Laramie, and was delivered into northwestern Wyoming. "We were on the trail four and one-half months, and had to stand guard every night."

Cattle herds and wagons crossed the Red River near the Doan's community because of the river's easy access and sandy riverbed. Sometime in the mid to late 1880s, a straw bridge was built across the river.
Photo courtesy of the Oklahoma Historical Society Research Center, Oklahoma City, Oklahoma.

Another reason Doan's was an ideal spot for crossing was that it provided a visual glimpse of the next phase of the drive. Mable Doan Igou stated that, "…the trail drivers when starting out from Doan's Crossing could see one of the Wichita Mountains which stood out from the rest and was in appearance like an Indian teepee, and they used this mountain as a landmark to guide them."[41]

After the cattle drives declined in number after 1886 and then halted completely, Doan's Crossing in the early 1890s declined. The Fort Worth and Denver City Railway did not make it to Doans, but instead went south through Vernon. Most of the businesses left Doans around 1893.

Today only the historic C. A. Doan's adobe and a few more recent houses remain at the town site. Several monuments tell the story of the famous crossing, and the Doan's May Day Picnic is celebrated annually in Watts Grove. Since 1884, relatives, friends, and loved ones of the trail drivers have met there to remember and honor those who went up the Trail.

There is one more route to acknowledge before leaving Texas.

---

[41] Keefe, Doan's 1978 May Picnic Program.

THE QUANAH DETOUR ROUTE OR GHOST TRAIL: (Map #3-3)

Another route, that is very little known, paralleled the Western Trail farther west. Skaggs referred to this route as the "Ghost Trail." It was part of the shift to avoid, or get out in front of, the westerly movement of settlements with the closing of open range in Texas. George W. Saunders alluded to this more westerly route when he wrote, "Later on the Southern herds quit the old trail...and intersecting the Western Trail in Kimble county, from where all followed the well defined and much traveled Western Trail to Doan's Crossing on Red River."[42] This later feeder route has already been discussed. (See Map # 1-4 — "Nueces River Feeder Route")

Some herds on this Nueces River Feeder Route that Saunders wrote about, did not continue to the Beef Trail Crossing in Kimble County and connect with the Western, but instead, "struck a more direct but obscure path northward through Quanah to the trunk route north of Doan's crossing."[43] In other words, the drovers left the south Llano River in Edwards County and pushed their herds straight north along the west edge of Kimble County to Fort McKavett, Fort Chadbourne, and Fort Phantom Hill, crossing the Red River just north of Quanah, Texas, thirty to forty miles west of Doan's Crossing. Again, Saunders referred to this later route in 1931 when he said — "I do not claim all northern cattle crossed [the] Red River at Red River Station [Eastern Trail] and Doan's Crossing [Western Trail]. I know quite a lot of cattle crossed at Quanah..."[44]

> We call this Quanah pathway a "detour" because it does rejoin the Western farther up the line. It is not a "branch," because, in our assessment, a branch does not rejoin the main trunk line. Recall that George W. Saunders wrote that the Nueces River Feeder Route, which was later part of this Quanah Detour, left the main trunk line of the Western Trail in Live Oak County and followed the Nueces River. Jimmy Skaggs, on the other hand, when writing of this path, stated that it pushed north from Uvalde in Uvalde County. Skaggs was using G. W. Scott as a source. Note the late date.

Looking at the Quanah Detour map, one can see this shift. This more westerly path was not formed until early to mid-1880s. (Within a couple of years, by 1885-86, these south Texas routes would cease altogether.)

G. W. Scott, who used and wrote about the Quanah pathway, was from Uvalde. A lad of nineteen, he hired out to Paul Handy to deliver a herd to Colorado. The outfit consisted of eleven men and a remuda of sixty-four horses and left the Leona Ranch south of Uvalde in March of 1890 with a herd of 2,221 two-year-old steers. They crossed the Nueces River and as Scott recalled:

> After six or eight days our herd was easily controlled, especially at night. Grass and water were plentiful, and we had an easy time until we reached Fort McKavett, where I accidentally caused the cattle to stampede one moonlight night. From here we drove to San Angelo [Fort Concho] and stopped one night near that town, which at that

---

[42]Emphases added by authors. George W. Saunders, "A Log of the Trails," in Hunter, 963.
[43]Jimmy Skaggs, thesis, 37.
[44]G. W. Saunders, "Trail Historian Corrects Errors," *San Antonio Express*, Oct. 17, 1931.

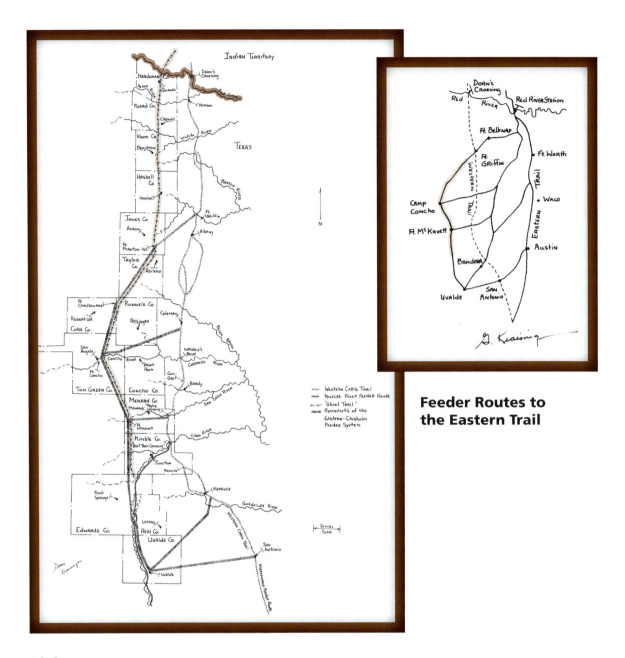

Feeder Routes to the Eastern Trail

#3-3
The Quanah Detour Route or "Ghost Trail":
This map shows the continuation of the Nueces River Feeder Route (Map #1-4) north of the Llano River following the outer extremities of the former feeder system to the Eastern Trail. This map also shows the comparison between the Ghost Trail and the Western Cattle Trail.

Before the Western Trail existed, various routes fed into the Abilene Trail, or after 1874, into the Eastern Trail. When the Western Trail replaced the Eastern Trail, these feeder routes ceased going into the Eastern, but were used to feed into the Western. The insert shows the network of routes east of the Western Trail that were abandoned when the Western Trail started.

The Quanah Detour Route, established in later years (in the early or mid-1880s) paralleled the Western Trail farther west, but used the old feeder routes that had been used since the time of the Eastern Trail to connect with the Western Trail. The dark lines in the Quanah Detour Route map represent the older feeder system network on the west side of the Western Trail.

time was a wide-open place. Several of the boys went in to see the sights and have a good time. We drove our herd across the plains to Quanah, where we were quarantined for several weeks on account of Texas fever. We held these steers for seven weeks before being allowed to proceed on to Colorado.[45]

G. W. Briggs, Jr. also wrote of this Quanah Detour. He had worked as a herd inspector at Doan's Crossing in 1880 and had been at the Waggoner Ranch, twenty-five miles south of Vernon. In a letter to H. S. Tennant in 1933, he wrote that the Western Trail was not known as the "Western" in those days "for the reason that there was a trail west of this trail, that was used extensively in the early eighties." In Briggs' mind, the Western Trail was not western because of another trail farther west. In 1881, he moved to Comanche Springs in the Territory "to inspect all trail herds that went up the trail" and he "stayed there until it was discontinued in 1889."[46] This was one of the locations where the Quanah Detour rejoined the Western. Briggs witnessed and knew of this more westerly pathway, and he stated that trail driving ended at Comanche Springs in 1889.

A mural on the wall of the Dodge House, Hotel and Convention Center in Dodge City, Kansas also shows this ambiguous route. This map gives some additional clues.[47] Even though the mural map has some geographical errors, it does show a trail west of the Western Cattle Trail in Texas. Bedish, the map maker, erroneously labeled this trail the "Fort Griffon [Griffin] - Dodge City Trail," which was the name that Corwin Doan used for the Western Trail that went by his store at Doan's Crossing. The map shows, however, this detour route starting at Bandera and intersecting the Western Trail at present-day Mangum, Oklahoma. This will be discussed fully in the next chapter on the Western Trail in Indian Territory. (Interestingly, however, P. P. Ackley, when he was marking the trail in the 1930s, placed a marker at Mangum.)

When the cattle drovers and their herds moved west to cross the Red River, the town of Quanah was being laid out. The Fort Worth and Denver City Railway survey team surveyed the townsite in 1884, and lots were sold a year later. The post office was established in 1886. When G. W. Scott came through with the herd of steers bound for Colorado in 1890, Quanah had been selected to be the county seat

---

[45]This account demonstrates the reason why the southern routes were being shut down. Actually by 1890, most of the herds were no longer coming out of south Texas, but were now being processed and staged in the Panhandle. (G. W. Scott, "With Herds to Colorado and New Mexico," in Hunter, 115-116) George Warren Scott was born in 1871. To be nineteen, the trail drive had to have been in 1891. Therefore, in the Hunter essay, there is a typographical error. The 1881 date on page 116 should be 1891. Scott died in 1922 before *The Trail Drivers of Texas* was published.

[46]Letter to H. S. Tennant, Okla. State Highway Department, dated July 6, 1933, included in article, "The Two Cattle Trails," which reports Tennant's research, *Chronicles of Oklahoma* Vol. 14, 1936, 104. Because of Oklahoma House Bill No. 149 in 1931, Tennant was investigating the location of the Western and Chisholm trails in Oklahoma in 1933.

[47]The mural (painted map) was done by Gabrial A. Bedish sometime around 1974-1975. It is unknown where he got his information, and an attempt to locate Bedish was unsuccessful. This source is used because there are so few references to this detour route. The hotel is currently owned by Justin and Charle Swift.

of Hardeman County, and was building the first of several stone buildings in its business district. *The Chief* newspaper was in its first year, and the town had a population of 1,400 people.[48]

The Quanah Detour was the last pathway used to move herds north from out of south Texas. The outlet from south Texas to buyers in the north was being choked out by settlers and barbed wire. The final Kansas quarantine of 1885 was one more roadblock for the industry.

---

[48]The town was named for the Comanche chief, Quanah Parker. (William R. Hunt, "Quanah, Tx," *Handbook of Texas Online* [accessed May 6, 2011])

THE WESTERN CATTLE TRAIL | 1874-1897

> *The prospect of entering an uninhabited wilderness was a source of great joy to the cowboys. Civilization and cattle trailing were not congenial, and we had been greatly annoyed in the settled districts of Texas. Depending entirely on free grass for forage for our cattle and horses, we had constantly come in collison with the farmers, who wanted the grass for their domestic animals.... The Indian Territory was the cowpuncher's paradise. Now we would have no more lanes, no more obstructing fences, but one grand expanse of free grass. It was a delightful situation to comtemplate.*

B. J. Fletcher
age 19, one of eight cowboys with a
Thomas Snyder herd, *Up the Trail in '79*, pg. 27

James Gibson made a trip up the Western Trail with a herd of cattle and on point with him was a lad by the name of John Williams. Near the Wichita Mountains, a bunch of Indians rode up behind Gibson and grunted in their Indian fashion, "How John?" and after lingering a while asked such questions as, "No cara swap horses?" They then went over to Williams and hailed him by "How John!" As soon as they rode away Williams came over and said "Jim, those d–ned Indians know me," and when Gibson expressed surprise and asked where he had met them, Williams said "I never seen the d–ned fools before, but they called me John." Later the circumstance was related in camp to the old trail hands, who whooped and yelled and seemed to consider it a good joke, and when they had quieted enough so as to be understood, they told Williams that Indians saluted all white men by, "How John!"

"Trail Life," in Hunter, *The Trail Drivers of Texas*, pg. 271

CHAPTER IV

Indian Territory: Military Forts, Feeder and Splinter Routes

THE WESTERN CATTLE TRAIL | 1874-1897

"Cowboys at dinner in the Territory"
This group of cowboys have gathered around the cook and chuckwagon for dinner while in Indian Territory. Another cowboy watches the herd.

Because the tent is pitched, it is either early in the day before the trail drive, after the bedrolls have been packed away, or it is the last camp of the day. A tent provided protection from wind, rain, or snow during the night. (Cowboy hats have changed over the last one-hundred twenty years.)

Photo courtesy of Research Division of the Oklahoma Historical Society, photograpic archives, Oklahoma City, Oklahoma.

In 1933 the Oklahoma Legislature in its House Bill No. 149 authorized a study of two cattle trails through its state. The results, circulated by the Oklahoma State Historical Society in 1936, presented a detailed map and essay which described the difference between the Western Trail and the Chisholm Trail. What was not presented, however, was the network of trails between the two cattle trail systems, although information on those trails was buried in the historical data collected by the Society. In a five-year period, 1875-1880, feeder routes merged into the Western from the Chisholm, and in turn, up until 1889, splinter routes from the Western fed into the Chisholm Trail. This chapter presents that information and examines the 1936 map that came out of the mandated study. But first, a review of the 1870s-1880s Indian Territory — its geography, its people, and the military forts — is in order.

During the early cattle driving days, Texas drovers and cowboys assumed that open range would continue indefinitely. The freedom to roam the open expanse of grass was to them a God-given gift. Thus, while trailing cattle for hundreds of miles through this vast America prairie, drovers did not welcome interruptions of their passage ways. Their goal was to deliver cattle to a buyer at a railhead in Kansas, to an Indian reservation in Nebraska or the Dakotas, or to ranches in the upper plains region.

Upon leaving Texas, drovers were leaving a place with increasing "settled districts" and entering a place where confrontations with the Indians was a possibility. However, in Indian Territory, as B. J. Fletcher recalled there was "one grand expanse of free grass" without any settlers to interfer with their passage through the region. The Red River boundary across the northern border of Texas was more than just another river to cross, cowboys knew that after fording its waters, they were passing into unfamiliar territory and were getting farther from their home ranches. The river represented a line in the sand, so to speak, where once crossed, anything could happen. To add to the suspense was knowledge that they were now in the Indian's domain — an area that had been selected by the Government on which to place numerous tribes with hope that they would undergo the process of being Christinized and civilized.

THE FIGHT OVER GREER COUNTY, TEXAS:
(Map #4-1)

Almost every story about trail drivers crossing the Red River at Doan's Crossing emphasizes how they "jumped off" into Indian Territory — the unknown land of Indians. The area north of Wilbarger and Hardeman counties and the Doan's community was a new venture to the drovers. Some drovers faced the non-white inhabitation of Indian Territory cautiously, others like B. J. Fletcher looked upon the other side of the river as an adventure and "a delightful situation to contemplate."[1] The outfits, however, were still in Texas — Greer County, Texas, to be exact.[2] The

---

[1] B. J. Fletcher, *Up the Trail in '79*, 27.
[2] "Old Greer County" is now present-day Jackson, Harmon, Greer, and part of Beckham counties in Oklahoma.

THE WESTERN CATTLE TRAIL | 1874-1897

#4-1
The Western Trail Through Greer County, Texas and the Western Part of Indian Territory:
This map shows the Western Cattle Trail from the Red River to the Kansas line.

county had been formed by the Texas Legislature in 1860, but remained unorganized throughout most of the trail driving days. When the county was organized in 1886, an election was held to choose a county seat, either Frazer, later Altus, or Mangum. Both towns had received post office status in order to be considered as a county seat candidate; local residents voted in favor of Mangum, or "Tin Can City," as the cowboys called it.[3]

Greer County lay between the North Fork of the Red River and the Red River and was claimed by Texas for thirty-five years, from the 1860 to 1896.[4] During the trail-driving days, the State of Texas fought with the United States government to retain its ownership of Greer County. The fate of the area was in limbo for years while the dispute languished in the courts. When Oklahoma Territory was created in 1890, the United States government filed a lawsuit against Texas to settle the boundry dispute once and for all. Texas' claim was based on a provision in the Adam-Onis Treaty of 1819 between Spain the United States. The provision identified the boundry of New Spain (later Texas) as the upper branch of the Red River. The Melish Map that was used in the treaty was in error, however, because it showed only one major branch in the river's upper course instead of the existing two. Texas claimed that the North Fork was the "Red River" of the 1819 treaty, but the United States interpreted the lower fork as the true "upper branch" boundary. Texas responded that the lower fork of the river was barely known by early explorers and Indians, as is reflected on the Melish Map; therefore the disputed territory should be awarded to Texas by right of possession and occupation. The argument that the North Fork was the main stream of the Red River was not accepted, and in 1896 the Supreme Court awarded the area to Oklahoma Territory.[5]

While most cowboy accounts of travel along the Western Trail relate that they crossed the Red River into Indian Territory, two cowboy accounts accurately state that when the cattle crossed the Red River, they entered Greer County, Texas. One is the 1876 journal of Lewis Neatherlin.

---

[3] The town was called Tin Can City because of a store that was covered with flattened tin cans. One of the first stores in Mangum was owned by Henry Sweet who was also the postmaster. ("Greer County," www.OKGenWeb.org, [accessed May, 2008] and Oklahoma Department of Libraries booklet, "The Early Day Friendship Area," Nov. 2002, 9)

[4] Even though Greer County was under the jurisdiction of Texas, the area was initially ruled by the Comanches and Kiowas. When the last free bands of Comanches and Kiowas were confined to the reservation at Fort Sill in 1875, the area became safe for cattle drives and white settlers. By 1876, ranches were being established in the area.

[5] Greer County was opened for homesteading in 1897. (Robertson & Robertson, *Cowman's Country*, 84, and Charles R. Goins & Danney Goble, *Historical Atlas of Oklahoma*, 122)

May 18:

After a long talk with the inspector, I give him a due bill and we crossed the Red River. Very wide and sandy but very little water. We took dinner on the bank of the North Fork of Red River, 2 miles from where we crossed the main river. The trail lay on the west side of the North Fork all the afternoon, and we camped near it tonight.[6]

May 19:

The trail still lies west of the river and we are on what is called the panhandle of Texas. The Wichita Mountains lie east and in front. Have been in sight of them 2 1/2 days. No timber in sight, except a small skirting of scrubby elm and cottonwood on the North Fork. Two to four miles in our right, a very fine valley of rich productive land, some 10 miles in length and seems to be 3 to 6 miles wide. Had a rainy night and could not hold the cattle. Both herds in one this morning but all in sight of the wagons. Camped in big valley. Had to carry wood a mile or more [with] our horses.[7]

This early 1876 account not only mentions the "panhandle of Texas" (Greer County) but reveals that the Western Trail had been established and used by this date, because the trail was visiable to Neatherlin. He states that the "trail lay on the west side of the North Fork." The brand inspectors were also in place.

In the second entry, Neatherlin comments that after the cattle had been mixed because of the rainy night, they were still "in sight of the wagons." As long as the supply and chuck wagons were in sight, the outfit felt comfortable. These wagons were the core of the operation. From the cook's camp, the business of driving cattle was conducted.

The second account is that of G. W. Briggs, Jr. He became a brand inspector in the area four years after Neatherlin wrote in his journal of the trail driving through the area. Briggs and some other men from North Texas ranches went to Doan's store in May of 1880 to inspect the herds that went up the trail that year. "We were known as trail cutters," Briggs wrote in his recollection, "but the trail drivers called us the dirty bunch, because we relieved them of thousands of cattle that did not belong to them." Briggs continued in a letter written in 1933 that "After leaving Doan's Crossing the

---

[6]Brand inspectors patrolled the Red River to check herds before they crossed. Every animal had to have a road brand that was verified by the trail boss or contractor. If an unbranded maverick wondered into the herd or if a cow from another herd with a different road brand was mixed into the herd, that animal was cut out of the herd. The trail boss then had to pay the inspector a per capita fee for examining the herd. The practice helped prevent stolen cattle from leaving the state. The Texas legislature in 1870 authorized the govenor to appoint cattle inspectors. Because the job of inspector often came with no salary, the local sheriff or another county officer inspected the herds for a fee. Neatherlin had to give the inspector a "due bill" before crossing the river.

[7]Leo Kelley, ed. *Up the Trail in '76, the Journal of Lewis Warren Neatherlin*, 18.

trail bore due north through old Greer county forty miles to Warren and crossed the North Fork of Red River, thence northwest to Comanche Springs…"[8]

Other routes traversed Old Greer County. To understand these routes and their connection to the Western Cattle Trail, each will be examined.

THE MOBEETIE TRAIL: (Map #4-2)

Sharing the crossing of the Red River where the Doans later built their small settlement was the Mobeetie Trail.[9] It was identified by that name because it led into the town of Mobeetie in the Texas Panhandle. The trail connected the three early communities of Mobeetie to the west with Henrietta and Gainesville, south of the Red River, to the east. With Mobeetie and Fort Elliott at the northwest end, the trail extended southeast through Greer County and the Mangum area, established in 1884, where a stage station was later established, to the Red River crossing that become Doan's Store in 1878 and where another stage station was located and continued eastward some ninety miles to Henrietta. From Henrietta's supply deport and stage station, the Mobeetie road extended on a southern route forty miles to Fort Richardson which completed the military connection between Fort Elliott and Mobeetie. Another sixty-four miles, farther east of Henrietta, wagons and stage passengers connected with the older commerce center of Gainesville.

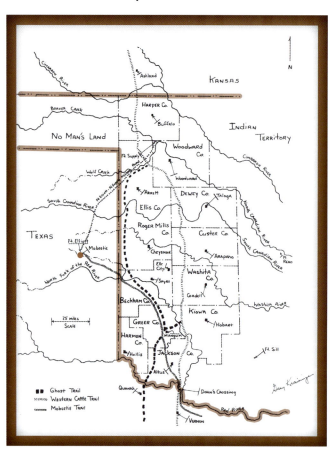

#4-2
Trails Across Greer County, Texas, and Beyond:
The Western Cattle Trail;
The Mobeetie Trail (Fort Elliott-Fort Richardson Military Road);
The Quanah Detour Route (Ghost Trail).

Mobeetie had started as a buffalo hunters' hide camp in 1875. It was originally known simply as Hidetown and was located on Sweetwater Creek. There, buffalo freighters, including Charles Rath, piled their hides until they could be hauled to warehouses. Rath was one of the biggest dealers in hides. He and his partners, Robert M. Wright, who operated the sutler's store at Fort Dodge, and A. J. Anthony, had an outfitting store on Front Street in Dodge City. In the years after the Atchison, Topeka, and Santa Fe had reached Dodge in September of 1872, the partners formed the

---

[8] Because of the practice of checking for road brands by inspectors, Doan's Crossing (which was established in 1878) later built furnaces and pens for the specific purpose of branding cattle for the road. (G. W. Briggs, Jr., to H. S. Tennant, Oklahoma State Capitol Building, letter of July 6, 1933. Letter printed in Tennant's article, "The Two Cattle Trails," *Chronicles of Oklahoma*, Vol. 14, 106) Tennant was researching the "two trails" for the State of Oklahoma and had asked for input from old timers.
[9] The crossing of the Red River for the Mobeetie Trail and the Western Trail was in Section 15, T2s, R20w.

Charles Rath Mercantile Company which traded, bought, warehoused, and shipped hides and meat east.[10]

At first, the buffalo hunters worked in central and western Kansas north of the Arkansas River, and Rath, an opportunist who was always on the move to feed his thriving hide business, sent his wagons out to the hide camps and, in turn, supplied the camps with needed materials. In the 1874 season, however, hunters and skinners ventured south of the Arkansas River, in violation of Indian treaties, to follow the buffalo. Thus, as the buffalo were depleted around Dodge and the hunters' camps moved greater distances from the hide-shipping terminal, the Dodge hide merchants decided in the early spring of 1874 to move their trading posts south. The first spot selected was to a hide camp near the old Adobe Walls ruins, located near presesnt-day Stinnett in Hutchinson County in the Texas Panhandle. However, on June 27, 1874, the newly established buffalo camp was attacked by a combined force of Kiowa, Comanches, and Cheyenne, and the hide merchants had to flee back to Dodge City. (more on this in the next chapter).

Not to be deterred by the Indians nor the losses incurred at Adobe Walls, Rath determined to set up another trading post. In the spring of 1875, before the herds migrated into the region, he and his partner Bob Wright approached W. M. D. Lee and A. E. Reynolds at Camp Supply to engage in another venture. While Rath was an entrepreneur in the dealing of hides, Lee and Reynolds were the biggest names in a freighting operation that connected Dodge City and the Texas Panhandle. The two men had established the sutler's store at Camp Supply in 1868 and had a government license to trade with the Indians. They handled government contracts which involved fifty or more teamsters on their payroll.[11]

After the attack on Adobe Walls the summer before, the atmosphere of the Panhande changed in the spring of 1875, and the military launched a campaign to move the Indians of the Southern Plains east into Indian Territory. Thus, the area became a war zone, and white settlers, cattle drovers, and freighters had to be mindful of the dangers. Rath wanted to establish three trading posts, and Lee and Reynolds, under the orders of Commander Lt. Col. William Lewis at Camp Supply, were in the midst of provisioning soldiers in the field. All the supplies for both the buffalo hunters and the soldiers came out of Dodge. Rath therefore concluded that by combining forces with Lee and Reynolds, there would be safety in numbers and both of their purposes could be accomplished.[12]

The freight route leading out of Camp Supply, a road that later became the Camp Supply-Fort Elliott Military Road, extended southwest along Wolf Creek where some buffalo hunters unloaded gear to prepare for the hunting of buffaloes that

---

[10]The hide business was so enormous that hunters made better than a hundred dollars a day. (Ida Ellen Rath, *The Rath Trail*, 79-80, 101)

[11]C. Robert Haywood, *Trails South*, 125-126.

[12]The offensive actions by the U.S. Army of 1874 and 1875 was recorded as the Red River War. Lasting less than a year, it officially ended in June of 1875. ("Red River War," online: www.texasbeyondhistory.net [accessed Dec. 2, 2011])

ranged to the south. It then continued to the boundary of Texas and from there south along the boundary to the Washita River. Farther south on Sweetwater Creek, Colonel Nelson Miles, who was in charge of the Indian Territory Expedition, organized his part of the campaign in July of 1874, and selected a camp for his troops. It was here that a permanent post — a military cantonment — would be established. To supply the post, Lt. Col. Lewis arranged to transport 650,000 pounds of contractors' goods with 106 mule teams and wagons. The supplies would be sufficient for 500 men and the same number of animals. By the end of January, 1875, the new Sweetwater cantonment was equipped, and Major James Biddle was its commander.[13]

Charles Rath's interest, however, was the hide camp established just south of the army cantonment. Buffalo hunters had established a camp early in the summer of 1874 and were now depending on Rath to establish a post and a freighting system for their hides. Rath's bullwackers (freight wagon drivers) used the heavily carved road the military freight wagons had used that ran from Dodge City by way of Camp Supply.

As the only settlement at the time in the Panhandle, Hidetown, with the Rath trading post as its nucleus, quickly attracted more buffalo hunters along with gamblers, outlaws, and bullwackers. Regular customers, of course, were the soldiers from the nearby cantonment. By the summer of 1875, there was also a respectable restaurant in addition to the many saloons and dance halls in a growing community now referred to as "Sweetwater."[14] In February of 1876, the Sweetwater Cantonment was renamed "Fort Elliott," and it consisted of an officers' quarters, barracks for six companies of enlisted men, a headquarters building, hospital, laundresses' quarters, storehouses, and cavalry stables.

The Mobeetie Trail on Map #4-2 is the bullwackers' path going southeast out of Mobeetie, formerly known as Sweetwater and Hidetown. The pathway that Neatherlin and other trail drivers on the Western Trail would have seen, led to and from Mobeetie across Greer County and followed an ancient migration route used by the buffalo and Indians for centuries, thus, the reason for the hide camp on the Sweetwater in the first place. It was recorded as an old wagon road as early as 1870 even before Mobeetie was founded,[15] but the "Mobeetie Road or Trail," was used by all — buffalo hide and bone wagons starting in 1874, the military moving between Fort Richardson in Jack County and Fort Elliott, cattle herds coming up from south Texas, and stage and freight wagons transporting goods through the region. The

---

[13]Robert C. Carriker, *Fort Supply*, 92, 103, 146.

[14]When Wheeler County was organized in 1879, Sweetwater was selected as the county seat, but when applying for a post office, the name was changed to Mobeetie. In 1880 a stone courthouse was built, the first one in the Texas Panhandle. Within a year, Mobeetie became the judicial center of the Thirty-fifty District which comprised of fifteen surrounding counties. Thus, within its first six years of existence, Mobeetie had boomed and was called the "Mother City of the Panhandle" and had evolved from a buffalo camp to a legal business center and social hub. (Kathy Weiser, "Mobeetie — Panhandle Mother City," Legends of America online http.www.legendsof america.com [accessed May 25, 2011] and Robertson and Robertson, *Cowman's Country, Fifty Frontier Ranches In The Texas Panhandle, 1876-1887*, 53-54)

[15]Jodean Martin, "Jackson County Oklahoma," http://flies.usgwarchives.org [accessed Oct. 7, 2009] Martin writes that the wagon road can be found on an 1870 government survey that is in the Jackson County Assessor's Office.

route connected with Henrietta in Clay County in extreme north Texas, south of the Red River. (see "Bosque County Feeder Route," Map #3-2)

Even though a settlement had been established at Henrietta in 1857 and a post office assigned in 1862, the community was abandoned because of hostile Indian attacks.[16] Settlers returned, however, in 1874. The post office was reopened and, like Mobeetie, the town became a buffalo hide center. Hunters bought their supplies in Henrietta and returned with full wagons of hides and bones.

The Mobeetie Trail also continued to Gainesville farther east in Cooke County. Gainesville had existed long before either Mobeetie or Henrietta and was a commerce hub. Even though Gainesville was not incorporated until February of 1873, it had existed as a community as early as 1850. Gainsville became the seat for Cooke County soon after it was organized in 1849, and in 1858, it hosted a stop on the Butterfield Stagecoach line. While Mobeetie had developed from its use by buffalo hunters and soldiers, Gainesville benefited economically as one of the several supply points in the area for the drovers from off of the early Arbuckle Trail, a predecessor of the later Chisholm Trail.[17]

The Mobeetie Trail was a convenient pathway for some cattle outfits — if it suited the direction they were trailing. Herds coming from Bosque County, on the Bosque County Feeder Route, through Hood, Parker, Palo Pinto, and Jack counties, used the Mobeetie Trail, or one might identify it as the "Fort Richardson-Fort Elliott military road," from Jacksboro (Fort Richardson) to the crossing of the Red River where this feeder route merged for a short distance with the Western Trail.

Whether coming from a feeder route or the Western Trail trunk line to Doan's Crossing, a trail boss had a choice at the river crossing. He could lead his herd straight north on the Western Cattle Trail to the North Fork of the Red River and beyond into Indian Territory, or the outfit could move from the main trunk approximately four or five miles north of the river crossing, or southeast of present-day Hess, over to Nine Mile Spring on the Mobeetie Trail and continue from there northwesterly across Greer County and on to Mobeetie (see Map #4-3). Nine Mile Spring was nine miles from Doan's Crossing and was the location of the L. V. Eddleman ranch headquarters in the early 1880s[18] Even before C. F. Doan established his store in 1878, the Mobeetie Trail was a viable choice for drovers. When James Gibson was in an outfit to deliver a herd of 500 horses to Dodge City, Kansas, he noted that at

---

[16]Because of the raiding Indians, Clay County, Texas, and areas to the west were inhospitable in the late 1850s and mid 1860s when settlers in Henrietta and Buffalo Springs were trying to create communities. In 1867, two companies of soldiers were deployed from Jacksboro to build a fort in Clay County to protect the area. Because an initial attempt to establishing Fort Richardson in Clay County proved unworkable, the fort was rebuilt ten miles south, in Jack County, near Jacksboro. Although attempts to settle Henrietta and Buffalo Springs proved unsuccessful during the 1860s, settlers returned to these communities to stay in 1874 and 1878. The fort was abandoned in 1878. ("Fort Richardson, Texas," http://en.wikipedia.org [accessed May 31, 2011])

[17]"History of Gainesville," http://www.gainesville.tx.us/Historical/HistoricalTour.html [accessed May 26, 2011]

[18]"Oklahoma Historic Survey, — Greer County," *Chronicles of Oklahoma*, Vol. 36, No. 1, Spring 1958, 294.

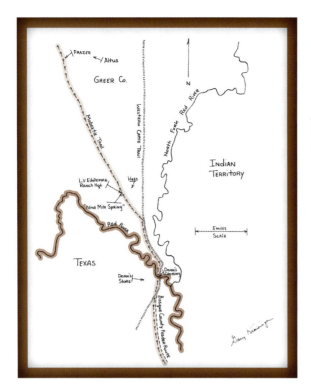

#4-3
The Mobeetie Trail, the Bosque County Feeder Route, and the Western Cattle Trail:
The Mobeetie Trail (having connected with Fort Richardson in Jack County, Texas) merged with the Western Cattle Trail south of Doan's Crossing. This trail and the Bosque County Feeder Route (Map #3-2) fed into Doan's Crossing. At Doan's Crossing, the Bosque County Feeder Route ended, but the Mobeetie Trail followed the Western Cattle Trail until it splintered off of the Western a few miles north of Doan's Crossing in Greer County in order to continue to Mobeetie and Fort Elliott.

"Doan's Store, an Indian trading store on Red River," the "trails forked, one going to Mobeetie and the other by the Wichita Mountains."[19]

In 1881, F. M. Polk hired on with William H. Jennings and John Blocker and was in the herd bossed by Bob Jennings. They left the Jennings ranch "near the San Marcos River (in the Austin area) on the first day of April for Kansas." Polk described how they made their way to Taylor, Texas, and "reached Lampasas County" and struck the Western Trail farther up the line "I don't remember just where...," he wrote. The outfit was using the San Gabriel-Brownwood Feeder Route.(see map # 1-11) Polk believed that after crossing the Red River at Doan's, they were in Indian Territory:

> We crossed the Red River into Indian Territory at Doan's Store, and here we struck the Indians by the thousands. We kept our eyes open and managed to keep peace by giving them a beef every day....we were not very badly frightened. We all had our guns and knew how to use them if we got in a fight.

The Bob Jennings herd then veered west onto the Mobeetie Trail. Soon afterward, the owners of the herd, Blocker and Jennings, "overtook us at Bitter Creek," which is just west of present-day Altus. Polk then noted, "They were to deliver the cattle at Mobeetie, a little town in the Panhandle." Polk, however, did not go to Mobeetie, but he and another cowboy were sent on up the trail to overtake another one of Blocker and Jennings' herds which was being delivered to Dodge City.

In the following year, Polk hired on with Mark A. Withers, who "sent several herds this time and I went with a bunch under Gus Withers." They crossed the Red River at Doan's Store and "there we found a large number of Indians camped, but they were peaceable, for they were fast finding out that it didn't pay to molest cattle drivers."[20]

What a difference a year made.

At the Red River crossing, owner M. A. Withers met the herd and instructed

---

[19] "Trail Life," essay about James Gibson who made eight trips with horses. The horses were sold to early settlers in job lots in Western Kansas and Nebraska. in Hunter, *The Trail Drivers of Texas*, 271-273.
[20] Polk did not realize that the area was Greer County, Texas. (F. M Polk, "My Experience on the Cow Trail," in Hunter, 141-142)

Gus Withers to continue to Dodge City on the Western Trail trunk line and moved Polk and his bother Cal to another herd under trail boss Tom Hawker. The herd had been sold to an English syndicate and was to be delivered to a Mr. Johnson at Mobeetie. Thus, "After leaving Doan's Store we traveled up Bitter Creek [on the Mobeetie Trail] for forty or fifty miles and then turned west to Mobeetie..." It is interesting to note Polk's next comment: "we turned our herd over to John Hargroves to hold on the LX Ranch until fall, as we could not take them on to Tuscosa [Tascosa] until after frost on account of a quarantine they had on at that time."[21] It was 1882, and cattle drovers from south Texas were adjusting to the ever-growing pressure from the settlers and the quarantines. The Quanah Detour Route, discussed in the former chapter, was a response to that pressure. The Mobeetie Trail to Mobeetie, in the Texas Panhandle, and from there north to Dodge City was another route over which to trail cattle to the railhead. It was not a direct route, however, and was not as straight a pathway as the Western Trail, and its disadvantage, as revealed in Polk's narrative, was the cattle quarantines imposed in the Texas Panhandle. Using the Western Trail through Indian Territory, and later the Quanah Detour Route, did not pose the problem of a quarantine

FRONTIER FORTS AND THE MILITARY ROADS:

During the mid 1870s to the late 1880s, Texas drovers on the Western Trail crossed Greer County, Texas, and Indian Territory passing through the Comanche-Kiowa-Apache Reservation and the Cheyenne-Arapaho Reservation. (Map #4-1) What had once been a homeland for free-roaming Indian tribes that followed the migrating herds of buffalo was now an organized system of reservations. A network of forts in Indian Territory and the Texas Panhandle area, established during the Indian wars, were now responsible for maintaining the peace on the reservations. The forts' primary function shifted from protection of the military roads to providing medical and subsistence needs for the reservation residents. Since the establishment of the reservations, a stage system linking the forts was introduced, and the old military roads became civilian pathways that had to be patrolled to keep them safe from marauding outlaws, thieves, whiskey peddlers, and other undesirables who had entered Indian Territory after the Indians were subdued.

Fort Dodge supplied Camp Supply, and, in turn, freight wagons from Camp Supply replenished Fort Elliott, Fort Reno, and Fort Sill. Fort Elliott in the Texas Panhandle was also connected to Fort Dodge by its own military road and provided many services not attainable anywhere else in her area such as hospital care. The first postal service in the Texas Panhandle was provided through Fort Elliott, and in

---

[21]Polk finishes his account by saying that Mr. Johnson, after receiving the herd at Mobeetie, traveled to Dodge City with Mark Withers to meet the Gus Withers' herd. In a violent storm, "Mr. Johnson was struck and killed by lightning while returning to camp. Mr. Withers was knocked from his horse, but wasn't hurt further than receiving a bad fall and shock." (Polk, Ibid, 146)

THE WESTERN CATTLE TRAIL | 1874-1897

October of 1879, telegraph lines were completed from Fort Sill, Fort Reno and Fort Supply to Fort Elliott. The patrolling of the Texas Panhandle border along the west boundary of the Cheyenne-Arapaho Reservation was Fort Elliott's main task. The garrison's primary duties was to stop small hunting parties of Indians from crossing into the Texas Panhandle. The soldiers escorted truant Indians back across the border to their reservation, hunted down renegade Indians, and settled disputes. After various cattle ranches were established in the region in the mid 1880's, the garrison policed the border trying to keep Panhandle stock from crossing over into the reservation.[22]

East of the Western Trail was Fort Sill on Cache Creek, near in the center of the Comanche-Kiowa-Apache Reservation. Its new role was as a law enforcement post.[23] Fort Reno in central Indian Territory on the eastern edge of the Cheyenne-Arapaho Reservation was adjacent to the Darlington Indian Agency and helped protect the tribes from white horse thieves and settle disputes among tribesmen.[24] Camp Supply, which became a fort in December of 1878, was located in the Cherokee Outlet north of the Cheyenne-Arapaho Reservation. It had always been a supply post since its creation in November of 1868. During the trail days, it supplied the cattle drives on their way north. For most trail herds upon leaving Doan's Crossing, the next major supply depot was Fort Supply.[25]

Over the military trails among these forts, soldiers traveled from stronghold to stronghold, crisscrossing Greer County and Indian Territory performing their various duties. The cattle drives moving out of Texas added to their task and complicated the situation.

In 1874-1875, when the Western Trail was in its infancy, to avoid possible confrontations between the cowboys and the Indians, escorts were offered to cattle herds moving through Greer County and Indian Territory. After the Indians were settled on reservations, however, many acres of rich tribal grazing lands encompassed the cattle trails, and the domain was now designated as belonging to the Indians, under the army's protection. Therefore, by the 1876 season, soldiers served as escorts through the reservations for a different reason; namely that the military needed to protect Indian farms from damage and to make sure that the longhorns were not grazing off the trail. Drovers, as a general rule, often didn't respect the reservation boundaries, and without an escort, their cattle might graze at length on the reservation grasslands in violation of the laws. Indians resented the vast numbers of Texas-based

---

[22]"Fort Elliott,: www.fortwiki.com [accessed May 30, 2008]

[23]Unlike Fort Elliott, Fort Sill, established in 1869, remained open after the Indian wars were concluded, and it changed from a cavalry base to a field artillery center, eventually becoming home to a field artillery school in 1911. Of all the historic forts, Fort Sill is the only active Army installation remaining on the South Plains; The U.S. Army Field Artillery School remains in operation in 2013. ("The History of Old Fort Sill," www.army.mil/pao/pahist.htm [accessed June 6, 2008])

[24]After Indian Territory became the state of Oklahoma in 1907, Fort Reno was abandoned The old fort site served as a U.S. Cavalry remount station from 1908 to 1949. Today, the grounds of the old fort is the home of the U.S. Department of Agriculture's Southwestern Livestock and Forage Research Station. (online: http://en.wikipedia.org/wiki/Fort_Reno_(Oklahoma) [accessed June 12, 2008] and "Legends of America," http://www.legendsofamerica.com/OK-ElReno.htm, [accessed June 12, 2008])

[25]Robert C. Carriker, *Fort Supply Indian Territory*, 32-33, 107, 111.

Robby McMurtry, from graphic novel: **The Road to Medicine Lodge, Jesse Chisholm in the Indian Nations** *(2011), page 62.*

cattle on their land, and some confrontations resulted in near bloodshed. In 1876, therefore, the army quickly ordered the removal of any unauthorized cattle from the Indian reservations, and to keep the peace, soldiers from Fort Elliott, Fort Sill, Fort Reno, and Camp Supply escorted the cattle herds.

As the drives became larger and more often, soldiers ceased to accompany every herd. The cost of trespassing the Indian lands came in the way of a grazing toll from each herd. Representatives from each tribe expected a fee usually in the form of one to three head of stock. Not always was this unwritten expectation obeyed by trail bosses.

Bob Fudge told of such an incident in 1882 in Greer County when he worked for Ab Blocker. Blocker contracted to have two thousand "mature" head of cattle delivered to the Little Big Horn River in Montana, and Fudge was one of twelve cowboys to trail the herd. He recalled Doan's Store where "we could get supplies here for the cook, and also get tobacco and a new supply of ammunition for our six-shooters." After crossing the Red River, "we were given orders to be on the lookout for Indians day and night, which had the effect of making us 'some scared.' It sobered us down to the seriousness of our position anyway." Then they met the Indians:

> We were going along as usual one day when one of the boys saw dust raising in front of us and to our left. There was not a rider of any kind in this Territory but trail herds travelling north and soldiers and Indians. We could soon see mounted men through the dust coming on an angle toward us. We did not stop the herd until we found them to be Indians, sure enough, with all their war paint and decoration. There were about twenty of these Indians….
>
> Well, our boss and another cowboy advanced a short distance to meet the Indians. Their chief did the talking to our boss. He demanded

one hundred of our best beef cattle, cut from the lead of the herd. Indians were not fools when considering beef. The boss told him 'No,' but said that he could have some from the drags of our herd which were cripples and the ones that were getting foot sore, and as our boss stayed with this the Indians got mad. They insisted on cutting them from the lead. They said that we were on their territory and that the white man had killed all their buffalo and they were going to have good beef in return. I don't know how long this argument lasted. It seemed hours to me, but I don't suppose it was more than a half hour. The Indians left at a gallop, going back the direction from which they had come.

The boss had us corral the horses in our rope corral fastened to the wagon and told us that it was every man for himself and the Devil for us all. We threw our bed rolls on the ground and everything that we thought would stop a bullet or an arrow or protect ever a part of our bodies. We did not have to wait long for the Indians to come in sight again. They were traveling at about the same pace as when they first approached us. There wasn't much said between our little outfit until now — all but one man, who refused to do a thing but lie in the bottom of the wagon and hide like a lizard, had been preparing to make his last stand. It was some sort of relief that the Indians were coming in daylight.

When the chief got within about one hundred yards of us he stopped his outfit and raised a white flag on a stick which was to show us he had accepted our terms....the boss cut out about twenty head of footsore and crippled cattle and the Indians accepted them without ever a grunt. The Indians commenced butchering those cattle as soon as they were in their possession.

The next day some soldiers came into the outfit's noon camp, and the cowboys learned that they had dealt with a bunch of renegade Indians who were being hunted by the soldiers for killing four or five men who were on the trail with about five hundred horses. The Indians had not only stolen their horses but also killed the men. "The Indians knew they were being hunted or we would have met the very same fate that the horse men did," wrote Fudge. "We surely breathed easier after meeting those soldiers."[26]

By 1883, the numbers on the Western Trail were at their zenith and herds trailed one behind the other, and the single most important duty of the forts was to assist the cattle drives. Troops from Fort Supply worked closely with Fort Reno and Fort Elliott to assure proper conduct by whites and Indians on the trail. In order to keep the cattlemen from cutting across Indian farms and to encourage the drovers to stay on the trail, Fort Supply kept a small detachment of soldiers posted during the summer where the Western Trail crossed the Washita River. A sergeant, ten privates, and a few Indian scouts maintained the post for twenty-day periods before being

---

[26]Jim Russell, *Bob Fudge, Texas Trail Driver Montana-Wyoming Cowboy, 1862-1933*. 33-34.

relieved. By 1887, signs were posted at the Washita River crossing informing drovers of northbound herds of their choices of trails, because the destination into Dodge City, Kansas was off limits as a result of the quarantine, and drovers now had to splinter off toward Colorado or go east on a cut-off to the border towns of Caldwell or Hunnewell, Kansas and ship their cattle from there.

By 1888, a revised strategy was implemented. Fort Sill troops picked up Texas herds at Comanche Springs on the North Fork of the Red River and escorted them to the Washita. From there Fort Elliott troops picked up the herds and led them to the Canadian. From there, troops from Fort Supply took over. The crossing point on the Canadian River also offered a cut-off to Caldwell, on the Deep Creek Trail to be discussed later, which appeased the Indian tribes because it by-passed their farms, which before had been crossed and trampled on by herds using the old cut-off. Cattlemen eventually came to depend on the troops and welcomed their presence. Drovers realized that it prevented harassment and loss of cattle as they passed through Indian Territory. Not every herd was escorted, of course, but just knowing of the possible presence of Army troops relieved tension.[27]

THE TRUNK LINE OF THE WESTERN CATTLE TRAIL, GREER COUNTY NORTH TO COMANCHE SPRINGS:

(Map #4-4 "Lower Portion of the Tennant Map")

The best source for an accurate map of the Western Trail through present-day Oklahoma is the one reprinted by the Chisholm Trail Heritage Center in Duncan, Oklahoma with permission from the Oklahoma Historical Society. It is an excellent map and has withstood the test of time. A companion map of the Chisholm Trail appears on the reverse side. These two maps are the result of a mandate of the 1931 Oklahoma Legislature that provided for "the locating, tracing, and mapping" of the two main cattle trails that crossed their state — the "Chisholm" and the "Texas Cattle Trail." The research was assigned to the Engineering Department of the Department of Oklahoma State Highway Commission — and in particular to H. S. Tennant, an employee of that agency. We refer to the map that emerged from this effort, published by the highway commission in 1933, as the "Tennant Map." Without the research provided by the report and Tennant's interviews, we would not have this valuable information on the trail. What is especially appreciated today, over 80 years later, is the Texas Cattle Trail (Western Trail) map shows by "x" marks "where the trail may be plainly seen (1933)." All the supplemental information collected by the Highway Commission was filed with the Oklahoma Historical Society. The maps produced by the Commission were copyrighted by the Society, and Tennant's report was published in The Chronicles of Oklahoma *in March of 1936.*

---

[27]Robert C. Carriker, Ibid, 169-175 & 177. H. S. Tennant, "The Texas Cattle Trails, *Chronicles of Oklahoma*, March, 1936, 106 Kraisinger & Kraisinger, *The Western, the Greatest Texas Cattle Trail, 1874-1886*, 82-85.

EXAMPLES OF PETER P. ACKLEY TRAIL MARKERS ON THE WESTERN TRAIL

Trail driver Peter P. Ackley, Elk City, Oklahoma, organized a trail-marking project around 1930-1931 and placed an unknown number of markers along the Chisholm and Western Cattle trails. The largest of his markers is at Doan's Crossing which was unveiled on October 21-22, 1931. It is an impressive twelve-foot tall gray granite marker. George W. Saunders and fellow trail drivers, who were in attendance, were astonished to read the words "Longhorn Chisholm Trail" on the marker. Over the next three years, Saunders argued with Ackley about the incorrect name. Some time around 1936, the incorrect name was cut off the face of the stone.

This red granite marker, which points north, was placed by Ackley probably around 1931 in a roadside park located on Highway 283 north of Vernon, Texas. It also reads "Chisholm Trail." Ackley was convinced that the Western Trail was a part of the Chisholm Trail system. Even though George W. Saunders and the Old Time Trail Drivers Association tried to convince him otherwise, Ackley continued to mark the Western Trail improperly.

Co-author Margaret Kraisinger stands next to a P. P. Ackley sign at the Tri-Marker Park in Ogallala, Nebraska. The metal sign reads: "Going Up the Texas Chisholm Trail, 1867." Two other signs like this were discovered in Scranton, North Dakota, showing the distance that Ackley traveled to place signs. George W. Saunders, in a letter to Ackley, sarcastically called these signs "yellow butterfly markers."

To read more about P. P. Ackley and the George W. Saunders' debate, read Chapter 1 and 14 in The Western, the Greatest Texas Cattle Trail, 1874-1886.

Undoubtedly the Oklahoma Legislature in 1931 mandated the research because of the personal debate between George W. Saunders, and the Old Time Trail Drivers' Association, and Peter P. Ackley over the mis-naming of the large granite monument at Doan's Crossing that was later dedicated and placed at the site on October 21-22, 1931 and the improper marking of the Western Trail by Ackley as the "Longhorn Chisholm."[28] This controversy involved Saunders undertaking a campaign to debunk the words "Longhorn Chisholm" on trail markers. As president of the Old Time Trail Drivers' Association, Saunders also spearheaded a resolution at their 17th annual association reunion in October of 1931 that resolved that only the Western Trail crossed at Doan's Crossing. Saunders continued to provide newspaper interviews, write scores of letters to county judges to try to stop the placement of trail markers by Ackley, and appealed to Ackley, himself, to correct his error. Saunders also sent out circular letters to all of his trail-driving friends and asked for support affirming that the Western, not the "Chisholm," used the Doan's River Crossing. Meanwhile, Ackley continued to place his "Longhorn Chisholm" markers up and down the trail.

One issue the authors have with this 1933 Oklahoma State Highway Commission map (the Tennant map), however, is the labeling of Doan's Crossing. In print it says, "Doan's Crossing first used in 1874 by Maxwell and Morris, Doan's Store est. 1874, P.O. est. 1879." This is an error. As discussed in Chapter III, Doan's Crossing did not exist until 1878. In his attempt to gather reliable information on the trail, Tennant interviewed an old timer, N. J. McElroy from Blair, Oklahoma, who was seventy-five years old in 1933. In the front of Tennant's report it states that McElroy told him that he drove "cattle over this trail in 1874 and to 1887." McElroy was around sixteen in 1874. McElroy also told Tennant that "Maxwell and

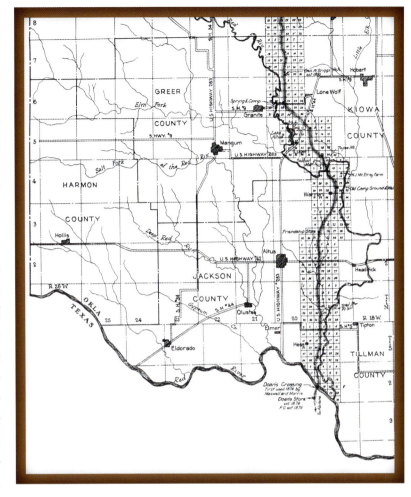

#4-4
The Lower Portion of the Tennant Map:
This map, showing the "Texas Cattle Trail" (Western Trail), was created from research done by H. S. Tennant and the Engineering Department of Oklahoma State Highway Commission. The research was started in 1933 under the direction of House Bill 149 of the 13th Session of the Oklahoma Legislature. The final data and this map were turned over to the Oklahoma Historical Society in 1936. The report was printed in The Chronicles of Oklahoma in March of 1936. In this study, this map is referred to as "the Tennant Map."

---

[28] See Kraisinger and Kraisinger, Chapter I, "The Controversy" and Chapter 14, "Conclusion & Authors' Comments" of *The Western, the Greatest Texas Cattle Trail, 1874-1886*.

Morris drove the first herd of cattle over this trail in 1874 coming from southern Texas...," *which apparently was part of the interview. This led Tennant to identify the date on the* *map. Later in Tennant's report, concentrating on McElroy's interview, Tennant provided a* *good description of an established route that went through "Vernon, which was then called* *Eagle Flat." McElroy explained that "after leaving Doan's Store we came on up through* *old Greer County close to North Fork...." McElroy was apparently with Maxwell and* *Morris, and he asserted: "This was in 1871 and Doan's Store was not established in 1871.* *I later knew C. F. Doan." McElroy would have been about thirteen years old in 1871.[29]*

The authors believe that a typographical error may have occurred or the elderly *McElroy had a fuzzy memory. Because of the hostile Indian situation in 1871, this Western* *Trail, so accurately described by McElroy, was not in existence. It is possible, of course, that* *McElroy was with Maxwell and Morris in 1874, the first year of the trail when Capt. John* *Lytle took his herd over the trail, but we feel that the drive McElroy is actually referring to* *was in 1877 or later. Also, McElroy referred to Vernon, Texas on that drive as "Eagle Flat,"* *which was there in the late 1870s (established post office in 1880), but not any earlier.[30]*

The only other source we have found referring to Maxwell and Morris was in Harry *Sinclair Drago's book* Great American Cattle Trails. *According to Drago, Maxwell and* *Morris drove a big herd of stock cattle from South Texas, using the Belton Feeder Route from* *the Eastern Trail to the Western Trail in 1877. Could this have been the year that McElroy* *meant? 1877 — not 1871, an easily misread number.[31] The year 1877 was still before the* *Doan's Store establishment (1878) and before Vernon (1880), so that would work.*

For years the authors have sought more information about Maxwell and Morris and *their trail drive. McElroy and Drago are the only two references we can find. Drago used the* *1920 edition of Marvin Hunter's* The Trail Drivers of Texas *(no page) as a source, but a* *thorough search of that rare volume was in vain.*

Obviously, the 1874 date for the establishment of Doan's Crossing is incorrect, and we *feel that Maxwell and Morris used the crossing in 1877 — not in 1874, which also means* *that they were not the first to use that crossing.*

After crossing the Red River, drovers trailed straight north — "in the direction of the north star. Hour by hour, step by step and day by day we pursued our way, not knowing the hardships that were in store for us," wrote T. J. Burkett of his 1883 drive. Burkett had been stationed in a line camp on the R2 Ranch in Wilbarger County when he was told that he was to hit the trail.[32] His outfit may have used the

---

[29]In more than one source, N. J. McElroy told how he was kidnapped by Comanche Indians in 1869 and held until his father paid a ransom for him. He was eleven years old at the time. That means that in 1874, McElroy would have been around sixteen, but in 1871, only thirteen, which is a very young trail cowboy. H. S. Tennant interviewed McElroy in about 1933 when McElroy was 75, putting his birthdate at 1858. (H. S. Tennant, *Chronicles of Oklahoma*, online, http://digital.library.okstate.edu [accessed July 3, 2008]

[30]Jimmy M. Skaggs in his thesis, "*The Great Western Cattle Trail to Dodge City, Kansas*," (1965) referred to the settlement on the Pease River as "Eagles Crossing." pg. 33.

[31]Harry Sinclair Drago, *Great American Cattle Trails*, 172.

[32]T. J. Burkett, Sr. "On the Fort Worth and Dodge City Trail," in Hunter, 927. Burkett described this part of the trail as long and tiresome and the hardship ahead was to be a stampede of the herd in the Wichita Mountains. "After three days of hard work" to gather 1800 steers, they were again on "their way to a distant clime beyond the sands of the Cimarron."

Location: According to Chronicles of Oklahoma, *Vol. 38, 1960, 11-12, a marker was located from Hess, Oklahoma, one mile east, 4 miles south, and 1/4 mile back east.*

Authors' commentary:
During the trail-driving days, herds and outfits crossed the Red River into Greer County, Texas, not into Indian Territory. The next line seems to have been taken from the H.S. Tennant map which states that the crossing was "first used in 1874" and the "Doan's Store est. 1874." The crossing was used by Captain John T. Lytle in 1874, but the Doan's Store was not established for another four years (1878).

The ending date of 1895 is not accurate if one remembers that after 1886, this portion of the trail was used very little because of the shift of cattle traffic farther west to the Texas Panhandle. 1889 would be more acceptable.

We do not know where the number 19 million cattle comes from. The Western carried approximately six million cattle during the entire period of its existance, 1874 to 1897. The other 13 million cattle could not represent the other three cattle trail systems because they did not go through Doan's Crossing. It is a gross over statement.

upper end of the Bosque County Feeder Route to merge into the Western Trail north of Vernon. The herds and their outfits trailed the west bank of the North Fork of the Red River. On the other side of the river lay the Comanche-Kiowa-Apache Reservation. They passed through the area where one of the Hess brothers would later establish a community bearing the Hess name. The homestead of Carter and Elvira Hess was established late in the trail-driving era of the Western Trail.[33]

Eleven miles into Greer County, the Western Trail crossed the Fort Elliott-Fort Sill military road. In Section 29, T 1n, R19w, the Tennant map notes: "Trail to Ft. Sill,." indicating that the military road intersected the Western Cattle Trail. George Boyd noted this road in his recollection of an 1877 trail drive when he was seventeen years old. The outfit was driving a large herd of cattle from Fort Griffin, Texas, to Dodge City when they came upon a military road running from Sweetwater Cantonment (Fort Elliott) to Fort Sill. The outfit did not use the military road, but

---

[33]The three Hess brothers, William Carter, James Buckhanon (Buck), and Robert C. Brackenridge (Brack), were from Arkansas and settled, along with many of their friends, in Johnson County, Texas (near Fort Worth) and also in Greer County. The brothers made several trips to Texas after the Civil War always encouraging others to follow. They owned land in different locations, leaving one part of the family at a homestead and then taking older children to squat elsewhere. In 1886, William Carter and his wife Elvira were in Greer County. Their home was established as the Hess post office in May of 1889 and was on the mail run from Vernon to Mangum. (Linda Gayle Wilson Heuckendorf, "How Did Hess, Oklahoma Begin," online: http://www.southerngrace.com [accessed June 14, 2011] According to Tennant, the Western Trail was two miles east of Hess. Ibid., 87.

2
THE GREAT WESTERN CATTLE TRAIL
CIRCA 1876 - 1895

BEGAN IN SOUTHERN TEXAS AFTER QUANAH PARKER AND THE COMANCHES SURRENDERED AT FORT SILL IN 1875. DUE TO THE FAILING POST-CIVIL WAR ECONOMY IN TEXAS, RANCHERS DEVELOPED A 1,000 MILE TRAIL TO DODGE CITY, OGALLALA, AND OTHER NORTHERN MARKETS TO RECEIVE REWARDING PROFITS. WITH FAITH IN GOD, COWBOYS DROVE MILLIONS OF LONGHORNS OVER THE PRAIRIE THAT HAD BEEN CONSERVED BY THE PLAINS INDIANS IN INDIAN TERRITORY. THE COMANCHES AND OTHER TRIBES BECAME SKILLED AS DIPLOMATS AND OFFERED RIGHT OF PASSAGE FOR BEEF FROM THE CATTLEMEN. MANY OF THE HUMAN EXPERIENCES WE CALL "THE WILD WEST" THAT CAPTURED THE INTEREST OF THE WORLD EVOLVED HERE ON THE GREAT WESTERN CATTLE TRAIL.

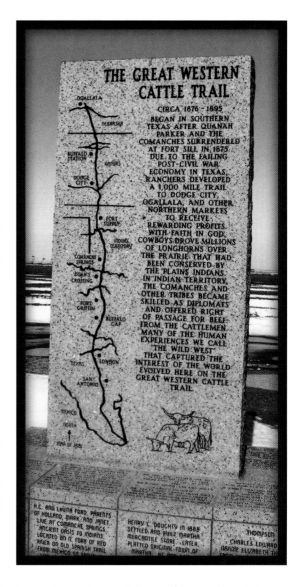

Location: four miles east of Altus, Oklahoma, Jackson County, outside of the Altus Air Force Base, on Highway 62.

Authors' commentary:
This is an impressive and very fine monument. We particularly like the map. It shows major points along the Western Trail's pathway, and beyond Dodge City, including Buffalo Station on the Kansas Pacific Railroad.

The dates are mis-leading, however. The trail started in 1874 and had ceased to be used through the Altus and Friendship area by 1889, as indicated on the Friendship marker five miles northeast of this marker. Trail driving continued from Texas until 1897, but drovers used a route farther west.

The "1,000 mile trail to Dodge City, Ogallala, and other northern markets" is not correct. From south Texas, it was around 900 miles to Dodge City, Kansas, and another 900 miles to the northern territories — a much longer trail than indicated.

This marker was erected after 1965 because of the use of the term: "Great Western Cattle Trail," which was coined by trail historian Jimmy Skaggs in 1965.

Boyd wrote that the road was a sign of activity because other than the military road, "the only signs of human life they saw were a few wagon tracks and old camps of buffalo hunters."[34] (Note: Side Bar Box)

The trail continued north passing between the North Fork of the Red River and present-day Altus.[35] A stage station on the Salt Fork River next to the Mobeetie Trail, that connected Fort Elliott (Mobeetie) to Henrietta, was located approximately two and one half miles west of present-day Altus. The Sand Station was established in 1879, but the cowboys called it "Buttermilk Station." Another small settlement, Frazer, later developed "on the waters of the Frazer (the Salt Fork of the Red River)..., West near Sand Station."[36] One of the very early settlers to Greer County was P. H. Holt who located in Frazer in 1884.[37]

Moving north up the trail, following Tennant's map, a location labeled "Friendship Store" appears. There was no community of Friendship there during the cattle-driving days. Refer to the marker.

It was in this general area that Lewis Neatherlin, in 1876, met a group of Indians requesting a toll. Neatherlin did not argue:

May 20:
Everything all right this morning. I got an early start and made good time until 11 o'clock when we met a body of Wichita Indians, who treated us friendly but wanted 2 cows. Not feeling disposed to the contrary, I gave the cows to them. Then they wanted sugar, coffee, flour and soap, but I was getting a little tired of them and wanted to be on the march, so I give the chief 1 1/2 lbs. of coffee and a very small piece of soap. Told them that was all I would let them have, so they left and we went on our way. Made a good evening's drive.[38]

> The authors have found no evidence that this Fort Elliott-Fort Sill military road was used as a splinter route from the Western Trail. The only time this would have been convenient would have been after 1880 when the Kansas border towns of Caldwell and Hunnewell opened up, and the Chisholm Trail was revived as a main trunk line. Cattle outfits destined to deliver herds to Fort Sill or to these Kansas border towns, could have left the Western Cattle Trail, traversed across the Comanche-Kiowa-Apache Reservation to Fort Sill, then used the Fort Sill-Fort Reno military road on to the Cheyenne Arapaho Reservation before connecting with the Chisholm Trail.

S. H. Tittle recalled his trail drive of 1879 to Tennant who interviewed him in the early 1930s. He used the names of places in the present day, even though the locations were not there in 1879:

---

[34]Jodean Martin, "The Empire of Greer County, Texas," online: http://files.usgwarchives.org/ok/jackson/history/greerhistory.txt [accessed Oct. 14, 2009]

[35]H. S. Tennant: the Western Trail was five miles east of Altus where it crossed Highway 62. Ibid, 87.

[36]Buttermilk was one of the favorite products that cowboys could get from road stands and homesteaders. Perhaps, on occasion, this Sand Station furnished buttermilk, thus the name. In 1891 the Frazer settlement was flooded and the settlers moved two and one half miles east to higher ground and changed the town's name to Altus — meaning in Latin "high ground." (http://countyest.okstate.edu [accessed June 17, 2011] and http://files.usgwarchives.org [accessed Oct. 14, 2009]

[37]Pioneer Edition of 1935, July 21 *Mangum Daily Star*, Sec. A, Pages 1-4. Also online at http://www.rootsweb.ancestry.com [accessed Oct. 11, 2009]

[38]Leo Kelly, ed. *Up the Trail in '76*, 19.

From Doan's Store the trail went along the West side of North Fork until it got to Navajo. From Navajo the trail went on up to where it crossed the North Fork of Red River which was at a ford due north of old Warren.[39]

Navajo, about four miles east of Alfalfa (Friendship), was established in 1886. Arthur Yeakly and his mother built a home at the location in 1884,[40] but the town officially started when two brothers-in-law, W. H. Acers and H. P. Dale established a general store in expectation of engaging in some Indian trade and to provide supplies to outfits on the Western Trail. Located in a valley of the Navajo Mountains, part of the Wichita Mountain range, the partners built their store within a couple of miles of the North Fork, and three miles outside of the Comanche-Kiowa-Apache Indian Reservation, and four miles east of the cattle trail. When Acers and Dale petitioned a post office, the Post Office Department insisted on adding an "e" to the Navajo name

3

WESTERN CATTLE TRAIL

IN 1875 THE LAST FREE BANDS OF COMANCHES AND KIOWAS WERE CONFINED TO THE RESERVATIONS AT FORT SILL, ALLOWING REGULAR CATTLE DRIVES OVER THE WESTERN CATTLE TRAIL, WHICH CONTINUED UNTIL ABOUT 1888. BY THE TIME THE DRIVES ENDED, MILLIONS OF LONGHORNS HAD PASSED THIS WAY, THROUGH WHAT IS NOW FRIENDSHIP, BOUND FOR DODGE CITY. THIS AREA WAS GREER COUNTY, TEXAS UNTIL 1896, WHEN THE SUPREME COURT DETERMINED IT WAS A PART OF OKLAHOMA TERRITORY. AFTER IT WAS OPENED FOR HOMESTEADING IN 1897, SETTLERS POURED IN, SEEKING FREE LAND AND A NEW LIFE.

OKLAHOMA HISTORICAL SOCIETY AND FRIENDSHIP HISTORICAL PROJECT

Location: on the northeast corner of the intersection in Friendship, across the road from the Friendship Baptist Church. Next to this marker is the white concrete post inscribed "Gr. Western Tr." erected by Rotary Club International in 2004.

Authors' commentary:
When referring to Tennant's map (Map #4-4), we wonder why he and the Department of Oklahoma State Highway Commission put "Friendship Store" on the map. There may have been a road house on the trail in that locale, which, so far, we have not been able to find any evidence of, but the community of Friendship and post office (Alfalfa, 1903) were not there during the trail-driving days. The marker correctly states that.

If there were a road house, dugout, or refreshment stop for the cowboys in this area, it probably was not called Friendship. The town's name seems to come from the Friendship Baptist Church that was located here in 1908.

The marker is very well done. Even the date 1888 is accurate, for after that date, the Western Trail had moved west. We just wish these markers would indicate that cattle herds went beyond Dodge City!

---

[39]S. H. Tittle, interview by H. S. Tennant. "The Texas Cattle Trails," *Chronicles of Oklahoma*, Vol 14 (March, 1936) 103.
[40]*Mangum Daily Star*, July 25, 1935.

in order to avoid confusion with another post office by that name.[41] John and Lum Bennight built a long, red building providing a stock of general merchandise, and Ed Clark opened a saloon that housed gambling tables and a bar complete with brass rail. W. H. H. Cranford operated a drug store where he sold drugs, notions, cosmetics, and toiletries. Many of his customers were the Indians from the reservation who bought his patent medicines with high alcohol content because federal law prohibited the sale of liquor to Indians. There were also John Brown's grocery store, the home of Dr. H. C. Redding, a small unpainted church, and the City Hotel.

Navajoe grew and became a small retail center for incoming squatters who were taking the chance that their claims would later be honored after the Greer County dispute was settled. It was also the nearest trading post for the Comanche and Kiowa who had "grass money" to spend from leasing their land to cattlemen, and it was a supply point for chuck wagons from off of the Western Trail.

Even though the Western Trail went by Navajoe for only about three years, it continued to thrive for another twelve or so years. However, Navajoe eventually came to an abrupt end. Edward Everett Dale has written:

> it was young, lusty, and vigorous with hopes and dreams for a future that were never to be realized….Navajoe was never a large town as Oklahoma regards size now but for many years it was the largest and most important one which a traveler would pass near in a journey north over the Western Cattle Trail from Vernon, Texas to Woodward, a distance of some two hundred miles. Moreover, it was the trading center for the people of an area far larger than is the so-called trade territory of almost any Oklahoma town today with a population of upwards of ten thousand.[42]

In 1901, when the Comanche-Kiowa-Apache Indian lands were opened up for white settlement and 13,000 acres of land were taken up in 160-acre tracts by hopeful settlers, the town of Navajoe collapsed and soon disappeared.[43]

Warren, to the north, was a settlement just south of the North Fork river crossing. Settlers appeared in this locale around 1886. The post office was established on February 25, 1888. Tennant recorded that the trail went "3/4 miles east of Warren, Oklahoma, in the NW1/4 of Section 27, T4N, R19W." A well and a camp ground was located here. From this resting spot the trail continued northwest through the "sand hills to the crossing of North Fork of Red River."[44] The town

---

[41]H. S. Tennant and the Oklahoma State Highway Commission chose to not place Navajoe on their map. At the time of their research (1931-1933) the town was gone and its foundations had given away to farm ground.

[42]Edward Everett Dale, "Old Navajoe," *Frontier Times*, Vol 24, No. 5, Feb. 1947, 307-320.

[43]Map, "Historic Sites in the Friendship Area," from website "History of Friendship, Oklahoma," http://www.rootsweb.com [accessed June 18, 2007]

[44]H. S. Tennant, "The Two Cattle Trails," *Chronicles of Oklahoma*, Vol 14 (March, 1936) 103. As mentioned before, one of the old timers that Tennant interviewed and gleamed information from about the trail was Nathaniel Jacob McElroy. He and his family were early settlers of the Warren community, and their farm was near the North Fork of the Red River. The McElroy farm was noted on the Tennant map. (Sec. 14, T4N, R19W)

had a school, grocery store, blacksmith shop, a doctor, and a few other businesses.[45] Because Warren was established at the end of the Western Trail era, the community was a trail town for only one or two years. By 1889, few herds, if any, used this portion of the Western Trail.

Cattle herds and their outfits left Greer County and forded the North Fork of the Red River at a crossing known as "Trail Crossing" or "Warren Crossing." Cowboys remembered a small store on the west bank of the river at the crossing before leaving Greer County. It was on the east side of the trail and was owned by Tom Wilson and John Passmore. The two had opened for business in 1883 and sold cartridges, tobacco, and other last-minute supplies to the drovers before they entered Indian Territory and the Comanche-Kiowa-Apache Reservation. Like Navajoe, the Wilson and Passmore store was a favorite spot for the Indians. It has been reported that the partners engaged in an enjoyable and profitable pastime of playing monte with the Indians.[46] The store is not shown on the Tennant map.

After fording the river and passing through the gap in the Wichita Mountains between Mt. Soldier and Mt. Tepee, herds stretched out into a valley. Neatherlin described the valley at some length:

May 21:

Drove some 2 miles and crossed the North Fork of Red River. Soon after crossing, we come to the foot of one peak of Wichita Mountains. I [climbed] about halfway to the top. Getting tired, I turned back. At the foot is as pretty [a] running spring branch as I ever seen and as good water I ever tasted in [my] life. Some post oak in the valley between the river and mountains. After dinner, our trail lay in a gap or valley with peaks on both sides. The Valley was about one mile wide and some 2 or 3 long. Mesquite grass and timber on it. While at dinner one of the men shot a bear but did not get it. The valley gradually widened out until the mountains were soon at a considerable distance on each side, but extending farther on our left. By night we were on a smooth prairie but found no water for the cattle and grass shorter than usual. Camp on a plain. No timber in sight.[47]

---

[45]Warren's post office was closed in 1920. Today there is no official city government, but residents live scattered in a thirty-square mile area that is considered Warren, Oklahoma. Jackson County Extension Service, "Warren," online: http://countyext.okstate.edu [accessed June 26, 2011]

[46]J. O. Tuton, news editor, "A History of the Empire of Greer," *The Mangum Daily Star*, Golden Anniversary issue, October 13, 1937, 17.

[47]Leo Kelly, *Up the Trail in '76*, 20. The taller peak had been visible since crossing the South Fork of the Red River at Doan's Crossing. At first, this mountain was named Mt. Webster, but because it looked like a tepee and became a drover's landmark, the name was changed to Mt. Tepee. Mt. Soldier had been the location of a confrontation on Christmas Day in 1868 between a band of Comanches and a troop of soldiers led by Col. Evans. One soldier was killed and thus, the encounter became known as the Battle of Soldier Spring and the Mountain, as Soldier Mountain. Today these mountains are called the Quartz Mountains. (Cecil Chesser, "Battle of Soldier Springs was 120 Years Ago Today," *Altus Times*, Dec. 25, 1988, and "The Great Western Cattle Trail," online at http://rebelcherokee.labdiva.com/cattletrail.html [accessed June 17, 2008]

N. J. McElroy recalled on his trail drive through the gap between the mountains that "There were some soldiers stationed in the Wichita Mountains near a big spring." (most likely in 1877)[48] This is the spring that Neatherlin had enjoyed a year earlier.

In this valley of the Wichita Mountains, the Comanche half-breed Indian Chief Quanah Parker was born. He had given up his war ways in 1875 and accepted reservation life and stayed close to his birth place on Elk Creek next to Soldier Mountain.[49] Quanah would often meet the cattle drives as they passed through the gap to demand payment for crossing into his tribal lands.

John Wells remembered Quanah Parker in his 1883 trail drive:

> …we came to Wichita Mountains, where we crossed the North Fork of Red River. There we found Quanah Parker and his friend waiting for us. He wanted a yearling donated, and said, 'Me squaw heap hungry.'… Quanah was dressed like a white man. His friend wore breech cloth and hunting shirt with a Winchester to his saddle. Quanah had on a hat and pants with a six-shooter in cowboy style. I made friends with Quanah, but I didn't like the looks of his friend. When the boss returned to the herd after dinner he gave Quanah a yearling and by that time four or five other warriors had appeared. They drove the yearling to their camp.[50]

T. J. Burkett also mentioned Quanah Parker in his recollection. When the Indian approached, he asked for "wohaw, plenty fat, heap slick." A yearling was cut out of the herd and given to Quanah Parker. Burkett commented further that "There were about 500 Indians camped near the trail, and nearly every herd that passed gave them a beef. Hundreds of cowboys knew Quanah Parker, and he had scores of friends among the white people."[51]

The Indians preferred to hunt and eat buffalo, but by 1876, buffalo herds had been greatly depleted and so the Indians now accepted beef into their diet. It appears that most outfits gave one or two cows for the privilege of crossing the Indian lands, but in Neatherlin's situation in Greer County, the group of Indians was hoping to get more — coffee and soap.

Another cowboy, Jeff Connolly, remembered the Indians at the Wichita Mountains. He was with a John Blocker outfit going to Colorado in 1886. According to Connolly, they had "shaped up ten herds" for the trail that season, but by the time they reached the Red River, the cattle had been cut and condensed into two large herds. He recalled:

---

[48]H. S. Tennant, "The Two Cattle Trails," 101.
[49]Quanah Parker (1850 (52) - 1911) was the son of War Chief Peta Nocona and Cynthia Ann Parker, a white woman who had been captured at the age of nine by Quahada warriors in 1836. She lived with the Comanches and had Quanah and two other children. Quanah was known as the "last chief of the Comanches." He had eight wives and 25 children. (Quanahparkerfamilyhistory@groups.msn.com)
[50]John Wells, "Met Quanah Parker on the Trail," in Hunter, 165.
[51]T. J. Burkett, "On the Fort Worth and Dodge City Trail," in Hunter, 927.

When we reached the Wichita Mountains, in Indian Territory, the Indians met us there and wanted beef. I had a big black range steer I had picked up in Texas, and when I got up in the roughest part of the mountains I cut this steer out and told them to go after him. The steer outran them and got away and directly I saw them coming back, one after another, like they travel, but without any beef.[52]

After trailing through Indian encampments, the herds and drovers continued north, over a "very hard land, it being a general camping place. (level ground) We drove until 4 in the afternoon before we found water for the cattle at which time we reached a small, deep creek. The water very bitter," recorded Neatherlin that evening. They were at Gyp Springs.[53]

The trail continued west of present-day Lone Wolf and by Comanche Springs. The springs provided an area for camping near the North Fork of the Red River.[54]

4
THE GREAT WESTERN CATTLE TRAIL SOUTHWEST OKLAHOMA

QUANAH PARKER AND THE COMANCHES SURRENDERED AT FT. SILL IN 1875. TEXAS RANCHERS, BEGINNING IN 1876, CREATED THE 1000 MILE TRAIL FROM SOUTHERN TEXAS TO DODGE CITY, OGALLALA AND OTHER NORTHERN MARKETS. IN INDIAN TERRITORY, PLAINS INDIANS WERE SKILLED AS DIPLOMATS OFFERING RIGHT OF PASSAGE FOR BEEF. THE PEAK YEAR WAS PROBABLY 1881 WHEN 301,000 HEAD IN ABOUT 100 HERDS CROSSED THIS SITE. EACH HERD REQUIRED 10 MEN AND EACH COWBOY REQUIRED ABOUT 7 HORSES. DURING THE NINETEEN OR TWENTY YEARS OF THE TRAIL'S EXISTENCE, OVER SEVEN MILLION LONGHORNS CROSSED THE PRAIRIE MARKING IT THE LARGEST OF ALL CATTLE TRAILS.

SPONSORED BY KIOWA COUNTY HISTORICAL SOCIETY 2007

Location: three miles south of Lone Wolf, Kiowa County, Oklahoma on State Highway 44, east side of the road

Authors' commentary:
This attractive marker has a map that shows Lugert, Lone Wolf, Hobart, and Comanche Springs in Indian Territory north of Doan's Crossing. Even though 1876 was a big year for ranchers in Texas to head north to the newly established railhead at Dodge City, Kansas, and beyond, Texas herds were crossing over at Doan's Crossing to head north as early as 1874.

Some of the "other northern markets" were much farther than 1,000 miles. On specific information on the marker: the numbers, 1881 was the peak year; 7 million longhorns probably made the trip; and the Western Trail was the largest of all the cattle trails. These are all accurate. High marks for this one!

ref: Chronicles of Oklahoma, Vol. 38, 1960

---

[52] Jeff Connolly, "Hit the Trail in High Places," in Hunter, 193.
[53] Leo Kelly, (Neatherlin journal) May 22, 1876 entry. Tennant shows Gyp Springs in Section 7, T5N, R19W.
[54] Tennant does not mention "Comanche Springs" in his descriptions or his map, but instead says there were two "spring and camp ground" locations in Section 21, T5N, R19W and another in Section 21, T6N, R20W.

Here about a day's drive after passing through the gap, inspectors were waiting to check the herds. The purpose of this second inspection station that drovers faced after leaving Doan's Crossing was to not only inspect northbound herds on the Western Trail, but, later on, to also check the herds coming in from the southwest off of the Quanah Detour Route. Jeff Connolly, who was on the Western Trail, alluded to the inspection station when he wrote: "The next day [after going through the Wichita Mountains] the trail cutters looked us up and did not find anything."[55]

George W. Briggs was an inspector at the Springs. He had gone there in 1881, a year after serving as an inspector at Doan's Crossing. As stated previously in Chapter III, Briggs continued "to inspect all trail herds that went up the trail." He stayed there until 1889 when "it [trail driving] was discontinued.," Recall, that it was Briggs, who worked and lived at this junction, and referred to the Western Trail as the "Dodge Trail" because "there was a trail west of this trail that was used extensively in the early eighties." That trail, of course, was the Quanah Detour Route, a branch that rejoined the Western at Comanche Springs. Briggs, in 1881, had established a ranch just north of the Springs on Elk Creek where cattle could get water. S. H. Tittle recalled: "in order to obtain water for the cattle the trail swung in through George W. Briggs's ranch."[56]

Comanche Springs was also a main headquarters for soldiers who were stationed to escort the herds to the Washita River.[57] To assure protection of the Indian farms and to make sure there was no harassment of the trail drivers by the Indians, U.S. soldiers, starting in 1886, had a presence and provided an excort to the next soldiers' station.[58] Thus, Comanche Springs was a major location, not only because drovers were now accompanied by soldiers on their trek north, but also because this was one of the few locations where the Quanah Detour Route (Ghost Trail) intersected the Western. A review of this later route is in order.

---

[55] Jeff Connolly, in Hunter, 193. "Trail cutters" were inspectors who could cut out from the herd unbranded cattle or animals that did not have the correct herd brand.

[56] "Statement of S. H. Tittle with reference to location of Western Trail," in Tennant, "The Two Cattle Trails," *Chronicles of Oklahoma*, Vol 14 (March, 1936) 103. The Briggs ranch is identified on the Tennant map. Briggs' statement about trail driving being discontinued in 1889 is repeated because it verifies that the Western Trail and the Quanah Detour Route ceased to be used in that area after 1889.

[57] Briggs letter to Tennant, Ibid., 106. Briggs described Comanche Springs as on the "North Fork passing about four miles east of the present town of Lugert and about one mile east of the bridge of Highway No. 9, on North Fork." Ethel Taylor writes that "In 1888 Fort Sill troops met the cattle herds at Doan's crossing at the Red River, then escorted them north to the Washita River." ("The Great Western Cattle Trail," www.geocities.com [accessed Dec. 26, 2000]) We feel, however, that even though U.S. soldiers were visible at Doan's Store and in the Washita Mountains, most of the soldier escorts started at Comanche Springs around 1886.

[58] After the Indians were settled on reservations, government agents encouraged them to be less normadic and become involved in farming. North of Comanche Springs, cowboy outfits and their herds were no longer in Greer County, Texas, but were now on reservation lands and, in a way, were trespassing on the farms of the Indians.

THE WESTERN CATTLE TRAIL | 1874-1897

THE QUANAH DETOUR ROUTE (GHOST TRAIL) THROUGH GREER COUNTY AND INDIAN TERRITORY: (Maps #3-3 and #4-2)

In the later years of the Western Trail from south Texas, a relative little known route was established farther west of the main trunk line of the Western. It crossed the Red River above Quanah, Texas. Once into Greer County, its pathway passed west of present-day Duke, on Deep Red Run Creek, and on into Mangum on the Salt Fork of the Red River. At Mangum, the outfits had a choice. They could continue to drive northeast toward the North Fork of the Red River where at Comanche Springs there was an inspection station for herds leaving the state of Texas — and, at that point, merge with the Western Trail trunk line. Or, the herds and their drovers might continue north following the established Mobeetie Trail for a short distance, perhaps to avoid the inspection station at Comanche Springs, and ford the North Fork of the Red River on the northern border of Old Greer County. Trail drivers who opted not to rejoin the Western Trail at Comanche Springs either continued on the Mobeetie Trail into the Panhandle of Texas or used the Quanah Detour Route to rejoin the Western Trail farther up the line near Fort Supply.[59] To say it another way: Later herds that were on the Quanah Detour Route, after 1882-1883, could pick up the Mobeetie Trail at Mangum (established in 1884) and follow it for a ways before leaving the Mobeetie farther up the line to continue on its own path.

Walter Cynthia Ford homesteaded at Hext in Beckham County, Oklahoma Territory, in 1899. In his family history, *Our Niche in History*, he described using an established cattle trail from their homestead to Mangum, the closest town at the time. It was "one of the old cattle trails in western Oklahoma at the point where it crossed the Ford's farm between Sayre and Erick (Hext), Oklahoma," wrote his grandson in a letter to *The Sayre Record and Beckham County Democrat* in 2006. The grandson, LeRoy Ford of Fort Worth, had asked Harry Sinclair Drago, author of *Red River Valley*, about the trail. Drago answered that there were many diversions from the main Western Trail and "That [the] trail which crossed today's Beckham County, south of Sayre and north of Erick, was an integral part of the Western Trail cannot be doubted." — in other words, it was a branch of the Western Trail. Drago described this route as:

> An alternate route avoided passing through the Kiowa-Comanche reservation by keeping in Greer County, which was then in Texas jurisdiction, and passed the present towns of Altus and Mangum,

---

[59]An obsure map, discovered in *The Junior Historian*, shows this latter portion of the Quanah Detour Route as a split in the main branch of the Western Trail. This map is mentioned because it is one of the few pieces of evidence that shows that there was another more westerly route or, as Jimmy Skaggs named it: "Ghost Trail." The map does not show, however, the lower part of the Quanah Detour Route or Ghost Trail in Texas or its route through Quanah. Thus, to an observer of the Oklahoma map, the route appears to be a left fork of the Western Trail. ("Historic Trails of the Cattle Kingdom," imformation compiled from Gard, Webb, Dobie, and Potter. *The Junior Historian*, Sept. 1967, 15. We do not know who created this map using the four historians' work.)

THE WESTERN CATTLE TRAIL | 1874-1897

crossing the North Fork into the Cheyenne-Arapaho reservation west of present Sayre and the Washita at Red Moon. This route passed above Antelope Hills to cross the Canadian and continued up Little Robe and Commission Creeks about five miles from the 100th Meridian.[60]

What Drago is describing here is the Quanah Detour Route of the Western Trail system. (See Map #4-2) Once the herds reached the Sweetwater Creek where it joins the North Fork of the Red River and where Walter C. Ford later homesteaded, the cowboy outfits turned off of the Mobeetie Trail, going north, instead of west to Mobeetie, picking up the Fort Supply military road[61] and following it to a point south of the fort where it rejoined the Western trunk line. When LeRoy Ford posed his question to Dorothy Williams of the Oklahoma Historical Society, she responded by identifying the trail as the old Camp Supply Road that tied into the Fort Elliott and Fort Sill road system north of Hext.[62]

In summary then, the Quanah Detour Route crossed the Red River above the town of Quanah, Texas, where herds were inspected and moved through Greer County to Mangum. From Mangum, some trail herds turned northeast to go to Comanche Springs and rejoin the Western Trail. But other herds picked up the Mobeetie Trail and continued north for some distance, left that trail, and picked up the Fort Supply military route a short distance from Sweetwater Creek, and then continued on to Fort Supply on its military road. The detour did not go into the Texas Panhandle because of the quarantine.

THE TRUNK LINE OF THE WESTERN CATTLE TRAIL — COMANCHE SPRINGS TO EDWARD ROCK CROSSING: (Map #4-5)

North of Comanche Springs, trail drivers crossed a number of small streams. Neatherlin remarked in his entry on May 24: "Crossed 3 creeks. Do not know the name of any of them, but one thing I do know, they are troublesome to get the wagons over. Made some 10 miles."[63]

N. J. McElroy, in his interview with H. S. Tennant, described the streams as the trail continued north. After Comanche Springs, the herds turned "to a East course, then turned northeast and crossed Elk Creek west of Hobart about four or five miles."[64]

---

[60]LeRoy Ford, "Western Trail cuts through Erick area in late 1800's," letter and map submitted to *The Sayre Record and Beckham County Democrat*, January 4, 2006. Red Moon was a school built later on the Cheyenne Arapaho Reservation.

[61]Goins and Goble, *Historical Atlas of Oklahoma*, 93.

[62]*The Sayre Record and Beckham County Democrat*, January 4, 2006.

[63]Leo Kelly, Neatherlin journal, 20.

[64]"Statement of N. J. McElroy," in Tennant, "The Two Cattle Trails," 101-102. Briggs described the route using towns instead of creeks. He said that after leaving Comanche Springs, the trail went "due north to Elk Creek, thence north passing a little to the east of the present town of Canute. Thence north near the town of Butler, thence slightly west, passing a little to the east of Leedy." 107.

THE WESTERN CATTLE TRAIL | 1874-1897

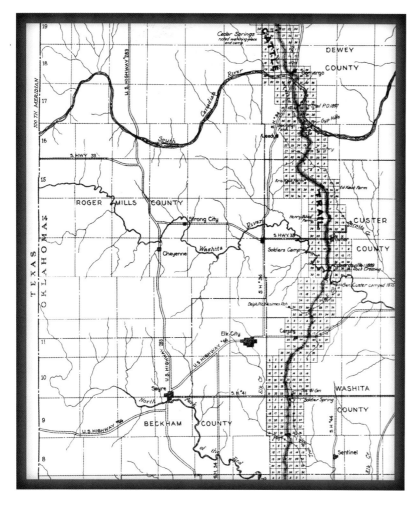

#4-5
The Center Portion of the Tennant Map:
This portion of the Tennant Map shows the Western Cattle Trail from Soldier Spring to north of the crossing of the South Canadian River.

At Big Elk Creek Crossing a horseshoe bend in the creek made it an ideal crossing place for cattle and wagons alike. The natural curve, carved by nature from red sandstone bluffs, assisted drovers in pointing the herds into the rock-bottom creek from the south. Cattle waded upstream around the bend and exited into a small fertile valley of bottom land between Elk Creek and just west of Trail Elk Creek. Here bands of Cheyenne and Arapaho hunted and camped on both sides of the trail. Chuck wagons, and other wagons as well, entered the water at the same location but drove farther upstream in the creek to a place with a more gradual upward incline to exit. The wagon pathway became a mail freight and local wagon crossing and was used for years after the cattle crossings. Eventually a wooden bridge was constructed close to the original crossing.[65]

Two of the creeks that Neatherlin may have referred to were Soldier Creek and Little Elk Creek, and the trail went west of another spring referred to as Soldier Spring. A spring gushed from a sandstone bluff into a large pool at its base, and, at the time, a lone cottonwood tree graced the site. The surrounding lowlands with its abundant tall bluestem and the cooling spring made for a popular resting spot for soldiers and their horses and drovers with their trail herds.[66]

After resting at Soldier Spring, the herds trailed up "Trail - Elk Creek," and according to McElroy, "...we continued down Tenth Cavalry Creek [Cavalry Creek] on the north side thereof, then turned north along a little creek called Dear

---

[65] The crossing later became known as the "Big Four Crossing" because it was located on land that was leased from the Kiowa by the Big Four Cattle Company. Their brand the #4 represented the four largest ranches in North Texas, at the time. The crossing was a mile north of old Highway 9 west of Hobart. (Ethel Taylor, "The Great Western Cattle Trail," on line at http://rebelcherokee.labdiva.com/cattletrail.html [accessed June 17, 2008])

[66] According to H. S. Tennant, Soldier Spring was located on the east side of Section 3, T9N, R20W. Over time, the high rock bluff has eroded away to a few outcroppings of red rock, and only a small spring-fed pool remains. When early settlers first arrived, they found the names of soldiers and their ranks carved into the bluff and surrounding rocks. Thus, the name, "Soldier Spring."

Man's Creek. After this we went down a Canon [sic] called Poker Creek. Next we crossed the Washita...."[67]

Neatherlin didn't know the names of the creeks in 1876, but again noted in his May 25th journal entry, "Crossed small, high-banked, muddy creeks and arrived on Washita River in time to go down and find 6 other herds, all waterbound."

The crossing at the Washita was referred to as Edward Rock Crossing ("Rock Crossing" on the Tennant map).[68] Later, the community of Edwardsville was established in 1889 in Section 26, T13N, R17W, near the site. The crossing was the second major junction and soldier station in Indian Territory on the Western Trail. At this point soldiers from Fort Elliott, stationed at the crossing, relieved the Fort Sill soldier escorts and accompanied the herds to the Canadian River.[69]

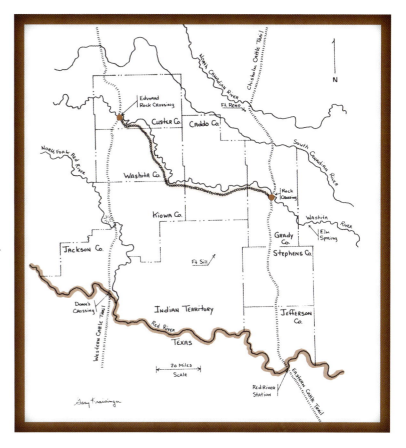

#4-6
The Washita River Feeder Route:
This map shows the feeder route following the south side of the Washita River from Rock Crossing on the Chisholm Trail on the Chickasaw Reservation, in present-day Grady County, to Edward Rock Crossing on the Western Trail in Cheyenne-Arapaho Reservation in present-day Custer County.

THE WASHITA RIVER FEEDER ROUTE: (Map #4-6)

As Comanche Springs, other routes used the Washita Rock Crossing. Throughout most of the life of the Western Trail in Indian Territory, a feeder route and two splinter routes used this location. Neatherlin alluded to this when he wrote about the "6 other herds, all waterbound" at the Washita.

The "other herds" that Neatherlin mentioned in his journal were likely from the a feeder route coming in from the Chisholm Trail. Leo Kelly, who edited Neatherlin's journal, verifies this when he observed that, "Most of these herds had probably turned west off the Chisholm Trail."[70] The year 1876 would have been the first season, or perhaps the second, that this route was being used. The last herds were trailed into eastern Kansas on the Chisholm Trail during the 1876 season, but

---

[67] "Statement of N. J. McElroy," in Tennant, "The Two Cattle Trails," 101-102 and the Tennant map.
[68] Both H.S. Tennant (map) and Wayne Gard (*The Chisholm Trail*, 80) refers to the crossing as "Rock Crossing." Goins & Goble (*Historical Atlas of Oklahoma*, 117) and Jimmy M. Skaggs (*Ranch and Range in Oklahoma*, 4) refer to the crossing as "Edward Rock Crossing." Ethel Taylor, local historian of the area, on her home page identifies it as: "The Washita River Crossing near Edwardsville Rock." (http://www.geocities.com:0080/Heartland/Hills/1263/cattletrail.html [accessed Dec. 26, 2000]) Betty Miller, a long-time resident of the area, says it has been called the Edward's Rock Crossing for as long as she can remember. (interview with Lyle K. Miller, Clinton, OK, son of Betty, July 13, 2011)
[69] "Soldiers Camp" is marked on the Tennant map as being three miles northwest of the Washita crossing.
[70] Leo Kelley, *Up the Trail in '76*, 21.

THE WESTERN CATTLE TRAIL | 1874-1897

E. C. Abbott, aka Teddy Blue, (1860-1939) with a FUF cattle outfit from Texas in 1883, used the Washita River Feeder Route to connect with the Western Cattle Trail in Indian Territory. He would later tell of his experiences on this trip to Montana to Helena Huntington Smith who published We Pointed Them North *in 1939.*

Photo courtesy of Montana Historical Society Research Center, Helena, Montana.

many outfits and their herds were still using the familiar trail in 1877, at least for a portion of their northbound journey. They used the familiar trail but veered off to the west in either Texas or Indian Territory and used the Western Trail. The Washita River Feeder Route provided the first opportunity in Indian Territory for herds to connect with the Western Trail.

Drovers and their herds on the old Chisholm Trail on the Chickasaw Reservation, in current Grady County, trailed to the Rock Crossing on the Washita River down river from the Edward Rock Crossing on the Western. At this point they turned northwest and followed the Washita River along its south side until reaching the Edward Rock Crossing of the Washita on the Cheyenne-Arapaho Reservation, in current Custer County, and crossed the river there.[71]

---

[71]Wayne Gard, *The Chisholm Trail*, 228; Goins and Goble, *Historical Atlas of Oklahoma*, 99.

E. C. Abbott, Teddy Blue, in his trail drive of 1883 from San Antonio, used this Washita River Feeder Route. His outfit for the FUF, a New England owned ranch, was hired to deliver a herd to the Yellowstone River in Montana. The drovers, including Teddy Blue, crossed the Red River at the confluence of the Washita River and the Red River near Preston Bend on the old Shawnee Trail and continued northwest along the Washita until they came to the Edward Rock Crossing where they joined the Western Trail.[72]

Neatherlin described the fording of the rocky-bottomed Washita.

May 26:

Early this morning we were making preparations to cross. Rafted over our baggage and pulled the wagons through the water by hand. Set the cooks to getting dinner and at 12 o'clock everything was over and dinner ready. The Washita here is about 50 feet wide.[73]

THE RED FORK RANCH SPLINTER ROUTE AND CALDWELL, KANSAS: (Map #4-7)

North of the crossing of the Washita, a splinter route was established during the 1881 season. On June 2, 1880, the Atchinson,.Topeka, & Santa Fe extended its line to Caldwell, Kansas, and the small trading post town suddenly became a railhead from which to ship cattle.

From its beginning in 1871 to the close of the trail in 1876, it had been a stopover for cowboys on the Chisholm Trail headed into Abilene, Ellsworth, Wichita, and Newton. The group of frame houses and rough shacks that paralleled the cattle trail was in Kansas, but it was close enough to the border that the quarantine law could be circumvented. Stockyards were built on the state line about two miles southeast of Caldwell, "designed to accept cattle from Indian Territory" and where the cattle could be loaded into stock cars without entering Kansas.[74]

At the same time, the Kansas City, Lawrence and Southern Railroad built a line straight south of Wellington and platted the border town of Hunnewell, Kansas, fourteen miles east of Caldwell. The two neighboring railheads revived the Chisholm Trail in 1880, causing a reversal of recent cattle trail traffic patterns. For the previous

---

[72]E. C. Abbott (Teddy Blue) and Helena H. Smith, *We Pointed them North*, map on vii. The map, "The Texas Trail," in *We Pointed them North*, shows the herd crossing the Red River north of Dallas, which would have been the old Shawnee Trail, and using the Washita River to connect with the Western Trail. The route goes all the way to Montana; it was Teddy Blue's last trail drive in 1883. The text does not support this map very closely, however, which posses a problem. To use this eastern crossing of the Red River in 1883 would have been a very difficult task because of settlements and fencing. A route farther west would have made more sense at that late of a date., but the map does show the feeder route to the Western Trail.

[73]Leo Kelly, Neatherlin's journal, 21. S. H. Tittle told H. S. Tennant that they crossed the Washita River in 1879 about at the mouth of Oak Creek, just south of Butler. (Tennant, "The Two Cattle Trails," 103)

[74]Bill O'Neal, *Border Queen Caldwell*, 75-77.

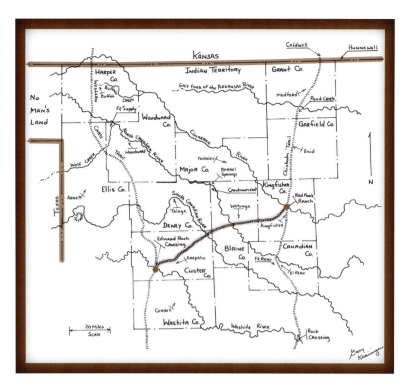

#4-7
The Red Fork Ranch Splinter Route:
This map shows the splinter route from north of the Washita crossing on the Western Trail (Edward Rock Crossing) on the Cheyenne-Arapaho Reservation in present-day Custer County, Oklahoma, going northeast across Indian Territory, crossing the South Canadian River and the North Canadian River to connect with the Old Chisholm Trail at the Red Fork Ranch on the Cimarron River.

three years, 1877-1879, the Chisholm Trail had ceased to be a trunk line into Kansas to deliver cattle to northern markets and had become a feeder to the Western Trail. (However, cattle were still trailed north to stock ranches in Indian Territory and the Outlet.) Now, with Caldwell and Hunnewell serving as new, active railheads, the Chisholm trunk line in Indian Territory was reopened and accepted herds from feeder routes from the Western.[75]

Caldwell's and Hunnewell's appeal and marketing strategy to Texas cattlemen was their proximity to Kansas City and other eastern markets. The shorter rail time saved money, especially in the initial year of 1880. Caldwell, with the AT & SF, and Hunnewell, with the KCL & S, carried on a fierce rate war that year which drove rail prices down. When railroad officials realized that they were losing money because of the battle over rail prices, the AT & SF bought out the KCL & S. By the end of September the Santa Fe was building a roundhouse south of its new depot in Caldwell, and from then on the Santa Fe controlled the shipping prices from Dodge City, Caldwell, and Hunnewell.[76]

During the spring of 1880, Caldwell prepared for the connection with the Santa Fe railroad by building numerous saloons, gambling houses, brothels, and mercantiles, and its population tripled almost overnight. On June 16, 1880, the first shipment of cattle was made from its stockyards, which were still under construction. When the season was over, *The Caldwell Post* bragged that the town had shipped more cattle than its rival — 25,531 to Dodge's 17,957.[77]

---

[75] The lower part of the Eastern/Chisholm Trail system was conjested with ranches, fences, and people, but the the portion in Indian Territory to the Kansas border could still be used. When we refer to the entire Eastern Trail system, from Texas to Nebraska, we use the term "Eastern/Chisholm." When we discuss that portion of the trail in Indian Territory and Kansas, we use the term "Chisholm Trail" because that is the home of the original term. Many Texans do not consider the term "Chisholm" as correct in their state.
[76] Bill O'Neal, 75-77.
[77] John L. Lillibridge, *The Red Fork Ranch and Its People*, 47, and Goins and Goble, 117. In the 1880 season, 394,784 head of cattle were trailed out of the state of Texas. If Dodge shipped out only 17,957 and only 25,531 were splintered off the Western Trail and shipped out of Caldwell, then that gives one an idea of how many cattle continued beyond Dodge. Even considering the sales of stock to local ranchers, to Indian agents, and to those who wintered cattle in Indian Territory, it still proves our point that a vast majority of the cattle were driven north of Dodge City.

Since 1876, Texas cattlemen had turned off of the Chisholm Trail at Red Fork Ranch on the Cimarron River to divert their herds from the eastern Kansas cattle towns, which were behind the quarantine line, and trailed herds instead to Dodge City over lands in the Cherokee Strip. But now there was a choice. Luther A. Lawhon, a trail hand for Cal Mayfield who was driving "one thousand head of ML horses," wrote of their decision upon reaching the Cimarron in 1880:

> We left the Hill pasture in Live Oak County for a long and arduous drive to Dodge City, Kansas…. after many hardships and exciting experiences, we again enjoyed the comfort of "God's land," in the frontier town of Caldwell, Kansas. [The year] was one of the worst ever known on the trail. Storms, rain and lightning…. it was a run night after night, with but short intermissions. We had crossed the Cimarron River, out of the Indian Territory, and came to where the *Dodge [Cimarron Cut Off] and the Caldwell trails forked, Mr. Mayfield decided to follow the latter trail, as Caldwell was somewhat nearer.* After resting at Caldwell for a few days, the herd was "split up" and I was assigned to go with a bunch which was loaded on the cars and shipped to Kansas City.[78] (italics added)

In the spring of 1881, as Caldwell braced for its first full season of Texas cattle herds and cowboys, the Cherokee Strip Live Stock Association met in Caldwell with the purpose of "realigning the cattle trails" in Indian Territory. The association's cattlemen, who leased land from the Cherokees in Indian Territory, actually wanted to confine the Texas herds to the old Chisholm Trail. Now that the Chisholm Trail in Indian Territory had been revived, herds would come across the Cherokee Strip and through the leased lands and to the border near the closest supply depot. With the arrival of the Santa Fe rails at Caldwell, the Cherokee Strip Association members felt that the trails through Indian Territory needed adjustment. They were loyal to Caldwell[79] and wanted herds funneled into that community, where they had business interests, and not use the Cimarron Cut-Off to Dodge City, Kansas which also went through their grazing lands in the Strip. Therefore, the association appointed J. W. Chastain to "superintend the laying out of new cattle trails through Indian Territory." A specific directive to Chastain was as follows:

> A new trail is to be laid out to accommodate the cattle driven from the Western Trail, Pan Handle and Northwestern Texas to Caldwell and Hunnewell, leaving the Western Trail in the vicinity of the Washita River and will intercept the Caldwell and Hunnewell Trail at the Red Fork crossing of the Cimarron.

---

[78]Luther A. Lawhon, "The Men Who Made the Trail," in Hunter, 201.

[79]Caldwell was the closest town to the "people down in the Territory" or "down below." Some families who lived in the Strip (Outlet) also had homes in Caldwell, and their children went to Caldwell for schooling. (Lillibridge, *The Red Fork Ranch and Its People*, 50)

In other words, Chastain was asked to create a feeder route from the Western to the old Chisholm Trail for the benefit of Caldwell. Another goal of the Livestock Association was to see that:

> All parts of the old trail north of the Cimarron River and known as the Dodge Trail that leaves the eastern trail at Red Fork Ranch, following Turkey Creek and Eagle Chief Creek, then to the Cimarron at the mouth of Buffalo Creek, is to be permanently closed and abandoned.

In other words, to make sure that the herds continued on to Caldwell and not splinter off on the Cimarron Cut Off to Dodge, the cut-off would be closed. They wanted to limit the number of herds coming across the Strip and to prevent exposure to infected cattle with Texas Fever from south Texas. Another directive given to the association's superintendent was that he lay out

> A new trail in the place of the one abandoned [Cimarron Cut-off to Dodge] to be opened for the accommodation of herds that are on the Eastern or Caldwell Trail and whose destination is Dodge or points north of there. This trail will leave the Eastern Trail south of the [North] Canadian River [in the Fort Reno area], crossing the North Canadian west of the Cantonment Post and intercepting the Dodge Trail at Buffalo Creek.[80]

Thus, to keep the Texas herds farther south of the Strip and away from the association members' ranches, a new feeder route to the Western Trail was to be developed for those herds and trail drivers who had contracts or buyers at Dodge City or farther up the trail.

The splinter route to the Chisholm may have been identified by various names. It has been referred to as the Red Fork Ranch Splinter Route. Some cowboys called it the Caldwell Route, or the Hunnewell fork, as Ernest Fletcher did. Fletcher was fourteen in 1884 and started north with a herd under the brand of LIL. They were trailing "about 3,000 head, all beef cattle" to be "trailed north to Honey Wells, Kansas." They "started by way of Vernon, [Texas], crossing the Red river at Doan's store." Fletcher then wrote: "When we got to where the trail forked, [Edward Rock Crossing] one fork going to Honey Wells and the other to Dodge City, we were between two Smith and Elliott herds." Wanting to see the Powder River in Wyoming, "where one of the Smith & Elliott herds were headed," Fletcher secured a job with one of their herds and continued north on the Western Trail trunk line to Dodge City, while the LIL herd went to Hunnewell on the splinter route.[81]

---

[80]Notice here that the association used the term "Eastern" to refer to the Chisholm Trail in Indian Territory. (Lillibridge, Ibid, 49-50)

[81]Ernest M. Fletcher, Forbes Parkhill, ed, *The Wayward Horseman*, 33-35. Fletcher was released at Dodge from the Smith & Elliott herd. He hired on with the Pryor Brothers, under Col. Ike T. Pryor, and continued on to Colorado. The Pryor Brothers were moving fifteen herds, with 45,000 head, northward over the trail to Colorado in 1884.

This Red Fork Ranch Splinter Route ran from north of the Washita crossing on the Western Trail, northeast across Indian Territory, crossing the South Canadian River and the North Canadian River to connect with the old Chisholm Trail at the Red Fork Ranch on the Cimarron River at the mouth of Turkey Creek. This splinter route was the one that J. W. Chastain had plotted under the direction of the Cherokee Strip Association in the spring of 1881.

The Red Fork Ranch had been a vital location in the old days. It was a drover's camp that catered to the cowboys. Located in a natural break or narrow opening of the Cross Timbers, a thick belt of trees running from the Arkansas border to central Indian Territory, the ranch continued to service trail traffic after the Kansas 1875 quarantine.[82] To many seasoned trail drivers, the Red Fork Ranch destination was a familiar one. After resting at the ranch, drovers and their herds continued north on the Chisholm, or Caldwell Trail, to the Kansas border and the Caldwell holding pens. The herds grazed in Indian Territory while the cowboys rode into Caldwell for supplies and entertainment.[83]

With the new branching of the feeder and splinter routes, the Red Fork Ranch lost a portion of the Chisholm Trail business from those that had been using the Cimarron Cut-Off, but it gained some business from the new splinter route from the Western Trail. The 1881 season actually turned out to be a fairly good year at Red Fork. John W. Hood, manager of the ranch, reported that seventy-eight cattle herds, totaling 110,792 head, and thirteen horse herds, totaling 4,585 head, had passed through the ranch that season. Of that number, Caldwell shipped out 31,644 head. It is not known how many head shipped out of Hunnewell that season. It had been a better season than 1880.[84]

THE WASHITA SPLINTER ROUTE TO CANTONMENT: (Map #4-8)

Another splinter route created by the cowboys and their herds started from the Washita Edward Rock Crossing. With the aim of getting their cattle to Caldwell, drovers pointed their longhorns on a straight path directly to Cantonment in Blaine County on the Canadian and then on to Caldwell.

The first Cantonment had been established in March 1879 as a mid-way point between Camp Supply and Fort Reno.[85] It had been established at Barrel Springs,

---

[82]The Red Fork Ranch continued to service the trail traffic after the Kansas quarantine of 1875 because it was the last opportunity in Indian Territory for cowboy outfits to turn off of the old Chisholm Trail to connect with the Western Trail. This Cimarron Cut-Off will be discussed shortly.

[83]Kraisinger & Kraisinger, *The Western, the Greatest Texas Cattle Trail*, 32-35. The Red Fork Ranch was located near present-day Dover, Oklahoma.

[84]Lillibridge, *The Red Fork Ranch and Its People*, 50.

[85]Cantonment" is a word for a temporary military fortification. The post on the North Canadian was simply known as "the Cantonment on the North Fork of the Canadian." As the result of the panic caused by Dull Knife and his band of Northern Cheyenne when they escaped from the reservation near Fort Reno in September of 1878, Lt. Col. Richard I. Dodge and four companies of the Twenty-third infantry from Fort Leavenworth, Kansas, established Cantonment midway between Fort Reno and Camp Supply on March 6, 1879. (Jon D. May, "Cantonment," Electronic Publishing Center of Oklahoma State University. http://digital.library.okstate.edu/encyclopedia [accessed July 24, 2011])

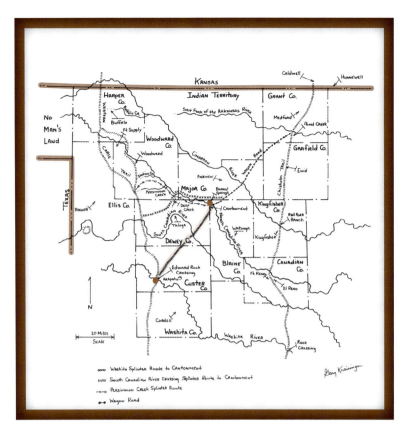

#4-8
The Washita Splinter Route to Cantonment:
This map shows the splinter route from north of the Washita crossing on the Western Trail (Edward Rock Crossing) on the Cheyenne-Arapaho Reservation in present-day Custer County, Oklahoma, going northeast to connect with Cantonment, (the military camp), on the North Canadian River in the Cheyenne-Arapaho Reservation in present-day Blaine County. From there, drovers and their herds could continue on the Wagon Road, crossing the Cimarron River and continuing northeast to Pond Creek on the old Chisholm Trail, crossing the Salt Fork of the Arkansas River, and trailing their herds to Caldwell on the Atchison, Topeka, Santa Fe Railway or to Hunnewell on the Kansas City, Lawrence & Southern Railroad, on the Kansas border. This splinter route opened up in 1881 after these two towns received rails in 1880.

eight miles north, northwest of the present-day Canton, next to the Camp Supply-Fort Reno military road.[86] Perhaps the post was located there because a wagon road from Wichita on the Arkansas River in Kansas by way of Pond Creek had been laid out in 1877 to connect with the military road at this point. Theodore Baughman in his book, *The Oklahoma Scout*, writes that in January of 1877, "Edward Finlan telegraphed to me at Dodge City to come to Wichita and join a party to lay out a trail from Wichita to Barrel Springs. On reaching Wichita I found the party all ready for service and awaiting my arrival."[87]

The party consisted of a detachment from the 24th Infantry, under the command of Lieut. Hyle, Benjamin F. Wilson, Cyrus Beard, and scout Theodore Baughman. The group also had with them a government ambulance, one escort wagon, and two four-horse baggage wagons. Baughman wrote that the weather, which, at first, produced a "a driving blizzard" and "continued cold and disagreeable," caused frequent "obstructions to our passage." At Salt Fork and Turkey Creek in the Territory, "our wagons broke through the ice, causing us a great deal of delay and trouble in extracting the wagons and horses, and giving us a good dunking."

The party angled southwest in Indian Territory, "experiencing much difficulty in finding a trail which would be passable and afford pasturage for cattle." They named one creek after Lieut Hyle and crossed the Cimarron River at a "good crossing" that

---

[86] Barrel Springs was located in Section 6, T19N, R13W. "Military Map of the Indian Territory, compiled under direction of 1st Lieut. E. H. Ruffner, Engineers Chief, Engineer Dept. of the Missouri, January, 1875." (Western History Collections, University of Oklahoma Libraries, Norman, OK., Box 2, Folder #4, 8614)

[87] Theodore Baughman was born in Ohio in 1845. The frontiersman was a scout for the US Army for twenty years, mostly in Indian Territory. When he guided the 24th Infantry to establish the Canton Trail, he was 32 years old. (Theodore Baughman, *The Oklahoma Scout*, (1886) 138)

Baughman had located a year before on another commission. After establishing the route to Barrel Springs, the party returned to Wichita in March of 1877.[88]

This wagon road provided "pasturage for cattle," and fed into the military road from the northeast. It later became a convenient feeder route to the Chisholm Trail for those cowboys and herds that came from the west off of the Western Trail toward Caldwell and Hunnewell. Even though, as Baughman reported, they forged a route from Wichita to Barrel Springs, the "Contone Trail" on the Sollers' map of the 1880s frontier shows this route only from Pond Creek on the old Chisholm Trail to Contonment.[89] Because the road was established after the Kansas quarantine of 1875 and Wichita was, therefore, no longer a railhead for Texas through cattle, the road was originally established to freight goods from the Wichita railhead into Indian Territory.[90]

By the time Henry C. Keeling was appointed to the position as post trader at Cantonment in the winter of 1879, the post had just been relocated to the south bank of the North Fork of the Canadian River.[91] Keeling explained, in his memoirs, that the post had originally been located in the hills eight miles north, shortly after the Dull Knife raid through Western Kansas in 1878, at a place known as Barrel Springs, but when Col. Dodge and his 23rd Infantry marched into Barrel Springs a few months later, he did not like the location in the sand hills and relocated the cantonment to the river.

Keeling, who became aquainted with and befriended many of the Indians who camped around the post, later recalled how the Indians "were really starving on the short rations furnished by the Government. They would not eat wild turkey, which was plentiful at the time, as they claimed it would make cowards of them, nor would they eat fish; nothing but beef or buffalo."

Therefore, during 1880 and 1881, when this splinter route from the Washita Crossing was first used, there was a great deal of trouble with the Indians because the Interior Department's cut in rations. A group of angry, young warriors were poised to go on the warpath. Even old Stone Calf, a Southern Cheyenne chief, raised his teepee "within five feet" of Keeling's front door "and ornamented it with a string of scalps hung on a rawhide lariat," to show that he was not afraid of the soldiers. The chief told Keeling and Capt. Charles Wheaton, the post commander, that "unless the

---

[88]Baughman, Ibid, Chapter XVI, "The Trail from Wichita to Cantonment," 139-141.

[89]Map, by W. Sollers, "Southwestern Frontier in the 1880's," Angie Debo, ed. *The Cowman's Southwest, being the reminiscences of Oliver Nelson*, and.Goins and Goble, *The Historical Atlas of Oklahoma*, shows this road from the Salt Fork of the Arkansas (Pond Creek) intersecting the Fort Reno - Camp Supply military road about midway. It is labeled "Wagon Road," 121.

[90]Robert L. (Bob) Klemme of Enid, Oklahoma, Chisholm Trail historian, has found references to this Cantonment Trail in his extensive research of the Chisholm Trail. Ruts of this wagon road were once visible, and still may be, one mile west, two miles south, and one quarter mile back east of Hillsdale, Oklahoma, next to the radio tower. The location is now used for agriculture. Also, ruts were once visible two miles west and one half mile north of Ringwood near Highway 412. Interviews and emails between Klemme and Gary Kraisinger, January - May, 2011.

[91]Colton's Atlas of 1882 labeled the encampment as "New Cantonment." It was near the south bank of the North Fork of the Canadian River. In today's geography that would be in the northwestern part of Blaine County, Oklahoma, about four miles west and a mile north of the town of Canton, its name a derivative of Cantonment.

Government issued rations he would go on the warpath. That he would rather die fighting than to starve to death."[92]

This uneasiness was happening in and round Cantonment while Caldwell was laying in provisions and preparing for its first big season of the Texas cattle trade. Wagons of supplies from Caldwell merchants were attacked by the renegades, and when Texas cattle herds came across the reservation, trail bosses were faced with demands for cattle by the Indians. In the summer of 1881, the situation became so intense that the post commander instructed his Indian scouts to go to the cattle crossing on the South Canadian as herds entered into the Cheyenne-Arapaho Reservation to "tell the cattlemen that if they wanted any protection to send [word] to the post." Henry Keeling was also the post's interpreter and took his turn going to the South Canadian to help negotiate the price for the Indian toll. He wrote later, "I had to have the cattlemen give the Indians two or three head from each herd that crossed, and it seemed to satisfy them."

When the cowboys and their herds reached Cantonment on their way to Caldwell in 1880 and 1881, they saw a military encampment somewhat more advanced than the expected temporary post of tents and hastily erected log huts. The soldiers' barracks were made of logs or pickets placed vertically as closely as possible, with one end buried in the ground, and the exposed logs then cleated with a mortar made of a mixture of clay and grass. The roofs were a flat layer of logs covered with brush "which, in turn, was covered with a layer of course grass." Later on, however, shingles were added to the earth roofs, and even though the camp was to be temporary and never officially named, three permanent buildings of stone masonry construction were erected. These were used for a hospital, post bakery and commissary, and officers' quarters.

In the later seasons of trail driving, drovers passed by the abandoned cantonment that was eventually rehabilitated as a mission and Indian school organized and maintained by the Mennonites.[93]

The Caldwell short-cut from the Washita caused a great deal of resentment by the Indians because the cowboys and their herds damaged the Indian farms in and around Cantonment. As the most direct and shortest route, drovers and their herds left the Washita crossing, drove to Cantonment on the Canadian River, passed over the Indian grounds, and followed the old wagon road that was blazed in 1877. The wagon road already had well-established crossings on the Cimarron and the Salt

---

[92]Henry C. Keeling, "My Experience with the Cheyenne Indians," *Chronicles of Oklahoma*, Vol. 3, No. 1, March, 1925. Republished by permission of the Kansas State Historical Society of the address by Henry C. Keeling, of Caldwell, Kansas, before the thirty fourth annual meeting of the Kansas State Historical Society, Dec. 7, 1909. Acquired online July 1, 2011, http://digital.library.okstate.edu/Chronicles

[93]Cantonment was abandoned by Capt. Charles C. Hood and Companies B and F of the 24th Infantry on June 14, 1882. The buildings and grounds were turned over to the Interior Department and it, in turn, allowed the Mennonite Church to occupy and establish a mission and school for the Cheyenne and Arapaho Indians at the site. When the Darlington Agency for the Cheyenne and Arapaho, near Fort Reno, was subdivided into three agencies in 1903, Cantonment was selected as one of these subdivisions. (Joseph B. Thoburn, "The Story of Cantonment," *Chronicles of Oklahoma, Vol. 3, No. 1*, March, 1925, 72. on line: http://digital.library.okstate.edu/Chronicles)

Fork of the Arkansas and connected to the old Chisholm Trail south of Caldwell near Pond Creek.

It was the intention of the area's military personnel that the Texas drovers use the Red Fork Ranch Splinter Route rather than the shortcut by way of Contonment to Caldwell. Troops were even placed at the Washita Edward Rock Crossing to point herds in that direction or escort them on to the South Canadian River over the main trail. (See Map #4-7) It is not known how successful the military was in forcing use of the Red Fork Ranch Splinter Route.

"CATTLE TRAILS ACROSS INDIAN RESERVATION:" (Map # 4-9)

In the Western History Collections at the University of Oklahoma Libraries in Norman, Oklahoma is a hand-drawn map that shows the Western and Chisholm trails and the splinter and feeder routes described previously. It is an "1881 official map app'd by Sec. of Interior Commissions of Indian Affairs H. Price sent to Mr. P. B. Hunt at Kiowa Agency, Anadarko."[94] This map, reproduced here, in part, was sketched at the time when J. W. Chastain, under the direction of the Cherokee Strip Live Stock Association, was charged to chart a new route for the Texas drovers. It was also the first full season for Texas herds coming from the south to head toward the newly established railheads of Caldwell and Hunnewell.

This very early map is unique and significant in that it shows the "cattle trail to Ft. Dodge, Ks" (the Western Trail) from the Red River, going through "Disputed Territory, Greer Co. Texas," continuing through Cheyenne-Arapahoe Reservation and going through the Cherokee Strip toward the Kansas line. On this map the trail goes around the east side of Camp Supply. The camp was actually a designated fort by 1881.

The "Abeline Cattle Trail," (the Chisholm) is shown from the Red River, going through the Chickasaw Reservation on north to the Kansas line. Missing from the map is the North Fork of Canadian River. Only the South Fork of the Canadian River is shown.

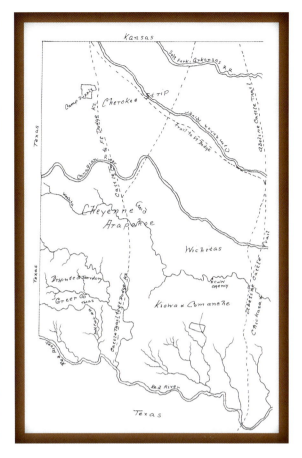

#4-9
"Cattle Trails Across Indian Reservation, 1881 official map app'd by Sec. of Interior Commissions of Indian Affairs H. Price sent to Mr. P. B. Hunt at Kiowa Agency, Andarko:"
This hand-drawn map was sketched by an unknown person during the time when J. W. Chastain, under the direction of the Cherokee Strip Live Stock Association, was re-defining pathways for the Texas drovers. It shows the "cattle trail to Ft. Dodge, Ks," (the Western Trail), the "Abeline Cattle Trail, (the Chisholm Trail), and an unmarked trail from north of the Washita River, connecting the Western Trail to the Chisholm Trail or what this study refers to as the "Cantonment Feeder Route" and the Wagon Road.

Map courtesy of the Western History Collection, University of Oklahoma Libraries, Norman, Oklahoma.

---

[94]This old map was discovered after our Map #4-8 was developed. It agrees with our research except it shows the Cimarron River Cut-off route south of the river and the Western Trail trunk line as going around the east side of the Camp Supply. Both of these issues will be discussed later in the chapter. (Western History Collections, University of Oklahoma Libraries, Norman, OK., Box 2, Folder #96, 8626)

Connecting these two systems is a feeder route from the "Cattle Trail to Ft. Dodge," just north of the Washita River, or the Cantonment Feeder Route and the wagon road, to the "Abeline Cattle Trail," joining together somewhere in Kansas. The map-maker did not label this route, but merely shows the splinter route as going, it is assumed, into Wichita, Kansas — which is the wagon road that Theodore Baughman helped blaze in 1877.

The other connecting route is the splinter route from the Chisholm Trail to the Western Trail, along the south side of the Cimarron River, which in this study is referred to as the Cimarron Cut-off. On the 1881 map, the route is labeled as the "Trail to Ft. Dodge."

THE TRUNK LINE OF THE WESTERN CATTLE TRAIL TO THE SOUTH CANADIAN RIVER:

After the Kansas quarantine of 1885, the Washita Edward Rock Crossing took on a different role. The location became a separation point for herds coming from the south. Only a portion of the total number of herds went to Caldwell, or Hunnewell. Texas cattlemen also sold their herds to Indian agents farther up the line, moved their own herds on to northern ranches, delivered herds to ranchmen on the northern plains, or drove the herds to railheads to be shipped east. Those herds that did not turn off on the Red Fork Ranch Splinter Route or the Caldwell route continued on the Western Trail, which was destined to detour around Kansas by trailing through Colorado. As a consequence, some drovers referred to the trail north of the Washita crossing as the "Colorado Trail."

As troops from Fort Supply, Fort Reno and Fort Elliott continued to monitor the trail herds, additional measures were undertaken to keep herds on the correct paths in order to prevent intrusions on Indian lands. By the spring of 1887, signs were posted at the Washita informing trail bosses of the northbound herds their choices--to continue on the Western Trail which would branch off to Colorado farther north or to shift to the splinter route to Caldwell to market their cattle.[95]

After crossing the Washita River on the Western Trail, the herds continued north. Again Neatherlin in 1876 recorded in his journal:

May 26:
We drove some 5 miles this afternoon over a beautiful, rolling prairie, but late in the evening we crossed the worst creek that we have seen. Had to unload the wagons, wading in soft mud to the knee to do it and broke one tongue. Bogged about 20 cattle but got them all out except 2.

The creek that the Neatherlin herds crossed, which he called the "worst creek" yet, was Barnitz Creek. The herd continued north through the Gyp Hills and McKenzie

---

[95]Robert C. Carriker, *Fort Supply, Indian Territory, Frontier Outpost on the Plains*, 174-75.

Flats, also called the South Canadian River low lands. Neatherlin's next day's journal told of more woes.

May 27:
Another bad creek in front by 9 o'clock. We had our wagon tongue spliced with rawhide and continued on our march. We had to turn left and head the creek going west. Got into some more real rocky hills, worse than those we passed on the 25th, with occasionally a deep ravine heading on either side of the trail. We drove until 3 in the afternoon before we found a place to get dinner. We again struck some high, gray-sandy prairies with skin oak, but no water. Cooked the last bread stuff we had for dinner. Started on but had to turn back on account of some hills and gullies that we could not hold the cattle on at night.[96]

---
[96]Kelly, Neatherlin's journal, 21.

Approximately six miles north of the Washita River crossing, herds crossed the California/Beale Wagon Road (See Commentary Below). Neatherlin and those who followed him crossed this old road and descended into the Canadian River valley. Neatherlin wrote in his journal that after driving "some 4 miles through steep hills and deep gulleys" the river came into view. The crossing area was "about 600 yards wide but the water was not exceeding 40 yards and not more than 12 inches deep." The location did not afford any comfort for the Neatherlin herds. After crossing, there was "no timber" and little water "that we can water the cattle at" and "as is common on sand the grass is very poor." The drovers camped in a dry ravine and had to dig in the sand to find enough water "to use in camp."[97]

Location: two miles north of Leedy, Dewey County, Oklahoma on Highway 34

Authors' commentary:
This marker points out a location on the Western Cattle Trail in Oklahoma. Like so many other markers, the text mentions Dodge City as if it were the end of the trail.

The California - Beale Wagon Road:
In 1858, Lt. Edward Beale was hired to improve a wagon road from Fort Smith, Arkansas to Albuquerque, New Mexico Territory. The War Department allocated $50,000 for this portion of the route. Beale's route was predominately along the South Canadian River in Indian Territory from present-day Eufalla (North Forktown) to Chouteau's Trading Post. From that point on, the route was along the south side of the river to the Antelope Hills.

The Western Cattle Trail crossed the California - Beale Road in Sec. 35, T 14n, R 19w. It appears that the two paths ran together for approximately five miles north, northwest separating in Sec. 3, T14n, R19w in current-day Custer County.

The California - Beale Wagon Road was the first federally funded highway to be constructed in the southwest going from Fort Smith, Arkansas to Los Angeles, California. The years of construction were from 1857 to 1860 at a cost of $210,000.[1]

---

[1] Interview and correspondence: Jack Beale Smith, Oklahoma City, Oklahoma, with Gary Kraisinger, Sept. 5, 2008.

---

[97] Neatherlin's journal, 21.

During the trail-driving days in Indian Territory, 1874-1889, there were long distances between sources for supplies. After leaving Doan's Store, the next "town" was Navajoe, and after that trail-drivers looked forward to Fort Supply, several days' drive to the north. Between Doan's Store and Fort Supply, there might be a lone stage station on the Mobeetie Trail if a cowboy wanted to ride his horse off the beaten path to the west. There may have been single dwellings here and there along the trail that have vanished from written memory. Fledging towns did not come into existence until the end of the trail-driving days, when the Indians lands were opened for settlement in the late1880s through the early 1900s. Therefore, when G. W. Briggs described the trail between the Washita and the Canadian, he used the present-day towns of 1933 as reference:

> [The trail proceeded] north passing a little to the east of the present town of Canute [established 1902]. Thence north near the town of Butler [established 1898], thence slightly west, passing a little to the east of Leedy [established 1900]; thence northwest to the present town of Trail [established 1898], crossing the South Canadian at the west end of Burns Flat, thence northwest to the head of Persimmon Creek. The trail crosses Highway No. 34 near Camargo [established 1892].[98]

They then went up to Cedar Springs, a "big watering place."

S. H. Tittle was more specific. He wrote, "We crossed South Canadian close to Trail and then crossed Trail Creek at Camargo."[99] Briggs had written that they crossed the South Canadian "at the west end of Burns Flat."

Between the crossing of the South Canadian at present-day Camargo and the crossing at the head of Persimmon Creek, there are three trail markers: one is at the Johnston Murray Bridge on the South Canadian River near Camargo; one is referred to as Elephant Rock which is three and one half miles southwest of Vici; and the other is three miles west of Vici on Highway US-60. Note inserts.

THE SPLINTER ROUTES IN NORTHERN INDIAN TERRITORY: (Maps #4-10 and #4-11)

As the cattle-trail network in Indian Territory — feeder and splinter routes between the Western and Chisholm — was honed, manipulated, and supervised by the troops of the area forts, the northbound herds followed the direction of the soldiers. At the South Canadian River crossing, Fort Supply escorts took over the supervision. The crossing was the third checkpoint after leaving the Red River. By 1887, however, Indian agents at Cantonment and the Darlington Agency informed

---
[98] G. W. Briggs, Jr. letter to H. S. Tennant, July 6, 1933, "The Two Cattle Trails," 107.
[99] "Statement of S. H. Tittle with Reference to Location of Western Trail," to Tennant, Ibid, 103.

THE WESTERN CATTLE TRAIL | 1874-1897   203

6
DODGE CITY TRAIL CROSSED HERE

OVER THIS FAMOUS WESTERN TRAIL 11,000,000 CATTLE AND HORSES WERE DRIVEN FROM TEXAS THROUGH INDIAN TER. TO KANSAS. FIRST DRIVE, 1874, THE LAST, 1893, WITH THE OPENING OF THIS COUNTRY AS PART OF THE CHEROKEE STRIP. THE HERDS SUPPLIED SHIPPING FROM DODGE CITY, BESIDES THOUSANDS OF HEAD DRIVEN TO RANCHES IN THE NORTHWEST AND CANADA.

Location: at the Johnston Murray bridge across the South Canadian River near Camargo, Oklahoma.

Authors' commentary:
This marker was introduced along with the opening of the Johnston Murray Bridge in 1959. The marker was sponsored by the Vici Road Boosters. According to the *Vici Beacon*:

> "Wednesday the opening of the Johnston Murray bridge across the South Canadian river near Camargo will mark the big step in completion of the Old Trail route."

We do not know the mission of the Vici Road Boosters in 1959, but apparently they were promoting the cattle trail through their area, and had done so, according to the picture caption, "for 30 years." They may have also been responsible for the marker placed five miles west of Vici on US-60 also entitled "Dodge City Trail." The Boosters used the old term, "Dodge City Trail," while later markers use the "Western Trail."

Like the marker three miles west of Vici, which was placed at least a decade later, it uses the number of 11 million cattle and horses driven over the trail. This is a great exaggeration. Again, the ending date should be 1889.

"Vici Road Boosters' Dream Come True," picture and caption, *Vici Beacon*, 1959 (month unknown). Interview and article from DeWayne Brown, Vici, Oklahoma to Gary Kraisinger, February, 2011.

7
ELEPHANT ROCK

Location: one and one half miles west on Highway US-60 of Vici, Oklahoma, Dewey County and then two miles south and two miles southwest on County Road D2058.

Authors' commentary:
Alongside the county road is a white concrete post marked "Gr. Western Trail," which was erected by the Rotarians. It marks where local legend identified the location at Elephant Rock, a landmark to Texas cowboys and their herds as they followed the Western Trail going north.

Location: three miles west of Vici, Oklahoma, Dewey County, on Highway US-60.

Authors' commentary:
This fine-looking marker deserves an "A" for appearance and for mentioning that the Western Trail went beyond Dodge City. Additionally, it accurately states that the trail went into Canada. It also has the beginning date of the trail, 1874, correct. Because of the adjective "Great," this marker dates after Jimmy Skaggs' research in the mid 1960s.

We would like to know where the number 11,000,000 comes from for this trail. In our research, we find that 11 to 12 million cattle went up the four cattle systems after the Civil War, 1867-1897, and that the Western carried half of that amount. We do not believe the Great Western alone carried 11 million.

The Western Trail in Indian Territory ceased to be used around 1889, after Kansas quarantined its entire state against Texas longhorns. By that time, the cattle trail had moved west into the Panhandle of Texas, bypassing Indian Territory and Kansas. The marker is right, however, in that homesteading also become a barrier which brought an end to cattle drives. The sponsor and author of this marker is unknown.

According to Bruce E. Joseph and Bob Burke in A field Guide to Oklahoma's Historical Markers, published in 2005, page 42, there was another marker five miles west of Vici on US-60 entitled "Dodge City Trail." It read:

> From 1874 to 1893, millions of cattle and horses were driven from Texas through what became western Oklahoma over the westernmost of the famous cattle trails. The trail crossed the Red River at Doan's Crossing in Jackson County and continued north to Dodge City, Kansas. A series of markers throughout Oklahoma preserve the memory of the trail.

Was this marker replaced by the one above? This marker is believed to be an older one because of the use of the term "Dodge City Trail." We were unable to find this marker, even though Joseph and Burke's field guide indicates it was still standing in 2005.

THE WESTERN CATTLE TRAIL | 1874-1897

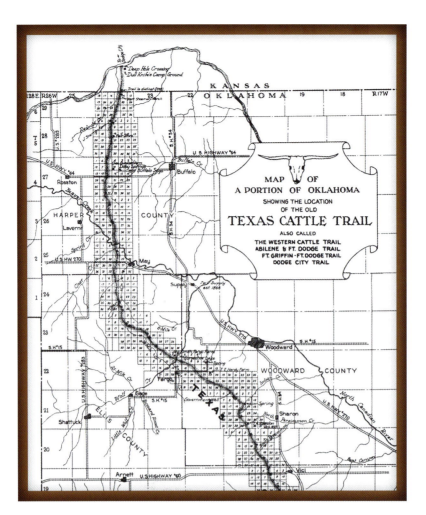

#4-10
The Upper Portion of the Tennant Map:
This portion of the Tennant map shows the Western Cattle Trail from Vici to the Kansas line.

Map courtesy of the Oklahoma State Historical Society, Oklahoma City, Oklahoma.

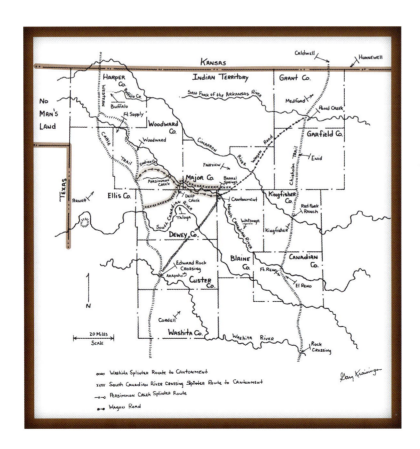

#4-11
The Splinter Routes in Northern Indian Territory:
South Canadian River Crossing Splinter Route and the Persimmon Creek Splinter Route.

Col. Zenas R. Bliss at Fort Supply that the cowboys were again taking the Washita Splinter Route shortcut from the Washita to Cantonment, cutting across the Indian farms. The resentful Indians were retaliating by stealing cattle and horses. In June, as the heavy trail traffic was underway, Colonel Bliss ordered a detail of troopers from Cantonment to locate another splinter route to bypass the heavy concentration of Cheyenne farms. This route started at the crossing of the South Canadian River, paralleled Deep Creek northeastward, crossed the North Fork of the Canadian near the mouth of Deep Creek, and followed the river until it connected with the wagon road that fed into the Chisholm Trail.[100] *Deep Creek was not shown on the Tennant map.*

G. W. Briggs, Jr. wrote of another route that was used in addition to the South Canadian River crossing splinter route. He explained that cattle herds left the main trail at the head of Persimmon Creek, which was another day's drive north, went down Indian Creek to the North Fork of the Canadian, and continued down that river to Cantonment. At this location the herds crossed the river and headed north to the Cimarron River. After crossing the Cimarron, they trailed northeast, crossing Turkey Creek, and then picked up the old Chisholm Trail, or Caldwell Trail, at Pond Creek and delivered herds to Caldwell or Hunnewell on the Kansas border. According to Briggs, some herds also ended up farther east on "the Arkansas River, for finishing before sending to market."

Also at the head of Persimmon Creek another route "branched off from the main trail," according to Briggs. This route went straight north to the North Canadian River where herds "drifted up the stream from Woodward past Supply and joined the main trail again."[101]

CAMP (FORT) SUPPLY: (Map #4-12)

On the trunk line of the Western Trail, as herds and their drovers trailed north down into Wolf Creek valley, they approached the Fort Supply twelve-mile military reserve limit and intersected with the Fort Supply- Fort Elliott Military Road just north of the Wolf Creek crossing.[102] Because of Fort Supply's reservation boundary, herds had to turn northwest in order to swing out around the military grounds. The military road ran along the north side of Wolf Creek, so this intersection, at

---

[100]Robert C. Carriker, *Fort Supply, Indian Territory, Frontier Outpost on the Plains*, 176-177.

[101]G. W. Briggs, Jr. letter to H. S. Tennant, July 6, 1933, "The Two Cattle Trails," 107. Fort Supply's military compound embraced one township — 36 square miles or 23,040 acres. In 1883, the reservation was enlarged by an additional 27 square miles to the north. A barbed wire fence was erected around the reserve. (Carriker, 159) Thus, when herds went "past Supply" on the east side, they either skirted the outer limits of the military compound, which would have been out of the way, or were allowed to go across the reservation. One could theorize that perhaps this branch was for those herds and drovers who were actually delivering part of a herd to the fort.

[102]Camp Supply had been established as a temporary "camp of supplies" in November of 1868. Supplies were moved to the camp from Fort Dodge as the camp became an operational base for General Sheridan during the Indian Wars, and it served as a supply depot for other cantonments and forts to the south. In December of 1878, however, it was awarded permanent status as a fort. The Fort Supply post commander had issued orders for drovers with their herds to stay at a 12-mile distance from the post or face the penalty of being arrested. See Robert C. Carriker, *Fort Supply, Frontier Outpost on the Plains*

THE WESTERN CATTLE TRAIL | 1874-1897

the perimeter of the military reservation was a pathway for stagecoaches, wagon freighters, and military personnel as well as herds of longhorns coming up from the south. It was also in this general area that the Quanah Detour Branch (Ghost Trail) of the Western Trail rejoined the trunk line from the southwest (see Map #4-2) Therefore, it was not uncommon for wagons or stagecoaches on the military road to wait for hours while a herd of Texas longhorns passed by.

Six miles southwest of this intersection, on Buzzard Creek where it converged with Wolf Creek, a camping spot by the name of Buzzard's Roost was established. Later on, it became a stage stop that offered the comforts of a picket house, a corral, dugouts and a blacksmith shop.

It is very likely that cowboys from off of the Quanah Detour Branch or the Western Cattle Trail visited this camp.

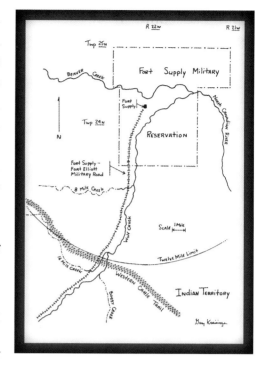

#4-12
The Western Cattle Trail in Relationship to the Fort Supply-Fort Elliott Military Road and the Twelve-mile Limit:
This map shows the Western Cattle Trail in the Wolf Creek and 16-Mile Creek vicinity on the outer limits of the Fort Supply Military Reservation and the intersection of the Western Trail and the Fort Supply-Fort Elliott Road.

Also southwest of this intersection was the town of Gage. It was established in 1887. Eleven miles north of this community, close to the Trail, is another marker.

Throughout the life of the trail, Fort Supply was the major supply stop for Texas drovers. For Lewis Neatherlin in 1876, two years before the Doan's Crossing store was established, supplies had not been replenished since Fort Griffin in the first week of May. He did note in his journal, however, that "Brother Jim killed one (buffalo)" on May 16, just south of the Pease River in northern Texas. Upon approaching Camp Supply, supplies were very low. Neatherlin had noted in his journal two days earlier that they had "cooked the last bread stuff we had." Thus, by the morning of May 29, as the herds worked their way toward Wolf Creek, Neatherlin and a Mr. Pond "mounted our horses and started to hunt Camp Supply." It would take them all day.

After purchasing one hundred pounds of flour the next morning from the Camp's sutler, the two men rode back to the herds. Neatherlin wrote that evening:

> **May 30:**
> We drove on down a few miles and camped on Wolf Creek, a large, sandy stream, some 60 feet wide and very shallow. Fine grass. We struck the first road today that we have seen in 200 miles.

They had come upon the military road from Fort Elliott. Neatherlin again rode into the post "for flour and bacon to do us to Dodge." The outfits rested their herds for a day. By evening Neatherlin was back and wrote in his journal:

May 31:
Returned late in the evening and found herds at the crossing of Wolf Creek, 18 miles above the post where we have to leave the road [Fort Elliott military road] and turn north. The post commander [had] issued orders for no herds to come nearer than 12 miles of the post under penalty of being arrested.[103]

Even after the Doan's store at the Red River crossing was established, trail bosses had to make sure their chuck wagons could sustain the trek to Fort Supply. The Navajoe and Warren stores would not be in existence until 1886 and 1888 respectively, and the stretch across Indian Territory to the post was one hundred and fifty miles of open prairie. The Doan's store and Fort Supply both stockpiled flour, bacon, beans, and coffee for the trail drives. While the Doans freighted their supplies in from Gainesville, the supply post on the North Canadian relied on freight wagons coming from Fort Dodge.

Flour to make the daily biscuits was a staple, and Neatherlin made two trips to the post to supply his three outfits with the necessity. The outfits' cooks must have looked forward to the supply camp. Even Andy Adams remarked about the stop when writing about his 1882 trail ride:

> There was never very much love lost between government soldiers and our tribe, so we swept past Camp Supply in contempt a few days later, and crossed the North Fork of the Canadian to camp for the night. Flood and McCann went into the post, as our supply of flour and navy beans was running rather low, and our foreman had hopes that he might be able to get enough of these staples from the sutler to last until we reached Dodge.[104]

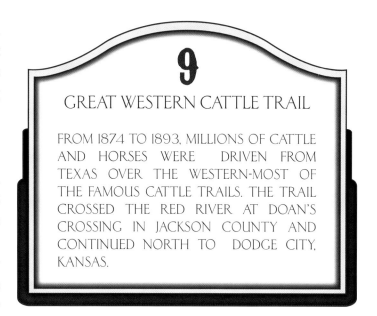

9
GREAT WESTERN CATTLE TRAIL

FROM 1874 TO 1893, MILLIONS OF CATTLE AND HORSES WERE DRIVEN FROM TEXAS OVER THE WESTERN-MOST OF THE FAMOUS CATTLE TRAILS. THE TRAIL CROSSED THE RED RIVER AT DOAN'S CROSSING IN JACKSON COUNTY AND CONTINUED NORTH TO DODGE CITY, KANSAS.

Location: on OK-46, eleven miles north of Gage, Ellis County, Oklahoma.

Authors' commentary:
Little is known about this marker. We guess that it is fairly recent. The ending date is not correct for that part of the Western Trail. In this area, trailing ceased in 1889.

The message is short and to the point. The reader has to assume, however, that the Western Trail must have crossed near by even though it does not say so.

Bruce E. Joseph and Bob Burke, *A Field Guide to Oklahoma's Historical Markers*, (Jan. 2005), 44.

---
[103]Leo Kelley, ed. Neatherlin's journal, May 30 - May 31 entries.
[104]Andy Adams, *The Log of a Cowboy*, 177.

The foreman "had hopes" of getting the flour and beans. With so many herds passing by Camp, later Fort Supply, there was the chance that the sutler could be out of the food stuffs. Only two days out from the post, Neatherlin remarks about the procession of herds:

June 2:
Being camped last night very near 2 herds that was ahead of us, we made a short drive today in order to let them get farther from us for, in case of bad weather as the clouds indicate, we might mix and that would be worse than laying up 2 days.[105]

The trail north of Fort Supply became increasingly difficult. The treeless, wide open terrain to the Cimarron River in southern Kansas offered little chance for water. After crossing the North Canadian River (also known as Beaver Creek) above the fort, drovers had to push their herds hard over thirty-eight miles to water on the Cimarron. It had to be done in under four days.

Between Fort Supply and the Kansas line, however, two more feeder routes joined the Western Trail.

THE NORTH CANADIAN RIVER FEEDER ROUTE: (Map #4-13)

On Buffalo Creek, east of the trail, was Buffalo Springs, a swamp-like area that offered a possible source of water. The camp area was the destination of another feeder route — the North Canadian River Feeder Route This feeder route was established by J. W. Chastain in 1881 under the direction of the Cherokee Strip Live Stock Association to replace the abandoned Cimarron (Cut-off) Feeder Route to accommodate "herds that are on the Eastern or Caldwell Trail and whose destination is Dodge or points north of there."[106] The Canadian River Feeder Route splintered or diverged from the Chisholm Trail upon reaching the North Canadian River near Fort Reno; it followed the river on its north side in a northwesterly direction, (The Fort Supply - Fort Reno military road was on the north side of the river.) and continued on until reaching the vicinity east of Fort Supply in the Cherokee Outlet. Here it turned north to connect with the Western Trail west of Buffalo Springs on Buffalo Creek.[107]

Charles Moreau Harger referred to this feeder route in his 1892 Scribner's Magazine article on "Cattle-Trails of the Prairies." Because his article is one of the first essays written about the subject, historians have relied heavily on its facts. However, Harger made a couple of major errors. Not only did he say that the Chisholm Trail was named after John

---

[105]Leo Kelly, ed. Neatherlin's journal.
[106]John L. Lillibridge, *The Red fork Ranch and Its People*, 49-50.
[107]James W. Cloud, "Ft. Supply - Darlington Trail Traced," *Pioneer Tele-Topics*," Sept., 1979, 15.

Chisholm, "an eccentric frontier stockman" from Paris, Texas, but he also made a mistake regarding the North Canadian River Feeder Route to the Western Trail. Therefore, for the historical record, we would like to explain and point out important issues that need to be noted.

First, Harger did give historians valuable information about a route of a lesser-known branch, or feeder route, to the Chisholm Trail. As discussed in Part I, Chapter IV, it was an earlier route that is seldom seen on maps and few people know about today. This route, west of the Fort Arbuckle Trail, needs to be mentioned again on the subject of the Western Trail feeder routes in order to explain Harger's error related to the North Canadian River Feeder Route. Again, to repeat Harger's quote in 1892 describing the route in Indian Territory:

> *…forded the Red River near the mouth of Mud Creek, followed that stream to its head, kept northwest to Wild Horse Creek, to the West of Signale Mountains, and crossed the Washita at Elm Spring. Due north… to the Canadian River….*[108]

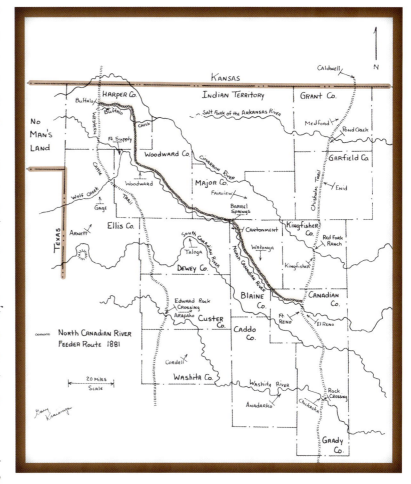

#4-13
The North Canadian River Feeder Route:
This map shows the feeder route following the north side of the North Canadian River from near Fort Reno in Cheyenne-Arapaho Reservation, in present-day Canadian County, to west of Cantonment (military camp), and continuing northwest across the Cherokee Outlet to east of Fort Supply and on to Buffalo Springs on Buffalo Creek, in present-day Harper County, to eventually connect with the Western Trail.

Elm Spring was a stage stop on the Fort Sill - Fort Arbuckle road on the Washita. A large elm tree grew behind the stage depot and a natural spring ran between the depot and the river — thus its name. Later, the stage stop was changed to Erin Springs, in honor of a sister to a local homesteader, Frank Murray.[109]

---

[108]Charles M. Harger, "Cattle-Trails of the Prairies," *Scribner's Magazine*, 1892, 734-735, and 1883 Indian Territory map, showing Signale Mts. in the Chickasaw Nation next to Wild Horse Creek near Ft. Arbuckle. online: http://alabamamaps.ua.edu/historicalmaps/us_states/oklahoma/index.html 2nd map from the top of the list. [accessed Aug. 16, 2011]

[109]Frank Murray built the first home in Erin Springs in 1871. In 1879-1880, he began construction of a large stone house which is still standing. It is the Murray-Lindsay Mansion. ("Erin Springs," on line, www.okgenweb.org [accessed Dec. 31, 2010]) C. Roeser, Government Printing Office, 1879 map showing "Elm Spr. (south of the Washita River) on the Ft. Sill & Ft. Arbuckle Stage Road." located in the Government Documents Dept. in the McCasland Maps Collection on the 5th Floor in Map Case B at Oklahoma State University at Stillwater. Copy acquired with the help of John Phillips, map curator. Interview and emails between Phillips and Gary Kraisinger, September, 2011.

Then Harger referred to a splinter route from the Chisholm Trail to the Western, the one we call the North Canadian River Feeder Route, in his statement, "In later years the Chisholm trail gave off a western shoot which left it near Elm Spring, and passing near Fort Reno, went on northwest into western Kansas, stricking Dodge City on the Arkansas." This western shoot or splinter route did leave what he called the Chisholm Trail in later years (1881), but not from Elm Spring. Harger did not tell his readers that this earlier pathway had moved west in the intervening years to its well-known path--the one we see on maps today. The later path went through Red River Station, crossed the Washita at Rock Crossing, and continued on to Fort Reno. The older route, used before 1870, that had entered Indian Territory at the mouth of Mud Creek on the Red River and continued on to Elm Spring had been abandoned and, by many, forgotten.

When the Government Land Office made a survey in 1872 of the Chisholm Trail, the pathway they put on the map was the one through Red River Station and on to Fort Reno--not the older route discribed by Harger. Harger's mistake in writing about the North Canadian River Feeder Route, which he called a "western shoot," was in describing it as leaving the older pre-1870 "Jesse Chisholm Trail" route. Neither the route that later became the well-known Chisholm Trail nor the feeder route existed in 1870.

Because of this issue with the two "Chisholm Trail" routes, we discovered two maps that show both of these pathways. As mentioned earlier, one, entitled "Indian Territory," is from the United States Indian Bureau of 1889, and the other, also from 1889, is from Cram's Unrivaled Atlas of the World 1889. *The latter is titled, "Map of the Oklahoma Country in Indian Territory," by George F. Cram. These two maps differ from Harger's description in that they show the earlier route about fifteeen miles east of Elm Spring.*

By 1881, when the Cherokee Strip Live Stock Association was adjusting splinter routes because they wanted to limit south Texas herds, possibly infected with the Texas Fever, from crossing the Cherokee Strip, they platted the substitute feeder route starting from the Fort Reno area.

THE CIMARRON (CUT – OFF) FEEDER ROUTE:
(Map #4-14)

According to Jimmy Skaggs, who was one of the first to research this feeder route, a pathway from the Red Fork Ranch on the Chisholm Trail followed the Cimarron River and cut over to the Western Trail. Skaggs called it the "Camp Supply-Chisholm Feeder Route." He described the route as feeding into the Western Trail near present-day May, Oklahoma, established in 1896, on Beaver Creek.[110] This route, as described by Skaggs, crossed the Cimarron River and trailed directly toward Camp (Fort) Supply and may have been used so drovers could cut animals out of their herd and deliver the beef to the fort. *May was also the location where, starting in*

---

[110]Jimmy Skaggs, "The Route of the Great Western (Dodge City) Cattle Trail." *The West Texas Historical Association Year Book*, 140. Map created by Gary Kraisinger, 2004, for *The Western, the Greatest Texas Cattle Trail, 1874-1886*, 35.

1885, outfits turned west to detour around quarantined Kansas to use the National Trail. (see Part III)

Other references, however, have been made to what became known as the "Cimarron Cut-Off." B. J. Fletcher, who helped drive a Thomas Snyder herd north in 1879 wrote: "…now southern Kansas, due north of us, had been settled so thickly with homesteaders that we would be forced to abandon the old trail [Chisholm] and detour to the west." Fletcher was referring to the 1875-1876 Kansas quarantine that had closed down the railhead of Wichita. The Snyder herd was trailed along the north side of the Cimarron River, but upon nearing the Saline Reservation, the outfit stampeded the herd across the river to the south side and forced it on in order to keep the cattle away from the deadly briny waters of the Saline Reservation.[111] The outfit then recrossed the river and connected with the Western Trail trunk line near Dodge City.[112]

Two other sources describe the Cimarron Feeder Route (also called the Cimarron Cut-Off) as connecting with the Western Trail at a different location. John F. Vallentine, who relied on old Cherokee Outlet maps, writes in his book, *Cattle Ranching South of Dodge City*, that the "northwest branch of the Chisholm trail forked near the Salt Plains" where the "western prong crossed the southeast corner of Comanche Co. [Kansas] and supposedly intercepted the Western Cattle Trail somewhere in Clark Co."[113] Harry S. Drago, in *Great American Cattle Trails*, described the "Cut-Off Trail" as following the Cimarron "for a hundred miles to Longhorn Roundup, where it intersected the new Western Trail." The Longhorn Roundup was a roadhouse in southern Clark County,

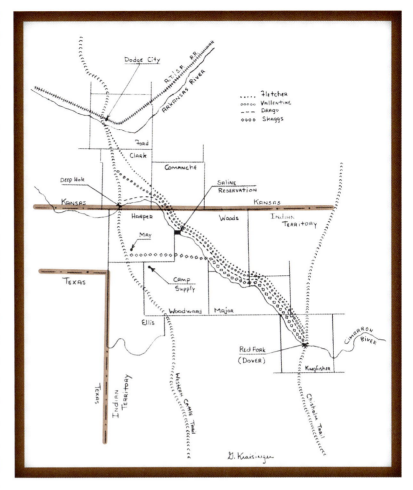

#4-14
The Cimarron (Cut-Off) Feeder Route:
This map shows four different routes used by trail drivers to cut over to the Western Cattle Trail from the old Chisholm Trail. The drovers and their herds left the Chisholm Trail at Red Fork Ranch in present-day Kingfisher County, followed the north bank of the Cimarron River, and connected with the Western Trail either at May, Deep Hole, somewhere in Clark County, Kansas or at Dodge City.

---

[111]Saline Reservation is another name for Big Salt Plains and Great Salt Plains. This vast salt-flat in northcentral Oklahoma, north of the Cimarron River, has been a source of salt since its discovery by white explorers in early 1800.
[112]B. J. Fletcher, *Up the Trail in '79*, 20-45.
[113]John F. Vallentine, *Cattle Ranching South of Dodge City, The Early Years (1870-1920)*, 21.

THE WESTERN CATTLE TRAIL | 1874-1897   213

Kansas, on the Cimarron River. The location was referred to as "Deep Hole" by the cowboys.[114]

These four sources, as well as others, agree that the Cimarron (Cut-off) Feeder Route to the Western Trail was used from about 1875 to 1881.[115] It was also this cross-over that the Cherokee Strip Live Stock Association was concerned about in the spring of 1881. Not only did the association direct J. W. Chastain to lay out a new trail to feed herds into the Caldwell area from the Washita Crossing, but they also insisted that "the old trail north of the Cimarron River" be "permanently closed and abandoned." According to the association, however, the Cut-Off (or splinter route) went to the source of Buffalo Creek which is about fourteen miles north of May.

The Cherokee Strip Live Stock Association actually referred to the splinter route as being "north of the Cimarron River." B. J. Fletcher, in his account said that they crossed the Cimarron and followed the river along the north side. Our research, based on other sources as well, supports the assertion that the outfits with their herds crossed the Cimarron River, went up Turkey Creek, and proceeded northwest along the north side of the Cimarron River. The old 1881 map, "Cattle Trails Across Indian Reservation" (Map #4-9), however, shows the route on the south side of the river.

THE YELTON STORE:

A few miles east of the Buffalo Springs campground is present-day Buffalo, Oklahoma. The "Hart Shoeman Ranch" was located in the last sections of Harper County, on the Kansas border, next to the trail. (See the Tennant Map #4-10) Also at this point, the map, produced in 1936, relates that the "Trail is distinct."

At one time there was a trail marker approximately one mile west of the trail on the ranch. According to the stone monument, there had been at one time a store and campground at the location. The "Yelton Store" was established by Theodore A. Yelton who was the first postmaster of a post office at the location. However, the post office did not come into existance until February 6, 1902. It was common, however, to find a road house catering to trail traffic in existance many years before application was offered or accepted for a federal post office. The store was located in Indian Territory and may not have been qualified for a post office until there was talk of statehood. The Yelton Store, and campground close by, probably consisted of one or two dugouts. It catered to the cowboys on the Western Trail and perhaps even to travelers on the Fort Dodge-Fort Supply Military Trail, some four miles to the east.[116]

When trail drivers pushed their herds across the Indian Territory line into Kansas, they knew that they were exchanging dealings with Indians and soldiers with

---

[114]Harry S. Drago, *Great American Cattle Trails*, 175-176. Drago probably got his information from an account by G. W. Mills in *The Trail Drivers of Texas*.
[115]Read a full discussion of the Cimarron Cut-off in Kraisinger and Kraisinger, *The Western, the Greatest Texas Cattle Trail, 1874-1886*, 33-40.
[116]Sarah Moore, ed. *Sage and Sod, Harper County History*, Vol. II. c. 1975, 279.

dealings with Kansas homesteaders. Trail bosses would now have to be aware of an ever-changing quarantine line and instruct drovers that the "nesters" of Kansas would often get in their way. For most cowboys, however, the thought of seeing a "civilized" town of substantial size with its imagined delights was foremost on their minds.

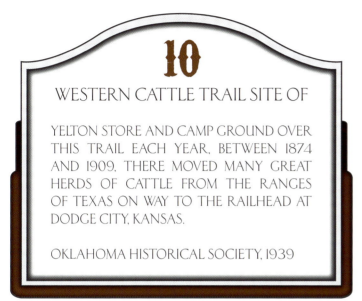

Location: About 9 miles north and 8 and three quarter miles west of Buffalo in Harper County, Oklahoma.[1]

Authors' commentary:
We had to search to find this engraved stone. It was dismantled and covered with debris in a ditch. Fortunately we took a picture for today the marker is no longer there.

The 1874 date is correct, but we do not know how the Society came up with the ending date of 1909. Drovers and their herds ceased using the Western Trail in this area in 1884 because of the state-wide Kansas quarantine of Texas cattle. Also, like so many other markers, it mentions only Dodge City as the destination. Most herds went beyond Dodge.

Yelton Store was located three miles west of Willard. The post office operated from February 6, 1902 to June 13, 1918. There were several postmasters during its existence. Eventually, the post office was moved to the Girard location, but the name was not changed. The location is S28, R24W, T20N.[2]

---
[1]Muriel H. Wright, George H. Shirk, and Kenny A. Franks, *Mark of Heritage*, Oklahoma Historical Society, 1976, Marker #56, 197. This source says that the marker is located on the Sherman's Ranch. Tennant's map uses the name, "Hart Shoeman Ranch."
[2]Sarah Moore, ed. *Sage and Sod, Harper County History, Vol. II*, c. 1975, 279.

> *I have seen herds so long that if a person was on a horse in the center of the herd they could not see the cattle in the lead or those in the rear of the herd, even though the land [was] very level.... The cattle marched along about twenty abreast, following in single file the paths worn deep through the buffalo sod, made by the passing of un-numbered herds.*

Recollections of an early Thomas County, Kansas, trapper Samuel Grout, *Golden Jubilee of Thomas County*, pages 27-30.

CHAPTER V

Kansas Homesteaders & Kansas Quarantines

> *When we got into Kansas we had all kinds of troubles with the new settlers. They would plow a furrow and if we crossed over that they would have us pulled [arrested] and fined unless it was time to bed the cattle and then they would give us all kinds of inducements to camp on their land, so they could use the buffalo [cow] chips for fuel the next winter. They would guard them like a Texan man does a watermelon patch, until they were ripe enough to haul in. We never saw a stick of wood for days in Kansas and had to use buffalo [cow] chips to cook with.*

James Shaw, 1879 trail drive with the Ellison and Sherrill outfit. The furrows were south of Dodge City in Ford County. James Shaw, *North from Texas, Incidents in the Early Life of a Range Cowman in Texas, Dakota & Wyoming, 1852-1883*, pg. 46.

THE WESTERN CATTLE TRAIL | 1874-1897   217

The Mead family *is pictured here sometime between 1875 and 1889 in Ford County, Kansas, near the town of Bloom. The dugout was close to the Western Cattle Trail, and these homesteaders would have been aware of the Texas cattle herds going north.*

Because of the lack of wood, dugouts and sod houses were common dwelling places on the high plains of Kansas.

Cowboys often times did not see these dugouts until they and the herd were almost on top of the dwelling.

This family was more affluant than many homesteaders because there is a smokestack and glass-pane windows.

Photo courtesy of "Kansas Memory," Kansas State Historical Society, Topeka, Kansas.

The Kansas Territorial and State Legislatures had passed quarantine laws directed against Texas herds ever since the Shawnee Trail days as early as 1859. Unlike other states, however, the Kansas laws were severely enforced, and drovers were always aware of the most recently drawn deadline and respected its enforcers. Because of the periodically re-aligning of these deadlines by the state, there was a westerly shift of the cattle trailing systems, the Shawnee, the Eastern/Chisholm, and the Western, from 1859 through 1885. Thus, one could say that Kansas controlled the cattle-trailing industry. By the time the Western Trail extended into Kansas, the western movement of settlers was at its peak, and Kansas passed four more quarantines — 1876, 1877, 1881, and 1885. The last quarantine was a major factor in causing the collapse to the entire trailing industry.

THE TRUNK LINE OF THE WESTERN CATTLE TRAIL, SOUTH OF DODGE CITY: **(Maps #5-1 and #5-2)**

Trail drivers and their herds crossed the Indian Territory - Kansas line and had to trail only three miles to water on the Cimarron River. Herds followed the east side of Redoubt Creek into present-day Clark County.[1] Between the mouth of Clark Creek, (which became Redoubt Creek in Indian Territory), and Deep Hole, travelers crossed the Cimarron River. The location was a natural, well worn spot used by the military on the Fort Dodge - Camp (Fort) Supply road since 1868. It was at this location that trail drivers became aware of the increased road traffic. The military road, which had been located east of the trail, now became part of the same route to Dodge. North of the river, stage coaches and freight wagons moved almost daily between Fort Dodge and Camp (Fort) Supply and created a deep track in the center of a wider path. Herds and their drovers could follow the path on either side of the ruts to Mulberry Creek. *(We feel that they mostly stayed to the west of the military road.)*

Cowboys knew that Fort Dodge was one of the most important forts of the area and that it sat at the apex of a triangle. (see map #5-1) Its right angle road connected to the camp on the North Canadian (Camp Supply), and its left angle consisted of various freight roads coming from the Texas Panhandle and the military roads from Fort Bascom and Fort Elliott, all of which funneled into Dodge. The final portion of the triangle, its bottom base, was completed by the military road between Fort Elliott and Camp (Fort) Supply. At Deep Hole, the Western Cattle Trail merged into the trunk line of the Fort Dodge - Camp (Fort) Supply road on the right angle of this "imperfect triangle." Historian, C. Robert Haywood, said it very well this way:

> In the 1870s and 1880s the nation's pressure to expand the West created a recognizable region that included the Texas and Oklahoma

---

[1]Clark County, Kansas, was part of Ford County until 1885. The trail entered Kansas (Clark County) through the W1/2 Section 13, T35S, R23W, 6th Principal Mer. After entering Kansas, Redoubt Creek became "Clark Creek." (Tennant map of 1936 and map in John Franklin Vallentine, Cattle Ranching South of Dodge City, the Early Years (1870-1920) 20.

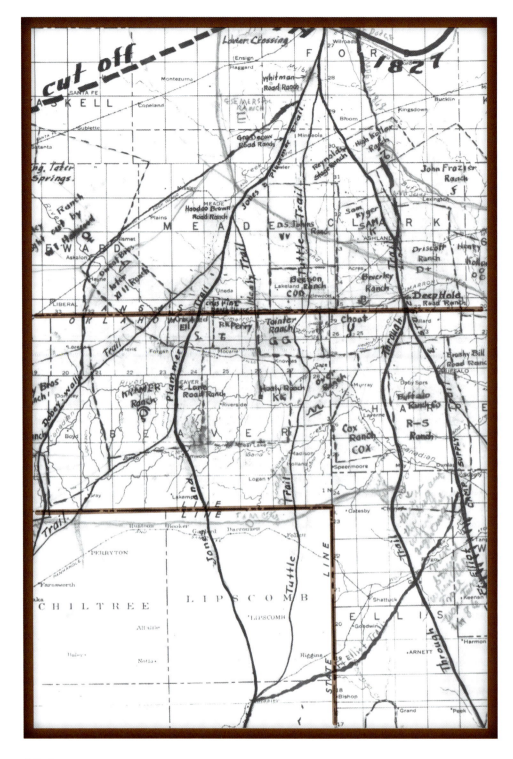

#5-1
The Imperfect Triangle:
This heavily annotated map created by M. W. Anshutz and Frank A. Webb in the 1930s shows the "imperfect triangle" described by trail historian C. Robert Haywood in 1986. The "Through Trail" is the Western Cattle Trail that blends into the "Camp Supply Trail and Stage Road" at Deep Hole Ranch on the Cimarron River. Other buffalo hide roads, freight trails, and local cattle trails connect with the Western Trail at or near Whitman's Road Ranch on Mulberry Creek.

Map Courtesy of No Man's Land Museum, Goodwell, Oklahoma.

[No Man's Land] panhandles and southwestern Kansas, best described as a ragged, imperfect triangle with Dodge City the hub and anchor.[2]

The Deep Hole location was a camp area that provided rest and water for soldiers and trail drivers alike who were preparing to cross the Cimarron. It must have been a social opportunity as well for not only did herds coming from the south on the Western Trail and soldiers coming to and from Camp (Fort) Supply cross at Deep Hole, but, according to Harry S. Drago, herds coming from the southeast on the Cimarron River Feeder Route from the old Chisholm Trail also blended into the Western at Deep Hole Crossing (see Map #4-13).[3] The other prongs of this feeder appears to have merged with the Western farther up the line. Historian of the Clark County ranching industry, John F. Vallentine, has written:

> Just where the intercept with the Western Trail was made is uncertain since no designated trail entering the southeast corner of Clark Co. is now known. Exact routes for cattle entering Kansas over the prongs of the northwest extension of the Chisholm trail may well have been left to the convenience of the cattle drovers and the approval of early resident stockmen in line with Texas fever quarantine lines.[4]

There was at least one road house on the banks of the Cimarron to provide service, first to the soldiers and then later on to the trail drivers. The road house remembered by most of the cowboys was "Red Clarke's Longhorn Roundup."

The Longhorn Roundup consisted of a framed building and corral built by John (or Red) Clarke on the south side of the river with lumber hauled down from Dodge City. The charismatic Clarke was a jokester and entertained all who entered his eating and drinking establishment. By May of 1881, the road house became the first post office in the county under the name of "Deep Hole." Whether the building was referred to as Deep Hole or simply Clarke's Place, it was a favorite stop for the cowboys.[5]

Across the river between the Big Sandy Creek and the Little Sandy Creek was another road house. According to Bob Lauderdale, who was on a cattle drive in 1877, in addition to Red Clarke's Longhorn Round Up there "on the opposite side was old Julia's 'Dead Fall.'"[6] It is speculated by locals that the name comes from the quick sand in the area, but the actual name of the road ranch was "Clem's Place." The stockade-like abode had been built by Clem Nitchie and was located on the trail in Section 26.

---

[2]C. Robert Haywood, "Jones and Plummer Trail," Oklahoma Historical Society article online, http://digital. library.okstate.edu/encyclopedia/entries/J/JO017.html [accessed Oct 13, 2011]

[3]Harry S. Drago, *Great American Cattle Trails*, 175.

[4]John Franklin Vallentine, *Cattle Ranching South of Dodge City, the Early Years (1870-1920)*, 21.

[5]When Clark County was established in 1885, it was not named after John Clarke, the proprietor of the Longhorn Round Up. It was named after Charles F. Clarke, a captain in the 6th Kansas Cavalry and Adjutant General in the US Volunteers who died in 1862. The "e" was dropped. ("Clark County," Kansas State Historical Society online: www.kshs.org/Kansasapedia/clark-county-kansas [accessed Oct. 24, 2011]

[6]Bob Lauderdale, "Reminiscences of the Trail," in Hunter, *The Trail Drivers of Texas*, 409.

Drovers and contractors, who were experienced hands on the trail in Kansas, knew where the road houses were. About a day's drive north at the next crossing, where Red Hole Creek meets Bear Creek, was a "so called ranch a little way off the side of the road" called Red Hole Ranch House. The adobe shack built of the local red dirt made "it literary a red hole," according to Father Verheyan who visited it on one of his journeys in 1876.[7]

As the traffic on the trail grew, local stockmen north of Red Hole, in order to keep the Texas cattle from coming in contact with their herds, enforced their ranch boundaries and limited the main trail to no wider than six miles, or three miles on either side of the central pathway. At the three-mile limit on the east side of the trail was a wire fence which marked the west line of Doc Day's D-Cross Ranch.[8] At the three-mile limit on the west side of the trail, the Beverly Brothers used line riders to patrol the boundary of their ranch to make sure that trail cattle were within their designated area and that ranch cattle stayed behind the line.[9]

Another three miles up Bear Creek along the east branch from Red Hole, was Bear Creek Station. At first it was a small adobe shack built on the creek bank by John Glenn, just as the cattle trailing was getting under way in 1875. Later on it was taken over by J. W. Driskill who improved the accommodations by building a framed structure. Because two soldiers were killed by Indians nearby, it was also known as Soldiers' Grave.[10]

Road houses and their postal services came and went. North of Soldiers' Grave, later Ashland post office, another post office was established in 1883 and named Klaine in honor of Nicholas (Nick) Klaine, Dodge City's newspaper editor and post master. For a short time it was operated under the name Baker's Store, but in the late season of 1884, cowboys found the same postmaster and store another mile northwest in the newly established town of Clark City. By the 1885 season, the post office/store had moved again — to Ashland, a mile and a half southeast.[11]

In northern Clark County, on Bluff Creek, was one of the longest running road houses. The eighteen-by-thirty-six foot soddie was built by Charles Kaufholz and a Mr. Beauregard during the early years of Fort Dodge. Here the partners served food, drink, and maintained a general store. In 1872, they sold out to George Reighard who expanded the business and added a stockade to the north side because he felt they needed protection from the Indians. In 1877, Salis Maley took over the operation. To the cowboys, the stop became known as "Maley's." In the next season,

---

[7]*Notes on Early Clark Co.* Vol. I., 54.

[8]J. M (Doc) Day established a large ranch on Wolf Creek in Lipscomb County, Texas in 1877, and also had extensive range rights in the Cherokee Outlet. In 1882, he purchased J. L. Driskill & Son's range privileges on the Cimarron River together with all the cows and spring calves on the range. The Clark County acquisition became known as the D Cross Ranch. (Vallentine, 70)

[9]Henry Mason Beverly, Sr. had three sons, William, H.M., Jr., and James R. Beverly Sr. and his wife moved from Kent. The Ashland post office was later established in July of 1885.

[10]The story about the death of these soldiers can be found in *Notes of Early Clark Co.*, Vo. I, 1 and 53, or in Kraisinger & Kraisinger, *The Western, The Greatest Texas Cattle Trail*, on page 98. The Ashland post office was later established in July of 1885.

[11]Kraisinger & Kraisinger, *The Western, the Greatest Texas Cattle Trail*, 100.

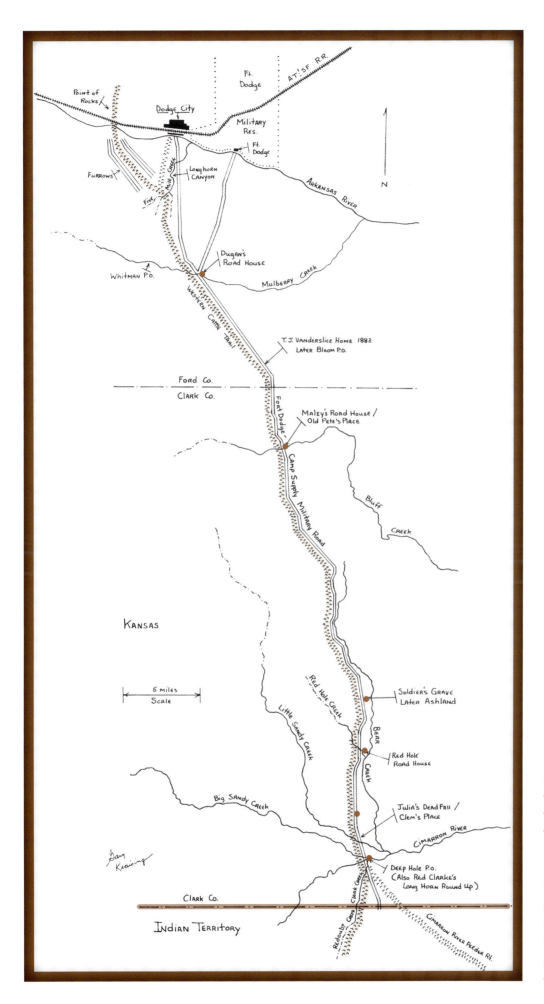

#5-2
The Western Cattle Trail from Indian Territory Border to Dodge City, Kansas: *This map shows the Western Trail trunk line across Clark and Ford counties, Kansas, to Dodge City. Various road houses appear along the way.*

THE WESTERN CATTLE TRAIL | 1874-1897

1

FORT DODGE - CAMP SUPPLY MILITARY ROAD

THE FORT DODGE-CAMP SUPPLY MILITARY ROAD PASSED SEVERAL HUNDRED FEET WEST OF THIS MARKER. THE ROUTE WAS ESTABLISHED IN 1868 DURING GENERAL PHIL H. SHERIDAN'S WINTER CAMPAIGN AGAINST INDIANS IN TEXAS AND THE INDIAN TERRITORY. THIS UNGRADED PRAIRIE TRAIL, APPROXIMATELY 90 MILES LONG, WAS IMPORTANT FOR TRANSPORTING SUPPLIES FROM FORT DODGE AND DODGE CITY TO CAMP (LATER FORT) SUPPLY, IN PRESENT OKLAHOMA, AND WAS AN IMPORTANT LINK IN THE COMMUNICATIONS SYSTEM OF WESTERN OUTPOSTS. IN THE 1880S, A GOVERNMENT TELEGRAPH LINE WAS ERECTED ALONG THE ROUTE OF THE TRAIL. IN CLARK COUNTY, TWO 50-FOOT SQUARE FORTIFICATIONS (REDOUBTS) WERE BUILT TO HOUSE CAVALRY PATROLS ASSIGNED TO KEEP THE MAIL AND SUPPLY ROUTE OPEN. IN THE 1870S AND 1880S, THE MILITARY ROAD SERVED AS A BRANCH OF THE WESTERN TRAIL OVER WHICH CATTLE WERE DRIVEN FROM TEXAS TO DODGE CITY AND BEYOND. THE PRESENT ROAD BETWEEN BLOOM AND ASHLAND FOLLOWS THE ROUTE OF THE FORT DODGE-CAMP SUPPLY MILITARY ROAD.

ERECTED BY KANSAS HISTORICAL SOCIETY AND DEPARTMENT OF TRANSPORTATION

Location: Roadside park at the east edge of Bloom, Kansas, Ford County. North of Highway 54 and south of the railroad tracks.

Authors' commentary:
The historical markers erected by the Kansas State Historical Society are complete and accurate. This marker mentions the Western Cattle Trail that ran parallel to the military road and specifies that the cattle went "beyond" Dodge, which, in our opinion, gives this sign high marks. The words "the military road served as a branch of the Western trail," however, is unclear, The two pathways blended together into basically one road at the Cimarron crossing in Kansas at Deep Hole which is about fifty-five miles south of Dodge. The older 1868 military road to the east into Fort Dodge was used less and less after the Western Trail became established in 1874. We feel that the military used the well-worn, more convenient Western Trail trunk line to Dodge City until 1882, when the fort was abandoned. Consequently the military road should not be referred to as a branch of the Western Trail. The actual dates of the trail in this region were 1874 to 1885.

1878, when cattle trailing was even heavier, the old favorite stopping place became known as "Old Pete's Place" after another owner, Pete Henderson. Under Pete, the road house became one of the three major stops for stagecoaches on their way to Fort Supply. Old Pete served meals, offered a bar, maintained a post office, and stayed in business through the duration of the cattle trailing in Kansas.[12]

Between the Bluff Creek crossing and the next water crossing at Mulberry Creek, trail drovers, and the military before them, passed by present-day Bloom, Kansas. Vallentine writes that the trail passed by "present-day Bloom on the northeast corner of town," and then "veered northwest."[13] The Kansas State Historical Society trail marker at Bloom, located on the east edge of town, states that the military road "passed several hundred feet west of this marker."

The Anshutz map shows the military road east of Bloom and the Western Trail west of town. The two paths were actually only one or two miles apart. Before reaching Mulberry Creek, the military road split, one branch going to Fort Dodge and another branch to Dodge City. The Western Trail paralleled the military road to Dodge City. The Reynolds stage stop, or Dugan's Road House, was located at the Mulberry Crossing, twelve miles south of Dodge City.

During the trail-driving days, the Vanderslice brothers and their families moved from Bloomsburg, Pennsylvania and homesteaded the entire Section 25 of T29S, R24W in Ford County. In 1882, T. J. Vanderslice started to build his two-story frame house in the middle of the section where he later maintained a store. On December 23, 1885, the location became the Bloom post office. Even though the Bloom store was located on the well-traveled Fort Dodge - Fort Supply military road and somewhat east of the Western Trail, it appeared too late to benefit from the trail traffic. Trail driving to Dodge was over in 1885, and Fort Dodge, as a military post, had been abandoned in June of 1882.[14]

The most notable road house in the journey north to Dodge was on Mulberry Creek, eight miles into Ford County and a day's drive, eleven miles, from the Bluff Creek crossing. Dugan's Store or road house was not popular for its accommodations or its owner's charm, but because of its location. A. H. Dugan ran a fairly uncomfortable abode on the nouth bank of Mulberry Creek, but located only ten miles south of Dodge City, it became the junction of numerous trails. In Indian Territory, military roads and stage routes had been established between the frontier forts, but in the Texas Panhandle through No Man's Land, outside of the Indian reservations, other freight routes and local cattle trails had also been blazed, and they all, one way or the other, went to Dodge City and passed by or stopped at Dugan's Store.

---

[12]Kraisinger & Kraisinger, Ibid, 101-102. According to John F. Vallentine, Clark County historian, Old Pete's road ranch was located in Section 20, T30S, R23W, page 20. The M. W. Anshutz map simply notes "Reynolds Stage Ranch" (Map #5-1), referring to P.G. Reynolds who came to Dodge City in 1875 and developed a network of stage lines in the Dodge City - Panhandle region. (Haywood, *Trails South, The Wagon-Road Economy in the Dodge City - Panhandle Region*, 15)
[13]Vallentine, Ibid, 20.
[14]Ethel E. Watkins, *Annie: Child of the Prairie*, 46 and map, page 38.

THE WESTERN CATTLE TRAIL | 1874-1897

FEEDER ROUTES FROM THE TEXAS PANHANDLE, ACROSS NO MAN'S LAND, TO JOIN THE WESTERN CATTLE TRAIL AT MULBERRY CREEK: (Map #5-3)

Four early freight trails, with the exception of the Tuttle Trail which was strictly a cattle route, ran by Dugan's Store on Mulberry Creek, approximately ten miles south of Dodge City, Kansas. These early routes were established before or at the same time the Western Cattle Trail extended into Dodge City. At first, the freight routes, extending south out of Dodge City, served the buffalo hide industry. Later, the same pathways were used as cattle trails and became feeder routes to the Western Trail.

When Captain John T. Lytle blazed the Western Cattle Trail in 1874, Dodge City was a railhead for buffalo hide freighters. The Atchison, Topeka and Santa Fe reached

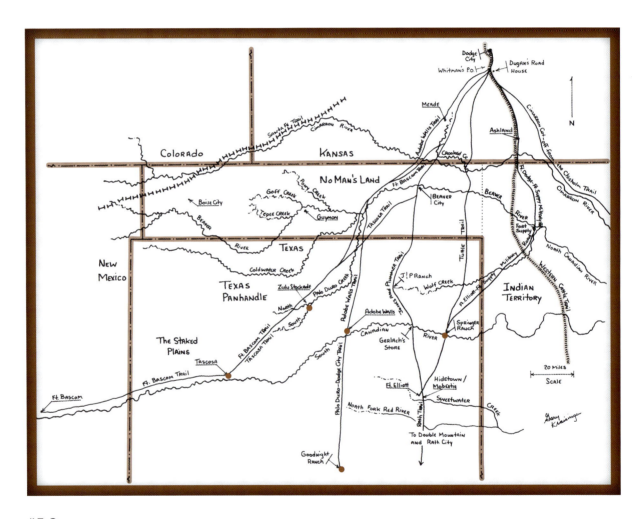

#5-3
Feeder Routes from the Texas Panhandle, Across No Man's Land, to Join the Western Cattle Trail at Dugan's Store on Mulberry Creek:
This map shows four freight or local cattle trails that fed into the Western Trail:
Fort Bascom (Military Road) / Tascosa Trail (originally a freight route);
Palo Duro / Adobe Walls Trail (cattle route from JA Ranch that used an old freight route);
Rath Trail / Jones and Plummer Trail (buffalo-hide and freight route);
Tuttle Trail (local cattle trail from Springer Ranch).

the town two years earlier during the onset of the buffalo hunts. When Lytle passed through the area with his herd, on his way to the Red Cloud Indian Agency in Nebraska, he saw a town bustling with soldiers, buffalo hunters, and a thriving hide business. Dodge hide dealers were immersed with the buying, trading, warehousing, selling, and shipping of hides and bones to large eastern markets. Saloons and merchants stocked wares to please the bullwhackers who freighted the hides and the hunters who killed the buffalo. Within a year, their thoughts would turn to supplying the Texas cattlemen. Stockyards were not yet fully built, and the Kansas quarantine law that would close down the central Kansas railheads to Texas cattle, was not yet a certainty.

The Santa Fe railcars brought in supplies from the east for the neighboring fort's military needs and merchandise for the town merchants. The cars were then loaded with thousands of buffalo hides and meat for the return trip. Indeed, Dodge City was bursting at the seams with commerce rarely seen in a frontier town in the middle of the Plains. In the years 1872 through 1874 alone, the Santa Fe shipped 459,453 buffalo hides from Dodge City.[15]

THE ADOBE WALLS TRAIL: (Map #5-3)

To take advantage of the economic rewards from marketing buffalo hides, Dodge merchants A. C. Myers, Fred Leonard, Robert M. Wright, and Charles Rath decided in March of 1874 to place a trading center closer to the hunters who had followed the buffalo south into the Panhandle.[16] The site the foursome selected was on the Canadian River about one and one half miles south of the old ruins of Fort Adobe.[17] Partners Myers and Leonard started the two hundred mile trek south in March of 1874 with thirty heavily loaded wagons of merchandise and building materials for their store. Fifty workmen and hunters, who were anxious to locate camps for the spring kill, traveled with them. Soon to follow, in April, was Rath and his company with another convoy of wagons and accompanying hunters with skinners.

The pathway blazed for Myers, Leonard and Wright, by teamsters, Charles Edward (Ed) Jones and Joseph H. Plummer, to Adobe Walls ran due south out of Dodge City, and crossed Mulberry Creek. About ten miles south of Mulberry Creek, the trail turned southwest, skirted Crooked Creek, which it crossed near the present-day Meade-Ford County line. The path crossed the corner of present-day Seward County angling south toward the Cimarron crossing. The route continued southwest

---

[15]Ida Ellen Rath, *The Rath Trail*, 101.

[16]The buffalo hunters were breaking treaties that had been made with the Indians in the region. In the Medicine Lodge Treaty of 1868, the Peace Commission provided that the area south of the Arkansas River was to be set aside for the Indians hunting grounds, and whites were granted safe passage but no other privileges. The hunters were taking buffalo from the Indians, and the merchants knew that to cross the "dead-line" and to build permanent structures in No Man's Land and the Texas Panhandle was illegal and extremely risky. (Rath, 102)

[17]Around 1845 or 1846, William Bent and partner Ceran St.Vrain built a satellite post to trade with the Indians in the area. This permanent structure, of adobe, was eighty foot square with nine-foot walls and only one entrance. After a battle with the Comanches, Fort Adobe, as it was called, was blown up and abandoned in 1849. The remaining walls (ruins) became a landmark.

THE WESTERN CATTLE TRAIL | 1874-1897

across No Man's Land, crossed the Beaver River, and entered the Panhandle just east of Palo Duro Creek. Straight south from there, the route went east of Horse Creek, entered the breaks of the Canadian River west of Adobe Creek, and followed that stream to one and one half miles south of the old Fort Adobe ruins[18].

Shortly after they arrived, these merchants built three sod structures on the site, closely placed together, with three-foot walls at the base of the structures tapering to eighteen inches at the top. The roofs were cottonwood logs and poles covered with sod. The Myers and Leonard Store, a twenty-by sixty-foot structure, included an eating house and an added corral. Next to it was the Rath and Wright store, and soon thereafter James N. Hanrahan and Rath opened a saloon. Tom O'Keefe started a blacksmith shop. One historian noted that, "By the end of spring [1874], 200 to 300 buffalo hunters roamed the area, and trade at Adobe Walls boomed."[19] The stores were referred to as Adobe Walls and the route to Dodge City was called the Adobe Walls Trail, but it didn't last long.

> Refer to "the Mobeetie Trail" section in Chapter IV about Charles Rath's activies after Adobe Walls.

On June 27, 1874, as the buffalo herds were thundering in from the south, an estimated 300 Indians led by Comanche prophet Isa-tai and Chief Quanah Parker attacked Adobe Walls, first killing some skinners in their camp on Chicken Creek and then advancing to the "Walls," as the hunters called the post. The Indians' planned early-morning surprise attack designed to overpower the white merchants and hunters did not materialize. Although vastly outnumbered, the twenty-eight men and one woman defended themselves in the unfinished, ill-equipped fortification. After the Indians withdrew from their attempted annihilation of the trespassers, the merchants and hunters scattered, some fleeing back to Dodge, and abandoned the trading post.[20]

The route established by these merchants between Dodge City and Adobe Walls was used for only about four months. It would be used later, however, as a portion of a cattle trail blazed by Charles Goodnight from his Palo Duro Ranch in the Texas Panhandle to Dodge City — and a feeder route to the Western Trail.

THE JONES AND PLUMMER TRAIL: (Map #5-3)

Shortly after the Adobe Walls fight in June of 1874, Ed Jones and Joseph Plummer decided to establish a camp at the head of Wolf Creek in Ochiltree County, Texas.[21] Knowing that there was a need for a trading post for hides and a store of

---

[18]C. Robert Haywood, "Adobe Walls Trail," *Handbook of Texas Online*, [accessed Oct. 19, 2011] Harry E. Chrisman, *Lost Trails of the Cimarron*, 40.

[19]H. Allen Anderson, "Adobe Walls, Tx," *Handbook of Texas Online*, [accessed Oct. 20, 2011]

[20]The success of the defenders was attributed to not only the thick walls of the adobes, but also to the new Sharps rifles that some of the hunters had with them. "Adobe Walls Trail," Ibid, and Rath, 109)

[21]Plummer was in transit with a wagon of supplies when the Second Battle of Adobe Walls occurred on June 27, 1874. He also missed being killed at the hide camp which was raided, and his companions murdered and scalped. Jones rushed to supply the traders and hunters with ammunition before the battle at Adobe Walls. (H. Allen Anderson, "Plummer, Joseph H.," *Handbook of Texas Online* and C. Robert Haywood, "Jones, Charles Edward," *Handbook of Texas Online* [accessed Nov. 1, 2011 and Nov. 5, 2011])

supplies for the hunters, Jones and Plummer ended their careers as buffalo hunters and became merchants and freighters. They built a cottonwood-picket-and-dugout store. Jones then marked out a 160-mile trail from there to Dodge City, and the partners freighted hides and meat north to Dodge and returned with supplies for the hunters.

As for the Mulberry Creek crossing south of Dodge City, where the feeder trails joined the Western Trail, it is doubtful that any road house was at the crossing as early as 1874. The following description of the Jones and Plummer route is taken from Robert Haywood's study, Trails South, *and the M. W. (Doc) Anshutz and Frank Webb map, created by Anshutz who was there and used the trail. The Anshutz memoirs by Doc and wife Carrie.* The Cimarron Chronicles, *is also referenced. The Haywood and Anshsutz sources differ somewhat. Haywood writes of Dugan's Store at the Mulberry Crossing while Anshultz shows the "Whitman Road Ranch" at the crossing (see Map #5-1). On this point, it appears that Doc Anshultz was in error; the Whiman's post office was located approximately four miles west of the later Dugan's Road House and crossing.*[22]

Anshutz and Webb also penciled on their map four other road houses, three of which are discussed by Haywood in his book. Whitman's Road Ranch and post office, and the other four road houses that Anshutz remembers were established later in the life of the trail — around 1885.

Doc Anshutz did not come to Kansas until 1877, after these trails had been established. His recollection of the Jones and Plummer Trail, therefore, is of the trail ten years after it was established. To substantiate this, Carrie Schmoker, future wife of M. W. (Doc) Anshutz, wrote that in 1879, only four years after the trail was established, she traveled down the Jones and Plummer Trail to a new homestead claim in what would later be Meade County (established Nov, 1885): "In all that distance, from Dodge to about three miles from the site of Meade," she wrote, "we saw not a single house, fence, field or tree, nothing but the brown trail and on every side as far as the eye could reach, just grassy prairie land..."[23]

The Jones and Plummer became a commercial highway after the hide business ended, and the road houses and post offices came and went according to the whims and financial or personal situations of the owners. Ranchers had staked out land in the Texas Panhandle and squatted in No Man's Land, present-day Oklahoma Panhandle, starting in 1876, but it was not until 1885 that homesteaders, in great numbers, came into the area. At this point, the Jones and Plummer was in its height of activity of a different kind. Instead of heavily laden wagons of buffalo hides, meat, and bones going to Dodge City from the Panhandle, there were wagons filled with merchandise and building materials for ranches, homesteaders, and new towns leaving Dodge and heading for the Panhandle and No Man's Land. In 1879 the trail was used by mail contractors, and by 1886, P.G. Reynolds made it a major stagecoach route from Dodge to Mobeetie.[24]

---

[22]The Whitman post office or "Whitman Road Ranch" was established on Feb. 27, 1885 and lasted until January 31, 1889. Charles W. Whitman was the post master. (Robert W. Baughman, *Kansas Post Offices*, 138 and 182). According to *The Kansas Everts Atlas of 1887*, the post office was located south of Mulberry Creek in SE 1/4 Section 16, T28S, R25W, page 326.

[23]Carrie and M.S. Anshutz, *Cimarron Chronicles*.

[24]C. Robert Haywood, "Jones and Plummer Trail," *Handbook of Texas Online*, [accessed Oct. 13, 2011]

So there are two time periods for the Jones and Plummer Trail — the era of the hide business starting in 1874 to the development of the early frontier ranches starting in 1876 — and the latter part of its life starting in 1879 when "civilization" started moving into the panhandles. The Anshutz map depicts this second time period.

We include the Jones and Plummer Trail, as well as the others, in this book to show that these trails were part of a network connected with the Western Cattle Trail, and that connection was at, or nearby, Mulberry Crossing. At first, it was the buffalo hide freighters that blended in with the Texas cattle herds on the Western Trail, in that last ten miles to Dodge. Subsequently traffic from mail wagons, stage coaches, and cattle herds from the Panhandle and No Man's Land ranches merged into the Western Trail. After 1885, when herds from south Texas no longer went into Kansas because of the quarantine, the Panhandle and No Man's Land ranchers had to share their space with the herds of Texas longhorns going north. (Part II) M. W. Anshutz, himself, in a letter in 1939 wrote:

> *The Jones & Plummer trail was more a feight than a cattle trail altho many herds from Texas panhandle ranches were driven over it to Dodge in the old days. But the main cattle movement from the Coast Country & Southern Texas was over the old "Texas" or "Through" trail as it was called in those days.[25]*

Thus, the Jones and Plummer Trail was a freight route until 1888, when the Atchinson, Topeka, and Santa Fe and the Rock Island railroads extended their services southwest and created rail centers and railheads for freight, but it was also used for cattle herds. The following description based on Haywood's research and Anshutz's recollections, includes the road houses and towns that later appeared several years after the trail was founded.

The Jones and Plummer Trail left Mulberry Creek going southwest, somewhat east of the old Adobe Walls Trail, passing the "Geo. Decow Road Ranch" (Anshutz, Map #5-1) a few miles south of the Mulberry. This was the approximate location of Wilburn, established in 1885, at the "swell of the Crooked Creek," just north of the current-day Ford-Meade county line. The town did not survive because the Rock Island Railroad "missed" the town.[26]

The trail continued from there paralleling Crooked Creek and skirting its east bank to keep to the edge of the sand hills. Fowler, established late in 1884, was the next town, eight miles southwest of Wilburn, where the trail turned west. Another twelve miles, just east of the future Meade City, put the freighters at George W. "Hoo-doo" Brown's road ranch, established in 1879-1880, (Anshutz, Map #5-1). On the creek, Hoo-Doo put up two sod buildings, one for a dwelling and the other one for a store.[27] South of Brown's road ranch at the confluence of Skunk Arroyo and

---

[25]Kansas Historical Society, letter dated August 11, 1939 from M. W. Anshutz, Nye, Kansas, to George Root Topeka, Kansas, item #222161, Trails correspondence 23. and, http://www.kansasmemory.org
[26]Haywood, 93.
[27]Carrie and M. S. Anshutz, *Cimarron Chronicles*, 117.

Crooked Creek, C. Pratt built a road-side store which later became known as O'dee, established post office, 1881. The road ranch was later managed by John Marts who moved to Crooked Creek with his family in 1879.[28]

At the crossing of the Cimarron River, two road houses existed, one on the north bank and one on the south bank. Charles Heinz's place was located on the north side along with "a spectacular prairie dog town on the flats."[29] Anshutz noted on his map: "Chas. Heinz Road House." On the south side was a station named Miles City, built and maintained by Captain and Mrs. Henry A. Busing. It consisted of a store and post office along with sheds and corrals. Neither Anshutz nor Haywood mention when these two road-side establishments started. The crossing, however, was called by various names. Haywood used "Miles Landing" in his text and "Busing Crossing" on his map. Anshutz used "Heinz's Place." The crossing was located east of Highway 23 in present-day Meade County.

In No Man's Land, fourteen miles south of Miles City, the route crossed the North Canadian (present-day Beaver) River at what would later become the location of Beaver City, established in 1880. The town company built the town right on the trail, and it survived the following years of rapid change when other early frontier towns did not. Before that, Jim Lane had built a large sod house for himself and family on the spot and had a store in one room. It served as the only road-side canteen until the town company placed its Main Street on the Jones and Plummer Trail.[30] Lane relinquished his squatter's claim, but continued to sell to the freighters; on the Anshultz map, it shows: "Lane Road Ranch."

South of the North Canadian (Beaver) River, freight wagons had to cross a stretch of sandy road that was the most dreaded part of the journey. The heavily loaded wagons bogged down in the deep sand, and freighters had to double team the wagons to get through. South of that point, it was open prairie. From Jim Lane's road house to the Jones and Plummer ranch on Wolf Creek was fifty-seven miles. The trail crossed into the Texas Panhandle north of current-day Booker and continued south to the campsite and store (located just east of present-day US Highway 83).

THE RATH TRAIL: (Map #5-3)

Not to be deterred by either the Indians or the abandonment of Adobe Walls, Charles Rath, who had been in Dodge City unloading hides and loading supplies in his wagons at the time of the Adobe Walls battle, established another store in 1875 on Sweetwater Creek at Hidetown, another buffalo-hide camp. Hostile bands of Indians, who were angered by their failure to annihilate the white intruders at the Walls, spread across the southern Plains, killing any white trespasser they encountered. In response, the military authorities were determined to remove all surviving Indians in the Panhandle and force them into Indian Territory.[31]

---

[28]Carrie and M. S. Anshutz, *Cimarron Chronicles*, 183.
[29]Haywood, 83.
[30]Haywood, 86.
[31]The Army offensive of 1874 and 1875 and the Indian resistance has been labeled the "Red River War."

In June of 1875, an army camp appeared on a low plateau overlooking Sweetwater Creek in order to observe the western boundary of Indian Territory. As construction of a permanent military facility was initiated, Rath unloaded his wagons at the neighboring Hidetown. The hide yard covered many acres of ground and the location became known as Sweetwater.[32] Rath, savvy about buffalo and their hunters, knew that the Sweetwater camp sat on the buffalo herds migration path. It became a strategic spot on a wagon road to the Red River Crossing, later to be known as Doan's Crossing, and on southeast to the railhead at Wichita Falls. (see the Mobeetie Trail section in Chapter IV and Map #4-2)

In the following fall of 1876, Rath joined forces with William McDole Lee and E. E. Reynolds to build another trading post and hide agency. From the Sweetwater Creek camp, Rath blazed a route south, and in Ida Ellen Rath's words:

> Rath rode ahead with a compass in his hand, heading straight south, following a trail where there was one, his pick and shovel crew making one where none existed….The trail they followed, with Charles Rath in the lead,…was called The Rath Trail.[33]

Rath City, (also referred to as Reynolds City), was located on the Double Mountain Fork of the Brazos River, 14 miles northwest of present-day Hamlin. The town was on the trail to Fort Griffin, another major buffalo hide center. By 1877, there were also two saloons, a dance hall, and several tents and dugouts.[34]

The trail between the Sweetwater camp and the Jones and Plummer ranch was extended south during this early period. When Fort Elliott was being established, supplies were brought in from Dodge City via Camp Supply. Using a military road to the new fort, wagons headed southwest, crossed the South Canadian River and traveled another thirty miles to Fort Elliott. When Mobeetie acquired a real foothold in the scheme of the network, however, freighters realized that the Jones and Plummer Trail was easier and more direct than routing their wagons through Camp Supply. Also in 1884, another road house was built about halfway on the extension between Wolf Creek and Mobeetie. John and George Gerlach built a log and plaster store on the South Canadian. Thus, the Jones and Plummer became the route of choice because it was convenient. The watering places were spaced closer together, the terrain was flatter, and road houses were established to serve the traveler.[35]

---

[32]Charles G. Davis, "Rath City, TX," *The Handbook of Texas Online*. [accessed Nov. 2, 2011] and Frederick Nolan, *Tascosa*, 33.

[33]Ada Ellen Rath, *The Rath Trail*, 144.

[34]Devon E. Kyvig, "Fort Elliott," *The Handbook of Texas Online*, and Ada Ellen Rath, Ibid, 154.

[35]Some people, including Ada Ellen Rath, considered the trail from Mobeetie to Dodge as the Rath Trail. The Haywood and Anshultz maps, however, correctly show it as the Jones and Plummer Trail from Fort Elliott (Mobeetie) to Dodge. They do not mention the Rath Trail, which was from Mobeetie south. On the other hand, Ada Ellen Rath shows the Rath Trail as coming out of Rath City, Texas, going through Mobeetie and on north to Dodge City, and she does not mention the Jones and Plummer Trail. (Haywood, Ibid, 4-5, 86-88 and Rath, Ibid, viii).

THE TASCOSA TRAIL: (Map #5-3)

Then there was Tascosa. Located one hundred miles west of Adobe Walls on the Canadian River, it became a trading center for surrounding ranchers in 1876. Because it was more isolated, Tascosa depended almost entirely on freighters arriving from Dodge City located two hundred and forty miles away. In spite of its distance from Dodge, which took an ox team with supplies four to six weeks to make the round trip, Tascosa became an important cowtown.

Two factors helped develop the route to Dodge. The old Fort Bascom military road had passed north of the town on its way to Fort Dodge in the late 1860s, and its route continued to be used occasionally by local traffic. Also, northeast of Tascosa, two hide hunter brothers, James H. and Robert Cator, and their party had established a camp on North Palo Duro Creek in 1873 in wait for an abundant herd of buffalo. On Christmas Day, a severe snowstorm moved in, and the party had to hastily build a crude dugout shelter with cottonwood pickets and buffalo hides in order to keep alive. They waited out the winter huddled in their shelter. In the following spring, the brothers moved to where the action was at Adobe Walls and established their camp on Aroja Bonita Creek, twelve miles from the Walls. After the Indian attack, as a result of which they claimed to have lost hides that were burned or stolen by the Indians, the Cator brothers returned to their shelter on Palo Duro Creek.

For the next three years the brothers worked out of their hide camp and ranch. Bob Cator established the best route for their hide wagons using the old military road and his own improvisation. In 1878, the brothers, realizing that the hide business was over, replaced their dugout on Palo Duro Creek with a three-room structure and established a store in order to sell and trade with local traffic. They called it Zulu Stockade because they considered the area as wild and isolated as the Zululand in southern Africa. Travelers coming out of Tascosa used their route and visited their stockade.[36]

The upper portion of the Tascosa Trail was actually the Jones and Plummer. Thus, the route south from Dodge followed the common road for all the trails, including the Western Trail, to the Mulberry Creek crossing at Dugan's Store. Travelers using the Jones and Plummer Trail or the Tascosa Trail turned southwest at Mulberry Creek and Dugan's Store, went by Hoo-Doo Brown's Soddy, south of Meade, crossed the Cimarron River at Heinz Crossing, and on to Beaver City in No Man's Land. At Beaver City, the Jones and Plummer Trail continued straight south to its Wolf Creek store, while the Tascosa Trail crossed the border into Texas and branched southwest to Chiquita Creek, in the northwest corner of present-day Ochiltree County, Texas. The trail continued southwest to Zulu Stockade and on to Little Blue stage stand, south of Dumas, Texas. Here the trail branched. The northern branch went to Tascosa by way of present-day Hartley County, and the southern branch entered Tascosa after turning south and then west through present-day Potter County.[37]

---

[36]H. Allen Anderson, "James Hamilton Cator," *The Handbook of Texas Online* [accessed Nov. 6, 2011]

[37]C. Robert Haywood, "Tascosa-Dodge City Trail," *Handbook of Texas Online* [accessed Oct. 13, 2011]
While Haywood indicated that the Tascosa Trail lead into Mulberry Crossing, (Map 1, Trails South), Ethel E. Watkins on her map in *Annie: Child of the Prairie*, page 38, shows the Tascosa Trail blending into the trunk line of the Western Trail north of Mulberry Crossing.

THE WESTERN CATTLE TRAIL | 1874-1897

THE TUTTLE TRAIL: (Map # 5-3)

Another Texas Panhandle - No Man's Land route that came into the Mulberry Crossing at Dugan's Store was the Tuttle Trail. In the spring of 1875, A. G. (Jim) Springer selected a spot on Boggy Creek just north of its junction with the Canadian River and built a ranch and store.

Springer chose wisely. His multi-room dugout served as a store, saloon, and hotel on the military road between Camp Supply and Fort Elliott. The roadhouse became a favorite stop for buffalo hunters, soldiers, and cowboys who could enjoy games of cards with Springer and purchase refreshments and supplies. Springer took in a young man, Tom Leadbetter, and the two decided in 1877 to construct a better roadhouse from cottonwood pickets with a thatched roof. In the following year, however, the two were killed over a poker game. The ranch was sold to John F. Tuttle and Frank (Bud) Chapman from Dodge City. Tuttle bought out Chapman's interest and continued to operate the ranch. In about 1880, Tuttle blazed a more direct route to Dodge City in order to deliver his cattle. It became known as the Tuttle Trail and was used by other cattlemen as well.[38]

THE PALO DURO — DODGE CITY TRAIL:

When Charles Goodnight came into the Texas Panhandle in the fall of 1876, he was one of the very first settlers to venture into the area after the Indians surrendered and moved to reservations.[39] With the financial backing of John Adair, Goodnight was able to buy up land for ranching and expanded the Palo Duro Canyon Ranch. (Refer to Part I, Chapter III)

Soon other ranchers followed Goodnight's lead into the Texas Panhandle. By 1877, a rough trail was laid out to deliver "a small bunch of cattle" from the JA Ranch to Dodge City. Goodnight wrote in 1926 that Leigh Dyer, his brother-in-law

> laid off the Dodge Trail, but he really didn't make much trail. He went haphazard until he struck the main freight road at the Canadian [Adobe Walls Trail]. We laid off the regular trail in 1878, and kept west of this route and the freight road until we got to within about four miles of Dodge. It was a straight route, and kept away from the Texas

---

[38]A post office was established at the ranch in September of 1879 under the name of Springer Ranch and lasted until February of 1885. In 1881, Tuttle sold his ranch to the Rhodes and Aldridge Company, a Denver horse ranch operation. (H. Allen Anderson, "Springer Ranch," *Handbook of Texas Online* [accessed Oct. 19, 2011]

[39]Many cattlemen, including Charles Goodnight, had lost their fortunes and herds in the nation-wide financial crash and panic of 1873. After seven years of hard work including the establishing of four cattle trails in Colorado, and investing in a southern Colorado ranch on the Arkansas River near Pueblo, Goodnight was left with only a mixed herd of 1,600 longhorns and his dignity. In late 1875, at the age of forty, he was looking to start again in the Panhandle. (Robertson and Robertson, *Cowman's Country*, 18, 23)

trail [Western]. We had to keep away from the Texas cattle to keep from getting Texas fever into our herds.[40]

The route from the JA Palo Duro Ranch to Dodge was "pretty near a straight course," according to Goodnight. "I know I was just thirty-five miles west of the hundredth meridian....The north star was all the compass I needed." Trail drivers basically used the Adobe Walls Trail to Beaver City and then roughly followed the Jones and Plummer Trail, or as Goodnight wrote, "We crossed it three or four times, but kept a straighter course than it did."

Goodnight herds, with the JA brand, started where Spring Creek and Mulberry Creek run together about three miles southeast of what would later become Goodnight, Texas (established in 1888). Here Goodnight built large receiving pens for the herds to be driven to Dodge City. After the first day's drive, which took herds through the present-day Goodnight area, the cowboys camped on the Salt Fork of the Red River. On the second day, the herds were driven to White Deer Creek, and on to the Arkansas River at Dodge City.[41]

DEVELOPING RANCHES IN THE TEXAS PANHANDLE CHANGE THE CATTLE – TRAILING INDUSTRY:

Starting in 1877, many large ranches were developed in the Panhandle. When the Indians were confined to Indian Territory on reservations, the Panhandle and No Man's Land became a tempting region for ranches. The buffalo had been drastically

For the reader who wants to delve deeper into these other trails in the Texas Panhandle and No Man's Land, we recommend C. Robert Haywood's *Trails South* (1986), Ida Ellen Rath's *The Rath Trail* (1961), Carrie and M.W. Anshutz's *Cimarron Chronicles* (written in the 1930s and published in 2003 by a granddaughter), and M. W. Anshutz's and Frank A. Webb's annotated map created in the 1930s.[42] We have included a portion of the Anshutz and Webb map in this study.

We mention these trails, Fort Bascom / Tascosa, Palo Duro / Adobe Walls, Rath Trail / Jones and Plummer, and the Tuttle because they all joined with the Western Trail south of Dodge, and it could be said, they fed into the Western and for the last few miles into Dodge were using the Western Cattle Trail.

Some of these trails were created at the same time as the Western Cattle Trail, 1874-1875. The military road from Fort Bascom (1863-1870) to Dodge City, that also traversed across the Texas Panhandle and No Man's Land, however, was pre-Santa Fe Railroad and pre-Western Trail. The fort, located just over the Texas border in New Mexico Territory, was abandoned only seven years after its establishment, but its military road later continued to be used, in part, as the Tascosa Trail by local Panhandle and No Man's Land ranchers. Therefore, the Fort Bascom Trail is shown on our map as part of the network of local routes that fed into the Western Trail at Mulberry Creek south of Dodge.

Remember that these well-known routes were originally created as hide and freight routes. They were a way to get the buffalo hides to market, but during their use by the teamsters and bullwackers and after the short-lived hide business, the wagon roads continued to be used by the local civilian traffic and cattlemen to trail their herds to Dodge.

---

[40]Goodnight later became the leading advocate in the Panhandle measures to protect stock from the Texas Fever. He played a major leadership role to keep herds clean after the Kansas quarantine of 1885. (Letter written by Charles Goodnight, Goodnight, Texas, to J. Evetts Haley, November 18, 1926, in the Haley Collection, Haley Memorial Library and History Center, Midland, Texas)

[41]The course of this trail to Dodge was described to Goodnight biographer, J. Evetts Haley, in two letters from Goodnight in November of 1926 and August of 1928. Both documents can be found at the Haley Memorial Library and History Center in Midland, Texas. E. Ethel Watkins in her book, *Annie: Child of the Prairie*, shows the "Goodnight Trail" as blending into the Western Cattle Trail a few miles north of Mulberry Creek, map, page 38.

THE WESTERN CATTLE TRAIL | 1874-1897

thinned out if not eliminated by the hide-hunters, whose camps disappeared or were replaced with fledgling communities. There was now a vast region of free grass. Within three years, eighteen ranches were established in the Texas Panhandle alone and some of them were as large as small European countries.

As Charles Goodnight was getting established in the Palo Duro Canyon, the freighting routes used by the buffalo hunters of the region were no longer used as freight routes to Dodge City, but were becoming civilian routes or cattle trails. As cattle ranchers followed Goodnight's lead into the Texas Panhandle, they also looked to Dodge City as an outlet for their cattle. The already established "hide trails" were used to trail their herds to market. In the same period, 1874-1876, the Western Cattle Trail was in its infancy; however by 1876, had become a substantial cattle trail into Dodge.

In the summer of 1877, two Chicago gentlemen who wanted to experience the West, W. H. Bates and D. T. Beals, set up a crude ranch headquarters in the vacant, unorganized landscape twenty miles down river from Casimiro Romero's Atascosa store.[43] Their ranch simply became known as **the LX**.

W.M.D. Lee and the Reynolds brothers, government contract freighters, decided to go into the cattle business in 1879 and established the **LE Ranch**. It was located west of Tascosa, (established in 1878), along the New Mexico border. When the Reynolds bought out Lee in 1881, Lee took on another partner, Lucien B. Scott, a wealthy banker from Leavenworth, Kansas, and they established the **LS Ranch**, Lee-Scott Cattle Company. Their first headquarters were located on the Rita Blanca Creek southeast of Tascosa. For a few years the LS was the largest ranch in the Texas Panhandle; it was almost as large as the state of Connecticut.[44]

The **Frying Pan Ranch**, headquartered about twenty miles southeast of Tascosa, was established in 1881. The Panhandle Ranch, as it was officially named, was owned by J. F. Glidden, the 1873 inventor of barbed wire, and his sales agent, H. B. Sanborn. The sales of barbed wire had gone so well in the lower part of Texas

---

[42]M. W. (Doc.) Anshutz (1861 -1840) at the age of 16, accompanied his aunt and small cousins from Ohio to Spearville, Kansas, "a mere station on the Santa Fe" in April of 1877. He soon found his way to Dodge City and eventually went to work for Fred Tanitor on his ranch in No Man's Land. In 1892, he married Carrie W. Schomoker (1868-1944) and they homesteaded on the north side of the Cimarron River in Meade County. In the 1930s both Carrie and Doc wrote about their lives and experiences. The fading manuscript was discovered in an attic and published in 2003 as the *Cimarron Chronicles*. Doc also dictated the markings for a map to his son-in-law, Frank A. Webb, who meticulously penciled out a more detailed map of the area that Doc knew so well — No Man's Land and southwest Kansas. The original map can be found at the No Man's Land Museum in Goodwell, Oklahoma.

[43]The first settlers to venture into the Texas Panhandle after the Indians surrendered were Spanish and Mexican sheepmen who knew about the rich grazing land of the Canadian River. Led by Casimiro Romero, the sheepmen trailed their flocks from New Mexico Territory to the present-day Tascosa vicinity and colonized by building plazas along the river. When Charles Goodnight came into the Panhandle in the fall of 1876, he and Romero entered into a pact. Goodnight agreed to not move into the Canadian Valley if Romero would agree to stay off of the headwaters of the Red River and out of the canyons of the Palo Duro. When other cattle ranchers came into the area, however, and started buying and leasing land, the sheepmen trailed their flocks back to New Mexico.

[44]To help to persuade the sheepmen to leave the Canadian valley, W.M.D. Lee, put $35,000 in a valise, hitched up a team and buggy, and drove down the Canadian River, buying out Mexican plazas, one by one. (Robertson & Robertson, 112)

that with part of the fortune they made, they purchased an enormous tract of land in the Panhandle, covering almost the entire western half of present-day Potter County and portions of Randall County. Also to demonstrate their wares, the ranch was enclosed with their extra heavy No. 9 barb wire--some 120 miles of fence.

Farther north on the Tascosa - Dodge City Trail, at Zulu Stockade, was, as noted above, the Cator brothers' ranch. In 1878, they dispensed with buffalo hunting and freighting and purchased cattle from the LX and started ranching. Robert Cator's brand was **the VP** and James Cator had the **Diamond C** brand. Just east of the Cators was the **Three Sevens Ranch**, started by Henry S. Boice and his financial partner, a Mr. Berry, in 1881. Boice's steer operation ran along the North Palo Dura Creek in present-day Ochiltree and Hansford counties.

Tascosa, established in 1878, was the center for the ranchers and cowboys from these ranches.

In the center corridor of the Texas Panhandle, west of the JA Palo Duro Ranch, was the **T Anchor Ranch** owned by Jot Gunter, Jule Gunter, and William B. Munson. By the fall of 1882, they began trailing cattle to the Dodge City railhead.[45] Northeast of the T Anchor and JA ranches was the **Diamond F** lands. The ranch was owned by an English company chartered as the Francklyn Land and Cattle Company in 1882. Managed by B. B. Groom and his son Harrison, the total holdings included 529,920 acres of leased grassland in Hutchinson, Gray, Roberts, and Carson counties where steers were fattened to prepare for market. They also had a stock ranch in Greer County. The Groom ranch had a Jones and Plummer stage stop located on the spread. The Grooms' neighbors and friends to the north were Henry Whiteside (Hank) Cresswell of the **Bar CC** and J. M. Coburn of the **Turkey Track Ranch**. Cresswell, who had been a dairyman and rancher in Colorado and neighbor to Charles Goodnight, came to the Panhandle in 1877. With partners J.A. and M.D. Thatcher and O.H.P. Baxter, Cresswell created the Cresswell Land and Cattle Company (the Bar CC) on a small creek north of the Canadian in Ochiltree County, to be known subsequently as Home Ranch Creek. Robertson and Robertson write that: "Eventually, the ranch extended from the Canadian River north to the state line, approximately a million and a quarter acres."[46] Later on, when Cresswell decided to move his headquarters farther south to a more centralized location on the ranch, he bought the old Jones and Plummer picket stockade that had been used to storehouse buffalo hides. From the front door of the picket house was the well worn path to Dodge City which Jones and Plummer and other buffalo hunters had used to deliver hides. It had became a cattle trail, convenient for the Bar CC as well as its neighbors to trail herds to Dodge.[47]

One of the Bar CC neighbors was James M. Coburn. He was an American Scotsman and Kansas City banker. In the six years following the removal of the Plains Indians, Coburn noticed the rush to the Panhandle by ranchmen and knew that a great amount of foreign money was backing those developing ranches. Thus,

---

[45]Robertson & Robertson, 146.
[46]Robertson & Robertson, 78.
[47]When Jones and Plummer moved away from the stockade in about 1876, Al and Doc Barton lived in the house. Cresswell bought the picket house from them. (Robertson & Robertson, 78)

in 1882, he went back to his native Scotland and persuaded a number of his country-men to invest in the ranching business. Coburn founded the **Hansford Land & Cattle Company** by buying up smaller ranches and herds. In January of 1883 he purchased the Turkey Track Ranch which had been started by R. L. McAnuity in 1879. He bought out T. S. Bugbee's Quarter Circle T at Adobe Walls, which was only the third ranch to be established in the entire Panhandle after the JA Ranch in 1876, and the Scissors Ranch from W. E. Anderson, who had established a ranch at the Adobe Walls site in 1878. Coburn chose to keep the Turkey Track brand for the expanded ranch which encompassed most of Hutchinson and Hansford counties. He then wisely hired the experienced C. B. (Cape) Willingham to manage the ranch which included 85,000 acres owned and 350,000 acres leased.

The **Seven K Ranch**, established by George Anderson in 1878, a smaller spread by comparison to the others, was developed early in Lipscomb County, south of Wolf Creek. The Jones and Plummer route went through the Seven K.[48]

These ranchers and others eventually changed the trajectory of the cattle-trailing industry. In the early years of ranch developent in the Texas Panhandle, the established buffalo hide trails were used by the local Panhandle cattle barons. When the state of Kansas attempted to quarantine Texas cattle out of the state in 1885, Charles Goodnight lobbied legislators to include in the legislation a loophole. These ranchers received special treatment in the Dodge City yards. The purpose of the law was to keep cattle from "communicating the Texas, splenic or Spanish fever," and, thus, bar longhorns entering Kansas. Goodnight made it clear to his Kansas legislative friends that the ranchers in the Panhandle and No Man's Land had policed their herds, and they were clean of the Texas Fever, and besides, the herds had wintered through the pre-season. Therefore, in Section 5 of the "Protection of Cattle Against Disease" Act, it stated:

> *Provided, however,* That if the owner or owners, or person in charge of such cattle, shall show by such certificate or certificates as shall hereafter be designated by the live-stock sanitary commission of this state, that the said cattle had been kept since the first day of December of the previous year west of the east line of the Indian Territory and north of the thirty-sixth parallel of north latitude, or west of the twenty-first meridian of longitude of north latitude, the provisions of this section shall not apply thereto.[49]

These boundaries were outside of the Texas Panhandle. The 36th parallel is basically the Red River.[50] However, the concession would not be a benefit for long. When the

---

[48]Robertson & Robertson, 137.

[49]*State of Kansas Session Laws of 1885*, published May 1, 1885, Chapter CXCI, "Protection of Cattle Against Disease," 310.

[50]Because of experience, it was believed in 1885 that north of the Red River, approximately the 36th parallel, cattle that had gone through a winter of freezing weather would be free of the Texas Fever. Therefore, if an owner could produce a certificate to show that his herds had "been kept since the first day of December" north of that line, it was assumed that the disease was eradicated. Winters were not considered harsh enough south of the 36th parallel. Since Charles Goodnight and his neighbors' ranches were north of the 36th parallel, the Act's provisions "shall not apply thereto."

trail system shifted west in 1885, the Texas Panhandle became the new gathering area for cattle for the industry. No longer were the majority of the trail herds coming out of south Texas. These Panhandle ranches, that were developed in the mid-1870s, took on the role of providing the cattle for the northern market. This will be discussed in length in Part III.

THE TRUNK LINE OF THE WESTERN CATTLE TRAIL INTO DODGE CITY, KANSAS:

As noted earlier, in the Mulberry Creek Crossing vicinity, Panhandle cattle trails, stage lines, the Western Trail, one branch of the Cimarron Cut-off from the Eastern Trail, and the Fort Supply - Fort Dodge military road merged. The combined trail became more conjested as it approached Dodge City. In 1882 another factor changed the complexion of the area. In June, Fort Dodge was suddenly closed. One company each was sent to Fort Reno, Fort Supply, and Fort Elliott, where they would be closer to the Indian reservations. What had once been the most important fort in the area — one that had supplied and provisioned other forts, cantonments, and soldiers since 1865 — was partially demolished.[51]

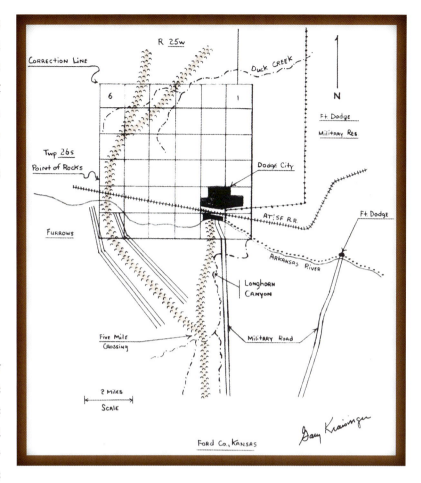

#5-4
The Western Cattle Trail Going Into and Around Dodge City, Kansas:
This map shows the Western Cattle Trail approaching Dodge City, Kansas from the south. Herds destined to be shipped out went straight into the Santa Fe loading pens. Some herds were held in "Longhorn Canyon," a natural corral before entering Dodge. Herds destined to continue on north went around Dodge City on the west side, using Point of Rocks as landmark.

Meanwhile, herds and their cowboys continued north toward Dodge City. Two miles south of Dodge City on Five Mile Creek was a canyon (Longhorn Canyon) and holding area. Here herds could be corralled and held while drovers rested or the owner/contractor could conduct business in Dodge City.[52]

---

[51] "Fort Dodge, Ford County, Kansas," Ford County Historical Society site, taken from Ida Ellen Rath's *Early Ford County* (1964), www.skyways.org. [accessed Oct. 20, 2011]

[52] Interview: Charles Meade, Dodge City, Kansas, owner of the Longhorn Canyon Ranch, and Gary Kraisinger, December 12, 2011. The location is in NW 1/4 of NE 1/4 of Section 14, T27S, R24W. The pathway is still partially visible today from the canyon toward Dodge City. In 2010, the Kansas chapter of the Great Western Cattle Trail Association placed a "GR Western TR" marker (post) on US Highway 56, one half mile west of the junction of Highway 56 and 283. The marker is on the south side of the road in Section 11, T27S, R25W.

THE WESTERN CATTLE TRAIL | 1874-1897

Point of Rocks: *Drovers on the Western Trail used this landmark as a signal to turn their Texas herds north toward Ogallala, Nebraska and beyond. This old photo, taken from the southeast between 1914 and 1922, shows Point of Rocks as it appeared at that time. The DAR (Daughters of the American Revolution) placed their marker here in 1907-1908, recognizing that the Point was an important landmark on the Santa Fe Trail (1822-1872). Soldiers on routes to Fort Mann (1846-1848) and Fort Atkinson (1850-1854), travelers on the Cherokee Trail (1849-to early 1890s), and drovers on the Western Trail (1874- 1885) all used this point as a landmark.*

Photo courtesy of Stan Trekell, Lawrence, Kansas.

Point of Rocks: *Four-miles west of Dodge City, this out-cropping of rocks is still quite noticeable. Since the early Santa Fe Trail days, almost 200 years ago, this landmark has been a point of reference to travelers. As of this writing, there is concern that the point will again be reduced in order to widen US Highway 50 to Cimarron. The City of Dodge City placed the now-famous cowboy metal sculpture on top of the point around 1997. The picture was taken from the west.*

Longhorn Canyon: *Two miles south of Dodge City on Five Mile Creek, a natural canyon was used by drovers to corral and hold their herds while in camp and resting from the long trip from Texas or while negotiations were in process for selling the longhorns in Dodge City. In the background of this 1878 photo is Five Mile Creek.*

Photo courtesy of landowner Charles Meade, Dodge City, Kansas.

The first herds from off of the Western Trail usually reached Dodge the first part of June. Drovers had already been on the "Dodge City Trail," as they sometimes called it, and away from home for eight to ten weeks. To the drovers, Dodge offered excitement, entertainment, and a time to let loose. For the trail boss and/or contractor, the railhead meant business. If the herd had been sold and was to be shipped back east, Dodge City marked the end of the trail. The trail boss negotiated the final price, ordered his outfit to load the cattle, and paid off the men upon completion of the job. Most of the time, however, Dodge was not the end of the trail. Over eighty to eighty five per cent of the cattle coming up the trail continued beyond Dodge. The trail boss/contractor then had to replenish his supplies, perhaps hire more cowboys, replace worn-out horses, repair wagons, and return to the northbound trail as soon as possible.

If the herds had been contracted to be sold farther up the trail, or if the trail boss's plans were to continue beyond Dodge to another destination, the Texas herds were not brought into Dodge. The cowboys would take turns riding into Dodge for entertainment, but the herds were held in camp south, west, and north of the community. Since the Fort Dodge military reservation was on the east side of Dodge, cattle herds could only bypass Dodge City on the west. Some herds started this western detour around Dodge as far south as Five Mile Crossing. This way the through-herds would not mix with other herds along the banks of the Arkansas River that were waiting to be loaded into railcars. From this location Kansas farmers/homesteaders had dug furrows to guide the trail drivers around Dodge. This labor-intcnsivc job was not done for the sake of the Texas drovers, but for the local famers' own purpose. Drovers were encouraged to keep their herds within the furrows and out of the way of the homesteaders' ground to protect settlers' crops and away from domestic cattle to prevent infection by Texas Fever.

KANSAS HOMESTEADERS AND STATE QUARANTINES:

The peak years of the Western Cattle Trail were also the peak years of homesteader migration into western Kansas. The forces propelling that migration were the Homestead Act of 1862, that offered almost free land to hard-working settlers, and the aura of manifest destiny that seemed to offer succcss to those who pushed west after the Civil War. The Union Pacific Railroad, Eastern Division, renamed the Kansas Pacific in 1869, had established numerous water stops and rail sidings across western Kansas by 1868, and the Atchinson, Topeka and Santa Fe Railway completed its rails to Dodge City and beyond in 1872. Therefore, after the winter of 1875 when Indians surrendered after their war of resistance, and were placed on assigned reservations, land hungry settlers, following the railroads, started arriving in western Kansas in waves, filing for homesteads to be cultivated and fenced.[53] By 1878, the largest surge of migration to ever hit Kansas poured into the state's western counties from the east and Europe, and the Texas cowboys with their longhorns headed north. It was inevitable that the two would collide. The fenced homesteads with plowed fields for crops and planted gardens were in the way of Texas drovers and their open-range ideas. The vast herds of longhorns, one after another, created, each succeeding year, a grazing swath across the landscapes which antagonized the "nesters."

To add to the antagonism on both sides was the Texas Fever. The Kansas Legislature had been dictating to the cattlemen for years, through quarantines, where they could and could not trail the herds. Beginning in 1859, the Kansas Territorial government had drawn a deadline through its eastern territory to keep the Texas herds well to the west of the oncoming settlements. Eventually the state had shut down first the Shawnee Trail and later the Chisholm Trail.

By 1876, when the Western Trail via Dodge City had replaced the quarantined Chisholm, the westward movement of the settlers had accelerated. Therefore, the

---

[53]James R. Shortridge in his *Peopling the Plains* states that two factors temporarily delayed the movement of people into western Kansas: the financial panic of 1873 and the grasshopper invasion of 1874. In 1875, however, the Kansas Pacific and the Santa Fe railroads initiated their major efforts to promote their railroad property and the advantages of settlement into the western counties of the state. By 1878 the "farming frontier [was] pushing westward" very rapidly. 72-77

Kansas Legislature had to revisit the deadline issue of its quarantine law again. As settlers continued to move rapidly west, cattle herds entered into the state from the south numbering 200,000 to 300,000 per season, and, over a nine-year period, the Kansas Legislature altered its deadline three times. This dynamic situation created five pathways across northwestern Kansas.

From 1876 to 1885, the deadline changed so many times that Texas cowboys needed to keep appraised about the Kansas law. The experienced cowhand could find himself following a different pathway than he did the season before, and, of course, there were always the settlers to worry about. Because Dodge City was a profitable business center, serving a growing population of settlers and ranchers in the region, the state's ever-changing deadlines spared the area, but west and north of Dodge was a vast region that fell victim to the sharpened pencils and decisions of the legislature.

After the 1875 quarantine, many Texas cattlemen assumed that the Dodge railhead would be safe from the unpopular quarantine line for many years, and that the western Kansas community would be their gate of opportunity to the northern territories. Just one year later, after Dodge City had established permanent corrals and holding pens, another quarantine deadline was breathing down the backs of the drovers. As a review, these five routes are as follows.[54]

NORTH OF DODGE: THE HAYS CITY — ELLIS TRAIL: (Map #5-5) CLOSED BY THE 1876 KANSAS QUARANTINE

In the early years of the Western Trail, cattlemen closely followed the military roads. This was for protection and, of course, these trails were where the early road houses were located. In the first years of the Western Trail through western Kansas, the drovers continued to parallel the military road north of Dodge — the Fort Hays-Fort Dodge Road. The railheads that catered to the Texas cattlemen beyond Dodge City were Hays City and Ellis on the Kansas Pacific. Ellis, Kansas, however, was particularly active in attracting the drovers away from Dodge City, convincing them to come to town. In 1876 when an estimated 200,000 cattle trailed up the Western Trail, Ellis merchants, the *Ellis County Star*, in Hays City, and the Kansas Pacific Railroad all boasted of their services, giving drovers a choice. Waiting on available trains in Dodge became a problem for trail drivers; consequently, the approximately seven-day drive to Ellis or Hays City was rewarded by good service and all the amenities a cowboy would want in a less crowded environment.

Ellis and Hays City were no stranger to cattle trailing. Even before Dodge City had thought of being a cattle center, herds were entering Ellis's railhead. In 1873, L. B. Harris had driven cattle, using his own route, from south Texas to Ellis by way of military roads between forts. There is also evidence, during the 1872-74

---

[54]These five routes, based around the quarantine laws, are presented in detail in Chapters 7 - 11 in Kraisinger & Kraisinger, *The Western, the Greatest Texas Cattle Trail, 1874-1886*. (pub. 2004)

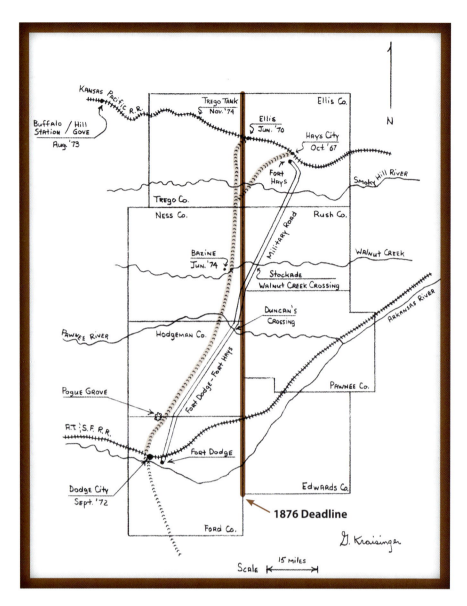

#5-5
The Hays City-Ellis Trail North of Dodge, and the 1876 Kansas Quarantine Deadline:
This map shows the Hay City-Ellis Cattle Trail and the Fort Dodge-Fort Hays military road from Dodge City, Kansas to Hays City and Ellis. This cattle trail was used, in part, as early as 1873 by L. B. Harris who followed the military road with a herd of longhorns he trailed from Fort Dodge to Fort Hays.

After Dodge City built its stockyards and was recognized as a railhead for cattle in 1875, this Hays City-Ellis Trail was used by Texas drovers to reach the Kansas Pacific railroad until 1877. Even though the quarantine line caused the trail system to move west in 1876, some drovers still used Ellis as a railhead in 1877 because the town was on the line.

period, that cattle had been driven into the Hays City and Ellis area from the east, off of the Chisholm Trail.

For three seasons, 1874 to 1876, drovers left Dodge City and pushed their herds slightly northeast paralleling the military road in Hodgeman County, continued across the eastern edge of Ness and Trego counties, and trailed to either Ellis or Hays City in Ellis County. In the spring of 1876, however, the Kansas Legislature enacted another deadline to be drawn along the western borders of Edwards, Pawnee, Rush, and Ellis counties, to take effect the following season. Only one year after shutting down Wichita and Ellsworth, the Kansas Legislature had drawn a new quarantine line — over fifty miles farther west than a year earlier — at the back door of Fort Dodge. Ellis and Hays City were behind the line. Dodge City was happy to be rid of its aggressive Ellis rival, but, at the same time, the quarantine line was now uncomfortably close.

Even with this drastic move of the quarantine line, it was not enough for some homesteaders. Ness County had been left out of the legislation. One homesteader let his disappointment be known in the Hays City newspaper in September of 1876:

…This wail I raise because of the glaring injustice done in Ness county by the legislature in not bringing her within the deadline. By this act our citizens have nearly lost their all; and if not remedied this fall, the most of us will leave. Each and every farmer who owns a few head of cows has lost over half of them by the pestilence — Texas fever….Not a man has escaped; and the effect is awful — we are in despair.[55]

NORTH OF DODGE: ROUTE 1, TO OGALLALA, NEBRASKA AND BEYOND: (Map #5-6)
CLOSED BY THE 1877 KANSAS QUARANTINE

The reason drovers trailed cattle to Ellis or Hays City was to use those Kansas Pacific railheads. However, because a large percentage of the trailed cattle were not to be shipped out of Kansas at either Dodge City, Ellis, or Hays City, an alternate route was used north of Dodge toward Ogallala, Nebraska. This other route, Route 1,[56] was basically the same for a short distance north of Dodge, then split south of Pogue Grove in Ford County. If cattlemen wanted to head toward Ogallala, Nebraska, they would cross Sawlog Creek west of Pogue Grove and trail another nine miles north to Buckner Creek. After crossing Buckner Creek, the trail angled west toward the northwest corner of Hodgeman County and continued north paralleling the Hays City-Ellis Trail. After crossing the Pawnee River in Hodgeman County, herds were trailed straight north through Ness, Gove, Sheridan, and Decatur counties. This route was a direct path to Ogallala. From the Sawlog just north of Dodge to Ogallala was 226 miles of open terrain. It was normally a fifteen to twenty day drive.

This is the route that Lewis Neatherlin used in 1876. He guided three of John H. Slaughter's herds over this route to Ogallala. Route 1 was used in 1874, 1875, 1876, and 1877 but because Ness County raised objection about being left west of the 1876 quarantine line, Route 1, like the earlier Hays City -Ellis Trail, was quarantined out of existence only four seasons after its initial use. In the spring of 1877, the Kansas Legislature slightly altered its 1876 deadline, to take effect in 1878, redrawing the line to place Ness County behind the line. The northern part of the deadline area remained the same, but the southern portion of the line was moved further west to the center of Ford and Hodgeman counties and then jogged around Ness County to include it under the new 1877 quarantine law.

---

[55]Minnie D. Millbrook, *Ness Western County Kansas*, 100.

[56]The routes across western Kansas, as described and mapped in detail in our book *The Western, the Greatest Texas Cattle Trail, 1874-1886*, were identified as the Hays City-Ellis Trail; Route I; Route II; Route III; and the Wallace Branch. These same labels are being used herein. Each subsequent route was farther west because of deadlines enacted by the state quarantine laws — because of the Texas Fever.

THE WESTERN CATTLE TRAIL | 1874-1897

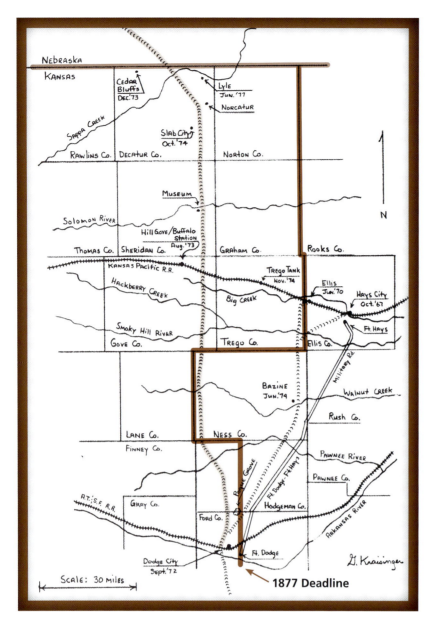

#5-6
Route 1 of the Western Cattle Trail North of Dodge, and the 1877 Kansas Quarantine Deadline:
This map shows Route 1 of the Western Trail from Dodge City, Kansas, across Kansas, toward Ogallala, Nebraska.

Starting in 1874, drovers and their herds trailed straight north from Dodge City toward Ogallala's Union Pacific rail yards during the same period that trail drivers were using the Hays City-Ellis Cattle Trail. When the Kansas cattle deadline was drawn in 1877, to appease Ness County, Route 1 ceased to be used.

NORTH OF DODGE: ROUTE 2, TO OGALLALA, NEBRASKA AND BEYOND: (Map #5-7) CLOSED BY THE 1881 KANSAS QUARANTINE

The 1877 law satisfied homesteaders in Ness County but created dissension in Lane and Gove counties. Trail drivers on a new Route 2 adjusted their route to the west and trailed through Lane and Gove counties, but settlers in those areas became upset and vocal. Immediately after the legislature's spring session, Governor George Anthony received a letter signed by 175 families in the Collyer, Kansas area of Trego County expressing their disappointment that Trego and Gove counties — located north and west of the newly drawn deadline — had been left out. The letter clearly expressed the sentiments of some Kansas homesteaders toward cowboys and their cattle:

246   THE WESTERN CATTLE TRAIL | 1874-1897

We the Chicago Soldiers Colony, at Collyer, Kansas, have been informed that Texas cattle are now enroute east, and that it has always been the custom to camp and graze along the course of Big Creek in Trego and Gove counties, and on the lands now occupied by the Colony as Homesteads, and as the damage to planted crops caused by the run of thousands of cattle upon it would be a very serious matter to us, utterly ruining us financially, as we have our all involved in the endeavor to obtain a home for ourselves and families, and as it is well those herders are composed of the outcasts of Society, unprincipled and lawless men, who disregard the rights of life of any person, we would most respectfully request that a detachment of military be sent to prevent the cattle from entering on the lands of Trego and Gove counties as we are not provided with arms to protect ourselves and families from such lawless men,…[57]

The resentment shown toward the cowboys in this letter did not result in any immediate changes. Homesteaders in Trego and Gove counties, west of the 1877 deadline, had to contend with their situation for another four years. The comment "now enroute east" hints, however, that the herds and their "unprincipled" cowboys were driving around Ness County, trailing back east across Gove and Trego counties, crossing the Smoky Hill River and delivering their stock to the Ellis stockyards which were about two miles behind the deadline. Perhaps this is why the homesteader called them "unprincipled and lawless."

Route 2 swung farther west after crossing Buckner Creek north of Dodge. It bypassed Ness County, trailing through Lane County. It still crossed Gove, Sheridan, and Decatur counties, only a few miles west of the former route. In some places the newer route was only eight to twelve miles farther west than Route 1, but different post offices, road houses, and watering holes were used. By 1879, this route was well established and carried the largest number of cattle in the Western Cattle Trail's years of existence. It had become as great as the Chisholm had been in its Abilene and Wichita days of the early 1870s.

In the Route 2 path was a small rail station on the Kansas Pacific, known, at first, as Buffalo Station. It was established as a water station in 1868 when tracks were laid. Five years later, in August 1873, a post office was established and named "Hill Gove." When Route 2 passed by the small station in the late 1870s, it was equipped to load cattle. If the owner or trail boss decided to cut out some animals to be shipped back east before continuing to Ogallala, Buffalo Park (renamed in 1878) was an option.

The local newspaper of Buffalo Park, *The Express*, reported mostly about the cattle going by Buffalo Park. According to the paper, in June of 1880, the town had twelve stores, three hotels, three livery stables, three restaurants, three saloons, one barbershop, two blacksmith shops, one harness maker, one bakery, a newspaper and

---

[57]Letter to the Governor found in Trego County history collection #732, Kansas State Historical Society, Library & Archives Division, Manuscript collection.

THE WESTERN CATTLE TRAIL | 1874-1897

a physician. It boasted about the regularity of train service. But the editor, J. C. Burnett, did not say that cattle were actually shipped from Buffalo Park. In the June 10, 1880 issue of the newspaper, he reported:

> It is estimated there will be 310,000 head of cattle, on trail, going north from Texas this year, larger than has been driven for several years, 50 percent greater than last year. Two hundred thousand will pass through Buffalo Park.[58]

Burnett continued to keep track of the cattle arrivals into Buffalo Park. In his July 22, 1880, issue he reported of 140,520 head "arriving" in Buffalo Park to date. Were some of the cattle shipped out and were the cowboys visiting the services of the town? A local homesteader, A. B. Brandenburg, also remarked about the cattle passing by Buffalo Park:

> What really made Buffalo Park a live town those days was the fact that the old cattle trail passed just west of Park, near the edge of town. There were from 100,000 to 200,000 head of cattle driven northward into the north western states. These were mostly cattle contracted for by the government.[59]

W. P. Harrington in his *History of Gove County* states that Buffalo Park was a railhead for cattle. He wrote:

> ....it is probably conservative enough to estimate that a quarter of a million head of Texas cattle passed through Gove county during the one season of 1880. Some of the cattle were shipped from the stock yards at Buffalo Park to the east or to the west, but most of the herds were driven on, to find their final stopping point in Nebraska or the territories of the northwest...[60]

Trail boss Bill Jackman recalled camping south of Buffalo Park in 1878 and related a confrontation they had with the local homesteaders. Jackman was in charge of one of the two herds belonging to Ellison & Sherill. The "country was dry, grass scarce and watering places for two herds at one time was hard to find," he wrote. A scouting by the two trail bosses discovered a creek "some distance north of Buffalo" that had "water sufficient to swim a good sized steamboat and the grass was excellent," but the "nesters of that section" had plowed a furrow on each side of the trail and

---

[58]*The Express*, Buffalo Park, Kansas, June 10, 1880.
[59]Quoted from W.P. Harrington's 1930 *History of Gove Co*, no page nos. When Brandenburg commented that the cattle were "contracted for by the government," he was referring to the contracts made between Texas cattlemen and the government to supply beef to the Indian reservations in the north.
[60]Harrington, *History of Gove Co.*

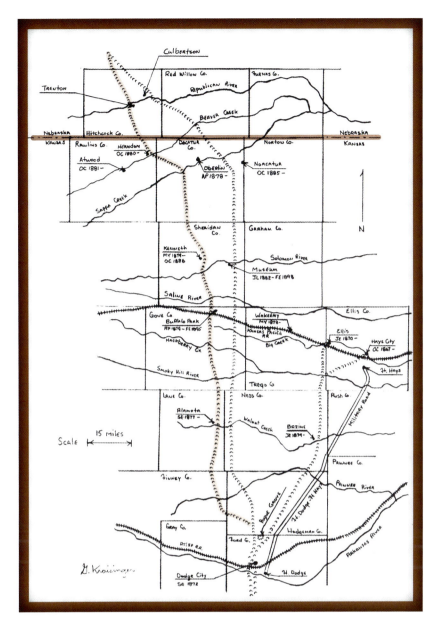

#5-7
Route 2 of the Western Cattle Trail North of Dodge:
This map shows Route 2 from north of Pogue Grove, across Kansas, toward Ogallala, Nebraska. Route 2 was possibly used as early as 1876, before the 1877 quarantine deadline was enforced. This route lasted longer than any of the other routes across Kansas and carried more cattle. Railhead destinations would have been Buffalo Station (Park) on the Kansas Pacific or Ogallala, Nebraska on the Union Pacific Railroad.

Route 2 ceased to be used when the Kansas quarantine of 1881 was enforced in the 1882 season.

posted signs reading: "Keep your cattle inside these furrows or be prosecuted."[61] Jackman continued:

> We had become enraged on reading these warning signs and Givens said, "Bill, suppose we put our herds into that fine grass and water and take the chances," to which I agreed. The cattle were now in sight and looked as though the two herds were strung out for a distance

---

[61] When a homesteader filed for ownership of land in Kansas, the parcel was taken out of the open range status and became the legal property of the settler. If Texas drovers and herds came upon the property, not knowing if it was open range or not, the owner could prosecute the trespasser. The rapid settling of the open range claimed the prime areas that contained water and good grass. Finding that pathways were blocked by new homesteaders angered the drovers.

THE WESTERN CATTLE TRAIL | 1874-1897

of three miles. My herd came first and Givens and I rode in front of the cattle until the water was scented and the cattle began running. The nearer the water, the faster they got, but now came the nesters, who were living in dugouts and could not be seen until they all mounted their old mares, bare-backed. They were bare-footed, bare-headed and all carrying double barrel shotguns yelling and demanding that we turn the cattle back to the trail. We said, "We cannot stop them — you boys stop them if you can." You never saw such maneuvers in your life, but the cattle went to the water just the same. The nesters went for the officers [sheriff] and we had to keep on the dodge for several days by riding on the high grounds and keeping a close lookout over the country for officers.[62]

In the following year, B. J. Fletcher, riding with a Snyder herd, met with perhaps the same group of what he called "barefooted homesteaders" on mules and brood mares insisting that the drovers turn west, out of their way, to avoid their settlement. Fletcher wrote: "so [we] turned out of their trail and made a detour of about fifteen miles to go around this settlement."[63]

In the same general area of Gove County, trail driver W. B. Hardeman told a story of trying to water cattle and running into an irate local homesteader.

In Kansas one day for dinner we bought some pies, eggs and milk from a granger. He informed Baylor that a certain section of land that had a furrow plowed around it, did not belong to his neighbor, but was railroad land and the number was 115. When I came to dinner Baylor told me about the section. He also told me we would not strike any more water that evening. This creek on Section 115 had fine water, and he asked me if I thought best to water there. I said, "Yes," knowing I had to herd that afternoon. Ham Bee protested, and said we should not treat that old man that way, but Ham did not have to hold the herd that evening, so I insisted, and Baylor said, "Get your dinner and fresh horses, I will start to the water." The old man lived in a dug-out on the side of a hill where he could see everything, so when he saw the cattle cross that furrow he came out with a shotgun, rolling up his sleeves, waving his arms and shouting, "Take those cattle off my land or I will have every damn one of you arrested." Baylor, being in the lead, came in contact with him first. He said, "Old man, there must be a mistake; we have some fat cattle and the agent of the railroad (some four miles to the depot) said he had no stock cars and for us to throw the cattle on

---

[62]W. T. (Bill) Jackman, "Where They Put a Trail Boss in Jail," in Hunter, *The Trail Drivers of Texas*, 856-857.
[63]B. J. Fletcher, *Up the Trail in '79*, 27.

Section 115." Well, sir, you should have heard that old man curse that (innocent) agent, as well as the country in general, stating he had moved his family out there, the drought came and it looked like starvation, so he was trying to save that little grass for winter. Baylor compromised by telling him he had a family and knew how it was, and would be willing to water on one-half of the section and would give him a dogie calf that had got into the herd several days before and we did not want it. The old man got in a fine humor, had us to send the wagon by the house to get a barrel of spring water — [64]

Farther up the trail, the herds and their drovers crossed Decatur County. Note Map #5-8 which shows Route 2 across Decatur County.

NORTH OF DODGE: ROUTE 3 AND THE WALLACE RANCH, TO OGALLALA, NEBRASKA AND BEYOND: (Map #5-9) CLOSED BY THE 1885 KANSAS QUARANTINE

The Kansas Legislature in its 1881 session again moved the quarantine line west. This time the distance was minor. Lane County, which lay directly west of Ness County, wanted the deadline moved to its western border, as the 1877 deadline had done for its Ness County neighbor, but the Legislature did not accomodate Lane County citizens and moved the line only a few miles west, placing only the east half of Lane County behind the line. The law did not change the boundary at the southern end of the quarantine line. It only affected the northern counties of Kansas. Gove and Sheridan counties still supported the cattle trail — allowing a third pathway to cross them since the Western Trail had begun crossing western Kansas.

Meanwhile, settlers continued to file for homesteads in western Kansas. Most could not afford to buy wire for fencing so they plowed furrows and posted signs to remind the drovers of their property rights.

After the 1881 quarantine law, drovers followed the same route north of Dodge until reaching Lane County where drovers split from the old Route 2 to establish another route. In so doing, they used different creek and river crossings, and scouted out new camp sites. At the Hackberry Creek crossing west of the Beve post office, established in March of 1881, the new route turned northwest cutting across the

---

[64]As compensation for the railroads' financial investment, the federal government awarded them alternate sections of land with in area ten to twenty miles wide on either side of the tracks. This land was sold to settlers by the railroad for a profit. Settlers' homesteads were naturally next to the railroad land in an adjoining section. This homesteader was protecting the railroad section for his own use. Section 115 that Hardeman refers to is probably in Township 11, Section 5, Range 28. This location would place the location four miles from Buffalo Park station in Gove County. Even though Hardeman does not state the date, we believe it to be 1881, based on other clues in his long narrative. (W. B. Hardeman, "Punching Cattle on the Trail to Kansas," in Hunter, 147-148)

THE WESTERN CATTLE TRAIL | 1874-1897   251

2
FRONTIER DAYS IN RAWLINS COUNTY

TRAVEL IS SO SMOOTH AND EFFORTLESS TODAY THAT IT IS HARD TO VISUALIZE ITS HAZARDS IN THE MID-19TH CENTURY. FOR EXAMPLE, IN JUNE, 1859, FOUR MULES PULLING A DENVER-BOUND PIKE'S PEAK EXPRESS STAGECOACH — SIX DAYS AND 450 MILES OUT FROM LEAVENWORTH — WERE TERRIFIED BY INDIANS A FEW MILES NORTHEAST OF HERE. PLUNGING DOWN A PRECIPITOUS BANK, THE ANIMALS UPSET THE COACH AND ITS BEST-KNOWN PASSENGER, HORACE GREELEY, EDITOR OF THE NEW YORK TRIBUNE. GREELEY WAS SOON RESCUED "AND TAKEN TO STATION 17, A FEW YARDS BEYOND, WHERE THE GOOD WOMAN DRESSED HIS GALLING WOUNDS."

THERE WERE OTHER, MORE SERIOUS ENCOUNTERS WITH THE INDIANS. ON APRIL 12, 1875, 40 MEN OF THE SIXTH U.S. CAVALRY ATTACKED 75 NORTHERN CHEYENNES ON SAPPA CREEK, 14 MILES SOUTH. TWO SOLDIERS AND MORE THAN A SCORE OF INDIANS WERE KILLED. A CHEYENNE RAID IN THE AUTUMN OF 1878 BROUGHT DEATH TO MORE THAN 30 SETTLERS ON SAPPA AND BEAVER CREEKS HERE IN RAWLINS AND ADJOINING DECATUR COUNTIES.

THOUSANDS OF CATTLE WERE DRIVEN THROUGH THIS AREA IN 1876-1885, PLODDING THE WESTERN CATTLE TRAIL FROM TEXAS THROUGH DODGE CITY TO OGALLALA, NEB. ATWOOD, ESTABLISHED IN 1879, IS THE SEAT OF RAWLINS COUNTY, ORGANIZED IN 1881.

ERECTED BY STATE HISTORICAL SOCIETY AND STATE HIGHWAY COMMISSION

Location: In the Atwood city park, north side of town, north of State Highway 36, Rawlins County, Kansas.

Authors' commentary: There were two routes of the Western Cattle Trail that passed through Rawlins County. This marker alludes to both with the dates of 1876-1885.
Route 2 traversed the northeast corner of the county from 1876 to 1881 and was closed down by the Kansas 1881 quarantine law.
Route 3 went through the east half of the county from about 1881 through 1884. Of course, the cattle trail did not end at Ogallala, but continued on to as far as Canada.

3
TEXAS OGALLALA CATTLE TRAIL BEAVER CREEK CROSSING 1869 - 1885

Location: Section 36, R33w, T2s five miles northeast of Atwood, Kansas on Beaver Creek, near Ludell, Kansas, Rawlins County.

Authors' commentary:
This bright sign was done by a local historical group to call attention to the crossing of Beaver Creek by Texas cattle. The "Texas Ogallala" Trail, of course, is the Western Cattle Trail. It is on Route 3 of the Western Trail in Rawlins County, Kansas, which existed from 1881 through 1884. The beginning date on this marker, unfortunately, refers to when the Chisholm Trail in eastern Kansas was active, not to this western route. Kansas Legislation stopped south Texas cattle from trailing into the state after the 1884 season — thus, the ending date. (To 1885 means up to that date, but not inclusive of 1885. The final quarantine law was passed in March of 1885.) We like this sign! Can't be missed.

252   THE WESTERN CATTLE TRAIL | 1874-1897

center of Lane County, traversing across the western part of Gove and Sheridan counties. The path crossed the extreme northeast corner of Thomas County and moved into Rawlins County, crossing Beaver Creek east of Atwood and continuing on to Nebraska.

The new route, midway in its course, also crossed the Kansas Pacific Railroad in northern Gove County. Whereas Buffalo Park on Route 2 had been an optional railhead for cattle, Grinnell on Route 3 served much the same function. The Western Trail crossed the rail line between Grainfield and Grinnell. Both communities had been established for only a short time. Settlers in the area had not "laid papers on the land," a common 1878 expression for filing land claims, until 1878 and 1879. Grainfield's way station, approximately five miles west of the trail, did not open for business until 1879, but within a year the community boasted about its stately twenty-room Occidental Hotel, a post office, and the first newspaper in the county. Grainfield and its surrounding land was heavily promoted by the Kansas Pacific Railway. The company advertised the area for homesteading and saw to it that a magnificent hotel was built to offer guests fine rooms, parlors, waiting rooms, and first class dining. The hotel also hosted groups for hunting the plentiful wild game in the area. Because of the railroad's support and its location along the Kansas Pacific line, Grainfield developed a lumber business. Lumber yards flourished, and lumber was hauled from here as far north as Oberlin and as far south as Dighton.[65]

Grinnell, located approximately four miles west of Route 3 of the Western Trail, had been the second station established on the railroad in Gove County in 1868. It was authorized the first post office in the county on June 6, 1870. By 1873 the town had a population of forty people, most of them associated with the railroad. The town used its railhead advantage for a different purpose. Extensive bone yards were built and later, holding pens for cattle, were constructed. For years, settlers gathered, delivered, and sold buffalo bones at Grinnell to be shipped back east, and by 1882, after the quarantine line had moved, Grinnell replaced Buffalo Park as an optional railhead for cattle.

The bone yards at Grinnell were a key to the local settlers' survival in the early 1880s. Along the Route 3 area a severe drought struck western Kansas. No grain was raised in Gove, Sheridan, Thomas, or Decatur counties. One early trapper, Samuel Grout, remembered that "The seasons from 1880 to '84 were very dry, and almost all the divide settlers moved away.… The settlers who remained picked buffalo bones and hauled them to Grinnell, selling them and buying provisions." Grout also remembered seeing "the millions of long-horn Texas cattle going to the northwest to feed the Indians, and to stock the great ranges left unstocked after the extermination of the buffalo."[66]

Thus, while Grainfield seemed to be interested in promoting homesteading, supplying lumber for new buildings, and catering to wealthy visitors from the East,

---

[65] Albert B. and Mary T. Tuttle, ed & comp., *History & Heritage of Gove County, Kansas*, 55-57.
[66] Samuel Grout recollection in *Golden Jubilee of Thomas County*, 27-30, 33.

THE WESTERN CATTLE TRAIL | 1874-1897   253

Grinnell catered to struggling settlers and encouraged Texas cattlemen to visit their less-sophisticated community. Because the trail passed between the two communities, drovers could visit either town. It is not known, however, how much the cattle facilities were used at Grinnell.

Because the early 1880s were desperate years for the dry-land homesteaders, they looked for any means to acquire money from the passing trail drivers. Sometimes drovers were asked to pay a toll by a settler when crossing his land, creek, or watering

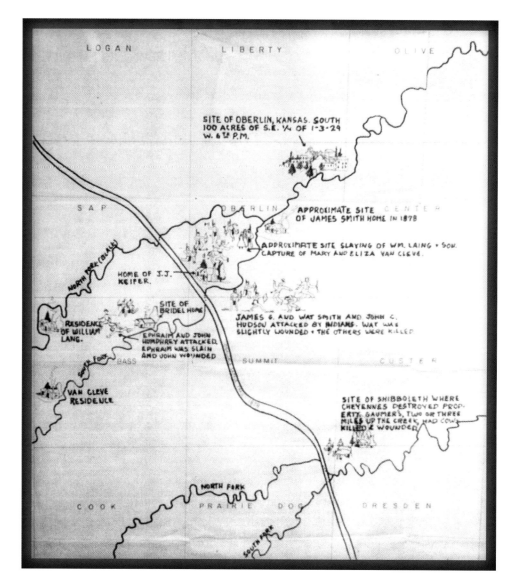

#5-8
Ogallala Cattle Trail, 1878:
This recently discovered map shows part of Dull Knife and Little Wolf's raid in 1878 in Decatur County, Kansas. Surprisingly, it also documents Route 2 of the Western Cattle Trail through that county. The creator and date of this map is unknown, but the "Ogallala Cattle Trail, 1878" is well defined. As suggested in The Western, the Greatest Texas Cattle Trail, *the Dull Knife and Little Wolf exodus from Indian Territory, that swept through Kansas, followed the Western Cattle Trail very closely. This map adds new evidence to that suggestion.*

Map courtesy of Decatur County Museum, Oberlin, Kansas.

hole. However, the land or creek did not always belong to the settler. At the Barney Sloey homestead in Gove County, Thomas L. Sturman wrote that Sloey "immediately started for the springs where the big herds always watered. Mr. Sloey would tell the boss that he could water at the springs for $15 or $20. The 'Trail Boss' always paid, not knowing that Sloey did not own the springs. They were on the quarter adjoining his."[67]

Contractors and trail bosses who had gone over Route 3 in 1882 found a barbed wire fence under construction in their pathway the following year. In 1882, several ranchers in northern Lane County realized that it would be feasible to pool their cattle onto a common range in order to cut down on operating costs. The cattlemen formed the Smoky Hill Cattle Pool by bunching their stock together on public land and hiring a few cowboys to manage the herds. Each member of the pool was assessed according to the number of cattle he owned in the pool in order to pay wages and other expenses. Fewer cowboys managing a conglomerate herd was more economical, and because public domain (un-homesteaded) was free, the costs were minimal. Once a year cowboys from the different ranches rounded up their own cattle for counting, branding, and selling.

A fence was built across the south end of the grazing range and a short distance up the east and west side to keep the cattle from drifting south during winter storms or from getting onto settlers' homesteaded land. The fence, which was built by a member family of the Smoky Hill Cattle Pool, Josh Wheatcroft, Sr. and his two sons, Link and

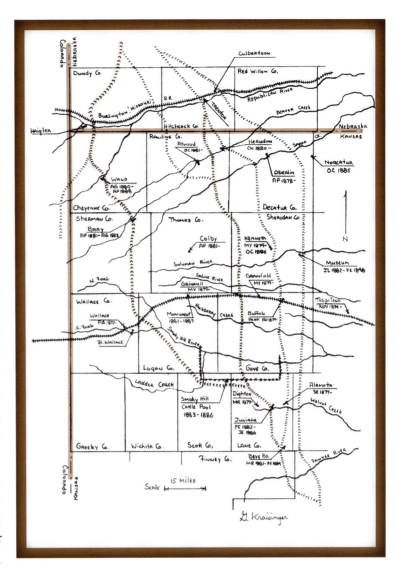

#5-9
Route 3 and the Wallace Branch of the Western Cattle Trail North of Dodge:
This map shows Route 3 from near the Beve post office in Lane County, across Kansas, toward Ogallala, Nebraska. Route 3 was probably used starting in 1881 and shared cattle traffic with the Wallace Branch. Cattle herds on this route were trailed through the Smoky Hill Cattle Pool area in Gove and Lane counties and possibly used the railhead at Grinneell on the Kansas Pacific. The Wallace Branch splintered off of Route 3 in Lane County and continued west, northwest across Kansas to Ogallala, Nebraska. This route was used starting in 1883 when the Smoky Hill Cattle Pool fence obstructed the Route 3 pathway. Instead of using Route 3, some trail drivers trailed their herds around the cattle pool and used the dryer, more risky Wallace Branch. When the Kansas Legislature passed its state-wide quarantine in March of 1885, both routes ceased to be used.

---

[67] Mrs. Thomas L. Sturman, *Pioneer Reminiscences*, 17. Martin Sutcliffe on his Gove Co. map wrote: "Barney Sloey homestead; good watering pond on the Hackberry creek where Texas cattle got water as long as cattle were driven over the Texas Trail. Barney Sloey charged per head for watering here." (Kansas State Historical Archives, Manuscript Collections)

Josh, started at the west end in St. John County, now Logan County, at the William Sternberg ranch and stretched south for about four miles, going along where the old Smoky Hill Trail had been and on down to where the Steele house was later built by the side of what later became Scott Lake. It then went east across Scott and Lane counties to two mile west of present-day Pendennis. Here it turned north, stretched across the Smoky Hill and Indian creeks and continued for about another four miles. The Wheatcrofts started building the sixty-eight mile drift fence in the spring of 1883, hauling the posts and wire from Grainfield. It took them one year to hand dig the post holes, four rods apart, and to stretch two-wire stays of four-point galvanized barbed wire between the posts. The fence was finished in the spring of 1884.[68]

The cattle pool fence created a difficult situation for both the Texas drovers and the cattle pool range riders. If the trail boss' intention was to drive his herd straight north to the Kansas Pacific Railroad at Grinnell or to continue directly north to Ogallala, Nebraska, then the fence was lowered to allow Texas herds through.[69] The pool riders monitored the range cattle and watched the trail cattle to make sure that they did not mix with the pool herd.

In 1883 and 1884, when trail drivers found the Smoky Hill Cattle Pool fence stretched across the trail in Lane County, some trail bosses chose to not trail their herds through the pool and to, instead, go around the west end of the barrier. This created the Wallace Branch. Herds turned straight west along the south side of the fence in Lane County, trailing into Scott County until reaching the west edge of the barrier. At the west end of the fence (S32-33, R32W, T16S) herds were pointed northwest and angled across Logan County, passed through the northeast corner of Wallace County, trailed a few miles north of recently abandoned Fort Wallace, and then continued north through Sherman and Cheyenne counties toward Ogallala, Nebraska.[70]

This final cattle route, leaving Route 3 in Lane County is referred to as the Wallace Branch because it angled toward Fort Wallace and Wallace County. It was a longer trip, but it also was in a less populated area. The quarantines had been drawn by the state of Kansas because of the westward movement of settlers, but in

---

[68]Josh Wheatcroft said he "was the best post hole digger in the bunch. I could dig a hundred post holes a day." He would unroll the wire and "Father stretched all the wire." The Smoky Hill Cattle Pool prospered until the blizzard of 1886. The storm killed most of the cattle in the pool and put the cattlemen out of business. Soon after, the Wheatcrofts sold the wire and fence posts. The government had also sued the ranchers for fencing government land, so the fence had to come down. With no cattle or fence, the cattle pool enterprise was over. For the exact location of the fence, see Kraisinger and Kraisinger *The Western, the Greatest Texas Cattle Trail*, 224-225. Ellen May Stanley, Early Lane County History, 176 and Ellen May Stanley, *Cowboy Josh*, 50-51.

[69]The 1881 quarantine law did not exclude the Buffalo Park railhead in Gove County. Therefore, some drovers and their herds could have swung to the east side of the cattle pool fence, picked up the old route (Route 2) and drove on to Buffalo Park. The small railhead sat on the edge of the 1881 quarantine deadline that had put the east part of Gove County under quarantine.

[70]Fort Wallace had served its purpose during the Indian wars and was officially closed on May 31, 1882. A detachment of soldiers remained for a couple of years to guard the buildings and to prevent encroachment, but by 1886, the cemetery was moved and settlers in the region began to dismantle the buildings for the lumber and stone. During the high point of the cattle driving days, the fort would have been standing, but basically inactive. (Oliva, *Fort Wallace, Sentinel on the Smoky Hill Trail*, 122)

the far western counties, settlement was still sparse. In the northerly drive from Fort Wallace to Nebraska, there was essentially no one to disturb the daily trek of cattle. The Wallace Branch, however, was also a gamble. Even though the years of 1880 to 1884 were dry years, the far west region of Kansas was dry to an extreme. There were stretches of forty and fifty miles without reliable water. Therefore, the route could be very risky.

COWBOYS AND "NESTERS:"

In reading the accounts and recollections of trail drivers, one notices that it was the homesteaders of Kansas that cowboys remembered. The waterways, for the most part, were there, for as Harry E. Chrisman observed, there was a ladder of rivers, and creeks, that the herds used going north to Nebraska.[71] As the 1880s progressed, however, it became increasingly difficult to work around the "nesters," as the cowboys called the settlers. Drovers witnessed the newcomers as they excavated dugouts in the side of hills for their families or labored to construct sod houses, called soddies, carried water from near-by creeks, and broke the virgin soil with a crude plow to try to plant and reap a crop. Although the homesteaders were often a nuisance, cowboys could see the bare fortitude of the young families surviving on a harsh ungiving land. Homesteaders had dreams for a better tomorrow, and only through their hard work could they realize this; few had any money.

Like the Soldiers Colony in Trego County, some homesteaders looked upon the drovers as unprincipled, lawless, and boisterous youngsters and wanted the herds removed from their area. After all, the drovers were rough looking, armed, and transient. Other settlers, however, knew that the cowboys were hard working and were only doing their job. They were out in the elements, pushing two to three thousand animals to a far destination.

Homesteaders and drovers, for the most part, tolerated one another. Even though they preferred to stay out of each others' way, each recognized the needs of the other. Even with their animosities, at times, toward each other, they often helped one another. Those homesteaders who lived next to the trail may not have wanted the cowboys and their disease-carrying Texas cattle in their vicinity, but in a number of ways they benefited from the cowboys' presence. Dugouts or soddies were turned into small mercantiles for liquid refreshment or temporary post offices. Farmsteads had eggs, buttermilk and sometimes fresh-baked pastries that the cowboy was glad to pay for. Those homesteaders, who later had wells, offered water to the trail cook or cowboys. Rexford Blume from Rawlins County recalled:

> My parents had a good well on their place, Whenever those cattle came through, the chuck wagon would drive to my folks place to replenish their supply of fresh water. The cook would take on a specified

---

[71]Harry E. Chrisman, *The Ladder of Rivers*, published in 1962.

amount of water to carry them to the next watering place. They got 50 cents for the water that they took. If any of the herders chose to water their ponies there, they would give my parents 50 cents also, which was a lot of money in those days.[72]

An even greater benefit to the homesteader was the calves that were given to them. The cattlemen's practice of killing the new-born calves on the bedground, because they slowed up the herd, eventually led to agreements between local homesteaders and the drovers.[73] If the settler was there before daylight with his wagon, he was often allowed to pick up the new-born calves. After all, the cowboys would rather see a farmer try to keep them alive than to have to kill the animals. If a milk cow was stubborn or sore footed in the herd, the settler could also acquire her for a small fee or trade.

Thus, the homesteaders had mixed feelings about the Texas cowboys. They certainly didn't want the Texas Fever being spread to their domestic cows, but they were willing to carry home new-born calves. They didn't want to share the grass with the Texas herds, but welcomed the cow chips that were deposited for fuel for their stoves. They protested, at times, when herds drank from the local streams and ponds, but they gladly pocketed any money that the trail boss gave them for the privilege. Trail drovers, in turn, sought out farmsteads hoping to acquire a favorite treat, buttermilk. A young "waddie," homesick for Texas, was able to post a letter to family back home in a makeshift post office; and a stiff drink was offered, now and then, at the road houses along the way.

THE 1885 QUARANTINE CLOSES THE WESTERN CATTLE TRAIL:

Route 3 and the Wallace Branch, were the last pathways of the Western Trail to cross Kansas, and the herds were large, and the total number of cattle going over the trail exceeded 200,000 animals in a season. But by the mid 1880s the massive wave of immigration had reached the far western counties of Kansas. The authors of *The History of Cheyenne County* described the atmosphere in their county: "In the fall of 1884 and spring of 1885, the settlers began to come in and sod houses sprang up over night, all over the country."[74] Therefore, the Kansas Legislature addressed the quarantine against Texas cattle one more time. In the 1885 session, lawmakers passed an act "for protection of cattle against Texas, splenic or Spanish fever." The new act repealed the 1881 law and affirmed that no one between the first day of March and the first day of December of any year could drive "any cattle capable of

---

[72]Letter to Anselm Sramek of Atwood, Kansas, from R. R. Blume, dated March 26, 1965, authors' files. Rexford Blume, next to the youngest child, was born Dec. 19, 1888, in Rawlins County. His parents and older siblings would have told him of the cattle drives. He was 76 years old in 1965.

[73]The herd was taken off of the trail and after allowed to graze, they bedded down for the night. This was referred to as "bedground." During the night the cowboys would sing to the herd to keep them quiet and content.

[74]*The History of Cheyenne County*, 11.

258   THE WESTERN CATTLE TRAIL | 1874-1897

communicating or liable to impart what is known as Texas, splenic or Spanish fever" into the state. The 1885 act differed from any other preceding law in that there were no stated quarantine lines within Kansas--instead, it covered the entire state. The penalty for anyone if found guilty of violating the act was a misdemeanor in the form of a fine not less than one hundred dollars and not more than two thousand dollars, or imprisonment in a county jail for not less that thirty days and not more than one year, or both. The law continued to affirm that if any cattle within the state were determined to be capable of communicating the fever, a local sheriff or any constable of the county could seize the cattle and keep them in his custody until the first day of December. The owner of the cattle was to be held responsible for "all the costs and expenses of taking, detaining and holding said cattle" and if the costs were not paid within ten days after the first of December, the officer was to advertise and sell the stock in order to recover the costs. Of course, any legal fees and expenses the officer incurred were to also be paid by the cattle owner, and the officer himself was to be compensated for his trouble. The owner of the cattle or "persons violating any of the provisions" was also liable to the people who felt violated. For example, any cattle owner who was "injured" by the fever could file a civil action suit to recover such damages and could receive a lien on a drovers's cattle for payment.

Diseased cattle who were capable of transmitting the fever were defined in Section 5 of the law as those from south of the thirty-sixth parallel of north latitude. If, however, the owners could show a certificate issued by a live-stock sanitary commission of the state where the cattle had been located since the first day of December of the *previous* year "west of the east line of the Indian Territory and *north* of the thirty-sixth parallel of north latitude, or west of the twenty-first meridian of longitude west from Washington and north of the thirty-fourth parallel of north latitude," i.e. the Texas Panhandle, then the law would not apply. Any cattle owned and kept in the state of Kansas were also exempt from the law. The law was approved on March 7, 1885 and was signed by the secretary of state, E. B. Allen.[75]

The stringent provisions of the law stopped the driving of cattle from South Texas into the state of Kansas. The law changed the complexion of trail driving. Texas cattlemen were not in the habit of holding their cattle in Indian Territory or the Texas Panhandle for a winter before trailing them north across Kansas. Some herds were grazed out over the winter south of the Kansas border, but, for the most part, drovers road-branded and trailed their herds in one season. Kansas' final deadline was at the Colorado border. Texas drovers had to go around Kansas starting in the 1885 season.[76]

---

[75] Chapter CXCI, "Protection of Cattle Against Disease," *State of Kansas, Session Laws of 1885*, Topeka, KS: Kansas Publishing House, May 1, 1885., 308-311.

[76] This study discusses "through" cattle herds that originated in Texas and were driven to northern markets in one season. The 1885 Kansas quarantine stopped that flow through Kansas. However, ranches in Indian Territory, south of the Kansas border, continued to stock their ranges with Texas cattle, graze, and deliver these herds to Kansas border railheads.

> *…and there, below us in the valley of the South Platte, nestled Ogallala, the Gomorrah of the cattle trail. From amongst its half hundred buildings, no church spire pointed upward, but instead three fourths of its business houses were dance halls, gambling houses, and saloons. We all knew the town by reputation, while the larger part of our outfit had been in it before.*

Andy Adams, *The Log of a Cowboy*, pg. 259,
an account of an 1882 trail drive to Montana.

> *The cook gave us a light breakfast owing to the wind blowing so hard that he could not cook well. We started at 5 and at one, I reached the Platte River with the rear cattle 2 hours behind the front cattle. We took a hearty dinner and drove 4 miles up the river valley to Ogallala, a small town on the Union Pacific Railroad, our destination.*

Journal entry of Lewis W. Neatherlin, July 8, 1876.
Leo Kelley, ed., *Up the Trail in '76*.

> *We arrived there [Ogallala] about August 1st, our cattle all in good shape — in better condition a long ways than when we left. They were there delivered to the various purchasers, who removed them to their respective ranches in that great cow country. Our faithful saddle horses, wagons and all were disposed of with the cattle.*

G. W. Mills, recollection of his 1877 trail drive,
in Hunter, *Trail Drivers of Texas*, pg. 235.

CHAPTER VI

Destination: Ogallala, Nebraska and Two Splinter Routes

Few people, other than Nebraskans, realize that Nebraska was an active cattle trail state. Because of the early dime novels and the later Hollywood western movies, Kansas cattle towns such as Abilene and Dodge City, became famous locations while Nebraska cattle towns like Schulyer, Kearney, and Ogallala were overshadowed by their neighbor's reputations. The fact is, however, that no other state, outside of Texas, had more cattle trails. The Shawnee Trail, the Chisholm Trail, the Ellsworth Trail, four routes of the Western Trail, the National Trail and, and the Texas-Montana Feeder Route extended into Nebraska. There were, as well, three major splinter routes from the Western Trail in Nebraska.

As the various Kansas quarantines lines moved westward during the trail-driving era, four different routes of the Western Trail formed across western Kansas, and those routes continued to Ogallala, Nebraska. Ogallala was the western-most railhead in Nebraska in a line of rail terminals, to receive Texas herds, that operated in the state. The quarantine laws in Kansas directly affected Nebraska, and as settlements spread across the midwest, those Kansas quarantine lines dictated the cattle movement into Nebraska as well. Thus, Ogallala inherited the cattle driving industry from its eastern neighbors, just as Dodge City received the honor after Abilene, Wichita, Newton, and Ellsworth were closed down in Kansas.

EARLY CATTLE TOWNS IN NEBRASKA:

Nebraska's major artery of water, the wide Platte River, ran across the state from the Missouri River on its eastern boundary to the western boundary lines with Wyoming and Colorado. Since the 1840s, freight wagons and pioneer conestogas destined for Oregon, Utah, and California followed pathways along its banks.[1] Along the North Platte River road, early river towns catered to this western flow of traffic and enticed the Union Pacific Railroad to lay tracks from Omaha westward starting in 1865, paralleling the river. Texas cattlemen soon discovered that if the Kansas rail terminals on the Union/Kansas Pacific and the Santa Fe Railway were not hospitable or accessible, the Union Pacific in Nebraska was an option for marketing their herds.

Also the river towns along the Missouri River were recipients of the overflow of herds from Kansas. At first on the East Shawnee Trail in 1866, drovers who hoped to find a more hospitable market than the one in Sedalia,. Missouri, swung west and north from Baxter Springs, Kansas to pass through eastern Kansas along the western

---

[1]The Oregon Trail began in 1841 when pioneers in covered wagons undertook the longest of the great overland routes, approximately 2,000 miles, from Independence, Missouri, to the Pacific northwest. The caravans traveled from fort to fort until reaching Fort Vancouver in Oregon Territory. The first leg of the journey was from Independence to Fort Kearney (Dobyville), then to Ogallala where they crossed to the south side of the North Platte River to Fort Laramie, present-day Wyoming. In 1847, Morman Joseph Smith led his followers from Nauvoo, Ill. along the north bank of the Platte River to Fort Laramie where their route joined the Oregon Trail to South Pass, Colorado. From there the Mormans turned south to the Salt Lake Valley. When gold was discovered in 1848 in California, Forty-niners traveled the same route to Fort Hall, Idaho then turned southwest to Sutter's Mill in California. There was also traffic along the South Platte River Valley to Denver. Nebraska gets its name from the Oto Indian word *nebrathka* meaning "flat water," their name for the Platte River.

fringe of the settlements to avoid trouble on the border passing Kansas City and Westport. The drovers and their herds continued north along the eastern border of Nebraska, paralleling the Missouri River to Brownville and Nebraska City. Later, herds continued on to Plattsmouth.

(Check the Shawnee Trail System map on the front endpage. One branch of the East Shawnee is shown going into Sedalia and another into the Westport/Kansas City, Missouri area. Later, the middle or more westerly branch referenced here, extended on into Nebraska.)

Cattle not ferried over into Iowa that year from Brownville or Nebraska City, were sold to Nebraska feeders or delivered to various Indian agencies. Of the 260,000 longhorns headed north in 1866, Nebraska historian Norbert Mahnken estimated that 15,000 ended up in Nebraska.[2]

As settlements in eastern Kansas and Nebraska moved west, the Texas drovers also adjusted their route farther west. The Middle Shawnee Trail, established in 1867, shifted west to adhere to the line established by the Kansas quarantine law revised in February of 1867, and to a new series of laws passed by the Nebraska Legislature in May of that year. Because of an outbreak of the Texas Fever in certain Nebraska localities in 1866, Governor David Butler, under pressure from the frontier farmers, called a special session of the Nebraska Legislature, and the lawmakers passed a series of laws that stated that no person was to drive any cattle "affected with any contagious or infectious disease through the state," and prohibited the running at large of stock in certain of the more populous communities. As in Missouri, however, the laws were not rigorously enforced, and Texas cattle drives continued into the state.[3]

As the West Shawnee Trail branch ventured into Junction City, Kansas and the Abilene Trail started its first full season to Abilene in 1868, the Texas Fever flared up again in several areas of Nebraska. The Nebraska Legislature revisited its inadequate 1867 law and enacted a new state law in February of 1869 stating that it was unlawful to bring Texas cattle into the state during July and August. It had appeared to the lawmakers that the disease was spread during the summer months when the Texas cattle were in the area. This law was also met with indifference. In those areas where officials did enforce the law and stopped the herds at the Kansas-Nebraska border, the drovers simply stopped, allowed the herds to graze on the prairie grasses, and waited until September when the provisions of the law no longer applied. Because the law was enforced mostly in the heavily populated areas of eastern Nebraska, the major effect of the legislation was to shift the route farther west.

In the mid 1860s, the more westerly route came north out of Abilene, Kansas, and headed slightly east to the Big Blue River just below the forks. From there the drovers and their herds followed the fertile valley of the Big Blue through Gage, Saline, and Seward counties in Nebraska. This Blue Valley Trail, as it became known,

---

[2]Norbert R. Mahnken, "Early Nebraska Markets for Texas Cattle," *Nebraska History, a Quarterly Magazine*, Vol. XXVI, January-March, 1945, 4-5.
[3]Mahnken, Ibid.

offered a choice for the drovers. They could sell their herds at Schulyer, or turn east and market their herds in Omaha or Nebraska City, or go north to the Indian reservations. This extension of the Abilene Trail, or Blue Valley Trail, met with immediate success and offered to Texas cattlemen an alternative to Abilene where the Kansas Pacific Railroad had a monopoly.[4]

Schulyer, Nebraska, located at the upper end of the Blue Valley Trail, became the new railhead in 1870. According to the *Omaha Herald*, between 40,000 and 50,000 head were sold at Schuyler that summer. It was estimated that one out of every six longhorns that left Texas in 1870 ended up in Nebraska.[5]

Schulyer's merchants and cattle dealers became excited over the prospects that their town would become a prosperous cattle town for the Texas herds. That excitement, however, was short lived. Homesteaders poured into the Platte River counties by the thousands in 1871. The state's overall population increased by 40,000 that year, and many of them settled in southern Nebraska and along the tributaries of the Big Blue River. Also, Nebraska passed its first herd law a few months before, which differed from a quarantine law in that it requried animal owners to restrain their animals or pay damages to the affected property owners.[6] This law, which replaced the flimsy 1869 cattle disease law, created a significant problem to drovers. As the area south of Schuyler filled up with settlements, stray cattle could be confiscated and fines levied toward the trail boss. The trail to Schuyler, as a result, became too risky, and trail drivers looked westward.[7]

In 1872, because of settlements and the herd law, cattle-driving shifted west again. Ellsworth on the Kansas Pacific replaced Abilene, and in Nebraska, Kearney replaced Schuyler on the Union Pacific. The Burlington and Missouri Railroad, which had been building a line west of Nebraska City, completed its junction with the Union Pacific at Kearney in the fall of 1872. New stock yards were built at Kearney.

---

[4]As noted earlier, sections of this Eastern/Chisholm System went by different names. In Indian Territory to the Arkansas River (later Wichita, Kansas) before 1871, it was the Abilene Trail. Sometime after that date, the route was referred to as the "Chisholm Trail." From the Arkansas River to Abilene, it was sometimes called the "McCoy or Abilene Trail," and from Abilene to the Platte River Valley, it was referred to, by some, as the "Blue Valley Trail." It was all the same trail or system.

[5]Omaha *Herald*, Omaha, Nebraska, August 24, 1870, and Mahnken, Ibid, 20.

[6]As homesteaders poured into the state, the practice of turning stock (hogs, sheep, horses, cattle) loose to graze on the open range became a problem. When the prairies began to fill up with settlers, free running stock got into neighbors' crops and gardens. The dispute arose between those who wanted all crops fenced but allow stock to run free — against those who wanted owners of stock to fence in their animals. Finally in 1870, in special session, the Nebraska Legislature passed its first herd law. Under this law everyone had "to restrain their animals from trespassing upon cultivated lands" of other people or pay damages, and if anyone found stock in crops, that person could hold the stock until damages were paid. It was called a "herd law" because the best way to keep stock from getting into other people's crops was to herd them. This law allowed poor homesteaders to plant a crop anywhere without the expense of a fence. Some Nebraska counties also had a "fence law," which required owners to fence their fields. (Addison Erwin Sheldon , "History and Stories of Nebraska — The Herd Law," online: www.olden-times.com/oldtimenebraska [accessed Dec. 19, 2008])

[7]According to *A Sandhill Century, Book I*, Schuyler became "the first real cowtown between 1870-72." 1870 was the banner year; 1871 was a bust for many cattlemen; and 1872 saw only a trickle of herds.

Another incentive for Texas drovers to seek out the Kearney area was the abandoned Fort Kearny military reservation.[8] The one hundred square miles of prairie, adjoining the Platte River southeast of Kearney was still intact. The reservation was a choice parcel from which settlement had been excluded for five years. It was a perfect situation for the Texas drovers. Trail drivers and herds coming up the Platte Valley from the Ellsworth cutoff of the Chisholm Trail could camp on the reservation grounds and the cattle could graze freely. Trail bosses did not have to be concerned about their cattle trespassing on any homesteaders' crops or gardens, or having to face a farmers' threat under the new Nebraska herd law. The few squatters who did settle on the old reservation grounds had no right or title to the land, so they could not press charges in cases of cattle trampling their crops. Thus, the grounds became a convenient delivery point for Texas herds. From 1872 through 1875, Kearney reigned as the most important cattle town of Nebraska. The saloons, gambling houses, and brothels that had made up old Dobytown, the off-limits den of vice for Fort Kearny, moved to town and continued to sell goods and services to the cowboys.[9]

When Kansas began enforcing its latest quarantine law in the spring of 1876, the Chisholm Trail closed down not only in Kansas, but it also brought an end to Kearney, Nebraska's trailing economy.[10] Dodge City and Ogallala, farther to the west, were now in line for the next generation of cattle driving activities. Even though Kansas continued to vigorously draw deadlines in western Kansas — in 1876, 1877, and 1881 — all the Western's various routes eventually led to Ogallala.

The four routes of the Western Cattle Trail that ran across western Kansas, north of Dodge City, entered Nebraska and headed toward Ogallala. Over the next few pages these four routes in Nebraska will be briefly described. For a detailed discussion of these routes, with maps, refer to our first book, The Western, the Greatest Texas Cattle Trail, 1874-1886. *In Nebraska, Route 1 and Route 2, which eventually obsorbed Route 3, joined together into one trunk line in Section 5, T6N, R35W in Hayes County.*

ROUTE 1 FROM KANSAS TO SECTION 5, T6N, R35W IN HAYES COUNTY, (1874–1877): (Map #6-1)

Route 1, by way of Dodge City, entered Nebraska in Red Willow County in Section 32, T1N, R28W. It angled across the southwest corner of that county leading into Hitchcock County. Approximately three miles into Hitchcock County (Section 22) the herds and drovers veered straight north and followed the ridge to the south of Culbertson. This small town had been established between the Frenchman River and Blackwood Creek, with a post office added in 1873, but it remained for

---

[8]The town of Kearney derived its name from the fort, but because of a postal error, the town's name contained an added "e." It was never changed.

[9]Mahnken, Ibid, 98.

[10]As stated before, there were some concessions made to drovers and their herds in the 1876 season. A few herds were allowed to trail to the Wichita railhead.

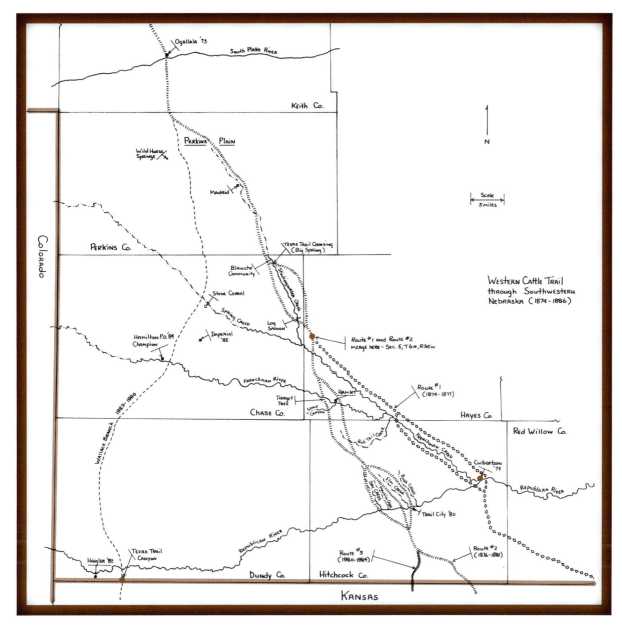

#6-1
The Western Cattle Trail Through Southwestern Nebraska, 1874-1884:
This map shows Routes 1, 2, 3, and the Wallace Branch of the Western Trail, coming out of Kansas toward Ogallala, Nebraska. Routes 1 and 2 merged into one trunk line in Section 5, T6N, R35W, north of the Frenchman Creek in Hayes County.

several years, a small and quiet place with only a few buildings. Some drovers pushed their herds across the Republican River east of Culbertson and followed Frenchman Creek on the north bank, while others crossed the Republican on the south side of the Frenchman and continued to trail up the south side of the creek, fording the creek some twenty miles upstream.

Lewis Neatherlin, guiding his three Slaughter herds northward in 1876, wrote of his journey up the Frenchman:

> **July 4:**
> This being the one-hundredth anniversary of American Independence,

it seems as if we ought to have rest and amusement, but it was to the reverse with us, as I believe we have had the hardest day's work that we have had on this trip. Drove 16 miles and crossed a very rough and brushy stream called the Frenchman; up and down steep hills and in deep canyons that was almost like a wall on either side, and could hardly see our horses' ears for [the] dust, and the day very warm.[11]

According to the entry, it appears the herds crossed the Republican west of Culbertson proceeding up the south side of the Frenchman and then crossed the river to its north side before Six-Mile Canyon. Charles Hester, however, who was on a trail drive a year later, recalled:

After the Republican crossing, we took to the high ground east of the Frenchman. We were under the hills and did not see Culbertson.

Location: At the Republican River Crossing, Sec. 33, T3n, R33w, one and one half mile west of the intersection of Highway 25 and 34, north side of Highway 34, Hitchcock County, Nebraska (north of old Trail City, on Route 2 of the Western Trail)

Authors' commentary:
This red granite monument is the shape and size of a grave stone. It stands in memory of Texas drovers who trailed cattle. There is confusion in the text, however. Just what the Southwest Nebraska Historical Society intended is unclear. According to the dates, 1869-1885, the stone seems to commorate all cattlemen who drove herds north on the Shawnee, Eastern/Chisholm, and the Western trails. The Shawnee and Eastern/Chisholm trails started before 1869, however. The trails did not go to Ogallala nor did the trails cross where this monument is located. Consequently, the stone is located in the wrong place.

The stone states that cattlemen "drove their herds from Texas to Ogallala," so it must be at this location to mark the Republican River Crossing and to recognize the Texas-Ogallala Trail (the Western). If that is the case, then the dates should read 1874 to 1885, for that trail did not exist before 1874.

The Southwest Nebraska Historical Society in 1934 either confused these trails as so many others had, or it mistakenly considered the Texas Ogallala Trail as an extension or branch of the Eastern/Chisholm. The Old Time Trail Drivers Association in the 1930s tried to explain to the public that there were two different trails. Obviously, the Southwest Nebraska Historical Society of 1934 was among the many who were confused about the location and dates of the two trails.

---

[11]Leo Kelly, ed. *Up the Trail in '76, The Journal of Lewis Warren Neatherlin*, July 4, 1876 entry, 27.

The Blackwood could be seen to the east but before long we lost it. We would drift down to the Frenchman for water and then locate a bedding ground away from it. We struck the Stinkingwater above present Palisade but kept away from the dangerous boggy bottoms.[12]

The trail continued in a northwesterly direction up the Stinkingwater Creek across the southwest corner of Hayes County to Section 5, T6N, R35W.

ROUTE 2 FROM KANSAS TO SECTION 5, T6N, R35W IN HAYES COUNTY, (1876–1882): (Map #6-1)

Starting in 1876, another route, Route 2, entered Nebraska in Hitchcock County in Section 31, T1N, R31W and pointed to the Republican River Crossing. Drovers worked their way across southwestern Nebraska's rugged terrain, deep canyons, and steep cliffs. Neatherlin's remarks about the "hardest day's work" so far on the trip in following the Frenchman, going "up and down steep hills and in deep canyons," confirms B. J. Fletcher's 1879 trail drive experience. Fletcher was on the route farther west, three years later, and recalled:

> [We] came to the deep canyons through which flow the Republican River and the Frenchman's River. As we approached a canyon, it was a strange spectacle to see the foremost cattle disappear suddenly from the level plain as they descended the steep sides of one of those deep gashes in the earth's surface. Upon the plain there is no slope to indicate the approach to the canyons through which flow the watercourses of that region, and the leaders of our herd seemed to go into the ground just as a prairie dog enters its burrow. Soon the entire herd had disappeared from our view.[13]

Before reaching the Republican River, the trail split into three smaller routes. Some herds were driven up Elm Creek; some up Bush Creek; and other herds up Dry (Canyon) Creek.[14] On the ridges above the creeks, about five miles north of the river, the three routes met again, and all Ogallala-bound herds were again on the same pathway. In this area the longhorns were allowed to graze, and the drovers camped on the divide overlooking the canyons.[15]

---

[12]Charles Hester, recollection of 1877 trail drive, in E. S. Sutton, *Sutton's Southwest Nebraska*, 160. Kraisinger & Kraisinger, *The Western, the Greatest Texas Cattle Trail*, 158-161. The crossing of the Stinking Water was in Sec. 23, T1N, R36W.
[13]Fletcher, *Up the Trail in '79*, 55. Fletcher was one of the drag men. He was on his first trail drive at the age of nineteen. Inexperienced drovers usually started their cattle-driving career by following a herd or being in the "drags." Therefore, he could see the whole herd in front of him.
[14]As of 2011, ruts were still visible along Dry Creek, also called Canyon Creek, on the Harold Pothoff Ranch. (Interview with Harold Pothoff by Gary Kraisinger, June, 2011)
[15]Kraisinger & Kraisinger, Ibid, 210.

THE WESTERN CATTLE TRAIL | 1874-1897

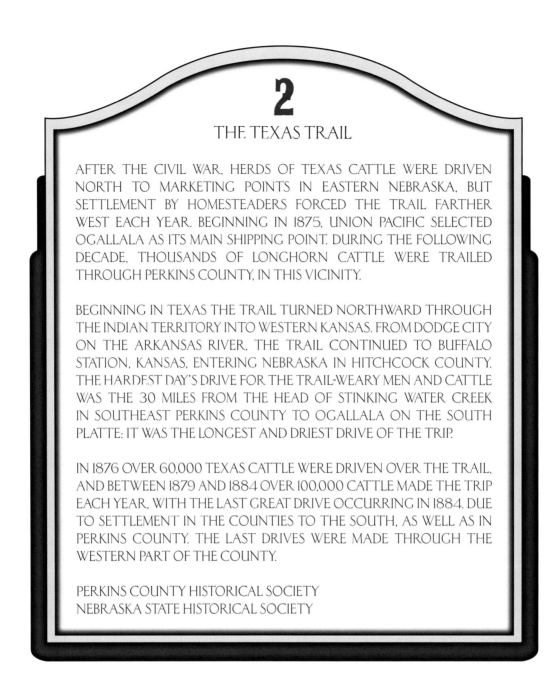

Location: east edge of Madrid, Nebraska, on Highway 23, Perkins County

Authors' commentary:
This is a great marker! What it does not say, however, is just as important as what it does say. The comment: "herds of Texas cattle were driven north to shipping points in eastern Nebraska" implies that cattle from off of the Shawnee, Chisholm, and Ellsworth trails came into Nebraska. Nebraska City (1866), Brownville and Omaha (1867), and Plattsmouth (1870) were all shipping points for the Shawnee. Schuyler (1870), on the North Platte River, was the shipping point north of Abilene, Kansas, on the Chisholm, and Kearney (1871) was north of Ellsworth, on an extension of the Ellsworth or Cox Trail. Nebraska had homesteader pressure just as Kansas did.

     The route described in paragraph two is Route 2, going from Dodge City, through Buffalo Station on the Kansas Pacific Railroad to Hitchcock County, Nebraska and beyond.

     The marker states that trailing was basically over in the Madrid area of Nebraska after 1884. The Wallace Branch of the Western Cattle Trail from Kansas and the splinter trail, the National Trail (that went around Kansas and came into Nebraska until 1886) were the last routes to cross Perkins County. They went farther west than Madrid, however — across the western part of the county. Thus, the comment: "the last drives were made through the western part of the county." Texas cattle were quarantined out of Kansas starting in 1885, thus, ending most cattle drives into Nebraska.

After breaking camp and continuing on the main trail for another seven miles, drovers came to another fork on the trail. On the ridge just south of Bobtail Creek in Hitchcock County, the trail split once again. Herds were either driven north — crossing Bobtail Creek, and fording the Frenchman east of present-day Hamlet — or continued in a northwesterly direction skirting the Bobtail and passing by present-day Hamlet on the west. The easterly route required the crossing of Bobtail Creek to the Frenchman, while the westerly route required maneuvering across Sand Canyon before crossing the Frenchman. At the Frenchman crossing was a landmark--three cottonwood trees appeared. One tree was larger than the other two, and it became known as the "Target Tree."[16]

After crossing the Frenchman River and struggling up the embankment to the flats, the drovers and their herds continued across the divide until they hit Stinkingwater Creek. There in Hays County, north of the Stinkingwater, the two routes joined together, and trail drivers picked up the well-traveled route of the former trail (Route 1) that had been used since 1874.

ROUTE 3 (1880–1884):

Route 3, which had moved west in Kansas in response to homesteader pressures and eventually the 1881 quarantine law, entered Nebraska in Section 34, T1N, R33W and joined Route 2 approximately six miles into Nebraska in Section 11, T1N, R33W. (note Map #6-1)

THE TRUNK LINE OF THE WESTERN CATTLE TRAIL FROM SECTION 5, T6N, R35W TO OGALLALA:

Routes 1 and 2 merged into one trail in Hayes County in Section 5, T6N, R35W. From that point, the trail continued in a northwesterly direction into Chase County to the Stinkingwater. Here again, drovers used both sides of the creek. Hester recalled that "the North [northern portion of the] Stinkingwater had a safe bottom, and we ranged both sides of the valley with its high hills to the east and sandhills to the west, up to the Big Spring."[17]

For those herds and drovers who chose to use the west side of the creek, they crossed the Stinkingwater in Section 23, T7N, R36W. Near where the trail forked and just a mile north of the crossing, a whisky dealer set up a portable-type saloon

---

[16]Two of these cottonwood trees are still standing today in 2012. They are located in SW 1/4 of Sec. 22, T5N, R35W on Kenneth Ham's ranch. (Interviews with Kenneth Ham by Gary Kraisinger, June and December, 2011)

[17]The authors feel that during the early years the east side route was used more, but as numbers of cattle increased, herds, one after the other, were driven up both sides of the creek. The Big Spring reference by Hester refers to a slough of water located farther north in the NW 1/4 of Section 8, T8N, R36W in Chase County, located at the Texas Trail Crossing.

THE WESTERN CATTLE TRAIL | 1874-1897

3

TEXAS TRAIL CANYON

AFTER THE SLAUGHTER OF THE BUFFALO AND THE LAST OF THE INDIAN HUNTS, RANCHERS MOVED INTO THIS PART OF THE REPUBLICAN RIVER COUNTRY IN 1875. AMONG THEM WERE I.P. AND IRA OLIVE, WHO WERE USING THIS CANYON ON THEIR RANCH IN 1876. HERDS OF TEXAS CATTLE WERE DELIVERED TO THEM HERE BEFORE BEING DRIVEN NORTH TO OGALLALA.

PRIOR TO 1880, THE MAIN TEXAS-OGALLALA TRAIL ENTERED NEBRASKA FIFTY MILES EAST OF HERE, BUT WITH THE INFLUX OF HOMESTEADERS, THE TRAIL WAS PUSHED WEST TO THIS AREA. BY 1881 THIS CANYON WAS KNOWN AS TEXAS TRAIL CANYON, AND A CHECKPOINT WAS ESTABLISHED HERE IN 1883-84, WHERE THE CATTLE WERE CHECKED FOR BRANDS AND DISEASE. IT IS SAID THAT 150,000 CATTLE WERE MOVED THROUGH HERE IN 1886, THE LAST YEAR OF THE TRAIL DRIVES.

A NUMBER OF PIONEER BURIALS WERE MADE IN THE IMMEDIATE VICINITY, BEGINNING WITH MEXICAN LEON, A COWBOY KILLED IN A FIGHT WITH IRA OLIVE. WHEN THE RAILROAD BUILT THROUGH IN 1881-82, A WORKER WAS KILLED AND BURIED 100 YARDS EAST OF HERE. REMAINS OF SEVERAL UNIDENTIFIED PIONEERS, ADULTS AND CHILDREN, HAVE BEEN DISCOVERED OVER THE YEARS, AND THEY WERE REINTERRED HERE IN 1971.

DUNDY COUNTY HISTORICAL SOCIETY
NEBRASKA STATE HISTORICAL SOCIETY

Location: four miles east of Haigler, Nebraska on Highway 34 south side of the highway; Dundy County

Authors' commentary:
The "main Texas-Ogallala Trail" that entered Nebraska fifty miles east of this marker, was, of course, the Western Cattle Trail. Nebraska historians call their part of this long trail the "Texas-Ogallala Trail."

This Texas Trail Canyon is on what we call the Wallace Branch that trailed through Wallace County and the vacinity of Fort Wallace and continued north exiting Kansas from Cheyenne County into Nebraska. Nebraska historian E. S. Sutton called this branch the "Texas Trail."

It is noted that the last year this route was used was in 1886. Which was after the final Kansas quarantine of 1885. This portion of Nebraska continued to receive cattle from off of the National Trail, which will be discussed later.

272   THE WESTERN CATTLE TRAIL | 1874-1897

under a large cottonwood tree. The peddler simply set up his wares on a board or log on a tarp under the tree. The distinct cottonwood, on the otherwise bare plains, marked the spot quite well where the cowboys knew they could buy their last refreshment before pushing up the Stinkingwater. This popular spot was referred to as "Log Saloon" or "Saloon Tree."[18]

The trail drivers and their herds on the east side of the Stinkingwater crossed farther up stream to the west side in northern Chase County in the NW 1/4 of Section 8, T8N, R36W, at a slough of water or a "fine springs of water," as Lewis Neatherlin called them.[19] By 1878, the crossing had become known as the "Texas Trail Crossing," or later, the "Blanche Crossing,"[20]

Charles Hester described the crossing:

> A willow-pole bridge crossed the creek--that's stretching the imagination. Three or four poles were stretched lengthwise across the bog and creek, then other pieces were laid crosswise. All lay on the ground and mud. Our chuckwagon got across, bouncing in great style. We could hear the rattle of pots and pans and old Prairie Dog Joe [the cook] cursing and laying on the blacksnake above the bawling of the cattle. Joe said it was the wildest ride in all his experience.[21]

Experienced drovers on this route knew that this watering hole was the last chance to allow the cattle to get their fill before reaching the Platte River. What lay ahead was the toughest forty-one miles on the route since leaving south Texas. Thirty three of those miles was across the Perkins Plain, an arid plateau with no running water. (The Stinkingwater Creek cut into Perkins County, but most of the time it was a dry draw.) Herds had to be pushed hard to the crest of the divide before they could descend into the Platte Valley where Ogallala was located. The distance usually meant three hard days of trailing with only a small chance of finding rain water in ponds or lowland lagoons. For cattle to go without water for three or more days was risky. They became skittish and hard to handle and were prone to stampede. If a scout did find water for his herd, it was common courtesy for the trail boss to point the way for any herds following behind. Neatherlin did just that:

July 7:
Drove 2 or 3 miles and turned off where Charley told us. Found plenty of good rain water in 2 large ponds among the sand hills. Good grass where we would have never looked for water. I put up a board directing

---
[18]The Saloon Tree was located in the center of a field northwest of the Maddux Cattle Company's feedlot in the SE 1/4 of Sec. 14, T7N, R36W. ("Historic Landmarks," *Chase County History*, Vol. 6, 31 and Kraisinger & Kraisinger, Ibid, 162-163)
[19]Kelly, Ibid, July 6, 1876 journal entry, 27.
[20]Immediately north of this slough or spring in SW 1/4 of Section 5, T8N, R36W, the community of Blanche would appear in a few years. Therefore, the trail crossing was also referred to as the "Blanche Crossing."
[21]Charles Hester as quoted in Sutton, Ibid, 160.

other herds how to find it. We drove some 8 miles further and camped on a vast, sandy plain with but little grass. The wind is blowing like a hurricane from the south and has been ever since yesterday morning, and feels like it was off of a furnace.[22]

THE WALLACE BRANCH OF THE WESTERN CATTLE TRAIL IN NEBRASKA TO OGALLALA, (1883-1884):

Another route of the Western Trail came out of northwest Kansas destined for Ogallala (see Map #6-1). At the state line, it was fifty miles west of Routes 1, 2, and 3, entering Nebraska in Dundy County in Section 32, TlN, R40W through Texas Trail Canyon. At this location inspecters checked the longhorns for road brands and disease before they crossed the rugged Republican River.

As explained earlier, the route started in 1883 because of a cattle pool drift fence erected across the trail in northern Lane County, Kansas. The Smoky Hill Cattle Pool was an obstacle to herds going north, consequently, herds destined for Ogallala, that didn't want to cut across the cattle pool grounds, could swing out around the obstacle in Lane and Scott County and detoured across western Kansas into Nebraska.

Nebraska historian E. S. Sutton referred to the route in Nebraska as the "Ogallala Trail" or "Texas Trail." This route was used more than Route 3 of the Western in the 1883 and 1884 seasons because the Kansas quarantine deadline had been moved farther west again in 1881. The Wallace Branch had the advantage of being out in front of the ever encroaching homesteaders, but the trail drivers often faced a shortage of water on the route.

The Wallace Branch, or Texas Trail in Nebraska, crossed the Republican River and skirted the canyons in Dundy County, forded the Frenchman east of Champion in Chase County, and then headed straight north toward Ogallala. This route merged with the main trail coming from the southeast in northern Perkins County in Sec. 25, T11N, R38W. The final seven miles into the Platte River Valley — the dry northern end of the Perkins Plain — must have been especially difficult with thousands of very thirsty animals.

DESTINATION — OGALLALA:

By the time the herds arrived in Ogallala, drovers from south Texas had trailed them some eleven hundred miles over a period of approximately four months. They had pushed across Texas, Indian Territory, Kansas, and into southwestern Nebraska. Most had hired on in February to prepare the cattle for the trail and reached Ogallala in late June. Trail drivers hadn't seen anything like Ogallala since leaving Dodge

---

[22]Kelly, Ibid, 27.

City. Ogallala was not as large as Dodge, supporting fewer saloons and dance halls, but its reputation was just as notorious. It became known as the "Gomorrah of the cattle trail." Sam Neill, a "mere boy" in 1880 when he made his first trip up the trail, wrote years later that we had been "not inside a house after we left Frio Town [Texas] until we reached Ogallala. The last house I was in before I left was Tom Bibb's saloon in Frio Town, and the next was Tuck's saloon in Ogallala. This was a mighty long time between drinks."[23]

As for the herds that arrived outside of Ogallala, they grazed on the south bank of the South Platte River, while negotiations were being finalized in town. If a contract had not already been made on a herd, the owners would often arrive in Ogallala by rail several weeks before the cattle arrived. Here they negotiated with a buyer for the best price. Col. J. F. Ellison was one of these principal buyers who remained "at Ogallala much of the time."[24] He was a middleman or broker who assisted ranchers in acquiring the kind of cattle they wanted. The bulk buying and selling of cattle at Ogallala went through a broker. The *American Agriculturist*, in 1878, described the scene:

> ...the cattle, while waiting to be sold and delivered on the north bank of the river, graze up and down the south side of the Platte over an area forty miles long and from one and a half to four miles wide. At one time this year (July 21st) there were fifty-five thousand head of cattle grazing in this valley. There is a space left between the herds a quarter of a mile or more wide, which the cow-boys utilize for camping purposes, they remaining on this [south] side of the Platte until the cattle are sold.

According to the *American Agriculturist*, there were 120,000 head "distributed to the ranchmen." In that season, the cash prices paid for cattle were yearling heifers, $8; yearling steers, $9; two-year old heifers, $11; two-year old steers, $13; cows, $12; three-year old steers, $16; and beeves, $19 to $20.[25]

After the cattle were sold, the drovers received $30 per month in wages and usually an extra $50 upon reaching the end of the drive for expenses to return to Texas. If a cowboy spent all of his wages with the Spanish Monte and Faro dealers in Ogallala and did not have enough money to pay his way back to Texas by rail, he was forced to mortgage his next season's wages to return home. Some of the cowboys continued on north of Ogallala to help deliver a herd. Others were not always willing to go beyond Ogallala. However, a cowboy who was not anxious to return to Texas, and wanted to see more country, could easily find work with another herd trailing

---

[23]Neill, "A Long Time Between Drinks," in Hunter, *The Trail Drivers of Texas*, 256,

[24]*American Agriculturist*, NY, Dec. 1878, as reprinted in the *Keith County News*, Ogallala, Neb., Sept. 18, 1996, 3.

[25]*American Agriculturist*, 3. If an owner found a demanding market at Ogallala or sold more cattle than he anticipated and needed more cattle than he had put on the trail, then his agent in Texas was ordered to put another herd on the trail for a "forced drive." These drives were often made in 90 days, rather than the typical 120 days.

north. The chance of seeing the Black Hills, or visiting Miles City, or Fort Buford was an exciting prospect for a young waddie.[26]

If an agreement was made with a rancher from the northern territories, the buyer often made arrangements with the cattlemen to deliver the herd to his ranch. Samuel D. Houston wrote years later about his trip up the trail in 1879. The outfit was owned by Head & Bishop, and Houston's trail boss was John Sanders. Houston recalled:

> We reached Ogallala August 10th, 1879, and there we met R. G. Head, who gave the boss, John Sanders, orders to cross the South Platte the next morning and proceed to the North Platte. He said he would see us over there and would tell us where to take the herd.[27]

Houston helped deliver Sanders' herd to a ranch on Pumpkin Creek, Nebraska, approximately "one hundred miles up the Platte." Upon his return to Ogallala, however, he was asked to join an outfit bossed by Tom Moore to deliver a herd of four thousand Texas steers to the "Red Cloud Agency in Dakota."[28] In most cases, herds destined for Indian agencies were on contract before the herd left Texas.

THE OPENING OF INDIAN LANDS TO SETTLERS AND CATTLE HERDS:

Ogallala was located at the base of one of the greatest grasslands in the world, where large ranches were being established to "finish out" herds for the beef markets in the East and at neighboring Indian reservations. The reservations were in a large parcel of land, encompassing approximately 43,000 square miles of arid plains extending from the Missouri River westward. The Great Sioux Reservation, as it became known, encompassed parts of Dakota, Nebraska, and Wyoming territories.

The Sioux people had migrated westward from the lower Ohio and middle Mississippi valleys, and their descendants emerged on the plains in the 17th century. The Teton Sioux (aka Lakota), one of three groupings of the Sioux, became nomadic buffalo hunters, and their territory extended throughout the Platte Valley, upper Missouri and Yellowstone rivers, and the eastern slope of the Rockies.[29] In 1851, the

---

[26]Also spelled "waddy," this term was used by cowboys to refer to a young cowboy who was on his first trail drive and inexperienced. On the ranch during a round-up, the extra cowboy needed to fill out an outfit for a week or so was a waddy. The word derived from "wad" or "wadding" —. anything to fill in. Ramon F. Adams. *The Cowboy Dictionary*, 338.

[27]Samuel Dunn Houston, "A Trying Trip Alone Through the Wilderness," in Hunter, *The Trail Drivers of Texas*, 78.

[28]The Red Cloud Agency had been in four different locations from 1871 to 1878: on North Platte River in Wyoming Territory, one mile west of present-day Henry, Neb. (1871-1873); on White River in northwest Nebraska, near Crawford, Neb. (1873-1877); moved to the Missouri River, (1877-1878); and relocated to present-day South Dakota in 1878 and renamed Pine Ridge Agency in 1889.

[29]The other two groups of the Siouan people were the Santee and Yankton. The Santee lived in present-day Minnesota, and the Yankton live in the area between Minnesota and Missouri River.

government via a Fort Laramie Treaty sought to concentrate the Sioux tribes in order to allow for white migration into the area, but the plan caused resistance because the Teton resented the intrusion into their hunting grounds. In 1868, the government adopted a Peace Policy with the Teton Sioux at Fort Laramie. This treaty included the creation of the Great Sioux Reservation, which the Teton accepted. The government also committed to abandon a trail and the military posts from Fort Laramie to Montana Territory and to keep whites from hunting and settling in the designated reservation. The Teton, as their part of the peace policy, were to remain within the boundaries of the reservation so they would not hinder immigration into the region.

The agreement, in addition, called for the establishment of various Indian agencies, each with an appointed agent. For administrative purposes and to receive government-issued rations and other goods promised by the treaty, the Teton Sioux reported to six separate agencies. On the Missouri River, the Hunkpapa, Blackfoot, San-Arc, Miniconjou, and Two-Kettle Sioux drew rations at Standing Rock and Cheyenne River agencies.[30] To the south and west, Oglala enrolled at Pine Ridge Agency, and the Brules reported to the Rosebud Agency. It was to these agencies that Texas cattle were delivered to fill out beef contracts for the government. Some sixteen thousand Tetons resided in the Great Sioux Reservation.[31]

The Peace Policy lasted only eight years. By the time drover Samuel D. Houston was asked to help deliver a herd of Texas cattle to the Red Cloud Agency in 1879, conditions had changed from what they had been in 1868. The Peace Policy, and treaty, had been broken.

In 1874, it was rumored that gold could be found on the Teton Sioux lands in the Black Hills of Dakota Territory. Thus, the government ordered Lieutenant Colonel George Armstrong Custer to lead an expedition to explore routes and possible sites for future Indian agencies and posts in the Black Hills (and to quietly see if the gold rumors were true).[32] Custer's entourage left Fort Abraham Lincoln near Bismarck, in present-day North Dakota, on July 2, 1874. When two prospectors in the group found gold in the southern Black Hills, a dispatch was sent to Fort Laramie saying: "For several days the miners have been successful in obtaining gold colors." Things would never be the same. By September, *Harper's Weekly* had published an article stating that gold had been discovered along the banks of a creek in the Black Hills. Within months, thousands of miners rushed into the Hills to pan for gold — on sacred Sioux land.[33]

---

[30]These tribes were five of the seven sub-divisions of the Teton Sioux.

[31]Robert M. Utley, *The Indian Frontier of the American West, 1846-1890*, 232. Howard R. Lamar, ed. "Sioux Indians," The *New Encyclopedia of the American West*, 1051-1054.

[32]In 1874, the post-Civil War boom had worn itself out, and the nation was facing a depression. Washington politicians reasoned that a gold strike would revive business and give hope to down-and-out citizens as it had done in 1849 in California.

[33]Custer's entourage in this expedition consisted of about one thousand men, comprising of ten companies of cavalry, two of infantry, and numerous scouts, teamsters, guides and interpreters. Their camp was set up on French Creek "about ten miles south of Harney's Peak, in the southern Black Hills." The gold was panned in this area. (John S. McClintock, *Pioneer Days in the Black Hills*, 19) Time Life Books, Inc. *The Miners*, 44-49.

THE WESTERN CATTLE TRAIL | 1874-1897

The government announced at once that no mining would be permitted until a new treaty could be negotiated with the Sioux and hastily formed a commission to meet with the Sioux in September of 1875. Meanwhile, anxious miners and merchants constructed a stockaded town, throwing up rows of shacks to wait out the negotiations. It is estimated that over the winter of 1875-1876, some 10,000 to 11,000 gold-seekers bided their time within the stockade, which they called "Custer City."[34]

The talks between the Sioux and the commissioners came to a standstill, however. The commissioners returned to Washington, and by November, the government renewed the order that all Sioux had to be within the confines of the Great Sioux Reservation and that non-agency Indians had to return to their own respective agencies by January 31, 1876 or be considered hostile and subject to military actions.[35] No longer was the Laramie Peace Treaty respected. Military leaders disregarded the treaty's Black Hills boundaries and ceased efforts to prevent gold-seekers from entering the Hills. Thousands of prospectors rushed into the sacred lands of the Sioux.

The government had issued an ultimatum. All military forts that lay in a band around the Great Sioux Reservation were placed on alert. The Sioux resisted and retaliated. By May, a repetitive chorus of raids and confrontations between the military and the Indians took place, which was, in part, the opening stages of what became known later as the Great Sioux War. Because of the government's ultimatum, General Phillip Sheridan ordered three army expeditionary forces to the Yellowstone River area in southeastern Montana to find and engage with free-roaming Lakota Sioux and their allies, the Northern Cheyenne, all of whom had not returned to their assigned agency. On June 25, 1876, part of the Seventh Calvary, led by General George Armstrong Custer, were killed at the Battle of the Little Bighorn.

By 1877 the U.S. government had forced a new treaty on the Lakota Sioux, announced that the Black Hills was no longer part of the reservation, and opened up 7.7 million acres of the Black Hills to homesteading and private interests.[36]

NEW MARKETS FOR TEXAS CATTLE HERDS:

Cattle ranches had been emerging in the northern Wyoming and Montana territories since the early 1870s, and many of them were stocked with Texas longhorns. Ogallala and Sidney, Nebraska, and Cheyenne in Wyoming Territory became the

---

[34] "History of Custer," www.custer.gov [accessed July 9, 2010] Harold Hutton, *The River That Runs*, 76, and www.custer.govoffice.com accessed June 27, 2010.

[35] Thomas R. Buecker, *Fort Robinson and the American West , 1874-1899*, 78-79.

[36] The new 1877 treaty resulted in the U.S. government taking a strip of land along the western border of Dakota Territory fifty miles wide, plus all land west of the Cheyenne and Belle Fourche rivers. Thus, the 1877 treaty, which was in violation of the original 1868 Fort Laramie Peace Treaty, removed all of the Black Hills from the Sioux control. The Lakota accepted the treaty in the fall of 1877 in order to get their rightful allotment of winter provisions. (Time Life Books, Inc. *The Miners*, 44-49) The remaining area of the Great Reservation was later divided up into seven separate reservations: The Cheyenne River Agency, Crow Creek Agency, Lower Brule Agency, Rosebud Agency, Sisseton Agency, Yankton Agency and the Pine Ridge Agency.

gateways to the north through which the cattle would flow into this region. Located along an extended 170-mile line, east to west, the three towns were well situated for benefiting from the cattle-trailing boom. Ogallala and Cheyenne were cow towns, and both Sidney (Sidney Barracks) and Cheyenne (Fort D. A. Russell) were adjacent to military forts that catered to the gold miners. After the Indians were forced to surrender, the Indian agencies needed cattle to fill the beef allotments to the Indians, and gold miners by the thousands needed supplies, including beef for consumption. After the Indian wars, the cattle herds were now able to venture farther north to fill government contracts, stock ranches, and meet other needs. Northwest of Ogallala, on the White River, was the Red Cloud Agency (near Camp Robinson), and farther up the river was the Spotted Tail Agency (near Camp Sheridan). Within two years, the Pine Ridge and Rosebud reservations and their related agencies would be established on the south border of the Great Sioux Reservation in Dakota Territory.

Over the next decade, a massive migration of people and trail herds penetrated into the non-Indian lands on the northern plains. The business and cattle operations at Ogallala, Sidney, and Cheyenne were the forces driving the economy of the region.[37]

Upon reaching Ogallala from the south, herds were delivered in all directions from the terminal. It is estimated that approximately 100,000 head were shipped out each season on the Union Pacific Railroad to the eastern markets, but the balance were trailed to various ranches and Indian agencies. The main trunk of the Western Trail crossed the South Platte at Ogallala and continued up the North Platte River to the mouth of Rawhide Creek and then turned north to pass through Wyoming and Montana territories and eventually entering Canada. There were, however, two splinter routes that left Ogallala.

THE CHEYENNE, WYOMING AREA AND THE CHEYENNE SPLINTER ROUTE FROM OGALLALA: (Map #6-2)

One hundred seventy miles west of Ogallala is Cheyenne, Wyoming. In the early days of territorial development, Cheyenne was located in Dakota Territory. The site was platted by General Grenville M. Dodge and his survey crew on July 4, 1867 as the location where the westward-building Union Pacific Railroad would cross Crow Creek, a tributary of the South Platte River. Dodge referred it as "Crow Creek Crossing," but friends of Dodge named the crossing after the prominent plains tribe, the Cheyenne.

Non-natives throughout southern Wyoming believed the coming railroad was a sign of assured prosperity. Therefore, white immigrants gathered around

---

[37]Yankton, Dakota Territory and Sioux City, Iowa, were also centers for prospectors coming from the east. (Barbara Fifer, *Bad Boys of the Black Hills*, 2) There was also a Niobrara river route going up the Niobrara "to the mouth of the Keya Paha River, thence along the Spotted Tail road to the crossing of the White Earth River, thence across to the Black Hills, or follow the Spotted Tail road to that agency, thence across to the Hills." (Hutton, ibid, 76)

THE WESTERN CATTLE TRAIL | 1874-1897   279

Crow Creek Crossing, and by the time the first tracks were laid into the new city on November 13, 1867, over four thousand hopefuls were in Cheyenne. Upon reaching Crow Creek, the Union Pacific found a ramshackle town of quickly thrown up saloons, gambling houses, restaurants, dance halls, and shacks and tents, populated by gamblers, roughs, troops, and bull-whackers. In fact, the town had appeared so quickly out on the empty plains that it would become known as the "Magic City of the Plains."[38]

Fort D. A. Russell was established at the same time as Cheyenne, three miles northwest of Cheyenne.[39] Created by an executive order, it was one of the forts built to protect the construction workers on the Union Pacific Railroad. It was not at all like

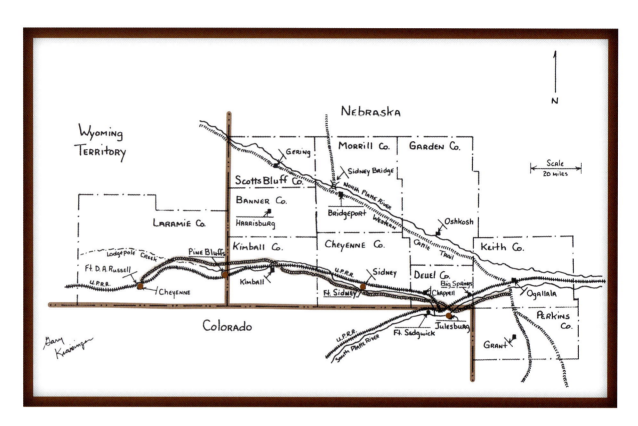

#6-2
The Cheyenne Splinter Route from Ogallala, Nebraska to Cheyenne, Wyoming.
This map shows the splinter route from Ogallala, Nebraska, to Julesburg, Colorado, near Fort Sedgwick. From there the splinter route follows closely the northern spur of the Union Pacific Railroad from the Julesburg Junction to Sidney, Nebraska, at Fort Sidney, continuing to Pine Bluffs, Wyoming, and ending at Cheyenne, Wyoming, next to Fort D. A. Russell.

---

[38] Bill O'Neal, Cheyenne, *A Biography of the "Magic City" Of the Plains*, 3.
[39] The fort was named for brigadier general David Allen Russell (1820-1864) who commanded a division for the Union Army in the Civil War at Shenandoah Valley. He was killed during the Third Battle of Winchester on September 19, 1864. In addition to protecting railroad construction workers, Fort D. A. Russell also served as protectorate and escort to overland mail stages, the telegraph line, and surveying parties. In 1930, the base was renamed Fort Francis E. Warren, after a Medal of Honor recipient who served as Governor of Wyoming. In 1949, it became Francis E. Warren Air Force Base. ("Fort D. A. Russell," www.wyomingtalesandtrails.com [accessed June 6, 2010]

the haphazard tent-and- shack town of Cheyenne, however. A large military center was constructed with lumber brought in by wagon trains. After the rails reached Cheyenne, top-grade building materials were brought in. Soldiers constructed nearly 100 framed buildings, stables, storehouses, a hospital and, of course, an elegant two-story officer's quarters for their commanding officer, Col. John D. Stevenson.

Nearly 900 soldiers, twenty-three officers, and a number of officers' wives resided at the fort. There were seven companies of the Thirtieth Infantry, four troops of the Second Cavalry, and a band. On February 22, 1868, only eight months after fort construction began, Colonel Stevenson invited the citizens of Cheyenne to the post to view a dress parade in honor of George Washington's birthday, and a few days later, invitations were extended to Cheyenne's leading citizens to attend the unveiling of his beautifully decorated headquarters. Officers and wives greeted the guests; fine wines and refreshment were served; and the post band provided music.

While Col. Stevenson and his officers were initiating a succession of balls, receptions, and band concerts with prominent Cheyenne citizens, a different kind of entertainment awaited the common soldier on the west end of the Magic City. Like all forts, Fort Russell had its camp town, off the military reservation, for the soldier's amusement; It was a sleazy hole of saloons, dance halls, and bordellos, and, like many other forts, the town had a pet name. This one was called, "Chicago."

Before long, military leaders at Fort D. A. Russell decided to add a quartermaster's depot. In August of 1867, soon after Fort Russell's location was determined, the military decided to construct "Cheyenne Depot" about half way between Fort Russell and Cheyenne on Crow Creek. The construction of what would become the nation's second largest quartermaster depot was overseen and built by its first commander Capt. Elias B. Carling of the Quartermaster Corps. Camp Carlin (the "g" was dropped) was another community, or fort-like establishment, with company barracks, guard house, commissary, mess hall, bunkhouses, and numerous shops and offices that catered to its personnel.

Sixteen large warehouses consisted the core of the post. They sat along the two parallel sets of railroad tracks built as a spur from the Union Pacific mainline. Out of these warehouses, the military supplied fourteen western forts, troops in the field, in addition to providing food and clothing to the Red Cloud and Spotted Tail Indian agencies. More than one hundred wagons and five pack trains delivered several million pounds of supplies to the post over the years.

Military equipment and uniforms were shipped to the depot from the east, but the majority of the supplies were acquired locally from farmers, ranchers, and Cheyenne merchants or brokers. These military contracts and purchases created a boom to the economy, and for the depot's civilian employees. Support personnel, which included teamsters, craftsmen, cooks, and stock tenders, often outnumbered the soldiers at the fort, and they created jobs with paychecks that were spent in Cheyenne.[40]

---

[40]As military forts became less important, the camp was abandoned in 1887. (Bill O'Neal, Ibid, 30-32 and "Camp Carlin," http://wiki.wyomingplaces.org [accessed June 6, 2010]

By 1875, when Texas herds were being trailed over the Western Trail to Ogallala, seven years after the construction of Cheyenne, Fort Russell, and Camp Carlin, the Crow Creek communities were in their second boom. Cheyenne had grown up and had become a sophisticated city with entrepreneurs of all types in addition to a core of respectable lawyers, doctors, editors, teachers, and preachers.

Then there were the cattle barons whose ranches dominated the vast vacant grasslands of Wyoming. The earliest of these cattle kings was John Wesley Iliff. Almost from the time the railroad reached Cheyenne, Iliff was fattening cattle on nearby open range. He had come west from Ohio to Denver in 1859, and, while a merchant there, saw the need for beef for the army posts. Later clients included the Union Pacific construction crews and the residents of the newly-created Indian reservations. He started to develope his own herd and by 1868 had several thousand head of cattle on the South Platte, fifty miles east of Denver.

In the spring of 1868, only a few short months after the arrival of the Union Pacific in Cheyenne, Iliff and a freighter named Fenton visited Goodnight at his Apsihapa Canyon ranch in south central Colorado Territory. Iliff agreed to buy Goodnight's herd if the owner would deliver it to Cheyenne. It was the season that Goodnight created another route farther east than the old Goodnight-Loving Trail that had been used by his deceased partner Oliver Loving to deliver cattle to Denver and became the pathway for trail drivers to Cheyenne. From his canyon ranch, Goodnight drove the herd due north, crossed the Arkansas River near Pueblo, climbed out of the Arkansas River basin, and followed the front slope north to the Platte river basin. At the confluence of Crow Creek and the Platte, near where Greeley now stands, he "swam his herd, recalling that those old Texas steers, with only a portion of their heads and horns above water, 'looked like a million floating rocking chairs.'"[41] From there, Goodnight trailed the herd up Crow Creek to Cheyenne. Goodnight, who often bought cattle from John Chisum, who trailed them from Texas to his New Mexico Territory ranch, drove only one other herd on to Wyoming and that was to the Chugwater. After that, Goodnight drove herds purchased by Iliff to his headquarters on Crow Creek in northern Colorado near Cheyenne.[42]

Iliff's holdings eventually extended more than 100 miles along the South Platte River from Colorado's eastern border and sixty miles northward into Wyoming. When the Black Hills opened up and gold seekers created their own camp and communities, Iliff sold cattle to the various Black Hills' butcher shops. Iliff also had butcher shops in Denver, and he opened a meat market in Cheyenne. Although Iliff died suddenly in 1878 at the age of forty-six, he had set an example to other cattlemen such as W. C. "Billy" Irvin, who drove Texas longhorns to a ranch on the North Platte River in 1876, and Alexander H. Swan, who organized the Swan Land and Cattle Company whose headquarters, the Two Bar Ranch, was forty-five miles north of Cheyenne.

---

[41]J. Evetts Haley, *Charles Goodnight, Cowman and Plainsman*, 206.

[42]According to J. Evetts Haley, Goodnight's delivery of cattle to Iliff "on Crow Creek in the early spring of 1868 is said to have been the first Texas herd in Wyoming, and the new owner [Iliff] was known as the first 'cattle king' of the northern Plains." (Haley, Ibid., 241)

Before Ogallala had inherited the cattle trade from its eastern neighbors, and before it became a railhead for Texas cattle on the Western Trail, Cheyenne, Wyoming[43] was a cattle center; and in future years, it would boast of the comings and goings of big ranchers and cattle shipments. On November 29, 1873, a year before the Western Trail headed into Kansas and Nebraska, ten ranches formed the Laramie County Stock Growers' Association. By 1879, the organization had expanded to become the Wyoming Stock Growers Association, headquartered in Cheyenne.[44]

After rumors of Black Hills gold spread in 1875, Cheyenne became one of the main gateways into the region. Because the city was an established center, it could outfit large parties of prospectors who, at first, came to Cheyenne to wait for the government to release the Hills to settlers and prospectors. Months later, when the area was declared open, Black Hills immigrants streamed through the city by the thousands.

Cheyenne was not at all like the small cow town of Ogallala. It had a metropolitan culture with theaters, high-end mercantile stores, classy hotels, saloons, and many large stately mansions built by some of the more prosperous residents. The streets of the city were filled with freight wagons coming and going and six-horse Concord stagecoaches that left the city almost daily for the Black Hills. During the gold-rush years when all roads seemed to lead to Cheyenne, the Western Cattle Trail splinter route from Ogallala was one of those roads.[45]

To reach this intriguing center of commerce with its cattle barons and frenzied gold seekers, Texas drovers followed the South Platte River from Ogallala to Julesburg, Colorado, and then trailed west to the adjacent areas of Sidney, Nebraska, Pine Bluffs, Wyoming, and on to Cheyenne. All of these communities had been surveyed and platted for the Union Pacific's rail stops in 1867.[46] General Dodge and his crew had not followed the more northerly Oregon Trail route but went almost directly west out of Nebraska in order to be closer to Denver and to have access to Wyoming coal supplies. For cattlemen to follow the rail route made sense, because each of the three towns had a railhead for cattle, and each was on a creek or next to a watering hole. Two, moreover, were protected by a military fort. Julesburg sat at the junction point on the Overland Trail where wagon trains and stagecoaches could either continue southwest to Denver or west to Cheyenne. Outside of Julesburg

---

[43]Congress created Wyoming Territory in 1868. President Grant appointed Brigadier General John A. Campbell as the first governor of the territory. A year later, the territorial legislature granted women the right to vote and hold office. The new law was the first of its kind in the United States. ("Wyoming," *The World Book Encyclopedia*, Vol. 21, (1982), 440)

[44]O'Neal, Ibid., 148.

[45]Stage coaches ran twice a week from Cheyenne to Custer City and then, starting in March of 1876, the Black Hills Stage Company ran daily coaches between Cheyenne, Custer City, and Deadwood. The last coach from Cheyenne to Deadwood left in February 1887. (Barbara Fifer, Ibid., 7, 46)

[46]Julesburg had been in the general locale before the railroad came through. A Frenchman by the name of Jules Beni had a trading post, blacksmith shop, a saloon, and a few other enterprises. When the railroad came through, the town moved closer to the river and railroad (1867). When a branch line of the Union Pacific was built to Denver in 1881, Julesburg made another move to be near the railroad at the point of junction. (http://townof julesburg.com [accessed June 6, 2010])

was Fort Sedgwick, and herds could water on either the South Platte River or on Lodgepole Creek.

Sidney, Nebraska was located on Lodgepole Creek, a good watering spot for cattle, and the town was connected to Fort Sidney, also called Sidney Barracks. Starting in 1875, it became the southern terminus to the Sidney-Black Hills freight route that carried military and civilian passengers and goods to Fort Robinson, to various Indian agencies, and to Deadwood, Dakota Territory. Like Cheyenne, Sidney outfitted gold prospectors. Of the two towns, however, Cheyenne had the advantage. Sidney had fewer goods in its stores, and its Black Hills route faced a difficult crossing of the North Platte River about forty miles north.[47]

Bob Lauderdale followed this Cheyenne Splinter Trail to the Cheyenne area in 1880. In the fall and winter of 1879, he and C. F. Carroll had made several trips "down the Rio Grande below Laredo and bought cattle from the Tortilla ranch in Mexico and from Pedro Flores, Juan Benavides, Jesus Pena and others for Camp, Rosser & Carroll." In the spring, Lauderdale and Carroll each started north with a herd, but they had to combine the two herds at Bandera (Texas) because several of Carroll's hands had quit. When they reached Ogallala, the herd was sold, but Lauderdale then delivered 1,000 head of the original herd to Pine Bluffs.

Lauderdale, who trailed cattle almost every year from 1876 to 1889, described the watering holes of the different routes he had used in his long trailing career. On this splinter route, he recorded that they trailed "to Ogallala on the South Platte, up the South Platte to Chug Water by Big Springs, Julesburg up Pole Creek [Lodgepole] to Sydney, Pine Bluff, Horse Creek, and to Chug Water." (Horse Creek and Chug Water are north of Cheyenne.)[48]

Henry D. Steele also wrote of his trip to Ogallala in 1883 and of delivering part of the herd to Cheyenne. He was under the employ of rancher Dick Head of Lockhart, Texas, and his trail boss was Monroe Hardeman:

> In the spring of 1883,...We gathered the cattle in Mason and Coleman Counties, The cattle were pretty thin, as the range was dry and had little grass. We passed through McCulloch County, through North Texas, and into the Indian Territory. Crossed the Washita River when it was on a big rise....
>
> When we reached Dodge City, Kansas, we remained there several days to allow the herd to rest, and from here we proceeded to Ogallala, Nebraska, where Mr. Head sold the cattle, and most of the crew came home, but Joe Lovelady, Pat Garrison, and myself and Charlie Hedgepeth, a negro, went on with the herd to Cheyenne, Wyoming, where we arrived in August. When we started back we bought our [train] tickets for Austin, and the price was $33.35 each.[49]

---

[47]O'Neal, Ibid., 94.
[48]Jasper (Bob) Lauderdale, "Reminiscences of the Trail," in Hunter, *The Trail Drivers of Texas*, 407-410.
[49]Henry D. Steele, "Played Pranks on the Tenderfoot," in Hunter, 138.

In the following year George W. Brock helped deliver a herd to "Julesburg Junction"[50] which was on this Cheyenne Splinter Route. In his long rambling narrative, Brock explained that he was working on the Blanks and Withers Ranch in La Salle County, Texas, in the spring of 1884, when herds were being prepared for the trail. Two herds were sent up the trail. Gus Withers was the trail boss of the first herd, which started with 4,000 head of three and four year olds. The herd to which Brock was assigned was with trail boss Sam Childress. The herds were shipped by rail to Wichita Falls, Texas, and then cowboys trailed the herd from there to Julesburg, Colorado.[51] Brock recalled:

> After we got to the top of the ridge I looked down in the valley of Washita River [Indian Territory] and the whole face of the country was alive with herds. I went back and stopped the herd until I could survey the route, and found that by going above the trail and crossing about five miles up and swimming the river we could get ahead of everything…in the lead of all other herds.

Over 300,000 cattle were on the trail in 1884. This comment, "the country was alive with herds," shows the congestion and bunching up of herds around the river crossings.

> At Dodge City every man, including the boss, except myself, celebrated in great style, while I was left to handle and hold the outfit. After disposing of our lame cattle we shaped up and moved on to Ogallala.
> We watered at the North Republican [Nebraska]. The lead cattle struck the Frenchman about sundown, and from then until next morning about 10 o'clock they kept coming in, and every once in a while a man would show up. The morning we started this particular drive I ate breakfast at daylight and the next meal I ate was at 10 o'clock the next day.

A large cattle herd strung out for miles during the day in their march. Here Brock writes of the long procession: "they kept coming in" and "every once in a while a man would show up." He alludes to the long hours of trailing the herd.

> Leaving Ogallala we went up the south side of the Platte River to Julesburg Junction, where we delivered our cattle to Governor [John Long] Rout[t] and ex-[actually future Lieut.] Governor [Jared L.] Brush of Colorado.

---

[50]Julesburg had moved from its former location two years before George W. Brock made his trail drive in order to be at the point of junction with the Union Pacific. It was also a junction on the Overland Trail where wagon trains and stagecoaches could either continue southwest to Denver or west to Cheyenne. Thus, people and cowboys called the location "Julesburg Junction."

[51]By 1884, a transitional period in the trail driving era, ranchers in south Texas were starting to ship herds part of the way by train. Cowboys and their horses would ride along with the herd, unload the herd, and continue the trip on the trail to their destination.

THE WESTERN CATTLE TRAIL | 1874-1897

Going up the river our only trouble was to keep our stock off the farmers. They had no fences and it took very carefull watching to keep them out of those patches. To let your stuff get on those patches meant the highest price grazing that a Texas horse or steer ever got. One night I woke up and heard the horse bell and I knew it was in the wrong direction, so I got up and found them grazing on one of those high-priced corn patches. I quickly drove them to camp, woke up everybody and moved everything away that night. I believe that corn actually did the horses good;…

If Texas horses or cattle were discovered in a farmer's corn patch, the owner could have the trail boss arrested and fined — a hefty amount. That is what Brock meant when he wrote about "high-priced corn patches."

After reaching Julesburg Junction we crossed the Platte and began delivering. I was sent to meet Gus Withers, [the owner] who had not yet come up with us. I had three horses, riding one and leading the others. When crossing the Platte my horses were so weak from the trip from Texas, and the quicksand so very bad, they could not carry me, so I led them, wading water up to my chin.

Not only was trail driving taxing for the cowboys, but the working horses suffered as well. That is the reason for a rumuda with a herd. A cowboy often switched horses during a trail drive.

Brock indicates that the cattle had been sold to Governor Routt and Jared L. Brush at Julesburg Junction, but the cattle had to be delivered north of the river to a certain destination, as was so often the case. As with cowboys on the other trails, those who went all the way to Cheyenne on the Cheyenne Splinter Route, delivered their herds, enjoyed the entertainment that the city had to offer, and then hired out to another outfit or returned to Texas.

Brock returned to Texas:

After all our cattle had been delivered we naturally felt that we could sleep as long as we cared to. So Childress and myself slept until 10 o'clock the next morning.

The dinner that Mark Withers gave us at the [train] station when we were ready to come home paid me fully for all the meals I had lost on the trip.[52]

---

[52]George W. Brock, "When Lightning Set the Grass on Fire," in Hunter, 219-225.

THE MISSOURI RIVER SPLINTER ROUTE:
(Map #6-3)

The splinter route west to Cheyenne, Wyoming was used to deliver herds to ranchers, but if a contract had been made with an Indian agency in southeastern Dakota Territory, herds were trailed northeast out of Ogallala. This was a difficult route. North of Ogallala between the North Platte basin and Dakota Territory lay a vast area of sandhills, which adjoined the southern border of the Great Sioux Reservation. On early Nebraska maps the area was referred to as "Sioux Country"

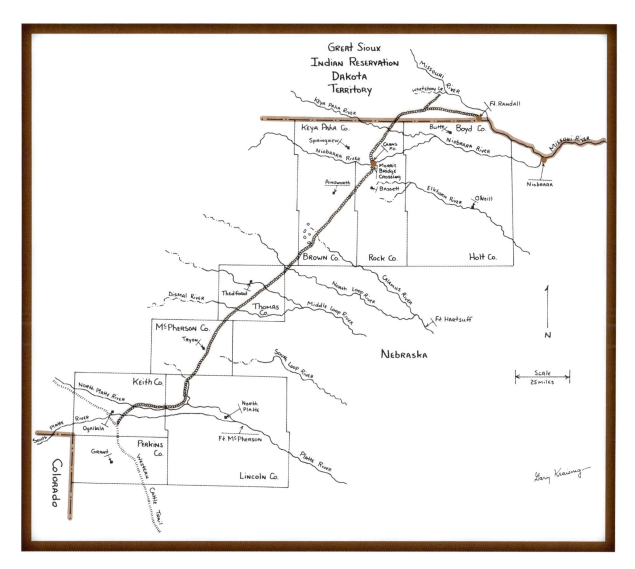

#6-3
The Missouri River Splinter Route From Ogallala, Nebraska to the Missouri River in the Great Sioux Indian Reservation, 1876-1879:
This map shows the splinter route from Ogallala, going northeast across the sandhills of Nebraska (Sioux Country), stopping at a group of small lakes in southern present-day Brown County, and continuing on to the Niobrara River. Drovers and herds crossed the river at Morris Bridge (Carns post office) and continued to the Keya Paha River, which marked the Nebraska state line. From there they drove through the Great Sioux Reservation to the Missouri River. Here herds were delivered to Indian agents in the Fort Randall area or the Whetstone Creek area.

THE WESTERN CATTLE TRAIL | 1874-1897

or "unceded Indian Territory" — in fact, it was Sioux hunting ground, where the Indians were allowed to leave their reservation to hunt the antelope, deer, and the few remaining buffalo and to summer their horse herds on the lush grasses of the valleys.[53] These sandhills and Sioux hunting grounds were to be avoided as much as possible by non-Indians.

Across the north edge of the sandhills runs the Niobrara River. It stretches across the entire width of Nebraska from the Seventy-seven Hills area west of Lusk, Wyoming to its confluence at the Missouri River. In the eastern part of the state, the river also, at this time, was the southern border of several Dakota reservations, separating Nebraska from the Sioux, Ponca, and Yankton reservations.

The town of Niobrara is located where the Niobrara River and the great Missouri River meet. During the 1870s, it was situated at the lower end of the Indian reservation complex, with the Santee Reservation to the south and the Yankton and Ponca immediately to the north. The original town site was started in 1857. There was a steam sawmill, and the first ferry boat began operation in about 1860 and was operated by horses walking on a treadmill.[54] Because of its access to the river and a ferry boat service, Niobrara became a logical place to cross herds of cattle destined for the Indian reservations north of the river.[55] Therefore, Niobrara was a cattle town not long after the time it had a river ferry.

Texas herds had been driven north of Schuyler, Nebraska into Niobrara, from 1870 to 1872. The *Platte County Journal* in Columbus reported on August 3, 1870, that "Jno. W. Bloomfield" (called Johnny Smoker), had constructed "about 6 miles from the head of Shell Creek west of the 6th P.M, a cattle crossing near his house to accommodate Drovers driving herds headed for the Indian Reserves up north by the most direct route." On August 17, the paper reported that "Shell Creek renamed Schuyler is scarely a year old. A Drover says 20,000 Longhorns are near Town."[56]

When the trail system moved west to Kearney in 1872, herds destined for reservations were driven from Kearney to Niobrara.[57] In an unpublished manuscript by Henry Tienken, a resident of Niobrara at the time, he noted:

> Great herds of longhorn cattle from Texas were driven through Oklahoma, Kansas and Nebraska. They crossed the Platte River at Kearney and had to swim the Missouri at Niobrara. Mr. Mayberry [Seth

---

[53]This large expanse of undeveloped land ran from present-day Holt County to present-day Sheridan County. Today there are twenty-six counties in the Sandhills which comprises of about one fourth of the area of Nebraska.

[54]The name "Niobrara" is from an Indian word meaning "running water."

[55]An 1875 map of Nebraska shows the northern border of Nebraska in this area as being the Niobrara River. ("Map of the State of Nebraska," by Geo. L. Brown, State Secretary of Immigration, Omaha, Neb., 1875) Another map that shows the river being the Nebraska state border is on page 91 of Harold Hutton's *The River That Runs*, and online: "Great Sioux Indian Reservation" map, (www.bing.com) Today that area north of the Niobrara River, south of South Dakota, is mostly Boyd County, Nebraska.

[56]*Platte County Journal*, Columbus, Nebraska, August 3, 1870 and August 17, 1870.

[57]The Kansas trails that led into Kearney from 1872 through 1875, were the Cox Trail from Ellsworth and the extension of the Ellis-Hays City route.

Mabry], a texan, and Bill Paxton of Omaha were interested in these cattle. The herds ranged in number from 2,000 to 3,500 and it was a big job to crowd these wild cattle into the river. The cowboys would construct a plank fence or wing into the river, and then crowd two or three hundred head at a time into the Missouri. They would have several men from town, who would use skiffs to keep the cattle away from the banks and to keep them from floating down the river too far, and also to keep them away from the soft, muddy sandbars. Quite a number of the cattle would drown and float on their sides downstream to be towed to the bank by a bunch of Poncas who would be on the watch for them…. When the cattle had been delivered to another outfit on the Dakota side of the river, those who had trailed the cattle from Texas would stay a few days and rest the men and horses, have a dance and paint the town red.[58]

Cattle herds continued to feed into Niobrara to meet Indian contracts by way of Kearney through 1875. In 1876, however, when the Kansas quarantine took effect and the Nebraska herd law became a reality, Niobrara ceased to be a cattle town. The demise of the cattle era in Niobrara was witnessed by its newspaper, the *Niobrara Pioneer*, in 1876 when it indicated that fewer herds were coming into their community. Only one herd crossed at Niobrara in 1877.

In its July 5, 1877, issue the *Niobrara Pioneer* noted:

> A herd of 2,200 Texas cattle commenced crossing the Missouri River on Tuesday afternoon. 9 of the herd were drowned and two or three of the remaining Poncas have taken them by the horns and invited the Santees to participate in the enjoyment of eating them. Very slow progress has been made in crossing them so far. *This is the only herd that will cross at this point this season, the others having been ordered to make their trail farther up the Niobrara.*[59] (authors' emphasis)

This whole shift in the routing system of delivering cattle into the Dakota Territory reservations required that another path be created in order to deliver beef to the Indians. That path had to come from Ogallala. Trail drivers and their herds who had "been ordered to make their trail farther up the Niobrara" because of the herd law would cross the Niobrara farther upriver.

Starting in 1876, the Black Hills had been opened up to settlers and prospectors who came from the east by way of Sioux City or Niobrara had to cross the river safely somewhere. After its cattle days, Niobrara was promoting itself as a supply point for

---

[58]This crossing by Mabry appears to be the same one described by the *Niobrara Pioneer* on October 6, 1874. Of the initial herd of about 2,400, about 225 animals were lost, according to the newspaper. "The loss is estimated at $6,000." wrote the *Pioneer*. (Hutton, Ibid., 100)

[59]According to Harold Hutton, who wrote about the Niobrara River, *The River That Runs*, this crossing "farther up the Niobrara" was approximately one hundred miles above Niobrara. This would put the crossing near present-day Carns, or southeast of Springville and north of Bassett.

THE WESTERN CATTLE TRAIL | 1874-1897

the Niobrara- Black Hills Trail. The river crossing at Niobrara had proven to be less than ideal for cattle, and heavily loaded supply wagons destined for the Black Hills were not going to try to float across the two-river confluence. A ferry farther up the Niobrara, however, had been established as early as 1873, and by 1876 a man by the name of Rickord had a more popular ferry in Range 18 — it became known as Rickord Ferry. Numerous freighters, who were trying their luck in hopes to make a profit selling their goods to the miners, used Rickord's Ferry along with prospectors headed west from Niobrara and up the Elkhorn River valley.[60]

The ever increasing flow of prospectors, freight wagons, and cattle herds was facilitated by a newly built bridge at the site of Rickord's Ferry. John A. Morris and his family arrived at this site sometime in 1876 and settled on a large unsurveyed island a couple of miles up river from the ferry. Because of the deep canyons along the south shore of the river, the area around Morris' island was the best place to ford the river, but a bridge was needed. So in the winter of 1877-78, Morris and his family — which consisted of three grown, unmarried sons and a son-in-law — set about bridging the Niobrara River. Hutton described the monumental feat:

> The Morrises built their own pile driver; the hammer was hewed from the trunk of a huge oak tree. They took their pile driver out on the ice in the winter, cut holes in the ice and drove the piling. When they put the floor on was not made clear; it may have been done after the break-up [of ice]. There were stringers of the native timber, held in place by mortise-tension joints; the floor was of the same native timber. On top of it was a layer of willows of fish pole size, topped by a layer of sod. There was not a sawn timber, or a bolt or spike in the entire structure.[61]

By the spring of 1878, the Morris Bridge was ready to receive traffic. From his log house on the island, Morris did a thriving business at a store and from the toll for those using the bridge. At a later time, a post office was added under the name of Carns, and the crossing became known as the Carns Bridge.[62]

According to Harold Hutton, the first trail drive from Ogallala to attempt a push across the Sandhills to the Niobrara Valley and on to the Missouri River was in 1876, and that herd was led by trail boss Mac Stewart.[63] The route he would follow

---

[60]In an interview with Carolyn Hall of Bassett, Nebraska, she stated that the Black Hills Trail crossed the Niobrara River approximately 15 miles northeast of present-day Bassett. In her family, a great grandfather ran the ferry across the river, and it operated about three years. Then the Morrises built their bridge. (September 19, 2011)

[61]Harold Hutton, *The River That Runs*, 80.

[62]The Carns post office was moved to Morris' Island in December of 1879. Its name was changed from Elm Grove to Carns, probably in honor of Lt. Gov. Edmund Crawford Carns. (Elton A. Perkey, *Perkey's Nebraska Place Names*, 114)

[63]Hutton, Ibid, 80.. The authors found no evidence that cattle were driven directly to the town of Niobrara from Ogallala. Yet, even after Kearney ceased to be a cattle town on the trail system in 1875, some cattle, according to the *Pioneer* newspaper, were being driven into Niobrara on the Missouri River in 1876 and 1877. At this time, the authors have been unable to determine where these herds were being driven from. If from Kearney, then the trail boss may have somehow addressed the Nebraska herd law.

would become the Missouri River Splinter Route. Trail herds were pushed northeast through the Sandhills — which at that time was Indian country — using the Dismal, Loup, and Calamus rivers for water. Even though the route seemed to be a long, arduous way to satisfy the government contracts, it avoided settlements, and it was the most direct route to the Missouri River. After crossing the Niobrara, the herds would be in Dakota Territory, on an Indian reservation, and within Fort Randall jurisdiction. The post was located in the midst of the reservations on the south side of the Missouri River approximately forty miles up river from the town of Niobrara. It had been established in 1856 to help keep the peace and to control the many Indian tribes in the area.[64]

The trail drive led by Mac Stewart in 1876 is the same one that James H. Cook talks about in his memoirs, *Fifty Years on the Old Frontier*. Cook wrote that he helped drive 2,500 Texas steers "from a point on the Nueces River, Texas, a short distance above the town of Corpus Christi, to what was then known as the Whetstone Bottom on the Missouri River, Dakota." The cattle were destined to "supply a number of Indian agencies with beef."[65]

There were ten men in the outfit, "including Mac Stewart and the cook," and when they arrived in the north, a guide, Aaron Barker, who had been employed at North Platte City was hired. The guide "knew western Nebraska probably as well as any man living in those days, having been associated with the Sioux Indians in that part of the country for years." A guide was needed because "all of us knew that we were to go into a country much of which was regarded as belonging to the Sioux Indians, by both inheritance and treaty rights." Cook recalled how the Sioux and Cheyenne were particularly antagonistic toward whites in 1876 because of the invasion of the Black Hills by white gold-seekers. The Clarke Bridge, north of Sidney, Nebraska, had just been completed across the North Platte River which "enabled thousands of fortune hunters to enter lands in which they seemed to think riches could be had by picking up gold with little labor or expense." *(This bridge was on another route of the Western Trail to be discussed later.)* Cook also asserted that this herd was "the first great herd of cattle to be driven through western Nebraska into Dakota." The outfit was prepared for trouble:

> Most of our outfit had had experience in trailing herds through a country infested with Indians of many tribes, who had all sorts of notions regarding the rights of white men to travel through or to make trails across their hunting grounds….Everyone went armed with a heavy revolver and a knife. But few carried rifles. One reason for this was that the added weight on one side of a horse, on those long, hard trips, was

---

[64]Fort Randall also served as a major navigation link on the river, but its main mission was to patrol the Indian reservation. It was the first fort in a chain of forts on the upper Missouri River. It closed in 1892.

[65]Whetstone Bottom is the river bottom area of Whetstone Creek on the Missouri River. It was located just north of the Fort Randall Military Reservation in Dakota Territory. Whetstone Agency was located there from 1869 to 1871. The Agency was not there, however, in 1876 when Cook's outfit delivered the herd.

THE WESTERN CATTLE TRAIL | 1874-1897

a great cause of saddle galls — something to be strictly guarded against on an eighteen-hundred-mile drive, for a horse with bad saddle sores cannot thrive, and much hinged on the condition of the saddle horses when handling those immense herds of wild cattle.[66]

The herd and outfit crossed the south and north Platte rivers a few miles east of Ogallala and was driven to Birchwood Creek and then to the headwaters of the Dismal and Loup rivers, before going on "north through the great chain of shifting sand hills."[67] Cook continues:

> Driving on north from the headwaters of the north fork of the Loup River, our guide escorted us to one of the sand-hill lakes, then unnamed. The weather was very warm, and we had a long drive without water before we reached the lake. The cattle scented the water long before we reached it, the direction of the wind being favorable, and they strung out for it at a trot. We tried to hold the leaders back, but when we arrived within half a mile of the water, the herd split into bunches and, in spite of all our efforts, rushed madly into the water. About a hundred head of them were mired down before we could crowd the others to a spot in the lake where the mud and guano were less deep.
>
> The task that confronted us, before we could expect anything in the shape of supper, was to save the cattle which had mired down. This proved to be a considerable task, for our saddle horses would mire down trying to get in close enough to the cattle for us to throw ours ropes over their horns and pull them out. As some of the best cattle in the herd were in the mire, we wanted to save them if possible.
>
> Fortunately there was a clump of willow trees growing at one side of the lake. We cut clumps of these, tied them into bunches, and used them to make a sort of corduroy road to those of the cattle which were farthest from shore. On these our horses or work oxen could get a secure footing from which to pull. Every head of cattle which we extricated was ready and willing to fight all mankind the moment they could get to their feet after being dragged out to solid ground. The horse of one of our men was badly gored by taking too many chances. Its rider thought his horse could outstart and outrun any steer.[68]

---

[66]Obviously, it was Cook's calculation that the trip from Texas to their destination to be eighteen hundred miles long. It was actually closer to being thirteen hundred miles.

[67]It is possible that the outfit was partially following an old military route from Fort McPherson to the Black Hills, before veering northeast.

[68]The lake that Cook talks about where the cattle were mired down was probably one of the group of lakes southwest of Ainsworth, Nebraska, including Willow Lake, Enders Lake, Long Lake, Twin Lakes, and Moon Lake. (James H. Cook, *Fifty Years on the Old Frontier*, 81-86) Cook's 1876 cattle drive is also printed in the *Nebraska History Magazine*, Vol X, 1927. The article, appeared four years after Cook's book, quotes: "There were ten of us, including our Trail Boss, Mr. Mack Stewart, and the cook, with the cattle and a band of saddle horses."

Another reference in the *Nebraska History Magazine* of 1938 is made of a herd that took this Missouri River Splinter Route. Although the writer does not identify the drovers or the herd, he states that in 1877 or 1878, the herd consisted of 2,600 steers driven by eighteen men "down the Platte to North Platte and across to the Loup [River]."[69]

Luther North, who had part ownership in a ranch "on the head of the Dismal River," made reference to this cattle route as well. In his book, *Man of the Plains*, he told of an incident where he and others were pursuing some stolen horses and said that "They did not follow the cattle trail leading north, but cut across the sand hills to the north fork of the Dismal, then followed down to where the trail crossed." The Dismal River merged with the Middle Loup River in central Nebraska, so the trail would have to have been west of where they merged.[70]

The Missouri River Splinter Route lasted for three years. In 1878 the government moved the Brule Sioux from the Ponca Reserve north of the Niobrara and created the new Rosebud Reservation farther west in Dakota Territory. In the following year the Oglala Sioux were placed on the Pine Ridge Reservation. To reach the agencies on these reservations, the trail drivers and cattle herds changed their route to one that would go north of Ogallala, a much easier route than traversing the Sandhillls of northcentral Nebraska.

---

[69] E. S. Sutton refers to this drive in a letter sent to the Nebraska State Historical Society, but does not say who was in the outfit. *Nebraska History Magazine*, Vol. 19, No. 3, 1938, 254.

[70] Luther North went into partnership with his two brothers and Colonel Buffalo Bill Cody in 1878. The Cody-North Ranch was located at the head of the Dismal River where a log ranch house was built. Their first cattle herd of 1,500 was bought at Ogallala from off of the trail. They "hired six of the men that had driven them up from Texas to help us take them to our range." (Donald F. Danker, ed, *Man of the Plains, Recollections of Luther North, 1856-1882*, 237, 254)

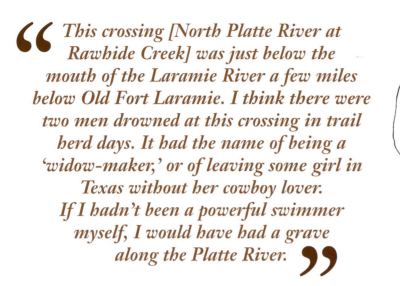

> *This crossing [North Platte River at Rawhide Creek] was just below the mouth of the Laramie River a few miles below Old Fort Laramie. I think there were two men drowned at this crossing in trail herd days. It had the name of being a 'widow-maker,' or of leaving some girl in Texas without her cowboy lover. If I hadn't been a powerful swimmer myself, I would have had a grave along the Platte River.*

Bob Fudge, 1895 trial driver to Montana in Jim Russell's *Bob Fudge, Texas Driver, Montana-Wyoming Cowboy*, pg.67

CHAPTER VII

The Western Cattle Trail, From Ogallala To Canada And More Splinter Routes

THE WESTERN CATTLE TRAIL | 1874-1897   295

"Beef Issue"
This photo was taken in the 1880s at the US Army post, Fort Yates (1863-1903) in present-day Sioux County, North Dakota. Fort Yates was the tribal headquarters for the Standing Rock Sioux Indian Agency.

On issue day, when cattle were released, Indian families came into the agency to claim their share of the allotment. The cattle may have been delivered via a Western Cattle Trail splinter route. (See page 321 of this chapter.)

Photo courtesy of Research Division of the Oklahoma Historical Society, photographic archives, Oklahoma City, Oklahoma.

From 1876 to 1885, the Western Cattle Trail reached its peak in numbers of cattle on the trail. Dodge City and Ogallala were established cattle towns and through them, drovers brought up the trail from Texas over 200,000 head each season, with the 1876 and 1880 seasons handling over 300,000 head each. The Texas cattlemen's hope of establishing a lucrative northern market for their cattle and a dependable pathway to that market had been realized. In these years, the Western Cattle Trail expanded out from Ogallala into the Dakota, Wyoming, and Montana territories and even into Canada. For ten seasons herds of longhorns were trailed from Texas to these northern destinations, a distance of over 1,800 miles.

In 1876 dramatic changes occurred in the lives of soldiers, settlers, and cattlemen on the northern plains. The destruction of Custer and his men in June of 1876 at the Battle of the Little Bighorn in Montana Territory, led to military actions that would force the tribes within the boundaries of their reservations. Gold found in the Black Hills only months before intensified the flow of gold seekers and settlers into the area.

By the close of 1877, most of the northern Plains Indians were reluctantly confined on newly established reservations, and the government was responsible for feeding them. And thousands of miners, in and around the Black Hills, constituted a significant market for beef. The Texas cattlemen were only too happy to satisfy the demands of both of these populations. These great markets, and the extension of the Western Cattle Trail, all lay north of Ogallala.

Ogallala was now a full-fledged cow town. In less than three decades many changes had occurred in the industry, but certain factors remained constant. One constant was the Texas cattlemen's desire to deliver their cattle to the buyers in the north and the continuous conflict between cattlemen and those who stood in their way, whether Indians or incoming settlers. The next decade would see the heaviest usage of the trail from the south. Texas cattle coming up the Western Trail through Dodge City, Kansas, to Ogallala, Nebraska were the engine driving this transformation. Cattle trails played a key role in this explosive period of western settlement. Texas trail drivers furnished the cattle to the ranches that took over the grasslands where the buffalo once grazed, and drovers watched the ranchers expand their holdings. It was the golden era for the Texas cattle-driving industry. The need to furnish beef to the Indian reservations, as well as the eastern cities, and to replenish and increase the herds of northern ranches became the main focus in the decade 1876 to 1886.

Since the new market was in the north, it was inevitable that Texas cattlemen would establish finishing ranches in the north. Texas was a good breeding ground for the longhorn, but not a good place for pasturing livestock. One author puts it this way: "The long sinuous lines of cattle moved in a solemn unwavering course from the short dead grass of Texas to the belly-high grass of the wild North."[1] The northern pastures offered cooler weather, water, plentiful grass, and fewer insect pests.

---

[1] W.T.M., "Preface" of *The End of the Long Horn Trail* by A. P. (Ott) Black.

From the the late 1860s to 1878, grazing pastures in New Mexico, Arizona, Colorado, Nebraska, and Wyoming were used. Well known examples included John Chisum's ranch in New Mexico and Seth Mabry's ranch in Nebraska. Ranches south of the Black Hills were established from 1877 to 1881, while those pasturing ranches north of the Black Hills came into existance starting in 1882. These ranches supplied the needs of the area, and, in turn, owners kept these finishing ranches supplied with cattle from Texas. Incoming herds consisted of yearlings and two-year olds that were double-wintered on the lush grasses to a marketable finish.[2]

Bert L. Hall, in his study of the Dakota region, recorded that in 1880 the aggregate number of cattle brought into the area was 89,000 head, with 30,000 delivered from Texas to the Indian agencies and another 31,800 Texas cattle destined for the Dakota ranches. The balance of 27,200 head was trailed into the region from Wyoming and Nebraska to fill the livestock need for the ever increasing number of ranches. Lewis F. Crawford recorded that in 1882 that 100,000 head had been driven into the Black Hills, and in 1883 the number of cattle driven into the area reached 250,000.[3] Thousands of animals were being moved from the home ranches in Texas to new satellite ranches in the north, and from those finishing ranches, the cattle were dispersed to fulfill government contracts for Indians reservations and to provide the beef to mining camps. Also, cattle fed the new markets in the north with less emphasis placed on shipping cattle to outside markets in the east. Contracts with Indian agencies, military posts, mining camps, and expanding ranches drove the demand for cattle from Texas cattlemen and local ranches. It was not until 1882 and 1883 that cattle were shipped out of these northern territories from its neighboring ranges. The finishing ranches were now ready to expand their deliveries beyond the immediate local needs, and they loaded cattle at Valentine, Nebraska, Pierre, South Dakota and, later in 1883, Dickinson, North Dakota, to be shipped east.

THE TRAIL NORTH OF OGALLALA:

Starting in 1874 and 1875, Ogallala was a wide open town and gateway to the exploding markets in the north. From the south, some 100 to 150 herds of Texas cattle were trailed north over the Western Trail in the months of June through September. For as far as one could see, the banks of the South Platte were crowded with cowboy camps and cattle herds. Edger Bronson, who had a ranch on the White River one hundred miles north of the South Platte River, wrote:

A wonderful sight was the Platte Valley about Ogallala in those days... That day, far as the eye could see up, down and across the broad,

---

[2]The term "double-wintered" means that cattle were allowed to graze on pastures for two winters, or two years, in order to be heavier and more marketable. Dakota Territory was not declared as the states of North Dakota and South Dakota until November 2, 1889. They became the 39th and 40th states. (Lewis F. Crawford, *Ranching Days in Dakota*, 17)
[3]Crawford, Ibid, 14.

THE WESTERN CATTLE TRAIL | 1874-1897

level valley were cattle by the thousands — thirty or forty thousand at least — a dozen or more separate outfits, grazing in loose, open order so near each other that, at a distance, the valley appeared carpeted with a vast Persian rug of intricate design and infinite variety of colours.

Approached nearer, where individual riders and cattle began to take form, it was a topsy-turvy scene I looked down upon.[4]

The in-coming Texas cattle season got everyone's attention. According to one neighboring rancher, Ogallala became "wide-awake, wild and sometimes wicked town with many saloons, dance halls and gambling dens, all running full blast both day and night."[5] Buyers and owners alike met the herds. Deals were made and orders given. Cattle were loaded on to trains, which headed east, or supplies were replenished to continue the next leg of the trip. The business end of the transfer of cattle herds was done at the Spofford House, for a time the only hotel in town, where the cattle kings met to buy and sell their herds. The cowboys, on the other hand, frolicked in town. Bronson described what he remembered about Ogallala:

The one store and the score of saloons, dancehalls, and gambling joints that lined up south of the railway track and formed the only street Ogallala could boast, were packed with wild and woolly, long-haired and bearded, rent and dusty, lusting and thirsty, red-sashed brush-splitters in from the trail outfits for a frolic.[6]

From the Ogallala hub, the majority of the northbound Texas herds crossed the South Platte River, trailed through or around the town of Ogallala, and continued north, crossing over the hills and descending into the floor of the North Platte River by way of Ash Hollow Creek. This was the main branch of the Western. It followed the old Oregon-California emigrant trail along the south side of the North Platte River and then split at the Sidney Bridge, some sixty miles up river. The main trunk line of the Western Trail continued on west, following the river, while a major splinter route to Fort Buford turned north.

Cowboy Samuel Houston later wrote of his exhilaration and excitement of being with a big herd that left Ogallala to head north. He had joined up with the herd under trail boss Tom Moore south of town on August 28, 1879. The large herd was "one of the old King herds which had come in by way of Dodge City, Kansas, from the old coast country down in Southern Texas," Houston wrote. As the herd approached Ogallala, Houston recalled:

---

[4]Edgar Beecher Bronson, *Reminiscences of a Ranchman*, 258. Bronson's book was first published in 1908.
[5]John Bratt, *Trails of Yesterday*, 245. In 1879, John Bratt established a ranch in Lincoln County, the next county to the east of Keith County. His ranch was located midway between Fort McPherson and North Platte City on the Birdwood. The John Bratt & Company cattle were known as the "Circle Herd." 180-181.
[6]Bronson, Ibid, 259.

Everybody in town was out to see the big King herd go through. I threw my hat back on my head and I felt as though the whole herd belonged to me.

When the lead cattle struck the foothills I looked back and could see the tail end coming in the river, and I told my partner, the right-hand pointer, that we were headed for the North Pole. We raised our hats and bid Ogallala good-bye. When the lead cattle got to North River it was an hour and ten minutes before the tail end got to the top of the hills.[7]

Dick Withers was also on this northern route from Ogallala in 1879. He and Bill Jackman had a combined "open Y" herd of 5,500 head belonging to Capt. James F. Ellison that they had trailed from the Ellison ranch in Caldwell County, Texas. Their boss had met them at Ogallala, sold the herd, and told the boys to deliver it to the Sidney Bridge on the North Platte. Withers wrote in his recollections:

---

[7]Samuel Dunn Houston, "A Trying Trip Alone Through the Wilderness," in Hunter, *The Trail Drivers of Texas*, 79.

After replenishing our grub supply, we pulled on and struck the North Platte which we followed up the Narrows. The "Narrows" is a name given to a ledge of hills which run from the divide to the North Platte River. A herd cannot be driven over these hills, but is forced to travel up the bed of the river for about a mile. The North Platte is a treacherous stream, and full of quicksand. We had to send our chuck wagon around over the hills, and it required all day for the wagon to make the trip…. From here we traveled up a beautiful valley all the way to Sidney Bridge, where we delivered the cattle,…[8]

John Wells described this sixty-mile trip, which he drove in 1883, as "a hike." The drovers had brought up a mixed bunch of about "four thousand cattle and one hundred and fifteen horses" to Ogallala that belonged to Hudson, Watson & Company, but upon reaching Ogallala, the cook quit, and Wells was "the only one of the bunch" who was qualified to fill the job. Wells — being responsible for the chuck wagon — "crossed the South Platte River and hiked out up the North River" and "proceeded to Sydney Bridge and crossed below the Block House." Wells wrote that at this point, they "took the right-hand trail" and went to "Fort Robertson [Robinson]."[9]

Wells is referring to the turn off on the Fort Buford Splinter Route, a northern path from the Western Cattle Trail trunk line (refer to Map #7-1). However, the role of Sidney Bridge, the junction of these two routes, needs to be reviewed before venturing up this splinter route.

The Fort Buford Splinter Route and its off-shoots is presented before the main trail of the Western Trail in the north because of proximity. Throughout this book, the authors have presented the location of the main trunk line of the Western Cattle Trail from its starting point in Texas northward, and when a feeder route or splinter route was established in the development of the trunk trail, a description was added for that pathway. The same is true here--only the Fort Buford Splinter Route is the largest and longest splinter route discussed so far, and within its system there are various off shoots (Map #7-1). The main trunk line of the Western Trail, from Ogallala, followed the south side of the North Platte River, and it turned north at Rawhide Creek to continue its route through Wyoming and Montana territories. By contrast to the Fort Buford Splinter Route, it lasted longer and went all the way to Canada. But before reaching Rawhide Creek on the trunk line, trail drivers had a choice. If their herd was to be delivered to any one of several Indian agencies in the Great Sioux Indian Reservation, or to miners in the Black Hills, or to ranchers located in northern Nebraska or in western Dakota Territory outside of the boundary of the reservation, they turned off of the main trail at Sidney Bridge.

The Fort Buford Splinter Route's most northern destinations were the Fort Berthold Indian Agency, and Fort Buford at the confluence of the Missouri and the Yellowstone rivers in northwestern Dakota Territory.

---

[8]Richard (Dick) Withers, "The Experience of an Old Trail Driver," in Hunter, 313.
[9]John Wells, "Met Quannah Parker on the Trail," in Hunter, 168.

THE FORT BUFORD SPLINTER ROUTE NORTH FROM SIDNEY BRIDGE, NEBRASKA: (Map #7-1)

For Texas drovers, the Sidney Bridge was an ideal spot to splinter north from off the main trunk line of the Western Trail to deliver cattle: (1) to ranches and the Rosebud Agency, using the Niobrara River Route; (2) to the Red Cloud Indian Agency (Camp/Fort Robinson); the Spotted Tail Indian Agency (Camp Sheridan); and the Pine Ridge Indian Agency, using the White River in northeastern Nebraska and southern Dakota Territory; (3) to the Cheyenne River and the Standing Rock Indian agencies, using an East Detour Route; (4) to the mining camps in the Black Hills; and (5) to Fort Buford at the confluence of the Missouri and Yellowstone rivers.

SIDNEY BRIDGE AND CAMP CLARKE:

To reach the Indian agencies, the mining camps, and the finishing ranches in the Dakotas or to deliver cattle to Fort Buford, trail drivers with their herds chose to cross the North Platte River at Sidney Bridge and continue north on what was called the Fort Buford Splinter Route. A large rock formation marked the general location of the turn off, and it was usually referred to as "Courthouse or Jail Rocks." Wells recalled the landmark as the "Block House."

The bridge provided easier access across the formidable North Platte River. When the Black Hills gold rush frenzy was at its height, several Omaha merchants, the Union Pacific Railroad, the town of Sidney, thirty-eight miles to the south, and entrepreneur Henry T. Clarke combined resources to construct a bridge across the North Platte River. The businessmen, in particular, knew that the only obstacle to a thriving direct trade route to the Black Hills was the North Platte. The bridge that Clarke built was about 2,000 feet long with sixty-one wooden trusses. The mammoth project was completed in May of 1876, just in time to take advantage of the flood of miners headed for the gold fields from Sidney and surrounding locations. At the south end of the bridge a small hamlet called Camp Clarke greeted the hundreds of freight wagons, stagecoaches, riders, and trail herds. There was a hotel, store, saloon, and a post office. Tolls to cross the bridge ranged from two dollars to six. The bridge's official name was Camp Clarke Bridge, but the hamlet and bridge became known, by those who used it, simply as the "Sidney Bridge."[10]

Like Cheyenne, Wyoming, to the west and Pierre City, South Dakota to the northeast, Sidney, became a major outfitter for the prospectors heading to the Black Hills. Sidney, Nebraska, located on the Union Pacific Railroad, had the advantage of being the closest town of any size to the mining camps, about 170 miles from Custer and 200 miles from Deadwood.

---

[10]When the gold rush waned and the railroad reached Dakota Territory, trail traffic over the Sidney-Black Hills Trail declined in 1886. The Sidney Bridge continued to be used by local travelers until about 1900. ("Camp Clarke Bridge and Sidney-Black Hills Trail," www.nebraskahistory.org [accessed July 8, 2010] and Norbert Mahnken, "The Sidney-Black Hills Trail," *Nebraska History*, Vol. 30, No. 3, 1949, 211)

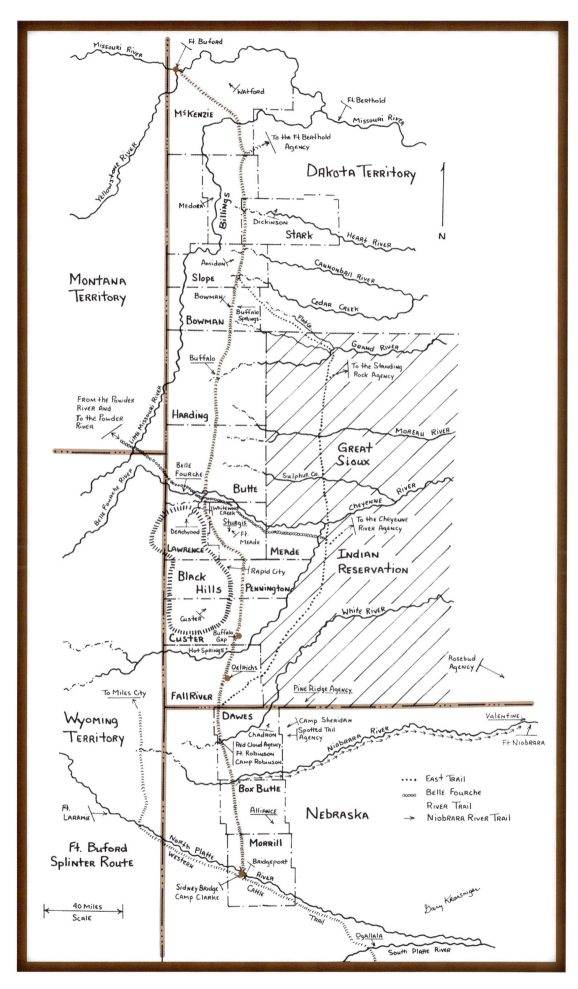

#7-1
The Fort Buford Splinter Route from Sidney Bridge on the North Platte River to Fort Buford on the Missouri River: *This map shows the main splinter route and the various offshoots from that route to deliver beef to the Indian agencies.*

The Fort Pierre-Deadwood Trail, that supplied prospectors from the east, was thirty miles longer,[11] and the rough Niobrara river route from Niobrara was longer still. Also, there was already an established military trail in place from Sidney Barracks, the military camp outside of Sidney, to as far north as the Red Cloud Agency (Camp Robinson) and to the Spotted Tail Agency (Camp Sheridan). This military route was well patrolled by troops from Sidney Barracks and Camp Robinson. Thus, when Clarke's bridge opened in the spring of 1876, the Sidney-Black Hills Trail became a very busy route.[12]

Freight wagons from Sidney to the mining town of Deadwood crossed over the bridge daily, and gold from the mines was returned south to Sidney. In 1876,

Sidney Bridge: *The 2,000 foot long wooden bridge, spanning the North Platte River, was completed in May of 1876, just in time to take advantage of the flood of miners headed for the gold fields in the Black Hills. Even though the bridge was officially named "Camp Clarke Bridge" after the main financier of the project, those who used it, called it Sidney Bridge because it was on the pathway from Sidney to the Black Hills. Texas drovers and their herds using the Western Trail from Ogallala, Nebraska, also turned north at Sidney Bridge in order to reach Indian agencies, mining camps, and ranches in the Dakotas. The photo shows the bridge looking south.*

Courtesy of the Nebraska State Historical Society, Lincoln, Nebraska.

---

[11]The Fort Pierre-Deadwood route was a little over 200 miles long starting from the Missouri River going west across the Dakota prairies. The stage and freight line started in 1876 at the outset of the gold rush and continued until 1908. (Shawn Werner, "A Trail Rediscovered, Celebrating the Fort Pierre-Deadwood Stage," *Deadwood Magazine*, August, 2009 and online at www.deadwoodmagazine.com. [accessed, July 13, 2010])

[12]As to which of the Black Hills routes was the busiest and most popular depends on who one reads. According to Harold Hutton and Norbert Mahnken, the Sidney Road had the most advantages. Hutton writes that the "Fort Pierre was a close second" to Sidney while Barbara Fifer in her book, *Bad Boys of the Black Hills*, writes that "Sidney, also on the Union Pacific Railroad, was Cheyenne's lesser competitor for passenger and freight access to the Black Hills." Writer Bill O'Neal in his book, *Cheyenne*, argues that the Magic City was, by far, the largest supplier of prospectors. Of course, the direction from which the prospectors were coming was the major factor.

Camp Clarke in 1876: *On the south end of Camp Clarke Bridge (Sidney Bridge) a small hamlet developed to greet the hundreds of freight wagons, stagecoaches, and riders headed for the mining camps and the trail herds. There was a hotel, store, saloon, and post office. The south end of the bridge can be seen in the background. Tolls to cross the bridge ranged from two dollars to six.*

Photo courtesy of the Nebraska State Historical Society, Lincoln, Nebraska.

major freighting companies gladly extended their route into the Black Hills, and by 1878 over 10,000 miners in this remote region needed an abundance of supplies. Fifty to seventy-five wagons left daily from Sidney, each capable of carrying 8,000 pounds of goods. Deadwood resident John S. McClintock, who arrived in the Black Hills in 1876, later wrote of the freight traffic to Deadwood:

> Up to the middle of June, 1876, much of the freight shipped into the Black Hills was brought in by outfits of two and four horse teams. Large trains of oxen were also used... After these trains, of from six to eight mules and from six to ten yoke of oxen of the long horn Texas variety, came in, it was not unusual to see Main Street [of Deadwood] completely blocked for hours and even half a day at a time, by one and sometimes two lines of these trains. There would invariably be at least two, and more frequently three, freight wagons heavily loaded and down to their hubs in mud slowly following each long string of oxen, the leaders of which would have a spread of horns from three to four feet.... the leaders of these bull trains, after being lashed and goaded by their merciless drivers and tortured by flies, became vicious and dangerous.[13]

---

[13] John S. McClintock, *Pioneer Days in the Black Hills*, 63. McClintock's book was first printed in 1939.

The Sidney - Black Hills Road, *as depicted by Robby McMurtry. A Texas cattle herd comes in close proximity to a freight wagon headed north to the mining camps in the Black Hills and a stagecoach returns from Deadwood, or another mining area, headed south toward Sidney, Nebraska.*

For a short time a pony express operation carried mail to the miners from Sidney, and two main stage lines used the route. Up to three large Concord stage coaches left Sidney every day, each carrying nine first-class passengers on the inside and as many as three to seven others on the top of the coach. The cost of a coach ride, which was the quickest way to the Hills, was $25. A cheaper ride, but slower, was by freight wagon. For those who could not afford the fare on a coach or freighter, traveled in a single wagon, on horseback, or on foot. It was very risky for the lone traveler because of possible attacks by Indians or road bandits.[14]

After the bridge was opened on the North Platte, Texas cowboys and their herds also used this busy route.

---

[14] In 1878, when bandits became so numerous, Luke Voorhees, manager of the Gilmer and Salisbury stage lines, arranged to have an armed coach built to carry gold from Deadwood to Sidney. The coach was lined with half inch steel and the windows were no more than portholes. The gold was placed in an 800 pound safe inside the coach and was guarded by six to eight armed guards. The coach became known as "old ironsides" and was in service for three years. It was robbed only once. (Mahnken, Ibid)

Sidney-Black Hills Road Stagecoach: *This coach to Deadwood, Dakota Territory, was one of two or three to leave Sidney every day. Up to nine people could ride inside and, according to this photo, eight people, not counting the driver, could ride on top. It is very likely that a Texas cattle herd could be spotted from atop the coach.*

Photo in owner's collection.

(1) The Niobrara River Route from the Fort Buford Splinter Route Map #7-1

From the Sidney Bridge turn-off to the Niobrara River was approximately fifty miles.

The three or four-day drive was over open prairies used by military and civilian traffic. After stage companies had established their daily schedules from Sidney to the Black Hills, stations were in place along the trail. Between the Sidney Bridge and the Niobrara River were the Red Willow Stage stop on Red Willow Creek, the Snake Creek Stage Station on Snake Creek, the Point of Rocks Station on Point of Rocks Creek, and the Running Water Ranche on the Niobrara River. Stage stops were approximately ten or twelve miles apart. At the Niobrara River, some trail drivers and their herds turned from the main Fort Buford Splinter Route and headed east along the Niobrara River.

The Niobrara River valley was open range in 1876 without homesteaders and ranchers because Indians from Dakota Territory still roamed the area and could be a

THE WESTERN CATTLE TRAIL | 1874-1897   307

threat to travelers. But by 1877 and 1878, the Sioux had been moved to the Rosebud Reservation in south-central Dakota Territory and to the Pine Ridge Reservation located in the greater Sioux Reservation north of the Red Cloud and Spotted Tail agencies. This left the former Sioux hunting grounds open for ranchers in the Sand Hills of Nebraska. By late 1878, sites all along the river valley were being taken up by incoming ranchers.

One of the first ranches was owned by the Newman brothers. H. L. Newman, a wealthy St. Louis banker and stock-raiser, eventually had ranches scattered from the Tongue and Powder rivers in Montana to west Texas. His brother E. S. "Zeke" Newman managed the business. When the Niobrara River valley opened up, J. S. (Billy) Irwin, foreman for the Newmans, and his crew trailed a herd of Texas cattle north in 1878 to the Newmans' new headquarters at the mouth of the Antelope Creek, along the Niobrara River.[15] The **N Bar Ranch** often bought two and three year old Texas cattle and wintered them out for two years, and then readied them for sale to the Indian agencies. A fenced pasture north of the river approxamately six to eight miles in size provided the grazing for the steers until they were driven to the agencies.[16]

Another herd to reach the Newman Ranch in 1878 came out of south Texas from the Smith and Savage outfit from Fort Mason in Mason County, Texas. Smith and Savage, which had more than one herd on the trail that year, upon reaching Dodge City, sold some of their cattle to E. S. Newman, who wanted 3,500 head trailed to his northwestern Nebraska ranch. Harper Cleveland and Jim Hastings were with the outfit when it left Texas, and although most of the rest of the crew returned to Texas, they continued with another outfit up the Western to Ogallala and then north to the Niobrara and on to an Indian agency. Years later Cleveland described their route:

> We went up the Platte past Ogallala to Camp Clark [Sidney Bridge]... crossed the river and hit a terrible storm. Jim Hastings was killed by lightning and we buried him there.
>
> We followed the Black Hills and Sidney freight road to the Niobrara River....turned down river to the mouth of Rush Creek...north to the head of the Antelope Creek and there we turned the herd loose.
>
> I think we were the first outfit to turn the herd loose [there]. From then until late fall other outfits came in down river. That winter we tried to hold the cattle north of the Niobrara and south of the state line. At the same time the government moved the Sioux back to the Rosebud....[17]

---

[15]According to James C. Dahlman, "The Newman ranch in 1878 was located at the mouth of Antelope Creek on the Niobrara twelve miles [south] east of where the town of Gordon now stands." (James C. Dahlman, "Recollections of Cowboy Life in Western Nebraska, *Nebraska History Magazine*, Vol. X, Oct.-Dec., 1927, 335)

[16]Marianne Brinda Beel, ed. *A Sandhill Century, Book I, the Land: A History of Cherry County, Nebraska, 1883-1983*, 8.

[17]Harper Cleveland wrote this account in 1932. from Beel, Ibid, 12.

Another very early ranch that occupied the former Sioux hunting grounds was the Hunters, R. D.(Bib) and David, with A. G. Evans, whose ranch was located on Deer Creek south of present-day Rushville and southwest of the Newman Ranch. The **H3** trailed several thousand head to the Niobrara in 1877.

Soon to follow was Texas cattleman Seth Mabry, who developed a ranch with headquarters along Leander Creek south of present-day Merriman, down river from the Newmans. It was his northern range for finishing cattle to be sold to the Indian Bureau and issued to the Indians. The brand was the **C-O Circle**. Mabry later bought the Boiling Springs Ranch, southwest of present-day Cody, Nebraska, because it was closer to the Rosebud Agency.[18]

The Newmans N Bar Ranch extended east of their headquarters for forty miles to the Mabry Ranch and then west to the Hunter and Evans H3 Ranch. These three ranches supplied most of the fresh beef to the Pine Ridge and Rosebud reservations. Within those ranches, the mature cattle were kept north of the river in large pastures to be handy for delivery. The N Bar Ranch furnished 250 head of these big steers to the Pine Ridge or Rosebud agencies every ten days during the summer and most of the winter. The N Bar Ranch and the H3 Ranch sold most of their cattle to the Pine Ridge agency, and Mabry, as mentioned earlier, sold most of its cattle to the Rosebud Agency.[19] These and other Texas cattlemen also sold herds from off the trail directly to the agencies.

Other early ranches along the Niobrara River were the **Double X Bar**, owned by D. J. McCann; the **Oxyoke and J**, owned by Ed Creighton, located at the mouth of Schlagel Creek, and the J. Peter Sharp Ranch at the mouth of the Minnechaduza. By 1878 and 1879, twenty cattlemen had created and stocked ranches, and their cattle were predominantly Texas longhorns.

These early ranches along the Niobrara were north of the river, for the most part, because the dreaded Sand Hills south of the river was considered unsafe for their cattle. According to Roy Ross, a Newman cowhand, line riders were stationed "at the edge of the high hills and kept turning back the cattle towards the river."[20] In the winter of 1879, during a bitter storm, several thousand Newman cattle drifted south, and Foreman Billy Irwin selected his own crew and horses and set out to retrieve the cattle. Among his twelve riders was a young Texan, James Dahlman, who had just arrived at the N Bar Ranch. He recalled that:

> The second day out we encountered one of the worst blizzards I had ever seen. All we could do was keep warm as best we could with what wood we hauled for cooking. After three days the storm let up and we made another start.
>
> We soon began to strike perfectly contented cattle in their new home amidst the splendid grass and water in the valleys. I remember

---

[18]Seth Mabry bought out Carpenter and Moorehead on Boiling Springs Flat around 1881.
[19]Beel, Ibid, 8-12. Robert H. Burns, "The Newman Ranches: Pioneer Cattle Ranches of the West," *Nebraska History Magazine*, Vol 34, No. 1, (March, 1953), 28.
[20]Roy Ross, letter printed in the Robert H. Burns article.

well the first bunch of native cattle Bennett and I struck. They were as wild as any deer, but those mavericks were fat as any brought out of a feedlot. One cow weighed at least 1,400 pounds so we butchered her, and the fat beef was a welcome change from fat bacon that was not of good quality.[21]

The outfit was gone for five weeks and ended up bringing in some 8,000 head that had drifted south. The experience proved that cattle could thrive in the Sand Hills.

During this open range period of approximately eight years, Texas longhorns were delivered to these and other ranches along the Niobrara. Each rancher had selected territory on government land, built a house of logs or sod, added a corral, bunk house, and barn, and went into the business of ranching. Each rancher recognized and respected his neighbor's territory. The land, however, was government owned and when the Fremont, Elkhorn and Missouri Valley Railroad extended west into the area in 1883 and 1884, and incoming settlers started to file on the land, under the homestead law, the ranchers had to respect those claims. By 1885, many of the Niobrara ranchers had moved north into Montana, Wyoming and Canada.[22]

Because of the influx of white ranchers along the Niobrara River and the close proximity to the Rosebud Indian Reservation to the north, the government

---

[21] Burns, Ibid, 12. Dahlman continued to work for the N Bar Ranch until 1883. In 1884, he married Harriett Abbott and the couple moved to Valentine where Dahlman was cattle inspector for the WSGA before moving on to become sheriff and then mayor at Chadron, Nebraska.

[22] James C. Dahlman, "Recollections of Cowboy Life in Western Nebraska," An address Given at the Annual Meeting of the Nebraska State Historical Society, Jan. 10, 1922. *Nebraska History Magazine*, Vol X, No. 4, (Oct.-Dec., 1927) 338. By 1892, seventy percent of the settlers who had homesteaded western Nebraska had given up and headed back home. *America, the Story of Us*, history channel presentation, July, 2010.

established Fort Niobrara, on April 22, 1880, on the Niobrara River four miles east of the present-day town of Valentine. It is probable that Texas trail drivers also delivered cattle to the fort for the soldiers, but within five years of its establishment, the cattle herds ceased to be in the area.[23] The Rosebud Reservation was due north in Dakota Territory (Map #7-1).

(2) To the Red Cloud Indian Agency, the Spotted Tail Indian Agency, and the Pine Ridge Indian Agency, using the White River in Northeastern Nebraska and Southern Dakota Territory: Map #7-1 White River

Before Texas herds were delivered to the ranches along the Niobrara River, pre-1878, drovers and their herds turned off of the Fort Buford Splinter Route at White River to deliver herds to the Red Cloud and Spotted Tail agencies in northwestern Nebraska. The Red Cloud Agency was created when the government relocated the

Camp Robinson *provided security for the near-by Red Cloud Indian Agency (1874-1877) and guarded the Sidney - Black Hills Road and surrounding region. The agency was moved in 1877, but the camp remained. It was to this camp and agency that Captain John T. Lytle and Tom McDaniel, along with eighteen cowboys including Frank Collinson, delivered 3,500 steers from the Lytle Ranch in Texas. The route that Lytle blazed to reach the agency became the Western Cattle Trail.*

Photo courtesy of the Nebraska State Historical Society, Lincoln, Nebraska.

---

[23] The Fort Niobrara military reservation consisted of fifty-four sections of land, and the first officer in charge was Major John J. Upham, in command of troops B. D, and F of the Fifth Cavalry and Company B of the Ninth Infantry. At first, the buildings were constructed of adobe. The fort was abandoned on October 22, 1906. A portion of the military reservation, a 16,000-acre tract, was retained by the government and is today a national game preserve. ("Fort Niobrara," www.memoriallibrary.com [accessed July 11, 2010])

Oglala Sioux to the White River in August of 1873.[24] A compound was constructed at the confluence of Soldier Creek and White River, near an ample supply of water, timber, and "bottomland considered sufficient for Indian farming."[25]

The agent appointed over the new agency was Dr. John J. Saville, a Episcopal Quaker who was well-intentioned but poorly equipped to handle Indian affairs. Immediately after arriving at the agency, Saville and his staff were harassed and faced the wrath of angry tribemen who had moved south from the Missouri River to draw the rations that the agency offered and to express resentment over the loss of the ability to follow their traditional ways. By February of 1874, the situation had deteriorated to the

"Driving Cattle into a Corral – Nebraska" *was sketched by artist V. W. Bromley sometime from 1875-1877. The corral was either at the Red Cloud Agency or the Spotted Tail Agency.*

Owner's collection.

---

[24]Chief Red Cloud and his people had been located some thirty miles below Fort Laramie in Wyoming Territory but needed an adequate source of firewood for thousands of tribemen and an area more isolated, further away from the white population. Therefore, a spot selected for the new agency was in unpopulated western Nebraska, off of the reservation land, but in the unceded hunting grounds area that had been granted to the Indians in the Fort Laramie Treaty of 1868. Joining with the Sioux were Northern Arapahos and Northern Cheyennes who also received rations and goods near Fort Laramie. (Thomas R. Buecker, *Fort Robinson and the American West, 1874-1899*, xvii)

[25]Buecker, Ibid.

point that Saville appealed to the commander of the Division of the Missoui, Lt. Gen, Phillip Sheridan, for help. As Sheridan hesitated, several hundred northern armed warriors terrorized the inhabitants of the unfinished agency stockade, roused Saville's chief clerk, Frank Appleton, out of his sleep on February 8, and assassinated him. Days later, the warriors killed two soldiers who were on a wood-gathering mission.[26]

The Spotted Tail Agency, forty miles east of the Red Cloud Agency, was created a few months after the Red Cloud Agency. Here Chief Spotted Tail and his Brule people had been settled. Their agent was Edwin A. Howard, who also was being harrassed by the northern dissidents. Howard appealed for help to the commanding officer, Colonel John Smith, of Fort Laramie.

The dire situation reached the desk of President Grant and soon troops were dispatched to various forts, each joining the forces at Fort D. A. Russell at Cheyenne. One thousand soldiers were divided into four companies, marched the ninety-three-miles in four days in bitter cold to Fort Laramie. On March 2, 1874, eight companies left Fort Laramie and headed for the agencies in Nebraska. Within a week, soldier camps had been established alongside both agencies. Agency Indians, realizing that Colonel Smith meant business, accepted the soldiers' presence. The northern Indians, on the other hand, broke camp and fled back to the north. The post at the Red Cloud Agency became Camp Robinson, and the camp at the Spotted Tail Agency became Camp Sheridan.

The routes into Camp Robinson and Camp Sheridan were either by way of Fort Laramie from the west or the Sidney - Black Hills Road from the south. On the Fort Laramie route, freighters had broken the way by hauling military goods, and later building materials, from the quartermaster depot at Cheyenne on the Union Pacific Railroad line. Requisitions were sent to department headquarters at Omaha, sent by rail to Cheyenne, hauled in wagons to Fort Laramie, and continued in wagons east to the Indian agencies. Commissioner Smith recommended that at least a sixty-day supply of goods be kept at Red Cloud and a thirty-day stock on hand at Spotted Tail. There were the tons of forage that had to be on hand for the some three hundred mules used to pull the wagons — plus the food, clothing, and other essentials needed by the troops.

The shorter route north from Sidney Barracks was laid out in the summer of 1874. It had the advantage over the Fort Laramie Route in that its more direct route was some forty-five miles shorter and its rail station was one hundred miles closer, thus saving on shipping. By summer's end, it had become the preferred route.[27]

Also during the summer of 1874, two Texas ranchers, Captain John T. Lytle and Tom McDaniel, trailed a herd to the Red Cloud Agency. The friction at the Indian agencies on the White River, which had almost erupted into war, had only been settled for a short time when Lytle and McDaniel arrived with their herd to fulfill their government contract.

---

[26]The chief clerk was Saville's nephew, and the two soldiers were Cpl. John C. Coleman and 1st Lt. Levi H. Robinson. Camp (Fort) Robinson was later named in honor of the 1st Lieutenant..
[27]Buecker, Ibid, chapter 2.

THE WESTERN CATTLE TRAIL | 1874-1897   313

Lytle and McDaniel's outfit included nineteen-year-old Frank Collinson, a lad who had been born in England but had begun his "Life in the Saddle" on the Circle Dot Ranch. George S. Noonan, district judge, had hired the young man two years earlier to work on his horse ranch in Medina County, Texas. "I was on a horse longer than I was off one during the day." Collinson recalled. His job was to gather horses, break bronchos, and brand colts.[28]

Captain Lytle had contracted with the government to deliver 3,500 head of big, aged steers to the Red Cloud Agency on the condition the herd arrived no later than August 1, 1874. Collinson was paid sixty dollars a month because he brought with him seven good horses. His would be the first herd to blaze the Western Cattle Trail across Indian Territory, western Kansas, and southwestern Nebraska and perhaps the first Texas herd delivered to the Red Cloud Agency.

Collinson later wrote, "We beat out a trail over sections of country that had not been traveled before, and over which thousands of cattle would later be driven." According to Collinson's memoir, the outfit started to gather cattle in the early spring of 1874, from the brush in Medina, Frio, and Uvalde counties. The outfit then herded them into the Lytle Ranch pasture. Most of the steers were from four to ten years old. They were road branded with a 7D on the left loin to ready them for the trail. On March 16, 1874, eighteen men, the herd of mature steers, and a remuda of one hundred horses started north. (During this same time period, soldiers from Fort Laramie were marching into the Red Cloud and Spotted Tail Indian agencies in northwestern Nebraska to reduce the threat of an Indian war and to establish military camps.)

The Lytle and McDaniel outfit and the herd of 3,500 passed through Fort Griffin, Texas, crossed Indian Territory, and followed the military trail from Camp Supply to Fort Dodge, Kansas. From there they passed by Fort Wallace, Kansas, and crossed the North Platte near what would later be Camp Clarke. The road from there to the agency was the newly established military route from Sidney Barracks to Camp Robinson. In two years, it would become known as the Sidney-Black Hills Road or the Sidney-Deadwood Road. Collinson wrote: "It was a relief to follow a well-marked government trail from that point to the Indian reservation, which we reached at the end of July." According to Collinson, the cattle were sold to the government for an average of thirty-six dollars per head.[29]

While Captain Lytle and most of the cowboys went back to Texas, Collinson and a few others stayed in a camp house near the corrals at Fort Robinson. They herded and moved cattle daily and issued about one hundred twenty five steers per week to the Indian agent. To control the large herd, two thousand head were kept on Niobrara River grazing pastures; eight hundred moved ten miles east of there, and the final eight hundred herded near the agency. Each morning a certain number of steers were driven into a separate pen and released for "issue on the hoof." Collinson described the scene:

---

[28]Frank Collinson, *Life in the Saddle*, 14.
[29]Collinson, Ibid, 31-40.

The bucks dashed up on their horses, which they had painted in Bizarre patterns. Behind them were the women with their knives, ready to skin and cut up the cattle.

Each morning the quartermaster told us how many cattle to issue. After counting the cattle, the big gates were thrown open and out ran those wild long-legged steers with savage bucks at their heels, screaming and yelling. It was a tossup which was the wildest. The bucks shot arrows into the steers, cut their hamstrings with long, sharp knives, lanced them, and often jumped from their horses to fight with a particularly rambunctious animal. In all this melee I never saw an Indian get hurt. This sport was second nature to him. It was his way to kill — had been for ages past.

Finally, when the steers were all down, the Indians gorged themselves on the entrails and until they could eat no more. Then the women had a feast and later skinned the animals and chopped up the meat. The hides, though badly damaged, were used for moccasin soles and ropes.[30]

---
[30] Collinson, Ibid., 41-42.

Frank Collinson stayed on the reservation well into November. He then sold his horses and went back to Texas.[31]

Four years after the Lytle and McDaniel outfit first delivered a herd to the Red Cloud agency, other herds followed. Red Cloud and his Oglala people, in 1878, were relocated to White Clay Creek in Dakota Territory.[32] Because the Fort Laramie Treaty of 1868 specified that agencies be within reservation lands that lie north of Nebraska's northern boundary, the Indian Bureau insisted that Red Cloud be moved. The Bureau wanted the agency moved to the Missouri River for ease of transporting supplies and troops to the agency, but the Oglalas would go no farther north than the White River forks, nearly two hundred miles from the proposed Missouri River site. The area became the last agency and was renamed the Pine Ridge Agency. (Map #7-1)

To deliver beef directly to the Pine Ridge agency,[33] herds and their drovers

---

[31] Because Camp Robinson was close to the Sidney-Black Hills Road, it remained functional and was designated a fort in 1878. When the Fremont, Elkhorn & Missouri Railroad line reached Fort Robinson on May 11, 1886, the town of Crawford was platted just off the east border of the military reservation. The fort ceased to be a military post in 1948. ("Fort Robinson History," Nebraska State Historical Society on line) In October, Spotted Tail's Brules were moved to the Ponca Reservation on the Niobrara, but within months again were moved into southern Dakota Territory where the agency became known as the Rosebud. Camp Sheridan was abandoned in May of 1881. (Hutton, 77 and "Camp Sheridan and Spotted Tail Agency," Nebraska State Historical Society, online)

[32] White Clay Creek starts in Sherdian County, Nebraska, and runs south to north until it enpties into the White River in Dakota Territory. The Pine Ridge reservation was located on White Clay Creek southeast of White River.

[33] Recall that Indian agencies received Texas cattle two ways. Independent contracts were made with Texas cattlemen, like Lytle and McDaniel, months before the drive was commenced with the understanding that the entire herd be delivered directly to the agency usually by a certain date. Or, herds were delivered to local ranchers or contractors, like the Newman Ranch on the Niobrara, who then "issued" cattle periodically to the agency in smaller lots. The smaller lots were usually referred to as "issue cattle."

could approach the Pine Ridge Agency from three directions. The one that seems to have been used the most was the Fort Buford Splinter Route to Fort Robinson as had been done since 1874. From there, cowboys pushed their herds along the military road south of the White River, passing present-day Chadron,[34] trailing through the Spotted Tail Agency (Camp Sheridan) and on to White Clay Creek at which point they turned northeast and followed that stream to the Pine Ridge Agency.[35]

Another path was from Fort Laramie, although this route was seldom used by cattle herds. The military road from the Fort ran northeast out of the fort, and was used prior to the Sidney-Black Hills route to connect with Fort Robinson and the Pine Ridge Agency. One year after the relocation of Red Cloud and his people, Samuel Dunn Houston, under the employ of D. R. Fant and his trail boss, Tom Moore, delivered 4,000 steers to the Pine Ridge Agency by way of this Fort Laramie route. It was late August 1878 and, according to Houston, rivers were flowing heavily because "The snow was melting in the mountains and the river was muddy and no bottom to the quicksand." Therefore, the outfit, "didn't cross the North Platte until we got to Fort Laramie, Wyoming." Saddles were pulled off of the horses and the drovers stripped off their clothing. The herd was strung out over a long line and pushed into the water. "Men and steers were up and under all the way across," Houston wrote. "We landed over all safe and sound, got the sand out of our hair, counted the boys to see if they were all there and pulled out to the foothills to strike camp."[36]

Upon reaching the White River, the drovers "crossed over and camped." Houston remembered:

> About the time we turned the mules loose [from the chuck wagon], up rode about thirty bucks and squaws, all ready for supper. They stood around till supper was ready and the old negro cook began to get crazy and they couldn't stay any longer. They got on their horses and left. An Indian won't stay where there is a crazy person. They say he is the devil. The next morning the horse rustler [wrangler] was short ten head of horses.

Upon arriving at the Pine Ridge Agency, Houston described the issuing of the cattle. *(Note that he still called it the Red Cloud Agency, instead of Pine Ridge, but they were in Dakota Territory.)*

---

[34]Chadron was created when the Fremont, Elkhorn, and Missouri Valley Railroad built a branch into South Dakota in 1884. The community was named after Louis Chartran, a fur trader who ran a trading post on near-by Boudeaux Creek in the 1840s. (Chadron Chamber of Commerce, "History of Chadron," www. chadron.com)

[35]The military road from Fort Robinson to Camp Sheridan was a portion of the longer military road from Fort Laramie in Wyoming to Fort Randall in eastern Dakota Territory. (Nebraska State Historical Society map, *Nebraska History Magazine*, Vol. 21, No. 4, Oct-Dec, 1940)

[36]Samuel Dunn Houston, "A Trying Trip Alone Through the Wilderness," in Hunter, 80. Houston made a point about "counting the boys" because he had lost a "good old friend who once started to cross that river and he was lost in the quicksand," just above Ogallala.

...the next morning we strung the old herd off the bed ground and went in to the pens at Red Cloud Agency, Dakota. There I saw more Indians than I ever expected to see. The agent said there were about ten thousand on the ground.

It took us all day to weigh the herd out, ten steers on the scales at one time. We weighed them and let them out one side and the agent would call the Indians by name and each family would fall in behind his beef and off to the flats they would go [to be slaughtered].

…The next morning we started back over our old trail to Ogallala. It was about October 16th and some cooler and all of the boys were delighted to head south.[37]

A third possible route for cattle herds to reach the Pine Ridge Agency was to use a military road from Sidney Barracks. A Nebraska State Historical Society map of 1940 shows a route, "Sidney to Spotted Tail Agency," crossing the Niobrara River in Dawes County from the south and going northeast by Antelope Springs and on to Camp Sheridan and the Spotted Tail Agency. From there, herds followed the trail northeast to the Pine Ridge Agency in Dakota Territory.[38]

(3) The East Detour Route from the Fort Buford Splinter Route to deliver herds to the Cheyenne River Agency and the Standing Rock Agency Map #7-1

On the Fort Buford Splinter Route, trail drivers who did not splinter off at White River to deliver herds to Indian agencies, pressed northward toward Dakota Territory. They trailed across the grass lands of northwestern Nebraska by the Big Cottonwood Creek (Carney's) Ranche station, within view of Benedict Buttes, and on to Horsehead Creek and Horsehead Springs where another stage station was located.

Just after crossing into Dakota Territory, south of present-day Oelrichs, an East Detour Route veered off of the Fort Buford Splinter Route. This route, which would eventually turn back into the main splinter route, left the Fort Buford Splinter Route for the explicit purpose of delivering cattle to the Cheyenne River Agency or to the Standing Rock Agency in the Great Sioux Indian Reservation. The route also detoured around the congested Black Hills mining camps and the busy Sidney-Black Hills Road. (see Map #7-1)

This East Route was described by Raymond Griffiths in a manuscript written in the 1930s and later published by Bert L. Hall in his book, *Roundup Years*:

The main route on this end [Dakotas] starting at Ogallala coursed thru the Nebraska Sand Hills, then between Oelrichs and the town of Pine Ridge [Pine Ridge Agency]. Continuing it crossed the upper reaches

---

[37]Houston, Ibid, 81-83.
[38]Nebraska State Historical Society map, *Nebraska History*, Vol. 21, No. 4, (Oct-Dec, 1940)

of feeder streams to the Cheyenne and White rivers, then bore north and slightly east to the mouth of the Belle Fourche R. [River] at its junction with the Cheyenne. From this point it ran north crossing Sulpher [Sulphur] or Cherry creek and the Moreau R. [River] and followed an angling route over the country east of Slim Buttes. The trail crossed Grand R. [River] near the junction of the north and south forks of the stream, then bore in a northeasterly [northwesterly] direction up Flat creek to south of Chalf Buttes, from where it threaded onto the Little Missouri in North Dakota [Territory] and eventually found its way into Canada. It had been laid out where there were water holes, streams and springs. The trail blazers had sought out good crossings, where banks were suitable, and not too steep. It was 700 lonely miles from Ogallala to Canada.[39]

To reach the Cheyenne River Agency, cowboys and their herds veered off of the Fort Buford Splinter Route onto the East Detour Route. About twelve miles south of the junction of the Belle Fourche and Cheyenne rivers,[40] they followed the high ground down the Cheyenne River some eighty miles to the agency on the Missoui River. The Cheyenne River Agency was located at the mouth of the Cheyenne River on the west bank of the Missouri River about six miles above Fort Sully. On May 17, 1870 the "Post at Cheyenne River Agency" was built next to the agency for use in subduing the tribes. This post's name was changed to Fort Bennett in December of 1878.[41]

> It appears that Raymond Griffths believed this easterly route was the "main route" for cattle herds trailed north by way of Ogallala, Nebraska. We contend that this route — we call the East Detour Route — was used primarily to deliver cattle to the reservations. Obviously, cattle herds also used the Fort Buford Splinter Route. We have not been able to find any evidence that cattle were ever trailed north of Fort Buford into Canada.

In 1879, C. C. French was in an outfit that delivered beef to the Cheyenne Agency. The cowboys had started from Kimble County, Texas, and, by December, were in Dakota Territory. In his memoir, French recalled the delivery:

The herd we drove to the Cheyenne Agency was for the United States government and were fed to the Sioux Indians. One day early in December an Indian courier came to our camp with a message from

---

[39]Raymond Griffiths, "Grazing in South Dakota," manuscript published in Bert L. Hall's *Roundup Years, Old Muddy to Black Hills*, 89.

[40]Raymond Griffiths also wrote that there was a "Belle Fourche River Trail" that angled off near the mouth of the Belle Fourche River, wound westerly past present-day Vale and between Horse and Indian creeks, and continued on into Wyoming and Montana. This approximately 200-mile trail, between the junction of the Belle Fourche and Cheyenne Rivers to the Powder River/Broadus, Montana area, would make sense in later years, after ranchers moved into Meade County and began to lease land from the Indians on the reserve. This river route would have been convenient for local ranchers to deliver their herds to the Belle Fourche railhead and beyond. (Griffiths, Ibid., 89)

[41]The Cheyenne River Sioux Reservation was not created until 1889 when the United States government broke up the Great Sioux Nation into smaller parcels. The reservation's eastern edge was the Missouri River and the Cheyenne River formed its southern boundary. In 1891, the agency was moved 56 miles up the Missouri River, opposite to Forest City. The Land Acts of 1909-1910 opened up part of the Cheyenne River Reservation to white settlement. Today the tribal headquarters is located at Eagle Butte, South Dakota. ("Cheyenne River Reservation,:" www.aktalakota.org [accessed April 30, 2012])

the commander of the post saying that if the mercury went 28 degrees below zero he wanted 250 steers that day to commence killing for the Indians' winter beef. We delivered the steers and the Indians killed them all in one day. The meat was exposed to the cold for a few days and then stored in an immense warehouse to be issued out to the Indians every week. During the killing period about 800 steers were slaughtered. About 7,000 Indians were present at the killing…. When the killing was completed we had about 600 steers that had to be crossed over the Missouri River on the ice, which was then about 28 inches thick across the channel…. At this time the government thermometer at Peeve [Pierre?] recorded 72 degrees below zero.[42]

Joseph Phillip Morris, with an outfit of nine cowboys, a cook, and a wrangler, also delivered a herd of steers to the Cheyenne Agency in 1879. Morris, a veteran trail driver, had been delivering cattle from DeWitt County, Texas, to Indian agencies in northwest Nebraska and into Dakota Territory since 1876.[43] He liked contracting with the government because they paid in gold or silver. Morris had a special way to hide his money, which could be as much as $100,000, according to John Becker:

> To avoid "problems" Morris took the coins and placed them in a green steer hide, which he nailed to the bottom of his chuck wagon. As the green hide shrank the bags of coins became securely fastened to the bottom of the wagon. They remained there (and out of sight) until Morris reached the nearest town with a Wells-Fargo office, from which he expressed his gold and silver to San Antonio.[44]

The Morris outfit trailed a total of 3,308 steers in 1879, acquired from over forty different ranches in South Texas. Morris and his partner, Willis McCutcheon, had over $31,000 invested in the herd. The drovers started north from Texas on February 16th and reached Dakota Territory five months later. Becker, in his research on Morris, described the trail as going in a "north-westwardly direction along the North Platte [the Western Trail] to present-day Bridgeport [Sidney Bridge]" and then "turned due north until it struck Hat Creek, which flows into the Cheyenne River." The outfit then followed the Cheyenne River to its mouth on the Missouri River to the Cheyenne Agency.[45]

This route that Morris took varies only slightly from the route described above except that the Morris outfit went a little farther west of the main splinter route and trailed the high ground east of Hat Creek until they reached the East Detour Route

---

[42]C. C. French, "When the Temperature was 72 Degrees Below Zero," in Hunter, 742.

[43]J. P. Morris bought his own ranch in 1884 in Coleman County and the brand "Rafter-3," which he operated for the rest of his life and for that of his descendants.

[44]John T. (Jack) Becker, "J. P. Morris and the Rafter-3 Ranch," Thesis in History at Texas Tech University, Lubbock, TX, 2001, 28.

[45]Becker, Ibid, 33-35.

where they followed it to the confluence of the Belle Fourche and Cheyenne rivers. From this point they turned east to follow the river to the agency.

After trailing for more than 1,500 miles, Morris found that he had lost only fourteen steers. He returned home by way of Cheyenne, Wyoming, because that city had the closest Wells Fargo office where he deposited his gold or silver coins. He then went to Denver, Colorado where he caught a train home.[46]

The drovers and herds that were headed for the Standing Rock Agency continued up the East Detour Route to approximately ten miles south of the Grand River and then followed the high ground down that waterway to the Missouri River. From there they went north to Fort Yates and the town of Winona that sat on the river's east bank. The fort had been established in May of 1870, but later was associated with the Standing Rock Agency which adjoined the fort on the north. The original Indian agency, Grand River Agency, had been established in the fall of 1868 at the mouth of Grand River on the Missouri River, but after being flooded in 1873, the agency was moved up the Missouri River some fifty five miles and rebuilt next to Fort Yates.[47]

According to A. P. (Ott) Black, the town of Winona "numbered about three hundred and fifty" people and consisted of "six saloons, two dance halls, one hotel, two stores, and a postoffice." The Fort Yates army post "had a garrison of about ten companies of soldiers, three companies of cavalry and seven of infantry."

Black had gone to work for the Millet Ranch in Texas in 1881 at the age of fourteen. At that time, the Hashknife ranch was owned by William E. Houghes and John Nicholes Simpson under the name of the Continental Cattle Company. When Houghes and Simpson purchased the Millet outfit in 1879, they established another ranch near present-day Alzada, Montana near the mouth of Box Elder Creek on the Little Missouri River. The ranch was usually referred to as the HS Ranch.[48] In 1883, the HS Ranch started contracting cattle to the Standing Rock Agency. Black recalled the issuing of cattle to Standing Rock agency:

> I never knew how much grub it took to feed the forty-four hundred Indians camped around the agency but they did manage to eat up three hundred and fifty fat beeves every two weeks. These cattle were all furnished by the different cow outfits in the country. The Hashknives had it [government contract] awhile in the early eighties and delivered somethin' like five thousand head till they lost the contract.

---

[46]The original interview with J. P. Morris is found in the National Live Stock Association's *Prose and Poetry of the Live Stock Industry of the United States*, published in Denver in 1905, page 715.

[47]Although the agency site was changed in 1873, it continued to be called the Grand River Indian Agency until December 22, 1874, when the name was changed to the Standing Rock Agency. The name was derived from a sacred rock that was carried by the tribe from village to village. (www.standingrocktourism.com [accessed April 30, 2012])

[48]According to Lewis F. Crawford in *Ranching Days in Dakota*, the HS Ranch was the largest cattle outfit to operate north of the Black Hills. "The maximum number run by them at any one time was about 60,000 to 65,000." Their cattle ranged over a vast territory including portions of North Dakota, South Dakota, Wyoming and Montana. (Crawford, 15)

THE WESTERN CATTLE TRAIL | 1874-1897

I guess practically every big outfit in the country had a "shot" at it.

A Boss-Herder and a crew of about eight or ten Indians took charge of the herds after they were turned over.[49]

According to the *Press & Dakotan* newspaper at Yankton, 1200 head of cattle were slaughtered at Standing Rock that winter to furnish the Sioux with frozen meat. The price paid was four cents per pound delivered.[50]

(4) The Fort Buford Splinter Route to the Mining Camps in the Black Hills:

South of the Black Hills is a vast prairie of grasslands with few trees and intermittent buttes.[51] In the mid 1870s, it was criss-crossed with animal and Indian trails and was lightly used until northbound miners poured across it enroute to the Black Hills. Texas cattle herds followed in the wake. The Black Hills were so named because their appearance at a distance as a dark forested area; they covered one hundred miles north to south and fifty miles in width. In 1868, these hills had been reserved for the sole occupancy and use by the Sioux Indians, but the Hills were now inhabited by gold prospectors and the people who provided services to them.

These included the butchers who supplied the eating establishments in the mining towns, and the ranchers who were raising cattle to furnish beef to the Black Hills butchers and the Indian agencies. And cowboys trailed herds that provided the beef for the butchers.

As ranches, stocked with Texas longhorns from off of the Western Trail, began to spread along the Niobrara River valley in Nebraska in 1878, a similar transformation was occurring at the south end of the Black Hills in Custer County, Dakota Territory. In 1879, E. W. Whitcomb established the Bar T Ranch on Hat Creek, a few miles south of the Cheyenne River by trailing 8,000 head of Texas cattle to the site from Cheyenne. Frank Burton saw to it that 10,000 Texas longhorns were trailed from Ogallala, Nebraska to the north side of Cheyenne River near present-day Edgemont, which became the TOT headquarters. George Holden started the TAN Ranch with headquarters on the Horsehead Creek near the Sidney-Black Hills Road in 1880 when he brought in 7,000 head of Texas cattle. Custer County was great cattle country, and the market was its next door neighbors to the north, the newly established Pine Ridge and Rosebud reservations, the Lower Brule and Crow Creek agencies at Fort Thompson on the Missouri River, and the Cheyenne River and Standing Rock reservations to the northeast.

The discovery of gold in the Black Hills in 1874 had become one of the greatest factors in hastening the development of the livestock industry in the area. It was five years or more, however, before the eastern and foreign capitalists woke up

---

[49]A. P. (Ott) Black, *The End of the Long Horn Trail*, 7, 8, 11, 14, 50-51.

[50]Raymond Griffiths in Bert L Hall, *Roundup Years*, 82.

[51]Today this grassland is the Oglala National Grassland in Nebraska and the Buffalo Gap National Grassland in South Dakota. The Buffalo Gap National Grassland lies adjacent to the Pine Ridge Indian Reservation.

to the economic bonanza the region offered. In the early 1880s, syndicates moved in. A Scottish syndicate owned the VVV ranch and controlled the Matador Cattle Company which leased 500,000 acres of reservation land in the lower Cheyenne River basin. In 1882, Harry Oelrichs, with the backing of English financiers and others, came to the area and purchased Burtons's TOT Ranch, Holden's TAN Ranch, and the Bar T. He incorporated them under the name of the Anglo-American Cattle Company. The parent company was based in London.

The practice of driving large Texas herds north to fatten in the northern climates on spreads like the Anglo-American Cattle Company, the Sturgis & Goddel Ranch, and the Continental Livestock Company continued for the next ten years. In 1882, "an estimated 100,000 were trailed into the Hills and the next year many more."[52]

Continuing north on the Sidney - Black Hills Road, or the Fort Buford Splinter Route (Map #7-1), herds spread out on the grasslands of Dakota Territory, crossing small streams along the way — Medicine Creek, Duck Creek, South and North Black Banks creeks. To the east was Lone Wells Ranche, another stage station, and then the town of Oelrichs. On Horsehead Creek, at a location of a railroad construction camp and what later became Siding Nine for the Chicago & Northwestern Railroad spur, Harry Oelrichs, president and general manager of the Anglo-American Cattle Company, decided to build his mansion on a hill a short distance east of the track, employing carpenters who hailed all the way from New York.[53] Over the next five years, Oelrichs managed the Anglo-American Cattle Company on the east side of the tracks, and a town, using his name, developed on the west side of the tracks.

Oelrichs had two immense stables built which together housed several hundred steers. Each animal had a separate stall, with feed and water boxes in front of each animal and hay racks overhead. The beeves were then taken directly, only 300 yards distant, to the shambles, an area of slaughter. By 1887 a fully equipped abattoir (slaughter house) with two adjoining ice houses and three butchers was operating at full capacity.

The town of Oelrichs grew almost as fast during this time period. In 1884, George Sweitzer operated a railway eating house while the railroad was being built. Sam Moscs, foreman for the Bar T Ranch located nearby, built a two-story hotel at the north end of Main Street and owned a saloon at the town's southwest corner. Moses received the appointment of postmaster in December of 1885. Norman Atcheson, who came to the area in 1880 and helped build the railroad, took an interest in the newly platted town. He built several buildings in and around town including the first store south of the hotel. A well was dug in the middle of town, and as a later history noted, the people soon came:

> the town was growing by leaps and bounds as settlers, encouraged
> by railroad advertising in the East and in Europe, poured into town.

---

[52]Raymond Griffiths in Hall's *Roundup Years*, 82-83.
[53]The Fremont, Elkhorn and Missouri Valley Railroad built across Nebraska and reached Chadron in 1884. Then from a junction point just west of Chadron, a branch line (the Chicago & Northwestern) ran north to Rapid City, South Dakota.

They came to find work, to take up homesteads, to start businesses, to begin a new life, to make a fast buck. Homes and hotels were built, tents and hastily constructed shacks served traveling vendors.... coming by rail, on horseback, in covered wagons, by stage and on foot.[54]

Within three years, there were over 3,000 people in Oelrichs.[55] The trail cowboys would have known about Oelrichs, particularly Sam Moses' saloon, located near Atcheson's mercantile/grocery store. In a letter, Atcheson later wrote:

Oelrichs was one cowboy's town that had no killing because the town was a sociable one. Grant Eastman, the marshal, and Blakely, saloonkeeper, both having been cowboys, said to them, "Shoot all you want to let us know you are coming to town, then park your guns until you start home. Bid us goodbye and shoot all you want to." So we always knew when the cowboys were coming and when they were leaving.[56]

The buttes in the area, south of the Black Hills, became landmarks for the cowboys heading north. The town of Oelrichs sat in the shadow of Limestone Butte some two miles east of the town. The trail passed west of town. Nancy Shaw, in an interview, said that the Texas trail herds crossed her grandfather's place located six miles west and two miles south of Oelrichs.[57]

Twenty miles north of Oelrichs was Hot Springs. It was one of those wonders of nature where spring water ran like soothing bath water. The original white settlers called the area "Minnekahta" meaning warm waters, but in 1886 the name was officially changed to "Hot Springs." The butte on the outskirts of the town is Battle Butte. Trail herds passed approximately four miles east of Hot Springs and then headed out onto the river flatlands. In the early years of the Sidney-Black Hills Road, there was a stage station in the area called Slate Springs Station, but with the coming of the Chicago & Northwestern Railroad, the springs created a draw, and the town developed bath houses, hotels, and restaurants.[58]

---

[54]Oelrichs Historical Society, *In the Shadow of the Butte, A History of Oelrichs and Surrounding Area*, 4-6.

[55]While the town of Oelrichs survived, the Anglo-American Cattle Company did not. The cost of shipping feed in; the competition for ice at the stops when the meat was shipped east; the encroaching of homesteads onto the open range where their herds were pastured, plus other factors caused the company to go into the red. When the genius behind the operation, Harry Oelrichs became ill and returned to the East for treatment in 1887, the company stockholders sold out. (Oelrichs Historical Society, Ibid, 8)

[56]Norman Atcheson letter written in 1937 to Mr. Eugene Coffield and Mrs. J. Williams. Oelrichs Historical Society, Ibid, 138.

[57]Interview between Gary Kraisinger and Nancy Shaw in Meade, KS, June 4, 2006. Nancy's grandfather was Frank Shaw.

[58]The cattle drives through this area were over by 1886, so the cowboys did not witness the ambitious project of turning the area into a health spa. Local businessmen, like Fred Evans (Evans Plunge), created elaborate sandstone buildings over and among the mineral water springs for incoming tourist. When the Chicago and Northwestern Railroad started to unload passengers in 1891, the town's future was secured. At one time, there were at least a dozen bath houses to provide all manner of services and goods. (http://visithotspringsnow.com [accessed Aug. 8, 2010])

John Wells mentioned the springs in his memoirs of his 1883 trail drive. He wrote that their outfit and herd went "past the famous Crow Burke [Butte] Mountain--and crossed the Cheyenne River three miles below Hot Springs...."[59]

East of the Fort Buford Splinter Route was the town of Buffalo Gap. It had been located near a "gap" of the southern foothills of the Black Hills. It was so named, it was said, because buffalo sought shelter and food during the winter in the small valley. When the Texas herds came through about one mile west, Beaver Creek Station served as a junction for the trail to Custer via the Gap, and another trail to Point of Rock (Pringle) and the Deadwood Trail via Rapid City.[60] The village of Buffalo Gap, founded in 1877 as a stage station, within a decade boasted of having a post office, bank, hotels, saloons, and stores that served over a thousand residents. The Fremont, Elkhorn and Missouri Valley Railroad spur arrived in the town in November of 1885.[61]

After heading north from Buffalo Gap, the Fort Buford Splinter Route swung around the east side of the Black Hills. Outfits crossed Lame Johnny Creek, French Creek, Battle Creek, and Spring or Sand Creek. Each of these creeks were from six to ten miles apart, and each had a stage stop which offered an exchange of horses, a place for the passengers to stretch, and perhaps refreshments if the travelers were lucky. Drovers, for the most part, avoided the stations although they might camp nearby. A letter could be posted to be delivered farther down the line by the stagecoach driver.

Several towns in the foot hills of the Black Hills were established soon after the gold strike. These included Rapid City, Sturgis, and Spearfish, located on the perimeter of the black forest and each had access to the mining camps such as Lead and Deadwood that had been built overnight along the streams in the Black Hills. Rapid City was laid out in early 1876 by a party of explorers wanting to establish a permanent camp and town. In the party was John R. Brennan and Samuel Scott, who selected an area in the Rapid Valley along Rapid Creek. The party measured out a square mile with six blocks in the center for their hope-for community. Committees were formed by the adventuresome leaders to solicit merchants and families to settle on Rapid Creek, and soon a small community was in place selling supplies to miners and pioneers.[62]

Sturgis came into existence a year later, in 1877. A couple of miles east of the community, Fort Meade was established in August of 1878. At first the military post was called Camp Ruhlen, and a nearby camp that housed the troops who were building the fort was Camp Sturgis. By December, 1878, however, the new post was renamed Fort Meade (in present-day Meade County). Its purpose was to protect the Black Hills mining operations from hostile Sioux Indians.

---

[59]Crow Butte is located five miles east of Fort Robinson. John Wells, "Met Quanah Parker on the Trail," in Hunter, *The Trail Drivers of Texas*, 168.

[60]Dick Lloyd, "Outlaw Country, A Map & Guide to the Cheyenne-Blackhills Express Route and the Sidney-Deadwood Trail," Alliance, Neb., 1990.

[61]"Buffalo Gap, South Dakota," online: http://buffalogapsd.org. [accessed Aug. 31, 2010]

[62]John S. McClintock, *Pioneer Days in the Black Hills*, 248.

Spearfish, located on the northern edge of the Black Hills at the mouth of Spearfish Canyon, was founded in 1876 during the beginning frenzy of the gold rush. A 640-acre tract was laid out for the town site and a stockade constructed to insure protection from the Indians. Like Rapid City, it grew to become a supplier of foodstuffs to the mining camps.[63]

It was into these communities and the surrounding ranches that cattle were destined for the mining camps. Among the first herds trailed into the Rapid City area in 1878 was one owned by Gregory & Frease that bore the Bow & Arrow brand. M. C. Conners, using the 21D brand, trailed in 3,000 head and established a ranch on the upper Belle Fourche River. Beef on the hoof came from these local ranches and others who had contracts with the butchers of Rapid City, Sturgis, and Spearfish, and these ranchers obtained their cattle from the Texas drovers.

(5) *The Fort Buford Splinter Route north to Fort Buford on the Missouri River*

The Fort Buford Splinter Route continued north of the Black Hills. The drovers and herds crossed Whitewood Creek and turned north to follow that stream to the Belle Fourche River, and according to trail drivers H. H. Floyd and Charles F. Decker, crossed "the Belle Fourche River below the outlet of Owl Creek."[64]

Trail drivers and their herds continued north across Dakota Territory. They trailed past present-day Buffalo, South Dakota (established in1909) and Bowman, North Dakota (established in1907) and watered the herds at nearby Buffalo Springs.[65] At Cedar Creek, the East Detour Route rejoined the Fort Buford Splinter Route. From there the drovers pushed their herds up the divide, forded the Cannonball River, crossed the Fort Keogh-Bismarck Road[66] and continued north passing east of Medora (established in1883) and west of Dickinson (established in 1880).

---

[63]McClintock, Ibid., 248 -251. Unlike most frontier forts, Fort Meade is still standing and in use today. During World War II, it served as a training camp and POW camp. In 1944, the post was turned over to the Veterans Administration and a new hospital complex was built north of the old post. Fort Meade is currently occupied by the VA and the South Dakota Army National Guard. ("Fort Meade," online: http://fortwiki.com/Fort-Meade [accessed Sept. 3, 2010])

[64]H. H. Floyd and Charles F. Decker, trail drivers for the "Hashknife" (Continental Land & Cattle Company), from the notes and interviews of Maude L. Beach for the Montana Writer's Project of the WPA, dated Nov. 5, 1940, in *Faded Hoof Prints — Bygone Dreams*, Powder River Historical Society, 1989, page 123. The town of Belle Fourche, established a few miles upstream on the Belle Fourche River, did not play a role in the Fort Buford Splinter Route. This route was active only until 1886. Belle Fourche was not established until the railroad arrived in 1890. After that, Belle Fourche became a major railhead for the local cattle market. Also at this crossing area of the Whitewood Creek and the Belle Fourche River, another route was later used to trail cattle into Montana. Cattle, driven in both directions along this route, also came from Montana into the new railhead town of Belle Fourche.

[65]Near present-day Scranton, North Dakota (established in 1907), close to Buffalo Springs, Peter P. Ackley, a trail cowboy, placed two road-side markers in the early 1930s to show the location of this route. The Pioneer Trails Regional Museum of Bowman has one of the signs that was erected along Highway 12 at Scranton. Ackley, however, mistakenly labeled the markers as the "Chisholm Trail, 1867." For full details read Chapter I in Kraisinger & Kraisinger, *The Western, the Greatest Texas Cattle Trail, 1874-1886*, pgs. 13-14.

[66]There was a direct route from Fort Keogh in Montana Territory (established in 1876) to Bismarck, (established in 1872) when the Northern Pacific Railway reached the eastern banks of the Missouri River. Bismarck became the capital of North Dakota Territory in 1883.

Both Medora and Dickinson had been established following the construction of the Northern Pacific Railway through the area, and ranchers followed the influx of settlers at a rapid pace in 1882 and 1883. The most colorful newcomer was Marquis de Mores, a 24-year-old French aristocrat who came to the Little Missouri Valley in April of 1883 to seek his fortune. He planned to go into the cattle business by raising and slaughtering range cattle and then shipping dressed meat back east in refrigerated rail cars. He selected a site on the east bank of the Little Missouri close to the newly established Northern Pacific Railway. With financial backing from his father-in-law, a wealthy New York banker, de Mores invested heavily in his dream town and built a spacious 26-room home, overlooking the new town, which he furnished lavishly. His wife, Medora von Hoffman, arrived in August along with their children, nurses, maids, and domestic help. For three years Medora, named after de Mores' wife, buzzed with activity. The de Mores and Hoffman families occupied the "Chateau" seasonally, returning to New York for the winters.

Under de Mores' direction, the family built a meat packing plant, a hotel, stores, houses, and a Catholic church. He also sought overland connections with the Black Hills gold fields to increase the importance of his town and empire. In the summer of 1884, de Mores established the Medora Stage and Forwarding Company, a stage route to Deadwood. Along with a manager and superintendent, de Mores developed the 215-mile route. He constructed a freight warehouse, built way stations, hired drivers, purchased teams and four coaches, and negotiated for shipping contracts.[67]

In September of 1883, a young New Yorker arrived in the area and enjoyed the company of the de Mores at their chateau. Theodore Roosevelt actually came to the badlands of the Little Missouri Valley to hunt buffalo but fell in love with the "stark, brooding beauty of the badlands." He established the Maltese Cross Ranch which was seven miles south of the newly established town of Medora. A year later he created a second ranch thirty-five miles north of Medora, which he called The Elkhorn. Roosevelt lived in the Little Missouri River Valley off and on from 1883 to 1887, but eventually left the ranching business and returned east where he married his childhood sweetheart in December of 1886. He remained in the east to pursue a political career.[68]

East of Medora in neighboring Stark County was the town of Dickinson. The Fort Buford Splinter Route passed between the two towns. (Map #7-1) Dickinson had an advantage over other railroad start-up towns because it became a railroad division

---

[67]Service began in October of 1884. The journey for the 11-passenger stages to Deadwood usually took 36 hours, stopping along the way at some thirteen road side stations. This stage line likely followed a very similar route as the cattle trail. The company, however, lasted only until May of 1885. Marquis de Mores was unable to acquire a mail contract, and other shippers preferred a less difficult route. ("The Medora Stage and Forwarding Company," flier produced by the State Historical Society of North Dakota, 1983)

[68]Theodore (Teddy) Roosevelt was the Assistant Secretary of the Navy when the Spanish American War broke out in 1898. He resigned his post and led a regiment in Cuba known as the Rough Riders, earning the Medal of Honor. After the war, he was elected Governor of New York and in March of 1901 became the Vice President of the United States. In September of 1901 when President William McKinley was assassinated, Roosevelt became the 26th president of the United State at the young age of 42. (Clay S. Jenkison, "What Roosevelt Learned in North Dakota," Medora Magazine, 30)

THE WESTERN CATTLE TRAIL | 1874-1897   327

point. When Stark County was organized in June of 1883, it also became the county seat. Cowboy outfits coming into the area observed the new towns that appeared on the new railroad line and witnessed the beginnings of small farms and ranches in 1882 and 1883. These new ranchers spread across western Dakota Territory and southeastern Montana Territory, that included the **Hashknife** on Box Elder Creek, the **OX**, on the west edge of present-day Marmarth in Slope County in present-day South Dakota; and the **777**, located ten miles farther north on the Little Missouri.[69]

These ranches supplied the beef for the government to supply the Indian agencies and for the soldiers at Fort Buford. The closest Indian agency to these far northern ranches was the Fort Berthold Indian Reservation. The Three Tribes,[70] on the reservation were not within the boundary of the Great Sioux Reservation, but they had negotiated a treaty in1866 with the United States government that gave them the right to live on both sides of the Missouri River in northern Dakota Territory. Herds were trailed to the agency south of the Missouri.

Our research has shown that trail drivers usually crossed individual streams before that stream converged with another stream or river in order to have an easier crossing. To avoid crossing the Missouri River after its confluence with the Yellowstone River, we contend that another route was used, approaching Fort Buford from the southwest. This easier route would have been to turn west at or near Watford City and drive northwest, north of Lonesome and Charbonneau creeks, and enter the military reserve. After crossing the Yellowstone River, north of present-day Cartwright, the trail drivers would then go due north, crossing the Missouri River west of its confluence with the Yellowstone. This would put the drovers and their herds north of the Missouri River and at Fort Buford.

There were two possible trail routes to reach Fort Buford. Darrell Dorgan, director of the North Dakota Cowboy Hall of Fame at Medora, North Dakota, believes herds were trailed along a route very close to that of present-day U.S. Highway 85. The drovers and their herds would have entered the future state near present-day Haley, (established in1898), in Bowman County, crossed the railroad tracks at Belfield (established in1883) and continued north through present-day Grassy Butte (established in 1914). The herds were then trailed along the ridge down to the Little Missouri crossing near present-day Long X Bridge on U.S. Highway 85. Dorgan and his colleagues feel that the route then went north to near present-day Watford City (established in 1913) and turned northwest to the Indian Hills and crossed the Missouri River between Trenton and Williston (established in 1887) and continued upriver to Fort Buford.[71]

Fort Buford sat at the confluence of the Missouri and Yellowstone rivers. It had been established on June 13, 1866. The fort's many companies of infantrymen and cavalrymen had guarded railroad crews, provided escorts for steamboats and wagon trains, and had played a role in the campaigns against the non-reservation Indians of the mid-1870s. Sitting Bull had surrendered at Fort Buford after four years of exile in Canada in July of 1881. By 1884, the fort was a noted supply depot for other posts farther west on the Missouri and Yellowstone rivers. Steamboats transported large quantities of supplies from the lower points on

---

[69]Lewis F. Crawford, *Ranching Days in Dakota*, 88-89.

[70]The Three Tribes were the Mandan, Arikara, and Hidatsa. Even though they had negotiated a treaty with the United States government in 1866, the Fort Berthold Indian Reservation and agency were not established until 1870. Through the years, starting in 1866, portions of their reservation land were taken away by the US government. ("Timeline of Historical Events Relating to the Three Tribes of the Fort Berthold Reservation," www.lib.fortbertholdcc.edu [accessed May 15, 2011]

[71]Interview with Darrell Dorgan, Medora, North Dakota, by Gary Kraisinger, August 6, 2011.

the Missouri. From Fort Buford, supplies were then transported farther westward by boats of lighter draft and by wagon trains.[72]

A mile north of the fort, the town of Buford supported the fort with civilian employees who fulfilled the wood and hay contracts. This was the end of the route for the Texas cowboys. At Buford, trail drivers prepared for their return to Texas.

The bonanza years and the Fort Buford Splinter Route ceased in 1886. When Kansas quarantined its entire state in 1885 and Nebraska passed its herd law in 1886, the pathway through Ogallala, Nebraska and into Dakota Territory was cut off. The gold rush into the Black Hills waned after ten years, and by 1886, ranches in Dakota and Montana territories had taken over the government contracts to supply cattle to the Indian reservations. Mother Nature provided the final blow in the winter of 1886-87 — a record-breaking blizzard hit the mid-west that brought many cattlemen to their knees.

THE TRUNK LINE OF THE WESTERN CATTLE TRAIL AND TWO MORE SPLINTER ROUTES, NORTH OF THE RAWHIDE: (Map #7-2)

While herds and cowboys were trailing north on the Sidney-Black Hills Road, the Fort Buford Splinter Route, delivering cattle to Indian agencies, miners, and ranches, other herds continued up the south side of the North Platte River on the trunk line of the Western Cattle Trail, beyond the Sidney Bridge, to another turn-off at the confluence of Rawhide Creek and the North Platte River, just west of the Nebraska-Wyoming line. From the Sidney Bridge to the Wyoming border had been some fifty-eight miles, and then another sixteen miles to the confluence of Rawhide Creek and the North Platte River. On the route, drovers and herds passed the Court House Rock landmark, trailed by Chimney Rock, and crossed the Wyoming border just west of present-day Henry where the Red Cloud Agency had been located from 1871 to 1873. This segment of the Western Cattle Trail followed the Oregon-California emigrant trail to Rawhide Creek.

In his book *The Log of A Cowboy*, Andy Adams, who was trailing a herd of Circle Dot cattle in 1882, described the trip up the North Platte to Forty Island Ford at Rawhide Creek:

> ...we trailed out up the North Platte River. It was an easy country in which to handle a herd; the trail in places would run back from the river as far as ten miles, and again follow close in near the river bottoms. There was an abundance of small creeks putting into this fork of the Platte from the south, which afforded water for the herd and good camp grounds at night. Only twice after leaving Ogalalla [sic] had we

---

[72]When the area became settled in the 1890s, Fort Buford's usefulness ceased. It was abandoned in October of 1895. In 1924, the location became a state historic site. ("Fort Buford," North Dakota State Historical Society brochure, 2006)

THE WESTERN CATTLE TRAIL | 1874-1897   329

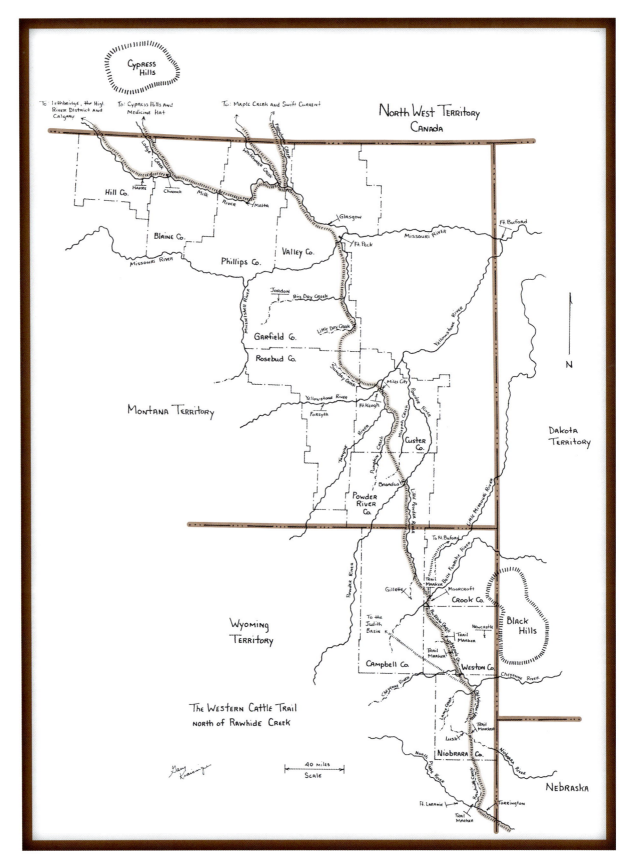

#7-2
The Western Cattle Trail Trunk Line from the Junction of the North Platte River and Rawhide Creek to Canada:
This map shows the Western Trail across Wyoming Territory and through Montana Territory to the Milk River and beyond.

At the age of 43, Andy Adams started writing about his life on the Plains. He had come to Texas in the early 1880s and worked as a cowboy and made many cattle drives from 1882-83 to 1889. However, Adams chose to use a fictional form for his writing which has resulted in the literary community to label his work as pure fiction. We would like to point out what www.americanliterature.com says:

> "Disgusted by the unrealistic cowboy fiction being published at the time, Andy Adams took it upon himself to provide a better account and drew heavily on his first hand experiences. His work is still widely considered the most compelling and accurate portrayal of cowboy life ever written."

Even though Adams used fictionalized characters in his novels, the circumstances he described was an autobiography of his own life. After in-depth study of the trail drives in his 1903 book, *A Log of a Cowboy*, and in his 1905 book, *The Outlet*, we affirm that there could be no way a writer could give such detail about landmarks and routes or describe a trail drive so accurately — unless he was there.

Photo courtesy of the Print Collection, Miriam and Ira D. Wallach Division of Art, Prints and Photographs, The New York Public Library, Astor, Lenox and Tiden Foundations.

been compelled to go to the river for water for the herd, and with the exception of thunderstorms and occasional summer rains, the weather had been all one could wish. For the past week as we trailed up the North Platte, some one of us visited the river daily to note its stage of water, for we were due to cross at Forty Islands, about twelve miles south of old Fort Laramie.[73]

The Forty Island Ford was one of the toughest and most dangerous river crossings on the trail. Horses and cattle had to swim the strong current of the river's main channel, a quarter of a mile in width. This particular spot had been selected as a crossing because two small islands in the river could be used as "stepping stones" before plunging into main-stream current. Within a mile and a half below the ford,

---

[73]The Circle Dot outfit started from the Rio Grande in Texas and delivered the cattle to the Blackfoot Agency in northern Montana, a trip of some 2000 miles. This trip is also depicted on a map in the book by Mark H. Brown and William R. Felton, *Before Barbed Wire, L.S. Huffman, Photographer on Horseback*. (Andy Adams, *Log of a Cowboy*, 288)

there were over thirty of the forty islands or sand bars after which the crossing received its name.

Herds stacked up at the crossing waiting for favorable conditions like a fall in the river flow. Trail bosses fretted about losing several days of trail time if cattle were caught in the muddy bogs along its shore, causing a loss of stock.

The Adams' outfit decided that it was better to swim the fast current than to try to cross after the river had receded, leaving dangerous sand traps. He described the crossing of Forty Island Ford and swimming the river channel:

> With the addition to our force of [foreman Wade] Scholar and nine or ten of his men, we had an abundance of help, and put the cattle into the water opposite two islands, our saddle horses in the lead as usual. There was no swimming water between the south shore and the first island, though it wet our saddle skirts for some considerable distance, this channel being nearly two hundred yards wide. Most of our outfit took the water, while Scholar's men fed our herd in from the south bank, ...The second island lay down the stream some little distance; and as we pushed the cattle off the first one we were in swimming water in no time, ...and our lead cattle struck out, and, breasting the water, swam as proudly as swans. The middle channel was nearly a hundred yards wide, the greater portion of which was swimming, though the last channel was much wider.... With our own outfit we crowded the leaders to keep the chain of cattle unbroken, and before Honeyman could hustle his horses out of the river, our lead cattle had caught a foothold, were heading up stream and edging out for the farther shore.[74]

The chances were better for a successful crossing if the herds could be double teamed by two cowboy outfits (as mentioned by Adams).[75] Ealy Moore, one of the trail bosses from the XIT Ranch, noted in his journal of 1892, the arduous task of getting the herds across the North Platte, and working with other outfits to ford the river — for four days:

June 20	Camped three miles North Platte, helped a N-N herd and Chris across that day.
June 21	Assisted Jim Vaughn to cross his herd in the forenoon, and tried to cross mine in the afternoon, but failed.

---

[74]According to Adams, the character of Wade Scholar was the trail foreman for the Prairie Cattle Company. They were headed for their northern range in the Badlands near the mouth of the Yellowstone in Montana. Their herd had been "waterbound over a week already with no prospect of crossing without swimming." (Ibid, 289-292)

[75]"Double teamed" means that two cowboy outfits from different herds joined to push a herd across the river. The added man power was then used to push the second herd across, thus one outfit helping the other.

June 22   Assisted Jack Horn to Cross.

June 23   Helped to cross Mil's [Milt's] my own and Dan's herds,
                 Camped one mile from river.[76]

Cowboys knew that the cattle had to be pointed and coaxed toward the farther shore in hopes that the lead steers would not take a sudden notion to turn back. If the herd did panic and started to mill in mid-river, there was nothing more dangerous to the life of a cowboy on his horse than trying to straighten out a milling herd in a river. Ralph F. Jones explains:

> The cattle could become weak and exhausted from swimming against the strong current to the point where they could be sucked under by the turbulent river and swept downstream, taking any unfortunate cowboy who happened to be on the downstream side of the herd with them. When this occurred, unless that cowboy happened to be an exceptionally good swimmer, he would have made his last trail drive.[77]

In 1882, numerous herds crossed the North Platte at the Rawhide. Adams mentioned that some twenty herds had gone ahead of them, and the herd directly in front of them by a few days was from western Nebraska where the outfit had wintered on the Niobrara River. It was headed for Alberta, Canada.[78]

In 1882, Ab Blocker was the owner of an outift trailing two thousand cattle destined for Little Bighorn River in Montana. Some of the cattle were to go to the government for "Indian beef," and others were to be delivered to cattle companies. The trail boss was John Hawk and Bob Fudge was one of the members of the twelve-man outfit. Fudge helped drive the Blocker cattle across the North Platte in 1882, and thirteen years later, in 1895, faced the river crossing again, this time with the XIT Ranch cattle. He was with one of five outfits trailing two thousand two-year-old steers in each herd destined for the company ranch in Montana. The five herds left the Panhandle ranch "just far enough apart so that one herd would be on water and out of the way before the next herd came." The herds were kept one or two days ahead of one another — except at river crossings. At the North Platte crossing, four of the XIT herds were stacked close together. Fudge was a powerful swimmer and was not afraid of any river. He later said, "At the time I weighed under one hundred sixty pounds and was six feet, three inches tall and could swim like a muskrat. I was also one of the oldest trail drivers, or had been up the trail about as many times as any man in the four outfits."

---

[76]Chris Gish was in charge of the fourth (out of five) XIT herd. Milt Whipple and Dan Cole were bosses for the fifth and third XIT herds. Ealy Moore was leading the second herd. Here at the North Platte, they were all helping each other cross. The other names mentioned were bosses from other herds. (Ealy Moore's 1892 journal in J. Evetts Haley, *The XIT Ranch of Texas*, 234)
[77]Ralph F. Jones, *Longhorns North of the Arkansas*, 12.
[78]Adams, Ibid, 309.

Fudge volunteered to swim point in crossing the herds, and arrangements were made with each trail boss to supply Fudge with a fresh horse for each crossing. Fudge later recalled: "We generally picked a big powerful horse for our swimming horse, as we called them. We took good care of these horses and did not ride them for a few days before coming to a swimming river." Fudge was quite proud of his "big fine sorrel" that was an experienced swimmer. The second day of crossing the herds, however, did not go well for Fudge:

> We had some trouble getting into the river. After the lead cattle started to wade out on the bank, I looked back to see how the line in the current was coming. They were getting scattered and drifting a long ways downstream. I turned my horse and swam him below the

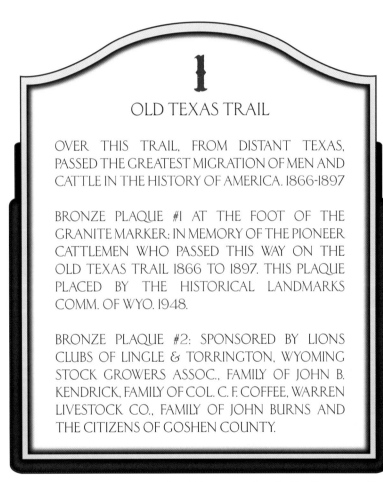

Location: At a rest area about 1.1 miles east of Lingle, Wyoming on the north side of U.S. Highway 26, Goshen County.

On the reverse side of the monument are numerous brands of herds that passed through this area. The four longhorns bear the brands of the Kendricks (OW), the Coffees (OIO Bar) Warren Livestock Company (JK), and the Hill family (HILL).

Authors' commentary:
The beginning year of 1866 on the sign is incorrect. Even though there may have been a couple of very early cattle drives into Wyoming, the trail was not established and trail traffic did not occur until after 1875. Until the Sioux were moved out of the area and the Black Hills were opened to settlers and miners, pioneers and cattle drives did not come into this area. Again, the 1866 date represents the date of origin of earlier Shawnee Trail and should not be used here. The Western Cattle Trail was called the Texas Trail in Wyoming. It is the same trail, and it did last until 1897, and it did represent the "greatest migration of men and cattle in the history of America."

NOTE: Where the Union Pacific Railroad crosses Rawhide Creek, there are two switch stations. Signs on the stations: "East Texas" on one and "West Texas" on the other denote where the cattle crossed.

Susan Carlson, *Wyoming Historical Markers at 55 MPH*, 41.
Mike Jording, *A Few Interested Residents: Wyoming Historical Markers & Monuments*, 115.

cattle where they were being carried downstream. This was somewhere about the center of the river. I swam back and forth on the lower side of the line of swimming cattle, urging them in a more direct course across the river, when my sorrel of which I had been so proud turned on his side and swelled his chest and stomach until he looked like a small balloon. He did not try to swim a stroke, just went floating down the Platte like a biscuit. I kept hold of him for about a hundred yards and decided I would swim to shore. As soon as I left that horse and started to swim he started for me, striking and doing his best to get on top of me. The only thing I could do was to dive, for if that horse had hit me with his front feet, I would have been crippled and would surely have drowned. When I dived, my hat was left on the surface of the water which the horse kept after, and that saved my life…. I swam to shore coming out on the north bank. My underwear was heavy with mud, and there was mud settled in places between my flesh and underwear, and my hair was a mat of mud and sand. My horse pawed that hat under and after it had disappeared, turned over on his side again and went floating down the Platte like a log. [79]

> Today there is a marker paying tribute to the drovers who crossed the North Platte River and trailed to the north on the Western (Old Texas) Cattle Trail, east of present-day Lingle and west of Rawhide Creek. The crossing and trail were also approximately eight miles west of present-day Torrington, Wyoming. Torrington, a water tower and coaling station on the Chicago, Burlington & Quincy Railroad, was established in 1889 with a post office and a few businesses.

The river did take a few unfortunate cowboys. Adams tells the story of how Wade Scholar and his outfit were asked to go back to the river to help another herd across. The foreman and his horse suddenly disappeared in the fast current and did not surface. They found him the next day on one of the sand bars below the ford.[80]

While the cowboys maneuvered herds across the river, the outfit cooks got an early start after breakfast, drove the twelve miles toward Fort Laramie,[81] restocked their wagons at the outpost's store, crossed the river on the fort's iron bridge, and drove back downstream on the north side along the old Mormon Trail in time to have camp set up and a hot meal ready for the trail drivers as they came up out of the river.[82] But not always did plans go as expected. If the sutler's store was busy or if the fort's bridge was clogged with wagons and livestock, a cook might be delayed.

---

[79] The horse was found about a half a mile downriver where he had climbed out on the south shore. Fudge explained that sometimes when horses and cattle become too exhausted, "they will turn over on their sides and float downstream seemingly without a care in the world until the current carries them to the bank where they get to their feet and wade out." (Russell, Ibid, 67-70)

[80] Adams, Ibid, 294-303.

[81] Fort Laramie had been founded by two fur trappers in 1834 at the confluence of the North Platte and Laramie rivers. They named their trading post after a well-known trapper to the Indians, Jacques Lorimier. Eventually, hundreds of Oglala, Brules, Miniconjous and Sans Arcs were camped more or less permanently around the post. The post was purchased by the U.S. Military in 1849 and became a protectorate and supplier to emigrant wagon trains for the near-by Oregon Trail. During the 1870s of Indian uprising, the fort served as a staging area and command post for troops. The fort ceased to be used in March of 1890. In 1937 it became a national monument and is maintained by the National Parks Service. (Struthers Burt, *Powder River*, 57 and "The Oregon Trail Fort Laramie," www.historyglobe.com [accessed May 20, 2012])

[82] Adams, Ibid, 288 and Sue Flanagan, *Trailing the Longhorns*, 126.

He would then have to cut across country coming up from the southwest as his outfit progressed north and had camped somewhere along the Rawhide.[83] The cowboys waited in camp for their cook and a meal and hot coffee.

To cut across country toward the Rawhide, a cook could push his team and restocked wagon north from Fort Laramie on the Deadwood Trail (Cheyenne Stage Route) to Old Government Farm,[84] south of Rawhide Butte, and then continued northeast along the Laramie's Fork-Fort Pierre Military Road to Rawhide Creek where he meet up with the herd. The military road connected with Fort Pierre in South Dakota, some 323 miles to the east, but the wagon master and his team used the road for only about six miles before reaching the Western Trail at the Rawhide.

In their journals, cowboys noted the soft sand along Rawhide Creek. Ezra Soar was in this area in 1880, driving a herd of cattle from Colorado. Upon reaching Rawhide Creek, "a very nice little creek [that] heads up into the bluffs," and he noted in his journal that the "roads [were] very heavy & sandy" and that they drove "about 8 miles over a very sandy road." On the following day, he wrote: "drove about 5 miles [.] road very hard & Sandy" [and] "had to haul one wagon at a time for quite a distance." It appears that the outfit had to double-team the wagons in order to get them through the deep sand. Soar also commented that: "There is thousands of cattle on the North Platte on both sides [and] if there should ever be a railroad through here this will be the country."[85] The year 1880 was before the Texas-Montana Feeder Route through Colorado was used (1884-1897) and the Union Pacific Railroad branch was completed up the North Platte River. (Part III, Chapter III) These "thousands of cattle" would had to have been trailed up the Western Trail from Ogallala, Nebraska, or up from Cheyenne, Wyoming.

Another reference to the sand along the Rawhide is found in Perry E. Davis' 1894 account of his outfit's return to Texas from the north. Davis was in charge of the chuck wagon. The outfit also considered double teaming the wagons:

| September 5: | Move about three miles down Rawhide; Camp at nice spring which flows from white sand bank. |
| September 6: | Move down about six miles and camp in a sandbed for dinner, grass green. After pulling |

---

[83]Bob Fudge relates that after he had helped with all the herds to cross the North Platte, he "started immediately for my own outfit, as they had pulled on up the trail." He stopped at another camp, ate, and since "the moon was out" started "to catch my own wagon" which he estimated was some ten miles on up the Rawhide. (Russell, Ibid, 70)

[84]This junction (Old Government Farm) was where the stage route and Laramie's Fork-Fort Pierre Road crossed. East of here is present-day Jay Em. The stage route was actually named the "Cheyenne and Black Hills Stage Route, but because it went to Deadwood, in Dakota Territory, it was more commonly called the "Deadwood Trail." (Paul & Helen Henderson map, May 1970, Gering Public Library, Gering, Nebraska, vertical files)

[85]Soar had driven his herd through Colorado, over what later would become the Texas-Montana Feeder Route from Pine Bluffs to the Rawhide. He did not stay on the main cattle trail, but instead, trailed straight east from the Niobrara River to connect with the Sidney-Black Hills route, and then on north. (May 21, 1880 entry, Ezra Soar's diary. Transcript owned by the City of Greeley Museums, Greeley, Colorado)

down for about three miles, we began to think of putting on another team. The sand was so soft it was almost impossible to pull through it. Here the valley was broken with wall rock, sand banks, and blowouts.

The stench of the river was also remembered. Perry Davis continued in his entry:

When the country opened out into a large, flat valley covered with stinkweed and boar weed. Here the water stinks. It is about five miles to where it empties into the Platte. [86]

And Bob Fudge recalled:

If cattle do not get scared before they get to swimming water and are dry, they take to swimming quite naturally; but if they get scared, it is sometimes hard to get them into a river, especially one that smells as the Platte did at this time. [87]

Cowboy journals recorded the locations of camp sites from the North Platte crossing to the Niobrara River. A couple of days' drive north of the North Platte, according to J. E. Moore, was Coffee Ranch. It was a location that was used for cowboy camps. Moore wrote on June 25, 1892: "Made a cut off [from the trail] of about four miles and camped just below Coffee's ranch."[88] Perry Davis also mentioned this camping spot:

September 5, 1894:   Move about three miles down Rawhide; camp at nice spring which flows from white sand bank. Green meadows close to Coffee's pasture at O1O ranch.[89]

---

[86]Wayne H. Gossard, Jr. (ed.) *Life on the Trail, the 1894 Diary of Perry Eugene Davis*, (http://coloradohistory. org /westerntrails[accessed July 22, 2007] and Colorado Historical Society, *Colorado Heritage Magazine*, 1981)

[87]Russell, Ibid, 68.

[88]J. E. Moore's 1892 journal in J. Evetts Hales, *The XIT Ranch of Texas*.

[89]Gossard, Ibid. Davis and his outfit were coming from the north. C. F. Coffee had a ranch on Box Elder Creek just south of present-day Torrington, Wyoming. According to the Chadron State College archives materials, Coffee established his Wyoming ranch in approximately 1873, but moved his herds across the border into Nebraska in 1879 to Hat Creek approximately twelve miles north of present-day Harrison, Nebraska where he established a ranch headquarters, and subsequently helped establish the Nebraska Stock Growers Association and the Omaha Stock Yards, and, in 1889, purchased the Commercial Bank in Harrison. As late as 1894, however, Perry Davis was still referring to the Wyoming location as the Coffee Ranch. (www.sandozcenter.com [accessed May 25, 2012])

THE WESTERN CATTLE TRAIL | 1874-1897

The Western Trail continued north toward Rawhide Buttes, a grouping of small round hills that were visible from a great distance. South of the Buttes, Rawhide Creek intersected the Deadwood Trail, and the Rawhide Stage Station of the Cheyenne and Deadwood Stagecoach and Express Line was located there. The Western Trail passed east of the Buttes.

Jay Em Creek was another camping spot. Davis recorded: "Pull down below [at] JM and camp in a grove; a pretty place, nice running stream, nice soft meadows [and] green grass."[90]

The next overnight camp and supply point was at the headwaters of the Niobrara River. The crossing of the Niobrara was about five and one half miles east of Silver Cliff, a tent and shack town connected to the Great Western Mining and Milling Company that operated a large stamp mill on Mining Hill. It operated from 1880 to 1898. When the Fremont, Elkhorn, and Missouri Valley Railroad reached the site in 1886, a camp of about two hundred people moved a mile and one half east to the new town site of Lusk. The rails were laid in July of 1886 and in the same month, Frank Lusk sold lots to create the town.[91] By 1892 when the XIT outfit, with Ealy Moore in charge of herd number two, and the Hashknife horse herd outfit, with Perry Davis as cook, came through, the town was thriving. The trail was east of Lusk, but the town was a supply point for chuck wagons, and provided refreshments and entertainment for cowboys.

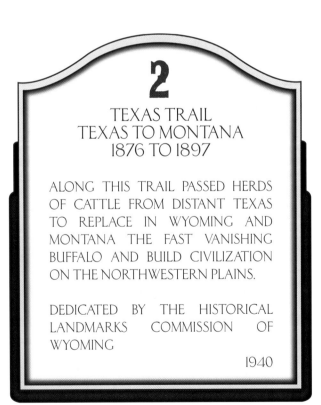

2

TEXAS TRAIL
TEXAS TO MONTANA
1876 TO 1897

ALONG THIS TRAIL PASSED HERDS OF CATTLE FROM DISTANT TEXAS TO REPLACE IN WYOMING AND MONTANA THE FAST VANISHING BUFFALO AND BUILD CIVILIZATION ON THE NORTHWESTERN PLAINS.

DEDICATED BY THE HISTORICAL LANDMARKS COMMISSION OF WYOMING

1940

Lower plaque: Sponsored by the Lusk Lions Club, Wyo. Stockgrowers Ass'n, and Stockmen of Eastern Wyo. Plaque by Bill Harwood

Location: Approximately 3.4 miles east of the junction of U.S. Highways 20 and 18/85, in Lusk, on the south side of U.S. Highway 20, Niobrara County, Wyoming.

Description: Bronze plaque on a native agate, jasper, and quartz boulder, typical of those found in the area.

Authors' commentary:
This marker's text is short but to the point. The dates are correct, one of the few that are. The portion of the Western Trail System in Wyoming is called the Texas Trail.

Susan Carlson, *Wyoming Historical Markers at 55 MPH*, 63.
Mike Jording, *A Few Interested Residents: Wyoming Historical Markers & Monuments*, 144.

[90]Gossard, *Life on the Trail, the 1894 Diary of Perry Eugene Davis*.
[91]There is a road side trail marker 3.4 miles east of Lusk. (Map: "Historical Sites," published by Niobrara County Library Foundation, Lusk, Wyoming, by May Ellen Smith, 1986)

Early Moore mentioned Lusk in his journal:

> June 26: Camped 10 miles of Lusk.

> June 27: Passed through Lusk, Wyo. and camped six miles beyond.

The Moore outfit and herd had traveled sixteen miles that day.

Davis noted their stay in Lusk:

> September 2: Camp at stockyards on Running Water or Niobrara. At Lusk paid ten dollars for watering horses. One man under the influence of Lusk whisky, very sick.

> September 3: Pull into Lusk for chuck and grind ax, etc. Camp for dinner two miles south of town.

North of the Niobrara River, the trail again crossed the Deadwood Trail or the Cheyenne-Black Hills Stage Route. Adams recalled the route in 1882 when he wrote that after a four-day trip from the North Platte, they came to the "main stage road connecting the railroad on the south with the mining camps which nestled somewhere in those rocky hills [Black Hills] to our right."[92] At the junction of the Western Trail and the Cheyenne-Black Hills Stage Route was the Fort Hat Creek Stage Station. It had originally been established as a fort in 1875 by Captain James Egin, but a year later became the stage stop on the Cheyenne-Black Hills Stage Route. It was actually located on Sage Creek, and the barracks had been built to connect with a tunnel to the creek so water could be obtained during a time of siege. Eventually, the post was not only a stage stop, but also served as a hotel, blacksmith shop, telegraph station, and post office.[93]

The next stage stop was on Old Woman Creek, a dry fork of the Cheyenne River. Here at Old Woman's Stage Station on the Cheyenne-Black Hills Stage Route, the trails split. Adams noted this fork: "the two thoroughfares separated, the one to the mining camp of Deadwood, while ours the Montana cattle trail bore off for the Powder River to the northwest."[94]

Andy Adams and his outfit were told at the stage station that after passing the next fork of the Big Cheyenne (Lance Creek), they would find no water for their Circle Dot herd until striking the Powder River. It was an eighty-mile dry drive.

---

[92]Adams, *Log of a Cowboy*, 308. The Cheyenne-Black Hills Stage Route connected Cheyenne, Wyoming to the mining camps in the Black Hills, Dakota Territory.
[93]Map: "Historical Sites," Ibid. According to Sue Flanagan, this army post was built on the wrong creek in the wrong state. Soldiers were sent in 1875 to establish an outpost on Hat Creek in Nebraska, but, instead, built "Fort Hat Creek" on Sage Creek in Wyoming. (Flanagan, 134.)
[94]Adams. Ibid, 309.

After crossing Lance Creek and continuing up the Cheyenne River to where Lodgepole Creek enters the Cheyenne River from the north, the cattle trail forked. Those outfits and herds on the trunk line of the Western Cattle Trail headed for Miles City, Fort Peck, Montana Territory, and into Canada continued north up the Lodgepole (refer to Map #7-2), while those who were delivering cattle into the Judith Basin, the Sun River Valley, and other ranges in the west-central part of Montana Territory turned northwest. This northwest route is referred to as the Judith Basin Splinter Route.

THE JUDITH BASIN SPLINTER ROUTE FROM THE WESTERN (TEXAS) CATTLE TRAIL: (Map #7-3)

At the Fort Hat Creek Stage Station, the Circle Dot outfit was warned of the harsh drive to the Powder River. The 1882 summer had been one of the driest in years. Adams recalled:

> ...we set our house in order for the undertaking before us. It was yet fifteen miles to the next and last water from the stage stand…. [Cheyenne River] The situation was serious, with only this encouragement: other herds had crossed this arid belt since the streams had dried up, and our Circle Dots could walk with any herd that ever left Texas.[95]

In his account of this parched drive, Bob Fudge, who was also on this route in 1882, wrote that they had been told at Fort Laramie that from the Cheyenne River to the Powder, there "was likely to be no water." In his memoirs he described the drive:

> The worst suffering I have ever seen in my seventy years with cattle was on this drive from the Cheyenne to the Powder River. This suffering cannot be told in words. The weather was terribly hot and at the end of the second day these cattle commenced to grind their teeth in their suffering, and when they were lying down their groans were something to make a wooden Indian's hair raise. At night those groans and the grinding of their teeth was the most horrible thing I have ever listened to.
>
> We travelled at night — whenever the cattle would move a bit we urged them on. We knew that we had to get to water or we would lose every one of them. We did lose between one and two hundred from thirst. This was the most pitiful thing I have ever seen. Every one of those cattle that died, died with their heads pointed toward Texas, I suppose they thought of the last water they had had, and maybe they thought of their native home in Texas. Anyway, they turned their heads south before kicking their last.[96]

---

[95]Adams, Ibid.
[96]Russell, *Bob Fudge, Texas Trail Driver*, 37.

THE WESTERN CATTLE TRAIL | 1874-1897

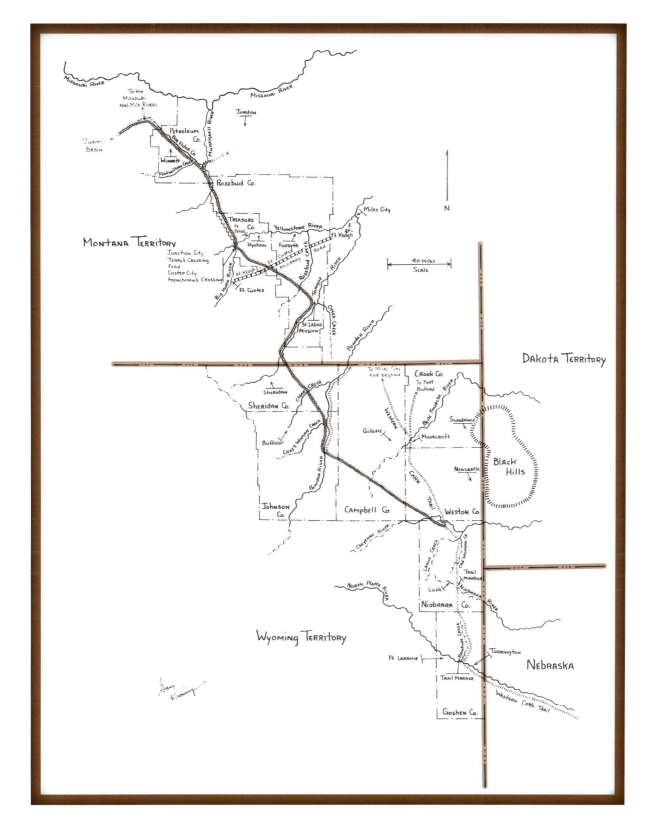

#7-3

The Judith Basin Splinter Route from South of the Cheyenne River in Wyoming Territory to the Judith Basin in Montana Territory:

This map shows the splinter route from the Western Cattle Trail trunk line going west across Wyoming Territory to the Powder River, following that river for a short distance, and then going northwest again to the confluence of Big Horn River and Yellowstone River. From there the route goes north, northwest to the confluence of Box Elder Creek and Musselshell River. The splinter route follows Box Elder Creek to the Judith Basin.

Cowboys and cattle reached the Powder River exhausted, going over twenty-five miles a day, and weak from lack of water. They had pushed across the eighty miles in three days. The surviving cattle not only needed water, but also required a long rest. The river was "paradise after what we had gone through," Bob Fudge remembered. The cattle rested, and the cowboys bathed in pools along the banks of the river.

For more than twenty miles, there was a cattle trail on both sides of the Powder River. Herds that were destined for north central Montana Territory and the Tongue River stayed on the west side of the Powder, grazed down it for four or five days, and then left its tributary to turn northwest. Drovers and herds that were headed for the Badlands and the lower Yellowstone country, continued to follow the Power River northeast. Adams indicates this division in the trails when he made reference to the "left-hand trail:"

> we took a left-hand trail. While large trails followed on down the Powder, their direction was wrong for us, as they led towards the Bad Lands and the lower Yellowstone country. On the second day out, after taking the left-hand trail, we encountered some rough country in passing across the saddle in a range of hills forming the divide between the Powder and Tongue rivers. We were nearly a whole day crossing it, but had a well-used trail to follow, and down in the foothills made camp that night on a creek which emptied into the Tongue. The roughness of the trail was well compensated for, however, as it was a paradise of grass and water. We reached the Tongue River the next afternoon, and found it a similar stream to the Powder — clear as crystal, swift, and with a rocky bottom.[97]

Range riders from off the ranches along Crazy Woman Creek and the Tongue River appeared occasionally. The area was cattle country that had been stocked with Texas cattle. The range riders' job was to be sure that none of the range cattle came near the Texas cattle on the trail because of the Texas Fever.

The trail drivers and their herds continued to follow the Tongue River north/northeast for several days, and then turned northwest again at approximately where St. Labre Mission is located today. By 1884 there would be a three-room log cabin built by the missionary, Father Emmett Hoffman, who wanted to help the local Northern Cheyenne and Crow tribes who lived up and down the Tongue River Valley.[98] A short day's drive put the herds facing the Rosebud River, and, farther on, the herds crossed the Fort Keogh- Fort Custer Military Trail. This trail was still active in 1882.

---

[97]Adams, Ibid, 328.

[98]From its beginnings as a small log cabin, St. Labre is now a series of schools for the Northern Cheyenne and Crow tribes. The main campus of the high school is located in Ashland, Montana, on the Northern Cheyenne Reservation. The Roman Catholic institution has over 780 students in three schools, a church, and a museum. ("St. Labre" on line, [accessed Aug. 9, 2009])

Fort Keogh and Fort Custer had been established in the summer of 1877 because of the warfare between the military and various bands of the tribes in the region in the aftermath of the Battle of the Little Bighorn on June 25, 1876. Troops poured into the area after the battle, with Fort Custer on the Bighorn and named for Lt. Col. George Armstrong Custer, and Fort Keogh farther downriver on the Yellowstone and named for Myles Keogh, an adjutant to Lt. Col. Custer, also killed at the Battle of the Little Bighorn.[99] Five years later, Texas cattle were being trailed within a few short miles of the battle site.

The Circle Dot herd and the Adams' outfit crossed the military trail and continued in a northwesterly direction, but the Ab Blocker outfit, that Bob Fudge was with, turned west, climbed the divide to Little Bighorn River and delivered its herd to the Mat Murphy ranch located on that river "about ten miles below Custer's battlefield." Fudge remembered that after the sale, which included their horses and saddles as well, the outfit was escorted in Murphy's mountain wagon "almost due east from Murphy's ranch, and then down the Tongue River to Miles City," which, according to Fudge "was nothing much... but a fort."[100]

The Circle Dot herd followed a creek[101] down to the Yellowstone River. Trail herds probably forded the river above the junction of the Bighorn River and the Yellowstone — or crossed the Yellowstone River above the confluence to take advantage of a more shallow crossing. According to R. D. Palacios' map, "Ranches and Cattle Trails of Early Montana," the town of Custer sat on the south side of the Yellowstone, and Junction City sat on the north side of the river.[102] Approximately ten miles east of Junction City or approximately seven miles downstream from the mouth of the Bighorn River had been the site of Fort Pease, established in June of 1875 by Gallatin Valley traders, hoping to become an important riverboat site. F. D. Pease with two partners built the a series of log huts connected by a palisade of cottonwood logs.[103] By the next year, however, the trading post was used by troops during Brig. General Alfred H. Terry's Indian campaign, but the area between the fort's stockade and the river is still referred to by the locals as Pease Bottoms.

---

[99]Fort Custer was abandoned in April of 1898. Fort Keogh was closed in 1908. ("Fort Custer," www.wkipedia.org [accessed Aug. 9, 2009] and "Fort Keogh," www.ultimatemontana.com, [accessed August 9, 2009])

[100]Russell, Ibid, 38.

[101]Tallocks Creek, a fork of the Bighorn, empties into the Bighorn River about a mile before it empties into the Yellowstone River. Adams said the creek that they followed was the "Sweet Grass." He must have been mistaken because the Sweet Grass is not in this area, or the term was used locally and has not survived to the present.

[102]Brown and Felton, *Before Barbed Wire*, map on inside cover. George F. Cram's map of 1883 "Montana," (authors' collection) and interviews by Gary Kraisinger with local citizens verify that the Junction City Store was on the north side of the river and Custer was on the south side.

[103]The trading post was built on land claimed by the Sioux as their hunting ground. A year later during the warfare between the military and the Sioux, the post was revived and occupied by the U.S. Army and was called Terry's Landing. After the military abandoned the post in the spring of 1876, the stockade which was 100 foot by 100 foot square was burned to the ground by the Sioux and Cheyenne. ("Fort Pease," www.fortsandfights.com [accessed August 10, 2009], and "Montana Forts of the Old West," www.legendofamerica.com [accessed Aug. 2, 2013])

THE WESTERN CATTLE TRAIL | 1874-1897

Steamboats, by way of the Missouri River, came up the Yellowstone as far as Junction City and Custer and unloaded their wares and troops. Homesteaders from the north side of the river flocked to the Junction City store for items of clothes, household goods, food, and furniture.[104]

The fur trade business had been flourishing in this area since the beginning of the 19th century. Manuel Lisa, one of the founders of the Missouri Fur Company, upon hearing of Lewis and Clark's report of the plentiful beaver along the Missouri River, left St. Louis in 1807 with a brigade of boats and men and ascended the Missouri and Yellowstone Rivers to the mouth of the Bighorn where he established a trading post. It was the first outpost in the upper Missouri region and became known as Fort Manuel Lisa. Even though Lisa himself was not French, the fur trade was dominated by Frenchmen.[105] By the mid 1830s, steamboats were being used to transport the furs out of the region.

When Adams came through this area with the Circle Dot herd in 1882, he prepared to cross the Yellowstone at the Bighorn; he referred to the crossing as "Frenchman's Crossing." It is not clear why he used that term — perhaps it related to the early role of the French trappers and fur traders. He called the village that sat next to the crossing "Ford," and described the "squatter type" village:

> The town struck me as something new and novel, two thirds of the habitations being of canvas. Immense quantities of buffalo hides were drying or already baled, and waiting transportation as we afterward learned to navigable points on the Missouri. Large bull trains were encamped on the outskirts of the village, while many such outfits were in town, receiving cargoes or discharging freight. The drivers of these ox trains lounged in the streets and thronged the saloons and gambling resorts.[106]

He noticed that among the throng of humanity "almost every language could be heard." There were not only buffalo hunters, but freighters, plainsmen, Indians, and a camp of engineers working on the survey of the Northern Pacific Railroad. Included in the drinking establishments were Yellowstone Bob's and The Buffalo Bull. Adams continued his description:

> Tying our horses in a group to a hitch-rack in the rear of a saloon called The Buffalo Bull, we entered by a rear door and lined up at the bar for our first drink since leaving Ogallala. Games of chance were running in the rear for those who felt inclined to try their luck, while in front of the bar, tables, around which seated the patrons of the place,

---

[104]Interview of Betty Cunningham, Myers, Montana, by Margaret Kraisinger, August 14, 2009.

[105]The Fort Manuel Lisa trading post was likely in the vacinity of current-day Custer. ("Manuel Lisa," http://mman.home.att.net/Lisa.htm, and Struthers Burt, *Powder River*, 19)

[106]Andy Adams, *A Log of a Cowboy*, 334.

playing for the drinks. One couldn't help being impressed with the unrestrained freedom of the village, whose sole product seemed to be buffalo hides. Every man in the place wore the regulation six-shooter in his belt, and quite a number wore two. The primitive law of nature known as self-preservation, was very evident in August of '82 at French-man's Ford.

The place called "Ford" by Adams was on the south side of the river. When crossing, Adams commented: "a number of spectators had come up from Frenchman's to watch the herd ford, the crossing being about half a mile above the village," and "when we reached the farther bank, we waved our hats to the group on the south side in farewell to them and to Frenchman's Ford."[107]

The R. D. Palacios map shows the crossing of the Yellowstone River as being called "Terry's Crossing," and Ralph F. Jones in his book, *Longhorns North of the Arkansas*, also called the crossing, "Terry's Crossing."[108] This was a newer term that had been used since Brig. General Alfred H. Terry's campaign of 1876, six years before Adams' crossing of the Yellowstone. Terry had directed an 1876 campaign to force the Lakota and their allies onto reservations after the Dakota Territory treaty had been breached by gold miners. In maneuvering for this campaign, some of Brig. General Terry's troops used the Yellowstone crossing — thus the name "Terry's Crossing."[109]

According to Andy Adams, the Circle Dot herd then followed a creek called "Many Berries," one of the tributaries of the Yellowstone. They paralleled it "mile after mile." Along the creek "grew endless quantities of species of upland huckleberry," and the outfit "feasted as we rode along." Adams continued:

> The grade up this creek was quite pronounced, for before night the channel of the creek had narrowed to several yards in width…after a continued gradual climb, we made camp that night on the summit of the divide within plain sight of the Musselshell River.[110]

The outfit crossed the Musselshell River about twelve miles above the entrance of Flatwillow Creek. The old crossing had been used for generations by herds of buffalo and migrating elk. It had also been "an old Indian ford," so it was "one of the easiest crossings" the herd had encountered. The trail drivers continued down the Musselshell to near the confluence of the Musselshell and the Flatwillow. Here the trail turned northwest.[111] At this point, herds from the main trunk line of

---

[107]Adams, Ibid, 335, 347-348..

[108]R. D. Palacios, *Ranches and Cattle Trails of Early Montana*, and Ralph F. Jones, Ibid, 15.

[109]The campaign that Brig. General Terry commanded was called the Centennial Campaign because it occurred during the country's 100th year since independence. ("Alfred Howe Terry," www.pbs.org/weta/thewest, and "Little Big Horn Battle (1876)" www.custerbooks.com and "Centennial Campaign (1876)" www.custerbooks.com)

[110]Adams, Ibid, 348.

[111]Present-day Mosby is located approximately three miles farther north down stream on the Musselshell.

the Western Trail came in from the east up the Big Dry Creek to continue on to the Judith Basin. Drovers and their herds from both forks continued up Flatwillow Creek until coming to the junction of Flatwillow Creek and Box Elder Creek. They continued in a northwest direction up Box Elder Creek to its head source in the Judith Mountains. Herds were then driven into the Judith Basin or straight north to the Missouri River and on to Fort Kelknap on the Milk River and into the North West Territories, Canada, later the provinces of Alberta and Saskatchewan. Adams wrote: "Our foremen…reported that the trail turned a due northward course towards the Missouri, and all herds had seemingly taken it."[112] Adams and the Circle Dot herd did not turn north, however, for their destination was the Blackfoot Agency in northwestern Montana Territory.[113]

For the most part, the Judith Basin in north central Montana Territory, was the destination for the cowboy outfits and their herds that followed this splinter route.

THE TRUNK LINE OF THE WESTERN CATTLE TRAIL CONTINUES TO THE NORTHERN RANGES:

Like trail drivers on the Judith Basin Splinter Route, drovers and their herds used the trunk line of the Western Cattle Trail that followed the Cheyenne-Black Hills Stage Route (Deadwood Trail) passed Fort Hat Creek Stage Station, trailed down Old Woman Creek, crossed Lance Creek, and climbed the divide before descending to the Cheyenne River. Drovers then followed the Cheyenne River to the confluence of that river and Lodgepole Creek where the Judith Basin Splinter Route broke away and headed northwest. The main trunk line, however, crossed the Cheyenne River at the Lodgepole and continued north up that creek continuing on through Wyoming Territory, into Montana Territory, and on into Canada.

In 1881, Richard Withers followed this trail. He had been engaged in Ogallala, Nebraska by James F. Ellison to deliver 6,500 head to the Belle Fourche. In his recollection, he said that they "went from Lodge Pole down the canyon [Buffalo Creek] to the Belle Fourche River, and within a week had the cattle branded and delivered." In 1881 "there was nothing there [three miles downstream from the mouth of Buffalo Creek] but a ranch, but now [in 1920-23] there is a railroad and the town of North Craft [Moorcroft]."[114]

---

[112]Adams, Ibid, 351. The authors speculate that some herds may have also headed north to the Missouri from the junction of Flatwillow and Musselshell creeks. They could trail into Fort Musselshell on the Missouri and beyond. (Palacios map, Ibid)

[113]The outfit and Circle Dot cattle continued on to Fort Benton by going west to intersect the Fort Maginnis Military Road that led to Fort Benton. From Fort Benton, they trailed on west about another 120 to 130 miles to the Blackfoot Agency. When the drovers continued west from the headwaters of the Big Box Elder and Judith Basin, they left the Judith Basin Splinter Route.

[114]At the time of Dick Withers' writing (between 1920-1923), he was living in Boyes, Montana "about one hundred miles from where I delivered those cattle on the Belle Fourche River below the old ranch." (Richard (Dick) Withers, "The Experience of an Old Trail Driver," in Hunter, 316)

Trailing cattle on this main trunk line is also recorded in J.E. May's journal of 1884. May drove cattle up the trail for the LS Ranch which had a finishing ranch in Montana. The home ranch, unfenced and almost as large as the state of Connecticut, since 1881, was one of the pioneer ranches of the Texas Panhandle. The owners, W.M.D. Lee and Lucien B. Scott, the Lee-Scott Cattle Company, had leased pastures along Cedar Creek in Montana in 1884 and, for four years thereafter, sent outfits up the trail to that finishing ranch. May simply recorded in his log book, without any comment, the exact route and the number of miles between each point, starting from Buffalo Springs in the Texas Panhandle to Cedar Creek, Montana.[115]

Another record of this route is from Ealy Moore's journal of 1892. Moore worked for the XIT Ranch, a neighbor to the LS Ranch. Starting in 1892, Moore led herds up the trail to the XIT's finishing range also located on Cedar Creek in Montana. For four years, starting in the spring, Moore took two-year-olds over the 850-mile trail to the Montana range. Moore's narrative starts when he left the XIT headquarters at Channing, Texas on April 20, 1892. Moore bossed one of five herds that were sent up by XIT that year. The other four herds were headed by Ab Owings, Chris Gish, Dan Cole, and Milt Whipple. Col. A. G. Boyce, general manager of the XIT, and George Findlay, business manager, tallied out 2,500 head to each trail boss and advised each one to "Keep your eye on the north star and drive straight ahead until you wet your feet in the waters of the Yellowstone."[116]

Both the May and Moore journals record basically the same route from the Texas Panhandle, trailing across No Man's Land, (western Oklahoma), through Colorado, and on into Wyoming to the Cheyenne River crossing. In 1884 and 1892, the dates of these journals, the pathway across Kansas and Nebraska was soon to shift (1884) or had been realigned west of those states (1892). (This is discussed in Part III.) Moore records that the XIT herds reached the Cheyenne River on June 30, 1892, and had been on the trail since April 20th, a total of 72 days. They had replenished their supply wagon in Springfield, Lamar, Hugo, and Brush in Colorado and at Lusk in Wyoming.[117]

The five herds of the XIT took three days to cover the several miles up the Lodgepole before starting down to Buffalo Creek.[118] On the 3rd of July, 1892, Moore wrote: "Lay over, so as the four herds that was right with me could get a little ahead. And camped on the head water of Lodge Pole."[119] After crossing the divide between the Lodgepole and Buffalo Creek, drovers and herds trailed down Buffalo Creek to

---

[115] May's log is printed in the Appendix of J. Evetts Haley's book, *The XIT Ranch of Texas*, 230-231 and in *The Herald* of Lusk, Wy., on July 18, 1940. May's log reads like a road map — camping stops and mileage between each daily drive are meticulously recorded. In Haley, however, there is a line left out of the log. *The Herald* show that line to be: Cross Platte — at Mouth of Rawhide Creek, follow up Rawhide Creek" — to mouth of J.M. Creek.

[116] Moore's 1892 log is also printed in Haley's book, *The XIT Ranch of Texas*, Appendix, 230-240 and in the Lusk *Herald*. Since J. E. May's journal is presented alongside Ealy Moore's journal in these two sources, some assume that the May journal was used as a guide by Moore. (Hans Gautschi, "Texas-Montana Trail," *The Herald*, Lusk, Wy, July 18, 1940

[117] Haley, Ibid, Moore journal, 238-240.

[118] There are two markers in this area of Weston County. One is just west of Lodgepole Creek on Highway 450, about twenty three miles west of Newcastle, Wy. The other is approximately three miles north of the Lodgepole on Highway 116, or about nineteen miles south of Upton, Wy.

[119] Moore journal in Haley, Ibid., 234.

THE WESTERN CATTLE TRAIL | 1874-1897

3

WYOMING

TEXAS TRAIL - 1866-1897

FOLLOWING THE CIVIL WAR, CONSTRUCTION OF THE TRANSCONTINENTAL RAILROAD OPENED THE WEST, ENSURING ELIMINATION OF VAST BUFFALO HERDS AND FORCING NATIVE AMERICAN INDIANS ONTO RESERVATIONS WHERE THE MILITARY PROVIDED FOOD.

LEGGY TEXAS LONGHORNS WERE MOVED AS FAR NORTH AS CANADA TO TAKE ADVANTAGE OF OPEN RANGE GRAZING AND LUCRATIVE GOVERNMENT CONTRACTS. THESE ROUTES BECAME KNOWN COLLECTIVELY AS THE TEXAS TRAIL. ONE ENTERED WYOMING NEAR CHEYENNE, HEADED NORTH PAST FORT LARAMIE, NEWCASTLE, AND UPTON, INTO MOORCROFT AND THEN WEST TO POWDER RIVER WHERE IT UNRAVELED LIKE A POOR PIECE OF ROPE. COWHAND BOB FUDGE RECALLED A DRIVE IN NORTHEAST WYOMING. "WE HAD BEEN TOLD THAT FROM THE CHEYENNE RIVER TO POWDER RIVER THERE WAS LIKELY NO WATER, WHICH WE SURELY FOUND OUT....THE WEATHER WAS HOT AND AT THE END OF THE SECOND DAY THE CATTLE COMMENCED TO GRIND THEIR TEETH IN THEIR SUFFERING.... THEIR GROANS WERE ENOUGH TO RAISE THE HAIR ON A WOODEN INDIAN."

DROVERS LEARNED THE BEST SIZE HERD TO MOVE A LONG DISTANCE WAS 2,500 HEAD. THE HERD STRETCHED OUT FOR A MILE OR MORE WITH COWBOYS PLACED ALONG THE EDGES DEPENDING ON THEIR SKILL. EXPERIENCED COWBOYS RODE POINT TO DIRECT THE HERD. OTHERS RODE DRAG AT THE BACK, EATING THE DUST OF THOSE AHEAD. THE REST WERE SPACED IN-BETWEEN AT FLANK AND SWING. HERDS MOVED SLOWLY TO AVOID STAMPEDE. CATTLE COULD BE MOVED 10-15 MILES A DAY, 300-500 MILES A MONTH AND COULD GAIN WEIGHT IF SKILFULLY MANAGED. COWBOYS WERE PAID AT THE END OF THE RIDE AND USUALLY RETURNED HOME WITH THE WAGONS AND HORSES. SOME STAYED BEHIND AND STARTED RANCHES OF THEIR OWN. ONE COWBOY, JOHN B. KENDRICK, COME TO WYOMING WITH A TEXAS HERD, MARRIED THE CATTLEMAN'S DAUGHTER, AND EVENTUALLY BECAME GOVERNOR. SUCH IS THE STUFF OF LEGEND.

WESTON COUNTY HISTORICAL SOCIETY & ANNA MILLER MUSEUM

Location: on Highway 450 in Weston County, Wyoming, 23 miles west of Newcastle, Wyoming

Authors' commentary:
The wording on the marker is well done, but the traveler should not jump to the conclusion that Texas cattle started coming into Wyoming right after the Civil War in 1866. It is true that "Texas Longhorns were moved as far north as Canada to take advantage of open range," but not until a decade later (1876).

The marker mentions "routes," and that they were "collectively known as the Texas Trail," and at the Powder River, "it unraveled like a poor piece of rope." All of these comments allude to the different splinter routes that are discussed in this book. In fact, the quote from Bob Fudge is about his 1882 trail drive in which the drovers used the Judith Bason Splinter Route that left the main trail at the junction of the Cheyenne River and Lodgepole Creek.

The third line of the second paragraph needs to be corrected and should read instead: "One entered Wyoming near Pine Bluffs, headed north, east of Lusk, west of present-day Newcastle and Upton, into present-day Moorcroft and then west to the Powder River..."

According to the *News Letter Journal*, this marker and the one 20 miles south of Upton, were placed there as a project of Leonard Cash, local historian and president of the Weston County Historical Society, who oversaw the project for eight years to its completion. The Weston County Travel Commission provided the funding for the project.[1] It is a good looking marker, and we are pleased that the ending date (1897) is correct.

---

[1] "Along the Texas Trail, Longhorns, Cowboys passed through Weston," picture and article, *News Letter Journal*, Newcastle, Wyoming, Nov. 2, 1995.

348   THE WESTERN CATTLE TRAIL | 1874-1897

the Belle Fourche River. The journey from the mouth of the Lodgepole, down the Buffalo, and to the Belle Fourche was sixty miles, according May's journal.

A roadhouse/saloon called LaBelle, established in 1892 and run by Jacob Kaufman was located at the Belle Fourche crossing. Kaufman was known as "Jew Jake." The roadhouse and crossing was at the mouth of Donkey Creek and the Belle Fourche River, one mile west of present-day Moorcroft. The Chicago, Burlington and Quincy Railroad laid rails toward the area in 1891, and a 159-acre plot of ground was purchased from a homesteader in order to establish a town along the line. By the following May of 1892, Lucian H. Robinson established the first store in a twelve by fourteen walled tent, and the town site became known as Moorcroft. Soon afterwards, there was a mail route between Moorcroft and Sundance and the stage made three trips a week to the location.[120] When Moore crossed the Belle Fourche a couple of months later in 1892, "Jew Jake's" roadhouse would have been at the crossing, and Robinson's tent store at the new town of Moorcroft would have been under way.

Within a couple of seasons, the LaBelle roadhouse was gone. By 1894, when Bob Fudge came through, only the town of Moorcroft was mentioned. Fudge was now a trail boss for the XIT:

> ...we came up the trail which I had travelled four times before. We joined this old trail not far from where Brush, Colorado is now. We kept the old trail as far as the Cheyenne River where we took off in a northeast [north, northwest] direction for the head of Little Powder River. We crossed the Belle Fourche River a few miles above where Moorcroft, Wyoming is now. In taking this northeast [north, northwest] route from the Cheyenne River, we saved many miles of trail from the way I went in '86 [the Judith Basin Feeder Route].[121]
>
> [I] remember the Burlington Railroad was graded a few miles west of the Belle Fourche River that summer [1894]. Our cattle were afraid of the grade. We had to put the remuda across in front of the herd before they would cross that freshly moved dirt. This railroad brought thousands of settlers to the country. Their homes are now scattered everywhere over the vast country which in 1882 I thought no one would ever live in. There was nothing in that whole country then but rattlesnakes, rabbits and cactus.[122]

---

[120]LaBelle was located where the trail crossed Highway 16, one mile west of present-day Moorcroft. (http://townofmoorcroft.com/History.htm [accessed August 28, 2009] and Margaret Bowden, *1916 Wyoming*, no page no.)

[121]To Fudge this route was "northeast" of the west route (Judith Basin Feeder Route) he had "travelled four times before." His actual direction from the Cheyenne River was northwest. In 1894, Fudge was with one of five herds that the XIT sent up to Cedar Creek that year. (Russell, Ibid, 61)

[122]The Burlington & Missouri Railroad actually arrived in Moorcroft in the summer of 1891 and continued on west. Here Fudge is simply commenting that he noticed a railroad at the location, where before, in 1886, there had not been a railroad. Bob Fudge also moved to Wyoming in his later years. To Jim Russell, his biographer, he commented: "This trail which we travelled down Little Powder River went across the land which I own now. As we grazed two thousand steers down that river in '94, I never dreamed that some day I would have a comfortable home along that trail." (Russell, Ibid, 61-62)

4

WYOMING

TEXAS TRAIL - 1866-1897

FOLLOWING THE CIVIL WAR, CONSTRUCTION OF THE TRANSCONTINENTAL RAILROAD OPENED THE WEST, ENSURING ELIMINATION OF THE BUFFALO HERDS, FORCING NATIVE AMERICAN INDIANS ONTO RESERVATIONS WHERE THE MILITARY PROVIDED FOOD. THE RAILS TRANSPORTED RANGE FATTENED CATTLE TO EASTERN MARKETS. THE RANGE CATTLE INDUSTRY SPREAD OVER THE CENTRAL AND NORTHERN PLAINS, AND BECAME ONE OF THE MOST SIGNIFICANT ECONOMIC DEVELOPMENTS IN LATE 19TH CENTURY U.S. HISTORY.

WITHIN A DECADE, CATTLE WAS KING, PROVIDING: JOBS FOR VETERANS, EXOTIC INVESTMENT OPPORTUNITY FOR FOREIGN INVESTORS, MARKETS FOR EXCESS GRAIN PRODUCED BY IMPROVED FARMING METHODS, FOOD FOR EASTERN INDUSTRIAL CENTERS AND ROMANTIC VISIONS OF LIVE IN THE WEST.

LEGGY TEXAS LONGHORNS MOVED AS FAR NORTH AS CANADA TO TAKE ADVANTAGE OF OPEN RANGE GRAZING AND LUCRATIVE GOVERNMENT CONTRACTS. THESE ROUTES BECAME KNOWN COLLECTIVELY AS THE "TEXAS TRAIL." ONE ENTERED WYOMING NEAR CHEYENNE, HEADED NORTH PAST FORT LARAMIE, NEWCASTLE, UPTON, INTO MOORCROFT, AND THEN WEST TO POWDER RIVER WHERE IT UNRAVELED LIKE A POOR PIECE OF ROPE. COWHAND BOB FUDGE RECALLED A CATTLE DRIVE IN NORTHEAST WYOMING. "WE HAD BEEN TOLD THAT FROM THE CHEYENNE RIVER TO POWDER RIVER THERE WAS LIKELY NO WATER, WHICH WE SURELY FOUND OUT.... THE WEATHER WAS HOT AND AT THE END OF THE SECOND DAY THE CATTLE COMMENCED TO GRIN THEIR TEETH IN THEIR SUFFERING... THEIR GROANS WERE ENOUGH TO RAISE THE HAIR ON A WOODEN INDIAN."

EVENTUALLY, PIONEERS SETTLED THE OPEN RANGE AND POOR BUSINESS PRACTICES COMBINED WITH HARSH WEATHER FORCED THE CATTLE BARONS TO CHANGE THEIR WAYS. BY 1888 THE VOLUME OF CATTLE DRIVEN FROM TEXAS NORTH TO THE OPEN PLAINS DWINDLED, AND BY 1900, THE DRIVES HAD CEASED ALTOGETHER.

WESTON COUNTY HISTORICAL SOCIETY & ANNA MILLER MUSEUM

Location: on Highway 116 in Weston County, Wyoming, 20 miles south of Upton, Wyoming

Authors' commentary:
This marker was one of two markers in Weston County erected in 1995 under the leadership of Leonard Cash, local historian and president of the Weston County Historical Society. The other marker (23 miles west of Newcastle) is only slightly different in wording than this one.

Again, there could be some confusion in the information in the first paragraph. The cattle industry that developed in this region did not occur until some fifteen years after the end of the Civil War (1866).

The Union Pacific Railroad did not reach this area until 1881. The phase: "Within a decade, cattle was king," probably means that in the decade of 1876 to 1886, the cattle industry in Wyoming was flourishing.

The third line of the third paragraph needs to be corredted and should read instead; "One entered Wyoming near Pine Bluffs, headed north, east of Lusk, west of present-day Newcastle and Upton, into present-day Moorcroft and then west to the Powder River…"

The last cattle drive to the north from Texas was in 1897, as correctly indicated in the title of this marker. The overland trek of through cattle from Texas did not last until 1900, as stated in the last line.

350   THE WESTERN CATTLE TRAIL | 1874-1897

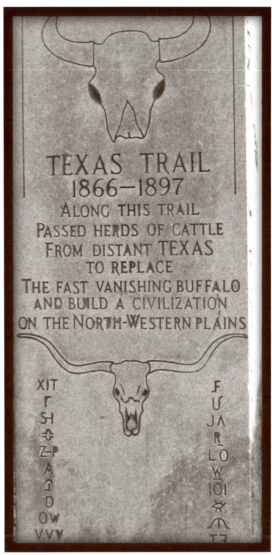

Location: *In rest area on the north side of Highway I-90, west of Moorcroft, Crook County, Wyoming*

Authors' commentary:
This is an attractive stone marker. The Texas Trail (Western Cattle Trail), in Wyoming, however, existed from 1876 to 1897. The 1866 date that most of these Wyoming markers used was the beginning date for the Shawnee Trail System through Kansas immediately after the Civil War. The Texas Trail, as labeled here, came into existence a decade later.

In August of 1894, Perry Davis, who was with an outfit driving a herd of horses from South Dakota to the home ranch in Texas, came through the Belle Fourche valley from the north, and, in his journal, he spoke of Moorcroft and Jew Jake:

> …we proceeded on our journey to the south…. After pulling over a long slope for about three miles, we reached the divide which brings us in plain view of the Belle Fourche valley with its beautiful groves of cottonwood. Some distance to the right, we saw a large smoke which proved to be the dust rising from the cattle trails which led to the river, where hundreds of cattle were going and coming from water. Camped on the river opposite Moorecroft [sic]. Locomotive whistle stampedes the mare herd. First whistle heard for eleven months. Horses were unaccustomed to the snort of the iron horse. Nothing left of the old Jew Jake ranch but the well and cellar.[123]

---

[123] Wayne H. Gossard, Jr., the Colorado Historical Society, "Life on the Trail: the 1894 Diary of Perry Eugene Davis," *Colorado Heritage Magazine*, 1981 serials collection, 26.

THE WESTERN CATTLE TRAIL | 1874-1897

Moorcroft in the mid 1890s became the largest cattle shipping point on the Chicago, Burrlington, and Quincy Railroad and a major stop-over for cattle herds headed on north to Miles City and beyond. In 1894, thirty two herds passed through Moorcroft. The Belle Fourche valley was an ideal location to allow herds to graze and rest whether the cattle had been trailed or hauled in by cattle cars. Texas Panhandle ranches could either trail herds to the Belle Fourche valley and beyond or ship cattle to Moorcroft and then unload the herd to be driven on to their satellite ranches in the north.

Sue Flanagan in her work, *Trailing the Longhorns*, states that from this crossing of the Belle Fourche, "the trail spread fan-like to the Dakotas; the Indian agencies; northern Wyoming; eastern, central, and western Montana; and the Canadian border."[124] The trunk line of the Western Cattle Trail continued north toward Miles City, and it is likely that some herds were trailed east, northeast from Moorcroft to the Sundance area (parallel to today's highway 90) north of the Black Hills to be delivered to ranches. One of the major splinter routes that Flanagan alludes to, from the Belle Fourche crossing, however, went northeast to deliver cattle along "the Belle Fourche River or some of the other tributaries of the Little Missouri in the good cattle country north of the Black Hills."[125] The trail continued as far north as Fort Buford at the confluence of the Yellowstone and the Missouri rivers in northwestern Dakota Territory.

THE LITTLE MISSOURI SPLINTER ROUTE TO FORT BUFORD — FROM THE BELLE FOURCHE RIVER IN WYOMING TERRITORY TO THE MISSOURI RIVER IN DAKOTA TERRITORY:

(Map #7-4)

A splinter route left the Western Cattle Trail to the northeast from the Belle Fourche crossing and followed the Little Missouri River into northwestern Dakota Territory. We refer to that route as the "Little Missouri Splinter Route." The best sources to describe this well-used splinter route are Andy Adams' narrative and Perry Eugene Davis' diary. Adams wrote about his experiences on the Judith Basin Splinter Route in 1882 to the Blackfoot Agency in northern Montana in his book, *The Log of a Cowboy*, published in 1903. Two years later, Adams published another book, *The Outlet*, in which he described his trail drive up the Western Cattle Trail to the Belle Fourche River in 1884 and then, leaving the main trunk line, delivered herds to Fort Buford on a splinter route. As in the 1903 *The Log of a Cowboy*, Adams wrote *The Outlet* in novel form with fictional characters, but the pathway that Andy Adams had taken as a trail cowboy is based on his own experience.

---

[124]Sue Flanagan, *Trailing the Longhorns*, 126.
[125]Ralph F. Jones, *Longhorns North of the Arkansas*, 14.

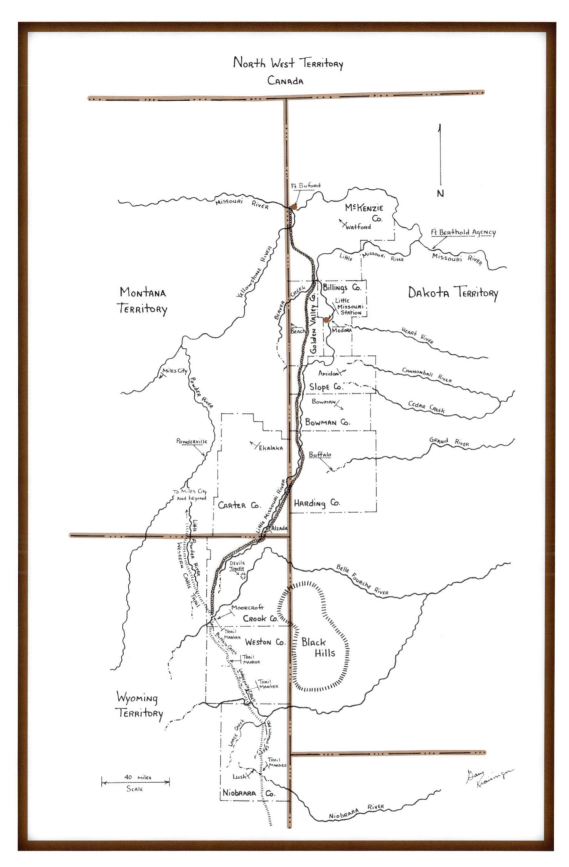

#7-4
The Little Missouri Splinter Route from the Belle Fourche River in Wyoming Territory to Fort Buford on the Missouri River in Dakota Territory:
This map shows the splinter route going north, following the Missouri River across Montana Territory into Dakota Territory, then continuing on north to the confluence of the Yellowstone River and the Missouri River.

THE WESTERN CATTLE TRAIL | 1874-1897

In *The Outlet*, Adams described himself, in the character of Tom, as twenty-eight years old, mustached, and six foot tall. The Medina County, Texas ranch where he worked had acquired a contract for "five million pounds of beef on foot" to be delivered to Fort Buford. To fill the contract, it would take three herds or ten thousand head, which had to be delivered by September 15, 1884. Adams explained, however, that his employer, Judge Noonan, owner of the Circle Dot Ranch, was putting a total of six herds on the trail that year: three herds for various Indian agencies in Dakota Territory and three for the government contract at Fort Buford, which was five hundred miles further north. The herds were mostly Circle Dot Ranch cattle with others mixed in. Cowboy Adams (Tom) was the foreman in charge of one of the three herds destined for Fort Buford on the Missouri River.

To prepare to drive these six herds north, ninety cowboys were hired at fifty dollars a month for six months. All the cowboys on this drive were unmarried. Great care and time was taken to select the finest horses, ones that could endure over 1,500 miles of travel.[126] Each drover was allotted ten horses, the foremen, twelve each, plus five extra horses for each herd to allow for horses that had to be left along the way.

The six herds left the ranch in Medina County, Texas on March 27, 1884, and followed the old Eastern Trail to the Red River Station Crossing and then crossed over to the Western Trail in Indian Territory and continued up the Western through Kansas and Nebraska. (Kansas had not yet closed its borders in 1884.) From Ogallala, the herds continued north to Moorcroft. After crossing the Belle Fourche River, the outfits turned northeast and followed the Little Missouri toward the Montana Territory border. To their right, drovers saw Devil's Tower looming in the distance, rising to 1,267 feet above the surrounding terrain. It could be seen from a distance of over fifty miles.[127]

Perry Eugene Davis was the cook responsible for the chuck wagon for an outfit driving a herd of 400 horses from the Hashknife horse ranch, located in southeastern Montana along Box Elder Creek, to the home ranch in the Texas Panhandle. Davis wrote a detailed diary of his trip in 1894 trailing from the north to the south. The drovers used this Little Missouri Splinter Route to the trunk line of the Western Cattle Trail. While Adams wrote his novel some twenty-one years after the fact, Davis' diary provides a meticulous record of his trip, including information on the weather, the scenery, and exact location on the trail.

Davis carefully recorded the camp stops between the Belle Fourche River crossing and Alzada on the Montana Territory border. By following the diary from north to south, however, we learn that the outfit left the Little Missouri, in the "sight of Devil's Tower," and camped "near oil wells at night" on South Deer Creek.[128] The

---

[126]Judge Noonan was credited as having some of the finest horses in Texas. His herd numbered three or four thousand head. Many of the horses were half thoroughbreds, but the small light Spanish ponies were used for trail work, "because wherever cattle were driven it took the Spanish horse to do the work." (Frank Collinson [cowboy on the Noonan Ranch], *Life in the Saddle*, 13-14)

[127]The monolith is located in Crook County, Wyoming, above the Belle Fourche River. The area of the sacred Bear Butte (Devil's Tower) and the Black Hills was very significant to the plains tribes. President Theodore Roosevelt declared Devil's Tower a U.S. national monument on Sept. 24, 1906.

[128]The oil wells that Davis refers to were part of the Osage Oil Fields which extended from the region of the Missouri Buttes and Devils' Tower to Newcastle, Wyoming. The first of these wells was drilled in 1890, four years before the Hashknife horse herd came through. (Wayne H. Gossard, Jr., Ibid, 26)

day before, the outfit had camped for the night at the mouth of Poison Creek, "which heads near the Little Missouri Buttes which loom up in the distance on the divide of the Little Missouri and Belle Fourche to the east." At noon they had stopped at the mouth of Prairie Creek, seven miles above the Elkhorn. The evening before that, they camped at the mouth of Elkhorn Canyon at an old TL bull camp where they corraled the mares, and their mid-day stop was at the forks of the North Little Missouri. The day before that, Davis had stocked his wagon at Alzada and drove to the mouth of Government Canyon for the night. It had taken five days from Alzada to Moorcroft on the Belle Fourche River, where the outfit "camped on the river opposite Moorecroft [sic]."[129]

Going north, drovers and their herds trailed on the west side of the Little Missouri River to the Montana Territory border and on to Alzada, likely camping at some of the same stops described in Davis' diary. Alzada was originally settled as a military telegraph relay station called "Stoneville," after the local saloon owner, Louis Stone. Stone had set up his depot in approximately 1878 for the soldiers on the Deadwood Road between Fort Keogh and Fort Meade, which also served as the stage route between Miles City and Deadwood, Dakota Territory. The area around Stoneville had been settled by cattle ranchers in the 1870s, especially after the gold rush of 1876. In the valleys of the Belle Fourche and Redwater rivers, for hundreds of miles in all directions, Texas cattle grazed on the open plains. The stage route to and from Miles City, Powderville, and the Deadwood area started around the same time. Thus, at the crossing of the Little Missouri, Louis Stone had picked an ideal spot to serve passing soldiers and travelers.

Stoneville's short-lived fame came in 1884, the same year that the Circle Dot herds and Andy Adams came through the area. The small town's locals stood up to a group of outlaws who called themselves the Exelby Gang. The incident sounds like a plot for a Hollywood western — when the locals, resentful of being harassed by the cattle and horse rustlers, had a shoot out with the ruffians and put them out of business. It became known as the "Shootout at Stoneville." In 1885, the town changed its name to the first name of a local pioneer rancher's wife's — Alzada.[130] By this time, the small town on the Little Missouri River crossing also found itself on the path of the Little Missouri River Splinter Route of the Western Cattle Trail in Montana Territory.[131]

---

[129]Wayne H. Gossard, ed., *Life on the Trail: the 1894 Diary of Perry Eugene Davis*, August 21 - August 25, 1894 entries. (http://coloradohistory.org/westerntrails [accessed July 22, 2007] Also found in *Colorado Heritage Magazine*, 1981.

[130]Stoneville probably had to change its name because a post office contract will not accept a duplicate or very similar name for a town in the same state. Stoneville must have filed for a post office in 1885. The settler's name was Laura Alzada Shelden. ("Alzada, Montana," http://www.ultimatemontana.com [accessed Sept. 14, 2009])

[131]The well-traveled Deadwood Road going southeast from Alzada to the Deadwood area and the Black Hills gold mines was used by Texas drovers as well. This route was used after the implementation of the Nebraska herd laws of 1886. When the pathway through Nebraska was no longer used, drovers used the more westerly route approaching the mining camps from the west, rather than from the east on the formerly described Fort Buford Splinter Route.

THE WESTERN CATTLE TRAIL | 1874-1897

According to Andy Adams, a half a million dollars' worth of native stock was lost in the fall of 1883 due to Texas Fever. In response to the severe Texas Fever outbreak, in which heavy losses were sustained, Montana Territory officials in 1884 tried to confine Texas cattle, driven through the southeast corner of the Territory, in order to isolate them for the winter or until heavy frost. Officials knew that if herds experienced a freezing-cold winter period, the Texas Fever was eradicated. To keep the local cattle separated from the in-coming Texas herds, camps of enforcers were established in the southeast corner of Montanta Territory along the Wyoming Territory border demanding that all Texas herds trail down the east side of the Powder River. Local range riders, in turn, were to keep all native cattle to the west of the river. Texas cattle were to be "controlled" east of the river and south of a deadline drawn from Powderville eastward to the Dakota Territory line. The quarantine area was open grazing ground that could accommodate half a million cattle for the winter or at least until a frost released the quarantine hold. However, if papers could be produced that herds wintered north of the 37th degree of latitude, they were allowed to pass. To avoid the quarantine, the cattle destined for Fort Buford went east and "grazed across [into] Dakota [Territory] from the Little Missouri to the mouth of the Yellowstone." The "quarantine was working a hardship to herds along the old Powder River route," reported Adams in *The Outlet*.[132]

After leaving Alzada, the main pathway of the Little Missouri Splinter Route of the Western Trail continued on north, following the Little Missouri and crossing over into Dakota Territory.

Perry Davis, August 19, 1894:

> Camped for dinner on the head of Lo Creek. Pulled across to the Little Missouri in evening and hobbled saddle horses. Camped ten mile above Stoneville.

Once into Dakota Territory, the outfits and herds stayed on the divide between the Yellowstone and the Little Missouri even though it "was a narrow one, requiring little time to graze across it." The Circle Dot herds bound for Fort Buford continued up the Little Missouri "crossing and recrossing it frequently" The river led the trail drivers through the Dakota Badlands. Adams described their descent off of the divide into the settlement of "Little Missouri," near present-day Medora, North Dakota:

> Sponsilier held the lead all the way down the river [Little Missouri], though I did most of the advance scouting, sometimes being as much as fifty miles in front of the herds. Near the last of the month [August] we sighted Sentinel Butte and the smoke of railroad trains, and a few days later all three of us foremen rode into Little Missouri Station of the Northern Pacific Railway....for as we approached the straggling village, our employer was recognized at a distance, waving his hat, and a minute later all three of us were shaking hands...

The herds crossed the railroad about a mile west of Little Missouri Station. A great deal of freighting was taking place at Little Missouri. Adams saw "numerous ox and mule trains coming in and also leaving for their destinations."[133]

The small settlement of Little Missouri was on the west side of the Little Missouri River opposite to the future Medora. Spawned from a military camp known as Badlands Cantonment, the post was established in 1879 to protect the surveying and construction crews of the Northern Pacific Railroad. Between the Cantonment and the river, the settlement had developed and continued to thrive even

---

[132]Adams, *The Outlet*, 276-277, 286.
[133]Adams, Ibid, 262, 274.

after the Northern Pacific was completed and the Cantonment was abandoned in early 1883. As described earlier, French aristocrat, Marquis de Mores, with his financial backing, moved to the opposite side of the river, next to a railroad siding and started the town of Medora, named after his wife. When Medora began to flourish, many of the Little Missouri businessmen and tavern owners moved across the river.

The trail to Fort Buford was ninety miles north of the settlement of Little Missouri. The three Circle Dot herds had grazed across the divide and down into the Missouri River valley in order to meet the contract's deadline of September 15. But Tom (Adams) and three others had been delayed by officials and quarantine issues and had had to travel the trail all night in order to reach their herds in time. They continued to follow the Little Missouri River for about ten miles and then "bore directly north until Beaver Creek was reached near midnight." Adams described the push across the divide between the Beaver and the Yellowstone River:

> The pace was set at about an eightmile, steady clip, with an occasional halt to tighten cinches or shift saddles. The horses were capable of a faster gait without tiring, but we were not sure of the route and were saving them for the finish after daybreak....
>
> Day broke about five in the morning. We had been in the saddle nearly ten hours, and were confident that sunrise would reveal some landmark to identify our location. The atmosphere was frosty and clear, and once the gray of dawn yielded to the rising sun, the outline of the Yellowstone was easily traced on our left, while the bluffs in our front shielded a view of the mother Missouri. In attempting to approach the latter we encountered some rough country and were compelled to turn towards the former, crossing it, at O'Brian's roadhouse, some eleven miles above the mouth....The outfits were encamped on the eastern side of the Yellowstone; and before leaving the government road [Ft. Keogh-Ft. Buford Road], we sighted in our front the flag ascending to greet the morning, and the location of Fort Buford.[134]

Fort Buford, at the confluence of the Missouri and Yellowstone rivers, had been established in 1866, but by 1884 when the Circle Dot herds reached the fort, it was a noted supply depot for other posts farther west on the Missouri and Yellowstone rivers. The fort was the end of a long trip for the Texas cowboys and their herds.[135]

The trail drivers visited the small town of Buford above the fort and prepared for their return to Texas. Some drovers, however, wintered out in the northern Dakota Territory, and one of these was Andy Adams.[136] He called it "the winter of our discontent." A boy from the south, he described his first Dakota winter:

---

[134]Adams, Ibid, 311-313.

[135]When the area became settled in the 1890s, Fort Buford's usefulness ceased. It was abandoned in October of 1895. In 1924, the location became a state historic site.

[136]The government contract was not completed at Fort Buford so one outfit of drovers had to winter out the cattle on a Little Missouri ranch. In the following spring, the fort's agent again contracted for beef which gave reason for the continued existence of the northern ranch.

To that long winter on the Little Missouri a relentless memory turns in retrospect. We dressed and lived like Eskimos. The first blizzard struck us early in December, the thermometer dropped sixty degrees in twelve hours, but in the absence of wind and snow the cattle did not leave the breaks along the river. Three weeks later a second one came, and we could not catch the lead animals until near the railroad; but the storm drove them up the Little Missouri, and its sheltering banks helped us to check our worst winter drift. After the first month of wintry weather, the dread of the cold passed, and men and horses faced the work as though it was springtime in our own loved southland.[137]

The Little Missouri Splinter Route of the Western Trail continued to be used to Fort Buford for about four more years. The Circle-Dot ranch sent three more herds up in 1885 to their Little Missouri ranch for distribution to the fort and for shipping out. The herds and drovers "followed the same route as our herds of the year before," wrote Adams, and "The first of the through cattle arrived early in September," but the cattle were not mixed on the ranch because of the fear of the Texas Fever. The 1885 season was so successful with cattle prices reaching $60 to $65 per head, that the owner "was a quarter-million dollars to the good."[138]

According to his book, Adams stayed as foreman of the Little Missouri Ranch in North Dakota Territory for five years. In 1889 —

the stock, goodwill, and range were sold to a cattle syndicate, who installed a superintendent and posted rules for the observance of its employees. I do not care to say why, but in a stranger's hands it never seemed quite the same home to a few of us who were present when it was transformed into a cattle range. Late that fall, some half-dozen of us who were from Texas asked to be relieved and returned to the South.[139]

The cattle driving industry of through cattle was rapidly slowing down. Syndicates and foreign-owned empires were taking over the family ranches in the north, including those at the mouth of the Beaver on the Little Missouri. The farther eastern route to Fort Buford, the Fort Buford Splinter Route via Nebraska, even though it was an easier route, dryer and faster than the Missouri River route, was not used after 1886. Even though Circle Dot herds were driven into Fort Buford only until 1888, other Texas herds may have been driven to the fort to 1894, before it was abandoned in 1895.

---

[137]Adams, "The Winter of Our Discontent," last chapter of *The Outlet*. The quote is from page 366.
[138]Adams, Ibid, 370.
[139]Adams, Ibid, 366. In 1890 Andy Adams left the cattle business and ventured to Colorado to follow the gold mining boom. He also went to Nevada and Kentucky to look for gold. After being unsuccessful at this venture, he went back to Colorado Springs, Colorado and started writing about his life. He died there in 1935. He never married. (C. D. Merriman, "Andy Adams," www.online.literature.com [accessed Oct. 25, 2013])

THE TRUNK LINE OF THE WESTERN CATTLE TRAIL CONTINUES FROM THE BELLE FOURCHE RIVER CROSSING, WYOMING TERRITORY TO MILES CITY, FORT PECK, MONTANA TERRITORY AND TOWARD CANADA: (Map #7-2)

A few miles north of the Belle Fourche River crossing near the town of Moorcroft, the Little Missouri River Splinter Route left the main trunk line of the Western Cattle Trail and followed the present-day "D" Road straight north to the Little Missouri River and then went downriver northeast to Fort Buford. The trunk line of the Western Trail, which was a heavily-used pathway, continued north on the "D" Road a few miles, but then turned northwest to cross over the divide to the Cottonwood Creek, and from there continued down the Cottonwood to the Little Powder River, some thirty-two miles away. It was a three-day trail drive. On the Little Powder, the trail continued in the valley for sixty miles before reaching the big Powder River. Some twenty miles of this stretch of the trail was through the Powder River badlands. Ealy Moore, with the XIT herds in 1892, noted in his journal: "Drove through a rough piece of country and camped on L. P. [Little Powder] about 10 miles below [the Powder River badlands]."[140]

Maude L. Beach, in her "Historical Outline of Powder River Country," in a 1942 article described where the trail crossed the Powder River: "the Old Texas Trail, which on its last lap into Montana led through the whole length of present Powder River Country, down the Little Powder to its mouth (just below the present site of the County Seat, Broadus) where it crossed [the Powder over] to the Tongue,…"[141]

The Powder River was a very dangerous river to cross with a reputation of being a mile wide and an inch deep. It was not a deep river, but quicksand was a threat in addition to flash flooding. Robert E. Straborn, author of Wyoming's first guidebook in 1877, wrote that "we have nothing good to say of Powder River…Its waters are darkly mysterious and villianously alkalied."[142] Struthers Burt who wrote of the Powder River in 1938, said that the river was "by no means a mile wide and considerably over an inch deep," but that the "narrow, yellow, winding little river" was fierce "in the spring floods, coiling torpid and slow in the summer heat like a rattlesnake." It was spotted with "the horrid blackness of quicksands." But the Powder River is a famous river and Burt asked:

> How, then did this river, short, ugly, unvirtuous, almost anonymous, born to every handicap, become the most famous river in a state filled with lovely rivers?

---

[140]J. Evetts Haley, *The XIT*, Moore's July 11, 1892 journal entry, 235.

[141]Maude L. Beach, comp. article, "Historical Outline of Powder River Country," Feb. 19, 1942, in *Faded Hoof Prints — Bygone Dreams*, 20.

[142]As quoted in Struthers Burt book, *Powder River, Let'er Buck*, 11.

Famous now all over the country, its name familiar to thousands who haven't the faintest idea where the river is, or whether it's an actual river or merely an exclamation. A river spoken of with contempt by all who first saw it, whose name has become a battle cry. A shout of encouragement. A cry of derision. A password to a secret society. And above all a symbol of an American way of living…[143]

Two more creeks had to be crossed before reaching the Yellowstone. According to May's journal, it was another fifteen miles to the Mizpah and then on to the Pumpkin Creek, some eighteen more miles. Upon approaching the Pumpkin, the trail drivers followed the Pumpkin downstream toward the Tongue River. Moore, leading the XIT herds in 1892, recorded that they camped near the "Beebe P. O. on Pumpkin Creek," on July 19.[144] The journey down Pumpkin. Creek to the Tongue and then to the Yellowstone was, according to May's journal, sixty miles in length. As herds approached the Yellowstone, they were within a few miles of Miles City, a destination point for some Texas herds.

The trail continued north of the Yellowstone River, and herds crossed the river above the confluence of the north-flowing Tongue River and the east-flowing Yellowstone River. Moore pointed out in his July 22 journal entry that they "watered on Tongue river and camped on the breaks of the Yellow Stone."[145] Approximately two miles east on the Yellowstone was Miles City.

On the south side of the Yellowstone just west of its confluence with the Tongue River sat Fort Keogh. General Nelson A. Miles had established the "Cantonment Tongue River" in the summer of 1876. The site provided easy access to the boats that brought supplies up the Yellowstone River. As noted previously, the purpose of the cantonment was to bring the Indians under control and to move them onto reservations.[146]

Miles City started like so many other fort towns. Whiskey peddlers followed the soldiers and soon set up "shop" on the military reservation to provide soldiers liquid refreshments. One such establishment was started by Mat Carrol who merely placed some barrels under a tarp and started to sell whiskey. When these peddlers became a problem because of the number of soldiers sent to the guard house for drunken behavior, General Miles ran the vendors off of the reservation. Shortly afterward, John Carter squatted just beyond the reservation boundry on a flat piece of ground

---

[143]Struthers Burt, *Powder River, Let'er Buck*, 10-11. The yell of "Powder River!" was a battle cry of Teddy Roosevelt's Rough Riders when they went up San Juan Hill during the Spanish-American War and also during World War I in Europe. (Ralph F. Jones, *Longhorns North of the Arkansas*, 15)

[144]The Beebe Post Office was established in 1890. It is located at the intersection of Highway 59 and Beebe Road #203 on Pumpkin Creek. Highway 59 closely follows the Western Trail from the Little Powder to Rock Springs.

[145]Ealy Moore journal entry in Haley, Ibid, 235. The Tongue River is a tributary of the Yellowstone and empties into the Yellowstone in the Miles City area.

[146]Not only was General Miles a well respected leader among his soldiers, but he also gained trust from some of the Sioux and the Crow. He was able to bring some tribesmen to reservations with a promise of a better life.

on the south side of the Yellowstone. He built a log hut of driftwood and started to sell whiskey. Other merchants soon joined Carter, and "Milestown" was born, named after the military post's commander. Subsequently, General Nelson Miles moved the stockade a couple of miles southwest hoping to distance the soldiers from this rowdy den of temptation. The cantonment officially became Fort Keogh on November 8, 1878. General Miles' strategy to isolate the troops from the grog shops didn't work. The town peddlers simply moved their shacks closer to the reservations' edge — to the city's current location, and its name evolved to Miles City. The Northern Pacific Railroad arrived in Miles City on November 21, 1881.[147]

After crossing the very swift and cold, treacherous Yellowstone River above Fort Keogh, the herds belonging to the LS Ranch[148] and the XIT[149] left the trail and delivered their cattle to those two ranches' northern ranges along Cedar Creek. Cattle destined for the extreme northern portions of Montana and Canada, however, continued in a northerly direction a few miles to North Sunday Creek, then trailed up to its headwaters, some forty miles north of the Yellowstone River crossing.[150] George W. Huss, a local Miles City historian, asserts that trail drivers and their herds continued on north of Miles City, "up Sunday Creek, up [down] the Little Dry [Creek], and along the Big Dry to the Missouri...." or they turned up the Big Dry and continued "to the Musselshell."[151] Herds crossed the Missouri near the Fort Peck Indian Agency.

The Fort Peck Indian Agency was not a military post. The old Fort Peck had been a stockade built on the Missouri River in 1867 by Abel Farwell of the Durfee and Peck firm who operated trading posts up and down the Missouri River. In 1871, the Milk River Indian Agency purchased the post from Durfee and Peck and moved it from the mouth of People's Creek on the Milk River to a location on the Missouri. It became the Fort Peck Indian Agency.

The agency served the Assiniboine, Brule, Teton, Hunkpapa and Yankton Sioux tribes, and it continued to be a trading post and an Indian agency for another eight years. It also served at times as temporary headquarters for the military when the government was negotiating with the Indians. Its stockade, perched on a narrow ledge of shale about thrity five feet above the Missouri River, was built with twelve-foot cottonwood logs set vertically in the ground, with three bastions and four gateways. The rear walls laid against the hillside. Although it was in convenient proximity to the river and the steamboats, and although it possessed a good wharf,

---

[147]Sue Flanagan in her book, *Trailing the Longhorns*, stated that Texas herds first arrived at Fort Keogh in 1880, page 136. Troops withdrew from Fort Keogh in 1907 and, in 1909, Fort Keogh became a remount station for the U.S. Army. The station supplied thousands of horses for World War I. The Army relinquished the land and withdrew in 1922 and 1924 and the ownership was transferred to the U.S. Department of Agriculture. It is now a Livestock and Range Research Laboratory. ("Fort Keogh," www.ars.usda.gov/Main and "Fort Keogh," http://fortwiki.com [accessed Aug. 30, 2009 and Sept. 7, 2009])
[148]Reference: J.E. May 1884 journal.
[149]Reference: Ealy Moore 1892 journal and the Bob Fudge 1894 trip.
[150]Flanagan, Ibid, 138.
[151]George W. Huss. Miles City, Montana. Speech at the dedication of the Western Cattle Trail marker in Miles City, Miles City Club, August 7, 2010.

the river continued to cut away at the bank near the fort. During the mid 1870s, "the front of the stockade was so close to the edge of the ledge that there was barely room to turn around with a team and wagon," one visitor wrote.[152]

Finally, because the stockade was subject to flooding each spring and was in danger of being washed away by the river, a new Fort Peck Agency was relocated to Poplar Creek in 1878 or mid 1879. Cowboy outfits and their herds crossing the Missouri River near the old Fort Peck Agency in the 1880s and 1890s would have seen an abandoned stockade surrounding the remnants of log buildings, shops, stables and a corral, all were gradually being eroded away by the river.[153]

After crossing the Missouri River, herds proceeded up the Milk River, passing the town of Glasgow, established in 1887, which came into existence when the Great Northern Railroad came through. At the confluence of the Frenchman Creek or Whitewater Creek, drovers could then follow either creek into present-day southwest Saskatchewan, Canada, or continue up the Milk River to present-day southeast Alberta.[154]

THE WESTERN CATTLE TRAIL TO THE NORTH WEST TERRITORIES, CANADA:

Just as the northern territories of the Dakotas, Wyoming, and Montana were rapidly changing from predominantly Indian hunting grounds to farms and ranches developed by whites starting in 1876-1877, the same transformation was occurring across the border in the North West Territories of Canada. Less than a decade earlier, in 1869, the Canadian government had purchased Rupert's Land from the Hudson's Bay Company and the vast region — which includes present-day Alberta, Saskatchewan, Manitoba, and other provinces — became the country's "North West Territory." In order to establish sovereignty and to encourage settlement for farming and ranching, the Canadian government enacted the Dominion Land Act in 1872 which allowed for grazing leases, but the leases could be canceled for any reason with six months' notice. This land policy was not successful in promoting settlement, and the Plains Indians continued to occupy the region. After the area had been relinquished by the Hudson's Bay Company, lawlessness was rampant. Buffalo and wolf hunters were killing, to the point of extermination, the buffalo and wolves, and hide traders roamed at will throughout the region exchanging alcohol for valuable furs, robes, and horses from the Indians. The Hudson's Bay Company had banned trade in alcohol and had the power to enforce the ban, but by 1873, with the Bay Company no longer in charge, alcohol had become the principal trade commodity in the exchange for furs.[155]

---

[152]"Old Fort Peck," http://www.fortpeckdam.com/history [accessed Sept. 10. 2009]

[153]"Old Fort Peck," http://www.fortpeckdam.com/history and http://www.fortpecktribes.org. Camp Poplar was established in 1880 at the newly located Fort Peck Agency on Poplar Creek. The river channel changed in 1918 and destroyed all traces of the site of old Fort Peck.

[154]The huge area was known then as the North-West Territories. Alberta and Saskatchewan did not become provinces until 1905.

[155]"Royal Canadian Mounted Police History," http://www.essortment.com/royal-canadian-mounted-police-history-21218.html [accessed June 19, 2012]

In order to get control of the situation so that a planned trans-Canadian railroad could push into the newly organized region, and so that homesteaders and ranchers would be willing to risk settlement, the Canadian Parliament established a police force for the region in May of 1873, appropriately named the North West Mounted Police. By the following summer almost 300 mounted, uniformed policemen marched into the North West territory in search of whisky forts and rogue traders. In October of 1874, a permanent post, Fort Macleod, was built on the banks of Oldman River in present-day Alberta. Within months Fort Calgary was established on the Bow River in present-day Alberta, and Fort Walsh was established in the Cyprss Hills. The North West Mounted Police, later called the Royal Canadian Mounted Police, wiped out the illicit whisky trade, brought law to the region, and established generally friendly relations with the Indians.[156]

To continue with their initiative to facilitate settlement in the region, the Canadian government revised the Dominion Land Act in 1876 to extend the time period of the low-rate leases from six months to several years, and in the following year signed the Blackfoot Treaty which relocated Indian tribes into reserves. In the same years that the Black Hills in the Dakotas was opened up for settlement, and mining, and the Texas cattle herds were pushing farther north into recently opened grasslands in Wyoming and Montana, the North West Territories of Canada found itself in the same situation. Homesteaders and ranchers took advantage of the government leases. The production of livestock would help feed the relocated Indians. Marketing of cattle in the east would be facilitated by the Canadian Pacific Railroad which was working its way across the continent, and the North West Mounted Police provided protection in the region.

George Emerson, a former trader for the Hudson's Bay Company, introduced the Texas longhorn to western Canada in 1876 when he trailed a small herd from Montana into present-day Alberta. In 1879, he brought in an additional 1,000 head.[157] Also, Peter E. Slaughter "drove two herds of cattle to Cypress Hills on the line of Canada and Northern Montana [Territory]" sometime during the 1876 to 1878 trail driving seasons. He was in partnership with his father, George W. Slaughter, and the cattle were driven north from their ranch in Palo Pinto County in northern Texas.[158]

Researchers at the Western Heritage Center on the Cochran Ranch, one of the first ranches established in southern Alberta in 1881, assert that: "Though the original cattle herds arrived in Alberta from Montana in the 1870's, the ranching era really began in 1881."[159] It was in 1881 that the Canadian Parliament again extended the time period on the leases, this time to twenty-one years. A rancher could lease up to 100,000 acres of land at one cent per acre annually. The lessee could then purchase

---

[156] "Royal Canadian Mounted Police History," http://www.canadaka.net/content/page/53-royal-canadian-mounted-police-history [accessed June 19, 2012]

[157] The Alberta Texas Longhorn Association, "Longhorn History in Canada," http://www.albertatexaslonghorn.com/home.html [accessed April 6, 2006]

[158] "P. E. Slaughter," in J. Marvin Hunter's *The Trail Drivers of Texas*, 787.

up to five per cent of the leased land for a cattle station at a cost of $2.00 per acre. Between the leases, the unclaimed land was taken up by homesteaders, who, as in the United States, moved westward in search of open, free land.[160]

According to historian Simon M. Evans, herds that were trailed into Canada were "purchased in Montana and Idaho at the northern terminus of the trail drives from Texas and Arizona." In 1880, about one thousand head were trailed into North West Territory, with 6,000 arriving in 1881, and 16,000 in 1882.[161] The Saskatchewan Stockgrowers reported that in 1881, there were 9,000 cattle in all of the North West Territories.[162] This would account for the 7,000 head trailed in during 1880 and 1881, the few herds brought in during the mid-to-late 1870s, as well as the native British cattle brought in by homesteaders from the east. By 1884, only eight years after the first herd was trailed into present-day Alberta Province, the cattle census recorded 40,000 head.[163] The Saskatchewan Stockgrowers, on the other hand, stated that "by the time the railroad reached such places as Moose Jaw, Swift Current, Maple Creek, Medicine Hat, and Calgary, in the mid-1880s, cattle production in the Puliser [Palliser] Triangle exceeded 50,000 head."[164]

Most of the cattle that were trailed into Canada came through Montana, They were from two different sources: longhorns from Texas from off of the Western Trail, and Durham-Shorthorn-cross cattle from Oregon. Many of the emigrants who had gone to Oregon in the great migration in the decades before, became stockmen. By the 1870s, the Oregon ranchers had a surplus of stock and began to drive their cattle back east to Idaho, Nevada, Utah, Montana, Wyoming, and the Dakotas, as well as to livestock markets in Omaha and Kansas City. One source tells the story:

> Back over the Oregon Trail the herds went. Beginning in 1875, thousands of cattle started their eastward trek from Oregon along the same ruts carved by the wagons and livestock of the pioneers more than 30 years before. Baker City and Oregon City became major cattle towns, and were two of the largest cities in the state. The railroad town of Winnemucca, Neveda, rivaled comtemporary Dodge City.
>
> Cattle were driven down the Oregon Trail past Baker City, across western and southern Idaho in sight of old Fort Hall, then into Wyoming. Some drovers cut off the trail before reaching Fort Hall and worked their way north-ward along the immigrant trail to Montana; others entered Wyoming over the Lander cutoff and followed the Overland route to the ranches or winter pastures on the

---

[159]Museum Display, Western Heritage Center, Cochrane, Alberta on Cochrane Ranch, July, 1996.
[160]Boyd M. Anderson, "Plows or Pastures? The Stockmen Take a Stand," *Beyond the Range*, as printed in *The Saskatchewan Stockgrowers Magazine*, January, 2006, 25.
[161]Simon M. Evans, "Stocking the Canadian Range," *Alberta History*, 26:3 (summer, 1978) 11.
[162]Anderson, Ibid, *The Saskatchewan Stockgrowers Magazine*, November, 2005, 28.
[163]The Alberta Texas Longhorn Association, "Longhorn History in Canada," Ibid.
[164]Boyd M Anderson, "The Golden Years," *Beyond the Range*, as printed in *The Saskatchewan Stockgrowers Magazine*, November, 2005, 28.

Laramie Plains. After a season on the range, the cattle were shipped by Union Pacific Railroad from Cheyenne, Ogallala or Sidney to Omaha and Chicago. Large herds trailed past Fort Laramie and were turned northward to become the foundation stock for ranches on the Powder River and in the Black Hills. Other herds made the more difficult eastward crossing over the old Mullan Road from Oregon into Montana and pushed east to ranches on the Madison, Gallatin, Yellowstone and other rivers.

Some 60,000 cattle moved out of Oregon in 1878 and more than 100,000 in 1879. The peak of the phenomenon was 1880, when 200,000 Oregon cattle trailed east. Montana continued to be a major market for Oregon cattle until hard winters in the late 1880s decimated the Pacific Northwest. Soon, the surplus of Oregon cattle was gone.[165]

The quality of the imported Oregon cattle taken into Montana Territory in significant numbers after 1876 was higher than that of the Texas longhorns, but the Texas cattle had some advantages to the Wyoming and Montana ranchers as well as to the Canadian ranchers. Stockmen were impressed by the range-rugged stock. The animal had proven to be a resilient beast — highly fertile and disease resistant. The longhorn cow gave birth unassisted to calves that could get up quickly to nurse; thus, calving problems were minimal. The longhorns also had longer life spans. Many cows produced calves regularly past twenty years of age and, on occasion, calved past the age of thirty. The stockman did not have to worry about isolated cows and their calves — few wolves wanted to face a longhorn cow with calf. Since the Texas longhorn also had the ability to adapt to almost all weather conditions, including the frigid Montana and Canadian winters, they were often favored over the more vulnerable Durham and Shorthorn breeds.[166]

Texas cattle on the Western Cattle Trail were trailed up the Milk River toward the Canadian border. Those headed for the present-day Saskatchawan Province area branched off from the Milk River pathway and followed the Frenchman Creek or Whitewater Creek across the border to destinations like Maple Creek, Swift Current, and Moose Jaw. Herds destined for Cypress Hills and Medicine Hat, Alberta, left the Milk River and continued up the Lodge Creek into North West Territory. The Milk River pathway continued on to Lethbridge, the High River District, and Calgary, also in present-day Alberta. Cattle herds driven in from Montana stayed mostly south of present-day Calgary and the Saskatchewan River.

Some Texas longhorns, though not large numbers, walked the entire south-to-north width of the continental United States. The Western Cattle Trail had become international. Longhorns from South Texas, some of which had been acquired in

---

[165] "Cowboys Then and Now" museum exhibit and museum flier, "On to Oregon," Union County Museum, Union, Oregon. Also map in Garnet M. and Herbert O. Brayer, *American Cattle Trails, 1540-1900*, page 70.

[166] The Alberta Texas Longhorn Association, "Breed Advantages," http://www.albertatexaslonghorn.com/breed_advantages.html [accessed April 6, 2006]

THE WESTERN CATTLE TRAIL | 1874-1897

Mexico, ended up on the grasslands of Canada. Others had been pastured in Montana Territory for a season or two, after their trail drive from Texas, and subsequently were trailed into Canada. Only longhorns could travel such long distances. When the vast plains of North West Territory, Canada were fully stocked with cattle from the south, the Western Cattle Trail had come to an end.

THE WESTERN CATTLE TRAIL | 1874-1897

PART III
THE RE-EMERGENCE OF THE CATTLE-TRAILING INDUSTRY VIA THE NATIONAL TRAIL AND THE TEXAS-MONTANA FEEDER ROUTE TO THE WESTERN TRAIL
1885–1897

> *"Longhorns laid a foundation of an industry that grew in the 1870s, boomed in the 1880s, collapsed in 1886-87, and re-emerged in modified form..."*

Norbert Mahnken "Early Nebraska Markets for Texas Cattle,"
Nebraska History, a Quarterly Magazine,
January-March, 1945

CHAPTER 1

Change And Turmoil Brews In The Cattle-Trailing Industry

> *For twenty years that widly imaginative venture that pushed millions of cattle throughout the virgin range of the West along the Texas Trail had been at its height. Then Dodge City was closed to the trail drivers from Texas in 1885, when the quarantine line was extended to include southwestern Kansas. Thereafter, the great trail movement entered upon its declining decade.*

J. Evetts Haley
The XIT Ranch of Texas, 1953, page 126.

In the quote on the introductory page of this section, historian Norbert Mahnken wrote, in 1945, that the cattle-trailing industry had "collapsed in 1886-87." In his native Nebraska, the state legislature had issued a herd law in 1886 that essentially prevented the Texas herds from trailing across the state. And J. Evetts Haley in 1953 alluded to the 1885 Kansas quarantine law as the final blow to the industry, and "thereafter, the great trail movement entered upon its declining decade." Both states' laws contributed to the industry's decline. It was never the same after 1885. Texas cattlemen hoped to regain the momentum of the decade before, and trail drivers created another pathway around Kansas and Nebraska in order to deliver their herds to the northern markets, but other factions also stood in the way.

By the mid-1880s, times were changing and the cattle-trailing industry was on the wane. For thirty years Texas drovers had pushed their longhorns north to be shipped to eastern slaughter houses. For over ten years, drovers on the Western Trail had delivered cattle to the railheads, to the Indian agencies, and to ranches on the northern plains. As has been described, a line of movement from Texas, across Indian Territory, Kansas, and Nebraska had occurred during the 1870s and 1880s. Every so many years, the Kansas Legislature drew another quarantine line and the cattle trails were adjusted westward out in front of the settlements. In 1883 and 1884, the dependable pathway through Dodge City, Kansas and on to Ogallala, Nebraska was nearing a close for the Texas cattlemen and their drovers. They may not have known it, but the bonanza years for the Texas cattlemen in their endeavor to make handsome profits on trail cattle were coming to an end.

The reason for the changing trail conditions was the settling of the west. The peopling of the plains brought homesteads and barbed wire, both of which contributed to the end of the open range. As homesteaders moved west to stake claims for farms, trail herds that formerly grazed across their land were unwelcome, especially if they carried the deadly disease to local cattle. This peopling of the plains was often referred to as the "settling up" of the open range, which caused the old trail to be "fenced up." George Saunders in 1931 said that it was "immigration [that] forced them [the cattle trails] west...."[1] This migration of people had been going on for years in central Texas and in western Kansas and Nebraska, but by 1883 and 1884, people had pushed so far west that there was no more room for intruding trail cattle.

Railroads were also changing the complexion of trail driving. In the early 1880s, just ahead of the largest wave of immigration, new rails and trains pushed west. At almost every station and water stop, a town was created. For example, in 1881, the Texas and Pacific Railway reached Lone Wolf Creek, what had been a ranger camp on the Colorado River, and the small settlement soon became the cattle-shipping center known as Colorado City located in the southern portion of the Texas Panhandle. Wichita Falls, in north Texas, east of the Panhandle, received in September of 1882, its first of many railroads, the Fort Worth and Denver City

---

[1]George Saunders interview, "Trail Historian Corrects Error," Fort Worth newspaper, between Oct. 21 and Dec. 31, 1931.

Railway. Because of these and many other stations along the rails, people arrived in the area in increasing numbers.

The new settlements became an obstacle to cattle driving, making it more difficult to drive herds out of the south Texas ranches. Therefore, the nursery grounds and gathering area for longhorns that had been used for many years — the south Texas triangle — gradually shifted to the Texas Panhandle, an area west of the wave of immigration. For the Western Cattle Trail to survive, the cattle industry had to establish another route for moving herds out of the Panhandle and trailing them to Rawhide Creek in Wyoming where trail drivers re-connected with the old trunk line of the Western Trail.

Between 1876 and 1884, several cattle ranches were established in the Panhandle that included the JA (Goodnight) Ranch (established in 1876), the LIT (Littlefield) Ranch (established in 1877), the LX (Bates & Beals) Ranch, (established in 1877), the LS (Lee & Scott) Ranch (established in 1881), and the XIT (established in 1884), and others. By the mid 1880s, these ranches were supplying a major portion of the cattle being prepared for the trail. Some ranches continued to drive herds north during this period, but with difficulty.

There were two advantages to this gradual shift. Not only was the new gathering area closer to the markets in the north, the Panhandle ranchers were diligent about keeping their herds clean of the Texas Fever. The disease, carried by the southern longhorns, was prevalent along the southern Texas border, but in the Panhandle, the cattle herds could be kept free of the disease provided they were kept isolated from infected southern cattle.[2] This made the herds marketable. By the beginning of the 1880s, when large herds were being driven farther north into the Wyoming, Montana, and Dakota territories, the Panhandle ranches could advertise that their herds as free of the Texas Fever.

This was not easily done. In order to secure control over the fever issue as well as other stock interests, Charles Goodnight and his Panhandle neighbors met in Mobeetie, Texas on July 23, 1880, to attack the problem of the infected southern Texas herds. The group chose Goodnight as their president. A year later, the Panhandle Stock Association of Texas was officially organized. Over the next four years, Goodnight spent a great deal of time and money to protect the Panhandle herds and to represent the interest of the Panhandle ranches in persuading Kansas lawmakers, as well as the northern buyers, that their area of Texas was not a source of the dreaded Texas Fever.

One of Goodnight's first actions was to write to the cattlemen in the lower Texas country to warm them to not take herds through the Panhandle. One of Goodnight's friends, George T. Reynolds of the Long X Ranch, turned his letter

---

[2] The South Texas or Mexican tick that was found later to be the cause of the Texas Fever was not a problem in the Panhandle, provided herds coming up from the south were not allowed to mingle with the Panhandle herds. Charles Goodnight and the other ranch owners vowed to protect their herds from coming in contact with each other.

over to the editor of the *Fort Griffin Echo*.[3] On August 20, 1881, the letter was printed as a blanket warning to drovers trailing herds up the trail to Fort Griffin:

> I send Mr. Smith to turn your cattle so they will not pass through our range. He will show you around and guide you until you strike the head of this stream [McCullum Creek?] and then you will have a road. The way he will show you is nearer and there are shorter drives to water than any route you can take. Should you come by here you will have a drive of 35 miles to make.
>
> I hope you will take this advice as yourselves and I have always been good friends, but even friendship will not protect you in the drive through here, and should you attempt to pass through, be kind enough to tell your men what they will have to face as I do not wish to hurt men that do not understand what they will be sure to meet.
>
> I hope you will not treat this as idle talk, for I mean every word of this, and if you have any feeling for me as a friend or acquaintance, you will not put me to any desperate actions. I will not perhaps see you myself, but take this advice from one that is and always has been your friend.
>
> My cattle are now dying of the fever contracted from cattle driven from Fort Worth, therefore do not have any hope that you can convince me that your cattle will not give mine the fever, this we will not speak of. I simply say to you that you will never pass through here in good health.
>
> Yours truly,
> C. Goodnight[4]

The letters mailed out and posted by Goodnight reiterated the resolutions that had been in the articles of The Panhandle Stock Association adopted a few months earlier. In order to stop the spread of the Texas Fever "communicated by cattle drives from points south and east of us," the Panhandle ranchers agreed and resolved on four points:

That said cattle be confined to certain definite lines of drive,

That all drovers are requested to call on local stock men for information as to said trails, and that we pledge ourselves to render all needed help information or assistance when called upon.

---

[3]The Reynolds brothers had worked with Goodnight since the early trail days. William D. Reynolds had been on the trail with Goodnight and Oliver Loving, in 1868, and had helped take Loving's body back to Texas. The Reynolds Cattle Company had ranches in Texas and Colorado. (C. L. Douglas, *Cattle Kings of Texas*, 187-189)

[4]J. Evetts Haley, *Charles Goodnight, Cowman and Plainsman*, 361-362.

That all parties holding cattle in this section not wintered west of the Wichitas and north of the Brazos, at a point above Baylor County, are requested to hold the same under herd and separately from all range cattle until after frost.

That we further pledge ourselves to ignore and withdraw all assistance in any way whatsoever from all parties who disregard the above requests.

Two alternate routes, or "definite lines of drive," defined by the association were the old Rath buffalo trail[5] and a more westerly route, which bypassed Panhandle ranges, by extending "up Blanco canon, head of canon Tile, head of Cononcito Blanco, head of Palodura [sic], Tascosa to Colorado." The association "set aside one and one-half miles on each side of the Rath and Western trails for use and benefit of drovers." A large water tank was installed on Running Water Draw near the site of present-day Plainview, Texas, to furnish the herds with water, and the routes were marked out by "a common sod plow."[6]

To enforce use of these routes and to make sure drovers followed the association's instructions, armed riders were placed in strategic locations. This system of gun-toting enforcers to keep south Texas herds away from the Panhandle became known as the "Winchester Quarantine."

In 1882, the first full season for the Winchester Quarantine, Jack Potter helped deliver a herd of cattle to Cheyenne, Wyoming for the New England Livestock Company. Because the herd was destined for Wyoming, the drovers left the Western Trail near Fort Griffin and cut across the Texas Panhandle. Potter did not record the herd's exact route, but the young eighteen-year-old remembered the wild and bawdy town of Tascosa. No mention was made of an encounter with the Panhandle ranchers.

In the spring of 1883, Jack Potter was again assigned to deliver a herd, this time as a trailboss, to Cheyenne by his boss, Alfred T. Bacon, manager of the New England Livestock Company. Bacon instructed Potter to leave the Western Trail at Albany and blaze a cut-off that was shorter than his previous route. He later recalled that they "hit Tascosa, Buffalo Springs, the Ox Ranch on the Cimarron, Fort Lyons on the Arkansas, thence to the South Platte River at the mouth of the Bijou." (refer to the Potter-Bacon Trail — splinter route and Map #1-12 in Part II, Chapter I) But the trip was not without incident. This time, the herd and drovers ran directly into the Winchester Quarantine. Potter wrote of the ordeal:

I got through all right, but not before I had a run-in with the Goodnight people. I was forced to detour around their range on account of their cattle not being immune to tick fever, which had begun

---

[5]As mentioned earlier, the Rath buffalo trail was a feeder route to the Western Trail into Dodge City, Kansas.

[6]Pauline and R. L. Robertson, *Cowman's Country, Fifty Frontier Ranches in The Texas Panhandle, 1876-1887*, 52, and Jean M. Burroughs, *On the Trail, The Life and Tales of "Lead Steer" Potter*, 16.

to plague all the southern herds. Leigh Dwyer, Goodnight's brother-in-law, informed me that this herd which I was driving was the first one which had ventured through from the Western Trail, and since I had blazed it, others would surely follow and give them a heap of trouble.

After reaching his destination, Potter reiterated to his boss, "I was forced to detour [in Texas] and give in to them steel barrels pointin' in my direction. There warn't much else I could do."[7]

Other drovers followed Potter's lead. The short-cut to the north was too convenient to ignore, but this short-cut disregarded the request by Goodnight and the Panhandle ranchers. Letters were again written by the Panhandle ranchers to transportation agents who insisted on using the closed Llano Estacado ranges. A letter was also sent to Texas Governor Oran M. Roberts demanding a quarantine against south Texas cattle. The appeal was ignored, for South Texas lawmakers, who outnumbered the legislators from the Panhandle-Plains, were firm in their commitment to their free-grass constituents. The Panhandle ranchers and their quarantine enforcers stiffened their resistance. They were determined to not allow any more herds from the south or east onto their ranges.[8]

The Goodnight forces and their Winchester Quarantine were the first to draw a line in the sand between south Texas and the north. Even though the Texas Panhandle ranchers did not get any support from their state's own members of Congress, congressmen from states located north and west of the Panhandle ranches, in 1884, supported the call to stop the Texas trail drives. Kansans, many of them for the same reasons, joined in partnership with the Panhandlers. In the 1884 season, Kansas ranchers marked with furrows the limits of the Western Trail on either side a half mile wide trail from the state's southern boundary to the railhead at Dodge City. Armed riders were posted along the route, ready to shoot any cattle that strayed from the path. Other southern Kansas ranchmen sent manifests stating that no southern trail herds should be allowed to enter Kansas that year. Some tried to enforce the manifesto. In one June 1884 incident, a group of about one hundred fifty local ranchers, fully armed, formed a blockade at Campbell's Ranch in Ford County, Kansas to stop the herds coming from the south. When the drovers appeared determined to break through and drive their cattle to the shipping point, the Kansas ranchers appealed for help and soon their forces doubled in size. According to a newspaper account, "The drovers, seeing the odds against them, backed off, and, continuing along the southern boundary, proceeded to Colorado."[9] The ire of the southern Kansas ranchers was a prelude to the passing of a full Kansas quarantine nine months later.

To combat the anti-south Texas cattle sentiments, Texas trail agents in 1884 promoted the idea of a government sanctioned route or a national highway just for

---

[7]From an undated clipping from the *Union County Leader* about Potter--used and reprinted by Jean M. Burroughs in *On The Trail, The Life and Tales of "Lead Steer" Potter*, 15-16.

[8]Jimmy M. Skaggs, *The Cattle-Trailing Industry*, 106.

[9]*Albany [Texas] News*, June 20, 1884 as relayed by William Curry Holden, *Alkali Trails*, 41.

THE WESTERN CATTLE TRAIL | 1874-1897   377

Texas cattle. The idea had been discussed earlier. The editor of the *Ford County Globe* in Dodge City, Kansas had first promoted the idea for local ranch-owner readers in April of 1881. According to the editor, drovers, local stock raisers, and farmers had been talking of such a plan, for "it seems to be the only practical method through which this growing industry can receive that protection it deserves." He continued:

> ...since our supply of stock cattle is largely drawn from the State of Texas we see no valid reason why Congress should not so legislate as to protect this industry as it does all others. A well defined trail will protect our local stock growers, who have expended thousands of dollars in the improvement of their herds, and who have added much to the wealth of the State by so doing, and are deserving of a little more recognition then they have been in the past.[10]

The proposal envisioned a trail six to twelve miles wide staked off in the public domain on land in western Kansas taken out of homestead status, where through cattle herds could graze and "pass without trespassing upon their right [Kansas homesteads/ranches], thereby protecting all parties concerned," according to the *Globe*.

Cattlemen were not organized nationally in 1881, and not all stock raisers were in favor of the idea, so nothing was done at that time. However, in 1884, the idea was brought to the fore again, this time by Texans. A recognized route would serve two purposes for the Texas trail drivers: it would relieve them of having to deal with homesteaders and local ranchers with their fear of Texas Fever, and it would end the problem of drovers having to keep up with the changing quarantine lines by the states. In addition, a government highway would protect the local stock growers by keeping the Texas herds isolated and away from local herds.

Various beef producers decided to organize to discuss the national trail idea. A convention, the first of its kind, was held in St. Louis on November 17, 1884. Texas representatives, who attended in full force, sought quarantine relief and a national trail. They proposed a neutral strip of federal land extending through Colorado to lessen the chances of contact between domestic cattle and the Texas longhorns. The Texans also argued that a confined route would serve as a check on railroads so that they could not charge exorbitant rates in the shipment of cattle. Interested cattle buyers, such as the Chicago stockyard representatives and others, were on the Texans side in this matter. Cattlemen who trailed their herds didn't pay the train fares for cattle. This made the price of cattle cheaper at the end of the trail.[11]

Opposing the Texans were cattle growers north of Texas who wanted comprehensive quarantine laws and were vehemently against giving them any relief through a federal trail. They suggested that those who were for the national trail

---

[10]*Ford County Globe*, Dodge City, Kansas, as printed in *The County Gazettes*, California, Kansas (Lane County), April 1, 1881.

[11]The idea of a national route for stock was not a completely new concept. For years such "drover roads" had been used in Europe to aide stockmen to herd their cattle, sheep, pigs, etc. to market.

scheme were only interested in Texas money. Cattle herds in Nebraska and Wyoming were experiencing the affects of the Texas Fever at the time of the convention which caused representative from those states to adamantly oppose the proposed national trail. Many northern ranchers were not so concerned about the fever, but were against the proposed route because they no longer needed longhorns to stock their ranges.

In the debates at the convention southern cattlemen presumed that northern cattlemen were selfish and wanted to have all the northern grassland to themselves, sought to monopolize the northern market for their beef, and wanted to keep Texas cattle out of the market and off of their ranges. Joseph Nimmo, the Chief of the Bureau of Statistics of the United States, articulated this assessment of range and ranch cattle traffic in a report he prepared in response to a request by the Secretary of the Treasury. Nimmo's report was presented to the House of Representatives, and members of Congress found in that report the following:

> the northern ranges were originally stocked with young cattle, chiefly steers, driven from Texas. For several years it was supposed [sic] that Texas must continue to be almost exclusively the breeding ground, and that the northern ranges would for all time be the maturing and fattening ground for Texas cattle. But an important change has taken place in this regard [1884]. The raising of cattle on the northern ranges has met with an encouraging degree of success. At the present time many of the large cattle-owners and herdsmen of Montana, Dakota, Wyoming, Nebraska, and it is believed also of Colorado, are of the opinion that it is more profitable for them to raise their young cattle than to import them from Texas.[12]

From Nimmo's perception, the issue of the fever had become a political ploy. All through the years in trail-driving industry, the Texas Fever had been a problem — the reason the trail routes had been pushed west. The issue could be used to prevent Texas cattlemen from entering into lucrative contracts with northern buyers.

In regard to the issue of the Texas Fever, Nimmo concluded, after extensive research and interviews, that the "malady known as Texas Fever" was not as severe as northern cattlemen reported it to be. It was known that the "lowlands, bordering upon the Gulf of Mexico, are undoubtedly the locality of its origin," but the "general testimony appears to be to the effect that Texas cattle driven north have never communicated the disease to other cattle north of the South Platte River, nor to cattle in the State of Colorado." and that "the cause of the disease is eliminated from the systems of the Southern Texas cattle while "on the trail" from their place

---

[12]House of Representatives, Ex. Doc. No. 267, 48th Congress, 2nd Session, *Letter from The Secretary of the Treasury Transmitting a report from the Chief of the Bureau of Statistics*…a report on range and ranch cattle traffic of the western, southwestern, and northwestern states, in reply to a resolution by the House of Representatives., March 2, 1885, under the heading: "The Breeding of Cattle on the Northern Ranges," 26.

of nativity to the ranges of the north." Nimmo based his opinion on correspondence with the Hon. J. W. Carey, Delegate in Congress from Wyoming, and president of the Wyoming Stock Growers' Association, who stated that:

> …it is found to be perfectly safe to admit to our ranges Texas cattle which are driven on the trail. By the time they reach Wyoming and Nebraska, when moved in that way, they appear to lose entirely the liability to impart the so called Texas fever.[13]

Cattlemen in northern Nebraska and Wyoming Territory who suffered the effects of an 1884 epidemic of the fever disagreed with the Texans' on-the-trail theory and Nimmo's report. The Texas Fever had not been a real menace in the northern territories in the early days of trailing, but recently had become a severe problem. One reason was the practice of shipping cattle by rail part way, and then continuing the trail driving to the assigned range land. Disease-carrying cattle placed on a train in south Texas and railed to the north, bypassing the inspectors carried the disease north.[14] It was asserted that a diseased herd of 5,000 was trailed into Wyoming Territory from the railheads of Ogallala and Sidney in the summer of 1884. That herd had caused havoc, spreading the fever on the northern plains.

Secretary Sturgis of the Wyoming Cattle Association was overwhelmed with reports of losses. Local stock raisers reported from thirty to a hundred head dying daily as the 5,000 head moved northward across the state. In response to this devastation, the Wyoming and Montana territorial governors promised prohabitation against all Texas cattle coming up by rail. In his annual report of 1884, Secretary Sturgis "disclaimed any intention on the part of the northern growers to injure the Texas trade, but warned the Texas drovers that if the fever broke out on the northern ranges, it might stop the Texas drives altogether."[15] There had better not be any more Texas Fever in the 1885 season, he warned, or Wyoming and Montana buyers would cease to deal with Texas cattle.

The St. Louis convention ended with the Texans' position prevailing, and a proposal to the United States Congress for the creation of a national trail was drafted.[16] By the end of 1884, an appointed government committee on the proposed National Trail released its report. According to Joseph Nimmo, in his 1885 congressional report, the following points were made:

> The quantity of land which the Government of the United States is asked to donate for the purpose of establishing the proposed trail may

---

[13]Nimmo, Doc. No. 267, Ibid., "The Texas Fever," 29-30.

[14]One of these inspectors could have been Ernest Fletcher who, in 1883-1884, was an inspector at Texas Trail Canyon in Cheyenne County, Kansas. Here herds were held back for inspection before crossing the Republican River in Nebraska and continuing on to Ogallala. (Kraisinger & Kraisinger, *The Western, the Greatest Texas Cattle Trail, 1874-1886*, pages 252-254)

[15]Ernest S. Osgood, *The Day of the Cattleman*, 164-165.

[16]For a complete presentation of the convention and its arguments, see Chapter 13 of our book, *The Western, the Greateat Texas Cattle Trail, 1874-1886*.

be assumed to begin at the southern border line of Colorado, and to extend to the northern border line of the United States.

It is proposed that it shall be of variable width, from 200 feet at crossing places for "native cattle," to 6 miles at the widest part. Such a trail of an average width of 3 miles, and extending to the Dominion of Canada would be 690 miles in length and have an area of 2,070 square miles, or 1,324,800 acres. If it should be established only from the Southern boundary of Colorado to the parallel of 43 degrees north, which constitutes the northern border line of the State of Nebraska, it would have a length of 420 miles and an area of 1,260 square miles, or 806,400 acres.

The proposed trail would be located chiefly upon "range" land and not available for agricultural purposes, other than grazing. The intrinsic value of such lands, which now belong to the Government, cannot be accurately stated, but it is comparatively small.[17]

A feeder route to the proposed National Trail would start west of Fort Supply, after leaving the Western Trail, continue west across No Man's Land, angle toward the Colorado-Kansas border, and then continue north on the proposed National Trail route in eastern Colorado to Nebraska and beyond. The route was farther west than the existing trail that had been used for ten years and had proved to be adequate. The railheads of Dodge City and Ogalalla were well established and had a workable system of connections with buyers, but would be bypassed by the proposed National Trail. The new route through eastern Colorado was less accommodating because there wasn't an established railhead, the route had fewer watering places, and the added miles increased their overhead, diminished their profits, took more time, and was inconvenient. Even though the Texas faction had won the first round of their political battle to get their cattle to market, the end result was not ideal, but it was their only option if they wanted to trail their herds north.

Less than four months after the St. Louis convention, the Kansas Legislature voted to quarantine the entire state of Kansas with its "Act for the protection of cattle against Texas Splenic or Spanish fever." The law's *"Provided, however"* section was of particular interest. It stated that if the owner of such cattle could show a certificate "designated by the live-stock sanitary commission of this state" that the cattle had been kept since the first day of December of the previous year west of the east line of Indian Territory and north of the 36th parallel or "west of the 21st meridian of longitude west of Washington and north of the thirty-fourth parallel," then "the provisions of this section shall not apply" and also that the "provision shall not apply to cattle which are owned or kept in this state that may drift across the south line of the state."[18] In essence, the law recognized that the Indian Territory area (present-

---

[17]Nimmo, Doc. No. 267, Ibid, "Quantity of Land Necessary for the Proposed Trail," 32.

[18]The law stated that anyone guilty of breaking the law would face a fine and/or imprisonment. Kansas was the first to pass a comprehensive quarantine law. The words, "Provided, however," are in italics in the law. Chapter CXCL, "Protection of Cattle Against Disease," *State of Kansas Session Laws of 1885*, recorded May 1, 1885, 311.

day Oklahoma) to the 36th parallel and the Texas Panhandle to the 34th parallel, the south border of the Panhandle, were considered a disease-free zone. Concessions had been given to the ranchers in these areas, and their cattle could still be driven into Kansas and to its railheads--with certificates of inspection.

The Kansas 1885 quarantine law had addressed the efforts of Charles Goodnight and his neighbors in the Texas Panhandle. The ranchers could continue to drive their cattle to the Dodge City stockyards using the Palo Duro road established by Goodnight in 1877 or the Tascosa Trail, the Jones and Plummer Trail, the Rath, or the Tuttle. (see Map #5-3 in Chapter V in Part II) The lucrative market, however, was in the territories to the north. Government Indian agencies were still letting contracts for beef for their reservations, and some Wyoming and Montana territory ranchers still sought a continuing supply of cattle. The JA (Goodnight) Ranch, the LIT, the LX, and the LS, along with others, had now been established in the Panhandle for some seven years and were in a good position to take on the responsibility of being the breeding area and gathering area for Texas cattle. In 1884, however, another ranch had been established along the western boundary of the Panhandle, one that would become larger than any of the existing Panhandle ranches — the XIT. Over the next decade, the XIT would export thousands of head.

Within days of the Kansas quarantine law, on March 20, 1885, Colorado passed a law — also using the 36th degree of latitude as a demarcation line — requiring all cattle driven from below that line to be put in quarantine for sixty days in Indian Territory before entering into Colorado, or it required that trail drivers "procure from the State Veterinary board a certificate or bill of health to the effect that said cattle or horses are free from all infections or contagious diseases..."[19]

Other states also followed Kansas' and Colorado's lead. New Mexico passed a similar law in April of 1884, and Nebraska and Wyoming Territory passed laws in the spring of 1885. However, these quarantine laws were less restrictive. For example, New Mexico placed the responsibility of its law's enforcement on the governor. Nebraska and Wyoming Territory left the matter enforcing quarantine law entirely up to "responsible executive officers."[20] Under these conditions, there were always the possibility of loopholes and gaps that could be circumvented.

In addition to the above states and the Territory of Wyoming, the operators and cattle syndicates who were leasing land in the Cherokee Strip formed the Cherokee Strip Live Stock Association and announced that "it would oppose with every means possible the passage of Texas cattle through its region," giving fear of Texas Fever as the cause of its action.[21] The line of defense now seemed complete. Regardless of the concessions that Texas stockmen had received with their triumph at the November cattlemen's convention in St. Louis and the inclusion of the proposed national route

---

[19]The 36th parallel of north latitude is 1 degree, or 69 1/2 statute miles, south of the southern boundary line of the State of Colorado. (Nimmo, Doc. No. 267, Ibid, "The Quarantine Law of the State of Colorado," 36)

[20]Nimmo, Ibid, "Remarks in Regard to the Quarantine Laws of Kansas, Colorado, Nebraska, Wyoming, and New Mexico," 37.

[21]Osgood, *The Day of the Cattleman*, 166.

in the report of the U. S. House of Representatives, northern ranchers and state governments had formed a line of fences, blockades, and quarantine laws against the trail herds. Battle lines were drawn. The spring of 1885 would be a challenge for the Texas drovers, to say the least. Contracts had been procured by the stockmen of Texas, and they were determined to trail their herds north as usual.

The New York Times in July of 1885 reviewed the situation in its article entitled "The Cattle Blockade." On the one hand, it noted that:

> The Secretary of the Interior has undertaken to open a passage through Cheyenne and Arapahoe Reservation in the Indian Territory and the strip of public land lying north of the Texas Panhandle [No Man's Land] for several large herds of cattle on their way northward from the Texas breeding grounds.
>
> It is now proposed that the Texas herds before reaching the Kansas line shall turn to the left, pass through the strip north of the Pan Handle — called No Man's Land — and then enter Colorado at the southeastern corner of that State, continuing northward near the eastern boundary of Colorado to Nebraska and Montana. The sharp turn just before entering No Man's Land is a concession to the cattle barons of the Pan Handle, who not only breed but mature their cattle and are unwilling that their ranges shall be denuded of grass by the moving herds. If the Government shall clear the way through the Cheyenne Reservation the movement of cattle will then be checked in No Man's Land, which is held by cattle kings who are as independent as those of the Pan Handle. Moreover, there will be bitter opposition in Colorado, where quarantine laws are in force, along the Kansas boundary, where the people are talking about establishing a shotgun deadline and in the northeast corner of New Mexico, where many of the cattle have already strayed.[22]

The narrow corridor to the north had been publicized, but the cattle herds would be "checked" in No Man's Land. It remained to be seen what the outcome would be.

---
[22] "The Cattle Blockade," *New York Times*, July 13, 1885, p. 4. (accessed from the New York Times Archives online, archive.nytimes.com, Dec 19, 2008)

> *"We got along all right from here [Doan's Crossing] until we got to Wolf Creek at old Camp Supply, where they quarantined us, and we had to go down to No Man's Land, a strip between the Panhandle and Kansas, now a part of Oklahoma."*

**Jeff Connolly, in Hunter, *The Trail Drivers of Texas*, writing about a trail drive in 1885.
The drovers used the National Trail and sold the herd when they go to "this side of the Arkansas River, in Colorado." pages 191-192.**

CHAPTER II

No Man's Land & The National Trail 1885-1887

> *My last trip was made in 1887. We shipped our herd from Toyah to Big Springs, and from there we went the extreme Western Trail across the plains to Trails [Trail] City, Colorado.*

A. N. Eustace, in Hunter, *The Trail Drivers of Texas*, page 225.

In order to reach the newly proposed National Trail in Colorado, Texas trail drivers knew that they would have to trail through No Man's Land., seemingly the only open area left to reach the northern markets. Our research had lead to conclusions that there were three pathways across No Man's Land, each one used at a different period of time. The first route went across the northern part of the strip, but because of resistances from ranchers and homesteaders, Texas drovers were forced to move the trail south going through the middle of the strip, and finally, the pathway moved to the extreme south of the strip along the northern border of Texas. Our map shows these pathways and the sources used to identify these three routes.

In the spring of 1885, Texas trail contractors started some 300,000 head north from various ranches in Texas.[1] Among those were the Blocker Brothers and Jennings from Blanco County who outfitted approximately eight herds with a total of 25,000 head for contracts in the north,[2] and George West, working out of his Live Oak County ranch, who road branded several herds of contracted cattle. The planned course heading north was to follow the Western Trail to the Fort Supply area, leave the trunk line of the trail and turn sharply west into No Man's Land, south of the Kansas border, until reaching the corner of Colorado where herds would pick up the Nationsl Trail along the extreme eastern border of that state.

No Man's Land was to be used by Texas herds as a pathway through the barrage of blockades and quarantines, because it was the last public domain outside of any state or territorial law. The narrow strip of land, one hundred sixty-eight miles long and thirty-four miles wide, had been, by an unusual quirk of politics, left out of the alignment of state and territorial boundaries in the 1850s. The narrow strip had not been picked up by any state and, therefore, was a no man's land. In 1885, when Texas drovers used this open, unclaimed piece of ground to trail their herds from Fort Supply westward toward the Colorado border, it was void of any county divisions, local government, or organized law. Within a year, vigilantes would form the Respective Claim Board to combat the outlaws, and in the spring of 1887, emigrant settlers would organize and name the strip "Cimarron Territory."[3]

From the early 1880s, ranchers began to move into the strip because of the fine grazing and water in the valleys of the Beaver (North Canadian) River and Palo Duro Creek. No ranch boundaries could be established on the unowned land,

---

[1]This number comes from Ava Betz, *A Prowers County History*. According to Betz, over 300,000 cattle trailed through Trail City in the season of 1885. page 100. Goins and Goble, however, in their *Historical Atlas of Oklahoma*, 117, recorded 220,000 head. We support the former number.

[2]The 25,000 number for 1885 comes from *The Handbook of Texas Online* ("John Blocker"). Skaggs wrote, however, that the Blocker Brothers probably handled a total of 90,000 longhorns in 1885, citing Faun Vernon Strout, "The History and Development of Education in Wilbarger Country from 1858 to 1937" (M.A. Thesis, Southern Methodist University, 1937, p. 10) The Blocker Brothers (Bill and John) and, after 1874, the Blocker Brothers and Jennings Company (William Henry Jennings) bought, sold, and transported a considerable portion of the total number of livestock trailed north between 1871 and 1893.The operation is estimated to have handled 330,000 head of livestock driven north or about 7% of the total traffic. Abner and Jenx Blocker were younger brothers who trailed for the family business. (Skaggs, *The Cattle Trailing Industry*, 50, 136)

[3]Goins and Goble, Ibid. 99-137. No Man's Land, or Cimarron Territory, was added to Oklahoma Territory on May 2, 1890.

1

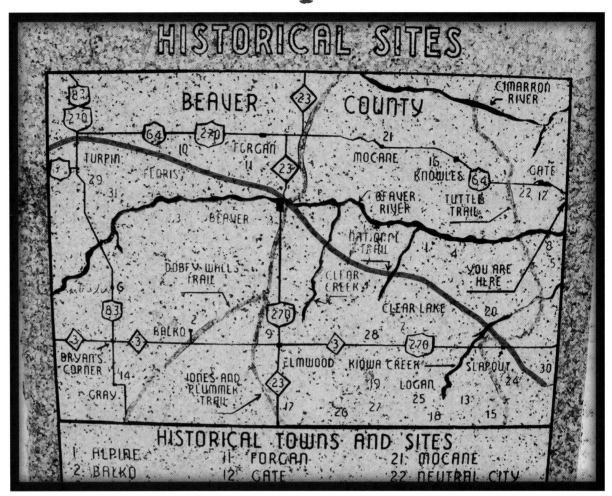

Map on the backside of the granite stone marker at Gate, Oklahoma. The front of the marker, "You Are Now Entering Old No Man's Land," is about the history of No Man's Land, the 37th Parallel, and Beaver County. Created and erected by the Beaver County Historical Society and the Oklahoma Historical Society.

Location: 5 miles east of Gate, Oklahoma at the Junction of Highways 64 and 283 Beaver County

Authors' commentary:
This is a handsome marker with extensive detail about the history of No Man's Land. It is the map, however, on the backside of the marker that is of particular interest to us. It shows the "National Trail" route starting across the northern portion of No Man's Land. In perspective, also identified are the Tuttle Trail and the Jones and Plummer Trail coming from the south, and the "Dobey Walls Trail" merging into the Jones and Plummer. All three of these trails were feeder routes into the Western Cattle Trail that then fed into Dodge City, Kansas.

Because of the spelling of "Dobey Walls," we suspect that the societies borrowed information from the Doc Anshutz's map that he created in 1935 (See Map #III, 2-2). This old Adobe Walls Trail was later used by the JA Goodnight Ranch to Dodge City. This map shows the traveler the location of these routes across No Man's Land. Citizens and cattle herds coming from the south were still using the Tuttle, Jones and Plummer, and Adobe Walls routes to connect with Dodge City when the "National Trail" route started. In 1885, the southern cattle herds, that came out of Texas below the 36th parallel started using this feeder route from the Fort Supply area to the east to push westerly across No Man's Land to connect to the National Trail in Colorado. As this marker shows, all these routes were being used at the same time.

and there was no written law pertaining to who controlled which range.[4] By the time Texas drovers decided to use the strip to reach Colorado, No Man's Land was checkerboarded by ranches.[5]

Under those circumstances, Texas drovers believed that No Man's Land was free of any legal encumberments and offered a way to slip by the barricades in the Cherokee Strip to the east and the Texas Panhandle Winchester Quarantine to the south. However, cutting across the parcel meant that Texas herds would be trespassing across a number of ranches. In an effort to connect with the National Trail, different routes were established across No Man's Land in the seasons of 1885 through 1887. These different routes were necessary in order to adjust to the protests from the ranchmen, and later homesteader squatters, who had settled on these public lands.

Different sources refer to the pathways taken by the Texas herds across No Man's Land by different names. The road-side marker at Gate, Oklahoma calls it the National Trail. Also, Jack Potter, on his map, "Map of Cattle Trail," labels the route as the "National Trail." The map, "Ranches of the Texas-Okla. Panhandle," in the 75th anniversary issue of the Oklahoma Panhandle in 1982 in Man and the Oklahoma Panhandle, *labeled the pathway as the "Montana or National Trail." Harry E. Chrisman on his map in* Lost Trails of the Cimarron, *identifys it as the "The National Cattle Trail." Doc Anshutz, who drew a map in 1935, called the pathway the "new Texas Through Trail 1886." Of course, these above sources show this pathway in three locations: a northern route, a middle route, and a southern route.*

According to Joseph Nimmo's 1885 congressional report, the National Trail was to be donated government land, on range land varying from 200 feet wide to 6 miles at the widest point, and was "to begin at the southern border line of Colorado and to extend to the northern border line of the United States." Therefore, we contend that the routes across No Man's Land are feeder routes to the National Trail — or splinter routes off of the Western Cattle Trail that fed into the National Trail.

THE NORTHERN FEEDER ROUTE TO THE NATIONAL TRAIL AND THE JACK HARDESTY WAR:

At first, herds trailing north left the Western Trail near present-day May and crossed No Man's Land through the northern portion of the strip, near the Kansas border. The road-side marker at Gate, Oklahoma shows the "National Trail" entering present-day Beaver County southeast of present-day Slapout, heading north, crossing Beaver Creek at present-day Beaver and then going northwest to enter present-day Texas County.[6]

---

[4] Homesteaders or ranchers, who settled on public land were known as "squatters." In No Man's Land, whoever first built a dugout or hut and set up residency, claimed the surrounding land.
[5] This is according to Boss Neff, cowboy and rancher in No Man's Land. (Colwell, Ibid, 156)
[6] Roadside marker, Gate, Oklahoma, Beaver County Historical Society; and Doc Anshutz map, Dec. 1935.

On this northern route, drovers also crossed the Tuttle Trail and the old Jones and Plummer Trail coming up from the south and the Palo Duro - Dodge City Road coming out of the JA (Goodnight) Ranch in the Panhandle, and they traversed the northern portions of the Kramer, Hardesty, and Dudley ranches.

In 1885, during the first season, trail drivers detoured around Kansas to connect with the proposed National Trail. When the Blocker Brothers and Jennings herds and the George West herd approached the east end of No Man's Land, there was a barbed wire fence, and cowboy guards were waiting.

Col. A. J. (Jack) Hardesty and his brother were the owners of the S-Half Circle (or Half Circle inverted S) Ranch located north of the Beaver (North Canadian) River, with its headquarters at the mouth of Chiquita Creek, south of the Kansas line, mid-way in the No Man's Land strip.[7] It was estimated that he ran some 20,000 cattle.[8] Hardesty, who was known for his fairness and dignity and had the respect of every cowboy who rode for him, however, was like Charles Goodnight to the south in the Texas Panhandle in that he opposed having infected Texas cattle herds coming across his ranch. Thus, he and Ludwig Kramer, his neighbor to the east, had met to discuss the matter.

Ludwig Kramer, of the Quarter Circle Q Ranch, had followed his two sons, Louis and Frank, into No Man's Land from Colorado in 1878. At first the two brothers headquartered their ranch about one mile west of present-day Beaver, near the Beaver River crossing of the Jones and Plummer Trail. In 1880 or 1881, the father and sons moved their headquarters south of present-day Beaver to the Elmwood vicinity at the bend of Clear Creek. The Kramers also had holdings in Kansas and Texas.[9]

Col. Hardesty and "old man" Kramer gathered a group of ranchers to stop the herds from passing through their ranches. Under Hardesty's leadership, the ranchers created a blockade by stringing barbed wire across the east end of No Man's Land to prevent the Texas herds from crossing the narrow span of land, the eastern boundary of present-day Beaver County. The ranchers then gathered a number of other cowboys and placed them along the wire to keep the Texas herds from crossing the line. The protest and blockade became known as the "Jack Hardesty War." Even though Hardesty and the other ranchers in the strip had no state or territory law to back them, they insisted they had a right to protect their own herds from the incoming Texas herds that might be carrying the Texas Fever.

Texas herds soon stacked up behind the wire barrier, and a stand-off between local cowboys and Texas drovers was imminent. Gunfire between the two factions was possible. John Blocker, on his ranch in south Texas, upon hearing of the standoff, telegrammed his younger brother Ab at Dodge City, who was returning by train from

---

[7]M.W. Anshutz wrote that the S-Half-Circle Ranch "ranged from the mouth of Sharps [Sharp] Creek to the mouth of Palo Duro and on Chiquita Creek." Carrie and M.W. Anshutz, *Cimarron Chronicles*, 126.

[8]As stated by Boss Neff in his autobiography written in 1939, and printed in *The Old Times News*, Vol. 1, No. 5, Dec., 1974.

[9]John Franklin Vallentine, *Cattle Ranching South of Dodge City, The Early Years (1870-1920)*, 97. Anshutz wrote: "Kramer and Sons came in on the Beaver River and ranged from the mouth of Clear Creek to the mouth of Sharps [Sharp] Creek." Ibid, 126.

Los Animas, Colorado, and asked him to get to the blockade as soon as possible.[10] Ab Blocker took the stage to Fort Supply while John Blocker and George West headed north to try to negotiate with the blockade defenders.

Ab later recalled:

> Fourteen armed men were riding fence to keep all herds from passing, and refused to meet any reasonable demands. Blocker and West went to Camp Supply and began wiring the authorities at Washington, sending several messages, one message alone costing them about $60.00, nearly all of the messages passing through the hands of Colonel Carr.... Things were looking pretty "squally," and I began to feel creepy. A ranchman friend of John told him that if he would give the word he would take his men and kill all of the fellows who had stopped the herds, but John told him that he thought he could beat them by law.[11]

After several days over 100,000 longhorns were being held behind the blockade.[12] Finally, word was received from Washington that the drovers could cut the fence and allow the herds to pass through, and "if there was further trouble troops would be ordered there," recalled Ab Blocker. Once the news was received and with the cavalry standing by, the herds were ready to move. Ab Blocker continued:

> A lot of the boys with axes cut the fence for a quarter of a mile, I took the lead and was the first to cross the line. In just a short time all the herds were on the move, and as far back as you could see the cattle, men, chuck wagons, horse rustlers and all were coming, all eager to get across No Man's Land.[13]

The No Man's Land blockade had been broken, and the Jack Hardesty War had come to an end without bloodshed. The Hardesty and Kramer group knew that their small armed force could not challenge the United State cavalry. Hardesty gracefully backed down and gathered his neighbors with another idea. If they could not prevent the southern herds from passing over the land and spreading the dreaded Texas Fever, then they would confine them to a designated route.[14]

---

[10] Dick Quinn, editor, "Herb Craig," *The Guymon Herald*, Vol. 21, No. 26, Page 1, Col. 6, Guymon, Oklahoma, Sept. 7, 1911. Craig was one of "Col. Jack's troops in what was known as the Jack Hardesty war," wrote Quinn. The editor knew Herb Craig personally and retold the incident about the protest and blockade in his newspaper in 1911. When he "quit riding," Quinn wrote, Craig became a saloon keeper in Hardesty.

[11] The telegrams were sent to the Department of Interior in Washington, D.C. which exercised authority over the Indian Territory and No Man's Land. (Ab Blocker, "The Man Who Had Hell in his Neck," in Hunter, *The Trail Drivers of Texas*, 507-508)

[12] "George W. West," in Hunter, 835.

[13] Ab Blocker who wrote his account for the Old Time Trail Drivers of Texas sometime between 1920 and 1924, mistakenly remembers this incident as happening in 1884. (Blocker, in Hunter, 508-509)

[14] George Rainey, *No Man's Land*, 103.

THE WESTERN CATTLE TRAIL | 1874-1897

The herds that had been blockaded were trailed en masse across No Man's Land. When they reached the corner of Kansas and the Colorado line, they encountered Jack Potter and his herd. Potter was headed for Ogallala, Nebraska, to deliver a herd for the New England Company. He had used the Potter-Bacon Trail and had cut over to Miles Camp, just nine miles northwest of the corner of Kansas and Colorado. Here he and his outfit laid over "for a few days to let some of the crush pass on," because where there were too many herds pressed together, there was danger of mixing.[15]

The No Man's Land ranchers were persistent in their cause. After the standoff with the incoming southern herds, they created a route around or through their ranches that was limited to two miles in width. They appointed line riders who made sure that the drovers and their herds kept within the bounds. The Western Kansas Cattle Growers Association had met on May 29, 1885, two months before the Hardesty War. Members of the association occupied ranch land in No Man's Land and decided to appoint an agent to direct the herds over the route from the Texas state line to Colorado. Martin S. Culver became the association's agent. During the first four weeks the route was opened, it was alleged that he guided four herds of Texas cattle numbering 10,000 head over the No Man's Land pathway.[16]

The editor of *The Guymon Tribune*, Richard Briggs Quinn, a few years later described this route in his paper:

> For many years the trail whipped in from over near the head of Fulton creek, or east of that locality, thence to water near the mouth of the Palo-Duro; thence to the mouth of Coldwater and on up the Beaver to a watering place not far from the present site of Guymon, then up to Tepee creek and across the divide to the Cimarron and into Colorado.[17]

In other words, the planned route went around the Kramer Ranch to the north and then "whipped in" from the north through the Hardesty Ranch to Fulton Creek to continue in a westerly direction across the Dudley Anchor D Ranch to Tepee Creek and on to Colorado.

THE 1886–1887 SEASONS:

When another season opened in the spring of 1886, the troubles of the former year had not gone away. The Texas Panhandlers and the Cherokee Strippers were planning another blockade of upcoming cattle herds. The opposing sides in the controversy decided to meet in Trinidad, Colorado, in May of 1886 in order to come to a compromise. It was decided that:

---

[15]Jean M. Burroughs, *On the Trail, The Life and Tales of 'Lead Steer' Potter*, 30.

[16]Alva Betz, *A Prowers County History*, 94.

[17]Richard Briggs Quinn, "The Old Cattle Trails Through Texas County," *The Guymon Tribune*, Vol. I, No. 2, Guymon, Oklahoma, June 23, 1921, p. 3.

Texas cattle from west of a line from Wilbarger County to Eagle Pass [Texas, on the New Mexico border] could pass through the Cherokee Strip without delay, provided they stayed on the trail; cattle east of this line and west of a line from Grayson County to Laredo by way of Cameron County could be driven through the Strip without stops, provided they had been driven all the way.[18]

The Pandandlers and Cherokee Strippers were aware that the south Texans could load herds into railcars and ship them part of the way bypassing inspectors and checking points. They decided to agree to conditions for trailing cattle through their area. For cattle shipped to the area, "forty-five days must elapse between the time they were unloaded from the cars and started through the Strip," and that "all cattle east of the last named line had to be on the trail fifty days before entering the Strip, or if shipped part of the way, seventy-five days must elapse."[19]

The year was a very dry and, according to trail driver, R. J. Jennings, "it was a very hard year for trail men, and many of them sustained heavy losses." Jennings was one of the trail bosses for the outfit of Blocker, Driscoll & Davis and wrote that the partnership had "about 20,000 cattle on the trail in different herds."[20] Ab Blocker, however, who was also a trail driver for Blocker, Driscoll & Davis in 1886, wrote that the partnership "had 57,000 cattle and 1,800 saddle horses on the trail that year."[21] And, W. B. Hardeman, a trail hand on another herd under Blocker, Driscoll & Davis, recalled that the partnership "drove forty thousand head of cattle, and had fourteen hundred horses."[22] Regardless of which old trail driver one believes, clearly the partnership of Blocker, Driscoll & Davis had thousands of head on the trail in 1886.

A severe blow to the cattle industry occurred in the winter of 1886. Blizzards and continuous freezing temperatures hit the mid-west from Montana to Texas in the latter part of December of 1886 and January of 1887. Thousands of cattle perished in the "Big Die Off."

By the summer, many cattlemen in several states were no longer in business. Ludwig Kramer & Sons lost over ninety per cent of their herd. They moved what cattle they had left to Colorado.

The tragic consequences of the 1886-87 winter may have influenced the change of the route in No Man's Land, but more likely, the shift in the trail took place because many settlers started moving into No Man's Land beginning in the fall of 1886. Towns were created and ranchmen, who had been squatting on the public lands, were pushed out. The settlers organized and by the spring of 1887 had passed laws that were detrimental to cattlemen. Thus, many cattlemen left the strip and moved their outfits, herds, and headquarters elsewhere. Within two years,

---

[18]*Taylor County News*, May 7, 1886 as referenced in William Curry Holden, *Alkali Trails*, 42.

[19]*Albany News*, May 20, 1886 and *Haskell Free Press*, June 18, 1886 as referenced in Holden, 42-43.

[20]R. J. Jennings, "My Third and Last Trip Up the Trail in 1886," in Hunter, 513.

[21]Ab Blocker, "The Man Who Had Hell in His Neck," in Hunter, 510.

[22]W. B. Hardeman, "Punching Cattle on the Trail to Kansas," in Hunter, 150.

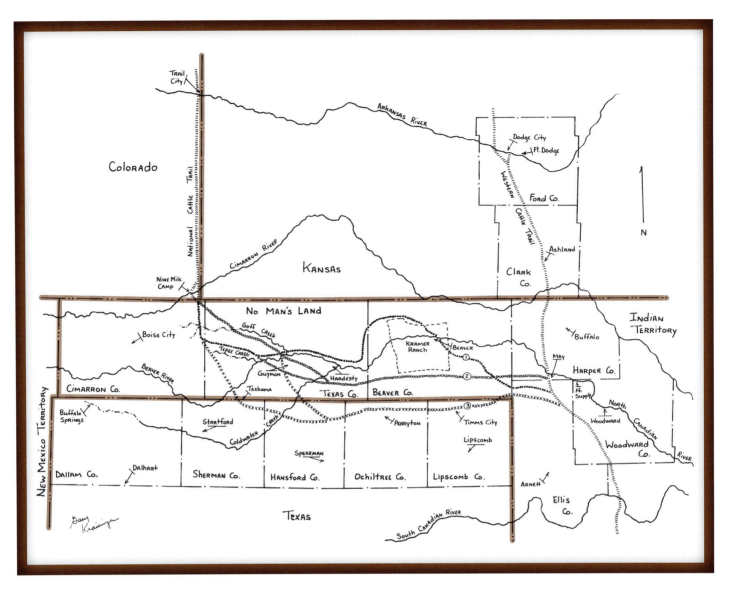

MAP #III, 2-1
No Man's Land:
This map shows the three feeder cattle routes from Fort Supply in Indian Territory to the southeast corner of Colorado to connect with the National Trail, 1885-1887.

The Northern Route (1): based on the road-side marker at Gate, Oklahoma, placed by the Beaver County Historical Society; and writings by newspaperman Richard (Dick) Quinn.

The Middle Route (2): based on a map from Man and the Oklahoma Panhandle, *by Jackson, Carlisle, and Colwell; and Harry E. Chrisman's map in* Lost Trails of the Cimarron.

The Southern Route (3): based on M. W. Anshutz map and the Jack Potter map in Cattle Trails of the Old West.

small cattlemen had come into the strip, and settlers acquired small herds.[23] The complexion of the area was changing.

Richard (Dick) Briggs Quinn, who has left a history of No Man's Land, arrived in the strip in January of 1887 as a lad of nineteen to visit his mother's brother Charlie Briggs. He stayed there for the rest of his life. Even though Quinn arrived two years after the Jack Hardesty War and the squabble over the pathway across No Man's Land, he became familiar with the cattle drives and the Texas drovers. His first recollections of the area were of the vast stretches of land and "all through the country were wide paths which the cowmen called trails," which were "worn down to the sod with no vegetation showing, to the width of a hundred yards."[24] He remembered the Johnny Fulkerson's Place, a family settlement being "a pretty good town in 1887 in No Man's-Land." The settlement had a store, a saloon, a wagon yard, and six or seven sod houses.

Shortly after Quinn's arrival in 1887, the Fulkerson settlement was renamed "Hardesty" after Colonel Jack Hardesty whose ranch headquarters was on Chiquito Creek nearby. A new "Farmers and Ranchers' Store" was owned and operated by W. A. Sullivan and his family. Dick Quinn and his uncle Charles Briggs homesteaded south of the Coldwater. The town was close to the Palo-Duro Trail and only a mile from one of the routes used by cowboys to cut across No Man's Land to the National Trail. (note Map Part #III: 2-1) Close by, at the mouth of Coldwater Creek, Texas cattle herds watered and camped, as "the bellowing of the cattle and the songs and shouts of the cowboys would be herd in the little settlement." Thousands of longhorns passed slowly along the trail in sight of the town.[25]

Quinn went on to become the *Hardesty Herald* editor for fourteen years, and then the editor of the *Guymon Herald* and the *Guymon Tribune*, and eventually became a United States Land Commissioner. After Oklahoma achieved statehood, he worked for the growth of Texas County and became a United States Marshal for the western district of Oklahoma.

Quinn was an eyewitness to the cattle drives and their cowboys. As the herds passed by the Hardesty area, he became acquainted with some of the drovers and understood their need to drive their herds across No Man's Land. He wrote that "for awhile," he was "employed to go along with the herds from the mouth of Coldwater to the next watering place on the Beaver, not far from Guymon," because "the trail herds were forced to keep within certain bounds. Through this section the route was limited to two miles in width."

---

[23]From the diary of Boss Neff written in 1939, Hooker, Oklahoma.

[24]From south to north the wide, well used trails included the Jones & Plummer freight trail and the Palo Duro-Dodge City cattle trail from the Goodnight Ranch. From east to west across No Man's Land were the cattle trails headed for the National Trail in Colorado. Then there were the mail routes and small settlement routes. (Elsie Cady Gleason, "Richard Riggs Quinn," *Chronicles of Oklahoma*, Vol. 18, No. 2, June, 1940, 118 and Richard Briggs Quinn, "The Old Cattle Trails Through Texas County," *The Guymon Tribune*, Vol. I, No. 2, pg. 3, June 23, 1921)

[25]According to Quinn, in the *Guymon Herald* of November 22, 1906, old Hardesty was first located on the south side of the creek, but was shortly moved to the north side. (Elsie Cady Gleason, "Richard Briggs Quinn," *Chronicles of Oklahoma*, Vol. 18, No. 2, June, 1940 and online)

On one occasion, the herd that Quinn was watching was being bossed by Ab Blocker. He wrote later:

> We had only one unpleasant encounter and that was not serious, although it could have developed into trouble. A herd dropped into water at the mouth of Coldwater. Alf [Ab] Blocker, a famous Texan, was in charge. When we rode up to Mr. Blocker he was mad clear through and had his war paint on. We told him our mission, and he called us to one side and pointed up the river. Said he, "Do you see that light streak up the river about two miles." When informed that we did, he exclaimed, "Well, right there, by God, is where I am going with these cattle." We knew that the place indicated was just two miles off of the designated route for trail herds and that argument would be of no avail, so we returned to town and advised the local men of conditions.[26]

The next morning twelve to fifteen men from the Hardesty and Kramer ranches, including Tom Hungate, Hardesty's foreman, rode out to Blocker's camp. They arrived there about noon.

Blocker was not surprised to see the group, for his outfit had heard "down the trail, even before we got to Fort Worth," that the "Neutral Strip" ranchers had organized. He later wrote, "It looked like every man had a Winchester rifle in his saddle boot and a six-shooter or two strapped on him. And even the boys were dressed that way! The way I remember it was that it looked like a place where the kids teethed on forty-five caliber cartridges!"[27]

Quinn, who was with the group, recalled the tense meeting. He recalled that Ab Blocker "came out smiling," and that his first words were: "Light, men, and have dinner."

Quinn continued his recollection:

> So every man dismounted and no word was uttered about our mission. After the meal, the crowd sat around and talked good naturedly and finally Blocker said, "Well, gentlemen, select some man to point this herd and we'll move out," and turning to the writer [Quinn], remarked, "Kid, you ride with me." And as we rode along he talked. Among other things he said, "Boy, I wasn't mad with you this morning, but that d_____ Kramer outfit and they tried to run it over me. You've put it over me in a way. Now these fellows with you are only trying to protect their little herds, but I know d_____ well they'll fight and mean business and I'm not looking for that kind of trouble." I told Blocker that the men with me had determined to make him follow the established route or escort his whole outfit back to the Texas line. His reply was, "Hell,

---

[26]Richard Briggs Quinn, "The Old Cattle Trails Through Texas County," *The Guymon Tribune*, Vol. I, No. 2, pg. 3, June 23, 1921.
[27]Harry E. Chrisman, *Lost Trails of the Cimarron*, 86.

I could see it when they rode up." We rode with Blocker for twelve or fifteen miles and during that time he told us many incidents of the trail, of the troubles and the pleasures connected with the work. We met him in after years as he came up the trail, likewise many others of his kind. They were all splendid men.[28]

This account by Quinn reveals that the northern route across No Man's Land was used for some time, from 1885 through, at least 1887. Hardesty had become a stopover for the trail cowmen and a refreshment stop for cowboys from the Hardesty Ranch. In 1891 when Quinn acquired the *Hardesty Times* and changed its name to the *Hardesty Herald*, the town leaders lobbied the Chicago, Rock Island and Pacific Railway (CRI&P) to go through their town. For years Hardesty was located on the railway's survey, and the town's people believed that they were destined to be a rail terminal and a great cattle shipping location, but in 1901, the railroad laid tracks twenty miles west, creating Sanford (present-day Guymon). Most of the Hardesty businesses and residents, including Quinn's *Herald*, moved to the new community.[29]

The summer drought of 1886 and the devastating winter blizzards created opportunities for the Texas cattlemen. For those ranchers who would continue to operate, more cattle would be needed to replenish herds that had been lost.

THE MIDDLE FEEDER ROUTE ACROSS NO MAN'S LAND:

According to the authors of *Man and the Oklahoma Panhandle*, there was a second cattle route across No Man's Land. Labeled the "Montana or National Trail" on their map, it tracked straight west from the east border of the strip across the south end of the Kramer Ranch, south of old Hardesty, crossed the Beaver River at the confluence of Tepee Creek due west of present-day Guymon, continued west, and then turned north after reaching the area straight south of the Colorado and Kansas corner borders.[30]

Harry E. Chrisman included this middle route on his map in *Lost Trails of the Cimarron*. He mapped the route across the middle of the "Neutral Strip" as going through the Hardesty Ranch and then turning north at the confluence of the Beaver River and Golf Creek, north of Present-day Guymon, and then followed that stream through the OX Ranch to the corner of Colorado.[31] It is not known how long this middle route was used, or it may have been used simultaneously with the lower feeder route.

---

[28]Quinn, *The Guymon Tribune*, June 23, 1921.

[29]Larry O'Dell, "Hardesty," Oklahoma Historical Society, http://digital.library.okstate.edu [accessed Nov. 8, 2009]

[30]Bernice Jackson, Jewel Carlisle, Iris Colwell, *Man and the Oklahoma Panhandle*, Diamond Jubilee (75th) issue, 1982. Map: "Ranches of the Texas-Okla. Panhandle," page 156.

[31]Chrisman, Ibid, 314-315.

THE WESTERN CATTLE TRAIL | 1874-1897

THE LOWER FEEDER ROUTE ACROSS NO MAN'S LAND: (Map #III, 2-2)

Because of the new "ownership" of the land with the arrival of settlers, another route farther south was created. Quinn wrote:

> Later on conditions forced the herds to travel along the south line of this county [present-day Texas County] to a Beaver crossing and watering place near the location of the old CCC ranch.[32]

The CCC ranch (the Cimarron & Crooked Creek Cattle Company) was organized by G.W.E. Griffith, a Mr. Cockins, and others in 1878. The headquarters of the "Chain C" brand was on the Beaver River near the southern boundary of No Man's

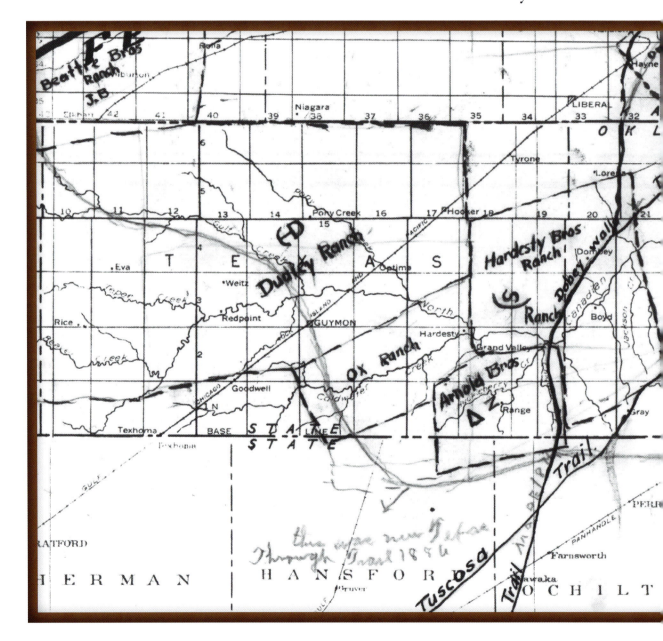

---
[32]Quinn, *The Guymon Tribune*, June 23, 1921.

Land, but the ranch's range stretched across present-day Texas County and into Kansas. The blizzards of late 1886 and early 1887, however, forced the ranch into an indebtedness of $50,000 with only dead cattle to back loans. After the Big Die Off, the ranch was reorganized and changed its brand to the Crooked L.[33] Quinn refered to it as the "old CCC ranch."

MAP #III, 2-2
A Portion of the M. W. (Doc) Anshutz Map of 1935, No Man's Land:
In 1935, Doc Anshutz showed on his map the "new Texas Through Trail, 1886" across the extreme northern boundary of the Texas Panhandle. The route crossed Coldwater Creek on the southeast end of the OX Ranch in No Man's Land and continued northwest toward the Colorado-Kansas border.

"Tim City" is also shown (penciled in) on the "Texas Through Trail" between the Tuttle Trail and Jones and Plummer Trail.

Map courtesy of No Man's Land Museum, Goodwell, Oklahoma.

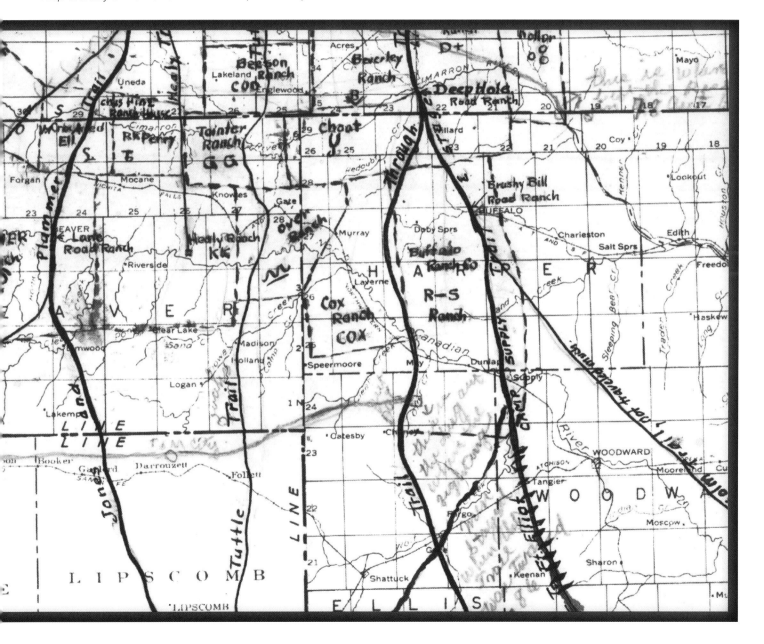

---
[33]Chrisman, Ibid, 94.

THE WESTERN CATTLE TRAIL | 1874-1897

This southern route is shown on the Anshutz map, as well. M. W. (Doc) Anshutz, came to Kansas in 1877 and was a ranch hand along the Cimarron and witnessed the development of ranches in the area in the mid-1870s and early 1880s. He called the southern route across No Man's Land the "new Texas Through Trail 1886." He had labeled the Western Trail from Texas to Dodge City, the "Through Trail," which is what the locals called the trail in those days.[34] Therefore, when cattlemen cut across No Man's Land to connect with the National Trail, a "new" route was established to replace the old one.

One could conclude from Anshutz's penciled comment on his map (created in December of 1935) that the feeder route across the northern edge of the Texas Panhandle, just south of No Man's Land boundary was actually started in 1886. He gives credibility to the third route by giving us a time line as well as the location of the route — especially by indicating the location of "Tim City" on the map.

George Timms, a Kansas capitalist, decided to develop a town along this new route, also assuming that the location would be the future site of a westbound railroad. Timms City, as he called his new townsite, was laid out sometime in 1886 in Section 1036, Block 43, near Kiowa Creek, three and one half miles southwest of present-day Darrouzett. The town quickly grew in 1887 to include a hotel, livery stable, W. F. Peugh's department store, a blacksmith shop owned by Martin Madison, several saloons, and even a newspaper. The town received its post office on December 2, 1887 with Josua T. Sedwick as postmaster. By this time, cowboys were camping with their herds on Kiowa Creek and enjoying the pleasures of Timms City saloons.[35]

Anshutz shows the southern route as leaving the "Through Trail" directly east of the northern boundary of the Texas Panhandle and hugging the Texas border, crossing the Tuttle Trail, passing by Timms City, crossing the Jones Plummer Trail, going by present-day Booker, and continuing to Fulton Creek. The route crosses Fulton Creek, passes over the Palo-Duro Trail ("Dobey Walls Trail" on his map), and swings slightly south to avoid the Arnold Brothers' Diamond Z range. South of Coldwater Creek, the route turns north angling across the Anchor D Ranch[36], by present-day Guymon, and follows Golf Creek to the corner of Colorado. (See Map #III, 2-2)

Jack Potter's map shows the "National Trail" also going across the northern boundary of the Texas Panhandle and turning northwest across No Man's Land to the Colorado-Kansas line.[37] Potter told Laura Krehbiel, his biographer that the route

---

[34]Anshutz, *Cimarron Chronicles*, 96.

[35]The deeded lots in the 160 acres of Timms City were recorded on January 3, 1888. However, when the feeder route to the National Trail ceased to be used, the railroad bypassed the town, and when the 1889 Cherokee Strip land rush occurred, its 400 residents abandoned the town. By 1890 the town was deserted. ("Timms City," vertical file folder located at the Wolf Creek Heritage Museum, Lipscomb, Texas, and *Amarillo Daily News*, Nov. 2, 1962)

[36]The Anchor D Ranch was established by Ezra C. Dudley and his son John around 1878. The Headquarters was on the Beaver (North Canadian) River about twenty miles west of present-day Guymon, Oklahoma. (digital.library.okstate.edu [accessed online, March 1, 2008] and Harry Chrisman, *Lost Trails of the Cimarron*, 79)

[37]"Map showing Cattle Trails as used from 1866 to 1895 for driving cattle on to shipping points or when trailing to northern markets," by Jack Potter, folded in the back of his book, *Cattle Trails of the Old West*, compiled and edited by Laura R. Krehbiel.

[went] up the northern tier of Texas counties to about where Texhoma is now located, entered No Man's Land, and crossed the Beaver River at or near the old Anchor D, Dudley ranch, and intersected the National Trail at Miles Camp, which was located on the Kansas corner.[38]

The Potter's map description is different from the Anshutz penciled route in that Potter extends the cattle route to the Texhoma area before turning north to reach the Colorado -Kansas border.

Evidence reveals that this lower route was used until the National Trail ceased to be utilized.

(Even though this lower route extended across the extreme northern portion of Texas, it started in No Man's Land and eventually crossed No Man's Land to connect with the National Trail. Therefore, this pathway is presented as part of the No Man's Land's three routes.)

THE NATIONAL TRAIL AND TRAIL CITY:

When it became evident that drovers were going to detour Kansas in the 1885 season and trail their herds through Colorado using a proposed government route, eastern Colorado cattlemen reacted. With strict quarantines now in place by their neighbors to the east (Kansas) and to the south (New Mexico), members of the Bent County (Colorado) Cattle and Horse Growers Association became vocal about the "vast herds coming from southern Texas."[39] The group announced that they had acquired land "at great expense" along the eastern portion of Bent County and wanted their right to this property protected. They further pointed out that Colorado law compelled herds to lay in quarantine north of the thirty-sixth parallel for ninety days before they could enter the state. However, they noted that the law "permitted [southern herds] to pass over our ranges after the rains cease and the grass matures," which would result in all the grass being eaten off, and "our native herds could not possibly live through the following winter." The association felt that without new regulations many of its members would have to give up cattle raising and lose a lifetime of building up herds and acquiring rights to the ranges.

The association resolved that its members would "cooperate in preventing the establishment of a cattle trail in Bent County." They vowed that they were not going to let any cattle enter the county. They would prosecute trespassers.[40] A message was sent out to all cattlemen along the state line that they were not to enter the county, and those that were already in the county, were ordered to not cross the Arkansas River because land along the river front to the Kansas line was owned by members of

---

[38]Krehbiel, Ibid, 47.

[39]The very large Bent County, named after Bent's Fort, that extended to the Kansas line, was created on February 6, 1874. In 1889, much of its territory was lost to the newly created counties of Cheyenne, Lincoln, Kiowa, Otero, and Prowers.

[40]From the preamble and resolution at the Bent County Cattle and Horse Growers Association meeting in West Las Animas on April 7, 1885. (Alva Betz, *A Prowers County History*, 92)

THE WESTERN CATTLE TRAIL | 1874-1897

the local cattlemen's association. They also informed the chairman of the up-coming convention promoting the locating of the proposed National Trail through Colorado that the Bent County Association would not allow the trail. Subsequently, the government committee proposed the route through Bent County anyway, but with controls and regulations. At that point, the Bent County cattlemen realized it was better to allow a six-mile path for the trail through the county than be exposed to the unregulated flow of cattle through their property, and they relented.

As soon as the National Trail route was announced and published in the summer of 1885, Martin S. Culver, a former Texan, obtained an easement from the government and, with partners, Howell P. Myton and W. S. Smith, selected a townsite in Bent County, Colorado, where the trail would cross the Arkansas River and the Santa Fe Railroad in section 17, township 23S, range 41W. The men, under the name of the Trail City Town and Improvement Company, invested $20,000 in capital stock in 200 shares worth $100 each to incorporate Trail City and claimed that it was going to be another "Cowboy Capital."[41]

As soon as the town was platted, Culver's Dodge City associates and supporters invested and started contructing buildings in the new town. Within days, merchants, brothels and saloon owners, and gaming-house operators from Dodge City joined the throng and moved to the site.

Businessmen in Coolidge, Kansas, just over the Kansas-Colorado line only three miles east of Trail City, became interested in the new town. Prohibition had come to Kansas, and saloons were disappearing in western Kansas, but liquor could be dispensed in Colorado. The chance to invest in a railroad town on a major cattle trail in a state that had no legal restrictions on drinking was an opportunity too good to pass up. Investors from Coolidge joined the rush to Trail City believing that easy money was soon to be theirs.[42]

Two factions emerged to embroil the area in controversy. Most occupants of Trail City, Colorado and investors in its businesses welcomed the Texas drovers and their herds. But cattlemen, who had claimed squatters' rights in No Man's Land, were preparing to throw roadblocks in the way of trailing herds. A new railroad town on the recently proposed national cattle route was exciting news, but the cattle blockade in No Man's Land meant that cattle were going to be stopped by fence riders.

In the summer of 1885, after facing Jack Hardesty and other ranchrs and being guided across No Man's Land, (with Martin S. Culver as one of the trail guides), trail drivers connected with the National Trail at the Colorado border in Baca County in Sec. 16, Twsp. 35S, Range 41W. At the corner of Colorado and Kansas, trail drivers

---

[41]Martin S. Culver, president of the improvement company, was a busy entrepreneur. He had moved to Dodge City in 1882 and opened a saloon. He placed himself among prominent cattlemen and became involved in local politics. Myton, the treasurer of the company, had served as deputy sheriff of Ford County in 1882 under Bat Masterson, and in 1883 had become the Registrar of the U.S. Land Office in Garden City. He was involved in the lumber business and was a vice-president of two banks. Smith, the secretary and kinsman to Myton, was interested in mercantile and land businesses and was involved in more than one developing town company. (Alva Betz, *A Prowers County History*, 93-94)

[42]Joseph W. Snell, "Trail City: A Note from the Record," 39, as reprinted in the *Kansas Quarterly*, date unknown, 39 and "Trail City, Ranches & Cattle Drives," www.usgennet.org [accessed Nov. 19, 2008]

had a choice. They could follow the proposed National Trail straight north along the border of Colorado or swing over to Nine Mile Camp on the Cimarron River, nine miles northwest. Water was the determining factor. The Cimarron River crossed the National Trail some six miles north of the border, but the river did not always carry water at this location. At Nine Mile Camp, water was usually available. A rider was typically dispatched to check out the river to the north and the Camp to the northwest, and then a decision was made.

Nine Mile Camp, or what Potter called "Miles Camp," was established as a line camp on the Beaty Brothers ranch sometime after 1884. John W. Beaty had established the Point of Rocks Ranch in Kansas in 1882 by filing a claim for a quarter section of land south of the Point of Rock landmark on the Santa Fe Trail in southwest Kansas. As the ranch expanded and extended into the open ranges of Colorado, line camps were established for the cowboys. Nine Mile Camp was one of those line camps and was nine miles west from the southwest corner of Kansas.[43] Jack Potter used the Beaty Ranch headquarters as a reference in his description of the National Trail. He wrote, "This trail [National] started from Point of Rock in the southwestern corner of the State of Kansas and left a gap of two hundred miles [actually 128 miles] between the Western [at Dodge City] and National Trails." Elsewhere in his book, he stated that cowboy outfits "intersected the National Trail at Miles Camp, which was located on the Kansas corner."[44] Potter considered the National Trail as starting at the corner of Kansas, on the Colorado side, and obviously used a cross-over from the Potter-Bacon Trail to Miles Camp (Nine Mile Camp) on the Cimarron. At Miles Camp, herds coming in from No Man's Land were joined by other herds coming from the west that had used the Santa Fe Trail off of the Potter-Bacon Trail. (see Map #III, 2-3)

A portion of the Ike Osteen map shows this cross-over from the corner of Kansas and Colorado through the "Sand Hills." Miles Ranch (Camp) was located on the Cimarron and the old Santa Fe Trail route. After herds were watered at the line camp location, they headed back to the National Trail along the Colorado border.[45]

Leaving Miles Camp, more than seventy miles from Trail City, the next possible water was at Bear Creek. If there was no water there, herds again swung off the main trail to Two Butte Creek to get water. From the Cimarron crossing to Two Butte Creek, a tributary of the Arkansas River, was a distance of fifty miles. It "was a semibarren, short-grass country which, during dry seasons, was completely without

---

[43]Nine Mile Camp or Miles Camp (Ranch) was located in Sec. 22, T34, R42. (Ike Osteen, *A Place Called Baca*, 143 & 154)

[44]Krehbiel, ed, and Potter, *Cattle Trails of the Old West*, 21-22. Because Jack Potter in his book stated that they picked up the National Trail at Miles Camp "located on the Kansas corner," we took him literally and wrote in our first book that the camp was located near the Kansas line. Since then, however, through interviews, further research, and a road trip, we discovered that the camp was nine miles west at a 45-degree angle from the southeast corner of Colorado.

[45]Osteen's map is located in the back of his book, *A Place Called Baca*. This detour from the proposed National to Miles Camp and back was somewhat longer by about ten miles, but Miles Camp was a destination.

THE WESTERN CATTLE TRAIL | 1874-1897

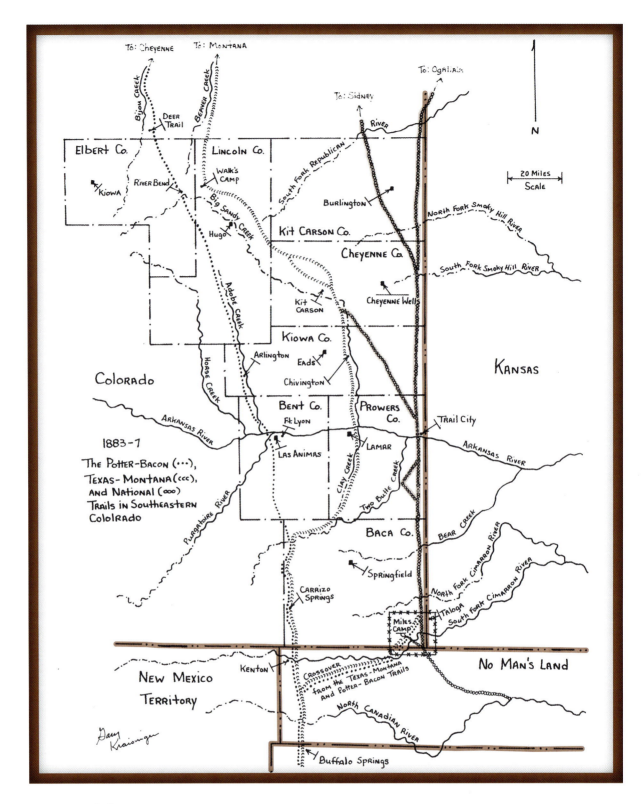

MAP #III, 2-3
Cattle Trails in Southeastern Colorado, 1883-1887:
This map shows: (1) the Potter-Bacon Trail from Buffalo Springs, Texas, across eastern Colorado to Cheyenne, Wyoming. Refer to Map #III, 2-4 for a close up of the southeastern corner of Baca County; (2) the Texas-Montana Feeder Route starting from Buffalo Springs, Texas going north across eastern Colorado toward Wyoming and Montana; and (3) the proposed National Trail along the eastern border of Colorado — used by herds coming from routes across No Man's Land and from a cross-over trail from the Potter-Bacon Trail (a section of the Santa Fe Trail).

water," according to Ralph F. Jones in his book, *Longhorns North of the Arkansas*. He described the drive:

> The trail boss would have a scout out looking for water in this barren country a couple of days in advance of the herd reaching the Cimarron. If there had been recent rains, water holes would be found and there would be no problem in crossing this country. However, if the scout had not found water, then it would be necessary to make the long fifty-mile drive without water and also to make dry camps between the two streams for the next couple of nights.
>
> …long before the break of dawn, the trail boss would shake out his riders and get the herd of thirsty cattle on up the trail, towards Two Butte Creek in an effort to get them on water before the hot part of the day. As they approached the small stream of Two Butte, and before they were close enough to the stream for the cattle to smell water, the herd would be broken up into small bunches. These bunches would then be led down slowly and allowed to go to the small stream only a few at a time, in order not to stir up and muddy the water for the cattle still to follow.[46][47]

Trail herds finally reached the Arkansas River where, on the far bank, the town of Trail City was extending its main street, called Trail Street, north from the Santa Fe tracks. Northbound herds were held along the river on the good river-valley grasses while the cowboys, who were usually paid upon reaching Trail City, took turns celebrating and enjoying the attractions of the over-night flash of a city.

The majority of the houses and businesses in Trail City had built along the main street, and those structures on the east side of the street had back doors that opened into Kansas. In the saloons, cowboys could sarcastically throw their empties into "dry" Kansas. The *Dodge City Globe Live Stock Journal* in August of 1885 noted that Trail City "is now looming up, and destined to become the rip roaring Texas cattle town of the west." However, it was still not known for certain that the national route would be accepted. The *Journal* commented: "Should this [the National Trail]

---

[46]Ralph F. Jones, *Longhorns North of the Arkansas*, 5-7.
[47]Six miles north of the Cimarron River on the Colorado-Kansas border inside the Kansas line in Kansas County (present-day Morton County), ground had been purchased and prepared in the fall of 1885 for a new town. The Topeka and Southwestern Land & Town Company wanted to locate a town as near to the southwest corner of Kansas as practical. Their reasoning was that a town in this locale would be in direct line of several proposed railroad lines. They purchased Sec. 16, T33, R43 and named the town "Taloga." The town would be close to the proposed National Cattle Trail. Even though Texas cattle were not allowed in Kansas, drovers could use the services of the community. Because of a severe winter, however, the town did not get platted and started until early the following summer. Fifteen families moved to Taloga, and a post office was established on June 1, 1886. By the later months of 1887, additional buildings had been erected and the town fathers were convinced that their community was on its way to becoming a railroad center. ("An Address Delivered by T. G. Shillinglaw, On the Occasion of the Laying of the Corner-Stone of the Public School House in Taloga, Sept. 25th, '87," as printed in the *Taloga Star*, Taloga, Kansas, Oct. 7, 1887)

2

TRAIL CITY

FACED WITH A KANSAS QUARANTINE ON THEIR CATTLE, TEXAS RANCHERS BEGAN DRIVING THEIR HERDS THROUGH EASTERN COLORADO IN 1885. THAT YEAR OVER 184,000 HEAD OF CATTLE PASSED THROUGH TINY TRAIL CITY, WHICH SAT ON THE KANSAS LINE JUST NORTH OF THE ARKANSAS RIVER. NORTHBOUND TRAIL RIDERS GOT THEIR FIRST PAYCHECKS HERE, AND THEY TOOK FULL ADVANTAGE OF THE THIRTY-ODD SALOONS, GAMBLING HOUSES, AND BROTHELS BUILT FOR THEIR ENJOYMENT. SHOCKINGLY SINFUL EVEN BY WILD WEST STANDARDS, TRAIL CITY PRODUCED ENOUGH DRUNKENNESS, VIOLENCE, AND DEBAUCHERY TO SHAME TOWNS MANY TIMES ITS SIZE. ITS LOCATION MADE TRAIL CITY A HAVEN FOR CRIMINALS, WHO COULD SLIP ACROSS THE STATE LINE AS NECESSARY TO ELUDE LAWMEN. BUT BY 1890 THE CATTLE DRIVES HAD ENDED, AND THIS SODOM ON THE PRAIRIE ABRUPTLY VANISHED.

KNIGHTS OF THE FRONTIER THEY WEREN'T. WITH ALL DUE RESPECT TO JOHN WAYNE, THE AVERAGE COWBOY WAS AN EXHAUSTED, HOMESICK LAD WHO COULD DO TWO THINGS EXCEEDINGLY WELL — RIDE AND HERD. USUALLY IN HIS TEENS OR EARLY TWENTIES, PERHAPS AFRICAN AMERICAN OR MEXICAN, THIS WELL-TRAINED, DISCIPLINED EMPLOYEE WAS CHARGED WITH MOVING $100,000 WORTH OF LIVE MERCHANDISE OVER ONE THOUSAND MILE OF WILDERNESS. THOUGH WATCHFUL FOR INDIANS AND OUTLAWS, THE COWBOY FOUGHT MOST OF HIS BATTLES AGAINST BOREDOM, FATIGUE, ORNERY STEERS, LIGHTNING STORMS, AND THE DUST KICKED UP BY TEN THOUSAND HOOVES. FOR HIS EXERTIONS HE RECEIVED FROM $25 TO $40 PER MONTH. TOWN STOPOVERS DID TEND TO GET ROWDY, BUT WHAT THE COWBOY CRAVED MOST — MORE THAN DRINK, MORE THAN WOMEN — WAS A BATH AND A SHAVE.

Location: On Highway 50 at the Colorado and Kansas state line, south side of the highway, three miles west of Coolidge, Kansas.
Prowers County, Colorado

Authors' commentary:
This is a very attractive marker with pictures. We don't know where the "184,000 head of cattle passed through tiny Trail City" comes from. Our sources (Goins and Goble, Betz, and Potter) all state that between 220,000 to 300,000 passed through Trail City in 1885.

The "thirty-odd saloons" is an exaggeration. Trail City was quite small and lasted only three years as a cattle town. Alva Betz, Prowers County historian, says, "there were never more than two whore houses in Trail City, and there certainly weren't as many as thirty [saloons]." (p. 100)

The date 1890 is mis-leading. After 1887, Trail City ceased to exist as a cattle town, and within one year, only 50 people still called Trail City their home. By 1890, Trail City disappeared.

The last paragraph describing the cowboy is a gem. We like it very much.

be made permanent, Trail City will become a city indeed. Lots are being disposed of very rapidly and people are fairly wild over their purchases."[48]

The building fever was wild at the end of August in Trail City. Lots were selling for one hundred dollars or more. Two saloons were up and going, a dance house was to be opened within a few days, and a general store and a livery stable were on the way. By the end of the following month, at the end of the season, lots were selling for as much as three hundred dollars, a newspaper moved in, and it

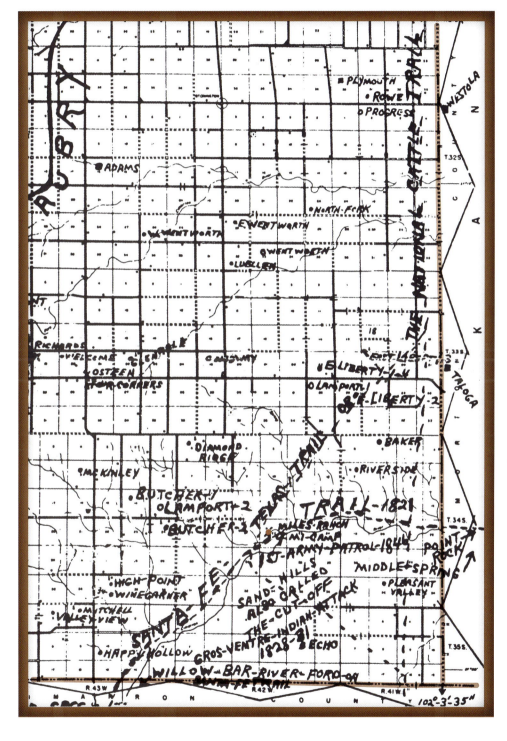

MAP #III, 2-4
Trails in the Southeastern Corner of Baca County, Colorado:
This is a portion of Ike Osteen's "Baca County Colorado" map from his book, A Place Called Baca (1973). It shows "Miles Ranch 9 Mi Camp" on the Beaty Brothers ranch and how it was accessed from the National Trail. Nine-Mile Camp (or Miles Camp) was on the Cimarron River on the old Santa Fe Route.

After visiting Miles Camp, drovers trailed their herds directly east or northeast to connect with the National Trail and eventually to Trail City.

They would have trailed their herds west to connect with the Potter-Beacon Trail, as Jack Potter related in his autobiography.

---
[48] Snell, Ibid, 39.

was rumored that some Texas cattlemen were planning to build a bridge across the Arkansas River at Trail City.[49]

Coolidge, Kansas merchants and businessmen, located a short hack's ride to the east, lived in a respectful dry Kansas town off the trail, but benefited from the wild speculations and money exchange of Trail City. While law enforcement was ineffective in Trail City because offenders crossed the line into Kansas or quickly made their way back to lawless No Man's Land, Coolige occupants sat outside of the "Hellhole on the Arkansas" and benefited from its growth.

In its first season of 1885, some 285,000 to 300,000 cattle trailed through Trail City. *(see footnote #1 of this chapter)* The processing of so many cattle created a bottleneck at the river where cattle piled up waiting to go through the trail checkpoint. Martin Culver not only guided herds up the trail to the city, he was also involved in town businesses, which included an agreement with the Santa Fe Railroad to collect two cents per head for each head of cattle that passed through their loading pens. Herds passed under the Santa Fe tracks over the dry Cheyenne Creek. The creek bed was deep enough for a man to sit on horseback and count the cattle as they passed through. Charles Goodnight recalled that it was not uncommon to have to wait for ten days to two weeks for the cattle to be processed. Jack Potter wrote that when he discovered that 285,000 head were ahead of him on the trail, he "bore off to the west and crossed the Arkansas about where new Fort Lyon is and continued north" in order to avoid the delay at Trail City.[50]

THE NATIONAL TRAIL NORTH OF THE ARKANSAS RIVER AND TRAIL CITY:
(Maps #III, 2-5 and 2-6)

North of the Arkansas River and Trail City is where Ralph F. Jones begins his excellent narrative about trailing longhorns out of the Texas Panhandle to the northern markets. He considered the Arkansas River as the natural division point between the southern and northern high plains country, "which extended for a thousand miles northward to the Canadian border." Jones was born on the Y Cross Ranch near Bushnell Creek in Colorado in 1895 where his father Frank E. Jones was the ranch foreman for the owner, H.B. Kelly. The younger Jones grew up hearing about the cattle herds that had been trailed by the Y Cross Ranch.

In later years, Jones wrote:

> After the perils of the river and particularly of Trail City, the trail boss would consider himself lucky if he moved out on the trail with a full crew. When the big herd was out of the valley, pointed northward and strung out on the trail for over a mile, the trail boss would probably ride his horse up on top of one of the rolling hills and, looking northward,

---

[49]Snell, Ibid, 40.
[50]Betz, Ibid, 100.

408   THE WESTERN CATTLE TRAIL | 1874-1897

give some thought to the problems which he might expect on the trail ahead. With his herd moving into that vast northern high plains country, referred to by the old trail drivers as the *Country North of the Arkansas*, he would know that in this big country, which extended northward a thousand miles from the valley of the Arkansas, emergencies could occur.[51]

Herds that were not shipped out on the Santa Fe rails from Trail City, continued north into the high plains north of the Arkansas. Which route the trail boss chose depended on his destination. There were three choices. Herds to be delivered into Wyoming and Montana cut over toward Kit Carson from Trail City and continued north to rejoin the Western at Rawhide Creek crossing in Wyoming. This route passed by the Y Cross Ranch.[52] This is also the splinter route from off of the National Trail that was referred to by two cowboys in J. Marvin Hunter's *The Trail Drivers of Texas*. Phil L. Wright, a drover for a Mr. Webb, mentioned earlier, was with a herd using the North Tom Green Feeder Route in Texas in 1885. Upon approaching the southern border of Kansas in this first year of that state's final quarantine, Wright wrote that his herd went:

> …out through the neutral strip known as No Man's Land, crossing the Arkansas River on the Kansas and Colorado line just above the town of Coolidge, Kansas, striking the Union Pacific Railway at Kit Carson, on to Hugo, Colorado,….[53]

It is striking that Wright mentions Coolidge, Kansas, and not Trail City. It was the first year that Trail City was building its cowboy town, and perhaps it was Coolidge that impressed Wright and his fellow drovers.

Jeff Connolly, also mentioned earlier, started up the trail in 1886 with cattle belonging to John Blocker. In his narrative, he does not name the trail, but it is understood that the herd was using the National Trail:

> Then we went on until we got to Camp Supply, where we had to go across the plains again [No Man's Land], and it was very dry…. We camped there that night and there came the hardest rain I ever saw fall, and it was so cold we nearly shook ourselves to death. It rained all the time from there on to Hugo, Colorado, where Blocker turned these cattle loose and where they were rebranded and turned loose again.[54]

---

[51]Ralph R. Jones, *Longhorns North of the Arkansas*, 8-10.

[52]J. Evetts Haley in his book *The XIT Ranch of Texas*, refers to this splinter route when he described the Texas-Montana Feeder Route going into Kit Carson. (This route will be discussed in the next chapter.) The Texas-Montana was "up the Sandy (Creek) to be joined by the eastern drive that came by Trail City, thence to Kit Carson." page 137.

[53]Phil L. Wright, in Hunter, 424. The Webb Ranch was located in Runnels County, Texas on the Colorado River adjoining the Blocker Ranch. In the first year that John Blocker delivered herds to Hugo, Colorado, the Webb herds "drove along the same trail with him."

[54]Jeff Connolly, in Hunter, 193.

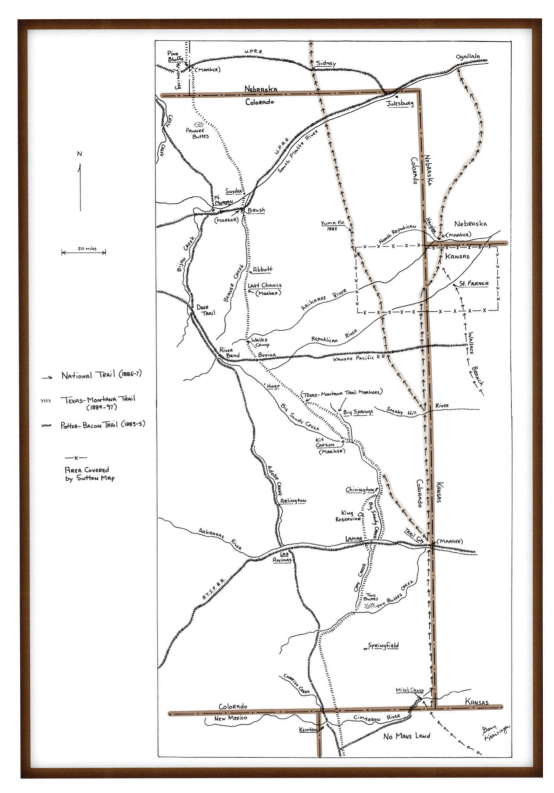

MAP #III, 2-5
The National Trail North of Trail City, Splinter Route and Branches:
This map shows: (1) the splinter route, north of Trail City, to connect with the Texas-Montan Feeder Route at Kit Carson, Colorado; (2) the branch, north of the Smoky Hill River, to Sidney, Nebraska. For a close-up of the boxed area, see Map #III, 2-6; and (3) the National Trail branch, north of the Smoky Hill River, to Ogallala, Nebraska before 1886.

If the herds were to be delivered into the Dakotas, then drovers continued north along the Colorado border until they reached the the South Fork Smoky Hill River. Here the trail split. The left fork of the trail to Dakota Territory veered off northwest to Sydney, Nebraska where it picked up the Sydney-Deadwood Road, then continued north to the Sydney Bridge on the North Platte River (present-day Bridgeport). Here herds re-connected up with the Western Cattle Trail.

The third splinter route began at the right fork at the Smoky Hill River and continued north until "about 100 miles beyond Trail City," it turned northeast cutting through the northwest corner of Kansas to reach Ogallala's shipping yards. According to trail driver Jack Potter:

> The drovers followed the state [Colorado] line for about 100 miles beyond Trail City and as the state line then headed across a high divide country which was not well watered, and as Colorado had no quarantine, the trail went farther west and did not touch the Kansas line until they made a turn northeast around the northwest corner of Kansas in order to get to the Ogalala [Ogallala] shipping point.[55]

According to E. S. Sutton, a Nebraskan historian, this National Trail splinter route, which he called the "West Texas Trail," crossed the Colorado line in Township 4 south, Range 42, into Cheyenne County, Kansas and joined up with the old Wallace Branch of the Western Cattle Trail in Township 1 south, Range 41, or in the Hackberry Creek area. Even though the route was in quarantined Kansas, that part of the state was very sparsely populated, so the few herds that slipped through did not matter to anyone. Trail drivers continued north on the Wallace Branch and followed the Texas Trail Canyon, a rugged Republican River side gulch, into Dundy County, Nebraska.[56] The route, which now carried cattle from the proposed National Trail, traversed across Dundy, Chase, and Perkins counties into Ogallala, Nebraska.[57] According to the roadside marker four miles east of Haigler, Nebraska (discussed earlier) "150,000 cattle were moved through here in 1886, the last year of the trail drives."

Texas cattlemen had delivered on foot just as many longhorns via the unsanctioned National Trail in 1885 as they had taken up the old Western Trail through western Kansas the year before. The big difference was that in 1885 they had to deal with the blockade in No Man's Land and comply with Colorado's quarantine stipulations. But, at least, there was a pathway to the north. If agreements could be made with the No Man's Land ranchers for a definite route through their ranches, and Colorado's quarantine requirements could be met, and if the National Trail were to

---

[55]Jack Potter, (Laura Krehbiel, ed), *Cattle Trails of the Old West*, 47.

[56]E. S. Sutton, map of cattle trails and historic sites in southwest Nebraska, created in 1953, located in the Dundy County Historical Society Museum, Benkelman, Nebraska.

[57]The Wallace Branch in Kansas and Nebraska is detailed in maps and narrative in our first book, *The Western, the Greatest Texas Cattle Trail*. Chapter 11, "North of Dodge to Ogallala: The Western Cattle Trail Wallace Branch Cut-off, 1883-1886, 239-263.

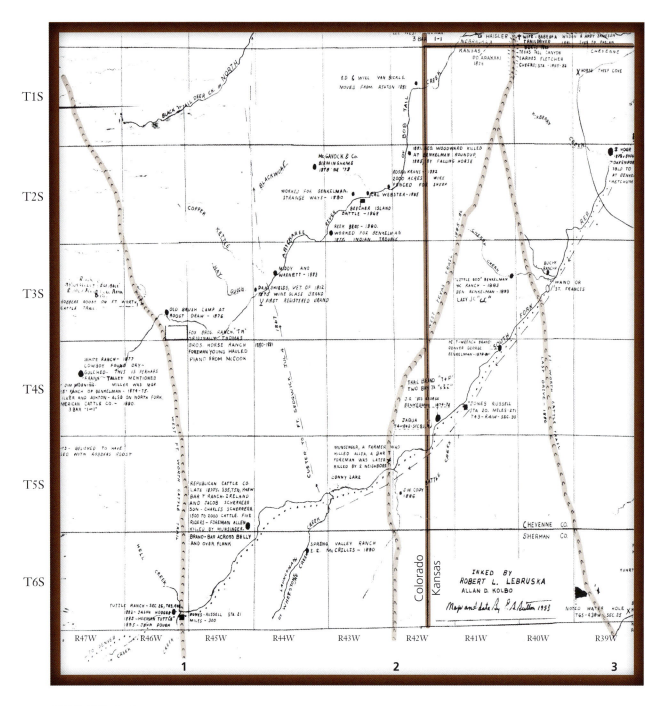

MAP #III, 2-6
Portion of E. S. Sutton Map (1953) of the National Trail in Northeastern Colorado and the Extreme Northwestern Corner of Kansas:
This map shows: (1) the National Trail route in Colorado to Sidney, Nebraska; (2) the National Trail route from Colorado across the northwestern corner of Kansas to Ogallala, Nebraska; and (3) the old Wallace Branch of the Western Cattle Trail.

Sutton called the National Trail in Colorado the "West Ft. Worth Cattle Trail." He labeled the National Trail route to Ogallala the "West Texas Trail, 1885-86," and he called the Wallace Branch from out of Kansas the "Ft. Worth Cattle Trail."

Map courtesy of the Dundy County Historical Society Museum, Benkelman, Nebraska.

be approved by the U.S. Congress, the following year could be back to normal and business as usual.

DEBATE OVER THE PROPOSED NATIONAL TRAIL CONTINUES:

When the first season of trail driving using the proposed National Trail came to an end, the future of that trail again took center stage. Bills authorizing a national trail were introduced into the U.S. Senate and the House of Representatives in December of 1885. Martin Culver rushed to Washington to lobby for the trail and his town. The Coolidge newspaper, the *Border Ruffian*, reported his return on January 30, 1886. "He says he feels sanguine that the Bill will become a law, and that Trail City will have a magnificent boom in the spring." The paper also printed a letter from someone in Trail City three days later, boasting about their growing community. In part, it bragged:

> Knowing the attitude of felicity you would arrive at in receiving news from Coolidge's suburb, we will mitigate your sufferings by informing you that the new opera house will be completed by March 1st, at which time Parcha Rosa will be on deck to warble to the unterrified of this community. A large delegation from your city is expected to be present….
>
> Our new church of Latter Day Saints and Sinners will be completed in a few weeks. The adobe frescoing is being manipulated at the present time, and bids fair to supersede that of St. Paul's Cathedral. It is suggested that your own Parson Painter be called on to shoot the inaugural address into the hearts of the Saints here….[58]

Residents and ranchers all along the proposed National Trail anxiously waited for Washington to make a decision throughout the winter of 1885-86. Culver had lobbied for the proposed route, but he had not been the only lobbyist. Since the moment the resolution had been initiated at the cattle industry convention in November of 1884 and throughout 1885 as trail drivers used the proposed National Trail, a wave of anti-trail sentiment had been increasing. Affected states had retaliated and passed quarantine laws, Kansas being the first to act immediately in March of 1885. Northern cattlemen, who didn't want any more Texas cattle and were openly against a sanctioned national trail, had lobbied all year to try to stall the introduction of the bill, and they had the voice of *The Breeder's Gazette* on their side.

Trail drivers, as they had done for years, pushed their longhorns north to market in the 1885 season, and promoters, investors, and merchants feverishly built a railhead on the Santa Fe in an open field in Colorado in the summer of 1885, which they named "Trail City," As this whirlwind of activity was occurring, the debate over the proposed cattle trail continued. The turmoil, which stemmed from the cattlemen's national convention in November of 1884, had not died down. Congress would soon vote on the proposed trail, and various interests would seek to effect the outcome. The Joseph Nimmo report to the House of Representatives, would have a significant impact on the debate.

---

[58]Snell, Ibid, 40.

THE WESTERN CATTLE TRAIL | 1874-1897   413

The journal had denounced the St. Louis convention of 1884 and angrily reported "that the session had been corrupted by Texans and by Kansas City cattle buyers." The *Gazette* announced that the convention had been "staged solely for the benefit of the stockmen of the extreme west and southwest."[59] Therefore, northern cattlemen, predominantly from north of Kansas and Colorado, formed another association, the "National Cattle-Growers' Association," and called for another convention to be held in Chicago. Meeting almost exactly a year after the St. Louis convention, on November 17, 1885, this group stated that they opposed the National Trail and called upon Congress to enact stronger controls over "the migration of diseased animals, so long as federal action did not infringe upon states' rights."[60]

Congressmen were being lobbied by the advocates of the trail as well. The Cattle Raisers Association of Northwest Texas knew that the fever epidemic of 1884 in the north had intensified bad feelings among northern cattle breeders. In response they passed the following resolution:

> Resolved that owing to the fact that Kansas and other States north and west of us have enacted quarantine laws which practically prevents Texas cattle from being driven through or into such States on account of what they allege to be splenic or Texas fever in Texas cattle, the effect of which is to make the market for marketable cattle in Texas inaccessible, we do therefore most earnestly request our State Legislature now in session to pass a law authorizing appointment of sanitary commissions….[to] suggest such a remedy for the existing evils as they think best.

The association then asked the U.S. Congress "to pass whatever laws were necessary to quarantine disease-carrying cattle but to exercise discretion so that the *trails would not be totally blocked*. [italics added]" Texas state Governor John Ireland and the Texas Legislature soft peddled the association's view and felt that a system should be adopted "to protect our stock system." They sent a resolution to the senators and representatives in Congress that Texas "respectfully requested aid in securing the establishment of a national trail for the outlet of Texas cattle."[61]

Finally, on December 2, 1885, Texas Senator Richard Coke introduced Senate Bill 721 authorizing a national cattle trail. A duplicate bill was presented to the House, eighteen days later, by Texas Congressman James F. Miller. Cattlemen on both sides of the issue had aired their views and it was now up to Congress to decide.

---

[59]Taken from *The Breeder'e Gazette*, VI (Nov. 27, 1884), 778. and (Dec. 18, 1884), 900, in Jimmy Skaggs, *The Cattle-Trailing Industry*, 113-114..

[60]Taken from the *Proceedings of the Third Annual Convention of Cattle Growers Held at Chicago, Ill, November 17 and 18, 1885* (Chicago: John Morris Company, 1886), 44ff, in Skaggs, Ibid, 115.

[61]Taken from "Minutes, [1877-1893] of the Cattle Raisers' Association of Northwest Texas, March 10, 1885," (Archives, University of Texas at Austin); Note the pointed comment: "what they allege to be splenic or Texas fever." Obviously the Texas cattlemen felt that the northern breeders were using the fever as an excuse to stop the flow of trail cattle. Skaggs, Ibid, 115-117.

The Senate committee, headed by Samuel J. R. McMillan of Minnesota, asked the Secretary of the Interior, L.Q.C. Lamar, to investigate the issues raised by the proposed bill. Lamar considered the issue of public domain, the overall state of the cattle industry, and the need for cheap beef in the north. He finally concluded at the end of the five-page report that the bill should be passed because he felt that it would "give people of all parts of the country food at moderate prices."[62]

The House had asked H. McCulloch, the Secretary of the Treasury, for information on range and ranch cattle. Under his direction, a massive report from the Chief of the Bureau of Statistics, Joseph Nimmo was placed in their hands.[63] The information in the 200-page report had been gathered over several months and included everything in regard to range and ranch cattle from the characteristics of the industry, and issues such as relations with the Indians, weather, quarantine laws, shipping and transporting, foreign ownership, business with Canada, and exportation. The massive report was augmented by over fifty pages of appendices containing letters, laws, maps, charts, and weather data "furnished by experts and others." The sections on the trailing of herds north and the Texas Fever were of particular interest to the House Committee.

Nimmo's report laid out three distinct reasons northern cattlemen opposed the continuance of the Texas cattle trade.

> It appears to be a fact beyond all controversy that a very large number of the present occupants of the northern ranges, constituting probably more than a majority of their total number, is openly and earnestly opposed to the driving of Texas cattle to the northern ranges upon considerations of a purely commercial and economic nature. First, they do not wish to be confronted by the competition of the Texas cattle in their midst. Second, they find that the Texas cattle in very many places "eat out" the grasses upon ranges which for years past they have regarded, as by prescriptive right, their own. Third, the contact of their herds with the Texas herds tends to depreciate the breed of their cattle….

The real reason the northern cattlemen did not want a Texas outlet was because Texans were flooding the market with their herds, the longhorns were inferior animals, and they "eat out the grasses." Nimmo reinforced his point with a quote from a Wyoming rancher, A. T. Babbitt:

---

[62]L. Q. C. Lamar presented his report to the Senate committee on January 19, 1886. It was during this time that Martin S. Culver was in Washington lobbying for the bill. Because of Lamar's favorable report, Culver returned to Trail City on January 30 and announced that the bill would probably pass. (quote from Skaggs, 116)

[63]On February 17, 1885, the House had ordered by resolution to H. McCulloch, Secretary of the Treasury, a report "calling for information in regard to the range and ranch cattle traffic in the Western States and Territories." *Letter from The Secretary of the Treasury: transmitting a report from the Chief of the Bureau of Statistics*, presented to the House of Representatives, 48th Congress, 2nd Session, Ex Doc No. 267 (Emporia State University, William Allan White Library, "Western American 1550-1900, Frontier History of the Trans-Mississippi West," Reel 41, No. 3894-3905 — report #3903)

We did not object to it [National Trail] on the ground of the liability of infection, or of cattle disease, because cattle driven from the south have never hurt us so far north, and we are not afraid of them. We have objected to the trail simply on the ground of safety of our investments. We have believed that if Government made an appropriation whereby a public highway for cattle was to be established, over which the immense herds of surplus cattle from Texas were to be invited to come and overwhelm us, we were in danger of obliteration and extinction.[64]

Northern cattlemen had made money on Texas cattle over the years but, according to Babbitt, they wanted "fair control of the ranges we desire to occupy."[65]

As for the Texas Fever, Nimmo felt that the introduction of a quarantine law "with the respect to the conditions of time and space, as has been done by the State of Kansas and Colorado, is of course a debatable question."[66] Nimmo felt the restrictions were too strict and harsh. Nimmo continued to say that "it would appear that the dangers...have been considerably exaggerated, and that the Texas cattle trail might safely be continued under proper sanitary regulations."[67]

Nimmo looked at the issue from an economic standpoint rather than its relation to the public domain as the Secretary of the Interior had. He did not take a stand on the issue one way or the other, but made it clear that a free open market, with controls, was necessary. He understood that there was a real concern from the northern herdsmen of receiving too many Texas cattle that resulted in overgrazing and dilution of herd bloodlines. To Nimmo, the Texas Fever was one of the ordinary hazards of life. It was not to be ignored, but controlled cautiously and during extreme epidemic conditions. Nimmo also stood on the side of states' rights — but expressed a disdain for states, like Kansas and Colorado, that took over too much control ("power") and stifled the course of the "purely economic nature" of the United States. He concluded his thoughts on the matter, but did not mention Kansas and Colorado by name:

The organic law of the United States establishes throughout all parts of the country absolute freedom of commercial intercourse.... That the freedom of commercial intercourse should be invaded or even threatened by indirection, through the exercise of the police powers

---

[64]Nimmo's report, 38. A. T. Babbitt had been the Wyoming delegate to the National Cattlemen's Convention in St. Louis on November 17, 1884.

[65]By the early 1880s, northern ranchers were importing cattle from Oregon and the Mid West. A more beefy animal was desired, and the lanky longhorn was no longer desired. As northern cattlemen tried to upgrade and improve the breed of cattle, the longhorn became considered unacceptable. Cows and bulls were intermingled on the ranges, and the Texas longhorn bulls interfered with efforts to improve the breed. The Indian agencies, however, continued to do business with the Texas cattlemen because they were not that particular with the quality of cattle consumed by tribesmen.

[66]The time frame of the Kansas law was from March 1 to December 1, and the "space" Nimmo refers to is the limitations for cattle from below the 37th parallel. (*Laws of Kansas*, 1885, 309)

[67]Nimmo's report, 37-38.

of a State for sanitary purposes, is repugnant to the cherished love of liberty which has from the beginning characterized the people of this country…. Those powers, in their application to sanitation, are designed to meet the exigencies of epidemics and unusual or extraordinary visitations, and not to protect against the ordinary and usual hazards of life. Pushed to the extreme, the exercise of such powers might arrest all enterprise and stop the wheels of commerce. It is inconceivable that the people of any State of the union would countenance such an unwise and unfair exercise of power, if convinced that it was not abundantly justified by an emergency demanding the interposition of a sanitary rule restrictive of commercial freedom. Any such action would meet the condemnation of the whole country, for it would be opposed to the fundamental principles of our institutions, and it would go in the face of all right, and all justice, and all magnanimity.[68]

In addition to receiving the Nimmo report from the Secretary of the Treasury, the House also placed the Congressional proposal for the National Cattle Trail in the hands of the Committee on Commerce. John H. Reagan of Texas, the chair of that committee, announced its approval of the proposal on March 23, 1886.

Just a week before the House proposal was approved in committee, the Senate unanimously passed the measure after receiving a favorable report from their commerce committee. Thus, both commerce committees from the House and the Senate gave their approval. The Secretary of the Interior was in favor of the proposed trail, but the Secretary of Treasury with Nimmo's Bureau of Statistics report was undecided. Nimmo had researched the issue and wrote a sound argument based on field work. To representatives on the Hill, Nimmo's carefully laid out points made sense. He struck down the argument from the northern cattlemen regarding the Texas Fever and had justified his argument on a constitutional basis. All through the months of March and April, Representatives reviewed Nimmo's comments.

The house bill did not make it to the floor of the House until April 23, and Reagan led the fight for passage. The bill received a favorable 69 to 29 vote, but a quorum was not present. Representative Reagan was forced to withdraw the bill. Was it because of Nimmo's report? It was expected that the bill would be re-introduced for a re-vote, but it never was.[69] In late April, Texas herds were already on their way to No Man's Land and would use the proposed National Trail. There was no longer a reason to push the matter. Ranchers in No Man's Land had created a guarded path across their lands, and Colorado had relented. The narrow strip of land along its extreme eastern border had been used successfully in 1885 to isolate the Texas longhorns. With regulations in place, it was now assumed that the path would be tolerated.

---

[68]Nimmo's report, 39.
[69]Skaggs, Ibid, 117.

THE WESTERN CATTLE TRAIL | 1874-1897

THE NATIONAL TRAIL AND TRAIL CITY, THE 1886-1887 SEASONS:

Even after the failure of Congress to pass the proposed National Trail, supporters of Trail City believed that the trail would eventually be accepted and continued to provide access to the north for Texas cattle. In the spring of 1886, construction of buildings in the town was underway, and a new lumber yard appeared. Optimism was so rampant that a telephone line to Coolidge was planned and a street car company incorporated.

I. P. (Print) Olive, a well-known Texas cattleman, established his Trail's End — a stable with corals, a wagon yard, and windmill. He also invested in a saloon called the Longhorn with partner Walt Hart. Culver owned a large limestone hotel which was said to be "second only to the Silver Star in Coolidge." H. M. Beverley, formerly from Dodge City, had a supply store which, according to the *Border Ruffian* on May 22, 1886, was "filled from top to bottom with goods of every description." It was one of the largest buildings "we have ever seen in the west."[70] Dodge City entrepeneur Bob Wright had a trail-outfitting store. There was Richmond and Dunbar's real estate office, and another saloon and dance hall owned by Joe Sparrow. Martin Culver also owned a saddlery and harness store which employed five full-time leather workers.

Many of the businessmen in Trail City lived in Coolidge, and four to six hacks hustled back and forth between the two towns daily. The fare was 50 cents round trip and, supposedly, dance hall women and pretty girls rode free. "Each hack had three seats and ordinarily carried six people, but when the driver had a dance hall girl sometimes as many as a dozen men would try to crowd in."[71]

The townspeople were expecting 200,000 to 350,000 head of cattle from Texas in 1886. The little town of about 200 residents more than doubled in size during the summer months and planned to be very busy that summer.

It didn't happen. During the summer of 1886, as noted earlier, the area suffered a severe drought. R. J. Jennings went "up the trail" from Texas for his last time in 1886 and reported that it was a very "hard year for trail men" because of the exceedingly dry weather. It was a "hard road" because "we found no grass and but little water." Jennings had started in south Texas with a herd of 2,500 head of Blocker, Driscoll & Davis cattle to be delivered in Colorado. (The Blocker brothers, J. W. Driscoll, and Davis had sent herds up in 1885 — they were apparently the first ones up the newly established National Trail and to arrive at Trail City.) Then, in 1886, Jennings said that the company had about 20,000 cattle on the trail in different herds. Trail boss Jennings traveled the Western Trail to Vernon, Texas, used the National

---

[70]Joseph W. Snell, "Trail City: A Note from the Record," as reprinted in the *Kansas Quarterly*, date unknown, 41.
[71]Betz, Ibid, 97.

Trail, and "delivered the herd on the north side of the Arkansas River at Coolidge, Kansas, or rather at Trail City, Colorado, there being only the state line between the two towns," he recalled.[72]

The *Coolidge Border Ruffian* reported on August 21, 1886, that 76,918 head of cattle had passed through Trail City between June 5 and July 19, 1886. By the end of August, the season was about over and, according to the *Ruffian*, businesses were starting to close down in Trail City for the season. Even if August numbers were added to the paper's tally, it would not equal the total number reported by *The Tascosa Pioneer*. On September 28, 1886, the *Pioneer* reported that 225,000 cattle had used the National Trail that year. Also, if the Haigler, Nebraska road-side marker is to be believed, that 150,000 head used that splinter route from National Trail to Ogallala, it still remains to be less than half of what was expected in Trail City.

The basic reason that Trail City received fewer herds in 1886 was because the Texas-Montana Feeder Route was now being used. J.E. May, who was a trail boss for the LS Ranch in the Texas Panhandle, had blazed a trail due north from Buffalo Springs, Texas in 1884, using, in part, the Potter-Bacon Trail, to the LS finishing ranch in Montana. It was a more direct route for the Texas Panhandle ranchers, and it by-passed Trail City.

The new XIT Ranch, that had stocked its ranges in the Texas Panhandle for the first time in 1885, had contracted fifteen thousand head to be trailed north in 1886. The herds were trailed through Colorado on "the Northern Trail" to Spearfish, South Dakota.[73] In its maiden year to trail cattle north, the LS Ranch's new neighbor would naturally follow this more direct route. So in 1886, there may have been 225,000 head on the trail, as the *Tascosa Pioneer* reported, but they all did not use the National Trail. The southern Texas cattle continued to be trailed through No Man's Land and over the National Trail, but the Texas Panhandle ranches had now taken their place as the new gathering area for trail cattle and would, over the next decade, deliver cattle to the northern ranges over a route farther west than Trail City.

Another reason for the decline of the National Trail was that quarantines were starting to make a difference. Northern buyers were more aware of the liabilities of Texas longhorns, because of the quarantines and negative press. Many of the cattle on the trail in 1886 were not sold. Between 1886 and 1887, steers dropped in price from $30 per head to $6 or $10 per head.

Another factor that worked against Trail City and the cattle-trailing industry was the Nebraska herd law that was passed in 1886. Different than a quarantine, the herd law did not prevent cattle herds from passing through its state, but made the trail boss accountable for every animal that caused damage while trailed through the state. If any part of the herd trespassed onto a homesteader's or rancher's property, the stock could be confiscated and the trail boss fined, delayed, and called into court.

---

[72]R. J. Jennings, "My Third and Last Trip up the Trail in 1886," in Hunter, 513-515.
[73]J. Evetts Haley, *The XIT Ranch of Texas*, 126.

Consequently, after the 1886 season, the two northern routes from Trail City into Sydney and Ogallala, Nebraska, ceased to be used.

Settlement of land in Colorado, western Kansas, and western Nebraska intensified during this time. Homesteaders continued to push west. On August 4, 1886, Congress authorized the establishment of the Bent Land District. The district was 145 miles long and 70 miles wide, with its land office in Lamar opening on January 1, 1887. Six months later, on July 25, Range 41 west through which the National Trail extended, was opened for settlement. Over one hundred filings were recorded on the first day. Scores of towns were developed wherever there was a railroad stop, a creek crossing, or a community settlement.

Over the winter of 1886 and 1887, the National Cattle Trail proposal was not revived and seemed to have been forgotten by Congress. Then in late December of 1886 and early January of 1887, the worst blizzard and cold spell in decades hit the mid-west. Thousands of cattle died or were rendered unmarketable, and many ranchers were financially devastated, never to recover their losses.

Trail City businessmen, however, would not give up. As the 1887 season rolled around, the local newspapers bragged about their town and pretended that the trail was still viable. The subject of the street car line between Coolidge and Trail City arose again. Both the *Bent County Register* and the Coolidge *Citizen* discussed its possibilities. But as July came around the editor of the *Citizen*, probably reacting to the fact that Range 41 west had been opened for settlement, wrote: "There is no longer a market for these Texas herds in the north.... The day of the range cattle industry is over. The granger has taken possession of the 'Great American Desert,' both in Kansas and Colorado. The territory composing the historic trail will now be dotted with farms, and no more Texas herds will be driven over it."[74]

A few herds used the National Trail in 1887. The one remaining route to Wyoming and Montana by way of Kit Carson was used. Herds still trailed through No Man's Land to connect with the National Trail in 1887 because Dick Quinn, who homesteaded on Coldwater Creek, recalled assisting herds trailing across the Strip.

The west branch of the National Trail, used in 1885-1887, re-connected with the Western Trail in Wyoming at Rawhide Creek. North of the Rawhide, the Western remained intact. Its pathway continued to be used to reach buyers and finishing ranches farther north. For three years, the National Trail had been a detour around Kansas, and in the last year of 1887, it detoured around Nebraska. As for the old Potter-Bacon trail, it was sparsley used because it only went as far north as Cheyenne, Wyoming.

After Range 41 west was opened to settlement, and the two Nebraska routes by way of the National Trail were no longer an option, Texas cattlemen shifted to the

---

[74]*Coolidge Citizen*, Coolidge, Kansas, July 31, 1887. Trail City was short lived and died a quick death. In the summer of 1886, Trail City had a population of 500 — 300 were transient. In 1888, the Colorado Business Directory listed Trail City as having a population of 50. By 1889, the railroad station and post office were gone, but there were still 50 people living there. ("Ranches & Cattle Drives," www.usgennet. org/use/co/county/prowers/hist/ranches.html [accessed Feb. 16, 2007]

newly established Texas-Montana Route. Trail City had boomed, thrived, and died in three years. The dreams of its promoters and local businessmen were shattered.

The failure of the federal government to authorize the national route for Texas cattle was the second major blow to the cattle-trailing industry. After the Kansas quarantine of 1885 and the demise of the National Trail, the Western Cattle Trail would continue farther north, but the industry itself was slowly coming to an end..

CHAPTER III

The Texas-Montana Feeder Route 1884-1897

&

The End Of The Cattle Trailing Industry

Two cowboys *pose for a cameraman. From their attire, we can assume they are somewhere in the northern territores. The cowboy on the left wears wooly chaps, and his partner has on a jacket, vest, and under-shirt.*

Photo in owner's collection.

In historical archives and on older trail markers in Colorado, the cattle trail (other than the National Trail) that detoured around Kansas and Nebraska starting in 1884 and 1885 has been labeled the "Texas-Montana Trail." It was called this for obvious reasons. Trail drivers pushed their herds from the Texas Panhandle across Colorado and Wyoming to their destinations in Montana. This "Texas-Montana Trail" has been viewed for years as a separate pathway, the last one to carry Texas herds north. We contend, however, that this route is part of the entire Western Cattle Trail System. It was a feeder route that connected with the older established trunk line of the Western Trail at Rawhide Creek near Fort Laramie in Wyoming. This assertion is the reason for this work — to show that the Western Trail System continued after the 1885 and 1886 Kansas and Nebraska quarantines and that Texas cowboys continued to trail herds north for another decade. This feeder route should be more accurately termed the "Texas-Wyoming Feeder Route," but we will use the historic term, "the Texas-Montana Trail." The following cowboy journals record the use of this pathway, the one trail drivers of Texas used in their last drives to deliver herds north.

A QUICK REVIEW:

The National Cattle Trail proposal was a possible solution for a detour around Kansas after its quarantine of 1885. The challenge for Texas trail drivers was to maneuver around the blockades and quarantines and to get their herds to a destination in the north. When the 1886 herd law in Nebraska was passed, however, the two eastern splinter arms of the National Trail were severed. (see Maps Part III, Chapter II, #3 and #4) The pathways into Nebraska ranch lands and the well-used routes to the reservations in the Dakotas, by way of Nebraska, were no longer available. Local northern stockmen had gotten their way. They now hoped to monopolize the contracting for the beef supply to government Indian agencies, in addition to shipping beef cattle east without any competition from incoming Texas cattle.

But the Kansas and Nebraska cattle laws had not closed down the upper portion of the Western Trail trunk line into the Dakotas (Part II, Chapter VII) by way of Rawhide Creek in Wyoming or into Montana and Canada. This destination became the new focus of Texas drovers. By the 1886 season, it had become obvious to trail drivers that the Trail City route was doomed, not only because of Nebraska's actions, but because Congress had not passed legislation regarding the National Trail. No narrow strip of land to trail Texas cattle along the Colorado eastern border would be sanctioned for Texas drovers.

The National Trail, during its short existence, had kept the cattle-trailing industry afloat while Texas cattle contractors re-aligned their industry for the years to come. Southern Texas ranchers faced an increasing problem of moving herds across Texas which was being filled with settlers and fencing. Texas herders were associated with the "offense," (as the Kansas quarantine law stated) of trailing herds with the Texas Fever. Therefore, a new trail direction and selling campaign had to be presented to northern buyers. The shift in strategy had not happened overnight. For years, Charles Goodnight, one of the first Panhandle pioneer ranchers, and his neighbors had worked tirelessly to distance their cattle from the southern herds. The carefully orchestrated Winchester Quarantine (Part II, Chapter V) had been successful, and

Goodnight's convincing argument to the Kansas Legislature and prospective buyers that the Texas Panhandle was not like south Texas with its infected herds, had reaped concessions from the State of Kansas and the respect of northern buyers.

As southern herds were being trailed through No Man's Land and up the National Trail, Panhandle ranchers were not only improving their herds through breeding, but they were also positioning themselves to become the new heartland and gathering area for Texas cattle. They promoted themselves as reputable dealers of upgraded clean cattle.

In the crucial years of 1884 to 1887, another influential ranch joined the ranks of the Panhandle group and helped develop this new direction for the cattle-trailing industry. The immense XIT was established in 1884, started to stock its ranges in 1885, and was ready to trail cattle through Colorado in 1886.[1]

The expansion of the railroad also affected the industry at this time. Starting in 1872, rail lines reached northern Texas and transported some cattle northward, but it wasn't until the early 1880s that railroads expanded their services into the western areas of Texas. Southern Texas stockmen, who now found their market choked off from the north by the rapid advancing homesteaders and their fences, could haul their herds part way by rail. (Drovers rode the train along with their herds to handle the cattle to and from the railcars.)[2] They then trailed the herds over the final stretch to their destination. Ranchers in the western part of Texas and the Panhandle located west of the encroaching immigration of settlers, continued, for the most part, to trail their herds. Expert contractors and experienced trail hands knew that cattle on the trail reached their destination in better condition than when they started; trail animals weren't stressed by the cramped quarters of a railcar or prevented from grazing and watering at crucial times of the day. The major factor was that cattle could be trailed from Texas to Montana for a fraction of the cost of a rail haul.

In order to compete with the northern suppliers of beef, it became prudent for large cattle ranches to establish finishing ranches in the north. Cattlemen had learned over the years that steers matured rapidly on the northern grasses, increasing in bulk and weight. After a year or two of growth these cattle were marketable and ready for delivery. By 1887, the days were coming to an end when government agencies and northern ranchers contracted for a certain number of head to be delivered in one season from the home ranch in Texas. Contracts and deals were now made between a buyer and seller, and the product — rather than being hundreds of miles away in Texas — was already located in the neighborhood of the buyer. The buyer no longer

---

[1]The Capitol Freehold Land and Investment Company, formed by a Chicago group, which became known as the Capitol Syndicate, obtained three million acres of Panhandle open range in exchange for building the largest state capitol building in the nation in Austin. The Syndicate members Abner Taylor, A.C. Babcock and John V. and Charles Farwell, had no ranching experience. They obligated themselves to building the grandiose state capitol and running a ranch twice as large as the state of Rhode Island. In 1887 they hired Colonel A.G. Boyce, an experienced cowman, to manage the XIT, who did so until 1905. The Syndicate spent $3,224,593.45 to build the magnificent Texas capitol which meant the ranch land cost the company $1.07 per acre, four times the price unwatered lands were selling for. It had been no bargain. Robertson and Robertson, *Cowman's Country*, 157.

[2]Douglas Branch, *The Cowboy and His Interpreters*, (p. 69) wrote that 30,000 were railed north in 1884.

had to wait for weeks to have cattle delivered; instead, a buyer was able to work directly with the manager of the northern satellite ranch to arrange delivery. Thus, cattle on the trail were now young two-year-olds destined for pastures in the north to be finished out for the market. Over the last decade of cattle trailing, the majority of the herds trailed (and partially hauled by rail) from south to north were destined for their owners' ranches in the north. In the mid 1880s, when the northern ranchers thought that the Kansas and Nebraska quarantines had eliminated or slowed down the flow of Texas cattle, Texas stockmen simply established finishing ranches in the north and were able to remain competitive.

The XIT, the largest ranch in the Panhandle, leased land in South Dakota in 1886 and in 1890 developed another finishing ranch between the Yellowstone and Missouri rivers on Cedar Creek, sixty miles above Miles City, Montana. Here, they adopted the policy of "double wintering" before shipping aged steers to the heavy-beef market in Chicago.[3] The LS (Lee and Scott) Ranch, established in 1881 and one of the pioneer ranches of the Panhandle with the second largest spread, also established, in 1884, a finishing ranch on Cedar Creek in Montana.

From 1884 to 1887 the LS cowboys drove thousands of head to their northern pastures.[4] The Mill Iron Ranch, established in 1881 in the lower part of the Panhandle, maintained a feeding ranch along the Powder River in Montana, and the Matador and the N Bar N ranches sent up herds annually to northern finishing ranches. These were only a few of the Texas ranches that followed this trend of the mid 1880s.

THE TEXAS–MONTANA FEEDER ROUTE BECOMES THE LAST OUTLET FROM TEXAS TO THE NORTH:

As traditional trails were closed off to Texas herds, alternative ways north had to be considered. As a consequence, Texas ranchmen paid closer attention to the route that Jim E. May, from the LS Ranch, had used to trail cattle in 1884 to Cedar Creek, Montana which was the ranch's finishing range. (See Map #III-3-1) There was still open range west of the National Trail, and two older trails were in the area. There was the 1875 New Goodnight Trail (refer to Part I, Chapter III) that went from around Fort Sumner, New Mexico, to Granada, Colorado a decade before, and the Potter-Bacon Trail that Jack Potter had blazed in 1883 from the Western Trail at Albany, Texas across Colorado, and on to Cheyenne, Wyoming. (See Part II, Chapter I) Jim May, following a path of least resistance, had used portions of these two trails in order to reach the LS Ranch in Ceder Creek. The new route, called here the Texas-Montana Feeder Route, lay between the Range 41 where, in 1886, the old National Trail strip had been opened to homesteading, and the settlements along the

---

[3]Haley, *The XIT Ranch of Texas*, 127.
[4]Robertson and Robertson, Ibid, 113. After the "big die-up" in 1886, Lee and Scott sold out their Montana herds in 1887.

THE WESTERN CATTLE TRAIL | 1874-1897   427

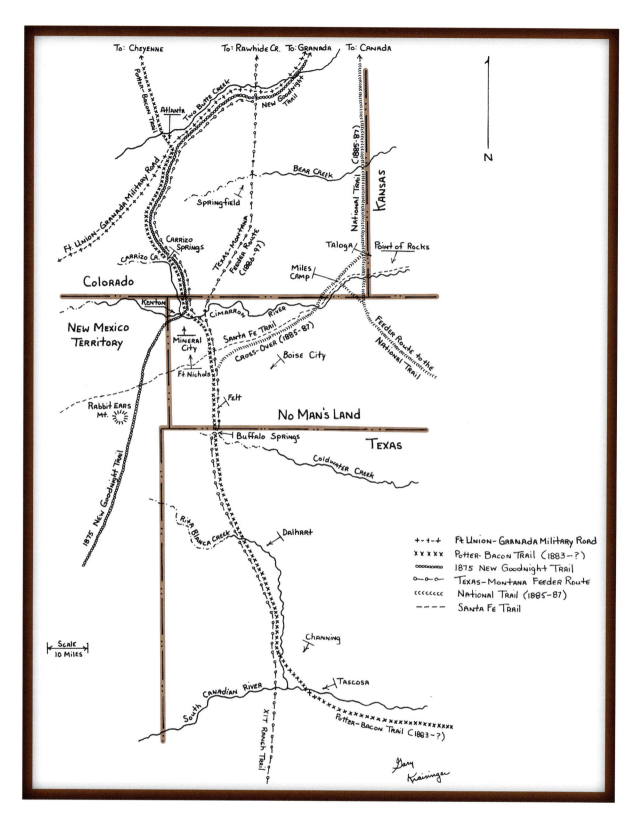

MAP #III, 3-1
The Various Routes Used to Trail Cattle North and Their Relationship to Each Other:
This map shows: (1) the 1875 New Goodnight Trail from Fort Sumner, New Mexico, across the northwestern corner of No Man's Land and through southeastern Colorado to Granada, Colorado (following part way the Fort Union-Granada Military Road); (2) the Potter-Bacon Trail (1883-1887) from south of Tascosa, Texas, across No-Man's Land and Colorado toward Cheyenne, Wyoming; (3) the Jim E. May route (1884-1885) starting at Coldwater Creek (Buffalo Springs); and (4) the Texas-Montana Feeder Route from Colorado City, Texas — after the route was straightened out through southeastern Colorado (1886-1897).

east slope of the mountains. The new route was in full use during the 1885 and 1886 seasons, at the same time that Trail City had high hopes of being the one and only cow town for cowboys on the trail north.

To fully understand the Texas-Montana Feeder Route and its pathway, two pre-existing trails need to be reviewed. In 1884 Jim May from the LS Ranch used Jack Potter's route (the Potter-Bacon Trail) and the 1875 New Goodnight Trail. He then struck out on his own in a northerly route to the Cedar Creek ranch in Montana. The earlier one — the 1875 New Goodnight Trail — will be reviewed first.

THE 1875 NEW GOODNIGHT TRAIL REVIEW:

In 1875, Charles Goodnight established a new route from his ranch in New Mexico Territory in order to get to the Santa Fe stockpens at Granada, Colorado to ship his cattle to market. Granada was the end of the line at that time for the Atchinson, Topeka, and Santa Fe Railway. (see Part I, Chapter III) He drove to the junction of Carrizo Creek and Cimarron River in No Man's Land, trailed north up Carrizo Creek, then traveled across country to the Fort Union-Granada Military Road and followed that road into Granada. Goodnight used this route for one or possibly two seasons.

THE POTTER-BACON TRAIL OF 1883-1884 REVIEW:

The Potter-Bacon Trail, that has been referred to many times in this study, was named after trail driver Jack Myers Potter and his employer, Alfred T. Bacon. In 1883, Potter, under the employment of the New England Livestock Company, was instructed by its manager, Alfred T. Bacon, to deliver a herd to Cheyenne. The Mexican cattle were picked up at Pena Station, near Hebbronville, Texas and driven to the Matamoros Feeder Route at Collins Station, near present-day Alice, and from there continued to Albany. At Albany, Potter received word from Bacon that he wanted his trail driver to leave the Western Trail and try a cutoff that might save some time. So Potter headed northwest, passed Rice Springs, crossed the Brazos River and the Matador Ranch, and continued north to Field's Crossing on the Red River.

In the Texas Panhandle, the Winchester quarantine was in force, so Potter, who was headed toward Colorado, detoured around the JA Ranch in Armstrong County and trailed to Tascosa. He passed by present-day Channing and Middle Water, both of which would later become part of the immense XIT Ranch, and continued to the headwaters of Coldwater Creek. The Potter herds entered No Man's Land just south of present-day Felt, Oklahoma.[5] He forded the North Canadian (Beaver) River in No Man's Land, crossed over the abandoned Santa Fe Trail (which would be used as a cross-over to the National Trail two years later), passed the ruins of old Camp Nichols and proceded on to the confluence of North Carrizo Creek and the Cimarron River.

---

[5]Felt, Oklahoma, was not established until the summer of 1925, when the Santa Fe Railway cut a line through.

When the Potter herd crossed the Cimarron River at the confluence of the river and Carrizo Creek, he picked up the 1875 New Goodnight Trail. (see Map #III, 3-1)

THE POTTER–BACON TRAIL IN COLORADO:

Trailing along the 1875 New Goodnight Trail into Colorado, Potter and his outfit followed Carrizo Creek north past what would later become the town of Carrizo Springs,[6] and continued upstream to the Carrizo Creek headwaters. At this point, Potter continued eighteen miles due north to the headwaters of Freezeout Creek. The outfit and herd followed this creek on the Goodnight Trail downstream until they intersected with the old Granada-Fort Union Wagon Road coming from the south. The cowboys and their herd left the Goodnight Trail and the Granada-Fort Union Wagon Road and picked up the old Penrose Trail of 1868 which had come from the north out of Fort Lyon.[7]

The Potter-Bacon Trail followed the old Penrose Trail north near where Atlanta would be platted four years later[8] and on to Las Animas, four miles west of Fort Lyon.[9] From the Las Animas area, the New England Livestock Company herd was pushed across the Arkansas River and trailed on north up Adobe Creek, past present-day Arlington,[10] continued north to North Rush Creek, and on to River-bend, six miles west of present-day Limon.

The cowboys and their herd continued northwest to Deer Trail where there was a Kansas Pacific rail station and a few dwellings.[11] Here they turned north to

---

[6]Carrizo Springs was founded in December of 1887 and grew to approximately four hundred persons supporting four saloons, a general store, one cafe, and a school. According to J. R. Austin, the town was "one of the most disorderly towns on the frontier," and was completely deserted by 1893. (J. R. Austin, *A History of Early Baca County*, 27-28)

[7]The Penrose Trail is not shown on our map to avoid congestion. This old military route was created by Captain William H. Penrose (who was stationed at Fort Lyon in 1867-1868) when Fort Lyon was part of the elaborate 1868 campaign by the war department to round up Indians and put them on reservations. The route ran southeast from Fort Lyon, built near Las Animas on the Arkansas River, to Beaver River in Indian Territory. Over a decade later, a small portion of the military road, from Atlanta to Las Animas, was used by Jack Potter

[8]Atlanta was started in May of 1887. Its main street was the Penrose Trail with stone buildings built on both sides of the trail. The post office remained as late as 1892, but the town had "long ceased to function as such." (Austin, Ibid, 29)

[9]In 1873, the Kansas Pacific Railroad decided to take part in the Santa Fe Trail trade by running a line south from Kit Carson, Colorado, to just west of the town "Las Animas" that had been established a few years earlier at a site four miles to the east. The new site was called *West* Las Animas. The citizens of (old) Las Animas picked up their town and moved to the new railroad site. Before long, West Las Animas was renamed simply Las Animas ("the spirits"). Two years later, in September 1875, the Atchinson, Topeka, and Santa Fe Railway came into town from the east, creating a boom for Las Animas. When the two railroads moved farther west in a race for LaJunta, the boom waned. The town was incorporated in September of 1882, a year before Potter came through. (www.nps.gov/safe/historyculture/map-timeline-intro.htm. and email from Frank Norris of the NPS, dated Nov. 30, 2012)

[10]Arlington was established when the Missouri Pacific Railroad came through in 1887. Its post office was opened on August 16, 1887. (wikipedia.org [accessed July 11, 2009])

[11]Deer Trail was another one of Kansas Pacific's created railheads. A railroad station was built in 1870, but the town lots were not granted and platted until 1875. Deer Trail became one of the important shipping points for eastern Colorado. (www.deertrailcolorado.org/history [accessed July 12, 2009])

430   THE WESTERN CATTLE TRAIL | 1874-1897

Trail Drivers on the Long S Ranch: Eight trail drivers from the Long S. Ranch, located in the Texas Panhandle, pose in front of their herd. An outfit of cowboys for a herd of 2,500 head often consisted of eight to fifteen cowboys, including the trail boss, wrangler, and cook.

Photo courtesy of the Texas State Library & Archives Commission, Prints and Photographs Collections, Austin, Texas.

pick up the Middle Bijou to Bijou, near present-day Wiggins, west of Fort Morgan.[12] The Potter herd was trailed north to cross the South Plate River and passed over the old Overland Trail. From this area they continued northwest to Cow Creek and followed it to its headwaters near Cheyenne, Wyoming. Jack Potter and his outfit delivered the heard and saw a city of several thousand with its opulant shops and fine entertainment. Cheyenne, at the time, was one of the most heavily used railheads.

---

[12] Fort Morgan had been built in 1864-1865 to protect emigrants traveling the South Platte River Road against Indian attacks. It sat on a strategic tract of land known as Morgan Flats and had a full view of the area for miles. It was the only army presence between Julesburg to the east and the regions of the Rockies in the west. The Fort Morgan Cutoff was established in 1864 to save about forty miles for travelers going to Denver. The fort was abandoned in 1868. In 1883, when Jack Potter and his outfit came through, Abner S. Baker was in the process of platting the ground for the new town of Fort Morgan. If Potter had gone into Fort Morgan, he would have seen a tent city around the new Union Pacific railroad station. Construction of permanent buildings started the following spring. (www.fortmorganchamber.org/history [accessed July 12, 2009])

THE JIM E. MAY ROUTE AND THE TEXAS–MONTANA FEEDER ROUTE TO THE WESTERN CATTLE TRAIL IN WYOMING:

The shift to a more western route was developing in 1883 and 1884, even before Kansas enacted its quarantine in the spring of 1885 and before the National Trail was enthusiastically promoted in 1885 and 1886. When Jack Potter, under the instructions of Alfred T. Bacon, created the cutoff from Albany, Texas and on across Colorado, he was breaking a path for a more westerly route. Then in 1884, Jim E. May blazed a trail from the LS Ranch in the Panhandle and meticulously documented his route. In 1885, when May again drove cattle up the trail for the LS Ranch, he had in his outfit nineteen-year-old, Sabastian "Boss" Neff, who later recalled that in their outfit that year were eight cowboys, a cook, and a horse wrangler, and that "He [May] had driven a herd for the LS in 1884 and of course knew the trail."[13]

The route to the north by way of Colorado, from May's perspective, started north of Coldwater Creek because the LS Ranch was in the Panhandle, and from the Coldwater Creek area May could pick up the Potter-Bacon Trail. In establishing another more-direct route to Montana, farther west than the proposed National Trail which would be initiated the following summer, May would use former (pre-existing) trails through No Man's Land and Colorado. Thus, following the 1883 Potter-Bacon Trail, May left Buffalo Springs (on Coldwater Creek[14], went "to Corrumpa [Creek] 15 miles, from Corrumpa to Carrizzo [South Carrizo Creek] 15 miles, from Carrizzo to Cimarron above 101 Ranch 15 miles."[15] South of the Cimarron River in No Man's Land, May also crossed over the old Santa Fe Trail just as Potter had in 1883, but in May's second drive in 1885, the old trail was now being used as a crossover to the National Trail. May did not mention roads or landmarks in his log. His account simply outlines his route from one creek or river to the next and the miles between waterings. In 1885, west of his pathway, Mineral City was being established five miles north of Old Camp Nichols.[16] By the next year, the Western Land and Mining

---

[13]Boss Neff wrote his memoirs in 1939.

[14]In Jack Potter's description of his route, he stopped at the headwaters of Coldwater Creek. A year later, Jim E. May starts at Coldwater Creek, but calls the location "Buffalo Springs." This ideal spot for watering herds and a cowboy camp later became the northern-most division headquarters and steer pasture for the XIT Ranch. In 1886, when the XIT started sending herds up the trail, Buffalo Springs became the starting point, not only for the XIT herds but for others as well.

[15]Corrumpa Creek is one of the streams that form the Beaver River. George Washington Miller leased land from the Quapaws in the Strip. He started using the 101 brand in 1881. (J. E. May log book in Haley, *The XIT Ranch of Texas*, 230)

[16]In June of 1865, Col. Kit Carson had selected and established the camp of troops "to give protection to trains passing to and from the States" on the Santa Fe Trail. The location was approximately three miles east of the New Mexico Territory line about half way between Fort Dodge and Fort Union. The three hundred soldiers, who were stationed at Camp Nichols, started the stone work to build an officers' quarters, hospital, and commissary, but suddenly abandoned the camp and marched back to Fort Union in September of 1865. (Frances Skelley Murdock, "Camp Nichols," article printed in *The Tracks We Followed*, 22-25)

Long S Ranch chuck wagon: *The chuck wagon and the cook were the hub of a trail-driving operation. The cook moved the wagon ahead of the herd and waited for the outfit to catch up for a mid-day meal and again for the evening meal. The campfire, tent, and food represented home base during the months the cowboys were on the trail. Not only did the cook prepare meals and dispensed coffee, he also administered medicine to the cow hands. Here Bob Simpson of the Long S Ranch stands next to his chuck wagon.*

Photo courtesy of the Texas State Library & Archives Commission, Prints and Photographs Collections, Austin, Texas.

Company from Kingman, Kansas opened two coal mines, and Mineral City was the home of the workers. Its main attraction, that trail cowboys would have been aware of, was a large two-story stone building that was erected during those early years. The 25-foot by 60-foot structure housed the post office, established in 1888, a store, a hotel, and a place where dances could be held.[17]

At the confluence of North Carrizo Creek and the Cimarron River (four miles east of present-day Kenton), Jack Potter, in 1883, and Jim May, in 1884 and 1885,

---

[17]The coal mines were abandoned after about two years, but the small community survived. In 1897, John Skelley purchased the stone building and became the new postmaster. By the turn of the century, Skelly's store was at its height of prosperity with a large inventory of groceries, dry goods, hardware, and ranch supplies. The store was completely destroyed and part of the Skelly home damaged in a 1908 tornado. Mineral (the word "city" was dropped) lost its post office in February of 1911. (Frances Skelly Murdock, "Mineral City," article printed in *The Tracks We Followed*, 160)

picked up the 1875 New Goodnight Trail. May wrote of the route: "from Cimarron to Carrizzo Springs via "from Cimarron to Carrizzo Springs via Road Cannon [Canyon] 18 miles."

Another landmark in this area of the Cimarron and Carrizo valleys was located at the confluence of the river and creek. Perched on a ridge of the mesa northeast of the confluence was a stone 16-foot by 30-foot fortress built by the outlaw Capt. William Coe sometime in the 1860s. Located in No Man's Land with no law or order, the hideout allowed Coe's gang a full view of both valleys. Even though Coe was captured and hanged in July of 1868, local historians kept the story alive. Trail drivers would have seen Robbers' Roost Mesa as they passed.[18]

After leaving Carrizo Springs and canyon road, May's outfit continued overland until the herds reached the head of Freezeout Creek, after another 18 miles. From Freezeout Creek to Two Butte Creek was another ten miles where they followed that creek down to the "mouth of Maverick [Mule Creek], 30 miles." When the May outfit started down Two Butte Creek, they left the Potter-Bacon Trail and struck out in a northerly direction separate from Potter's route. In his road-map approach, May continued to write down markers on his new pathway north to his final destination in south-eastern Wyoming:

> from Maverick [Mule Creek] to water on Clay Creek, 15 miles
> 30 miles to Lamar water half way,
> from Lamar 12 miles to water on Sandy (Big Sandy),
> follow up Sandy to Kit Carson, water twice on the way,
> Cross R. R. [Kansas Pacific] at Carson and follow up Wild Horse Creek two
>   waters on Creek, [watered herd twice]
> from Republican to Hell Springs 18 miles,
> from Hell Springs to Walker [Walks] Camp 18 miles,
> water in Arroyo 1 mile north, from there to water on Beaver 35 miles,
> from there to South Platte 30 miles,
> from South Platte to Pawnee 25 miles
> from Pawnee to Pawnee Buttes 15 miles
> from Pawnee Butte to Pine Bluffs 25 miles,
> from Pine Bluffs to horse creek 30 miles,
> follow down Horse Creek 35 miles and cross the divide to North Platte 12
>   or 15 miles.
> Cross Platte at Mouth of J.M. Creek [Rawhide] 30 miles.[19]

At the Rawhide Creek (J.M. Creek) May picked up the trunk line of the Western Cattle Trail in order to continue his route north to the LS Ranch's northern finishing grounds on Cedar Creek in Montana.

---

[18]Norma Gene Butterbaugh Young, ed. "Robbers' Roost," article printed in *The Tracks We Followed*, 20-21.

[19]J. E. May log in Haley, 230.

In 1884, May had blazed and chronicled a route north out of the Texas Panhandle through No Man's Land and Colorado that would later become known as the Texas-Montana Trail (Feeder Route). In the following year, May would use the route again with LS cattle. Herds were sent up over the new route from the LS Ranch through 1887, but other ranch drovers followed May's lead and continued to carry numerous herds each year into the northern territories, as the National Trail's use waned and eventually ended.

FURTHER DEVELOPMENT OF THE TEXAS–MONTANA FEEDER ROUTE TO WYOMING:
(Map #III, 3-2)

As May was establishing a route from Coldwater Creek (Buffalo Springs) in the northern Texas Panhandle to Wyoming Territory, trail drivers coming up from the south turned their direction farther west as well. Texas had become congested with settlements, and trailing was becoming increasingly difficult. When the Texas & Pacific Railroad arrived in Colorado City and Big Spring in 1881, it provided an option for the ranchmen located farther south of the Panhandle.

Colorado City, located on the Colorado River, and Big Spring, located on a tributary of the Colorado River on Beals Creek, were both south of the Panhandle. Because of the location of these new railheads, cattle from western and southern Texas ranches could be shipped to these two depots and then be trailed from there to a customer's destination or to a finishing ranch in the north. Two references to this new opportunity to use these railheads were recorded by Jerry M. Nance and A. N. Eustace. Nance, recalled that he became part owner of a ranch in Jeff Davis County in 1883 and ranched "with the Toyah Land & Cattle Company." They shipped 2,000 head in 1887 to Big Spring and from there trailed them to Trail City where they were sold. (It was Trail City's last season.) Cowboy Eustace, from a different outfit, wrote that they also shipped a herd from Toyah in Jeff Davis County in 1887 to Big Spring and "from there we went the extreme Western Trail, across the plains to Trails [sic] City, Colorado."[20] Also, Ab Blocker wrote that, in 1893, he picked up a herd of 2,997 "about seventy-five miles from Colorado City" and drove them to Deadwood, South Dakota, arriving with all but fourteen at the Franklin ranch.[21]

Basically, the Texas-Montana Feeder Route, or the extreme Western Trail as Eustace called it, didn't begin at Buffalo Springs where Jim May started up the trail with the LS herds, but rather, started farther south at Colorado City and Big Spring. The pathway angled north-westerly across present-day Mitchell, Scurry, Garza, Lynn, Lubbock, and Hockley counties to Yellow Houses (Casas Amarillas) in present-day Hockley County. J. Evetts Haley, who wrote about the XIT Ranch in 1929, drew a sketch of this pathway on his "Early Trails" map. He called the pathway,

---

[20]Jerry M. Nance, "Echoes of the Cattle Trail," in Hunter, *The Trail Drivers of Texas*, 110. A. N. Eustace, "Eight Trips up the Trail," in Hunter, 255.

[21]Ab Blocker, "The Man Who Had Hell in his Neck," in Hunter, 512.

THE WESTERN CATTLE TRAIL | 1874-1897   435

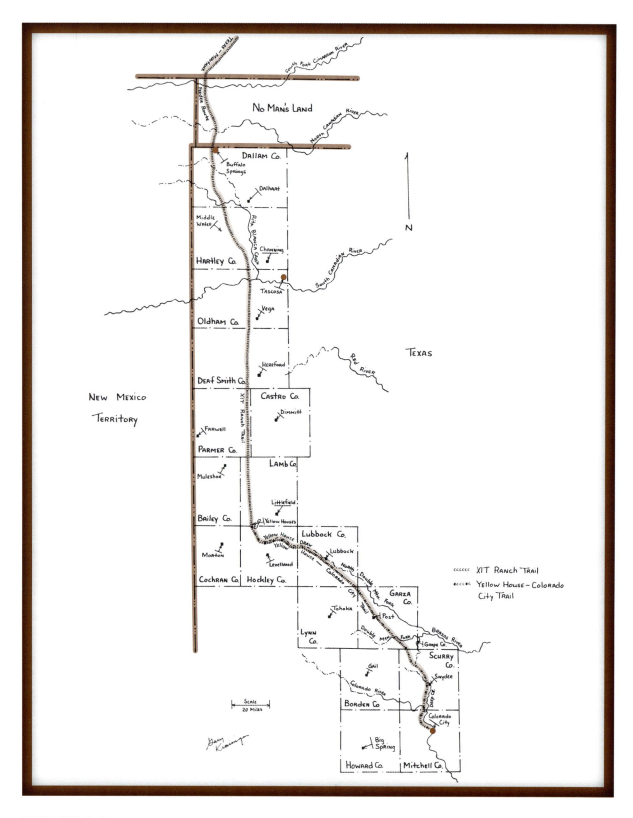

MAP #III, 3-2
Lower Portion of Texas-Montana Feeder Route From Colorado City and Big Spring, Texas Through No Man's Land:
This map shows what J. Evetts Haley called the Yellow House - Colorado City Trail south of Yellow House. From Yellow House, XIT Ranch's most southern division, herds were driven north over the XIT Ranch Trail to its most northern division, Buffalo Springs.

Information acquired from the J. Evetts Haley Collection, The Haley Memorial Library & History Center, Midland, Texas.

from Colorado City to Yellow Houses the "Yellow House-Colorado City Trail."[22] Yellow Houses was one of eight divisions established by the XIT Ranch, after its establishment in 1885, and was located at its most southern end of some 190 miles of ranch land from south to north. The ranch named this division headquarters after the yellow cliffs which from a distance resembled houses with open doors.[23]

After resting and watering at Yellow Houses, trail herds were driven straight north across the Panhandle, west of Tascosa, to Coldwater Creek. This spot, now noted as "Buffalo Springs," was the most northern division headquarters of the XIT. Haley called this part of the route the "XIT Ranch Trail." On this pathway, herds were trailed over portions of the XIT Ranch and other Panhandle ranches.[24]

J. W. Holston wrote in his reminiscence about traveling a similar route approximately thirty miles east of the XIT Ranch Trail. In 1886, the first year that the XIT started to trail cattle up this route, Holston was working for Moore & Krill Cattle Company, which had a "ranch out here at the Yellowhouse canyan [sic] and also had a Ranch up on the line of Wyoming & So. Decota [sic]." The outfit rounded up 3,000 head on the ranch and road branded them with an "O on the back." Holston's route in his own spelling was:

> …drove up on what is called the cap rock of the planes.
> …through whare canyon is now and waterd the herd in that spring.
> …Well we drove on and we heard some cowmen say there was a little settlement over there and they were starting to make a Town and they called it Amarillo. That was a pecular name to us cowboys.
>
> …Well we drove on and dident find any more water for 2 Days & nites for the cattle, they were getting fearfully dry & our Barrell of drinking water was almost gone too. Well one morning the cattle hoisted their heads and off they went off to the rite. They had smelled the water. Well we could not hold them….it was a spring branch running in to the canadian River.[25]

This route was east of XIT Ranch Trail but west of the Potter-Bacon Trail. Holston wrote that "there had only bin one herd of cattle a head of us starting this new Western Cow Trail." and that "There was no trail to see when that herd would be [unreadable] but when they would throw them back on the route and drive then we could see a dim trail." On the third stampede of the drive, during a big storm, the

---

[22]This "Yellow House-Colorado City Trail" roughly follows present-day Highway 84. (J. E. Haley, "Early Trails," from the J. Evetts Haley Collection, Haley Memorial Library and History Center Midland, Texas)

[23]The location and the bluffs after which the division headquarters was named are plural — Yellow Houses. But the nearby canyon, draw, ranch, and trail use the singular form. (Yellow House Canyon, Yellow House Draw, and the Yellow House-Colorado City Trail.).

[24]The "XIT Ranch Trail" roughly parallels present-day Highway 1055 / 385 North.

[25]J. W. Holston, "Life of J. W. Holston," owned by the Texas Library & Historical Committee, located at the State Library in Austin, Texas.

THE WESTERN CATTLE TRAIL | 1874-1897

trail boss, Tom Crowder, and his horse were killed by a "big flash of Lightning." His body was taken "in to Cooledge [Kansas] and shiped him back to Weatherford Tex. his home." The Moore & Krill drovers had picked up the National Trail. From Coolidge, near Trail City, Holston was sent back down the trail to find strays. On his way back to camp to catch up with his own outfit, Holston wrote: "Well to give you some idier of the cattle driving. I passed 5 or 6 big herds before I reached ours." This would have been on the National Trail.

In the early part of the 1886 season, the Moore & Krill outfit was one of the first to use the route. Holston called the route the "Western Trail" twice in his writing because to him, the trail through the Panhandle and up the eastern boundary of Colorado was the Western Trail. The herd was delivered to the finishing ranch "in sight of the Black Hills." When the cowboys went to Chadron, Nebraska to catch the train, "it was snowing and it [was] on the 4th day of September." The outfit had been on the trail for four months.

Charles Francis Randolph, the editor of *The Tascosa Pioneer*, recalled the new route through the Texas Panhandle to reach No Man's Land, Colorado, and beyond. In the spring of 1886, Randolph had moved his family and printing press to Tascosa, the second oldest community in the Panhandle. He observed the caravans of wagons coming in from Dodge City to stock the town's merchants who sold to the big cattle outfits in the area, and the cowboys, in turn, who shuffled among the drinking establishments.[26] He noticed the stage line which connected to Meade, Kansas, and the local cattle herds that were trailed the 240 miles to Dodge's shipping pens over the Tascosa-Dodge City Trail. In 1880, when Oldham County was organized, Tascosa became the county seat and supported a fine stone courthouse. Randolph, however, not only came to Tascosa because of its past accomplishments, but he was convinced that the town would soon be on the route of the Fort Worth & Denver City Railway or the Kansas City & Southern.

In the summer of 1886, when Randolph was initiating his *Pioneer* newspaper and working "hard to find its place and to express its commitment," the talk of the town was the incoming railroad. The Fort Worth & Denver City Railway had reached Vernon and was headed for Quannah. Meanwhile, Randolph left no stone unturned in reporting the local happenings around Tascosa. The twenty-seven-year old traveled for miles around and visited with any and everybody who could give him news about or related to his adopted town.[27]

On September 1, he reported that, after meeting with trail boss J. W. Millsap, who was in charge of 3,000 head from the Jesse H. Hitson Ranch in Stonewall County, that "opening up a trail across this part of the country and Mr. Millsap's ideas about it were considered worth taking down." Millsap was crossing the Canadian River just below Tascosa, trailing his third herd, the final number of a contracted ten thousand

---

[26]"Each of the larger stores in Tascosa freighted in 25,000 to 50,000 pounds of merchandise each month. As late as 1888 the *Tascosa Pioneer* noted that 119,000 pounds of freight had been delivered during the previous week." ("Tascosa-Dodge City Trail," *The Handbook of Texas Online*, accessed May 1, 2009)
[27]Frederick Nolan, *Tascosa, Its Life and Gaudy Times*, 208-209, 217.

headed for Denver, Colorado. He told Randolph that he preferred this route because it was "so much more direct" and that "the annual drive from west and south-west Texas out to Colorado and Montana" could reach as many as 325,000 head. Texas drovers coming up from west and south Texas via this route would pass by Tascosa for "the ranges to the south present no objections."

Randolph excitedly returned to his press office and wrote: "the addition to the life and business of Tascosa which would follow this trail would beat anything a railroad could do for the town…. The formal opening of this trail, we predict, would inaugurate an annual drive up this western portion of the Panhandle, that would surprise even the natives, and that would make Tascosa the livest stock town anywhere in the West."

Randolph had asked Millsap what the best route was north to Tascosa, considering convenient water and "taking advantage of the country." Millsap described to Randolph the following route. He began by telling Randolph that all southern stockmen should be able to reach Colorado City without specific directions:

> From Colorado City up Colorado river to the mouth of Deep Creek to the head of Grape creek, and cross Double Mountain Fork of the Brazos to the mouth of Yellow-House cannon; from Yellow-House cannon [Yellow House Draw] over to Catfish; up Catfish to the head of Blanco to Goodnight's tank in dry seasons and to Running water in rainy times; thence to upper water on Terra Blanco; thence to Palo Duro; from Palo Duro to Sweet La Cruce; from Sweet La Cruce [Sierrita DeLa Cruz Creek] to Canadian, from there to head of Tascosa creek and from there to Coldwater; from Coldwater to Big Beaver in the Neutral Strip; from Beaver to Tepee creek; thence to Cimarron twelve miles above Point of Rock[s]; from Point of Rock[s] to Bear Creek; from Bear creek to Arkansas; thence to [Wild] Horse creek, thence to Sheridan Lakes; thence to Battle-ground on Big Sandy; from Big Sandy to Kit Carson; then up railroad to Hugo, from Hugo across to Walk's camp, and on the open trail then to Montana.[28]

One can see that this "much more direct route" that Millsap used from the Tascosa area went straight north through No Man's Land to the corner of Colorado and Kansas where it connected with the National Trail. The Millsap route was somewhat different than the May route, which started at Coldwater (Agua Frio) Creek. May had blazed a route west of the National Trail, but Millsap chose to go straight north from Tascosa and trail directly to the National Trail. He did not mention Trail City, but because Millsap mentions the town of Kit Carson, Colorado, it is assumed that

---

[28]Goodnight's tank is referred to in Part III, Chapter I, footnote #6. Charles F. Randolph, "The Trail Question in Tascosa," *The Tascosa Pioneer*, Sept. 1, 1886. Both railroads bypassed Tascosa, and Randolph closed down his paper on February 28, 1891, writing that "today we lay down the saber and give up the fight; and the *Pioneer* is an institution of the past…" For a complete history of Tascosa and Charles Randolph, refer to Frederick Nolan's book, *Tascosa, its Life and Gaudy Times*.

he then left the National Trail north of Trail City and took the northwest splinter route to Kit Carson to connect to May's route of 1884, and from there northwest to Hugo, Colorado before resuming a northward course.

The 1886 Millsap route, as well as the J. W. Holston route, were not used by other trail herds in the following seasons because in that same year the Nebraska herd law was passed; Section 41 was opened for homesteading, and Trail City was in a rapid decline. The National Trail existed for only one more year. The high hopes of Tascosa becoming a cattle center were short lived. The XIT Ranch Trail, or the trunk line of the new Texas-Montana Feeder Route from Colorado City, did not pass through Tascosa. The cattle herds crossed the Canadian River west of the old community.

North of the Canadian River above Tascosa, trail herds coming up from the south by way of Colorado City picked up the Potter-Bacon Trail, that had come up by Tascosa from the southeast, and followed it to the headwaters of Coldwater Creek. The watering spot for herds on this path was now on XIT land and the site become the headquarters of the newly established ranch's most northern division. This division was now referred to as Buffalo Springs and was used to pasture young steers, before they were branded for the trail drive. By 1886, trail drives from south Texas, the Panhandle, No Man's Land, and New Mexico Territory arrived at well-known watering spot at the headwaters of Coldwater Creek. Buffalo Springs became the ideal gathering spot on what would be later called the Texas-Montana Trail to connect with the Western Cattle Trail at Rawhide Creek in Wyoming and to continue on to Montana, and in some cases, farther north into Canada.

During the seasons of 1885 to 1887, as noted above, the National Trail was also being used. If, during that time, the Texas drovers' destination was Nebraska or Dakota Territory, the drovers and their herds on the May route (the Texas-Montana Feeder Route) could leave that pathway south of the South Fork of the Cimarron River in No Man's Land and cross over to the proposed National Trail. Again, a pre-existing trail was used — the old abandoned Santa Fe Trail route.[29] (note Map #III, 3-1)

To repeat and emphasize, the Texas-Montana Feeder Route was the last pathway to be used by Texas cattlemen to trail their herds north. The mass movement of trail cattle had happened in the past. Herds trailed on the long drives in the last decade of trail driving, that used the Texas-Montana Feeder Route through Colorado, were mainly from large ranches, and these herds were destined for the northern grasslands controlled by their owners. Sue Flanagan, in her book, alluded to this fact when she commented that there was only a trickle of longhorns into Colorado in the summer

> The Jack Potter-Bacon splinter route that had gone through the Tascosa area in 1883 and 1884 had not been heavily used, but three years later, the area was becoming more active because of the Kansas quarantine which caused a westward shift in the cattle trail. An annual cattle traffic flow of over 300,000 head would be more than what Tascosa had ever seen before. The two alternate trails, other than the Yellow House-Colorado City Trail, mentioned here — the Holston route and the Millsap route — show that trail drivers were trying different pathways in order to reach Colorado. Only the main trunk line of the Western Trail, however, is shown on the map. The alternate paths, which may have been used only once, are not shown.

---

[29]Trail historian, Jimmy Skaggs wrote in his thesis that, "upon reaching the old Santa Fe Trail northwest of Boise City, [herds] either turned northeast to merge with the International [National Trail] at the common borders of Kansas, Colorado, and Oklahoma [No Man's Land], or turned northwest to join the eastern branch of the Goodnight-Loving Trail [the 1875 New Goodnight Trail] east of Black Mesa." (Jimmy M. Skaggs, "The Great Western Cattle Trail to Dodge City, Kansas," 38-39)

of 1887, but a shadow of former years, and that the 1887 season came "despite rumors that herds were being turned back, that Texas fever again was rampant, and that the trail was closed."[30]

The *Rocky Mountain News*, an advocate for preserving the trail as long as possible, strove to debunk the rumors. In July its agent interviewed the Texas representative of the Bureau of Animal Industry at Denver's Windsor Hotel to "ascertain facts" about the turning back of herds. He admitted that a few herds had turned back to Indian Territory to be wintered and another 35,000 cattle were being held for sale in Colorado. The author of the *Rocky Mountain News* article sought to prove that the rumor of the turning back of herds was unfounded by writing that Colonel John Simpson's 40,000 trail cattle had already passed out of Colorado on their way to Montana. To add to its case, the newspaper announced that "due to precautions taken by veterinary inspectors, not a single case of Texas fever had appeared."

In answer to the rumor that the trail was closed, the News printed a letter from a Colorado stockman. "The Texas Trail is not closed," he maintained. The rumors are the "same old funeral reports…that have been fired at the public every year that range has become scarce," he added.[31]

Despite rumors, for the next several years trail herds continued to move through Colorado headed north. The vast eastern plains of Colorado are a harsh steppe land of short grass and cactus, and, in some areas, austere badlands of yellow clay interspersed with streams and two major river valleys, the Arkansas and the South Platte. As XIT and other Panhandle herds trailed across these plains from the mid 1880s to the mid 1890s, the cowboys witnessed the homesteaders' struggle to settle in this dry, flat prairie landscape. With the Homestead Act of 1862, and the opening of the West by railroads, thousands of homesteaders flooded into the Plains, including eastern Colorado, in the mid-1880s. The wind-swept grasslands of eastern Colorado with its unpredictable weather could offer either 100-degree heat or a wicked snow storm in May. The XIT and Long X herds experienced the snow in May of 1892. By the time Texas drovers were trailing their herds across the eastern Colorado plains in 1892, many of the homesteaders had given up trying to make a living in the harsh conditions of bitter cold winters and summers of drought. Ralph F. Jones, a native of this area and author of *Longhorns North of the Arkansas*, estimated that at least four out of five of the original settlers lost hope and relinquished their homestead claims before they could "prove up" on their government contract. Some settlers sold their relinquishments to other incoming settlers, while many others, according to Jones, "simply abandoned the pitiful site."[32]

The only real tool which gave new settlers some hope in this environment was the windmill. Stubborn homesteaders managed somehow to get the money to dig a

---

[30]Sue Flanagan. *Trailing the Longhorns, A Century Later*, 164.
[31]Flanagan, 164 and *Rocky Mountain News*, July 27, 1887.
[32]Ralph F. Jones, *Longhorns North of the Arkansas*, 48. The northeastern portion of Weld County, encompassing 193,060 acres or an area 30 miles by 60 miles, is today the Pawnee National Grasslands. Also according to www.colorado.com this "sea of grass and sky was once littered with hopeful frontier families, but droughts and harsh winters crushed their hopes." [accessed March 17, 2010]

THE WESTERN CATTLE TRAIL | 1874-1897

well which provided water for gardens and livestock. For those who could not afford a well, barrels of water had to be hauled for long distances. The Chicago, Burlington & Quincy Railroad, the Colorado-Wyoming branch of the Burlington Missouri River Railroad which had consolidated with the Chicago, Burlington, and Quincy Railroad in 1880, gave hope and encouragement to homesteaders. Even though the drought years of the latter 1880s had emptied the eastern plains of Colorado, many homesteaders appeared suddenly along the incoming rail lines and created small towns.

The stuggles of homesteaders and the sudden re-appearance of Colorado newcomers in the rail line towns was witnessed by the Texas cowboys. They also experiences the harsh weather of eastern Colorado. Fortunately, other trail journals survive that describe trail drives using the last cattle trail, the Texas-Montana Feeder Route.

OTHER COWBOY JOURNALS SHOWING THE USE OF THE TEXAS-MONTANA FEEDER ROUTE:

J.Ealy Moore, XIT trail driver, 1892:

A journal written by a cowboy who took a herd over the Texas Montana Feeder Route in 1892 was left by J. Ealy Moore, who was working for the XIT. A trail boss, at the age of 26, Moore was managing one of five herds being sent north to the XIT's finishing ranch in Montana "north of the Yellow Stone river opposite Miles City," he wrote.[33] The XIT had been trailing herds north since 1886 when drovers had delivered cattle to near Spearfish to the Black Hills in Dakota Territory. In 1889 the XIT had sent up 15,000 head in six herds to the Black Hills. After that, herds had been sent to the ranch's finishing range on Cedar Creek where 20,000 to 30,000 head were pastured and after being "double wintered," shipped to the Chicago market via Miles City. By 1892, when Ealy Moore was trail boss, it had become the custom to drive 10,000 to 15,000 two-year-old steers each year to the northern ranch in order to replenish the Montana herd. There O. C. Cato, the XIT manager, received the home ranch's stock.

Tucked in front of Moore's pocket size notebook was Jim May's route directions. For eight years, trail drivers had followed May's lead. On the printed lines, Moore wrote on the first page of the notebook the names of his outfit and their wages for the trip. He was to receive $100, the cook, $40, and the drovers, $35 each per month. He used several pages to list the supplies and their cost. For the chuck wagon, he bought numerous items from H. Humphry at Channing, Texas,[34] on April 19, 1892, and he listed each item.

---

[33]The XIT finishing ranch was more precisely located 60 miles north of the Yellowstone River on upper Cedar Creek. (Haley, Ibid., 127)

[34]Channing in southeastern Hartley County was the location of the general headquarters of the XIT Ranch. It was platted as a town in 1891, a year before Moore trailed cattle north. During the 1890s, as Tascosa declined, many businesses were moved to Channing. The town replaced Hartley as the county seat in 1903. ("Channing, Texas," *The Handbook of Texas Online*, accessed May 3, 2009)

These XIT Ranch cowboys *appear to be gathering and preparing for the trail. This photo, taken in the 1890s, also shows a remuda (horse herd) and a cattle herd in the background.*

Photo courtesy of University of Texas at Arlington, Library, Special Collections.

Of the five XIT herds, Moore was in charge of the second. He records that Al Owens (The correct spelling was: Ab Owings) was overseeing the first XIT herd, and he had left two days earlier. Behind Moore were three herds bossed by Chris Gish, Dan Cole, and Milt Wipple. Col. H. G. Boyce, the general manager, who saw each herd off with a bit of final advice, had learned of a head tax being levied on all herds entering No Man's Land by self-appointed lawmen.[35] Since there was no government or official law enforcement in the neutral strip, some No Man's Land locals took advantage of the situation and administered their own law. Boyce told Owings, in charge of the lead herd, that if he was held up in No Man's Land because of the tax, he was to send a report back to the ranch so he could be rescued and to notify the trail boss, Moore, immediately behind him.

---

[35] Colonel A. G. Boyce was an experience cowman and had taken over as general manager of the XIT in 1888. He served in that position until 1905 when he was succeeded by Walter Farwell, the son of one of the owners, C.B. Farwell. (Robertson and Robertson, *Cowman's Country*, 157)

Boyce had learned that the tax was eight cents on every steer crossing over the strip. It was being collected by "officers" who met the herds, demanding five cents per head to enter No Man's Land and another three cents to exit the strip. On the twelve thousand XIT head, the sum would amount to $960. This was an expense not budgeted for by the XIT bosses. The cost of payroll and supplies along the way had been calculated to a fairly close margin and a tax in No Man's Land was not part of that cost. Owings had been warned by his superiors, and he was to be the one who was to test the waters.

Moore, the boss for the second herd, "had been instructed by Mr. Boyce not to try to pass the other herd in case it was held up." Owings was stopped on the Cimarron River by armed men who said they were United States marshals and demanded the tax. When he refused to pay it, he and his outfit were arrested and the herd was held until the tax was paid. A rider was sent back to the XIT for help. On his way, he informed Moore that Owings had been arrested. He then continued on to report to Boyce and George Findlay, XIT's business manager.

Moore had left for Montana with his herd from Coldwater Creek on May 4, but by the next day, when he was at the head of Cold Springs Creek in No Man's Land, he stopped the herd and stayed for four days, recording in his journal only about the rain. Writing in 1922, Moore provided additional commentary to the journal; "We were both held up for the tax and lost three or four days." In a letter to J. Evetts Haley in 1925, Moore wrote that after getting to Cold Springs,

> "an officer, at least he called himself one, came to my herd and told me that they had Owings and his herd under arrest down on the Cimarron river and were going to hold him until they collected the tax and if I wouldn't try to pass on thru but would stay where I was they wouldn't put a man with me."[36]

Boyce and Findlay rode up to No Man's Land and paid, under protest, the tax for the two herds. The other three herds turned west into New Mexico in order to avoid paying the tax.[37]

When Moore was allowed to continue north, he "moved to Wild Cat Creek" and then to the Cimarron River. On May 11, the herd and outfit were "four miles from head water on Auberry Canyon" in Colorado. Moore noted in his journal the next day that he had "Got off of the trail, went too far East." With May's route written in his journal, he realized that he was not on the right trail. However, he "stayed about 16 miles S.E. of Springfield [Colorado]." He later trailed the herd to Springfield where they obtained supplies, several hundred pounds of: potatoes, flour,

---

[36]Journal of J. Ealy Moore, copy acquired from The Dolph Briscoe Center for American History Collections, the University of Texas at Austin.

[37]Ranchers, who were conned by the bandits who guised themselves as U.S. officials, finally got the tax stopped by going into Federal Court. According to Moore's letter, "by 1894 we could drive thru without being molested." (Haley, Ibid, 133-134)

bacon, beans, bacon, corn, and currants, and on May 16th, "Watered on Butte and camped 2 miles East of Butte Mountains." On the 17th, the outfit "camped on Clay Creek." Again Moore commented about his course compared to his predecessor's route: "missed the upper water on Clay."[38]

The route through Baca County, Colorado was moved or straightened out sometime after May's drives and before Moore went through in 1892. (By 1892, Carrizo Springs and Atlanta were already ghost towns because the trail had moved east.) Drovers and their herds coming from the Panhandle chose a new route by crossing the Cimarron River approximately seven miles east of present-day Kenton, Oklahoma and entered Colorado at present-day Regnier.[39] J. Evetts Haley, who knew Charles Goodnight in his old age, wrote that this route, according to Goodnight, was "straightened by later drives, it was always known as the [1875] New Goodnight Trail."[40] Because this latter route was dry, several wind mills were installed in order to provide water for the cattle. Ike Osteen in his book, *A Place Called Baca*, has a map identifying the location of these wind mills, which were spaced about fifteen miles apart.[41]

Moore's 1892 journal reveals that his outfit trailed north from the Cimarron River toward Springfield, instead of going via Carrizo Springs as Potter, Goodnight, and May had done years before. On May 18, Moore wrote in his journal: "Watered at the 10 mile water on Clay [Creek] from Lamar, and camped four miles from Lamar that night." On the next day, they "passed through Lamar and crossed the Ark. river." (Map #III, 3-3)

Lamar was a young railroad town established after May first trailed the LS cattle through the area. It had been one of many of the towns established by promoters during 1886 in the exuberant drive to settle eastern Colorado. The town had been started on one day when the the railroad depot was moved from mile post 499 which sat on ground belonging to a rancher who refused to co-operate with town promoters, to mile post 502 where a landowner was more civic minded. The youngest town of consequence on the main line of the Santa Fe Railway, it soon secured a land office and eventually became the county seat of Prowers County.[42] The town supposedly supported sixteen saloons during the cattle trailing season. Alva Betz related that in 1888 a bunch of XIT cowboys and their herd trailed right down the main street of Lamar and was met by the local lawman who warned them to behave themselves.[43]

After crossing the Arkansas River, Moore and his cowboys drove eleven miles north to King Reservoir, arriving at noon. They stayed there for a day while a cold

---

[38]This second comment about his course compared to his predecessor's route shows that the trail normally was farther west. Moore's log in Haley, 232.

[39]Ike Osteen, *A Place Called Baca*, 95

[40]J. Evetts Haley, *Charles Goodngiht, cowman and plainsman*, 229.

[41]Ike Osteen, *A Place Called Baca*, map located in the back of the book.

[42]A. R. Black was the rancher who owned extensive holdings on either side of the mile post 499, the distance from Atchison, Kansas. On the site sat a depot and stock yard siding. It was called Blackwell. Black secured an injunction to prevent anyone from moving the depot. The injunction was to go into effect on a Monday. A crew moved the depot three miles west to section 31 on Sunday and renamed it "Lamar." ("History of Lamar," www.ci.lamar.co.us/history, [accessed Feb. 23, 2010])

[43]Ava Betz, *A Prowers County History*, 217.

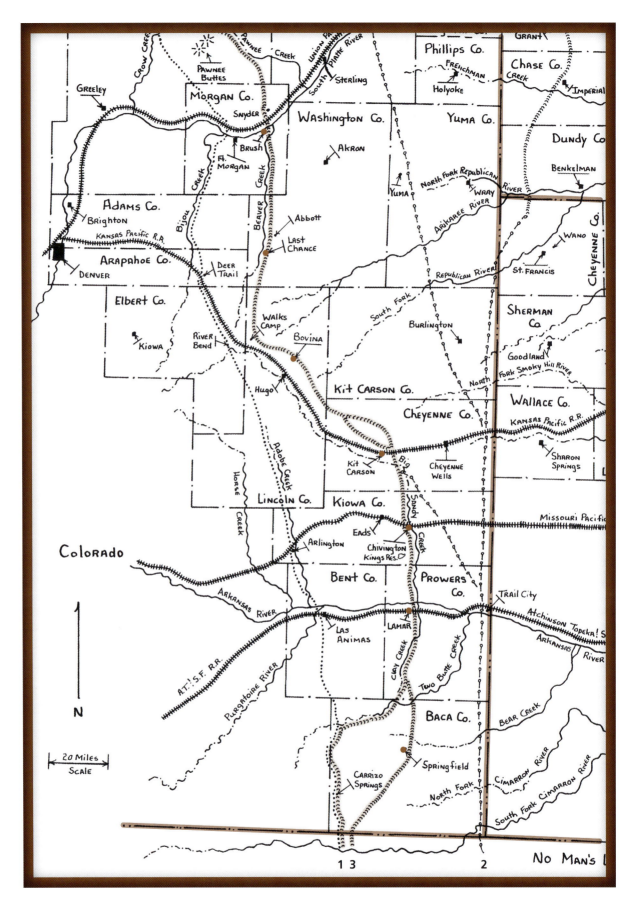

MAP #III, 3-3
Middle Portion of the Texas-Montana Feeder Route through Colorado:
This map shows the relationship of: (1) the Potter-Bacon Trail (1883-1887); (2) the National Trail (1885-1887); and (3) the Texas-Montana Feeder Route (1884-1897).

north wind blew. The men were, no doubt, dressed for warmer weather.[44] Moore wrote his May 21st entry:

> May 21: "Pretty cool cold north wind. Left K. R. [King Reservoir] after noon and went to Big Sandy."

For three days, the XIT cowboys and Ealy Moore pushed their herd along the Big Sandy Creek.

> May 22: "Watered five miles below Chivington on B.S. and Camped at Chiv. that night."

An elaboarate stage stop was located at the junction of Big Sandy and Rush Creek. It was called by different names — Stone City (because of the stone buildings), Swift City, and Alcorn Ranch. A supply depot and hotel and barn were located here. A holding grounds for cattle was provided north of the site, but south of the railroad at Chivington, they waited for the Missouri Pacific trains.[45]

Chivington was a quickly promoted Missouri Pacific railroad town. Towns along this line were named alphabetically and the "C" siding became "Chivington." The location was only nine miles from the Sand Creek massacre site of 1864, where Colonel John Chivington led a force of Colorado Territory militia who attacked and destroyed a village of Cheyenne and Arapaho encamped on Sand Creek. The brutal incident became infamous nationally, but not so much in eastern Colorado. When Moore came through with the XIT herd, the drovers became acquainted with the early days of Chivington and what the town could offer. Established only five years before, in 1887, the town supported a number of businesses and a very fine Queen Anne styled hotel called the Kingdom; it stood three stories and contained sixty-rooms.[46]

The XIT herd led by Ealy Moore in 1892 moved north to the Big Sandy Creek after leaving Chivington. They passed near the Sand Creek Massacre site and trailed by the old splinter trail from the mid-1880s cowtown of Trail City, as it intersected the Big Sandy. Just north of the confluence of the Big Sandy and Spring Creek, where Eureka Creek flows into the Big Sandy, one of the stage stops of the southern route of the Smoky Hill Trail was located — Dubois Station.[47] The station was near an open water hole along Eureka Creek that served as a watering spot

---

[44]King Reservoir, or King Lake was an artificial lake that was supplied by a canal from the Arkansas River, and is located some eleven miles north of Lamar.

[45]Betz, Ibid, 107.

[46]Chivington post office was established in Bent County on October 24, 1887, which became part of the new Kiowa County on April 11, 1889. The post office was located in the Kingdon Hotel. (Karlene McKean, Roleta Teal, Betty Jacobs, Mary E. Owen, and Terry W. Blevins (ed), *Tri-County History, A Centennial*, 77)

[47]The Smoky Hill Trail ran from the Missouri River to Denver, some 600 miles. The route was laid out by David A. Butterfield starting in 1865 and ran the full length of the Smoky Hill Valley and beyond. At the time, it was considered the most dangerous crossing of the plains until it was replaced by the Kansas Pacific Railroad in 1870. (Lee & Raynesford, *Trails of the Smoky Hill*, 6, 25, 48, 55)

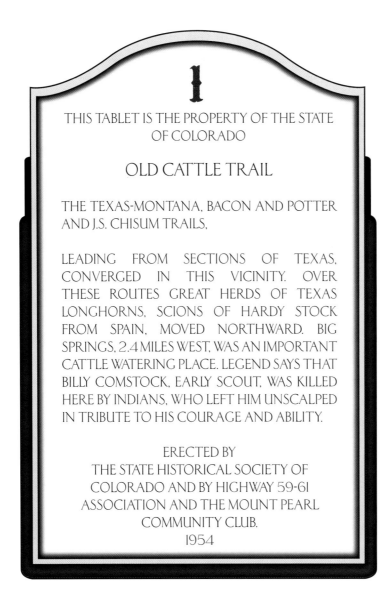

Location: Eleven miles north of Kit Carson, Colorado, Cheyenne County, on U.S. Highway 59. The monument shows signs of vandalism.

Authors' commentary: Starting in 1884, the Texas-Montana Feeder Route used a portion of the Bacon-Potter (Potter-Bacon) Trail and a portion of the 1875 New Goodnight Trail in order to go around Kansas and to feed into the Western Trail in Wyoming.

John S. Chisum was a cattle dealer and rancher who lived in Texas for eighteen years (1854-1872). In 1868, Chisum arranged to supply Goodnight, who was ranching in Colorado, with Texas cattle for markets in Colorado and Wyoming. For three years, Goodnight's outfits delivered Chisum cattle to northern markets. In 1872, Chisum moved his operation to New Mexico Territory. Chisum supplied cattle for trail drivings, but he did not drive cattle north, and there was not a "J. S. Chisum Trail."[1]

Billy Comstock, the chief scout at Fort Wallace, Kansas, according to Ron Field, "was killed by a Sioux warrior on August 16, 1868, near Big Spring Station on the Solomon River, 50 miles from Fort Wallace."[2] Big Springs is located 2.4 miles west of this monument on the old Butterfied Overland Dispatch Route.

The traveler might also be interested to know that cattle herds trailing by way of a Trail City splinter route went through Kit Carson, and this area as well, in 1885, 1886, and 1887. This large monument is a very fine tribute to the cattle trails. We do not, however, like the phrase "hardy stock from Spain." Some longhorns were bought in Mexico in the earlier years of cattle trailing, but the Mexican and Texas longhorns were many generations removed from the animals brought over from Spain. By the time drovers were using the Texas-Montana Feeder Route in Colorado, cattle herds originated mostly from the Texas Panhandle breeding grounds.

---

[1] "John Simpson Chisum," *The Handbook of Texas Online* (accessed August 14, 2007)
[2] "Ron Field, U.S. *Army Frontier Scouts, 1840-1921*.

for the cattle drives coming from Texas.⁴⁸ At this point, the Texas-Montana Feeder Route split for a short while into a northern route and a northwestern route. The northern route followed Big Spring Creek until it intersected with the Smoky Hill Trail. The northwestern route continued up Big Sandy Creek to Kit Carson, then up Wild Horse Creek. The two routes then reunited in the northwest corner of the Cheyenne County.

Moore and the XIT herd reached the Republican River on May 29th. He jotted in his journal that "an X herd over took me at noon." The Long X herd was owned by brothers George and William Reynolds from Albany, Texas.⁴⁹ That evening it started to rain.

The XIT herds led by Dan Cole, Chris Gish, and Milt Whipple — the ones that had been driven west of No Man's Land to avoid the head tax — joined up with Moore in Bovina on May 30. Two of the Long X herds had also halted at the location. Bovina, twenty miles east of Limon, became a townsite in the fall of 1888 when the Rock Island Railroad came through, but the Texas herds joined up here because Hackberry Springs, southeast of Bovina, was another ideal watering spot.⁵⁰

In his jounal, Moore reported that in the evening after the herds came together, it began to rain, turning to a hard rain by 9 p.m. and then to snow. The cowboys held the cattle during the night in order to not allow the herds to drift with the snow. Moore added in his commentary in 1922 that "It was bitter cold and we were dressed in summer clothing. We were suffering from cold ourselves."⁵¹ Finally at 2 a.m. Moore's outfit turned the herd loose and sought shelter for themselves at camp. At daylight, the cowboys crawled out from under their tarps in six inches of snow and found the four XIT herds and the two Long X herds all huddled against the railroad track — 15,000 in all. Twenty eight saddle horses belonging to the Long X froze to death in the night. Moore reported that he had lost three horses.⁵² For the next three days the outfits cut and separated the cattle, dividing the XIT cattle from the Long X cattle. Moore later wrote:

> We had to cut them into four herds and then separate one brand of steers from the other. It took us two or three days to do this as we had

---

⁴⁸The station was located near the north line of Section 21, T15S, R47W. In 1975, the only evidence of the station was an old caved-in well near the water hole. (*Tri-County History*, 37)

⁴⁹Brothers George T. and William D. Reynolds formed a partnership in 1868 and adopted the Long X brand. Their ranch, at the time, was located along the Clear Fork of the Brazos River in the vicinity of Fort Griffin. Trail drives to the north, as far as Canada, helped the ranch prosper, and by 1884 they incorporated having put together ranches in Haskell, Shackelford, and Throckmorton counties — headquartered at Albany. The following year, after Moore met the Long X on the trail, the Reynolds company established their Kent Ranch, after acquiring 232,000 acres in Jeff Davis County. ("Reynolds Cattle Company," *The Handbook of Texas Online*, www.tshaonline.org, [accessed March 5, 2010])

⁵⁰*Tri-County History*, 119, and telephone interview with Cora Freeman, Bovina nursing home, life-long resident, who said that "old timers used to tell of the watering spot [for Texas herds] southeast of town." Aug. 28, 2009. *Tri-County History* noted: "The trail followed the Big Sandy roughly to Hugo and north to Bovina where springs east of Bovina furnished ample water for the herds." 118.

⁵¹Moore journal, added notes from 1922.

⁵²Moore journal and letter to Haley in 1927, (*Panhandle-Plains Historical Review*, 50)

no horses that were trained to cut cattle and cattle that have been driven in a herd as long as these had are hard to separate.[53]

The storm had hit at the wrong time. Moore noted that if it had come only one day later, "we would have been scattered out more and would perhaps been able to have held our herds in better shape." It was the second major delay on the trip. They had lost three days in No Man's Land and this delay in Colorado. Finally on June 4th, the Moore outfit again started up the trail. The next reliable water source was Hell Springs, on Hell Creek, a little north between Bovina and Genoa.[54] May noted in his journal of a camp and watering spot at Hell Springs. Just north of Hell Springs was Dugout Creek. Here is where the Moore herd camped their first day out of Bovina. Moore jotted:

> June 4   Camped on dug out [Dugout Creek] 10 miles from Bovina. Came another storm that night, held my herd all O.K.

2

Location: Northwest corner of Cheyenne County, Colorado, approximately eight miles north of Aroya. From the intersection of State Highway 94 and U. S. Highway 40, two miles north, one mile east, and seven miles north.

Authors' commentary:
After the original plaque was stolen from this large stone monument, the local rancher made a substitute one out of sheet metal. One has to walk to this marker.

THIS MONUMENT STANDS ON THE SMOKY HILL TRAIL ON THE REPUBLICAN BIG SANDY DIVIDE, THE ROUTE, OF THE BUTTER FIELD STAGE 1866-1870. FIFTY YARDS EAST THE TEXAS MONTANA CATTLE TRAIL CROSSED THE SMOKY HILL TRAIL.

---

[53] The cowboys were using their saddle horses to do the roundup. (Moore jounral, notes from 1922)
[54] Harry Hansen, who owns the land today, verified that there is a spring on Hell Creek in the area of the trail that, in his memory, has never gone dry. Phone interview by Gary Kraisinger, August 28, 2009.

The next evening found the Moore herd and outfit three miles south of Walk's Camp. The camp, located at the headwaters of the Arikaree River, had been one of John Walk's buffalo hunting camps. He had furnished buffalo meat for the workers on the Rock Island Railroad. Walk chose this site because of the large cottonwoods and willows along the river's banks and the spring water.[55]

On June 7, Moore wrote in his journal that the outfit camped two miles south of Abbott, Colorado. Abbott had been platted in 1888 under the anticipation that a railroad would be built from Brush through Abbott and points east.[56] From there the trail followed Beaver Creek to Brush, Colorado, a community dating from 1882 that sat on the Burlington and Missouri Railroad which later became the Chicago, Burlington and Quincy Railroad.[57]

The Moore outfit stayed in the Brush area for two days. On June 9, they camped three miles south of Brush, and on the 10th, they "passed through Brush and crossed the South Platte River," and "Camped six miles north of Brush." Brush was one of the scheduled stops to replenish the chuck wagons. Moore noted in his journal that he purchased the supplies from Wm. Knearl. Billie Knearl was one of the first merchants in Brush. He had moved across the river from Snyder to the newly established railroad town.[58] Just below his list of purchased supplies, Moore noted that he had to pay Frank Stephens ten dollars for "crossing herd across South Platte." (Map #III, 3-4)

In addition to having to ford the river and paying to do so, cowboys and herds had to deal with irrigation ditches. In the seven miles between Brush and Snyder, irrigation ditches paralleled the South Platte River. As homesteaders and squatters settled along the river and built prospective railroad towns in the mid 1880s, they constructed irrigation ditches and fenced watering holes. When the Texas herds wanted to cross these ditches or water herds at the watering holes, they were charged a fee. In order to control the flow of the Texas herds and to restrict the cattle or

---

[55] Walk's Camp was located in the NE 1/4 of Sec. 20, T7S, R55W. During the late 1800s and early 1900s, this site was a meeting place for community picnics and gatherings. According to the current Lincoln County Historical Society's sign, "John Walk hunted buffalo here in 1872." (Laura Solze Claggett, *History of Lincoln County, Colorado*, 11)

[56] Abbott was originally located in the SW 1/4 of Sec. 3, T3S, R55W. It had a post office from 1887 to 1920. There were also, reportedly, a hotel, bank, school, a newspaper, blacksmith shop, lumber yard, saloons, various businesses. The trail town did not continue to grow, however, because the projected railroad never materialized. At first it was about ten miles northwest of Lindon. Then in 1918 Abbott was moved to about six miles north of Lindon. The post office was named after Albert Abbott who was a head of a land speculation company that was in the area. (Ray Shaffer, *A Guide to Places on the Colorado Prairie, 1540-1975*, 317, and Hildred Walters and Lorraine Young, "There Was A Town Called Abbott," *Colorado Prairie Tales*, 47)

[57] According to the *Historic Trail Map of the Greeley 1 x 2 degree Quadrangle, 1894 — 2336 — USGS*, by Glenn R. Scott and Carol Rein Schwayder, the town of Brush was established in 1882 and was originally called "Beaver Valley." Map used by permission from Research Curator, Peggy A. Ford, City of Greeley Museum, Greeley, Colorado.

[58] Expense pages in the back of Moore journal: "Brush, Colo., June 10, 92." Billie Knearl and his sister Polly had built the first store in Snyder, believed to have been near the railroad track. They also built and operated a hotel referred to by locals as the "Bee Hive" because of the many people who lived in it at the same time. ("History of Snyder, Colorado," *Morgan County History*, 9)

horses to a certain location, a fence was erected to form a lane or path so the herds would not disturb the ditches. Even eight years earlier, when May arrived at the north bank of the South Platte River at Snyder, he ran into two men who had built a fence across the trail and were charging a toll of five cents on every animal driven over the route. May was forced to pay the charge, approximately $125, but was not going to get caught paying the toll again in the following year. In 1885, May found a detour around the fence and broke the "swindlers' game."[59]

Snyder, located on the northern bank of the South Platte River, was the oldest town in Morgan County. Just one half mile south of the present town there is a natural ford across the river where old timers say the explorer John Charles Fremont crossed in his journeys to discover passage through the Rockies that was

3

TEXAS MONTANA TRAIL
1866 - 1897

Location: Intersection of U.S. Highway 36 and State Highway 71; roadside park in Last Chance, Washington County; north of Limon, Colorado

Authors' commentary:
As late as the 1960s, Last Chance was a lively stop for gas, food, and lodging for travelers. It was the last chance for rest and refreshment for quite a distance for those traveling in eastern Colorado. Even though the rest stop was not there during the trail-driving days, it sits on the Texas-Montana Feeder Route which State Highway 71 later closely followed.

At some time in the past, a group marked the trail here in Last Chance and placed this handsome marker in the roadside park. When this site was visited in 2007, the brass or bronze placque on the marker was gone. In 2011, a prairie fire burned some of the remaining buildings. It is not known in what condition the trail marker is in now, for Last Chance is now a ghost town with only remnants of buildings.

The ones who erected this marker may have been thinking of the Goodnight-Loving Trail that went through Colorado starting in 1866, for the beginning date for the Texas-Montana Trail (Feeder Route) is not correct. The route did not go through the Last Chance area until 1884. The feeder route used part of the 1875 New Goodnight Trail, not the Goodnight-Loving Trail. The ending date of 1897 is correct, one of the few markers that uses that correct date. Because of the cattle brands used on this stone marker, we assume that the people who erected this marker also placed the one at Brush, Colorado.

---

[59]Haley, *The XIT Ranch of Texas*, 135.

later used by the railroads. About one fourth of a mile west of Snyder, there had been a hunters' and trappers' camp as early as 1869 in what was called Beaver Territory at the time. This camp was the beginnings for the first community in Weld County, present-day Morgan County, with a general store, a saloon, and several houses. There had also been a stage station near Snyder on the south side of the river that was one of a series of such stations on the Overland Stage route. It was called the "Beaver Creek Station" because it sat near where Beaver Creek empties into the South Platte River. Mail was delivered to the station, and then someone had to ford the South Platte to take it across to the camp which, according to some historians, was called "Beaver Camp." By 1879, however, the settlement was renamed "Snyder" after J. W. Snyder, a cattleman from Georgetown, Texas, who was appointed to

4

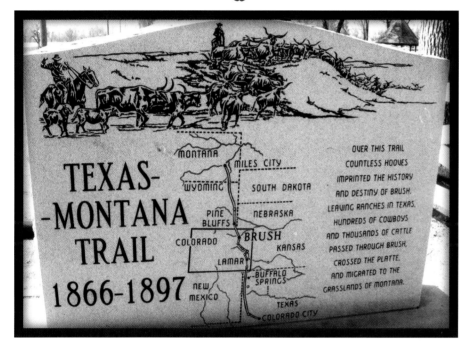

TEXAS-MONTANA TRAIL
1866-1897

OVER THIS TRAIL COUNTLESS HOOVES IMPRINTED THE HISTORY AND DESTINY OF BRUSH. LEAVING RANCHES IN TEXAS, HUNDREDS OF COWBOYS AND THOUSANDS OF CATTLE PASSED THROUGH BRUSH, CROSSED THE PLATTE, AND MIGRATED TO THE GRASSLANDS OF MONTANA.

Location: City Park in Brush, Colorado, Morgan County.

Authors' commentary:
This is a very handsome stone marker with a great map and artwork. There are thirty cattle brands cut into the back of this marker which we do not recognize. Some of the ranch brands that would have been on the trail were the XIT, N Bar N, 101, OX, and Long X. Perhaps the marked brands are local Colorado ranch brands.

The date 1866 is the beginning for the earlier Shawnee Trail System into Missouri and the Goodnight Trail System that started from south Texas and moved herds into New Mexico and Colorado, with some cattle perhaps ending at the Cheyenne, Wyoming railhead. The migration of "thousands of cattle" into the "grasslands of Montana" did not occur, however, until the Texas Trail (Western) came into use in 1876. Before that, the area was occupied by the Sioux.

The Texas-Montana Trail, that the marker addresses, did not cross Colorado headed for Montana until 1884. The excellent map on the stone shows the XIT Trail from Yellowhouse-Colorado City Trail, joining the Texas-Montana Feeder Route at Buffalo Springs and continuing across Colorado to Wyoming and beyond. Therefore, the accurate date for this marker should be 1884 - 1897.

This marker was dedicated on July 4, 1995.

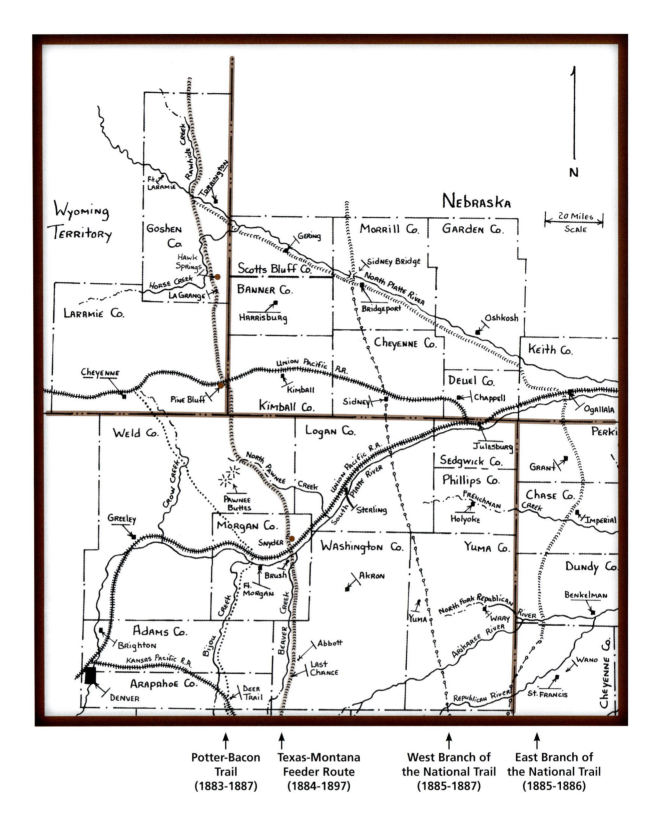

MAP #III, 3-4
Upper Portion of the Texas-Montana Feeder Route:
This map shows the relationship between: (1) the Potter-Bacon Trail to its terminus at Cheyenne, Wyoming; (2) the west branch of the National Trail to Sidney Bridge on the North Platte River; (3) the east branch of the National Trail to Ogallala, Nebraska; (4) the Western Cattle Trail along the North Platte River from Ogallala to Rawhide Creek in Wyoming; and (5) the Texas-Montana Feeder Route (until 1897) across Colorado and on across Wyoming to feed into and connect with the Western Cattle Trail at Rawhide Creek.

454 THE WESTERN CATTLE TRAIL | 1874-1897

administer the vast John Wesley Iliff estate.[60] The Union Pacific Railroad was built through the country in 1881, and a town began to be built around the depot. The Snyder Camp group moved closer the the depot, a new school house was built, and a post office, located in the railroad depot, was acquired in June of 1882.[61]

Moore wrote in his June 11, 1892 entry that they "camped at the Big Alkali lake 8 miles S. of Pawnee [Creek]," which was probably Hunter's Lake. It is believed to have been named after Samuel Dimmitt Hunter who was a wealthy sheepman and cattle rancher in the area who came to Greeley, Colorado, in 1870.[62]

Two examples of seedling towns north of Snyder were Raymer and Stoneham. When the Chicago, Burlington & Quincy Railroad constructed a line from Holyoke to Cheyenne in 1887, the Texas-Montana Feeder Route intersected with it between Raymer and Stoneham. John W. Carnhan, in his 1943 reminisce, recalled the railroad while he was on the trail. As a lad, Carnhan had trailed cattle from the Houston, Texas, area to Lincoln County, Colorado using part of the Texas-Montana Feeder Trail. Carnhan wrote:

> My first trip northward was before the railroad had been put through here in 1887. There had been talk of this road but up to that time not even a surveying stake had been driven in the ground. My next trip northward a year or so later the road bed had been laid and the town of Raymer was beginning to spring up. I don't recall but little of the town as a hand looking [out] for cattle so thought little of the many towns springing up along our trails.[63]

A 1894 USGS map shows two routes splintering from the Snyder, Colorado, area. One going in a northwesterly direction is labeled "Cattle Trail to Cheyenne via Crow Creek," and a northeasterly route labeled "cattle trail to Sidney, Nebraska." (see Map #III, 3-4) It does not show the Texas - Montana Feeder Route going north out of Snyder. The Texas trail drivers' journals, that are being used and followed in this narrative, however, describe the route as going straight north, northwest of Snyder toward Pawnee Buttes and the North Pawnee Creek — a route that continues all the way into Montana. According to Gladys Williams, a historian in Snyder, Colorado, the route led up "Dead Horse Draw on north, crossing the west edge of Snyder. They had to make 'Hunter's Lake' near New Raymer for the next watering place and rest." The USGS map does tell us that drovers trailed cattle via splinter routes that were destined for either Cheyenne, Wyoming, or Sidney, Nebraska, both of which were busy railheads where cattle could be shipped out to the east.

---

[60]As mentioned earlier, Iliff was one of Colorado's cattle barons who amassed a ranching empire along the South Platte River between Greeley and Julesburg. He was a supplier to Indian reservations and purchased herds from Charles Goodnight. Iliff died unexpectedly in 1878 at the age of 47, and J. W. Snyder was summoned to the area to operate the ranch.

[61]Aaron J. Woodruff was the first postmaster of Snyder in 1882 which was then in Weld County. The area became part of Morgan County in 1889. (Gladys Baughman Williams, *History of Snyder, Colorado*, 8 -10; and Tom Noel, "Iliff Crafted Kingdom from Cattle," *Rocky Mountain News*, 2008, http://www.rockymountainnews.com/news/2008/mar/01noel [accessed April 4, 2010] and "Snyder Post Office," http://webpmt.usps.gov [accessed March 17, 2010]

[62]Williams, Ibid, and Historic *Trail Map of the Greeley Quad*. and Moore's journal entry of June 11, 1892. In northeast Morgan County and southeast Weld County, there were a series of alkali lakes. To be approximately eight miles from the Pawnee, the cowboys would have been somewhere in southeast Weld County. Hunter Lake, one of the largest of these lakes, is located in Sec. 35, T7n, R57w. In the 1920s this lake was also known as the He-Lo Mystery Lake. The White Brothers bottled and sold waters of this lake as a mineral water, and the mud was put in jars and sold as a poultice cure for almost anything from sprains and sore muscles to canker sores. The "Denver Mud" was widely used as a cure-all. (Carol Rein Shwayder, ed., *Weld County, Old & New, People & Places*, Vol., 196, 216)

[63]John W. Carnhan, "Driving Cattle Northward," in Franklin M. Jones, *History of New Raymer*, Fort Morgan Heritage Foundation, 36-37.

5

OLD TEXAS TRAIL
OVER THIS TRAIL FROM DISTANT
TEXAS, PASSED THE GREATEST
MIGRATION OF MEN AND CATTLE IN
THE HISTORY OF AMERICA
1866 - 1897

BRONZE PLAQUE ON THE NORTH FACE
OF THE MONUMENT:
IN MEMORY OF THE PIONEER CATTLEMEN WHO
PASSED THIS WAY ON THE OLD TEXAS TRAIL
1866 - 1897
THIS PLAQUE PLACED BY THE HISTORICAL
LANDMARK COMMISSION OF WYOMING 1948

BRONZE PLAQUE AT BASE OF NORTH SIDE:
THIS MONUMENT SPONSORED BY THE LYONS
CLUB OF PINE BLUFFS, WYOMING STOCK
GROWERS ASSOCIATION, AND THE FAMILY OF
CAPTAIN D.H. AND J.W. SNYDER, TEXAS TRAIL
DRIVERS, WHO BROUGHT THE FIRST HERDS OF
TEXAS CATTLE TO WYOMING IN 1866.

Location: In Pine Bluffs, Wyoming, Laramie County, at the intersection of Highway 30 and Market Street, Second Avenue, and Lincoln Street, in a park adjacent to the Texas Trail Museum.

Authors' commentary:
This is one of seven markers erected in Wyoming honoring the Texas Trail cowboys. It was dedicated on August 1, 1948.[1] The Historical Landmark Commission also sponsored two markers seven years earlier at Lusk in Niobrara County (#2 marker in Part II, Chapter VII) and at LaGrange in Goshen County (#6 marker in Part III, Chapter III). On these markers the beginning date was 1876 for the Texas Trail — which is correct. Now on this marker, as well as others, they changed the beginning date to 1866. Perhaps the reason can be gleaned from the plaque at the base of the marker. The Snyder brothers may have driven herds to Cheyenne in the 1860s, but not on the Texas Trail.[2]

Perhaps the 1948 Commission concluded that the early Goodnight Trail System across Colorado toward Cheyenne was part of the Texas Trail network or they simply based the date on Snyder's narrative. The former markers of 1940 and 1941 were correct in that the Texas Trail did not go into Wyoming until 1876. The marker is very attractive and the map is excellent. The "Old Texas Trail" route shown occurred after the Sioux were removed to reservations and the area was opened for settlement. The lower part to the North Platte River is the Texas-Montana Feeder Route (1884-1897) and the upper portion is the Texas Trail or Western, (1876-1897).

---

[1] Mike Jording, *A Few Interested Residents, Wyoming Historical Markers & Monuments*, 1992, 115.
[2] According to Col. Dudley H. Snyder in Hunter's *The Trail Drivers of Texas*, the Snyder brothers after the Civil War, in 1866, drove a herd to Fort Union, New Mexico. They sold the balance of their herd to Charlie Goodnight around Trinidad, Colorado. Goodnight, in turn, may have trailed them to the railroad at Cheyenne, Wyoming, page 1030.

Raymer was platted by the railroad in 1888 and named for George Raymer, an assistant chief engineer for the railroad. The town site was then sold to the Lincoln Land Company which advertised that Raymer was part of "the rain belt." By the spring of 1889, several stores, a livery stable, a newspaper, *The Raymer Ranger*, and a post office, opened on June 27, 1888, was on site. Because of the drought and the lack of water, the town did not last long. Within a year, businesses started to close. In 1895 the post office was discontinued and by 1898 the town was abandoned.[64]

To the east of the Texas-Montana Feeder Route was Stoneham, which was populated by a Belgian immigrant colony, a few miles north and east of the present town. The Lincoln Land Company purchased the land site from Elenora B. Stone, after whom the town was named, and the Burlington Missouri depot was constructed in the town in 1887. A post office was opened in 1888. In 1889, the Belgian colony moved to the railside. Like Raymer, the town site dried up, was abandoned, and sold for back taxes in 1894. The town existed during the trail drives for only a short period. Moore may have seen its meager existence in 1892.[65]

As the trail herds moved up the North Pawnee Creek toward Pawnee Buttes, a prominent landmark, the drovers covered some fifteen miles per day, according to May.[66] As Pawnee Buttes came into view, they seemed to stand guard over the quiet spans of the Colorado badlands. There was an east butte, Gabriel's Castle, and a west butte, Devil's Smoke House, and the eroded columns of sandstone towered two hundred and fifty feet into the air. Moore's outfit trailed to within three miles of the buttes.[67] The trail continued to wind its way along the north fork of the Pawnee, east of the buttes among the Caulk Bluffs.

To reach Pine Bluffs, Wyoming, the herds trailed east of the bluffs across the extreme southwest corner of Nebraska. Herds filed down from the bluffs, crossed the Wyoming-Nebraska border, and continued toward the town of Pine Bluffs, on the Union Pacific Railroad. At Lodgepole Creek, there was a charge for watering the herd. Moore, in his journal, recorded his expenses of replenishing the wagon and that he "Payed to A. J. Elliott $15 for watering herd and driving through pasture."[68]

Pine Bluffs was so named because of the pines among the nearby bluffs. At first it was known as "Rock Ranch" and consisted of a tent, a slab shack with a stone chimney, and a square shed of canvas-covered poles, but when the Union Pacific Railroad came through in 1867, they renamed the location "Pine Bluffs." The small

---

[64]When another wave of immigrants came in 1909, the town was replatted and given the name of New Raymer because the post office would not accept just "Raymer." The New Raymer post office was opened on November 13, 1909. Note that Gladys Williams referred to "New Raymer" near Hunter's Lake in her comment about the Texas-Montana Trail. ("Raymer, Colorado," http://en.wikipedia.org [accessed April 9, 2010]

[65]When a second influx of homesteaders came in 1907, the Stoneham post office was reopened, the town replatted, and the town renamed "New Stoneham."

[66]Ralph F. Jones, who wrote *Longhorns North of the Arkansas* in 1969, discusses this route by saying that herds traveled toward the "north fork of the Pawnee." He is the only one to be specific about the "north fork" of the Pawnee. The journals of May and Moore only refer to the "Pawnee." (Jones, 9)

[67]Moore journal entry of June 13, 1892.

[68]Moore's journal — last recorded page of expenses.

railroad town was visited by Ezra M. Soar in 1880. He was driving a herd of cattle from the Wells, Colorado, area headed for the Black Hills. In his diary from March, 1880 to July 3, 1880, he describes for the reader his route. Starting at Pine Bluffs, Soar drove over a road that would later become the Texas-Montana Feeder Route.

In his May 13 entry, he wrote:

> ...on to Pine Bluff [s] Station a small place one store & saloon 2 or 3 houses drove 5 miles & camped for the night making (?) miles to day not very good feed we are now camped on Spring Creek 1 1/2 miles west of Pine Bluff [s] Station.[69]

By the time Jim May came through with the LS herds in 1884, Pine Bluffs was a cattle shipping point for local cattlemen.[70] Four years later, Dema Tremain arrived as a young girl and she wrote that Pine Bluffs was "a tiny place, one small store, a livery barn and a small hotel." From 1880 when Ezra Soar came through the town to 1888 when Tremain arrived, the town had not grown.[71]

The herds continued north over the high divide country that lies between Lodgepole Creek and Horse Creek. Coming off the divide, the trailsmen led their herds down to the headwaters of Bushnell Creek, a small stream that empties into Horse Creek. Widow Ellis's place was a watering spot for the herds on Bushnell Creek.

The next stop for water or camping was at the C. P. Ranch. The ranch was situated on the creek, a likely spot to rest. Soar wrote that they camped at "Cratons Ranch" on Horse Creek, "a good sized creek & very nice stream."[72] Starting in 1890, Milton Green became foreman of the ranch and was always hospitable to the trail drivers. Because of his kindness, trail bosses often saw to it that he received stragglers or young calves from their herds. Eventually, Green acquired a fine herd of Texas longhorns.[73]

As the trail progressed north, the herds started through what the cowboys called Horse Creek Gap. Horse Creek flowed between Bear Mountain on the west and Sixtysix Mountain on the east. Along this creek, a few more ranch houses became visible. The homes were of log or sod and had dirt roofs. One of these few ranch houses was built by Kale LaGrange about 1875 when he homesteaded on Horse Creek in the Gap. According to Soar's account in 1880, there was a bridge in this area:

---

[69]Ezra Soar's diary has very little punctuation. From a transcript owned by the City of Greeley Museums, Greeley, Colorado.

[70]"Pine Bluffs," Heritage Society web site: http:pinebluffs.org/heritage_society [accessed March 30, 2010]

[71]Dema Tremain, "Early Days of LaGrange Community," written in 1936 included in *Trails, Rails and Travails*, City of LaGrange, Wy., 5.

[72]Ezra Soar diary entry of May 14, 1880.

[73]The C.P. Ranch was owned at the time by General David Swearingen. Milton Green was under his employ from 1890 to 1898. ("Milton M. Green Family History," *Trails, Rails and Travails*, 66) A local by the name of Bump Miskimins wrote that there were only two places for the herds to water after leaving Pine Bluffs: the first water source was known as Johnson Place (the C.P. Ranch was later owned by Jelmer Johnson) and the next was at Hawk Springs.

May 16 Sunday: drove 6 miles & stopped for breakfast drove 4 miles and met Horse Creek again 2 miles on further to the bridge across Horse Creek then 4 miles further to Hawk Spgs.…

Neither May nor Moore mentioned the LaGrange location or the bridge. In 1889, with the encouragement of Kale LaGrange, Seymour J. Robb with partner, Nells Robertson, decided to build a mercantile store along the side of the Texas- Montana Feeder Route on the LaGrange site. The store was a two-story building with steps going up the outside to an upper room. During construction, Robb applied for and

1876 - 1897

IN REMEMBRANCE OF THE HARDY PIONEER STOCKMEN AND COWBOYS, WHO DROVE THEIR HERDS ACROSS THIS SPOT INTO CENTRAL AND NORTHERN WYOMING.

DEDICATED BY THE HISTORICAL LANDMARKS COMMISSION OF WYOMING JULY 1941

LOWER PLAQUE:
TEXAS TRAIL
CITIZENS OF LA GRANGE COMMUNITY AND WYOMING STOCKGROWER'S ASSOCIATION

Location: Opposite the Community Church in LaGrange, Wyoming in Goshen County.

Authors' commentary:
This is one of two markers erected in Wyoming honoring pioneer stockmen who drove herds to Wyoming on the Texas Trail. This one and the one at Lusk, both large boulders, (marker #2 in Part II, Chapter VII) were dedicated in 1940 and 1941 by the Historical Landmark Commission of Wyoming. They are to the point and have the correct dates of the trail, 1876-1897.

Seven years later in 1948, the Historical Landmark Commission dedicated two other markers: one in Lingle, in Goshen County, and one in Pine Bluffs, in Laramie County (markers #1 in Part II, Chapter VII and #5 in this chapter), also honoring pioneer cattlemen "who passed this way on the Old Texas Trail." But for some reason, the beginning date was changed to 1866. Another stone marker is at Moorcroft in Cook County (marker #5 in Part II, Chapter VII). Its dedication date is unknown. Its wording is somewhat different, but it also uses the incorrect dates of 1866-1897.

Two newer Wyoming markers west of Newcastle and south of Upton in Weston County were erected by the Weston County Historical Society in 1995 (markers #3 and #4 in Part II, Chapter VII). The society followed the lead of the 1948 markers and again used the dates, 1866-1897. They should have referred to the older 1940 and 1941 markers, the correct ones. The Texas Trail (Western Trail) did not reach Wyoming until 1876.

Mike Jording, *A Few Interested Residents, Wyoming Historical Markers & Monuments*, 1992, 92. Photo courtesy of LaDonna Friesen, Halstead, Kansas.

was appointed postmaster of a new post office — named LaGrange. The post office was in one corner of the store. Soon, mail was being delivered daily from Cheyenne. Within months the first school was built, a small log room with four small windows and a dirt roof, along with a large lumber yard and hardware store, an ice house, a frontier saloon, and a newspaper, (*The LaGrange Index*).[74]

The Y-Cross Ranch was located about three miles north of LaGrange in the Gap. The ranch buildings had been built on Horse Creek, at the mouth of Bear Creek, and were a very short distance from the Texas-Montana Feeder Route. H. B. "Hi" Kelley owned the ranch. In his employ was Frank E. Jones, who made extra money by repairing equipment and saddles for the trail drivers and trading horses with the trail bosses as they passed through the Gap. Jones took in the "beat-out" trail ponies and the broken saddles, pastured out the ponies, and repaired the saddles in his spare time, and then traded them with other trail hands coming up the trail. He, too, built up a small herd of cattle by taking part of his wages in cows.[75]

Hawk Springs, the second watering spot after Pine Bluffs, was a relief stop. Here the spring water bubbled out of the ground and formed a pool of water. Ezra Soar was impressed with its "fine springs [where] a few rods below the head it makes quite a good size creek good clear water."[76] Most herds probably stopped and rested here. One time at the Springs, a team of four mules broke away in a dead run from their master, and the cook's leg was broken in the process. The cowboys emptied a box of crackers and used the wood to make a splint for the leg. He was then taken to a near-by ranch and left with instructions that they would pick him up on their way back from Montana.[77]

According to May's journal, the trip from Pine Bluffs to Horse Creek was thirty-five miles. The herds crossed the divide to the North Platte in another twelve or fifteen miles. (The actual mileage from Pine Bluffs to the Rawhide Creek confluence is about sixty-five miles.) Herds stacked up at the North Platte River in 1892 when Moore was there. In addition to four XIT herds, there was an N Bar N herd, and at least one Long X herd in the queue. Crossing a river like the North Platte was always a concern. The congestion created an air of anxiousness. If a herd balked for some reason, it was difficult to coax them into the water. If the sun was not just right, cattle could not see the far shore and would not swim. If the herd suddenly panicked in midriver, they would turn and mill. Often in this situation, a herd was double teamed and pushed across with all cowboys available working the herd. In June of 1892, the North Platte was "brimming full." More than likely, the wagons were sent upriver some twelve miles to cross at the bridge at Fort Laramie.

On the first day, Moore helped the N Bar N herd cross and then helped Chris

---

[74]Tremain, Ibid, 7; and Bernice Chamberlain, "History of LaGrange, Wyoming," written in 1979 and appears in *Trails, Rails and Travails*, 9. Robb operated a store in the Y Cross ranch area about three miles downstream before he decided to move his business to LaGrange. (Jones, Ibid, 170)

[75]Frank E. Jones was the father of Ralph Jones who wrote *Longhorns North of the Arkansas*. Burt Jones, (brother of Ralph), "Frank E. Jones Family," *Trails, Rails and Travails*, 78. and Ralph Jones, 173.

[76]Ezra Soar diary entry, May 16, 1880. (City of Greeley Museums) Today the springs are covered by the Hawk Springs State Reservoir.

[77]Miskimins, Ibid, 13.

Gish, one of the other XIT trail bosses, to push his herd across. On the second day, Moore "assisted Jim Vaughn to cross his herd in the forenoon, and tried to cross mine in the afternoon, but failed." On the third day, Moore's cowboys helped Jack Horn with another herd. On the fourth day, the remaining three XIT herds, including Moore's, were pushed across the river.[78]

On the south side of the North Platte adjacent to the Rawhide Creek confluence, the Texas-Montana Feeder Route ended. At this point cattle merged with the old established Western Trail trunk line that had been in use since the mid 1870s. (see Part II, Chapter VII)

PERRY EUGENE DAVIS, TRAIL DRIVER/COOK FOR THE HASKNIFE, 1894:

Another diary of interest is an obscure one written by Perry Eugene Davis. During the summer and fall of 1894, two years after Ealy Moore's recorded trail trip, Davis was in a Hashknife outfit driving a herd of horses southbound from Camp Cook, South Dakota to the Panhandle of Texas. At the age of twenty-five, Davis was the trail cook for the outfit, and he recorded their trip on the Texas-Montana Feeder Route in vivid detail. The herd of forty saddle horses and 400 mares with the Hashknife ranch brand was owned by the Continental Land and Cattle Company. The horse camp, from which the outfit started, was located along Box Elder Creek about fifteen miles from where the creek empties into the Little Missouri River near the Montana-South Dakota lines. On August 19, 1894, the outfit "pulled from the ranch with chuck wagon" and the herd of horses under the charge of "Big Red or Mill Iron Red," the trail boss, and headed for the home ranch in the Texas Panhandle. In addition to the trail boss, Davis' comrades were Edd Lee, Buckskin Bill, Carl, the "Kid,"and Walter.

Davis faithfully wrote in his three-and-one-half-inch by six inch notebook with a pencil everyday and recorded not only the route they took but the weather, his impressions of the towns, the waterways, and people he encountered. Because he was the cook, he often noted the availability of wood and the conditions under which he had to work — in the rain, mud, or fierce wind — and his colorful descriptions and colloquial expressions are a pleasure to read. Even though the outfit was trailing down the trail — and thus opposite the usual flow of trail traffic — the reader still receives the benefit of his impressions of the Texas-Montana Feeder Route. This outfit followed the route to a point ten miles south of Lamar, where the horse herd was trailed east to follow the old National Trail; from there it went on south to the southeast corner of Colorado and into No Man's Land and on to the Texas Panhandle.

The following narrative quotes are from Davis's diary which mentions the locations of the Texas-Montana Feeder Route — south of Rawhide Creek in Wyoming — and a splinter route which the outfit took south of Lamar, Colorado. The diary is referred to north of Rawhide Creek in Chapter VII of Part I. Here the

---

[78]Moore journal, June 20, 21, 22, 23, 1892. Jim Vaughn was another trail boss, for perhaps either a Long X herd or some other herd. Also Haley, *The XIT Ranch of Texas*, 138.

THE WESTERN CATTLE TRAIL | 1874-1897

diary is presented starting at Rawhide Creek and on south.[79] Follow Maps #III, 3-4 and III, 3-3, and keep in mind that in 1894, more settlers were in the region, and the trail-driving era for through-herds was fast coming to an end.

Again, this route goes from north to south — over the same route that Ealy Moore had taken two years before, coming from the south.

Davis records:

September 7:   Leave the Rawhide and camp on the hill to the east in sight of the Platte at noon on big flat.... Camp on divide two miles from river on pinnacle. Snowstorm very cold. Edd [almost] froze to death on guard. Boys standing half the night; mares stampede.

September 8:   Camp on running stream called Wild Horse [Creek]. Horses stampeded.... short buffalo grass which looks as short and fuzzy as a schoolboy's beard.

Between the North Platte River Valley and Hawk Springs was a grass country known as Goshen Hole. Davis noted in his diary the bareness of the region. It was open country with gumbo flats and sagebrush. After he parked his chuck wagon at Hawk Springs:

September 9:   ...cross rough, sandy desert for about eight miles with lots of cactus, more than I ever saw in one place before... County as bare as bird's ass. Camp between Bear Mountain and Sixty-Six Hills; camp at Hawk Springs. Rain in mess box, pie box. After supper, take a trip to Nebraska, only a few hundred yards. The largest springs I ever saw. Large creek; no feed; poor cattle. Seventy-five miles from Cheyenne.

September 10:   Last night cold and frosty. Before Old Sol had risen his cranium over old Sixty-Six, we were on the road going through the pass between Bear Mountain and the Sixty-Six Hills. Pass through winding lanes in a settlement [LaGrange] for about three miles and cross a high bridge over a creek. Have trouble crossing horses.

---

[79]The Davis diary, edited by Wayne E. Gossard, Jr, can be found online: *Life on the Trail: the 1894 Diary of Perry Eugene Davis* (Colorado Historical Society). It is very detailed in descriptions of the places and people and especially of the cowboys that Davis worked with. To demonstrate the route of the Texas-Montana Feeder Route, however, this delightful diary will only be used in part. (http://coloradohistory. org/westerntrails/30000144.000.jpg [accessed July 22, 2007] Also, "P.E. Davis, trail cook, cattle drive from Camp Cook, SD through Montana, Wyoming, Nebraska. and Colorado," *Colorado Heritage Magazine*, 1981.

Ealy Moore, in 1892, did not mention the LaGrange location or the bridge, but in 1894 when Davis and the horse herd came through, he noted that they passed a settlement and crossed a high bridge over a creek (Horse Creek). LaGrange would have been there when Moore came through, but it had definitely become a recognized town two years later with a post office. Davis called the settlement by name when he later wrote that they had camped for dinner "on a hill two miles south of LaGrange." That night, the outfit camped about ten miles south of LaGrange "on the main divide between the two Plattes."

September 11: Cross a flat country about eight miles and camp at noon. Good grass. Pass homesteads and aermotors [windmills]; Move out after dinner along the ridge in sight of Pine Bluffs on the Union Pacific Railroad.… Cross Pole Creek [Lodgepole Creek in Laramie County, Wyoming], a nice stream, through a pasture where they charge twenty dollars for watering a herd. Watered before anyone sees us; no pay.… Cross the railroad track and pull into Nebraska. Camp on the line.

Ealy Moore had recorded in his journal that he had to pay A. J. Elliott fifteen dollars for watering the herds and crossing the pasture. Davis apparently refers to the same owner, only the price had gone up. Luckily, the cowboys and Davis slipped away before being seen.

September 12: Trail goes through a portion of Banner [present-day Kimball] County, Nebraska. Stop and fill barrel at a homesteader's well, 236 feet deep. Water is pumped out with an aermotor windmill. After moving along the [creek] about eight miles, we camp the wagon where there is good feed. Camp near Pawnee Buttes on the head of Pawnee Creek in Weld County, Colorado and get fence posts to burn.

The trail continued to wind its way along the north fork of Pawnee Creek, east of Pawnee Buttes among the Caulk Bluffs. Davis referred to these prehistorically-formed bluffs as "Cliff Hills." It is interesting that cowboys on the trail knew exactly where they were. To follow a beaten path through marked towns and across labeled creeks is understandable. It is known that trail drivers had maps of the area, but Davis recorded county and state names as well. On the night of September 11, Davis records that the chuck wagon was parked on the Nebraska line. He does not reveal how he knew that. Also, Davis marvels at the windmills. In 1894 in western Nebraska and eastern Colorado, windmills had become a necessary item of survival for the homesteader. Homesteaders also counted their fence posts. Davis did not get away with swiping fence posts for his camp fire:

...Picked up a couple of fence posts; granger follows me and uses very harsh language. He wants the post back and two dollars for his trouble. I told him I'd be hanged if I'd do it, and he said he would take it out in hide then and pulled my jumper. I thought I could knock him out and he'd leave, but if I had stayed with him a few minutes longer there wouldn't have been enough left of me to grease a flintlock gun. I said, "Say, partner, if you will just wait a while I will get your post and two dollars for your trouble."

The cowboys and the Hashknife horses "laid over at Pawnee Creek" on September 13. In the evening, Davis moved the camp to Agate Springs where they spent the night. The wind blew and Davis attempted to make breakfast the next morning:

September 14: At four o'clock it was cloudy as a stack of black cats, and the wind was blowing a terrific jimmycane [cyclone]. Had to pile up ovens, etc. to keep from blowing the fire out of the country while I got breakfast. After considerable effort I succeeded in making bread and fried meat and warmed up the beans and went gently to the boys and told them breakfast was now ready in the dining car.... After breakfast I find that some of the horses are gone. All but Kid go to look for them. Wait in the dust about two hours; move out about five miles and stop and get dinner. Move about eight miles; cross the railroad at Keota and camp five miles south of track.[80]

Two days later the outfit had reached the Union Pacific Railroad and its Snyder station. The following day was spent in Snyder where Davis purchased supplies. He observed the green fields, watermelon patches, and two railroad lines. The pens at Snyder were full of sheep, so the Hashknife horses could not use the Snyder stockyards. Trail hand Walton quit the outfit, and Buckskin Bill was hired. Trail boss Red and Edd crossed the South Platte River and visited Brush on the "B & M Railroad."[81] Davis had laid in chuck at Snyder. Ealy Moore, two years before, had

---

[80]Keota was originally a homestead established in 1880 by two sisters, Mary and Eva Beardsley. When the Colorado-Wyoming Division of the Burlington Missouri River Railroad came through in 1887, the sisters sold their land to the Lincoln Land and Cattle Company which promoted a station stop. A small town survived for a few years, but the post office was closed in 1890. Today the location is in the Pawnee National Grasslands, in Weld County on County Road 103 approximately fifty miles east of Greeley. The tracks were removed in 1975. ("Keota, Colorado," www.ghosttowns.com [accessed Nov. 19, 2012])

[81]Here Davis is referring to the Burlington and Missouri River Railroad which was consolidated with the Chicago, Burlington, and Quincy Railroad in 1880. It was the second railroad that Davis had observed, five miles in the distance. The Chicago and Burlington had reached Beaver Valley and the Beaver Creek Station in June of 1882. (www.brushcolo.com [accessed Nov. 5, 2012])

stopped to replenish the outfit's wagon at Brush. Both outfits had to contend with the irrigation ditches and fences. In his next day's diary entry, Davis commented about the troublesome fenced lanes:

September 17:   Pulled through long lane. Horses tore down wire fences, got badly cut and went through brush. Didn't pay for fences. Moved eight miles from Platte and camped for noon. Move about eight miles after dinner and water in Beaver [Creek] and pull into the hills a couple of miles and camp. Sheep here; feed short. Horses run into two bands of sheep, stampede.

When trailing horses or cattle, sixteen miles was a full day. It was common for cowboys to break up the daily push into two drives, one in the morning before noon camp and the other in the late afternoon or evening. Having to work a stampede, however, is an added irritation.

September 18:   Pull back to Beaver on the trails. See poor folk with wooden shoes…. Grasshoppers and sheep; no feed. Pull on a flat close to Beaver and camp…. Norwegians ask how is the times in Montana. When a Norwegian complains of hard times, it is time for everyone else to drift with the tide.

Davis points out in his diary that when the camp is off the trail, the wagon and herd are pulled back to the trail to continue the trip. The beaten pathway, used by previous trail drivers, was followed. The pathway, the Texas-Montana Feeder Route, for these cowboys was up Beaver Creek toward the Big Sandy Creek. Davis also noticed the area settlers and their plight to survive through the grasshoppers and drought. In 1886, a number of Danish families had moved into the region.

September 19:   Into Arapahoe County, Come to the county seat, Abbott. Small store; buy a big bale and lead pencils, six for five cents. Camp here for dinner…. Abbott is just simply a wide place in the road. Pull over to Plum Creek and water about five miles from Abbott. Good grass. Stay on the high flats.

September 20:   Cross middle fork of Beaver and water horses and pull about nine miles. Camp on a flat…. Pull the wagon back toward mountain about one mile and hunt a cactus bed to camp in…. Red talks of laying over a couple of days. Kill colts. Kid Carl and Edd Lee go out and get a fat antelope, which proved to be better than the common fat sow bosom that we were used to. This

THE WESTERN CATTLE TRAIL | 1874-1897   465

was the first fresh meat we had got since leaving the Cheyenne River in Wyoming.[82]

The trail boss (Red) appeared to have taken on the distasteful job of killing the new-born colts. This practice was common for both cattle and horse herds on the trail because the new-borns were too feeble to keep up with the rest of the herd and slowed down the drovers' job of moving on down the trail. Cowboys also took any opportunity they could to supply the cook with fresh meat. Here in his journal, Davis, for the first time, adds another name to just "the Kid and Edd." The outfit did not lay over for a couple of days, as Red suggested, but was on the move again the following morning.

September 21: …We are camped now on the high divide between the South Platte and the Arkansas River. This is a very elevated slope of country. Can see old Pikes Peak in the southwest….

September 22: We are on the trail before sunrise and in about two miles we came to a small creek called Spring Creek where we water the horses, fill the barrel, and coontail [swipe] a fence post a short distance from the creek. Over the first divide we came to Arikaree [River]…. It was eight miles from Young camp [probably Walk's Camp] to Dugout Creek. Six miles to Hell Creek camp for dinner and laid over in the afternoon….

The following day was Sunday, and the cowboys rested.

September 24: Pull out on the trail in a southeast direction and come to Dugout Creek in about five miles and water where there is a slew [slough]…. We pulled up on the divide toward Hell Creek about three miles where the wind blew about thirty or seventy miles per minute and camp where there is no grass. After dinner, we water in Hell Creek and pull across to Bovina, a flag station on the Rock Island Railroad, and camp at an old fellow's who tries to work trail out fits and who made one of the XIT bosses pay twenty-seven dollars for a fence post they had taken out of his fence. We had plenty of wood, but the boys went to his fence and took two white oak posts. D [7D] outfit pass us. The boss says he is glad to get ahead because we left a hard name and everyone

---

[82]Denver was the county seat of Arapahoe County until 1901. Abbot was in Washington County and had had a post office since 1887. It existed until 1926.

was watching him whenever he stopped fearing he would steal fence posts or water as we did.[83]

Bovina on the Rock Island Railroad was where the XIT and Long X herds had gotten pummeled with a spring blizzard two years before. The XIT and Long X herds had camped on Hackberry Springs southeast of Bovina at a well-known watering spot. Davis does not mention Hackberry Springs. Obviously, because of the scarcity of firewood, outfits on the trail used local fence posts for their campfires. A cook who had to feed his charge, would grab whatever he could to build a fire to cook a meal. He built up, broke down, and moved a camp twice a day. He started in the dark early every morning preparing biscuits, beans, or perhaps bacon, broke down the camp, packed, and was ready to move sometimes before sunrise. He and the trail boss selected a camping spot for mid-day, which Davis called dinner, where he again prepared a campfire and a meal, then on the move again. At evening camp, the cook might have the time to prepare a more extensive meal such as fresh meat or a cobbler. Of course, there was always hot coffee.

September 25: Moved almost direct east about twelve miles where we struck the Republican [River] and camped for dinner and watered…. Cross the old Smoky Hill Road…. After dinner, we pull out over a high country to the south…. Feed is no more here on account of grasshoppers and sheep.[84]

September 26: After a drive of about twelve miles down a long slope and past old bed grounds where you could have loaded up a wagon with leavings, etc. we came to the Bellyache Water Holes [Big-Springs] on a branch of the Big Sandy [Creek] about two miles down. We can see a few scattering trees and indications that we are rapidly going downhill to the Arkansas River which is about 100 miles distant. We have been going almost direct east all day…. We pull down to the trees…Here we find Sam Alexander, the D boss, just as he is pulling out of camp at a big spring where we water the horses and wait till he get in the lead…. We camp about five miles from Belly water holes on a flat.

Throughout most of the area on this trail drive, the grass is poor and both livestock

---

[83]The Seven-D Ranch was under five ownerships from 1869 to 1899. The headquarters was located on Comanche Creek four miles east of Fort Stockton in north central Pecos County, Texas. In 1894, the Seven D brand and ranch was owned by the Western Union Beef Company. (Julia Cauble Smith, "Seven-D Ranch," *The Handbook of Texas Online* www.tshaonline [accessed Nov. 8, 2012])
[84]Refer to footnote #47.

and homesteaders are feeling the hardships of a drought and a plague of grasshoppers. More than once Davis comments about the lack of feed. The horse herd outfit again crosses paths with the Seven-D cattle herd. In his next day's journal entry, Davis continues to jot comments about the nearby cattle herd.

> September 27: Find the 7D work mules in our horses…. In about five miles, we come to Kit Carson, a small town on the K.P.R.R. [Kansas Pacific Railroad]…. We fill the barrel at the tank and camp about two miles below town for dinner. As we pull down the creek about three miles we come to a pasture fence where one of the D herds rustled a fence post going up, which cost them thirty-seven dollars. Here we water the horses;… Camp sixteen miles below Big Sandy near a sheep ranch. Sheep and horses come on water about the same time. Two men come out and try to scare the horses. Edd knocks one down with my six-shooter and waters the mares.

According to Davis, there was more than one Seven-D herd. He wrote: "one of the D herds rustled a fence post." Edd is determined to water the herd even if a sheep owner tries to dominate the watering hole.

> September 28: …We follow down the creek about six miles to Massacre Springs, or Battlefield Water Holes,… Here there is a cutoff road over the divide south which we take and leave the Sandy. This creek was well named; it is almost impossible to pull a wagon through its bottoms. After leaving the creek, we pull direct south and over a high, sandy divide with here and there a bunch of sagebrush. About five miles from where we left the Sandy, we cross the Missouri Pacific railroad at Chivington, a small town of about thirty inhabitants. The main feature of this little hamlet is a fine, four-story, stone hotel surrounded by shade trees. About six miles south of Chivington, we strike the Sandy with plenty of running water and camp.

According to Davis, the outfit, for a short distance, used the old Trail City splinter route (cutoff road) and then returned to the Big Sandy Creek south of Chivington. Like Ealy Moore, Davis was impressed with the Kingdom Hotel.[85]

---

[85]When the Missouri Pacific Railroad realized that Chivington was not an ideal watering stop for their locomotive's boilers because of the high alkali content of the water, the line stopped at another location and the town's activity quickly faded. Since the Kingdom Hotel was directly connected to the railroad and its workers, it was eventually disassembled, and its materials sold and moved to other communities. ("Chivington, Colorado," http://en.wikipedia.org [accessed Feb, 23, 2010])

September 29:   Pull up to the D [Seven-D] wagon and wait till they find their horses…. Leaving the Sandy here, we bear to the right over the ridge and camp about ten miles south at an artificial lake called King's Reservoir, supplied by a canal from the Arkansas River which is fifteen miles south. As we leave the lake, about two miles, we cross an irrigation ditch and go into a lane and follow it about three miles with ditches on either side,… The horses run through the wire several times; killed two colts, cut others. I knew what would happen as soon as I saw the lane, which was eighty feet wide, and the fences nearly hid in sunflowers, which looked very scary to a bunch of wild horses….

Davis had stopped the chuck wagon and waited until sundown for orders from his trail boss as to where they would camp for the night. Then "About dark, Red came up and camped the wagon in two hundred yards of where I had been waiting for two hours. I was up till nine o'clock before I got my work done. I don't blame a cook for being cranky."

In 1894, cattle and horse herds had to contend with settlers and their fences. Here again, the Davis outfit was directed to use a lane in and around the irrigation ditches and fields of crops. Davis' frustration is sensed because of the loss of two colts and injury to others. Later in camp, the injured horses will have to be "thrown and doctored" with "wagon dope" applied to their cuts.

The wagon dope is axle grease carried on trail wagons and used to protect open wounds on the livestock or cowboys.[86]

September 30:   Hit the road bright and early. Pull through lanes about three miles till we come to the long bridge across the Arkansas River. Very sandy and dangerous to cross…. About one mile south of the river, we reach the town of Lamar, a very pretty place of about 1,000 people….

It appears that in the two years since Ealy Moore and his XIT outfit had stopped at Lamar to load up the chuck wagon, the town had grown. Their camp stay, however, was unpleasant:

Camp about one mile from town on a sand gulch. Wind blows hard; sand and gravel flies. Almost impossible to cook. The boys go back to town in the afternoon and wait for the wind to go down. About five o'clock,

---

[86]Wayne H. Gossard, Jr., editor of *Life on the Trail, The 1894 Diary of Perry Eugene Davis*, and diary entry by Davis on September 21, 1894.

pull out and up the creek about one mile and camp. Wind blowing a terrific storm. Stretch the wagon sheet around the wagon to break the wind. Strong smoke from the bull chips whips around in every direction around the wagon…. Wind blew cold all night.

Cook Davis could not escape the weather. He had to stay with the wagon while the other cowboys visited town.

October 1:   We move out on the trail behind the D wagon; about 10 miles to Clay or Wild Horse Creek on Big Sandy Creek with lots of timber…. Left the old trail and took a cutoff and stayed all night at Wolf Creek….

October 2:   Make a short drive in the forenoon and camp for dinner. Move to Butte [Two Butte] Creek, a running stream on a cutoff trail. Stay all night on Sanderoy, a big dry creek with plenty of dry wood. Had plenty of fire in Baca County, Colorado….

South of Lamar, the cowboys, trailing the Hashknife horses, left the Texas-Montana Feeder Route and two days later, Davis writes: "come into the old trail [National Trail] again which we had left at Big Sandy, which crosses the Arkansas about twelve miles [28] below Lamar where the cutoff trail crosses." By October 6, the outfit was in Kansas and headed south to No Man's Land and from there toward the Texas Panhandle. Davis's diary ended on October 19 after the horses were turned loose in the Hashknife pasture.

MAIN RANCHES USING THE TEXAS–MONTANA FEEDER ROUTE AND THE NUMBER OF CATTLE TRAILED NORTH, 1885 TO 1897:

As mentioned previously, in the last decade of trailing through-cattle to the north, only a few ranches were involved. Because of the changing attitude of northern ranchers toward the longhorn, the troublesome blockades and quarantines, and the rapid loss of open range because of homesteaders, fewer Texas ranchers put their herds on the trail. Large ranchmen, however, who raised thousands of cattle and still wanted to take advantage of the economics of trailing large cattle herds instead of using the railroads, continued to have drovers drive herds north to finishing ranches on the open plains of Montana and Wyoming. The journals of Ealy Moore, pushing an XIT herd in 1892, and Perry Davis, with a Hashknife horse herd in 1894, show the reader the problems that the drovers faced in the latter years of trailing. Moore's

470   THE WESTERN CATTLE TRAIL | 1874-1897

herd was stopped in No Man's Land by "officers" who were protecting a quarantine and demanding payoff, and Davis' outfit had to maneuver its horse herd through fenced lanes erected by homesteaders to protect their fields of crops.

After the collapse of the industry in 1886 and 1887, the trailing of cattle re-emerged in modified form for the next ten years,[87] but as illustrated in Chart #III-1, a significant number of cattle were trailed in the trail driving's final decade. The total annual numbers are elusive for that period because no sales were recorded as they had been before 1886. Because railing cattle by train had become more prevalent, numbers of cattle on the trail are not easily determined. Also individual ranches were trailing cattle to their own satellite ranches in the north, and those numbers were not recorded by those who kept tallies, such as newspapers and in rail records.

Goins and Gobel, in their *Historical Atles of Oklahoma*, estimated trail numbers starting in 1866 but ended their record in 1885. According to their chart, 300,000 animals were trailed north in 1884 and 220,000 in 1885. Goins and Gobel also write a disclaimer that their recorded numbers are "believed by many to be far too low."[88]

The Goins and Gobel chart does not show more specific trends. For example, the 1884 number represents herds still going through Dodge City, Kansas and on north, but probably does not include the LS Ranch herd lead by Jim May through Colorado. This was before the final Kansas quarantine law. The 1885 number of 220,000 represents herds on the National Trail in Colorado and perhaps those on the Texas-Montana Feeder Route. Starting in 1886, no more charts or tallies can be found. It was the period of the collapse after the Kansas quarantine, but J. Evetts Haley in his research stated that at least 225,000 head were trailed north in that year. This number would include the XIT's first year's numbers as well as others using the new Texas-Montana Feeder Route and the National Trail. This number does not appear to represent a collapse — but in the following years, the numbers decrease dramatically and did not reach that number again. By 1887, the National Trail was in its last year; Nebraska was no longer a viable option; and the trailing industry would never be the same.

This is not to suggest, however, that cattle herds were not being sent north in impressive numbers. It must be realized that while the trailing numbers decrease through the years, railed animals were increasing. These numbers are not addressed in this study.

In order to get an idea on just how many cattle or herds were put on the trail starting in 1885, the accompanying chart estimates the numbers on the trail starting in 1885. They were mostly from three ranches: the XIT in the Texas Panhandle; the 101 Ranch in No Man's Land; and the N Bar N in the Texas Panhandle. The LS Ranch also had a finishing ranch in Montana and drove herds from 1884 to 1887. They were bought out by the N Bar N in 1887-88.

---

[87]The terms of "collapse" and "re-emerge" were first used by Nebraskan historian Norbert Mahnken in 1945 when he wrote that the "industry collapsed in 1886-87, and re-emerged in modified form." (*Nebraska History, a Quarterly Magazine*, January-March, 1945)
[88]Charles Robert Goins and Danney Goble, *Historical Atlas of Oklahoma*, 117.

Other ranches, in addition to these three, were also on the Texas-Montana Feeder Route. Numbers from these ranches are only a guess. Narratives about these ranches' trail-driving activities do not mention actual trail numbers. For example, W. M. Pearce, who wrote about the Matador Ranch, simply says that the last year for the ranch to send herds north was in 1893.[89] If they had sent one herd of 2,000 head each year, that would add to the total. Only the two years (1887 and 1893) which can be actually documented are on the chart. The *Wyoming Tales and Trails* magazine states that the last year for the Mill Iron (Continental Land and Cattle Company) to drive herds north was in 1894.[90] The OX Ranch in Childress, Cottle, Hardeman, and Motley counties of Texas, owned by A Forsythe and D. D. Swearingen, according to John Leaky and Nellie W. Yost, trailed 5,000 head north in the years 1893 and 1894.[91] Again, it could be assumed that the Mill Iron and the OX Ranch also trailed herds prior to those years, adding to the total.

It is known, because of Davis' diary, that the Seven D Ranch had cattle on the trail as late as 1894. Moore, in his journal, mentioned the Long X herd in 1892. The 101 Ranch appears to have driven cattle north as late as 1895, and the XIT stubbornly continued to drive herds to their northern finishing ranch as late as 1897, with only one herd recorded for that year.

Using available statistics on a chart, therefore, suggests that well over a million longhorns were trailed north after 1885. Thus, it has become apparent that the Texas-Montana Feeder Route carried, in its thirteen seasons, an impressive number of cattle. It can truly be said that the cattle-trailing industry did re-emerge after the hard jolts of 1885 and 1886. Never again, were numbers equal to the ones recorded prior to 1885, but Texas cattlemen continued to trail cattle north until it became impossible to do so.

CHART #III-1:

This chart supports the assertation that over one million head were trailed north after the Western Cattle Trail System shifted west, going through Colorado. These numbers represent only herds on the trail. The numbers do not account for the herds that were shipped by train into the northern markets during the same time period.

The numbers on this chart come from cited sources and only record what is available in those sources. It is assumed, however, that ranches sent up herds in other years besides the recorded ones on the chart. For example, it is known from cited sources that the Long X had herds on the trail in 1888 and 1892 (which is recorded on the chart), but it makes sense that the ranch would have had herds on the trail in 1889 through 1891 as well. Proof to that is not available at this time. Most of

---

[89]W. M. Pearce, *The Matador Land and Cattle Company*, 30.

[90]"Brands and Branding," *Wyoming Tales and Trails*, pg. 5, www.wyomingtalesand trails.com [accessed Oct. 5, 2007]

[91]John Leaky and Nellie W. Yost, *The West That Was from Texas to Montana*, 96.

these ranches that trailed herds north, after J. E. May from the LS blazed the Texas-Montana Feeder Route in 1884, were trailing cattle to their own finishing ranches in the north — not to agencies or cattle buyers.

The numbers in this chart are based on the gathering of data piece by piece. Two major sources are Alva Betz and J. Evetts Haley. Betz wrote in *A Prowers County [Colorado] History*, that the Texas-Montana Trail handled from ten to thirty herds a year from 1887 to 1895.[92] Using the average size herd of 2,500, that would equate to 25,000 to 75,000 head per year, considerably less than in 1886. The "thirty" number is substantiated by the Western Texas-Trail Museum in Moorcroft, Wyoming which says that "32 herds came through the area in 1894."[93]

J. Evetts Haley, who studied the XIT Ranch, wrote that from 1886 to1896, "The usual drives [for the XIT] were from 10,000 to 12,000 head, though 20,000 head were driven one year."[94] The immense XIT Ranch, according to Ralph Jones, also drove additional herds for other ranches, and the 101 Ranch drove cattle every year until 1895.[95]

Two total lines have been charted. One is the accumulated annual numbers noted from the various sources, while the second total represents annual totals given in Betz, Jones, and by the Moorcroft Museum. The two totals are similar.

CHAPTER REVEIW:

During the years of the Western Cattle Trail, Texas herds had gone through western Kansas to Ogallala, up the south side of the North Platte from there, crossed the North Platte at the Rawhide, and journeyed on north to their destinations. The Texas-Montana Feeder Route came up through Colorado and joined the Western Trail at Rawhide Creek, thereby making it a feeder route to the larger Western Trail system.

The Texas-Montana Feeder Route has been presented in this chapter by using maps and four cowboy journals. This route across the open range of Colorado, west of the National Trail, was developed in 1884 by Jim E. May from the LS Ranch and was followed for the next thirteen years, with some modification, by other trail herds. The cattle trailing industry's westerly shift around Kansas and Nebraska occurred because of various reasons. (1) The Kansas state-wide quarantine law against Texas herds went into effect in the 1885 season. The route across Kansas was no longer available. (2) The National Trail, started in 1885 through Colorado, had not been sanctioned by the U.S. Government in the winter of 1885 which resulted in the opening of Section 41 to rapid homesteading in 1886, thereby blocking this route north. (3) The Nebraska Legislature passed a herd law which stopped the flow of Texas herds not only into Nebraska, but also into the Dakotas. (4) The Panhandle ranches, such as the JA, LS, and LIT, had worked for years to establish a reputation of healthy disease-free cattle and, by 1885, were ready to be considered the new gathering area

---

[92]Alva Betz, *A Prowers County History*, 74-75.
[93]Information flier and museum display, Western Texas-Trail Museum, Moorcroft, Wyoming.
[94]J. Evetts Haley, *The XIT Ranch of Texas*, 128.
[95]Ralph F. Jones, *Longhorns North of the Arkansas*, 93, 125.

Chart #III-1:
MAIN RANCHES USING THE TEXAS-MONTANA FEEDER ROUTE AND THE NUMBER OF CATTLE TRAILED NORTH: 1885-1897

RANCH	1885	1886	1887	1888	1889	1890	1891	1892	1893	1894	1895	1896	1897	TOTALS
XIT Capitol Freehold Land & Investment Co.			12,500 (Haley, 127)	12,500 (Haley, 127)	15,000 (Beach, 158)	20,000 (Haley, 136, 233)	10,000	10,000 (Fudge, 55)	12,500 (Fudge, 65)	10,000 (Haley, 143)	10,000	12,500	2,500	
Additional herds driven by XIT for others: (Jones, 93)			12,500	12,500	12,500	12,500	12,500	12,500	12,500	12,500	12,500	10,000		
101 Ranch The Standard Cattle Co. (Jones, 93)			10,000 to Wyoming	10,000 to Wyoming	10,000 to Wyoming	10,000 to Wyoming	10,000 8,000 to Montana	10,000 8,000 to Montana	10,000 8,000 to Montana	10,000 8,000 to Montana	10,000 8,000 to Montana	8,000 to Montana		
N Bar N The Home Land & Cattle Co.			15,000	15,000	15,000	15,000 (Mt. Mag. 16)	15,000	25,000 last drive (Mt.Mg, 18,19) (Haley, 138)						
LS Lee and Scott (1)	active	active	last year											
Long X Reynolds Land & Cattle Co.				8,700 (Stroud, 23)				5,000 (Haley, 136, 138, 233)						
OX Towns and Gudgell									5,000 (Leaky, 96)	5,000 (Leaky, 96)				
Matador Land and Cattle Co.			2,000 (Pearce, 30)						2,068 last drive					
Mill Iron Continential Land & Cattle Co.			40,000 (Flanagan, 164)							5,000 last drive (Wy Tales, 5)				
Seven D (7D) Western Union Beef Co.										7,500 (Davis diary)				

RANCH	1885	1886	1887	1888	1889	1890	1891	1892	1893	1894	1895	1896	1897	TOTALS
Others: Hashknife; Turkey track; the 777; etc.			15,000 (Hunter, 72, 255, 321, 601, 873, 920) last drive for Hashknife (Faded Prints 122-123) 35,000 held for market in Colorado (Flanagan, 164)	7,500 (Hunter, 72, 321, 920)	18,700 (Hunter, 72, 321, 409, 511, 873, 920)	12,221 (Hunter, 72, 115, 321, 873, 920)	5,000 (Hunter, 72, 321)	5,000 (Hunter, 72, 321)	17,494 (Hunter, 72, 321, 512)		2,500 (Hunter, 987)			
TOTALS Accumulated numbers	220,000 (Goins & Gobel, 117)	225,000 (Haley, 126) (Raine & Barnes, 230)	142,000 (Rocky Mt. News Flanagan, 164)	66,200	73,900	69,721	60,500	75,000	67,562	58,000	45,500	30,500	2,500 last herd north (Haley, 143) (Flanagan, 164) (Moorcroft Mus) (Raine & Barnes, 230)	1,136,883
COMPARED TO: **ESTIMATED YR. TOTALS** from Betz, Jones, and Moorcroft Museum	220,000	225,000	142,000	75,000 (Betz, 74)	75,000 (Betz, 74)	75,000 (Betz, 74)	87,500 32 herds cross N.Platte River, (Jones, 2)	75,000 (Betz, 74)	75,000 (Betz, 74)	80,000 32 herds came through in 1894 (Moorecroft)	75,000 (Betz, 74)			1,222,500"

The sources for the chart are as follows:

Beach, Maude L. (comp.) & Robert L. Thaden, Jr. (ed) *Faded Hoof Prints — Bygone Dreams*, Powder River Country, 1989 ed.

Betz, Alva. *A Prowers County [Colorado] History*, 1986 ed.

Bye, John O. *Back Trailing in the Heart of the Short Grass Country*, Davis Diary, Wayne H. Gossard, Jr. (ed.) *Life on the Trail, The [1892] Diary of Perry Eugene Davis*

Flanagan, Sue. *Trailing the Longhorns, A Century Later*, 1974 ed.

Goins, Charles Robert and Danny Goble. *Historical Atlas of Oklahoma*, 2006 ed.

Haley, J. Evetts. *The XIT Ranch of Texas*, 1929 ed.

Hunter, Marvin J. (comp. and ed.) *The Trail Drivers of Texas*, 1925 ed.

Jones, Ralph F. *Longhorns North of the Arkansas*, 1969 ed.

Leaky, John and Nellie W. Yost. *West that Was from Texas to Montana*, 1965 ed.

Montana — the Magazine of Western History, Spring, 2010.

Pearce, W. M. *The Matador Land and Cattle Company*, 1964 ed.

Raine, William MacLeod and Will C. Barnes. *Cattle, Cowboys and Rangers*, 1930 ed.

Russell, Jim. Bob Fudge, *Texas Trail Driver; Montana–Wyoming Cowboy, 1862–1933*, 1962 ed.

Stroud, Joseph G. *Memories of the Old Western Trails in Texas Longhorn Days*, 1932 ed.

Western Texas-Trail Museum flyer and display, Moorcroft, Wyoming

Wyoming Tales and Trails, "Brand and Branding," 5, online [accessed Oct. 5, 2007]

for trail herds from which herds would be sent north through Colorado. (5) The newly established XIT Ranch in the Texas Panhandle started sending numerous herds up the trail in the 1886 season. Its location, west of the National Trail and neighbor to the LS Ranch, helped to further establish that the Panhandle was the new breeding ground and supplier of Texas cattle, and (6) Panhandle ranches created finishing ranches in 1885 and 1886 in Montana and elsewhere. Numerous herds were being trailed to these ranches each season over a more direct route through Colorado.

The Texas-Montana Feeder Route was an extension of the Western Cattle Trail system. After the Western Trail was shut down in Kansas, another more westerly route had to be developed. This route, through Colorado, connected with the old trunk line of the Western Trail in Wyoming. Because of this, the Western Cattle Trail, north of the junction of Rawhide Creek and the North Platte River, remained intact and continued to be used until 1897.

The Western Cattle Trail System existed for twenty three years. In its first eleven seasons, the industry boomed, a time period when northern demands were at their peak for Texas cattle. The rise of the industry to meet these new requests resulted in a trailing of herds from south Texas averaging over 266,000 head per season. When Kansas enforced its 1885 quarantine and Nebraska followed with its herd law the following year, cattle-trailing over the old route collapsed. But by changing strategy and creating a more westerly route through Colorado, a few determined large ranches in the Texas Panhandle continued to trail herds north another twelve years. The trailing industry had revived.

EPILOGUE

"It ain't never goin' to be like it used to be"

> *A cowboy can ride down to Texas [from Wyoming] and back up to Canada and back again and get paid for it. It's a hell of a life!*

Monte Walsh
from the 2003 movie
Monte Walsh

> *Monte, the cattle life, as you know it, is dead. It died with the snow last winter."*
>
> *"It ain't dead. As long as there is one cowboy taking care of one cow, it ain't dead!*

conversation between
Shorty and Monte Walsh

THE WESTERN CATTLE TRAIL | 1874-1897

In the forward of *The Trail Drivers of Texas*, editor J. Marvin Hunter and his partner, George W. Saunders, dedicated the volume to the memory of the old trail drivers and all others who "fought manfully for proud, imperial Texas." The collection of remembrances was "brought forth" in order that the record be "kept straight and posterity is given a true account."[1] The final volume of 1,060 pages was released in 1925 and to his dying day on July 3, 1933, George Saunders, who was himself "an old-time cowboy, and one of the first to go up the trail,"[2] believed in keeping the record straight at all costs. In his last years of life he fought against misnomers and mis-understandings about the cattle trails.

In the intervening years since the last herds had been driven north and Saunders' retirement, many of the old trail drivers had passed on and the next generation had not experienced the short time span of the trail-driving industry. The challenges that Saunders faced in his final years to try to send out messages as to what it was really like during those trail-driving days, which trail was which, and the exact locations of the trails, continue today. A controversy arose in 1931 which caused the State of Oklahoma to mandate in 1933 in its House Bill 149 that research be done to map and explain exactly where the Chisholm and the Western trails were located in the state. Misunderstandings about the cattle trails is demonstrated, as well, on roadside markers that started appearing in the 1930s, and perhaps more damaging was (or is) the portrayal of wrong information in Hollywood movies, which people have a tendency to believe.[3]

In the last decade, the mis-understandings have surfaced again. There is renewed interest by old-trail enthusiast to mark the Chisholm and Western cattle trails. The location of the trunk lines of these two cattle systems is not completely understood by those promoters, and there is a great chance of more misinformation being repeated. This is understandable, of course. The cattle trail systems are complex and, as demonstratated in this book, require in-depth study to fully comprehend.

A clarity in the cattle-trailing systems north out of Texas has been our mission. By scanning old original maps, reading cowboy journals, and studying *The Trail Drivers of Texas*, in addition to scores of other documents, the authors have tried to carry on the mission of J. Marvin Hunter and George W. Saunders. Hopefully informed readers will be able to discern from the wrong information that continues to be relayed.

Not only have the authors read and written about cattle trail driving in the Old West, but we have followed the Hollywood movies and TV films, as well, depicting drovers trailing longhorns north. Most of us today who don't "sit a horse" nor know

---

[1] Foreward of *The Trail Drivers of Texas*, J. Marvin Hunter, editor.

[2] "Minutes of the First Annual Convention of the Old Time Trails Drivers' Association Held in the City of Houstin, Texas, March 21, 22, 23, 1916." in Hunter, 7.

[3] An example of a movie with a series of wrong information is "Dodge City," directed by Michael Curtis in 1939 and based on a story by Robert Buckner. Staring Errol Flynn and Olivia de Haviland, the movie was introduced as being about a lawless cattle town on the Chisholm Trail in 1872. Flynn, as the character of Wade Hatton, a Texas cattle agent, takes the job of sheriff to clean up the town. It was filmed in early Technicolor and was one of the highest grossing movies in 1939. Dodge City was on the Western Trail and was not an active cattle town until 1876.

anything about the nature of a steer, especially the longhorn, can't imagine being on the trail "pushing cattle to where they don't want to go" for over a thousand miles, but we can try to capture the experience by seeing a good trail-driving movie.[4] There are not very many films devoted to the topic. In the last couple of decades, Hollywood and TV producers have done their research, improved on costumes and props, and have presented plausible scenes for its audiences. A few of our favorites are as follows:

To get the feel of an Old West Montana town with its board sidewalks, dimly lit saloon and muddy streets, visited by a trail-driving outfit in approximately late 1880s or mid-1890s, view Kevin Costner's *Open Range*.[5] The loading of Texas steers into box cars to be shipped to Chicago in *Cowboy* is not realistically equaled in any other film.[6] The task of trailing a herd is presented with a different view in *Cowboys*, where it is shown that young boys in the 1870s were capable of driving a herd over a long distance. (Most trail drivers were twenty-five years old and younger.) The cook, Jebedioah Nightlinger, and his chuck wagon add authenticity to this 1972 film as well.[7]

The film *Lonesome Dove*, adapted from Larry McMurkry's novel, is perhaps the creme de la creme of trail-driving movies. The trail drivers followed the Western Trail via Dodge City, Kansas and Ogallala, Nebraska to Miles City, Montana. When Agustus McCrae dies in Miles City, his partner, Woodrow Call, promises to return his partner's body to Lonesome Dove, Texas. The idea of the journey back to Texas with a body in a wagon was borrowed by McMurkry from the Charles Goodnight and Oliver Loving true-life situation in 1867-68, when Goodnight promised Loving, his dying partner, at Fort Sumner, New Mexico, that he would take his body back to Weatherford, Texas. The movie has become a favorite with audiences world wide.[8]

The film that the authors particularly like is *Monte Walsh*. The storyline takes place from 1892 to 1900 and depicts the last years of trail life. It tells the story of the trail drivers' ultimate fate. Like so many Texas cowboys, the movie character Monte Walsh (Tom Selleck), had "no home, no property, except his horse and the line shack, no wife or kids, but had the freedom and pride and their rules that they lived by.

---

[4]The drama of the American cowboy to interested audiences started as early as 1883 when William "Buffalo Bill" Cody (1846-1917) started his outdoor extravaganze known as *Buffalo Bill's Wild West*. Very early films, in the late 1800s to early 1900s, depicted two popular topics: cops and robbers and the American cowboy. Quotes in the text are taken from the 2003 film, *Monte Walsh*.

[5]Kevin Costner co-produced, directed, and stared in this 2003 movie with Robert Duvall. It is about a former gunslinger and his partner who are forced into a stand-off with corrupt lawmen and a local cattle barron when members of their cattle-trailing outfit are killed and threatened.

[6]Chicago hotel clerk (Jack Lemmon) dreams of becoming a cowboy. He finally gets his wish when he joins Tom Reece's (Glen Ford) cattle-driving outfit. The entire film depicts the buying, trailing, loading, and selling of a cattle herd. There is no hint of a date, but it appears to be during the days of the Shawnee Trail. The 1958 movie is based on Frank Harris' semi-autobiographical novel, *My Reminiscences as a Cowboy*. Lemmon's character in the movie was Frank Harris.

[7]Rancher Wil Anderson (John Wayne) is in a dilemma when his cow hands run off to pan for newly-discovered gold in the Black Hills (probably in 1876). He goes to the school and recruits boys to help him drive his herd several hundred miles to Bell Fourche, Dakota Territory. Roscoe Lee Browne plays the part of the wise, experienced cook.

[8]The 1989 TV mini-series was based on Larry McMurtry's 1985 Pulitzer prize-wining novel by the same name. It is an epic story about two former Texas rangers who decide to trail a herd of cattle to Montana.

They don't work for anybody, but for a life." Even before the last herd was trailed to Montana, citizens knew they were facing not only the end of a century, but also the end of the Old West as it had been for so many years. The Wild West show owner in the story, tells Walsh:

> Times change; men change with them. Otherwise you get left behind. No more small operators; everything is amalgamated. Business is big and getting bigger. Machines do all the work…. It's the 20th Century!

As the populace excitedly looked forward to the new age, Monte Walsh resisted, "Things don't have to change. I ain't changin'." But on the Slash-Y Ranch, things did change. The Consolidated Cattle Company bought up all the ranchland, had fewer herds, needed fewer cowboys, and fenced their huge tracts of land. Monte Walsh finally loses his job. He hangs his head and says, "I don't know what else I can do." Monte Walsh is a dramatic film based on a true event in our history, and viewers feel saddened, in a way, that "things ain't never goin' to be the same."[9]

This sentiment relayed by the character Monte Walsh can be found in cowboy essays. C. H. Rust, in his essay to the Old Time Trail Drivers Association, wrote:

> The sad thought to this writer is the passing out of these scenes so well portrayed in the above [paragraphs]….
>
> I turn my face west. I see the red lines of the setting sun, but I do not hear the echo come back "Go west, young man, go west." I turn my face east and I hear the dull thud of the commercialized world marching west, with its steam roller procession, to roll over me and flatten me out.[10]

John C. Jacobs, who was a cattle inspector on the Clear Fork of the Brazos River near Fort Griffin, Texas, wrote that after "fifty years of life on the cow range:"

> It seems now as though it was all in some other world and under fairer skies. The cowboy as he was then is gone from the earth. The railroads and wire fences have got his job. His old sore-backed cow pony is aged and wobbly. The automobile has got his job and his old three-quarter rigged saddle, with its busted raw-hide cover, hangs out in the old rickety shed — a relic of former days — and soon the last of his tribe will sack his saddle, roll and light his last shuck as he bares his breast to the winding trail out over the Great Divide, where, we trust,

---

[9] Quotes taken from the 2003 film *Monte Walsh*. The movie originally produced in 1970 was based on a novel by Jack Schaefer, who also wrote *Shane*. It starred Lee Marvin as Monte and Jack Palance as his partner. The story was presented again in 2003 as a made-for-TV film on TNT with the same title, this time starring Tom Selleck as Monte and Keith Carradine as his partner, Chet Rollins. Both movies have the similar storyline: two aging cowboys and their fellow cowboys are finding it harder and harder to get work as civilization encroaches on the ranges they have ridden all their lives.

[10] C. H. Rust, "Memories of the Old Cow Trail," in Hunter, 209. His account was written around 1920-1924.

vast herds of long-horned cattle roam over fertile plains and slake their thirst from crystal streams.[11]

Frank Collinson, the Englishman who came to Texas in 1872 at the age of seventeen and who had ridden up the trail with Captain John T. Lytle in 1874, regretted in his old age to have to live in the city. After camping in the mountains for a few days with a companion, he wrote to a friend:

> It was like getting to Heaven, to hear the coyotes howl again and to smell the good cedar. Lord, I would not give two days like that for two years in town. The stars never shone brighter, and as I lay on my bedroll I thought I could hear again the old trail crew singing around a herd.[12]

The above are only glimpses into the trail driver's world, for most of the cowboys kept their personal feelings to themselves. Jim Russell, who compiled Bob Fudge's experiences, said that the old cowboy for years resisted from being interviewed because he felt that there was another man out there "whose life would make a better book."[13]

George W. Saunders, in his essays and articles, was usually concerned about the recognition of his fellow cowboys and the trails that they followed, rather than his own sentiments. In his presentation to the Old Time Trail Drivers' Association Reunion in 1917 he said, in part:

> Had these old-time trail drivers not looked for and found this market our vast herds would have died on the ranges and the vast unstocked ranges would have lain dormant and unproductive…. No one knows what would have happened had the Northern trail never existed, but it is plain that all commercial achievements, civilization, good government, Christianity, morality, our school system,… the building of railroads, factories,… and everything else pertaining to prosperity can be traced directly to the achievements of the old-time trail drivers. The many good things accomplished by the untiring efforts of these old heroes can never be realized or told, and it would be the father of all mistakes to let their daring and valuable efforts be forgotten and pass to unwritten history.[14]

The "Northern Trail" referred to all of the cattle trailing systems, and the heroes that Saunders referred to included Texas stockmen who didn't physically ride up the trail.

---

[11]John C. Jacobs, "Reminiscences of an Old Trail Driver," in Hunter, 665.

[12]Mary Whatley Clarke, ed. *Life in the Saddle*, by Frank Collinson, 241.

[13]Jim Russell, *Bob Fudge*, 133.

[14]George W. Saunders, "Origin and Close of the Old-Time Northern Trail," address to the assembly of the Reunion of the Old Time Trail Drivers' Association in 1917, in Hunter, 25.

In Saunders' mind, the cattle-trailing industry, which encompassed a wide variety of people involved in the beef business, developed the West.

Today this period of our history remains in our cultural memory. It represents another time which, as Saunders told us, would and did help create what we are today. One icon that represents this era, of course, is the cowboy. The recognition of this American hero in his hat, scarf, gun, and boots is one thing that has *not* changed.

At the end of the film, *Monte Walsh*, a little boy runs up to Monte in 1900, at the end of the aging cowboy's career, and asks: "Are you a real cowboy?"

And, Monte, who represents all the cowboys mentioned in this book, answers: "Yes, I am."

(Self Portrait)

ANNOTATED BIBLIOGRAPHY

Primary Sources:
First-hand accounts from cowboys, cattlemen, homesteaders, and newsmen:

BOOKS:

Abbott, E. C. ("Teddy Blue") and Helena Huntington Smith. *We Pointed Them North, Recollections of a Cowpuncher*. Norman, OK: University of Oklahoma Press, 1955.
>Abbott's trail account was first published by Farrar & Rinehart of New York in 1939.
>Helena H. Smith interviewed Abbott (1860-1939) numerous times in 1938 when he was seventy-eight years old. He was as "tough as whipcord, diamond-clear as to memory, and boiling with energy," she wrote.

Adams, Andy. *The Log of a Cowboy, A Narrative of the Old Trail Days*. Lincoln, NE: University of Nebraska Press, 1967. Third printing by Bison Books.
>The book was originally published by Houghton Miffin and Co. in 1903.
>Even though Adams' (1859-1935) work is often labeled "fiction" because he used fictitious names, his books are based on his own involvement as a cowhand trailing cattle from Texas north. This book refers to his experiences on a drive from Brownsville to Montana in 1882.

Adams, Andy. *The Outlet*. New York, NY: Houghton, Mifflin and Co., 1905.
>This is the third of Adams' books on Texas cowboys and trail driving. It followed his most well-known book, *The Log of a Cowboy* (1903) and *A Texas Matchmaker* (1904).
>This book narrates a trail drive in 1884 from Texas to Fort Buford in North Dakota Territory.

Anshutz, Carrie & M. W. (Doc). *Cimarron Chronicles, Saga of the Open Range*. Meade, KS: Ohnick Enterprises, 2003.
>This is a dual-autobiography written by a husband and wife, each with their own individual stories of homesteading and living in the Cimarron River Valley in southwest Kansas. The couple wrote their recollections in the 1930s, but the faded typewritten pages were discovered in an attic in the late 20th century.

Baughman, Theodore. *The Oklahoma Scout*. Chicago, IL: Homewood Publishing Co., 1886.
>Following the Civil War, Baughman went to Kansas and Indian Territory. He worked as a cattle drover on the Texas Trail and later became a government scout, serving in Arizona, Kansas, Texas, and New Mexico.

Black, A. P. (Ott). *The End of the Long Horn Trail*. Selfridge, ND: The Selfridge Journal, published date unknown.
>Ott Black was born in 1867 and wrote his memoirs around 1936. In this small book he describes ranches, early towns, cowboys, and cattle drives.

Bratt, John. *Trails of Yesterday*. Lincoln, NE: University of Nebraska Press, 1980.
>Originally published by the University Publishing Co. in Chicago in 1921.
>In 1879, John Bratt (1841-1916) established a ranch in Lincoln County, Nebraska. His ranch was located midway between Fort McPherson and North Platte City on the Birdwood. The John Bratt & Company cattle were known as the "Circle Herd."

Bronson, Edgar Beecher. *Reminiscences of a Ranchman*. Lincoln, NE: University of Nebraska Press, 1962. Bronson's book was first published in 1908.
>Bronson (1854-1917) was a professional writer, but came out west from New York and established a ranch north of the Platte River about five miles from Fort Robinson, Nebraska. Bronson's ranch appeared simultaneously along with the Newman and Hunter ranch and the Evans ranch farther east on the Niobrara River in Nebraska. Bronson was also active as a newspaperman.

Burt, Maxwell Struthers. *Powder River, Let 'er Buck*. New York, NY: Rinehart & Co., Inc., 1938.
>Burt (1882-1954) settled in Jackson Hole, Wyoming with his wife in 1908. He homesteaded the Bar BC Ranch near Moose, Wyoming in 1912. He was a writer of some eighteen books.
>This book is about the Powder River which, years earlier, so many cowboys had to cross with their longhorns.

Collinson, Frank. (edited and arranged by Mary Whatley Clarke) *Life in the Saddle*. Norman, OK: University of Oklahoma Press, 1963.
>Collinson (1856-1943) at the age of nineteen was in Captain John T. Lytle's outfit which blazed the Western Cattle Trail.
>His recollections and letters were written around 1934, but they lay unnoticed until Mary Whatley Clarke, with the help of Collinson's artist friend Harold Dow Bugbee, finally brought Collinson's experiences to print.

Cook, James H. Cook. *Fifty Years on the Old Frontier*. Norman, OK: University of Oklahoma Press, 1980. Originally published by the Yale University Press in New Haven, Conn, 1923.
>Cook (1857-1942) realized that his life in the post-Civil War American West was significant and put his memories to paper.

Cox, James. *Historical and Biographical Record of the Cattle Industry and the Cattlemen of Texas and Adjacent Territory*. Saint Louis, Ill: Woodward & Tiernan Printing Co., 1895.
>This original work is now in paperback.

Dale, Edward Everett. *The Range Cattle Industry*. Norman, OK: University of Oklahoma Press, 1930.
>Dale (1879-1972) was an American historian who was born in Texas. He worked as a cow rancher in old Greer County, Texas for several years. He became a longtime faculty member in the history department at the University of Oklahoma (1924-1952).

Fletcher, Baylis John. (edited by Wayne Gard) *Up the Trail in '79*. Norman, OK: University of Oklahoma Press, 1966.
>Fletcher wrote about his 1879 experiences on the Western Trail when he was an elderly man.

Fletcher, Ernest More. (Forbes Parkhill, ed.) *The Wayward Horseman*. Denver, CO: Sage Books, 1958.
>Fletcher narrated his story as a cowboy in Texas, Arizona, Nebraska, and Colorado.

Haley, J. Evetts. *Charles Goodnight, Cowman and Plainsman*. Norman, OK: University of Oklahma Press, reprinting of 1949 copyright.
>J. Evetts Haley published this book in 1936. At the time he was acknowledged for his excellent book on the XIT, which had been published seven years earlier. Haley, a historian and folklorist, spent a decade interviewing and researching the old cowboy and ranchman, Charles Goodnight.

Haley, J. Evetts. *The XIT Ranch of Texas, and the Early Days of the Llano Estacado*. Norman, OK: University Of Oklahoma Press, 1967.
>This work by Haley was first published by the Capitol Reservation Lands in Chicago, IL in 1929.

Hamilton, William Henry. *Dakota, An Autobiography of a Cowman*. Pierre, SD: South Dakota State Historical Society Press, 1941.
>Hamilton (1863-1945) originally wrote a series of letters to his son about his experiences as a young cowman in Dakota. His

THE WESTERN CATTLE TRAIL | 1874-1897

autobiography was then printed in the South Dakota Historical Collections, Vol. 19 in 1938, pages 475-637.

Hill, J. L. *The End of the Cattle Trail*, Long Beach, CA: approx. 1922.

Hill was in an outfit with trail boss Tim Driscoll in 1883 for cattlemen Schreiner and Lytle. (referred to in Part II, Chapter I)

Hough, Emerson. *North of 36*. New York, N.Y: Grosset & Dunlap, 1923.

Even though Emerson's book is a novel, it is included here because it is written by a man who witnessed the cattle drives and the Old West. Hough moved to New Mexico in the early 1880s and started writing about western life. This novel is about one of the first cattle drives after the Civil War and about Texas cowboys trailing into the unknown lands north of 36. The 36th parallel runs horizontally across Indian Territory approximately where Oklahoma City is today. It is a joy to read.

Kelly, Leo, ed. *Up the Trail in '76*, The Journal of Lewis Warren Neatherlin.

Booklet reprinted from the Oklahoma Historical Society's Chronicles of Oklahoma, Vol. LXVI, No. 1 (Spring 1988), 22-51. Neatherlin (1833-1909) went to Frio County, Texas in 1850 with his family. Near the family ranch was the large ranching operation of his cousin, John H. Slaughter. When Slaughter decided to "explore the new Western Trail" in 1876, he asked Neatherlin to supervise three herds (approximately 9,000 longhorns) to be delivered to Ogallala, Nebraska. Neatherlin's on-the-trail journal was discovered by a granddaughter in the 1980s in a dusty trunk in New Mexico.

Kennon, Bob. *From the Pecos to the Powder, A Cowboy's Autobiography* (as told to Ramon F. Adams). Norman, OK: University of Oklahoma Press, 1965.

Kennon was born in Cedar Hill, Texas in September of 1876. In 1896, he went up the trail with a herd from the Don Luis Terrazas Ranch in Old Mexico to the "Milestown" area in Montana. Kennon was in his eighties when he wrote and dictated his story to Ramon F. Adams.

Laws of Kansas - 1885 (or) State of Kansas, Session Laws of 1885, passed at the Twenty-First Regular, the Same Being the Fourth Biennial Session of the Legislature of the State of Kansas.

Laws Passed at the Special Session of 1884. Topeka, Kansas: Kansas Publishing House, May 1, 1885. Chapter CXCI, "Protection of Cattle Against Disease, An Act for the protection of cattle against Texas, splenic or Spanish fever and repealing chapter three of the Special Laws of eighteen hundred and eighty-four," pages 308-311. Approved March 7, 1885 and signed by E. B. Allen, Secretary of State.

Lemmon, Edward and Nellie Snyder Yost, (ed.) *Boss Cowman, The Recollections of Ed Lemmon, 1857-1946*. Lincoln, NE: University of Nebraska Press, 1969.

Lemmon wrote his remembrances at the age of 83 in 1940. He had been an all-around cowman in South Dakota who had the ability to manage a large group of cow men and had great knowledge of cattle. This book is a great source about ranches, towns, railroads, and people of early South Dakota.

Matthews, Sallie Reynolds. *Interwoven, A Pioneer Chronicle*. Austin, TX: University of Texas Press, 1958.

Sallie Reynolds' family settled in the Fort Griffin area from East Texas in 1866 when she was five years old. She was a daughter of a cattleman and married cattleman, John Alexander Matthews. She intented to write her family history for her children and grandchildren, but the journal has become a valuable Texas history chronicle, originally published in 1936.

McClintock, John S. (Edward L. Senn, ed.) *Pioneer Days in the Black Hills, by One of the Early Day Pioneers*. Norman, OK: University of Oklahoma Press, 2000. (originally printed by McClintock in 1939)

McClintock arrived at Deadwood, Dakota Territory, with a group of friends in 1876 and made the town his home until his death in 1942.

McCoy, Joseph G. *Historic Sketches of the Cattle Trade of the West and Southwest*. Kansas City, MO: Ramsey, Millett & Hudson, 1874.

This is a first-hand narrative from the "pioneer western cattle shipper" who opened up Abilene, Kansas in 1867 to Texas drovers. This book is one of the foundation sources in the research and study of the Texas cattle-trailing industry.

McKay, John. *Prose and Poetry of the Live Stock Industry of the United States, with Outlines of the Origin and Ancient History of Our Life Stock Animals*. National Live Stock Association, Denver, CO: 1905.

This massive work was issued in three volumes. McKay describes the Texas development of the range cattle industry, its revival after the Civil War, cow towns of the era, cattle trails, cowboys, and numerous other related topics.

North, Luther. (Donald F. Danker, ed.and archivist for Nebraska State Historical Society) *Man of the Plains, Recollections of Luther North, 1856-1882*. Lincoln, NE: University of Nebraska Press, 1961.

In about 1925, North (1846-1935) wrote about his experiences with the Indians and US Army on the plains of Nebraska. The manuscript was turned over to the Nebraska State Historical Society after his death.

Osgood, Ernest Staples. *The Day of the Cattleman*. Minneapolis, MI: The University of Minnesota Press, 1929.

University of Minnesota Assistant Professor Osgood (b. 1888) traced the rise and fall of the range cattle industry in Montana and Wyoming from 1845 to the turn of the century.

Rainey, George. *No Man's Land, The Historic Story of A Landed Orphan*. Enid, OK: by George Rainey, 1937.

This is a good historical account of the Cherokee Strip (Oklahoma Panhandle).

Records, Laban Samuel. (edited by Ellen J. M. Wheeler) *Cherokee Outlet Cowboy, Recollections of Laban S. Records*. Norman, OK: University of Oklahoma Press, 1995.

Records (1856-1941), the son of a Kansas Methodist minister, was a range rider from 1873 to 1887 in the Cherokee Outlet. He knew and mingled with Texas trail cowboys. He penciled his recollections on ruled notebook paper in 1937 and give it to his son, Dr. Ralph Records. The manuscript was eventually given to the Oklahoma State Library by his granddaughter Ellen J. M Wheeler, and published.

Russell, Jim. *Bob Fudge, Texas Trail Driver, Montana-Wyoming Cowboy, 1862-1933*. Lewistown, MT: News-Argus Printing, 1981.

Recollections of Bob Fudge as written by Jim Russell, who interviewed Fudge numerous times. This is one of our favorite books.

Shaw, James C. and Herbert O. Brayer (ed.). *North From Texas, Incidents in the Early Life of a Range Cowman in Texas, Dakota & Wyoming, 1852-1883*. College Station, TX: Texas A&M University Press, 1996. Originally privately published in 1931 as *Pioneering in Texas and Wyoming: Incidents in the Life of James C. Shaw*.

James Clay Shaw (1852-1943) tells of his life as a trail cowboy and range cowman in Wyoming.

Snyder, A. B. and Nellie Irene Yost. *Pinnacle Jake*. Caldwell, ID: The Caxton Printers, Ltd., 1951.

Born in 1872 in Nebraska, Snyder (Pinnacle Jake) told his story to his daughter Nellie Yost about his cowboys days with the Ogallala Land and Cattle Company, his trail experiences, and his later involvement with the 101 Ranch.

Stroud, Joseph G. *Memories of the Old Western Trails in Texas Longhorn Days*, 1932.

Stroud wrote his memories after friends urged him to do so. He said it was "impossible to make this narrative non-personal, since the West as I knew it was basically and intimately enmeshed in my own life."

Sweetman, Luke Decatur. *Back Trailing on Open Range*. Caldwell, ID: The Caxton Printers, Ltd, 1951.
Dedicated to his children, Sweetman wrote this book "as a lasting heritage of the lore and traditions of the old West as I knew it as a youth." It is written in first person, with dialogue, about his experiences in 1880s Montana Territory.

Taylor, T.U. *The Chisholm Trail and Other Routes*. San Antonio, Texas: The Naylor Co., 1936.
Printed for the *Frontier Times*, Bandera, Texas.
Thomas Ulvan Taylor (1858-1941) or better known as "T.U" by his colleagues and students, was born "within sight of the old cattle trail" in Parker County, Texas. He actually served for fifty years (1888-1936) as professor of engineering at the College of Engineering at University of Texas, becoming its "charismatic first dean" in 1906. He was instrumental in the design and building of Lake Worth and its dam and co-authored a book on trigonometry. His roots, however, were in rural poor Texas and even though "I did not go up the trail, I traveled along the trail and rode out to the sleeping herds." This book is a product of his love for that time and his knowledge of the "old trailers" he knew.

Watkins, Ethel Etrick and Annie Albright Scott. *Annie, Child of the Prairie, The Story of Bloom… An Early-Day Farming Community South of Famous Old Dodge City On the Kansas Frontier…* Colby, KS: Prairie Printers, Inc., 1968.
Scott, the daughter of Bloom's founder, tells her stories to Ethel E. Watkins.

Watkins, Ethel Etrick and Annie Albright Scott. *Annie's Story of Cowboys on the Prairie*. Dodge City, KS: Karla's Publications, 1983.
Scott was born in 1889 to Bloom founder Samuel Albright and his wife Josephine Leiper. Her parent's homestead was near the Rock Island Railroad line and its station stop at Bloom in southern Ford County, Kansas.

Webb, Walter Prescott. *History of the Great Central Plains*. New York, NY: Grosset & Dunlap, 1931.

From J. Marvin Hunter's *The Trail Driver's of Texas*. Austin, TX: University of Texas Press, fifth edition, 2006. Originally printed in 1924, under the direction of George W. Saunders, president of The Old Time Trail Drivers' Association. (actual accounts from and about cowboys and cattlemen)

The following essays were used as primary sources in this work:

Anderson, L. B. (Seguin, Texas). "A Few Thrilling Incidents in my Experience on the Trail," 203-207.
Blocker, Ab (San Antonio, Texas). "The Man Who Had Hell in His Neck," 504-513.
Brock, George W. (Lockhart, Texas). "When Lightning Set the Grass on Fire," 219-225.
Burkett, T. J. Jr. (Waelder, Texas). "On the Fort Worth and Dodge City Trail," 926-930.
"Captain Charles Schreiner," 359-362.
"Captain John T. Lytle," 322-323.
Connolly, Jeff (Lockhart, Texas). "Hit the Trail in High Places," 187-193.
Doan, C. F. "Reminiscences of the Old Trails," 772-779.
Ellison, J. F. (Little Jim), Jr. (Fort Cobb, Oklahoma). "Seven Trips Up the Trail," 92-93.
Ellison, J. F. (Little Jim), Jr. (Fort Cobb, Oklahoma). "Sketch of [father] Col. J. F. Ellison," 476-478.
Ellison, J. F. (Little Jim), Jr. (Fort Cobb, Oklahoma). "Traveling the Trail with Good Men was a Pleasure," 538-540.
Eustace, A. N. (Prairie Lea, Texas). "Eight Trips up the Trail," 253-256.
French, C. C. (Fort Worth, Texas). "When the Temperature was 72 Degrees Below Zero," 741-743.
"George W. West." 834-836.
Goodnight, Charles (Goodnight, Texas). "The Killing of Oliver Loving," 903-908.
Goodnight, Charles (Goodnight, Texas). "More About the Chisholm Trail," 950-952.
Hardeman, W. B. (Devine, Texas). "Punching Cattle on the Trail to Kansas," 146-151.
Houston, Samuel Dunn. (San Antonio, Texas). "A Trying Trip Along Through the Wilderness," 78-88.
Jackman, W. T. (Bill) (San Marcos, Texas). "Where They Put a Trail Boss in Jail," 851-862.
Jacobs, John C. (San Antonio, Texas). "Reminiscences of an Old Trail Driver," 662-665.
Jennings, R. J. (San Antonio, Texas). "My Third and Last Trip up the Trail in 1886," 513-515.
Lauderdale, Jasper (Bob). "Reminiscences of the Trail," 404-411.
Lawhon, Luther A. (San Antonio, Texas). "The Men Who Made the Trail," 193- 202.
Nagiller, W. M. (Williams, Arizona). "A Big Mixup," 669-670.
Nance, Jerry M. (Kyle, Texas). "Echoes of the Cattle Trail," 105-111.
Neill, Sam (La Pryer, Texas). "A Long Time Between Drinks," 256-257.
"Phil L. Wright," 423-425.
Polk, F. M. (Luling, Texas) "My Experience on the Cow Trail," 140-146.
Potter, Jack (Kenton, Oklahoma) "Coming up the Trail in 1882," 58-70.
"R. G. Head," 734-736.
Rust, C. H. (San Angelo, Texas) "Location of the Old Chisholm Trail," 37-41.
Rust, C. H. (San Angelo, Texas) "Memories of the Old Cow Trail," 207-212.
Saunders, George W., "Origin and Close of the Old-Time Northern Trail," address to the assembly of the reunion of the Old Time Trail Drivers' Association in 1917, pages 20-26.
Saunders, George W. (San Antonio, Texas) "A Log of the Trails," 959-971.
Saunders, George W. "John and Thomas Dewees," 940-942.
Scott, G. W. "With Herds to Colorado and New Mexico," 115-117.
Shipman, W. K. (San Antonio, Texas) "A Cowboy Undertaker," 881-883.
Slaughter, P. E. 786-788.
Steele, Henry D. (San Antonio, Texas) "Played Pranks on the Tenderfoot," 137-139.
"Trail Life," essay about James Gibson, 271-273.
Wells, John (Bartlett, Texas) "Met Quanah Parker on the Trail," 162-168.
"William C. Irvin," 619-621.
"William James Slaughter," 607-611.
Withers, Richard (Dick), (Boyes, Montana) "The Experience of an Old Trail Driver," 305-316.
Witter, Webster (Beeville, Texas) "Would Like to Go Again," 884-885.

Wright, Phil L., 423-425.

RECOLLECTIONS PRINTED IN OTHER PRIMARY SOURCES:

Atcheson, Norman. Letter written in 1937 to Mr. Eugene Coffield and Mrs. J. Williams about Oelrichs, Dakota Territory during the cowboy days. Atcheson had a mercantile/grocery store in Oelrichs.

Reprinted in Oelrichs *Historical Society's In the Shadow of the Butte, A History of Oelrichs and Surrounding Area*, page 138. (used in Part II, Chapter VII)

Boss Neff autobiography (written in 1939) printed in *The Old Times News*, Vol. I, No. 5, Dec., 1974.

Carnhan, John W., "Driving Cattle Northward," printed in Franklin M. Jones, *History of New Raymer*, Fort Morgan, CO: Fort Morgan Heritage Foundation, 1943.

As a lad, Carnhan had trailed cattle from the Houston, Texas area to Lincoln County, Colorado using part of the Texas-Montana Feeder Trail. (referred to in Part III, Chapter III)

Cleveland, Harper. Account printed in *A Sandhill Century, Book I, the Land: A History of Cherry County, Nebraska*. Published by the Cherry County Centennial Committee in 1986.

Cleveland was a Texas cowboy who was with the Smith and Savage outfit in 1878. They delivered a herd to the N Bar N (Newman) Ranch in Nebraska using the Niobrara River Route via Ogallala and the Sidney-Black Hills Road. Cleveland wrote his account in 1932. (referred to in Part II, Chapter VII)

Dahlman, James C. "Recollections of Cowboy Life in Western Nebraska," *Nebraska History*, Vol. X October-December, 1927.

Dahlman worked at the N Bar N (Newman) Ranch until 1883. The ranch was located on the Niobrara River Splinter Route of the Western Cattle Trail. (referred to in Part II, Chapter VII)

Floyd, H. H. and Charles F. Decker. From interviews by Maude L. Beach for the Montana's Writer's Project of the WPA, dated November 5, 1940, published in *Faded Hoof Prints — Bygone Dreams*, Powder River Historical Society, 1989, page 123.

Floyd and Decker were trail drivers for the Hashknife (Continental Land & Cattle Company). (referred to in Part II, Chapter VII)

Gossard, Wayne H., Jr. (ed). *Life on the Trail, the 1894 Diary of Perry Eugene Davis*. Printed by the Colorado Historical Society in *Colorado Heritage Magazine*, 1981 and online; http://coloradohistory.org/westerntrails.

At the age of twenty five, Davis was a trail cook with a horse drive for the Hashknife Ranch from Camp Crook, South Dakota to the Panhandle of Texas. His 1894 diary covered two months of the drive through eastern Montana, eastern Wyoming, and Colorado on the Texas-Montana Feeder Route, in eastern Colorado on the old National Trail, and in No Man's Land and the Panhandle of Texas on the Western Trail.

Grant, Ben O. "Life in the Town of Fort Griffin," as printed in *Tracks Along the Clear Fork*, 2012.

Griffiths, Raymond. "Grazing in South Dakota," manuscript written in the 1930s by Griffiths, published in Bert L. Hall's *Round Up Years, Old Muddy to Black Hills*.

About East Detour Route described in Part II, Chapter VII.

Hester, Charles, recollection of 1877 trail drive, in E. S. Sutton, *Sutton's Southwest Nebraska and Republican River Valley Tributaries*. Benkelman, NE: by E. S. Sutton, 1983.

Houston, Samuel Dunn. "A Drive from Texas to North Dakota," in *Frontier Times Monthly*, Vol. 3, No. 7. Bandera, TX: J. Marvin Hunter, April, 1926.

Keeling, Henry C. "My Experience with the Cheyenne Indians," *Chronicles of Oklahoma*, Vol. 3, No. 1, (March, 1925). Republished by permission of the Kansas State Historical Society of the address by Henry C. Keeling, of Caldwell, Kansas, before the thirty fourth annual meeting of the Kansas State Historical Society, Dec. 7, 1909. Also online: http://digital.library.okstate.edu/Chronicles.

May, J. E. - 1884 log of a trail drive, the original is in the Archives of the University of Texas, Austin. It is printed in the Appendix: "Logs of Early Trails," in J. Evetts Haley's *The XIT Ranch of Texas*, pages 230-231, and in *The Herold*, of Lusk, Wyoming, on July 18, 1940. It is also printed in full in *The Panhandle-Plains Historical Review*, Canyon, Texas: 1932.

May, of Vega, Texas, drove for the LS Ranch in 1884, and later for the N–N.

Moore, Ealy.- 1892 trail journal, printed in the Appendix: "Logs of Early Trails," in J. Evetts Haley's *The XIT Ranch of Texas*, pages 230-240. It was also printed in *The Herold of Lusk*, Wyoming.

(Hans Gautschi, "Texas-Montana Trail," *The Herold*, July 18, 1940)

Moore was a drover for the XIT Ranch.

"P. E. Davis, trail cook, cattle drive from Camp Cook, SD through Montana, Wyoming, Nebraska and Colorado," as printed in *Colorado Heritage Magazine*, 1981. (the Davis diary)

Starkey, J. J. "Pioneer History," *Kerrville Times*, November 19, 1931.

Recollection of Ernest Schwethelm who was with one of the Schreiner herds in 1885.

Tremain, Dema, "Early Days of LaGrange Community," written in 1936 and included in *Trails, Rails and Travails*, (Elizabeth Wilkinson Johnson, ed.) City of LaGrange, WY: 1988. (referred to in Part III, Chapter III)

PRIMARY DOCUMENTS:

Ezra Soar Diary. Written by Soar on an 1880 trail drive through Colorado. Transcript owned by the City of Greeley Museum, Greeley, Colorado.

Holston, J. W. "Life of J. W. Holston," owned by the Texas Library & Historical Committee, located at the State Library in Austin, Texas.

Holston worked for Moore & Krill Cattle Company which had a "ranch out here at the Yellowhouse canyon [sic] and also had a Ranch up on the line of Wyoming & So. Decota [sic]." He was on the trail in 1886. (used in Part III, Chapter III)

Jonathan H. Baker. Diary (1858-1918). Located at the University of Texas Library, Austin, Texas.

The typed manuscript of over 600 pages was originally secured from Baker's daughter by J. Evetts Haley in 1932. Baker wrote about three trail drives in the years of 1869, 1870, and 1871.

Journal of J. E. Moore. copy acquired from The Dolph Briscoe Center for American History Collections, the University of Texas at Austin. (used in Part III, Chapter III)

"Minutes, [1877-1893] of the Cattle Raisers' Association of Northwest Texas, March 10, 1885."

Archives at University of Texas at Austin.

Nimmo, Joseph. *Letter from the Secretary of the Treasury Transmitting a report from the Chief of the Bureau of Statistics…* a report on range and ranch cattle traffic of the western, southwestern, and northwestern states, in reply to a resolution by the House of Representatives, March 2, 1885.

Ex. Doc. No. 267, 48th Congress, 2nd Session.

(Emporia State University, William Allan White Library, "Western American 1550-1900, Frontier History of the Trans-Mississippi West," Reel 41, No. 3894-3905–report #3903)

Nimmo was the Chief of the Bureau of Statistics. His extensive report, with accompanying maps and charts, was presented to the House of Representatives in March of 1885.

Sub-sections of the report used, in particular: (Part III, Chapter I)

"Quantity of Land Necessary for the Proposed Trail,"

"Remarks in Regard to the Quarantine Laws of Kansas, Colorado, Nebraska, Wyoming, and New Mexico"

"The Breeding of Cattle on the Northern Ranges"

"The Quarantine Law of the State of Colorado"

"The Texas Fever"

Proceedings of the Third Annual Convention of Cattle Growers Held at Chicago, Ill, November 17 and 18, 1885. Chicago, ILL: John Morris Company, 1886.

PRIMARY PERIODICALS:

Harger, Charles Moreau. "Cattle-Trails of the Prairies," *Scibner's Magazine*, Vol. XI, No. 6, January - June, 1892, pages 732-742.

Harger, (1863-?) went to Kansas in 1879 and became a teacher and reporter and editor of the *Abilene Daily Reflector* for over twenty-five years. He contributed many articles on western topics to various magazines. John Rossel in February of 1936 said, "Probably no greater or more vivid description has ever been given of the Chisholm Trail than that of C. M Hargar, writing in 1892." *(Harger's description also works for the Western Trail. See the intro quote for Chapter V in Part I)*

PRIMARY NEWSPAPERS: (1867 - 1931)

"Abilene — The Cattle Market," *San Antonio Express*, San Antonio, Texas, April 29, 1868, page 2.

American Agriculturist, New York, Dec. 1878, as reprinted in the *Keith County News*, Ogallala, Neb., Sept. 18, 1996, page 3.

"An Address Delivered by T. G. Shillinglaw, On the Occasion of the Laying of the Corner-Stone of the Public School House in Taloga, Sept. 25th, '87." *Taloga Star*, Taloga, Kansas, Oct. 7, 1887.

"Brady, Texas," *Galveston News*, Sept. 18, 1877 and Sept. 29, 1877.

Coolidge Citizen, Coolidge, Kansas, July 31, 1887. ("The day of the range cattle industry is over.")

Ford County Globe, Dodge City, Kansas, as printed in *The County Gazettes*, California, Kansas (Lane County), April 1, 1881. Editorial about the idea of a government sanctioned route for the Texas herds, "thereby protecting all parties concerned." (see Part III, Chapter I)

Guymon Herald, November 22, 1906. about the town of Hardesty by editor Dick Quinn.

"Herb Craig," by editor Richard (Dick) Quinn. *The Guymon Harold*, Vol. 21, No. 26, page 1, col. 6, Guymon, Oklahoma, Sept. 7, 1911. Craig was one of "Col. Jack's troops in what was known as the Jack Hardesty war."

Martin, George W. "Texas Cattle," *Junction City Union*, Junction City, Kansas, Jan. 1867, reprinted in the *Junction City Union* on Sept. 8, 1991.

Nichols, Claude H. "The Triumph of Baxter Springs," *Cherokee Sentinel*, Baxter Springs, Kansas, March 26, 1870. (Reprinted in *The Citizen under* "Baxter Springs, First Cow Town in Kansas," 1964. Also includes a June 4, 1870 follow-up article.) Compliments of the Historical Museum and Heritage Center, Baxter Springs, Kansas.

Niobrara *Pioneer*, Niobrara, Nebraska, October 6, 1874.

Omaha *Herold*, Omaha, Nebraska, August 24, 1870.

Platte County Journal, Columbus, Nebraska, August 3, 1870 and August 17, 1870.

Saunders, George W. "Trail Historian Corrects Errors," *San Antonio Express*, October 17, 1931. Trail driver and founder of the Old Time Trail Drivers Association relates the facts and fiction of the cattle-trailing industry.

"The Cattle Blockade," *New York Times*, July 13, 1885, p. 4. [accessed from the New York Times Archives, online: www.archive.nytimes.com, Dec. 19, 2008]

The Express, Buffalo Park, Kansas, June 10, 1880.

"The Old Cattle Trails Through Texas County," by editor Richard Briggs Quinn. *The Guymon Tribune*, Vol. 1, No. 2, Guymon, Oklahoma, June 23, 1921, p. 3.

Quinn arrived in No Man's Land at the age of nineteen in 1887. He eventually became the editor of the *Hardesty Herald*, the *Guymon Herald*, and the *Guymon Tribune*. He was an eyewitness to the cattle drives and its cowboys.

"The Trail Question in Tascosa," by Charles F. Randolph. *The Tascosa Pioneer*, Sept. 1, 1886. (refer to Part III, Chapter III)

"Trail Historian Corrects Error," clipping from a Fort Worth newspaper, between October 21 and December 31, 1931. The clipping relates an interview of George W. Saunders. Authors' collection.

PRIMARY MAPS:

1883 Indian Territory map. Online: http://alabamamaps.ua.edu/historicalmaps/us_states/oklahoma/index.htmal (2nd map from the top of the list [accessed Aug. 16, 2011] This map shows Signale Mountains in the Chickasaw Nation next to Wild Horse Creek near Fort Arbuckle.

1885 U.S. Department of Interior Geological Survey map (1894 edition) showing the route of the Western Cattle Trail through Kerr and Gillespie counties, Texas.

Anshutz, M. W. (Doc) and Frank A. Webb. Heavily annotated map of a portion of the Texas Panhandle, No Man's Land, and southwest Kansas, created from the memory of Doc Anshutz and annotated by Frank A. Webb. The map was created in 1935. (Part III, Chapter V)

Located at No Man's Land Museum, Goodwell, Oklahoma.

"Cattle Trails Across Indian Reservation," an "1881 official map app'd by Sec. of Interior Commissions of Indian Affairs H. Price sent to Mr. P. B. Hunt at Kiowa Agency, Andarko." creator unknown.

Located in the Western History Collection at the University of Oklahoma Libraries in Norman, Oklahoma.

Colton, G. Woolworth. *Colton's Atlas of 1882*. NY: CB Colton, 1882.

Cram, George F. "Montana" map of 1883. Authors' collection.

Dull Knife and Little Wolf's Raid in 1878 in Decatur County, Kansas.

Hand-drawn map from an unknown creator that shows not only the distruction and attacks made by the Indians in 1878, but also shows the Ogallala Cattle Trail. Located at the Decatur County Museum in Oberlin, Kansas.

Engineer Bureau, War Department. "Indian Territory with part of the adjoining State of Kansas," 1866.

Located at the Oklahoma State University Library, Stillwater, Oklahoma.

Government Printing Office, C. Roeser 1879 map, showing "Elm Sp. (south of the Washita River) on the Ft. Sill & Ft. Arbuckle Stage Road." Government Documents Dept. in the McCasland Maps Collection, 5th floor in Map Case B at Oklahoma State University, Stillwater, Oklahoma.

"Great Sioux Indian Reservation," map online: www.bing.com. early map that shows the Niobrara River as the northern border of Nebraska.

Haley, J. Evetts. "Early Trails," from the J. Evetts Collection, Haley Memorial Library and History Center, Midland, Texas. (Part III, Chapter III)

"Map of the State of Nebraska," by Geo. L. Brown, State Secretary of Immigration, Omaha, Neb., 1875.

shows the Niobrara River as the northern border of Nebraska (refer to Part II, Chapter VI)

"Military Map of the Indian Territory," compiled under direction of 1st Lieut. E. H. Ruffner, Engineers Chief, Engineer Dept. of the Missouri, January, 1875. Located in the Western History Collections, University of Oklahoma Libraries, Norman, OK, Box 2, Folder#4, 8614.

Potter, Jack. "Map Showing Cattle Trails as used from 1866 to 1895 for driving cattle on to shipping points or when trailing to northern markets," map folded in the back of his book, *Cattle Trails of the Old West*, compiled and edited by Laura R. Krehbiel.

Scott, Glenn R. and Carol Rein Schwayder. *Historic Trail Map of the Greeley 1 x 2 degree Quadrangle*, 1894. USGS–2336.

Map used by permission from Research Curator, Peggy A. Ford, City of Greeley Museum, Greeley, Colorado. Shows the town of Brush, Colorado as originally called "Beaver Valley."

Sollers, W. map: "Southwestern Frontier in the 1880's." in *The Cowman's Southwest, being the reminiscences of Oliver Nelson*, Angie Debo, ed.

Sutcliffe, Martin. Gove County Map, Kansas State Historical Archives, Manuscript Collection.

Kansas State Historical Society, Topeka, Kansas.

The Kansas Everts Atlas of 1887 (The Official State Atlas of Kansas Compiled from Government Surveys, County Records and Personal Investigations). Philadelphia, PA: L. H. Everts & Co., 1887.

United State Indian Bureau map of 1889, "Indian Territory." Located in the Western Collection, Oklahoma University at Norman.

Ziegalasch, A. W. map: "The Old Chisholm Cattle Trail and Subsidiary Trails in Texas, 1873."

Property of the Harvey County Historical Library and Museum, Newton, Kansas.

SECONDARY SOURCES:

Books:

Anderson, Boyd M. and the Saskatchewan Stock Growers Association. *Beyond the Range, A History of the Saskatchewan Stock Growers Association*. Saskatoon, Canada: Modern Press, 1988.

Athearn, Robert G. *High Country Empire, The High Plains and Rockies*. New York, NY: McGraw-Hill Book Co., Inc., 1960.

Atherton, Lewis. *The Cattle Kings*. Lincoln, NE: University of Nebraska Press, 1972 Bison Book.

Originally published in 1961 by Indiana University Press.

Austin, J. R. *A History of Early Baca County*

Awbrey, Betty Dooley, Claude Dooley, and the Texas Historical Commission. *Why Stop? A Guide to Texas Historical Roadside Markers*. Lanham, MD: Taylor Trade Publishing, 2005.

Baughman, Robert W. *Kansas Post Offices*. Topeka, KS: The Kansas State Historical Society, 1961.

Beach. Maude L. (comp.) and Robert L. Thaden, Jr. (ed.), a Montana Writer's Project. *Faded Hoof Prints — Bygone Dreams*. Broadus, MT: Powder River Historical Society, 1989.

Bowden, Margaret Dillinger. *1916 Wyoming: Here We Come!* James H. Bowden and Jessie Outka, publishers, 2002.

Branch, Douglas. *The Cowboy and His Interpreters*. D. Appleton & Co. publishers, 1926.

Brayer, Garnet M. and Herbert O. *American Cattle Trails*. Lubbock, TX: Smith Publishing Co., 1952.

Brevet Press and N. Jane Hunt, (ed.) *Brevet's South Dakota Historical Markers*. Garretson, SD: Sanders Printing Co., 1974.

Bright, John D. (ed.) *Kansas: The First Century Vol. I*. New York, NY: Lewis Historical Publishing Co., 1956.

Chapter XI — "Cowtowns and Cattle Trails"

Brown, Mark H. and William R. Felton. *Before Barbed Wire, L. A. Huffman, Photographer on Horseback*. New York, NY: Bramhall House, 1955.

Larson Alton Huffman (d. 1931) went to Fort Keogh just outside of "Milestown" Montana Territory in 1878 as a post photographer. His candid pictures of life on the plains have become classics.

Brune, Gunnar. *Springs of Texas*, Vol. I. Fort Worth, TX: Branch-Smith, 1981.

Buecker, Thomas R. *Fort Robinson and the American West, 1874-1899*. Norman, OK: University of Oklahoma Press, 1999.

Burroughs, Jean M. *On the Trail, The Life and Tales of "Lead Steer" Potter*. Santa Fe, NM: Museum of New Mexico Press, 1980.

Caldwell, Clifford R. *John Simpson Chisum, The Cattle King of the Pecos Revisited*. Santa Fe, NM:Sunstone Press, 2010.

Carlson, Susan. *Wyoming Historical Markers at 55 MPH, A Guide to Historical Markers and Monuments on Wyoming Highways*. Cheyenne, WY: Beartooth Corral Publishing, 1994.

Carriker, Robert C. *Fort Supply, Indian Territory, Frontier Outpost on the Plains*. Norman, OK: University of Oklahoma Press, 1970.

Chapham, Walter C. *Western Movies, The Movie Treasury, The Story of the West on Screen*, Octopus Books, pub. date unknown.

Chrisman, Harry E. *Lost Trails of the Cimarron*. Athens, Ohio: Ohio University Press, 1990.

Originally published by Sage Books of Denver, Colorado in 1961.

Chrisman, Harry E. *The Ladder of Rivers, The Story of I.P. (Print) Olive*. Athens, Ohio: Sage Books, Swallow Press,1962.

Clayton, Lawrence and Joan Halford Farmer, (editors). *Tracks Along the Clear Fork*. Lubbock, TX: Texas A&M University Press, 2012.

Collection of stories about the Clear Fork Country, the land along the Clear Fork of the Brazos River in Shackelford and

Throckmorton counties.

Crawford, Lewis F. *Ranching Days in Dakota and Custer's Black Hills Expedition of 1874*. Baltimore, MD: Wirth Brothers, 1950.

Dary, David. *Cowboy Culture, A Saga of Five Centuries*. Lawrence, Kansas: University Press of   Kansas, 1981.

Dempsey, Hugh A. *The Golden Age of the Canadian Cowboy, An Illustrated History*. Calgary, AB, Canada: Fifth House, Ltd., 1995.

Dobie, J. Frank. *A Vaquero of the Brush Country: Partly From the Reminiscences of John Young*. 1957.

Dobie, J. Frank. *The Longhorns*. Edison, NJ: Castle Books, 1941.
> Dobie (1888-1964) was a native Texan who was on the faculty of the University of Texas at Austin for thirty years. He wrote a number of books and articles dealing with range life, rural Texas, and trail driving. He had been a newspaper columnist, as well.

Dobie, J. Frank. *Up the Trail from Texas*. New York, NY: Random House, Inc., 1955.
> Dobie's books are easy reading and entertain like a novel, but present the Old Texas as if he had been there. He was a contemporary to George Saunders and other aging trail drivers.

Douglas, C. L. *Cattle Kings of Texas*. Austin, Texas: State House Press, 1989.
> An excellant account of the men and families who created some of the vast ranches of Texas.

Drago, Harry Sinclair. *Great American Cattle Trails, The Story of the Old Cow Paths of the East and the Longhorn Highways of the Plains*. New York, NY: Bramhall House, 1965.

Dyer, D. B. Mrs. *Fort Reno, or Picturesque "Cheyenne and Arrapahoe Army Life," before the Opening of "Oklahoma."* Mechanicsburg, PA: Stackpole Books, 2005.

Field, Ron. *U.S. Army Frontier Scouts, 1840-1921*. New York, NY: Osprey Publishing, 2003.

Fifer, Barbara. *Bad Boys of the Black Hills...And Some Wild Women, Too*. Helena, MT: Farcountry Press, 2008.

Flanagan, Sue. *Trailing the Longhorns, A Century Later*. Austin, TX: Madrona Press, Inc., 1974.
> An excellant book on the different cattle trails out of Texas. Very well researched. One of our favorites.

Fletcher, Robert H. (Comp. by Glenda Clay Bradshaw). *Montana's Historical Highway Markers, Revised and Expanded*. Helena, MT: Montana Historical Society Press, 1999.

Fugate, Francis L. and Roberta B. *Roadside History of Oklahoma*. Missoula, MT: Mountain Press Publishing Co., 1991.

Gard, Wayne. *The Chisholm Trail*. Norman, OK: University of Oklahoma Press, ninth printing, 1988.
> Originally printed in 1954.
> A study of the Chisholm Trail has to include Gard's book.

Goins, Charles Robert & Goble, Danney. *Historical Atlas of Oklahoma*. Norman, OK: University of Oklahoma Press, 2006 (4th edition).
> Excellant history of Oklahoma via outstanding maps.

Hall, Bert L. *Roundup Years, Old Muddy to Black Hills*. Winner, SD: Western South Dakota Buck-A-Roos, 2000. Limited Centennial Edition #286.

Haywood, C. Robert. *Trails South, The Wagon-Road Economy in the Dodge City-Panhandle Region*. Norman, OK: University of Oklahoma Press, 1986.

Hoig, Stan. *Fort Reno and the Indian Territory Frontier*. Fayetteville, AR: The University of Arkansas Press, 2000.

Hoig, Stan. *The Sand Creek Massacre*. Norman, OK: University of Oklahoma Press, 1961.

Holden, Frances Mayhugh. *Lambshead Before Interwoven, A Texas Range Chronicle, 1848-1878*. College Station, Texas: Texas A & M University Press, 1982.
> Fourth Printing, 1997.

Holden, William Curry. *Alkali Trails, or Social and Economic Movements of the Texas Frontier, 1846-1900*. Lubbock, Texas: Texas Tech University Press, 1998.
> Originally published in Dallas by the Southwest Press in 1930.
> Holden (1896-1993) was a professor of history at Texas Technological College in Lubbock.
> He authored eleven books and many articles. He was also an archeologist and became dean of anthropological research at the the college. The "Cattle Kingdom" is only one aspect of this book, that covers a wide range of topics about the social and economic history of Texas.

Hutton, Harold. *The River That Runs*. Sioux Falls, SD: Pine Hill Press, 1999.
> Harold's fourth book relates the history of the land and people of the Niobrara River. The title is a translated name of the river from the local Indians. The rapid-flowing Niobrara River runs across norhern Nebraska.

Jording, Mike. *A Few Interested Residents: Wyoming Historical Markers & Monuments*.Newcastle, NY, Mike Jording publisher. Helena, MT: Falcon Press Publishing, 1992

Joseph, Bruce E. and Bob Burke. *A Field Guide in Oklahoma's Historical Markers*. 2005.

Jones, Ralph F. *Longhorns North of the Arkansas*. San Antonio, TX: The Naylor Co., 1969.
> The first line of the book is: "In any factual and authentic account of *the West as it was*, in the northern high plains country during the period from 1868 to 1908, it would be necessary to give proper recognition to the impact of the Texas-Montana Cattle Trail, upon this great and important area lying north of the Arkansas River…" Jones was born on the Y Cross Ranch in Montana alongside this trail in 1895.

Kraisinger, Gary and Margaret Kraisinger. *The Western, the Greatest Texas Cattle Trail, 1874-1886*. Newton, KS: Mennonite Press, Inc., (printer), 2004. Published by Gary and Margaret Kraisinger.

Lamar, Howard R. *Charlie Siringo's West, An Interpretive Biography*. Albuquerque, NM: University of New Mexico Press, 2005.

Leaky, John and Nellie W. Yost. *The West That Was from Texas to Montana*. Lincoln, NE: University of Nebraska Press, 1965.
> At the age of eighty-two, John Leaky dictated his life story to Yost. Born in 1873 in Texas, Leaky had been a cowboy all his life and worked for various ranches from Texas to Montana.

Lee, Wayne C. *Wild Towns of Nebraska*. Caldwell, ID: Caxton Press, 2008.

Lee, Wayne C. and Howard C. Raynesford. *Trails of the Smoky Hill*, From Coronado to the Cow Towns. Caldwell, ID: The Caxton Printers, Ltd., 1980.

Lillibridge, John L. *The Red Fork Ranch and Its People*. Ocala, FL: Greene's Printing.

McMurtry, Robby. *The Road to Medicine Lodge, Jesse Chisholm in the Indian Nations*. Morris, OK: Two Crows Studo, 2011.
> Graphic novel, illustrated, written and published by McMurtry while he was preparing illustrations for *The Western Cattle Trail, 1874-1897*, its Rise, Collapse, and Revival.

Nolan, Frederick. *Tascosa, Its Life and Gaudy Times*. Lubbock, TX: Texas Tech University Press, 2007.

Oliva, Leo E. *Fort Wallace, Sentinel on the Smoky Hill Trail*. Topeka, KS: Kansas State Historical Society, 1998.

O'Neal, Bill. *Border Queeen Caldwell, Toughest Town on the Chisholm Trail*. Waco, TX: Eakin Press, 2008.

O'Neal, Bill. *Cheyenne, A Biography of the "Magic City" of the Plains, 1867-1903*. Austin, TX: Eakin Press, 2006.

Osteen, Ike. *A Place Called Baca*. Springfield, CO: Ike Osteen, publisher, 1979.
> A fine history of Baca County, Colorado with accompanying map.

Palacios, R. D. *Ranches and Cattle Trails of Early Montana*.

Pearce, W. M. *The Matador Land and Cattle Company*. Norman, OK: University of Oklahoma Press, 1983.

Pelzer, Lous. *The Cattlemen's Frontier, A Record of the Trans-Mississippi cattle industry from oxen trains to pooling companies, 1850-1890*. Glendale, CA: The Arthur H. Clark Co., 1936.
> Pelzer was the president of the Mississippi Valley Historical Association and Professor of History at the University of Iowa.

Perkey, Elton A. *Perkey's Nebraska Place Names*. Nebraska State Historical Society publications, Vol. XXVIII. Lincoln, Neb.: J & L Lee, Co., 1995.

Raine, William MacLeod and Will C. Barnes. *Cattle, Cowboys and Rangers*. New York: Grosset & Dunlap, 1930.
> This work was originally published under the title *Cattle*.

Rainey, George. *No Man's Land, The Historic Story of A Landed Orphan*. Enid, OK: George Rainey, publisher, 1937.

Rath, Ida Ellen. *The Rath Trail*. Wichita, KS: McCormick-Armstrong Co., Inc., 1961.
> A biography of Charles Rath, buffalo hunter, merchant, hide buyer, and organizer of early day towns and trading posts.

Rister, Carl Coke. *Fort Griffin on the Texas Frontier*. Norman, OK: University of Oklahoma Press, 1956.
> Rister was a native Texan who wrote a dozen notable books. He was a member of the history faculty of the University of Oklahoma for more than two decades, and at the time of his death in 1955, was Distinguished Professor of History at Texas Technological College at Lubbock, Texas.

Robertson, Pauline Durrett and R. L. Robertson. *Cowman's Country, Fifty Frontier Ranches In The Texas Panhandle, 1876-1887*. Amarillo, TX: Paramount Publishing Co., 1981.
> Excellent book. This is one of our favorites.

Shaffer, Ray. *A Guide to Places on the Colorado Prairie, 1540-1975*. Boulder, CO: Pruett Publishing Co., no published date.

Sheffield, William J., Jr. *Historic Texas Trails: How to Trace Them*. Spring, TX: Absey & Company, Inc., 2002.

Shortridge, James R. *Peopling the Plains, Who Settled Where in Frontier Kansas*. Lawrence, KS: University Press of Kansas, 1995.

Skaggs, Jimmy M. (ed.) *Ranch and Range in Oklahoma*. Oklahoma City, OK: Oklahoma Historical Society, 1978.

Skaggs, Jimmy M. *The Cattle-Trailing Industry, Between Supply and Demand, 1866-1890*. Wichita, KS: The University Press of Kansas, 1973.
> As Professor of American Studies and Economics at Wichita State University, Skaggs wrote economic studies on various topics. The cattle-trailing industry was one of them. His research is top-knotch and very thorough, and his work is one of our favorite sources.

Soule, Gardner. *The Long Trail, How Cowboys & Longhorns Opened the West*. Published by Gardner Soule and printed by McGraw-Hill Book Company, 1976.

Stanley, Ellen May. *Cowboy Josh, Adventures of a Real Cowboy*. Newton, KS: Mennonite Press, Inc. (Printers), 1996. Published by Ellen May Stanley.

Stanley, Ellen May. *Early Lane County [Kansas] History, 12,00 B.C., A.D. 1884*. Newton, KS: Mennonite Press, Inc. (Printers), 1993.
> Published by Ellen May Stanley.

Stephens, A. Ray and Catrography by Carol Zuber-Mallison. *Texas, A Historical Atlas*, Norman, OK: University of Oklahoma Press, 2010.

Time-Life Books Inc., the Old West series: *The Indians*. Alexandria, VA: Time Life Books, 1975.

Time-Life Books Inc., the Old West series: *The Miners*. Alexandria, VA: Time Life Books, 1975.

Utley, Robert M. *The Indian Frontier of the American West, 1846-1890*. Albuquerque, NM: University of New Mexico Press, 1984. (page 232)

Vallentine, John Franklin. *Cattle Ranching South of Dodge City, The Early Years (1870-1920)*. Ashland, KS: The Clark County Historical Society, 1998.

Worcester, Don. *The Chisholm Trail, High Road of the Cattle Kingdom*. Lincoln, NE: University of Nebraska Press, 1980.

Wright, Muriel H., George H. Shirk, and Kenny A. Franks. *Mark of Heritage*. Oklahoma Historical Society: 1976.

Young, Norma Gene Butterbaugh, ed. *The Tracks We Followed*. Amarillo, TX: Southwestern Publications, 1991.
> Contains a series of articles written by Young and others, about places and times in No Man's Land.

Yost, Nellie Snyder. *The Call of the Range, The Story of the Nebraska Stock Growers Association*. Denver, CO: Sage Books, 1966.

SECONDARY PERIODICALS:

The Handbook of Texas Online, http://www.tshaonline.org
> "Abilene, Texas," [accessed Nov. 29, 2004]
> "Adobe Walls, Texas," by H. Allen Anderson, [accessed Oct. 20, 2011]
> "Adobe Walls Trail," by C. Robert Haywood, [accessed Oct. 9, 2011]
> "Albany, Texas," by Marilynne Howsley Jacobs, [accessed Jan. 10, 2007]
> "Amarillo, Texas," [accessed May 3, 2009]
> "Ashtola, Texas," [accessed May 3, 2009]
> "Bandera County," by Christopher Long, [accessed Oct. 9, 2007]
> "Bexar County," by Christopher Long, [accessed Oct. 4, 2007]
> "Brownsville, Texas," by Alicia A. Garza and Christopher Long, [accessed Dec. 2, 2007]
> "Butterfield Overland Mail," by Rupert N. Richardson, [accessed Nov. 29,.2004]
> "Camp Colorado," by Beatrice Grady Gay, [accessed March 2, 2008]
> "Camp Cooper," by Charles G. Davis, [accessed Dec. 8, 2010, April 19, 2011]
> "Camp Verde," [accessed Dec. 9, 2007]
> "Castroville, TX," by Ruben E. Ochoa, [accessed Dec. 2, 2007]
> "Cator, James Hamilton," by H. Allen Anderson, [accessed Nov. 6, 2011]
> "Channing, Texas," [accessed May 3, 2009]
> "Charles Goodnight," by H. Allen Anderson, [accessed April 22, 2007]
> "Charles Stillman," by John Mason, [accessed Jan. 25, 2011]
> "Chisholm Trail," by David E. Worcester, [accessed April 10, 2005]

"Clarendon, Texas," by H. Allen Anderson, [accessed May 3, 2009]
"Claude, Texas," [accessed May 3, 2009]
"Coleman County," by Rusty Tate, [accessed Oct. 9, 2007]
"Cowboy Strike of 1883," by Robert E. Zeigler, [accessed Jan. 31, 2010]
"Creed Taylor," by Dovie Tschirhart Hall, [accessed Feb. 23, 2008]
"Fort Elliott," by Devon E. Kyvig, [accessed Nov., 2011]
"Fort Griffin, Texas," by Lawrence Clayton, [accessed Dec. 27, 2004]
"Fort McKavett, TX," by Vivian Elizabeth Smyrl, [accessed Feb. 9, 2011]
"George Washington West," by Kurt House, [accessed Dec. 2, 2007]
"Goodnight-Loving Trail," by T. C. Richardson, [accessed Sept. 28, 2006]
"Goodnight, Texas," [accessed May 3, 2009]
"Hashknife Ranch," by H. Allen Anderson, [accessed Nov. 28, 2007]
"Haskell, Texas," [accessed April 29, 2009]
"Horsehead Crossing," by Glenn Justice, [accessed Nov. 28, 2010]
"John Simpson Chisum," [accessed Auguat 14, 2007]
"Jones, Charles Edward," by C. Robert Haywood, [accessed Nov. 5, 2011]
"Jones and Plummer Trail," by C. Robert Haywood, [accessed Oct. 13, 2011]
"King Ranch," by John Ashton and Edgar P. Sneed, [accessed Jan. 10, 2007]
"London, TX," by John Leffler, [accessed Dec. 12, 2007]
"Matador, Texas," by William R. Hunt, [accessed April 30, 2009]
"McCulloch County," by Vivian Elizabeth Smyrl, [accessed Oct. 9, 2007]
"Military Road," by Morris L. Britton, [accessed Sept. 26, 2010]
"Noxville, TX," by Anthony B. Gaxiola, [accessed Feb. 1, 2011]
"Old Preston Road, " by Jean T. Hannaford, [accessed Sept. 26, 2010]
"Parnell, Texas (Hall County), by H. Allen Anderson, [accessed Sept. 5, 2007]
"Pleasanton, TX," by Robin Dutton, [accessed Feb. 10, 2008]
"Plummer, Joseph H.," by H. Allen Anderson, [accessed Nov. 1, 2011]
"Potter-Blocker Trail," by C. Robert Haywood, [accessed April 17, 2007]
"Quanah, Texas," by William R. Hunt, [accessed May 6, 2011]
"Rath City, TX," by Charles G. Davis, [accessed Nov. 2, 2011]
"Red River Station, TX," by Brian Hart, [accessed Jan. 1, 2011]
"Reynolds Cattle Company," [accessed March 5, 2010]
"Robert Edward Lee," by Carl Coke Rister, [accassed April 19, 2011]
"Seven-D Ranch," by Julia Cauble Smith, [accessed Nov. 8, 2012]
"Shawnee Trail," by Wayne Gard, [accessed Jan. 4, 2005]
"Springer Ranch," by H. Allen Anderson, [accessed Oct. 19, 2011]
"Tascosa-Dodge City Trail," by C. Robert Haywood, [accessed May 1, 2009 and
        Oct. 13, 2011]
"Texas Fever," by Tamara Miner Haygood, [accessed July 24, 2009]
"Waldrip, Texas," by Vivian Elizabeth Smyrl, [accessed Dec. 16, 2007]
"Wilbarger County, by John Leffler, [accessed Oct 9, 2007 & April 24, 2011].

OTHER SECONDARY PERIODICALS ONLINE: (Listed by subject)
"Alfred Howe Terry," Online: www.pbs.org/weta/thewest [accessed August 12, 2009]
"Altus, Oklahoma," Online: http://conutyest.okstate.edu [accessed June 17, 2011] and http://files.usgwarchives.org [accessed Oct. 14, 2009]
"Alzada, Montana," Online: http://www.ultimatemontana.com [accessed Sept. 14, 2009]
American Life Histories: Manuscripts from the Federal Writers' Project, 1936-1940.
        Written recollection of G. F. Boone, [accessed Dec. 9, 2007]
"Andy Adams," by C. D. Merriman. Online: www.literature .com [accessed Oct. 15, 2013]
"Baxter Springs — First Kansas Cow Town," *Legends of America, Kansas Legends*, Online: www.legendsofamerica.com/OZ-BaxterSprings.
        html [accessed March 6, 2007]
"Baxter Springs, Kansas," Online: http://en.wikipedia.org/wiki/Baxter_Springs,_Kansas [accessed Oct. 13, 2010]
"Brands and Branding," *Wyoming Tales and Trails*, Online: www.wyomingtalesandtrails.com [accessed Oct. 5, 2007]
"Breed Advantages," by the Alberta Texas Longhorn Association, Online:
        http://www.albertatexaslonghorn.com/breed_advantages.html [accessed April 6, 2006]
"Brush, Colorado," Online: www.brushcolo.com [accessed Nov. 5, 2012]
"Buffalo Gap, South Dakota," Online: http//buffalogapsd.org [accessed Aug. 31, 2010]
"C. F. Coffee," Online: www.sandozcenter.com [accessed May 25, 2012] (Chadron State College archieves)
"Camp Carlin," Online: http://wiki.wyomingplaces.org [accessed June 6, 2010]
"Camp Clarke Bridge and Sidney-Black Hills Trail," Online: www.nebraskahistory.org. [accessed July 8, 2010]
"Cantonment," by Jon D. May. Electronic Publishing Center of Oklahoma State University. http://digital.library.okstate.edu/
        encyclopedia [accessed July 24, 2011]
"Centennial Campaign (1876)," Online: www.custerbooks.com [Auguat 12, 2009]
"Cheyenne River Reservation," Online: www.aktalokota.org [accessed April 30, 2012]
"Clark County," Kansas State Historical Society online: www.kshs.org/Kansasapedia/clark-county-kansas [accessed Oct. 24, 2011]
"Clyde, Texas," Online: http://texasescapes.com [accessed Feb. 11, 2011]
"Dale, E. E.," Bob L. Blackburn, Encyclopedia of Oklahoma History and Culture, Oklahoma State Historical Society. Online: http://
        digital.library.okstate.edu [accessed Feb. 12, 2012]
"Deer Trail, Colorado," Online: www.deertrailcolorado.org/history [accessed July 12, 2009]
"Erin Springs," Online: www.okgenweb.org [accessed Dec. 31, 2010]
"Fort Arbuckle," Online: http://digital.library.okstate.edu [accessed May 14, 2013]

"Fort Custer," Online: www.wkipedia.org [accessed August 9, 2009]

"Fort D. A. Russell," Online: www.wyomingtalesandtrails.com [accessed June 6, 2010]

"Fort Dodge, Ford County, Kansas," taken from Ida Ellen Rath's *Early Ford County* (1964), on Ford County Historical Society online
site: www.skyways.org, [accessed Oct. 20, 2011]

"Fort Elliott, Texas," Online: www.fortwiki.com [accessed May 30, 2008]

"Fort Keogh," Online: www.ultimatemontana.com [accessed August 9, 2009]
www.ars.usda.gov/Main [accessed August 30, 2009] http://fortwiki.com [accessed Sept. 7, 2009]

"Fort Morgan," Online: www.fortmorganchamber.org/history [accessed July 12, 2009]

"Fort Niobrara," Online: www.memoriallibrary.com [accessed July 11, 2010]

"Fort Pease," Online: www.fortsandfights.com [accessed August 10, 2009]

"Fort Richardson, Texas," Online: http://en.wikipedia.org [accessed May 31, 2011]

"Fort Sumner — Pride of the Pecos," by Kathy Weiser. *Legends of America*, *New Mexico Legends*, Online: http://www.legendsofamerica.
com [accessed Dec. 10, 2010]

"Greer County," Online: www.OKGenWeb.org [accessed May, 2008]

"Hardesty," by Larry O'Dell and Oklahoma Historical Society, Online: http://digital.library.okstate.edu [accessed Nov. 8, 2009]

"Harper, Texas," Online: www.realestate-harper.com/harpertexas.

"History and Stories of Nebraska — The Herd Law," by Addison Erwin Sheldon, Online: www.olden-times.com/oldtimenebraska
[accessed Dec. 19, 2008.

"History of Baxter Springs," Online: www.baxtersprings.us [accessed Oct.9, 2010]

"History of Chadron," Online: www.chadron.com [accessed April 27, 2012]

"History of Clyde, Texas," Online: www.clyde.govoffice2.com [accessed Feb 11, 2011}

"History of Custer," Online: www.custer.gov [accessed July 9, 2010]

"History of Fort Sumner, New Mexico," by Darla Sue Dollman. Online: http://www.suite101 [accessed Dec. 9, 2010]

"History of Gainesville," Online: http://www.gainesville.tx.us/Historical/HistoricalTour.html [accessed May 26, 2011]

"History of Julesburg, Colorado," Online: http://townofjulesburg.com [accessed June 6, 2010]

"History of LaBelle, Wyoming," Online: http://townofmoorcroft.com/History.htm
[accessed August 28, 2009]

"History of Lamar [Colorado]," Online: www.ci.lamar.co.us/history [accessed Feb. 23, 2010]

"History of Old Fort Sill," Online: www.army.mil/pao/pahist.htm [accessed June 6, 2008]

"History of Pleasanton, Texas," by Jack Keller. Online: [accessed July 8, 2005]

"Hot Springs, South Dakota." Online: http://visithotspringsnow.com [accessed Aug. 8, 2010]

"How Did Hess, Oklahoma Begin," by Linda Gayle Wilson Heuckendorf. Online: http://www.southerngrace.com [accessed June 14,
2011]

"Iliff crafted kingdom from cattle, Ohioan struck gold by buying up land, selling livestock," by Tom Noel. *Rocky Mountain News*, March
1, 2008. Online: www.rockymountainnews.com [accessed June14, 2009]

"Jackson County Oklahoma," by Jodean Martin. Online: http://flies.usgwarchives.org [accessed Oct. 7, 2009]

Jackson County Oklahoma Extension Service, "Warren," online: http://countyext.okstate.edu [accessed June 26, 2011]

"Jones and Plummer Trail," by C. Robert Haywood. Oklahoma Historical Society article online; http://digital.library.okstate.edu/
encyclopedia/entries/J/JO017.html [accessed Oct. 13, 2011]

"Keota, Colorado," Online: www.ghosttowns.com [accessed Nov. 19, 2012]

"Kimble County Historical Marker." Online: www.forttours.com [accessed Jan. 23, 2011]

"Las Animas History," Online: www.supporters-of-colorado-perservation-las-animas.org. [accessed July 11, 2009]

"Little Big Horn Battle (1876)," Online: www.custerbooks.com [accessed August 12, 2009]

"Longhorn History in Canada," by the Alberta Texas Longhorn Association, Online: http://www.albertatexaslonghorn.com/home.html
[accessed April 6, 2006]

"Manuel Lisa," Online: http://mman.home.att.net/Lisa.htm [accessed August 10, 2009]

"Missouri Beef History, Texas Fever," Missouri State University Online:

"Mobeetie — Panhandle Mother City," by Kathy Weiser. Legends of America online: http.www.legendsofamerica.com [accessed May
25, 2011]

"Montana Forts of the Old West," Legends of America online: www.legendsofamerica.com [accessed August 2, 1013]

"Old Fort Peck," Online: http://www.fortpeckdam.com/history [accessed Sept 10, 2009] http://www.fortpecktribes.org [accessed Sept.
10, 2009]

"Pine Bluffs," Heritage Society web site: http:pinebluffs.org/heritage_society [accessed March 30, 2010]

"Ranches & Cattle Drives," Online: www.usgennet.org/use/co/county/prowers/hist/ranches.html [accessed Feb. 16, 2007]

"Raymer, Colorado," Online: http://en.wikipedia.org [accessed April 9, 2010]

"Red River War," Online: www.texasbeyondhistory.net [accessed Dec. 2, 2011]

"Royal Canadian Mounted Police History," Online: http://www.essortment.com/royal-canadian-mounted-police-history-21218.html
[accessed June 19, 2012] and http://www.canadaka.net/content/page/53-royal-canadian-mounted-police-history [accessed
June 19, 2012]

"Snyder Post Office," Online: http://webpmt.usps.gov [accessed March 17, 2010]

"Soldier and Brave," Survey of Historic Sites and Buildings, Fort Bascom, New Mexico, National Park Service. Online: www.nps.gov
[accessed Dec. 18, 2010]

"St. Labre, Montana," Online: [accessed August 9, 2009]

"Standing Rock Agency," Online: www.standingrocktourism.com [accessed April 30, 2012]

"Texas Ghost Towns, Noxville, Texas." Online: TexasEscapes.com [accessed Feb. 5, 2011]

"Texas Road," Online: http://en.wikipedia.org/wiki/Texas_Road [accessed Sept. 26, 2010]

"The Empire of Greer County, Texas," by Jodean Martin. Online: http://files.usgwarchives.org/ok/jackson/history/greerhistory.txt
[accessed Oct. 14, 2009]

"The Great Western Cattle Trail," Online: http://rebelcherokee.labdiva.com/cattletrail.html [accesssed June 17, 2008]

"The Great Western Cattle Trail," Ethel Taylor. Online: www.geocities.com [accessed Dec. 26, 2000]

"The History of Baxter Springs," (Chapter XIII) from *History of Cherokee County, Kansas and representative citizens*, ed. and comp. by

Nathaniel Thompson Allison, 1904. Online: http://www.kansashistory.us/cherokee-ch13.html [accessed Oct 13, 2010]
"The Oregon Trail Fort Laramie," Online: www.historyglobe.com [accessed May 20, 2012]
"The Post on the San Saba," Online: www.texasbeyondhistory.net [accessed Feb. 9, 2011]
"Timeline of Historical Events Relating to the Three Tribes of the Fort Berthold Reservation." Online: www.lib.fortbertholdcc.edu
    [accessed May 15, 2011]
"Trail City, Ranches & Cattle Drives," Online: www.usgennet.org [accessed Nov. 19, 2008]

MISCELLANEOUS SECONDARY PERIODICALS:

Anderson, Simon M. "Plows or Pastures? The Stockmen Take a Stand," *Beyond the Range*, as printed in *The Saskatchewan Stockgrowers*
    Magazine, January, 2006.
Anderson, Simon M. "The Golden Years," *Beyond the Range*, as printed in *The Saskatchewan Stockgrowers Magazine*, November, 2005.
Borroum, B. A. "Pioneer Cattlemen and Trail Drivers," *The Pioneer*, V, No. 12.
Burns, Robert H. "The Newman Ranches: Pioneer Cattle Ranches of the West," *Nebraska History Magazine*, Vol. 34, No. 1, (March,
    1953).
Cloud, Jim. "Cloud Road: The Way From Texas," *War Chief of Oklahoma Westerners*, Vol. 13, No. 3, Dec. 1979.
Cloud, James W. "Ft. Supply - Darlington Trail Traced," *Pioneer Tele-Topics*, Sept., 1979, pgs 14-15.
Dale, Edward Everett. "Old Navajoe," *Frontier Times*, Vol. 24, No. 5, Feb. 1947, 307-320.
Dubbs, Emanuel, "Charles Goodnight," *Kansas Cowboy*, July-August, 2009, 23.
Evans, Simon M. "Stocking the Canadian Range," *Alberta History*, 26:3 (summer, 1978).
Gray, Jim. "Tracking Down an Old Trail-Driver — L. B. Harris," *Kansas Cowboy*, Sept/Oct., 2003.
Gray, Jim. "Those Wild Millett Cowboys," *Kansas Cowboy*, Vol. II, No. 1, Nov./Dec, 2006.
"Historic Trails of the Cattle Kingdom," information compiled from Wayne Gard, J. Frank Dobie, and Jack Potter. *The Junior*
    Historian, Sept. 1967, page 15. The compiler is unknown.
Jenkison, Clay S. "What Roosevelt Learned in North Dakota," *Medora Magazine*
Lamar, Howard R. "Sioux (Dakota, Lakota) Indians," *The New Encyclopedia of the American West*, New Haven, CT: Yale University Press,
    1998, pages 1051-1054.
Lovett, John R. "Major Cattle Trails, 1866-1889," essay in Goins and Goble, *Historical Atlas of Oklahoma*, 2006 edition, pages 116-117.
Merker, Sibylle, "Traildriving in Texas on the Western Trail," essay in *The Junior Historian*, from a Bellaire High School senior,
    September, 1967 issue, pages 14-17.
    This article contains the map, "Historic Trails of the Cattle Kingdom."
Nelson, Morgan, "First Among the First," James Patterson, 1833-1892, *Wild West History Association Journal*, Vol. II, No. 5, October
    2009, 4.
Niedringhaus, Lee I. "The N Bar N Ranch, A Legend of the Open Range Cattle Industry, 1885-1899," *Montana, The Magazine of*
    Western History, Vol. 60, No. 1, Spring, 2010, 3-23.
"San Antonio," *The World Book Encyclopedia*, Vol. 17 (1982), 81.
Skaggs, Jimmy. "Northward Across the Plains, The Western Cattle Trail," *Great Plains Journal*, Vol. 12, (1972), 55-56.
Walters, Hildred and Lorraine Young. "There Was a Town Called Abbott," *Colorado Prairie Tales*. Scottsbluff, NE: The Business Farmer
    Printing Co., 1974.
Werner, Shawn. "A Trail Rediscovered, Celebrating the Fort Pierre-Deadwood Stage," *Deadwood Magazine*, August, 2009. (also Online:
    www.deadwoodmagazine.com [accessed, July 13, 2010]
"Wyoming," *The World Book Encyclopedia*, Vol. 21 (1982), 440.

SECONDARY NEWSPAPERS:

"A History of the Empire of Greer," J. O. Tuton, news editor. *The Mangum Daily Star*, Golden Anniversary issue, October 13, 1937,
    page 17.
"Along the Texas Trail, Longhorns, Cowboys passed through Weston," *News Letter Journal*, Newcastle, Wyoming, November 2, 1995.
Amarillo Daily News, Nov. 2, 1962. Article about Timms City, Texas.
"Battle of Soldier Springs was 120 Years Ago Today," by Cecil Chesser. *Altus Times*, Dec. 25, 1988.
"Brady, Texas," *The Baird Star*, Dec. 10, 1937.
"Cattle Trail That Ended Here Will Be Honored With Oklahoma Marker," *Junction City Union*, Junction City, Kansas, June 19, 1970.
    Article about a dedication held at Cushing, Oklahoma, celebrating the West Shawnee Cattle Trail that went through that
    town and terminated at Junction City, Kansas.
"Historama," in "Museum Musings," by Gaylynn Childs. *Junction City Union*, Junction City, Kansas, July 8, 1996.
"Historama," in "Museum Musings," by Gaylynn Childs. *Junction City Union*, Junction City, Kansas, Sept. 8, 1991.
Fort Worth Star Telegram, Jack Potter's trail map. Oct. 30, 1949, page 2.
Mangum Daily Star, Pioneer Edition of July 21, 1935, Section A, pages 1-4.
    Also online: http://www.rootsweb.ancestry.com [accessed Oct. 11, 2009]
The Sayre Record and Beckham County [Oklahoma] *Democrat*, January 4, 2006.
Trail Map, *San Angelo Standard Times*, August 29, 1954.
Trail Map, San Antonio Express, October 16, 1931, page 7.
    This map was referred to by George W. Saunders as a "map with those four trails marked, showing their correct route."
"Western Trail cuts through Erick area in late 1800's," letter and map submitted by Leroy Ford. *The Sayre Record and Beckham County*
    Democrat, January 4, 2006.

SECONDARY MAPS:

American Cattle Trails map, by Garnet M. and Herbert O. Brayer in *American Cattle Trail, 1540-1900*, page 70.
Lloyd, Dick. "Outlaw Country, A Map & Guide to the Cheyenne-Blackhills Express Route and the Sidney-Deadwood Trail," Alliance,
    Neb.: 1990.
Nebraska State Historical Society map, *Nebraska History*, Vol. 21, No. 4, Oct.-Dec, 1940.
Henderson, Paul and Helen. 1970 map showing the Fort Laramie vacinity and the Deadwood Trail.
    Located in the vertical files of the Gering Public Library, Gering, Nebraska.

"Historic Sites in the Friendship Area," map on website: "History of Friendship, Oklahoma," http://www.rootsweb.com [accessed June 18, 2007]

"Historical Sites," by May Ellen Smith, Niobrara County Library Foundation, Lusk, Wyoming.

Oklahoma Historical Society, 1936 map, "Map of a Portion of Oklahoma Showing the Location of the Chisholm Trail," reprinted from *The Chronicles of Oklahoma*, Vol. XIV, No. 1 (March, 1936) from H. S. Tennant article, "The Two Cattle Trails," 84-122. This map has the Old Texas Cattle Trail or Western Cattle Trail map on the opposite side.

Oklahoma Historical Society, 1936 map, "Map of a Portion of Oklahoma Showing the Location of the Old Texas Cattle Trail, also called the Western Cattle Trail, Abilene & Ft. Dodge Trail, Ft. Griffin-Ft. Dodge Trail, Dodge City Trail," reprinted from *The Chronicles of Oklahoma*, Vol. XIV, No. 1 (March, 1936) from H. S. Tennant article, "The Two Cattle Trails," 84-122. Map made by the Engineering Department of the Oklahoma State Highway Commission from information obtained by its engineers during 1933, under the authority of House Bill 149 of the 13th Session of the Oklahoma Legislature.

STATE QUARTERLIES, YEAR BOOKS, COUNTY HISTORIES, CENTENNIAL EDITIONS:

Beel, Marianne Brinda, ed. *A Sanhill Century, Book I, the Land: A History of Cherry County, Nebraska, 1883-1993*. Cherry County Centennial Committee, Cherry County, Neb, 1986.

Betz, Alva. *A Prowers County History*. Lamar, CO: The Prowers County Historical Society, 1986.

Claggett, Laura Solze. *History of Lincoln County, Colorado*. Curtis Media Corp., printers, 1987.

Cook, James H. "Fifty Years on the Old Frontier," *Nebraska History Magazine*, Vol. X, 1927.

Felker, Rex A. *Haskell County [Texas] and Its Pioneers*. 1975

"Fort Buford," North Dakota State Historical Society brochure, 2006.

Gard, Wayne. "The Shawnee Trail," *The Southwestern Historical Quarterly*, Vol. LVI, No. 3, January, 1953, pages 359-377.

Gleason, Elsie Cady. "Richard Briggs Quinn," *Chronicles of Oklahoma*, Vol. 18, No. 2, June, 1940.

Golden Jubilee of Thomas County, Samuel Grout recollection (Chapter V)

Grant, Ben O. and J. R. Webb. "On The Cattle Trail and Buffalo Range, Joe S. McCombs," *West Texas Historical Association Year Book*, XI. (1935).

Harrington, W. P. *History of Gove County [Kansas]*, 1930.

"Historic Landmarks," *Chase County History*, Vol. 6. Chase County Historical Society, Nebraska, 1979, page 31.

Hodgeman County [Kansas] Museum. *Hodgeman County, From then Til..., The Continuing Saga*. Unpublished, in-house manuscript. Jetmore, Kansas.

Homesteaders and Other Early Settlers, 1900-1930, History of Western Cheyenne County, Colorado. Kit Carson, CO: Kit Carson Historical Society, 1985.

Jackson, Berenice, Jewel Carlisle, and Iris Colwell (comp.). *Man and the Oklahoma Panhandle (Beaver County, OT)*, 75th Diamond Jubilee issue, 1982. publisher unknown. Includes the map: "Ranches of the Texas-Oklahoma Panhandle," page 156.

Johnson, Elizabeth Wilkinson (comp. and ed.). *Trail, Rails and Travails*. Centennial issue for the City of LaGrange, Wyoming. Cheyenne, WY: Frontier Printing, Inc. (printer). Published by City of LaGrange, 1988. No. 1624 of 2,000 printed.

Lamar Centennial History Committee. Lamar, Colorado: I*ts First Hundred Year, 1886-1986, 100 All American Years*. Lamar, CO: 1986.

Mahnken, Norbert R. "Early Nebraska Markets for Texas Cattle," *Nebraska History, a Quarterly Magazine*, Vol. XXVI, January-March, 1945.

Mahnken, Norbert R. "The Sidney-Black Hills Trail," *Nebraska History, a Quarterly Magazine*, Vol. XXX, No. 3, 1949. pages 203-225.

McKean, Karlene and Roleta Teal, Betty Jacobs, Mary E. Owen, and Terry W. Blevins (ed.). *Tri-County [Colorado] History, A Centennial*. Limon, CO: The Tri-County Centennial Committee, 1989.

Moore, Sarah, ed. *Sage and Sod, Harper County History*, Vol. II, c 1975.

Notes on Early Clark County [Kansas], Vol. 1.

Oelrichs Historical Society. *In the Shadow of the Butte, A History of Oelrichs and Surrounding Area*. Oelrichs, SD, 1984.

"Oklahoma Historic Survey — Greer County," *Chronicles of Oklahoma*, Vol. 36, No. 1, (Spring 1958) Oklahoma Historical Society.

Owen, Keith R. "Doans: The Birth and Death of a Frontier Town," *West Texas Historical Association Yearbook*, Vol. 41 (1965) page 131.

Sherrill, R. E. *Haskell County [Texas] History*, Haskell, TX: Haskell Free Press, 1965.

Shwayder, Carol Rein (ed.). *Weld County [Colorado], Old & New, People & Places*, Vol. V. Greeley, CO: Unicorn Ventures, 1992.

Skaggs, Jimmy. "The Route of the Great Western (Dodge City) Cattle Trail," *The West Texas Historical Association Yearbook*, Vol. 41, 1965.

Snell, Joseph W. "Trail City: A Note from the Record," *Kansas Quarterly*, date unknown, p. 39.

Spiller, Wayne, comp. *Handbook of McCulloch County History*, Vol. I. Seagraves, TX: Pioneer Publishing, 1976.

Sturman, Mrs. Thomas L. *Pioneer Reminiscences*. Gove County Kansas Historical Association, 1986. This is a centennial project in memory of Mildred Cass Beason (1895-1971) who interviewed local people during 1937-1941. Their reminiscences appeared in various local weekly papers.

Sutton, E. S. article title unknown, about a 1877 or 1878 trail drive through Nebraska, *Nebraska History Magazine*, Vol. 19, No. 3, 1938.

Taylor, Virgina H. (State Archivist), "Notes on Coleman County History," *West Texas Historical Assoc. Yearbook*, Vol. 34, (1958), 128-129.

Tennant, H. S., "The Two Cattle Trails," *Chronicles of Oklahoma*, Vol. 14, No. 1 (March, 1936) Oklahoma Historical Society.

The History of Cheyenne County Kansas, Vol. I, (1987) Cheyenne County Historical Society.

"The Medora Stage and Forwarding Company," flier produced by the State Historical Society of North Dakota, 1983.

Thoburn, Joseph B. "The Story of Cantonment," *Chronicles of Oklahoma*, Vol. 3, No. 1, (March, 1925) Oklahoma Historical Society. Also online: http://digital.library.okstate.edu/Chronicles.

Tuttle, Albert B. and May T., ed & comp., *History & Heritage of Gove County, Kansas*. Gove County Historical Association, 1976. This is a bicentennial project.

Williams, Gladys Baughman. *History of Snyder, Colorado*.

THESES:

Becker, John T. (Jack). "J.P. Morris and the Rafter-3 Ranch," a thesis in history presented to Texas Tech University, Lubbock, Texas, 2001.

Haley, J. Evetts. "A Survey of Texas Cattle Drives to the North, 1866-1895," a thesis presented to the University of Texas, Midland,

Texas, June, 1926.

Skaggs, Jimmy M. "The Great Western Cattle Trail to Dodge City, Kansas," a thesis presented to Texas Technological College, Lubbock, Texas, August, 1965.

DOCUMENTS:

Anshutz, M. W. (Doc), Nye, Kansas, letter to George Root, Topeka, Kansas, dated August 1, 1939. Kansas Historical Society, Topeka, Kansas, item #222161, Trails correspondence 23.

Blume, R. R., Rawlins County, Kansas, letter to Anselm Sramek, Atwood, Kansas, dated March 26, 1965. authors' files.
    Reference: cowboys visited "my folks place to replenish their supply of fresh water."

Chicago Soldiers Colony, Collyer, Kansas, letter to Governor George Anthony, Topeka, Kansas, dated 1877. Trego County history collection #732, Kansas State Historical Society, Topeka, Kansas, Library & Archives Division, Manuscript collection.
    Reference: homesteads and planted crops in Trego and Gove counties are subject to damage because of the thousands of Texas cattle coming through the area, and families need protection "from lawless men."

"Cowboys Then and Now Exhibit," (notes taken) and "On to Oregon" article in the museum flier. Union County Museum, Union Oregan.

Goodnight, Charles, Goodnight, Texas, letter to J. Evetts Haley, dated Nov. 18, 1926.
    In the Haley Collection, Haley Memorial Library and History Center, Midland, Texas.
    Reference: blazing of a cattle trail from the JA Ranch in the Texas Panhandle to Dodge City, Kansas.

Goodnight, Charles, Goodnight, Texas, two letters to J. Evetts Haley, dated November, 1926 and August, 1928.
    In the Haley Collection, Haley Memorial Library and History Center, Midland, Texas.
    Reference: the course of the Palo-Duro Trail from the JA Ranch in the Texas Panhandle to Dodge City, Kansas.

Huss, George W., Miles City, Montana. speech given at the Miles City Club for the dedication of the Western Cattle Trail marker in Miles City, August 7, 2010. document in authors' collection.

Janzen, Myron. *Texas Post Offices*, an unpublished manuscript.
    A portion of this manuscript was acquired from Janzen by special permission.

Keefe, Maurine Igou, "Brief History of Doans," insert in the 1978 Doan's May Picnic Program.

Oklahoma Department of Libraries booklet, "The Early Day Friendship Area," Nov. 2002.

"Timms City," vertical file folder located at the Wolf Creek Heritage Museum, Lipscomb, Texas.
    Permission to borrow/copy that information for this study.

Steely, Skipper, unpublished manuscript, "Forty Seven Years," 1988. Commerce, TX: Texas A & M University, Special Collections.

Western Heritage Center, Cochran, Alberta on Cochran Ranch, museum display and notes taken.
    Opened July 1, 1996. notes in authors' files.

EMAILS AND INTERVIEWS:

Day, William Mark, Brady, Texas, with Gary Kraisinger, email: Feb. 22, 2011 and letter, March 28, 2011. in regard to the Dodge community and Dodge Crossing on Brady Creek.
    Interview: with Gary Kraisinger, March 24, 2011, about the remains of a rock corral near Katemcy in an area called "Peter's Prairie."

Dorgan, Darrell, director of the North Dakota Cowboy Hall of Fame, Medora, North Dakota, with Gary Kraisinger, August 6, 2011, in regard to the route of the trail to reach Fort Buford. (Part II, Chapter VII)

Cunningham, Betty, Myers, Montana by Margaret Kraisinger, August 14, 2009.
    In regard to Junction City Store on the north side of the Yellowstone River in Montana (Part II, Chapter VII).

Freeman, Cora, life-long resident of Bovina, Colorado, telephone interview with Gary Kraisinger, August 28, 2009. She said, "Old timers used to tell of the watering spot [for Texas herds] southeast of town." (Part III, Chapter III)

Hall, Carolyn, Bassett, Nebraska. Interview with Margaret Kraisinger, September 19, 2011.
    Hall states that the "Black Hills Trail" crossed the Niobrara River approximately fifteen miles northeast of present-day Bassett. Her great grandfather ran the ferry across the river, and it operated about three years. Then the Morrises built their bridge.

Ham, Kenneth, landowner, interviews with Gary Kraisinger, June and December, 2011.
    about the three cottonwood trees that were a landmark for the trail drivers, near the Frenchman River crossing in Hayes County, Nebraska. Two of these trees are still standing.

Hansen, Harry, current owner of the Hell Springs, Colorado, area. Phone interview with Gary Kraisinger, August 28, 2009.
    He verified that there is a spring on Hell Creek in the area of the trail that, in his memory, has never gone dry. (Part III, Chapter III)

Hurd, Bobbye, who lives near East Sweden, Texas, one mile south of the cemetery and has evidence of an east-west trail through his property, interview: with Gary Kraisinger, March 29, 2011.

Jordan, Judge V. Murray, landowner, Brady, Texas, with Gary Kraisinger, emails: Feb. 21, 2011 and Feb. 22, 2011.
    in regard to Brady Creek and the rock walls built by cowboys to enclose a space for their cattle

Klemme, Robert (Bob) L., Chisholm Trail historian. Interviews and emails with Gary Kraisinger, May, 2011, about the Cantonment Trail and once visible wagon road ruts in Oklahoma.

Maddux, Jack and Carol, Wauneta, Nebraska. interview with Gary Kraisinger, May 27, 2001.
    about the Saloon Tree (dispensary of refreshments) that lasted throughout the trail-driving days, located in a field northwest of the present-day Maddux Cattle Company's feedlot in Chase County, Nebraska.

Meade, Charles, Dodge City, Kansas, owner of Longhorn Canyon Ranch, with Gary Kraisinger, December 12, 2011, about the location of the canyon and the trail still partially visible today.

Miller, Lyle K., Clinton, Oklahoma, son of Betty Miller, long time resident of the Edward's Rock Crossing on the Washita River, with Gary Kraisinger, July 13, 2011.

Noack, Paul G., Austin, Texas. emails and interview with Gary Kraisinger, Dec. 29, 2010.
    in regard to Pegleg Crossing in Menard County, Texas.

Phillips, John, map curator at Oklahoma State University map department. Interview and emails between Phillips and Gary Kraisinger, September, 2011.

Pothoff, Harold, Trenton, Nebraska. interview with Gary Kraisinger, June 10, 2011.
    in regard to the ruts still visible along Dry Creek (aka Canyon Creek) on his ranch in Hitchcock County, Nebraska.

Rector, William R. MD, of Kerrville, Texas by Gary Kraisinger, email and phone interview, May 26, 2010, in regard to the route through Kerr and Gillespie counties.

Shaw, Nancy, granddaughter to Frank Shaw who had lived six miles west and two miles south of Oelrichs, South Dakota. interview with Gary Kraisinger in Meade, Kansas, June 4, 2006.
Trail herds crossed her grandfather's place.

Smith, Jack Beale, Oklahoma City, Oklahoma. Interview and correspondence between Smith and Gary Kraisinger, September 5, 2008, about the location of the California-Beale Wagon Road and its intersection with the Western Trail near Leedy, in Dewey County, Oklahoma.

Wright, D. D. ("Tex"), Santa Anna, Texas. Interview with Gary Kraisinger, March 15, 2011.
in regard to the Western Trail passing west of the present-day Colorado River Bridge and the Jinglebob Feeder Route going through Trickham and joining the Western Trail north of Coleman.

MAP INDEX

BY CHAPTER

PART II

Map # 1-1   "The Matamoros Feeder Route," by Gary Kraisinger 71

Map #1-2   "The Wilson County Feeder Route," by Gary Kraisinger 76

Map #1-3   "The 'Old Trail' Feeder Route," by Gary Kraisinger 78

Map #1-4   "The Nueces River Feeder Route," by Gary Kraisinger 91

Map #1-5   "McCulloch County, Texas," by Gary Kraisinger 94

Map #1-6   "The Fort McKavett Feeder Route," by Gary Kraisinger 97

Map #1-7   "The Mason-Gillespie County Feeder Route," by Gary Kraisinger 98

Map #1-8   "The Middle Colorado Feeder Route," by Gary Kraisinger..99

Map #1-9   "The Jinglebob (Trickham) Feeder Route," by Gary Kraisinger 105

Map #1-10   "The Southern Tom Green County-Concho River Feeder Route,"by Gary Kraisinger.........................106

Map #1-11   "The San Gabriel-Brownwood Feeder Route," by Gary Kraisinger 107

Map #1-12   "The Potter-Bacon Trail - Splinter Route," by Gary Kraisinger 111

Map #2-1   "Fort Griffin," compound layout. Courtesy of Lester W. Galbreath, Albany, Texas. 120

Map #2-2   "The Fort Griffin Area, Showing Feeder Routes to the Western Trail and Clear Fork River Crossing," by Gary Kraisinger 128

Map #2-3   "Belton Feeder Route," by Gary Kraisinger...129

Map #2-4   "Northern Tom Green County-Buffalo Gap Feeder Route," by Gary Kraisinger 131

Map #3-1   "The Western Cattle Trail Through Throckmorton, Baylor, and Wilbarger Counties," by Gary Kraisinger......139

Map #3-2   "Bosque County Feeder Route," by Gary Kraisinger 147

Map #3-3   "The Quanah Detour Route or 'Ghost Trial'," by Gary Kraisinger...154

Map #4-1   "The Western Trail Through Greer County, Texas and the Western Part of Indian Territory," by Gary Kraisinger 162

Map #4-2   "Trails Across Greer County, Texas, and Beyond," by Gary Kraisinger.....................................164

Map #4-3   "The Mobeetie Trail, the Bosque County Feeder Route, and the Western Cattle Trail," by Gary Kraisinger 168

Map #4-4   "The Lower Portion of the Tennant Map," created by H. S. Tennant and the Engineering Department of Oklahoma State Highway Commission, 1936...175

Map #4-5   "The Center Portion of the Tennant Map," created by H. S. Tennant and the Engineering Department of Oklahoma State Highway Commission, 1936...188

Map #4-6   "The Washita River Feeder Route," by Gary Kraisinger..189

Map #4-7   "The Red Fork Ranch Splinter Route," by Gary Kraisinger 192

Map #4-8   "The Washita Splinter Route to Cantonment," by Gary Kraisinger..196

Map #4-9   "Cattle Trails Across Indian Reservation," unknown creator...199

Map #4-10   "The Upper Portion of the Tennant Map," created by H. S. Tennant and the Engineering Department of Oklahoma State Highway Commission, 1936...206

Map #4-11   "The Splinter Routes in Northern Indian Territory," by Gary Kraisinger 206

Map #4-12	"The Western Cattle Trail in Relationship to the Fort Supply-Fort Elliott Military Road and the Twelve-mile Limit," by Gary Kraisinger	208
Map #4-13	"The North Canadian River Feeder Route," by Gary Kraisinger	211
Map #4-14	"The Cimarron (Cut-Off) Feeder Route," by Gary Kraisinger	213
Map #5-1	"The Imperfect Triangle," by M.W. (Doc) Anshutz and Frank A. Webb	220
Map #5-2	"The Western Cattle Trail from Indian Territory Border to Dodge City, Kansas," by Gary Kraisinger	223
Map #5-3	"Feeder Routes from the Texas Panhandle, Across No Man's Land, to Join the Western Cattle Trail at Dugan's Store on Mulberry Creek," by Gary Kraisinger	226
Map #5-4	"The Western Cattle Trail Goiing Into and Around Dodge City, Kansas," by Gary Kraisinger	239
Map #5-5	"The Hays City-Ellis Trail North of Dodge, and the 1876 Kansas Quarantine Deadline," by Gary Kraisinger	244
Map #5-6	"Route 1 of the Western Cattle Trail North of Dodge, and the 1877 Kansas Quarantine Deadline," by Gary Kraisinger	246
Map #5-7	"Route 2 of the Western Cattle Trail North of Dodge," by Gary Kraisinger	249
Map #5-8	"Ogallala Cattle Trail," by unknown creator	254
Map #5-9	"Route 3 and the Wallace Branch of the Western Cattle Trail North of Dodge," by Gary Kraisinger	255
Map #6-1	"The Western Cattle Trail Through Southwestern Nebraska, 1874 -1884," by Gary Kraisinger	267
Map #6-2	"The Cheyenne Splinter Route from Ogallala, Nebraska to Cheyenne, Wyoming," by Gary Kraisinger	280
Map #6-3	"The Missouri River Splinter Route from Ogallala, Nebraska to the Missouri River in the Great Sioux Indian Reservation, 1876-1879," by Gary Kraisinger	287
Map #7-1	"The Fort Buford Splinter Route from Sidney Bridge on the North Platte River to Fort Buford on the Missouri River," by Gary Kraisinger	303
Map #7-2	"The Western Cattle Trail Trunk Line from the Junction of the North Platte River and Rawhide Creek to Canada," by Gary Kraisinger	330
Map #7-3	"The Judith Bason Splinter Route from south of the Cheyenne River in Wyoming Territory to the Judith Basin in Montana Territory," by Gary Kraisinger	341
Map #7-4	"The Little Missouri Splinter Route from the Belle Fourche River in Wyoming Territory to the Missouri River in Dakota Territory," by Gary Kraisinger	353

PART III

Map #III, 2-1	"No-Man's Land," by Gary Kraisinger	394
Map #III, 2-2	"A Portion of the M. S. (Doc) Anshutz Map of 1935, No Man's Land," by M. W. Anshutz	399
Map #III, 2-3	"Cattle Trails in Southeastern Colorado, 1883-1887," by Gary Kraisinger	404
Map #III, 2-4	"Trails in the Southeastern Corner of Baca County, Colorado," by Ike Osteen	407
Map #III, 2-5	"The National Trail North of Trail City, Splinter Route and Branches," by Gary Kraisinger	410
Map #III, 2-6	"Portion of E. S. Sutton Map (1953) of the National Trail in Northeastern Colorado and the Extreme Northwestern Corner of Kansas," by E. S. Sutton	412
Map #III, 3-1	"The Various Routes Used to Trail Cattle North and their Relationship to Each Other," by Gary Kraisinger	428
Map #III, 3-2	"Lower Portion of The Texas-Montana Feeder Route from Colorado City and Big Spring, Texas through No Man's Land," by Gary Kraisinger	436
Map #III, 3-3	"Middle Portion of the Texas-Montana Feeder Route through Colorado," by Gary Kraisinger	446
Map #III,3-4	"Upper Portion of the Texas-Montana Feeder Route," by Gary Kraisinger	454

INDEX

Author comments included in the Table of Contents and Annotated Bibliography are not included in the index. Abbreviations D.T., I.T., and WCT stand for Dakota Territory, Indian Territory, and Western Cattle Trail, respectively. Page numbers containing the letter "n" indicate a footnote on that page. Page numbers for photographs are shown in *italics*. Map titles are contained in the separate Map Index.

A

Abbott, Albert, 451n56
Abbott, Colo., 451, 451 & n56, 465
Abbott, E. C. ("Teddy Blue"), *xxxvii*, 61, *190*, 191
Abbott, Harriett, 310n21
Abilene, Kans., xxi, xxxi–xxxii, 17–21, 45–54, 88, 191, 247, 263–65
Abilene, Tex., 131–33, 140n12, 140n14, 141
Acers, W. H., 180
Ackley, Peter P. ("Daddy"), 148–49, 155, 174–75, 326n65
Adair, John G., xxxiii, 37, 234
Adams, Andy (beef contractor), 31
Adams, Andy (cowboy/author), 3, 13, 96, 134, 209, 260, 329–46, 352, 354–58
Adobe Walls, I.T., 227–28 & n21
African Americans, 284, 317, 406
Albany, Tex., xxxiv, 62, 106–108, 110–11, 115, 133, 137–38, 142, 151, 376, 427, 429
Alice, Tex., 111, 429
Alkali Trails (Holden), 14–5
Allen, W. A., 112
Allen family (Claiborn, John, David and A. J.), *95*
Altus (Mangum, aka "Tin Can City"), Tex. (later Okla.), 162 & n3, 168, 178–79 & n36, 186–87
Alzada, Mont. (aka Stonveville), 321, 354–56
Amarillo, Tex., 113n105, 437
American Agriculturist, 275
American Indians. *See also* Indian reservation/agency; Indian Territory; *individual tribes*
  acculturation, 33, 138
  attacks on cattle herds, 31–32, 198
  attacks on settlers, 73, 75, 165, 167, 228, 233, 431n12
  Battle of Soldier Springs, 182n47
  Battle of the Little Bighorn, 343
  Cavalry attacks on, 252
  encounters/relations with whites, 27, 144, 165, 169–70, 176n29, 227n17
  government beef, 58, 70, 140, 279, 291, 298, 318–22, 329, 348, 350, 354, 357n136
  government rations, 197–98, 277, 312, 314–15
  "grass money", 181
  Red River War of 1874, 140–41
  Sand Creek Massacre, 59, 447
  treaties/land cessions, 15, 276–78, 312n24, 316
  U.S. Peace Policy, 277
Anderson, George, 238
Anderson, W. E., 238
Anshutz, Carrie W. Schomoker, 236n42, 279
Anshutz, M. W. ("Doc"), 220, 225n12, 229–31, 235, 236n42, 388–89, 390nn 7 & 9, 399–400
Anthony, A. J., 164–65
Anthony, George, 246
Apaches/Mescalero Apaches, 26, 29, 33
Appleton, Frank, 313
Arapaho Indians, 59n1, 198n93
Arbuckle Trail. *See* trail/trail branch
Arikara Indians, 328n70
Arkansas, 4, 12, 16, 202
Arkansas River, 12, 20–21, 28n10, 30, 33, 36, 53, 165, 196, 227n16, 265n4, 270, 401–402, 430, 447n44
Arlington, Colo., 430
Armstrong County (Tex.), 38, 113, 429
Ashland, Kans., 222
Ashland, Mont., 342n98

Ashtola, Tex., 113n104
Assiniboine Indians, 361
Atascosa River/Atascosa County (Tex.), 73, 236
Atcheson, Norman, 323–24
Atlanta, Colo., 430 & n8, 445
Austin, J. R., 430n6
Austin, Tex., 11, 46, 75, 77, 168, 426n1

B

Babbitt, A. T., 415–16
Babcock, A. C., 426n1
Baca County (Colo.), 402, 404, 407, 445
Backus, G. W., 148
Bacon, Alfred T., xxxiv, 110–11, 376, 429, 432
Baird, Matthew, 108n91
Baird, Tex. (aka Vickery), 100, 107n87
Baker, J. H., 49
Bandera/Bandera County (Tex.), 61–62, 73, 77–79, 82–86, 100, 115, 155, 284
Barker, Aaron, 291
Barrell Springs, I.T., 195–96
Bates, W. H., 236, 374
Battle of Palmito Ranch, 72 & n5
Battle of San Jacinto, 74–75
Battle of Soldier Springs, 182n47
Battle of the Alamo, 74–75
Baughman, Theodore, 196
Baxter, O. H. P., 237
Baxter Springs, Kans., xxxii, 10, 15n16, 17–21, 50, 52, 54, 263
Baylor County (Tex.), 139, 141–43, 376
Beach, Maude L., 326n64, 359
Beals, D.T., 236, 374
Beard, Cyrus, 196
Beaty, John W., 403
Beauregard (Mr.), 222
Beaver County (Okla.), 388–89, 394
Becker, John, 320
Beckham County (Okla.), 186
Bedish, Gabrial A., 155n47
Beebe Post Office, Mont., 350
Beeville, Tex., 46
Belfield, N.Dak., 328
Belle Fourche River/Crossing, 278n36, 319, 321, 326, 346, 349–55, 359
Belle Fourche, S.Dak., 319n40, 326n64
Belle Plain, Tex., 107n87
Belton, Samuel, xxx
Belton, Tex., 46, 123, 129–30
Bennight, John and Lynn, 181
Bent, William, 227n17
Bent County (Colo.), 401–402, 420, 447n46
Betz, Alva, 406, 473
Beverley, H. M., 418
Bexar County (Tex.), 75n14, 76
Biddle, James, 166
Big Blue River/Blue Valley Trail, 264–65
Big Cottonwood Creek Ranche (Neb.), 318
Big Spring, Tex., 435
Black, A. P. ("Ott"), 321
Black, A. R., 445n42
Black Hills, 47n19, 277–78, 279, 282–84, 291, 297, 302, 304 & n11, 322, 325–29, 345, 355 & n131, 480n7
Blaine County (Okla.), 195, 196, 197n91

Blair, Dave, 130
Blanco County (Tex.), 387
Bliss, Zenas R., 207
Blocker, Abner, 114n107, 171, 333, 343, 390–91, 393, 396, 435
Blocker, John R., x, 133, 168, 171, 183, 343, 386 & n2, 390–91, 409
Bloom, Kans., 224, 225
Bloomfield, Jno W. (aka "Johnny Smoker"), 288
Bluff Creek (Kans.), 50, 53, 222, 225
Blume, Rexford, 257
Boerne, Tex, 81, 82n28
Boggy Depot, I.T., 19
Boice, Henry S., 237
Booker, Tex., 231, 400
Boone, G. F., 85 & nn34–35, 89–90, 126–27
Borrum, James George, 15
Bosque Grande, N.Mex., 30–32, 34
Bovina, Colo., 449, 467
Bowman, N.Dak., 326
Boyce, A. G., 426n1, 443n35
Boyd, George, 177, 179
Boyd County (Neb.), 288n55
Brady, Peter, 94n56
Brady Creek/Mountains/Brady, Tex., 93–94, 96–98, 100, 103, 108, 115
brands/branding. *See also* cattle-trailing; ranches
    #4, 188n65
    21D, 326
    101 brand, 432n15
    Bow & Arrow, 326
    Chain C, 398
    C-O Circle, 309
    Crooked L, 399
    Diamond C, 237
    Hashknife, 141, 461
    HILL, 334
    horses, 461
    JA, 235
    JK, 334
    LIL, 194
    Long X, 449n49
    OIO Bar, 334
    OW, 334
    Seven D, 467n83
    Turkey Track, 238
    VP, 237
Brazos Island, 72n6
Brazos River, xxxiii, 3, 26, 101, 104n1, 108–10, 117, 119, 121, 124, 127–30, 137n2, 139, 142–43, 232, 376, 429, 439, 449n49, 481
Briggs, Charles, 395
Briggs, G. W., Jr., 155, 163, 185 & n56, 187n64, 203, 207
Britton, Alfred M., 112
Broadus, Mont., 319n40
Brock, George W., 285–86
Bronson, Edger, 298
Brooks County (Tex.), 73
Brookville, Kans., 19n26, 53
Brown, George W. ("Hoo-doo"), 230
Brown, John, 181
Brownsville, Tex., xxx, 62, 71–73, 77n21, 79, 115
Brownville, Neb., 19, 264, 270
Brule Sioux Indians, 293, 313, 335n81, 361
Brush, Colo., 451
Brush, Jared L., 285
Buckner, Robert, 479n3
buffalo
    hides, 108, 122, 164–67, 227, 235–36
    replacement by beef in Indian diet, 172, 179, 197
    U.S. extermination policy, 27, 59, 70, 133
Buffalo, Okla., 214
Buffalo, S.Dak., 326

Buffalo Gap, D.T., 325
Buffalo Gap National Grasslands, 322n51
Buffalo Park, Kans., 247–48, 251n64, 253, 256n69
Buffalo Springs, N.Dak., 326n65
Buffalo Springs, Tex., 167n16, 210–11, 347, 376, 404, 419, 428
Buffalo Springs (watering/pasture area). *See* Coldwater Creek (Tex.)
Buford, N.Dak., 329
Bugbee, T. S., 238
Burden, Kans., 20
Burke, Bob, 205
Burkett, T. J., 176 & n32, 183
Burlington, Iowa, xxxi, 16n18
Burnet County (Tex.), 107, 109, 151
Burnett, J. C., 248
Burton, Frank, 322
Buster, Charles W., 141
Butler, David, 264
Butler, Okla., 187n64, 203
Butterfield, David, 447n47
Butterfield, John, 28n9
Butterfield-Military Road. *See* military/stage roads
Byler, J. N., 15

C

Caie, J. W., 80, 81n25
Caldwell, Kans., xxxiii, 48, 61, 151, 173, 179, 191–200, 214
Caldwell County (Tex.), 109, 300
California, 3–4, 20, 47n19, 48, 137n2, 263 & n1
California-Beale Wagon Road, 202
Callahan County/Callahan Divide/Callahan, Tex., 106–108, 130
Camargo, Okla., 203–204
Cameron County (Tex.), 72, 393
Camp (Fort) Supply, I.T., 58, 60–61, 95, 123, 165–66, 169–71, 199, 207–10, 219, 232, 314, 384, 391, 409
Camp Carlin, Wyo., 281–82
Camp Clarke/Camp Clarke Bridge (aka Sidney Bridge), Neb., 302–306, 314
Camp Colorado, Tex., 101–104
Camp Cooper, Tex., 28, 31n21
Camp Nichols, Okla., 429, 432n16
Camp Poplar, Mont., 362n153
Camp Robinson, Neb., 60, 279, 304, 311, 313–14, 316n31
Camp Sheridan, Neb., 279, 302, 304, 313, 316n31, 317
Camp Verde, Tex., 83–84
Camp Wilson. *See* Fort Griffith
Campbell, Henry H., 112 & n101
Campbell, John A., 283n43
Canada
    cattle-trailing to, 333, 362–65
    Dominion Land Act, 362–63
    Hudson's Bay Company, 362–63
    Judith Basin splinter route, 346–52
Cannon, C. D., x
Canton, Okla., 196
Cantonmment (temporary military post)
    about the establishment, 195n85
    Badlands, 356–57
    Indian Territory, 194, 195–98, 203, 207, 211
    Sweetwater. *see* Fort Elliott, Tex.
    Tongue River, 360
Canute, Okla., 187n64, 203
Carhart, Lewis Henry (Rev.), 112
Carling, Elias B., 281
Carns, Neb., 290n62
Carrizo Springs, Colo., 430, 434, 445
Carroll, C. F., 83
Carson, Christopher H. ("Kit"), 432n16
Carson County (Tex.), 237
Carter, John, 360–61
Cartwright, N.Dak., 328

Cash, Leonard, 348, 350
Castroville, Tex., 77n22
Cato, O. C., 442
Cator, James H. and Robert, 233
Cattle (poem, Nance), xxiv, xliv
cattle companies. *See also* ranches
    Anglo-American Cattle Company, 323, 324n55
    Big Four Cattle Company, 188n65
    Blocker Brothers and Jennings Company, 387n2
    C. F. Doan & Company, 146
    Capitol Freehold Land and Investment Company, 426n1
    Cimarron & Crooked Creek Cattle Company, 398
    Consolidated Cattle Company, 481
    Continental Livestock Company, 141, 321, 323, 461, 472
    Cresswell Land and Cattle Company, 237
    Francklyn Land and Cattle Company, 237
    Hansford Land and Cattle Company, 238
    Hudson, Watson & Company, 301
    John Bratt & Company, 299n5
    Lee-Scott Cattle Company, 236, 347
    Lincoln Land & Cattle Company, 464n80
    Maddux Cattle Company, 273n18
    Matador Land and Cattle Company, 112, 112 & n101, 323, 427, 429, 472, 474
    Moore & Krill Cattle Company, 437, 438
    New England Livestock Company, xxxiv, 110–11, 114n107, 376, 392, 429, 430
    Prairie Cattle Company, 332n74
    Reynolds Cattle Company, 26n2, 112n100, 375n3, 441, 449n49, 453, 467, 472, 474
    Swan Land and Cattle Company, 282
    Toyah Land & Cattle Company, 435
    Warren Livestock Company, 334
    Western Union Beef Company, 467n83
Cattle Ranching South of Dodge City (Vallentine), 213
"Cattle Trails of the Prairies" (Harger), 18, 56, 210–12
cattle-trailing. *See also* feeder routes; fencing the open range; splinter routes; *trail system*
    1853 herds trailed north, xxx, 12
    1866-69 herds trailed north, xxxi, 17–18, 20, 43n2, 50–52, 130 & n24, 264
    1870-73 herds trailed north, xxxii, 18–19, 52–53
    1875-76 herds trailed north, xxxiii, 54, 85n35, 270, 272, 297
    1880-85 herds trailed north, xxxiii, xxxiv, 100, 184, 192n77, 248, 285, 297–98, 323, 387 & n1, 406, 408, 471
    1886-87 herds trailed north, 418–21, 439–40
    1885-1897 herds trailed north, 470–76
    about the chronology, xxx–xxxv, xliii, 4–6
    bedding down for the night, 258n73
    clearing up the confusion, xxi–xxii, 479
    cook's camp/supply wagon, *160*, 163, *433*
    cowboys/trail life, *ix–x, xxxvii*, 10, *24*, *42*, *58*, *95*
    defining the terms, xxxix–xl
    depiction in movies, 479–81
    double-team (wagons/river crossings), 231, 332–33, 336–37, 460–61
    double-wintering, 298 & n2, 427, 442
    "hair brand", 81
    head taxes, tolls and fees, 3n5, 12n4, 22, 32, 34–35, 163n6, 171, 179, 198, 254, 258, 290, 443–44, 449, 451–52
    herd inspections, 43, 117, 127, 139, 147, 151, 155, 163–64, 185–87, 380, 382, 393, 441
    organizing the drives, 69–70
    origins of the Texas longhorn, 3–4
    river crossings, 331–35
    road branding, xi, 73, 79, 81, 96, 163n6, 164n8, 259, 274, 314, 387, 437
    separating mixed herds, 127, 151, 163, 358, 449–50
    staging areas, 79–85
    stampedes, 14, 16, 31, 52, 81, 127, 137, 151, 153, 176n32, 213, 273, 437–38

    through-cattle, xl, 197, 259n76, 350, 358, 378, 470
    "trail cutters", 185n55
    trail width and daily progress, xxxviii
    "waddy", 276n26
cattle-trailing outfits. *See also* ranches/ranching
    Blocker, Driscoll & Davis, 92, 393, 418
    Camp, Rosser & Carroll, 284
    Ellison, Dewees & Bishop, 140n14
    Ellison & Dewees, 85n35, 93, 140–41, 144
    Ellison & Sherrill, 109n93, 126 & n19, 145, 217, 248
    Goodnight & Loving, xxxi, 25, 30
    Gregory & Fease, 326
    Head & Bishop, 276
    Hudson & Watson, 151, 301
    Lytle & McDaniel, 313–16
    Maxwell and Morris, 129, 175–76
    Millett & Mabry, 85n35, 93, 140, 141, 144
    Patterson & Franks, 25
    Smith & Elliott, 194
    Smith & Savage, 308
    Wheeler, Wilson & Hicks, 47–48
Chadron, Neb., 317
Channing, Tex., 114, 429, 442 & n34, 442n34, 3347
Chapman, Frank ("Bud"), 234
Charles Goodnight, Cowman and Plainsman (Haley), 22
Chartran, Louis, 317n34
Chase County (Neb.), 271
Chastain, J. W., 193–95, 199, 210, 214
Cherokee Indians, xxx, 15
Cherokee Outlet, 170, 210–11, 213, 222n8
Cherokee Strip, 193–95, 199, 204, 210, 212, 214, 382, 389, 400n35
Cherokee Strip Livestock Association, 193–94
Cherokee Trail, 240
Cheyenne, Wyo., 279–88, 302, 321, 336, 339n92, 376, 404, 420, 427–28, 431, 453–55
Cheyenne-Black Hills Stage Route. *See* Deadwood Trail
Cheyenne Indians, 59n1, 165, 188, 195n85, 198n93, 252, 278–79, 342
Chicago, Ill., 4, 19, 46, 50–51, 70, 378, 414, 427, 442, 480
Childress, Sam, 285, 286
Childress County (Tex.), 472
Chisholm Trail. *See* Eastern/Chisholm Trail System
Chisum, John S., 25 & n1, 32, 34–35, 47, 49, 105, 282, 448
Chisum, Pittser, 25, 32
Chivington, Colo., 447, 469–70
Choate, Monroe, 15
Choctaw Indian Reservation, xxx
Chrisman, Harry E., 257, 397
Chronicles of Oklahoma, 173, 175, 177
The Cimarron Chronicles (Anshutz and Anshutz), 235, 236n42, 279
Civil War, xxiii, xxx, xli, 3–6, 13, 17, 26, 43, 69, 72, 101n75, 280n39
Clarendon, Tex. (aka "Saint's Roost"), 112–13
Clark, Ed, 181
Clark County/Clark City, Kans., 213–14, 219 & n1, 221–23
Clarke, Charles F., 221n5
Clarke, Henry T., 302
Clarke, John ("Red"), 221, 221n5
Clark's Creek, Kans., 44
Claude, Tex., 113 & n105
Clay County (Tex.), 147
Clear Boggy Creek, I.T., 19
Clements, Joe, *95*
Cleveland, Charles, 1•9
Cleveland, Harper, 308
Cloud Trail, 47
Clyde, Robert, 108 & n91
Clyde, Tex., 61–62, 107–108 & n90-91
Coburn, James M., 237–38
Cody, William ("Buffalo Bill"), 293n70

Coe, William, 434
Coffee, C. F./Coffee Ranch, 334, 337
Coffee, Holland, 11
Coke, Richard, 414
Coke County (Tex.), 130
Colbert's Ferry, 11–12, 15n17, 61
Coldwater Creek (Tex.), 111, 114, 210, 395, 399–400, 428, 429, 432 & n14, 435–37, 440
Cole, Dan, 333n76, 347, 443, 449
Coleman County/Coleman, Tex., 61–62, 96n62, 99–103, 103 & n25, 105–108, 115, 284, 320n43
Collins Creek/Collins Station, Tex., 111, 122, 429
Collinson, Frank, 58, 60, 122–23 & n8, 314–16, 482
Collyer, Kans., 246–47
Colorado. *See also* National Trail System; Trail City, Colo.
    gold discovery, 27
    quarantine laws, xxiii, xxxii, 36, 382, 411
    resistance to National Trail, 401–402
Colorado City, Tex., 373, 405, 428, 435–39, 440, 453
Colorado River, 90, 94, 99–100 & n75, 103, 106, 130, 133, 373, 405
Colville, Silas Cheek, 11
Comanche County (Kans.), 213
Comanche County (Tex.), 129
Comanche Springs, I.T., 155, 164, 173, 184–87, 189
Comanche Springs, Tex., 30, 46
Comanches, 22, 27, 31–32, 34n27, 75, 140, 144, 162n4, 176n29, 182n47, 228
Concho River/Concho County (Tex.), 26–28, 97, 106, 133, 138n4
Conners, M. C., 326
Connolly, John, 183–84
Cook, James H., 291–92
Cooke County (Tex.), 167
Coolidge, Kans., 402, 406, 408–409, 413, 418–20
Coronado, Francisco Vásquez de, 3
Corpus Christi, Tex., 291
Cortés, Hernán, 3
Coryell County (Tex.), 126, 129
Cottle County (Tex.), 112, 472
Cow Gap, Tex., 94, 96, 98–100, 103, 115
Cowboy (movie), 480
Cox, William, 53n45
Cox's Crossing/Cox's Trail, 53, 270, 288n57
Cram's Unrivaled Atlas of the World 1889 (Cram), 212
Cranford, W. H. H., 181
Crawford, Alex, 87
Crawford, Lewis F., 298
Crawford, Neb., 316n31
Crawford, Samuel J., xxxi, 45
Creighton, Ed, 309
Cresswell, Henry Whiteside, 237
Crow Indians, 278n36, 322, 342, 360n146
Crude, W. F., 8
Culbertson, Neb., 266–68
Culver, Martin S., 392, 402, 408, 413, 415n62, 418
Cushing, Okla., 19
Custer, George Armstrong, 70n3, 277–78, 297, 343
Custer City, D.T., 278, 283n45, 325, 343–44
Custer County (D.T.), 322
Custer County (Okla.), 190

D
Dahlman, James, 309
Dakota Territory. *See also* Great Sioux Reservation
    Buffalo Gap National Grasslands, 322n51
    Indian reservations, 293, 296, 310–11
    ranches/ranching, 322–26
    splinter route to the Missouri, 326–28
Dale, Edward Everett, 61, 151, 181
Dale, H. P., 180
Dallas, Tex., 11, 46, 79
Daugherty, James, 16 & n20

Daughters of the American Revolution, 240
Davis, Jefferson, 84n32
Davis, Perry Eugene, 336–39, 351–52, 354–56, 461–72
Day, J. M. ("Doc"), 12, 222 & n8
Day, Jesse, 12
de Morès, Antoine (Marquis), 327
deadline, xl. *See also* quarantine/quarantine laws
Deadwood Trail/Deadwood, D.T., 283n45, 284, 304–307, 314, 325, 327, 336, 338–39, 346, 355, 435
Decatur County (Kans.), 247
Decker, Charles F., 326
Deep Hole (Kans., aka Longhorn Roundup), 213–14, 219–21, 224
Denison, Tex., 19, 146, 147
Denton County (Tex.), 16, 47, 48
Denver, Colo., xxxi, 28n10, 30, 33, 263n1, 282–83 & n46, 285n50, 431n12, 439, 447n47, 466n82
"Denver Mud", 455n61
desparados. *See* outlaws
Desperate Seed, Ellsworth, Kansas on the Violent Frontier (Gray), xxvi
detour route/trail, defined, xxxix
Dewees, Ann Irvin, 143n22
Dewees, John O., 140–141, 144
Dewees. Medina, 143n22
Diamond Springs, Kans., 20
Dickens County (Tex.), 112
Dickinson, D.T., 298, 326–27
Dimmit County (Tex.), 90
Doan, Calvin W., 145, 147
Doan, Corwin F., xxxiii, 119, 144–46, 148, 176–77
Doan, Jonathan, xxxiii, 144–46, 148–49
Doan's Crossing (Tex.)
    cattle-trailing from Ft. Griffin, 137–39, 151
    cattle-trailing north, 161–63, 169–73, 176–85
    establishment of the store, xxxiii, 123n8, 145–46, 176, 208–209
    establishment of the village, 148, 152
    feeder routes to, 146–52
    inspecting herds, 155, 163, 164n8
    McElroy interview, 175–76
    Mobeetie Trail crossing, 164–66
    Red River crossing, 61–62, 77, 90, 127, *152*, 153, 161, 205
    resupply at Doan's Store, 137, 142, 171, 203, 209
    stage station, 164
    trail markers, 100, 148, 149, 150, 174–75, 177
Dobbins, John, 16
Dobie, J. Frank, 3, 13–14
Dodge, Grenville M., 279, 283
Dodge, I. A., 96
Dodge, Richard A., 195n85
Dodge City, Kans.
    becoming a cattle town, xxxiii, 59–61, 79, 243, 263, 479n3
    buffalo hides and freighting, 165–67, 226–33
    cattle-trailing to, 96, 114, 123–24, 139–40, 168–69, 192–94, 237–38, 284–85, 471
    feeders and trunk lines, 212–13, 219–25, 233, 239–42, 388
    Point of Rocks landmark, 240, 403
    quarantine closure, 173, 245, 371, 373
    railroad connections, xxxiv, 59, 75, 119, 184, 381
    replacement by Trail City, 401–408
    trail markers, 88, 142, 150, 178, 180, 202, 204, 209, 215, 252, 270
    WCT to/from, 60, 93, 205, 225–26, 243–57, 297
Dodge City (movie), 479n3
Dodge City Trail, 79, 148, 204, 205
Dodge House Hotel & Convention Center, 155 & n47
Dominion Land Act of 1872 (Canada), 362–63
Donley County (Tex.), 112–13
Dorgan, Darrell, 328
double-team (wagons/herd river crossings), 231, 332–33, 336–37, 460–61
double-wintering, 298 & n2, 427, 442

Drago, Harry Sinclair, 129, 176, 186–87, 213, 221
Draper, W. F., 112n100
Driscoll, Tim, 96–97
Driskill, J. L., 222n8
Driskill, J. W., 222
Dubbs, Emanuel, 27
Dudley, Ezra and John, 400n36
Duffield, George C., 15
Dugan, A. H./Dugan's Store, 225
Dull Knife (Cheyenne), 195n85, 254
Dumas, Tex., 233
Dundy County (Neb.), 272, 274, 411
Durkee, John, 12
Durrett, Ryus, 112n100
Dyer, Leigh, 234

E

Eagle Butte, S.Dak., 319n41
East (Old) Shawnee Trail. *See* Shawnee Trail System
Eastern/Chisholm Trail System
 a brief history, xxi, xxiv, 42–44
 aka "McCoy" or "Abilene" Trail, 43, 265n4
 cattle-trailing to Kansas, 47–53
 creating Abilene railhead, 44–47
 as feeder route to WCT, 60–61
 government survey, 212
 quarantine/quarantine laws, 53–54
 revival of cattle-trailing, 61–62, 191–92
Eastman, Grant, 324
Edwards County (Kans.), 244
Edwards County (Tex.), 88, 90–91, 153
Edwardsville/Edward Rock Crossing, 189
El Dorado, Kans., 20
Ellis, Kans., xxxii–xxxiii, 60, 243–45, 247
Ellison, J. F., Sr., 49
Ellison, James F., Jr., 48–49, 85n35, 109, 140, 275, 300, 346
Ellsworth, Kans., xxxii–xxxiii, 19n26, 53–54, 129, 191, 244, 263, 265
Ellsworth Trail, 263, 266, 270
Elm Spring, Okla. (aka Erin Spring), 211
Emerson, George, 363
emigrant roads, xxi, 11, 299, 329, 335n81, 431n12
Ergin, James, 339
Eustace, A. N., 385
Evans, Fred, 324n58
Ewing, Alexander, 16

F

Faltin, August, 84
Farwell, Abel, 361
Farwell, Charles B., 426n1
Farwell, John V., 426n1
Farwell, Walter, 443n35
feeder routes. *See also* Western Cattle Trail
 about, xxxix, 6, 62, 69, 114–15
 Belton route, 127–30, 176
 Bosque County route, 167
 Cimarron Cut-off, 193–95, 200, 212–214, 239
 Eastern/Chisholm Trail, xxxiii, 60–61, 161, 191–97
 Fort Bascom Trail, 226, 235
 Fort McKavett route, 97–98, 100, 115
 Jinglebob (Trickham) route, 103–105
 Mason-Gillespie County route, 98–99
 Matamoros route, 62–63, 71–76n21, 79, 115, 429
 Middle Colorado route, 99
 North Canadian River route, 210–12
 Nueces River, 90–93, 100, 115, 130n25, 153–54
 Quanah Detour Route, xxxiv, 153–56
 San Gabriel-Brownwood route, 109–110
 Shawnee Trail/Old Trail, 11, 62–63, 77–78
 Texas Panhandle

Adobe Walls Trail, 227–28, 235, 388
Jones-Plummer Trail, 228–31, 235, 388
Mobeetie Trail, 164–69
Palo Duro-Dodge City Trail, xxxiii, 25, 38, 113, 228, 234–35, 382, 390, 395 & n24, 400
Tascosa-Dodge City Trail, 233, 235, 237, 382, 438
Tuttle Trail, 234, 388
Texas-Montana Feeder Route
 a brief history, xxxiv–xxxv, 425, 427–29
 connect to Goodnight Trail, 37
 cowboy storiess, 442–70
 extension through Colorado, 404, 407, 409–10
 extension to Nebraska, 263, 336 & n85
 extension to Wyoming, 435–42
 Holston route, 437–38
 Jim May route, 428, 432–35, 439–40
 Millsap route, 438–40
 Yellow House-Colorado City Trail, 435–40
 Tom Green County (Tex.), 26–28, 106, 115, 128, 130–33, 138n4
 Washita River route, 189–91, 197–99
 Wilson County (Tex.), 76–77
fencing the open range, 15, 56, 140, 147, 151, 191n75, 207n101n222, 237, 242, 255–56 & nn68-69, 265n6, 274, 308, 383, 390–91, 402, 426, 451–52, 463–69, 481. *See also* homesteading; ranching
A Field Guide to Oklahoma's Historical Markers (Joseph and Burke), 205
Fields, Jacob/Fields Crossing, Tex., 112
Fifty Years on the Old Frontier (Cook), 291–92
Flanagan, Sue, 352
Fletcher, B. J., 158, 161, 213–14, 250, 269 & n13
Fletcher, Ernest M., 62, 194 & n81, 380n14
Floyd, H. H., 326 & n64
Floyd County (Tex.), 112
Ford, LeRoy, 186–87
Ford, Walter Cynthia, 186–87
Ford County Globe, 377, 378
Ford County (Kans.), 217, *218*, 223, 224, 225, 227, 230, 245, 377, 402n41
Fort system. *See also* Camps; military/stage roads
Fort Adobe, Tex., 227n17
Fort Arbuckle, I.T., 47
Fort Atkinson, Neb., 240
Fort Bascom, N.Mex., 34 & n27, 37, 219, 226, 233, 235
Fort Belknap, Tex., 27–28, 34, 60, 101, 104, 137n2
Fort Bennett, D.T., 319
Fort Benton, Mont., 346n113
Fort Berthold Reservation, D.T., 328
Fort Brown, Tex., 72
Fort Buford, D.T., 301–303, 328–29, 352, 354–59
Fort Calgary, Can., 363
Fort Chadbourne, Tex., 28, 60, 137, 153
Fort Clark, Tex., 133
Fort Cobb, I.T., 47n19, 49n31, 60
Fort Concho. *See* San Angelo, Tex.
Fort Custer, Mont., 342–43
Fort D. A. Russell, Wyo., 279–82, 313
Fort Davis, Tex., 12
Fort Dodge, Kans., 60, 244
Fort Elliott, Tex., 37, 122n7, 164, 166, 166–73, 177, 179, 187, 189, 200, 232, 239
Fort Gibson, I.T., 12
Fort Griffin, Tex. (aka Camp Wilson), *116*, *120*
 beginning as outpost, xxxi, 119–22
 cattle-trailing through, 122–27, 151, 177, 232, 314, 375–76
 county seat relocation, 108–109, 122
 depot on WCT, xxxiii, 58, 61–62, 75, 80, 84, 115
 feeder routes to WCT, 127–33
 fort closure, 133
 trail marker, 142

THE WESTERN CATTLE TRAIL | 1874-1897   505

Fort Hall, Idaho, 263n1, 364
Fort Hays, Kans., 60, 243–44
Fort Kearney, Neb., 263n1
Fort Keogh, Mont., 326, 342–43, 355, 360–61
Fort Laramie, Wyo., 263n1, 277–78, 294, 312–14, 317, 335n81, 348, 350, 425
Fort Leavenworth, Kans., 12, 49n31
Fort Lyon, Colo., 408
Fort Macleod, Can., 363
Fort Maginnis, Mont., xxxvi, 346n113
Fort Mann, Kans., 240
Fort Manuel Lisa, Mont., 344n105
Fort Mason, Tex., 101 & n75, 104 & n1, 308
Fort McKavett, Tex., 60, 90n47, 97–98, 153
Fort Meade, D.T., 325, 326n63, 355
Fort Musselshell, Mont., 346n112
Fort Niobrara, Neb., 311
Fort Pease, Mont., 343
Fort Peck Indian Agency, Mont., 340, 361–62
Fort Phantom Hill, Tex., 28, 120, 137n2, 153
Fort Pierre, D.T., 304n12, 336
Fort Randall, D.T., 287, 291, 317n35
Fort Reno, I.T., 147, 169–72, 195–96, 198n93, 200, 210–12, 239
Fort Richardson, Tex., 127, 147, 164, 166–68
Fort Riley, Kans., 12, 20
Fort Sam Houston, Tex., 75
Fort Scott, Kans., 12, 15–17, 19
Fort Sedgwick, Colo., 280, 284
Fort Sidney, Neb., 280, 284
Fort Sill, I.T., 49n29, 60, 120, 144, 162n4, 169–71, 173, 179–80, 185n57, 211
Fort Smith, Ark., 202
Fort Stanton, N.Mex., 25
Fort Sumner, N.Mex., xxxi, 25–26, 28, 30–37, 114n107, 427–28, 480
Fort Supply. *See* Camp (Fort) Supply
Fort Terral, Tex., 60
Fort Thompson, D.T., 322
Fort Union, N.Mex., 456n2
Fort Vancouver, Oregon Territory, 263n1
Fort Walsh, Can., 363
Fort Worth, Tex., 43 & n2, 46, 79, 123–24, 129–30, 375, 396
Fort Yates, D.T., *296*, 321
Fort Zarah, Kans., 28n10
Forty Island Ford. *See* North Platte River
Fowler, George, 31
Fowler, Kans., 230
Frankel, E., 123
Franks, Bill, 105
Franks, William C., 25, 27, 31
Frazer, Tex., 162, 179 & n36
Fredericksburg, Tex., 88, 98, 103
freight routes, xxi, 6, 225–26, 230, 235–36, 263, 283–84, 305–306, 308, 313, 395n24
Fremont, John Charles, 452–53
French, C. C., 319
Friendship, Okla. (aka Alfalfa), 178–80
Frio County (Tex.), 77–79 & n23, 88, 314
Fudge, Bob, 171–72, 294, 333–37, 340–50, 482
Fulkerson, Johnny/Fulkerson settlement, 395
furs/fur trade, 317n34, 335n81, 344, 362

G
Gage, Okla., 208–209
Gage County (Neb.), 264
Gainesville, Tex., 47–48, 146, 149, 164, 167
Gard, Wayne, 8, 50, 51, 53
Garza County, Tex., 435
Gate, Okla., 388
George West, Tex., 73 & n12
Georgetown, Tex., 46
"Ghost Trail". *See* Quanah Detour Route

Gibson, James, 158
Giles, Alfred, 83
Girard, Okla., 215
Gish, Chris, 333n76, 347, 443, 449, 461
Glasgow, Mont., 362
Glen Rose, Tex., 147
Glenn, John, 222
Glidden, J. F., 236
Goble, Danney, 17, 50, 471
Goins, Charles Robert, 17, 50, 471
gold/gold discovery
    1849 California rush, 4, 47n19, 202, 263n1
    1859 Pike's Peak rush, 27, 30n16
    1874 Black Hills rush, 47n19, 277–78, 279, 282–84, 291, 297, 302, 304 & n11, 322, 325–29, 345, 355 & n131, 480n7
Gonzales, Tex., 46
Goodnight, Charles, xxxi, xxxiii, 24, 113, 137, 234 & n39, 234–37, 374 & n2, 382, 390, 425–26, 480
Goodnight, Tex., 113n104
Goodnight-Loving Trail, 30n34, 34n27, 130n25, 137–38, 282, 452
Goodnight Trail System
    blazing the trail, xxiv, 25–26, 32–33
    first drive, 326–32
    Palo Duro-Dodge City Trail, xxxiii, 38, 113, 234–35, 390, 395n24
    the trail of 1868, 33–35
    the trail after 1868, 35–37
    the trail of 1875, 37, 429
    the trail of 1878, 37–38
Gove County (Kans.), 247
Grady County (Okla.), 190
Grainfield, Kans., 253–54, 256
Granbury, Tex., 147
Grant, Ulysses S., 313
grasshoppers, 242n53, 465, 468
Gray, Jim, xxvi
Gray County (Tex.), 237
Grayson County (Tex.), 393
Great American Cattle Trails (Drago), 129, 213
Great Bend, Kans., 28n10, 54
Great Sioux Reservation, 70, 276–79, 287–88, 301, 318, 319n41. *See also* Indian reservation/agency
"Great Westerern", 72. *See also* Western Cattle Trail
Greeley, Colo., 100–11, 282, 455
Greeley, Horace, 252
Green, Milton, 458
Greer County (Tex./Okla.), 161–62, 180–82, 186–87
Grey, Zane, ix
Griffith, G. W. E., 398
Griffiths, Raymond, 318
Grinnell, Kans., 253–54
Groom, B. B. and Harrison, 237
Grout, Samuel, 216
Guadalupe River/Guadalupe County (Tex.), 16, 81–87
Gunter, Jot and Jule, 237
Guymon, Okla., 392, 395, 397, 400

H
Haigler, Neb., 272, 411, 419
Haley, J. Evetts, 22, 325n41, 371
Haley, N.Dak., 328
Hall, Bert L., 298, 318
Hall, Carolyn, 290n60
Hamilton, Tom and Mrs., 149n36
Hamilton County (Tex.), 129
Hamm, Kenneth, 271n16
Handy, Paul, 153
Hannibal, Mo., 11
Hanranhan, James N., 228
Hansford County (Tex.), 237–38

Hardeman, Monroe, 284
Hardeman, W. B., 92, 250–51, 393
Hardeman County (Tex.), 156, 161, 472
Hardesty, A. J. ("Jack"), xxxiv, 390–91 & n10, 395, 402–403
Hardesty, Okla. (aka Fulkerson settlement), 395, 397
Harger, Charles Moreau, xxxviii, 18, 47, 56, 209, 210–12
Hargroves, John, 169
Harlen, Wilhelm, 92
Harper, Tex., 87 & n37, 89
Harper County (Okla.), 211, 214–15
Harrington, W. P., 248
Harris, Frank, 480n6
Harris, L. B., xxxii, 59–60, 243–44
Harris, Tom, 114
Harrold, Ephraim, 149
Hart, Walt, 418
Hartley County (Tex.), 233, 442n34
Haskell, Charles, 112n100
Haskell County (Tex.), 139
Haskell Springs, Tex. (aka Rice Springs), 112, 429
Hastings, Jim, 308
Hawk, John, 333
Hawk Springs, Wyo., 460
Hawker, Tom, 169
Hayes County (Neb.), 266–71
Hays City, Kans., xxxii–xxxiii, 243–46
Hays County (Tex.), 12
Haywood, C. Robert, 219–20
Head, Dick, 284
Hebbronville, Tex., 429
Heinz, Charles, 231
Henderson, Pete, 225
Henrietta, Tex., 147, 164, 167 & n16, 179
herd laws. *See* Nebraska
Hess, James Buckhanon, 177n33
Hess, Robert C. Brackenridge, 177n33
Hess, Tex., 177
Hess, William Carter and Elvira, 177
Hester, Charles, 268, 271, 273
Hext, Okla. (aka Erick), 186
Hibbard, R. A., 10
Hidalgo County (Tex.), 73
Hidatsa Indians, 328n70
Hidetown, Tex. *See* Mobeetie, Tex.
Hill, J. L., 96
Historic Landmarks Commission of Wyoming, 334, 456, 459
Historical Atlas of Oklahoma (Goins and Goble), 130n24, 471
"Historical Outline of Powder River Country" (Beach), xxx, 359
The History of Cheyenne County, 258
History of Gove County (Harrington), 248
Hitchcock County (Neb.), 266–71
Hitson, Jesse H., 438
Hobart, Okla., 184, 187, 188n65
Hockley County (Tex.), 435
Hodgeman County (Kans.), 244
Hoffman, Emmett (Fr.), 342
Holden, George, 322
Holden, William Curry, 14–15, 61, 61–62
Holston, J. W., 437–38, 440
Homestead Act of 1862, xxx
homesteading. *See also* fencing the open range
    as barrier to cattle-trailing, 53n43, 70, 205, 213, 242–50, 264, 270, 274, 373, 426, 451–52
    dugouts, *218*
    herd law/fence laws, 265n6
    opening Range 41 for settlement, xxxv, 427, 440, 473
    railroads and, 251n64, 253–54, 349, 363
    relationship with drovers, 257–58
    removal of land for national trail, 378, 387
    settlement of Canada, 364
    settlement of Colorado, 420, 441–42
    settlement of Greer County, 162n5, 177 & n33, 180

settlement of Kansas, 59, 214–15, 229, 420
settlement of Nebraska, xxxv, 265, 272, 310 & n22, 323–24, 419–20
settlement of No Man's Land, 389, 395, 420
settlement of the Black Hills, 278
surviving drought and grasshoppers, 468
Texas land grants, 4n7
watering fees and tolls, 255 & n67, 452
windmills and fence posts, 463–64
Hood, Charles C., 198n93
Hood, John W., 195
Hood County (Tex.), 147, 167
Horsehead Creek/Horsehead Springs (Neb.), 318
Horsehead Crossing. *See* Pecos River
horses
    cattle-trailing remuda, xl, 69, 73, 79–80, 83, 87, 96, 125 & n15, 140, 153, 184, 286, 393, *443*
    herds trailed north, 92, 167, 168n19, 172, 195, 204, 205, 209, 301, 354, 461–71
    horse ranches, 234n38
    introduced by Spanish, 3, 354n126
    river crossings, 333–35 & n79
    stage stops, 137, 325
    stampedes, 351, 437–38, 462, 465
    swing stations, 33n25
    use by the army, 361n147
Hot Springs, D.T., 324–25
Hough, Emerson, ix
Houghes, William E., 321
Houston, Samuel Dunn, 276–77, 299–300, 317–18, 317n36
Houston, Tex., 455
Howard, Edwin A., 313
Hoy, J. D., 31
Hudson's Bay Company, 362–63
Huff, S. I., 26
Hugo, Colo., 440
Hull, Swoope, 107
Hulltown, Tex., 107–108
Humboldt, Kans., 44
Humphrey, H., 442
Hunnewell, Kans., xxxiii, 173, 179, 191–97, 199–200, 207
Hunt, P. B., 199
Hunter, J. Marvin, 176, 409, 479
Hunter, Samuel Dimmitt, 455
Hunter's Lake (aka He-Lo Mystery Lake), 455 & n62
Huntington-Smith, Helena, 61, 62
Huss, George W., 361
Hutchinson, Kans., 54
Hutchinson County (Tex.), 165, 237–38
Hutton, Harold, 289n59, 290, 304n12

I
Igou, Mable Doan, 152
Iliff, John Wesley, 30 & n16, 34, 282, 455n60
Illinois, 4, 12, 16–17, 27, 42–45, 51–52. *See also* Chicago, Ill.
Indian reservation/agency. *See also* American Indians; Great Sioux Reservation
    Blackfoot Agency, 331n73, 346n113
    Bosque Redondo Reservation, 26
    Cheyenne River Agency, 278n36, 318–19
    Cheyenne-Arapho Reservation, 169–70, 187, 189, 190, 192, 196, 198–99, 211
    Chickasaw Reservation, 189–90, 199
    Comanche Indian Reservation, 137–38
    Comanche-Kiowa-Apache Reservation, 169–70, 177, 179–83
    Creek Reservation, 12
    Crow Creek Agency, 278n36, 322
    Fort Berthold Reservation, 328
    Fort Peck Agency, 340, 361–62
    Grand River Agency, 321
    Lower Brule Agency, 277, 278n36, 293, 313, 316n31, 322, 335n81, 361

Northern Cheyenne Reservation, 342n98
Pawnee Indian Agency, 19–20
Pine Ridge Reservation, 276–79, 293, 302, 308–309, 311, 316–18, 322
Red Cloud Agency, xxxiii, 58, 60, 93, 122, 140, 276n28, 279, 302–304, 308, 311–18, 329
Rosebud Reservation, 277–79, 293, 308–309, 310–11, 316n31, 322
Sac and Fox Agency, 12, 19
Sisseston Agency, 278n36
Spotted Tail Agency, 279, 281, 302–304, 308–18
Standing Rock Agency, 277, 296, 302, 318, 321–22
Yankton Agency, 278n36
Indian Territory
about the fort system, 169–70
arrival of the railroad, 19
cattle-trailing across, xxx, 12n4, 170–73, 199–200
Arbuckle Trail, 43, 47–49, 140n12, 167
Quanah Detour Route, 186–87
Red Fork Ranch splinter route, 191–95
Shawnee Trail System, 19–20, 27
trail to Edward Rock Crossing, 187–89
trail to Fort Dodge, 199–200
Washita River feeder route, 189–91
Washita splinter route, 195–99
opening land to settlement, 70, 181
Yelton Store, 214–15
Indian Wars, 59, 140–41
Ireland, John, 414
Irvin, J. B., 133
Irvin, William C. ("Billy"), 143–44, 282
Irwin, John G., 137, 138
Isa-tai (Comanche prophet), 228

J
Jack County (Tex.), 147, 166, 166–68
"Jack Hardesty War", xxxiv, 390–91 & n10, 395, 402–403
Jackman, William J. ("Bill"), 110
Jacksboro, Tex., 147, 167 & n16
Jacksboro Frontier Echo, 124
Jackson, T. E., 108
Jacobs, John C., 117, 127, 139, 481
Janzen, Myron, 108n91
Jeff Davis County (Tex.), 435, 449n49
Jennings, Bob, 168
Jennings, R. J., 393, 418
Jennings, William Henry, 168, 387 & n2, 390
Jim Well County (Tex.), 73
Jobes, Samuel, *95*
Johnson County (Tex.), 177n33
Jones, Charles Edward ("Ed"), 227
Jones, Frank E., 408
Jones, G. W., 95
Jones, Ralph F., 345, 405, 408
Joseph, Bruce E., 205
Julesburg/Julesburg Junction, Colo., 280, 283, 286
Junction City, Kans., xxxii, 18–21, 44–45, 50, 52–53, 76n17n84, 264, 343

K
Kansas
1859 quarantine, xxx, 12
1861 quarantine, xxx, xxxi, 12–13, 17, 44–45
1875 quarantine, 59–60, 129, 195n82, 197
1876 quarantine, 70, 243–45
1877 quarantine, xxxiii, 245–46
1881 quarantine, xxxiv, 246–51
1884 quarantine, 215
1885 quarantine, xxi–xxii, xxxiv, 108, 200, 205, 230, 235n40, 238, 251–59, 266, 272, 381–82, 411, 421, 425
homesteaders and quarantines, 242–43

Jayhawker vigilantes, 16
Missouri border dispute, 15–17
Point of Rocks landmark, 240, 403
Protection of Cattle Against Disease Act, 238
quarantine law enforcement, 219
quarantine line moved west, 18–21, 79, 129
statehood, xxx
Kansas City, Mo., xxx, xxxii, 12, 15, 17–19, 70, 191–93, 264, 364
Kansas State Historical Society, 224, 225, 252
Karnes County (Tex.), 15
Katemcy, Tex., 98–99
Kaufholz, Charles, 222
Kaufman, Jacob ("Jew Jake"), 349, 351
Kearney, Neb., xxxii, xxxiii, 43, 263, 265–66 & n8, 270, 288–89, 290n63
Keeling, Henry C., 197–98
Kelly, H. B., 408
Kelly, Leo, 189
Kenedy, Miflin, 73n11
Kenton, Okla., 37n33
Keota, Colo., 464 & n80
Kerr County (Tex.), 76n17, 83–88, 96
Kerrville, Tex., 61–62, 73, 75–89, 91, 100, 115
Kimble County (Tex.), 66, 87–88, 90–91, 95, 115, 140n13, 153, 319
King, Richard, 73n10–74
King Reservoir/King Lake, 446–47 & n44
Kingman, Kans., 433
Kiowa County (Colo.), 447n46
Kiowa Indians, 27, 162n4
Kit Carson, Colo., 409–410, 420, 430n9, 434, 439n40, 448–49
Klaine, Kans., 222
Kramer, Ludwig, 389

L
La Salle County (Tex.), 285
LaBelle Roadhouse (Moorcroft, Wyo.), 349 & n120
LaGrange, Kale/LaGrange, Wyo., 458–60, 463
Lamar, Colo., 347, 420, 434, 445n42
Lamar, L. Q. C., 415
Lampasas County (Tex.), 99, 107, 109, 168
Lane County (Kans.), 247, 251
Laramie River, 294, 335n81
Laredo Trail/Laredo, Tex., 73n13, 284, 393
Las Animas, Colo., 430
LaSalle County (Tex.), 90, 92
Last Chance, Colo., 452
Lauderdale, Jasper ("Bob"), 82n28, 83, 145, 221, 284
Lawhon, Luther A., 192
Lead, D.T., 325
Leavenworth, Kans., 17
Ledbetter, W. H., 138
Lee, Robert E., 138 & nn5–6
Lee, W. M. D., 165, 236 & n44, 347
Leedy, Okla., 202–203
Leon Springs, Tex., 81, 82n28
Leonard, Fred, 227–28
Lewis, Gideon K., 73n10
Lewis, William, 165
Lewis & Clark Expedition, 344
Life in the Saddle (Collinson), 58
Light, John W., 76 & n18
Limon, Colo., 430
Lincoln County (Colo.), 455
Lipscomb County (Tex.), 238
Lisa, Manuel, 344
Little Missouri settlement, Mont., 356–57
Little Wolf (Cheyenne chief), 254
Live Oak County (Tex.), 73, 84, 90–91, 153, 193, 387
Llano Estacado. *See* Staked Plains of Texas
Llano River, 90–91, 115, 153–54, 887088

Lockhart, Tex., 46
The Log of a Cowboy (Adams), 134, 260, 329, 352
"A Log of the Trails" (Saunders), 90
Logan County (Kans.), 255–56
London, Tex., 92
Lone Wolf, Okla., 184
Lonesome Dove (movie), 32n22, 480
Longhorn Roundup. *See* Deep Hole, Kans.
Longhorns North of the Arkansas (Jones), 345, 405
Lost Trails of the Cimarron (Chrisman), 397
Loving, Jim, 34
Loving, Oliver, xxxi, 12, 25, 28–34, 43, 137, 282, 375n3, 480. *See also* Goodnight Trail System
Loving Trail, 30
Lowenthall, Louie, 149
Lubbock County (Tex.), 435
Lugert, Okla., 184, 185n57
Lusk, Wyo., xxix, 288, 338–39, 347–48, 350, 456, 459
Lynn County (Tex.), 435
Lytle, John T.
    blazing the WCT, xxxiii, 60–61, 75n15, 79, 93, 148
    cattle-trailing by, *58*, 75–76 & n19, 84, 97 & n64, 122, 141, 176–77
    delivering to Red Cloud Agency, 227, 311–16
    trail marker, *88*, 108
Lytle, Tex., 75–76

M
Mabry, Seth, 88, 140, 288–89, 298, 309
Madison, Martin, 400
Madrid, Neb., 268
Magnum, Tex. *See* Altus, Tex.
Mahnken, Norbert, 369, 373
mail/mail routes. *See also* military/stage roads; post offices/stores
    Overland Mail route, 26n4, 28–29, 127, 137 & n2
    pony express, 306
    writing/receiving letters on the trail, 101n76, 145, 375
Maley, Salis, 222
Man and the Oklahoma Panhandle (Jackson, Carlisle and Colwell), 397
Man of the Plains (North), 293
Mandan Indians, 328n70
Map of the Trail Drivers, 72n8
Marmarth, N.Dak., 328
Martin, George W., 44
Marts, John, 231
Mason County/Mason, Tex., 61–62, 98–100, 103, 140n13, 284
Matamoros, Tex., xxviii
Matthews, George T., 138
Matthews, John A., 112n100
Matthews, John Beck, 138
Matthews, Sallie Reynolds, 125
Mayfield, Cal, 192
May, James E., xxxiv, 347, 419, 427–29, 432–35, 445, 450, 452, 457–59, 471, 473
May, Okla., 212–13
McAnuity, R. L., 238
McBride, Dave, 149
McCanless, "Scandlous John", xxxv
McCann, D. J., 309
McCleave, William, 26
McClintock, John S., 305
McCombs, Joe S., 121, 123, 127
McCoy, Joseph, xxxi, 17, 20, *42*, 44–48, 50–53, 60
McCoy Trail. *See* Eastern/Chisholm Trail
McCuistion, Mary, 150
McCulloch, H., 415
McCulloch County (Tex.), 93–94
McCutcheon, William, 12
McCutcheon, Willis, 12, 320
McDaniel, Tom M., 58

McDonald, Eli, 87n37
McDowell, Kans., 44
McElroy, Nathaniel, 175–76, 181n44, 183, 187–89
McKinley, William, 327n68
McMillan, Samuel J. R., 415
McMullen County (Tex.), 73n12, 90
McMurtry, Larry, 32n22
McMurtry, Robert Wayne, vii, 171, 306, 483
McTaylor, George, 149
Meade, Kans., 229, 231, 233, 438
Meade County (Kans.), 227, 229–31, 319n40, 325
Medina River/Medina County (Tex.), x, 58, 60, 75–83, 88, 96, 314, 354
Medora, D.T., 326–28, 356–57
Menard County (Tex.), 92–93
Menger, William & Mary, 74
Mexico
    cattle introduced by Spanish, 3–4
    cattle-trailing to/from, 26, 72–73, 284
    independence from Spain, 75
    Texas independence from, xlii, 72
Meyer, Charles, 123
Middle Water, Tex., 114, 429
Miles, Nelson A., 166, 360–61
Miles City, Mont., 340, 343, 352, 355, 360–61, 442, 480
Miles City, Tex., 231
military units. *See also Forts entries*
    state militia
        6th Kansas Cavalry, 221n5
        32nd Texas Cavalry, 76, 140n13
        New Mexico Volunteer Cavalry, 26
    U.S. Army
        2nd Cavalry, 138, 281
        5th Cavalry, 311n23
        5th Infantry, 138
        6th Cavalry, 252
        9th Infantry, 311n23
        23rd Infantry, 195n85, 197
        24th Infantry, 196, 198n98
        30th Infantry, 281
military/stage roads. *See also* stage stations/routes
    about cattle trail use, xxi, 6, 99, 107, 243–44
    beginning of frontier fort system, 169–73
    Butterfield Mail/Military Road, 127, 137
    Fort Bascom, 233, 235
    Fort Dodge-various, 219–25, 239, 243–44
    Fort Elliott-Fort Richardson, 164–67
    Fort Elliott-Fort Sill, 177, 179, 187
    Fort Elliott-Fort Supply, 207–209, 232, 234
    Fort Griffin-Fort Belknap, 137 & n2
    Fort Griffin-Fort Richardson, 127
    Fort Laramie-Fort Pierre, 336
    Fort Laramie-Fort Randall, 317 & n35
    Fort Lyon-Indian Terrritory, 430n7
    Fort Maginnis-Fort Benton, 346 & n113
    Fort Mason-Fort Belknap, 101–102, 104 & n1
    Fort Reno-Fort Supply, 195–97, 210
    Fort Scott-Fort Gibson, 15
    Fort Scott-Fort Leavenworth, 12
    Fort Union-Granada, 37, 428–29
    Nueces River, 90n45
Miller, James F., 414
Millett Brothers, 16, 109–10, 139–42
Millsap, J. W., 438–40
Mineral City, Okla., 432–33
Miniconjous Indians, 335n81
Minter, I. F., 138
Missouri
    cattle-trailing to, xxx–xxxi, 4, 11–12
    cattle quarantine, xxiii, 12, 14–17, 36, 43–44, 140n12
    fears of Texas Fever, 5, 12

loss of Shawnee Trail access, 19, 26, 28
Oregon Trail origin, 263n1
overland mail route, 28n9, 137n2
Missouri River, 16n18, 19, 263–64, 276–77, 287–93, 303–304, 316, 319–22, 326–28, 344, 352–62, 427
Mobeetie, Tex. (aka Hidetown, Sweetwater), 164–69
Montana
cattle-trailing to, 171
quarantines and deadlines, 356
trials to northern ranges, 346–52
Monte Walsh (movie), 477, 480–81
Moorcroft, Wyo., 346, 348–55, 359, 459, 473
Moore, J. Ealy, 332–33, 337–39, 347, 349, 359–61, 442–61, 463–65, 470–71
Moore, Tom, 276, 299, 317
Moran, John J., 107n88
Mormon colony, 82n29
Morris, John A., 290
Morris, Joseph Phillip, 103, 129, 175–76, 320–21
Morris Bridge/Morris' Island, 287, 290
Morton County (Kans., aka Kansas County), 405n47
Moses, Sam, 323–24
Motley County (Tex.), 112 & n101, 472
Mountain Home, Tex., 87 & n36
movies, cattle-trailing depicted in, 479–81
Mulberry Creek (Kans.), 219–20, 225–27, 229–30, 233–35, 239
Munson, William B., 237
My Reminiscences as a Cowboy (Harris), 480n6
Myers, A. C., 227–28
Myers. J. J., 16
Myton, Howell P., 402

N
Nance, Bertha, xxiv, xliv
National Trail System
about the origins, xxxiv, 373–81
a brief history, 425–27
connecting WTC, 381–83, 387–89
creation of Trail City, 401–408
No Man's Land feeder routes
lower route, 394, 398–401
middle route, 394, 397
northern route, 389–97
north from Trail City, 408–13
settlement of Range 41W, xxxv
politics and controversy, 413–18, 420, 425
Navajo, 26, 33
Navajo(e), Okla., 180–83, 203, 209
Neatherlin, Lewis Warren, xxxiii, 79–82, 85, 87, 93, 101–103, 105, 124–25, 137, 143–44, 162–63, 166, 179, 182–84, 187–91, 200–202, 208–210, 245, 260, 267–69, 273
Nebraska. *See also* North Platte River; South Platte River
arrival of the railroad, 263
Eastern/Chisholm Trail, 43
extension of cattle-trailing to, 263–66
herd law, xxii, xxxii, xxxiv–xxxv, 5, 265–66, 289–90, 329, 355n131, 373, 419, 425, 440, 473, 476
Oglala National Grasslands, 322n51
settlement of Indian lands, 276–78
quarantine laws, xxii, xxxi, 264–65
Sidney Bridge/Camp Clarke, 302–306
Nebraska City, Neb., xxxi, 15, 16n18, 19, 264–65, 270
Nebraska Historical Society, 268, 270, 272, 318
Nebraska History Magazine, 293
Neff, Sabastian ("Boss"), 432
Neill, Sam, 275
Nelson, Hiram Louis, 87n36
Nelson, Morgan, 25
Ness County (Kans.), 247
"nesters". *See* homesteading
New Mexico

1680 Pueblo Revolt, 3
California-Beale Wagon Road, 202
cattle-trailing to, xxxi, 25–32, 43, 103, 137–38, 440, 444, 448
Goodnight Trail, 33–37, 429
introduction of Spanish cattle, 3
quarantines, xxxiv, 382–83, 401
ranches, 114n107, 236 & n43, 282, 298
New Spain, 3n2
New York
beef shipments to, 4–5
investment in cattle industry, 327
Panic of 1873, xxxii, 54n46, 69–70
refusal to buy Texas beef, 51–52
Newman, E. S., 308–309
Newton, Kans., xxxii, xxxiii, 19 & n26, 21, 53–54, 129, 191, 263
Nimmo, Joseph, 18, 61–62, 379–81, 389, 413, 415–17
Nine Mile Camp, Colo. (aka "Miles Camp"), 403
Niobrara County (Wyo.), 338, 456
Niobrara River/Niobrara, Neb., 122, 279n37, 288–93, 302–304, 307, 311, 314, 316n31, 318, 322, 333, 337–39
Nitchie, Clem, 221
No Man's Land, xxxiv
Adobe Walls Trail, 227–28
cattle-trailing across, 226–27, 347, 389–401, 401–12, 418–21
Goodnight Trail, 429
"imperfect triangle", 219–21
Indian removal, 235–39, 426
Indian unrest, 165, 228 & n21, 233
Jack Hardesty War, xxxiv, 390–91 & n10, 395, 402–403
Jones-Plummer Trail, 228–31
law enforcement, 408, 443–44
Mobeetie Trail, 164–69
National Trail, 381–84, 387–92, 412–17
Palo Duro-Dodge City Trail, 234–35
Potter-Bacon Trail, 114, 115, 429
Robbers' Roost, 37 & n33
"squatters" and homesteaders, 229, 402–403
Tascosa Trail, 233
Texas-Montana Trail, 432–42
Tuttle Trail, 234
Winchester Quarantine, 113, 376–77, 389, 396, 425, 429
Noonan, George S., 314, 354 & n126
Norris, Frank, xxvi
North, Luther, 293
North Dakota. *See* Dakota Territory
North from Texas (Shaw), 217
North of 36 (book, Hough), ix, 40
North of 36 (movie), ix
North Platte River, 270, 276n28, 279, 281–94, 284, 287, 299–304, 329–36, 454–56, 460–62, 476
The Northern Cheyenne Exodus in History and Memory (Powers), xxvi
Northern Trail. *See* Eastern/Chisholm Trail System
Noxville, Tex., 87, 89
Nueces Canyon, 90 & n45, 92
Nueces River, 3, 73 & n12, 77, 100, 291

O
Ochiltree County (Tex.), 228, 233, 237
O'dee, Kans., 231
Oelrichs, Harry, 323
Oelrichs, S.Dak., 318, 323–24
Ogallala, Neb.
becoming a cattle town, xxxiii, 263, 297–98
cattle-trailing to, 274–76
National Trail route to, 408–13
route extensions from Kansas, 245–57, 266–76
route extensions from Wyoming, 279–86
trails north from, 298–301
trails north - Ft. Buford splinter route, 302–29
trails north - WCT trunk line, 329–40

Oglala Indians, 335n81
Oglala National Grasslands, 322n51
O'Keefe, Tom, 228
Oklahoma Panhandle. *See* No Man's Land
The Oklahoma Scout (Baughman), 196
Oklahoma State Highway Commission, 175, 180
Oklahoma State Historical Society, 119, 161, 173, 175, 180, 202, 215, 388
Oklahoma Territory. *See also* Indian Territory; No Man's Land
    creation and boundary dispute, 162
    settlement of Indian lands, 181
    statehood, 170n24
Old Government Farm, Wyo., 336
Old Pete's Place (Clark County, Kans.), 225
Old Shawnee Trail. *See* Shawnee Trail System
Old Time Trail Drivers Association
    about the founding, ix–x
    drover recollections, 13, 43, 48, 481–82
    preservation of trail history, xlii, *174*–75, 268
Olive, I. P. ("Print"), 418
Omaha, Neb., 19, 263, 265, 270, 313, 337n89, 364–65
Omaha Herald, 265
Opelousas Trail, xxiii–xxiv
Open Range (movie), 480
Oregon City, Tex., 143–44
Osteen, Ike, 403, 445
Our Niche in History (Ford), 186
outlaws, 14, 16, 119, 121, 124, 139–40, 166, 169, 355, 406, 434.
    See also vigilantes
The Outlet (Adams), 3, 331, 352, 354, 356
Owings, Ab, 347, 443

P

Palacio, R. D., 343, 345
Palo Pinto County (Tex.), 12, 25–26, 27n7, 28n10, 31, 48, 79n23, 147, 167, 363
Panhandle Stock Association, 375
Panic of 1873, xxxii, 54 & n46, 234n39, 242n53
Paola, Kans., 17
Park, Kans. *See* Buffalo Park, Kans.
Parker, Cynthia Ann, 183n49
Parker, Quanah (Comanche), 156n48, 183 & n49, 228
Parnell, Tex., 112 & n102
Passmore, John, 182
Patterson, James, 25–33
Patterson, Tom, 25, 30
Pawnee County (Kans.), 244
Pease, F. D./Pease Bottoms, 343
Pease River, 110, 145, 208
Pecos River/Pecos County (Tex.), xxxi, 26–29, 31–32, 103, 105, 137, 141, 467n83
Peeler, Thomas M., 143n22
Pendennis, Kans., 256
Peopling the Plains (Shortridge), 242n53
Peta Nocona (Comanche chief), 183n49
Peugh, W. F., 400
Peyers, Emory, 103
Pine Bluffs, Wyo., 280, 456, 456–58
A Place Called Baca (Osteen), 407, 445
Platte River, 28n10, 263–66, 273–76, 282, 298. *See also* North Platte River; South Platte River
Plattsmouth, Neb., 19, 264, 270
Pleasanton, Tex., 73 & n13
Plummer, Joseph H., 227
Polk, Cal, 169
Polk, F. M., 168–69
Ponca Indians, 288–89, 293, 316n31
Pontotoc County (Okla.), 19
post offices/stores
    A. E. Ballou Groceries (Brady, Tex.), *95*
    Baylor County (Tex.), 141, 143

Black Hills, 325, 339
Camp Clarke/Sidney, Neb., 302, 305
Camp Cooper, Tex., 138n6
Carns/Carns Bridge, 287, 290
Castroville, Tex., 77n22
Clark County (Kans.), 213–14, 221–25
Coleman/McCulloch Counties (Tex.), 94, 101–108
Colorado Territory, 420n74, 430n10, 447n46, 451n56, 455, 457 & nn65–66, 464n80, 466n82
Doan's Crossing, 145 & n27
Donley County (Tex.), 112–13
Favorite Saloon (Kerrville), *83*
Ford/Meade Counties (Kans.), 229–32
Fort Griffin, Tex., 119–21
Gove/Lane Counties (Kans.), 247, 251, 253
Greer/Jackson Counties (Okla.), 162, 177n33, 180–82
Hall County (Tex.), 112n102
Harper, Tex., 87n37
Haskell County (Tex.), 112n100
Hitchcock County (Neb.), 266–67
Kendall County (Tex.), 81n27
Kerr County (Tex.), 85 & n33, 89
Koontz Grocery store (Baxter Springs), *10*
Menard County (Tex.), 92–93
Menger Hotel (San Antonio), *74*
Mineral City, Okla., 433
Montana Territory, 355 & n130
Morton County (Kans.), 405n47
Motley County (Tex.), 112n101
No Man's Land/Indian Territory, 166–67, 231, 234, 400
O'Brian's (N.Dak.), 357
Pleasanton, Tex., 73
Quanah, Tex., 155–56
Red River Station/Salt Creek, Tex., 49n28
roadhouses/road ranches, 180, 221–23, 225
Schreiner Department Store (Kerrville), *84*
temporary post offices, 257–58
Trail City, Colo., 418
Vernon, Tex., 146, 176
Wooten's at Raton Pass, 34
Wyoming, 335, 349, 460, 463
Yelton Store (Okla.), 214–15
Potter, Andrew Jackson ("Fightin' Parson"), 110
Potter, Jack Myers, xxxiv, 29, 62, 72n8, 93, 98, 103, 110–14 & n107, 376–77, 389, 393, 400–401, 403, 407–408, 411, 427–33
Potter County (Tex.), 113n105, 233, 237
Powder River, 319n40, 339–42, 348–50, 356, 359–60, 365, 427
Powers, Raymond, xxvi
Pratt, C., 231
Preston's Crossing/Preston Road/Preston Bend, Tex., xxiii, 11–12, 16, 19, 61, 191
Price, H., 199
A Prowers County History (Betz), 473
Pryer, Isacc ("Ike"), x
Pueblo, Colo., 28n10, 30, 33–34, 234n39, 282
Pueblo Revolt of 1680, 3

Q

Quanah Detour Route (aka "Ghost Trail"), xxxiv, 153–56, 164, 169, 185–87, 208
quarantine/quarantine laws. *See also individual states*
    about the origins, xxiii, xxxix
    deadlines, defined, xl
    early fears of Texas Fever, 43
    Kansas deadlines, 17, 19, 45, 54, 59, 219, 242–47, 249, 251, 256n69, 274
    Montana-Wyoming deadline, 356
    national trail proposal, 377–80, 413–16, 419
    New Mexico deadline, 383
    northern territories restrictions, 356
    politics and controversy, 378–80

trail system closure, 5, 266
vigilante actions, 14, 16
WCT closure, 258–59, 373
Winchester Quarantine, xxxiv, 113, 376–77, 389, 396, 425, 429
Quartz Mountains, 182n47
Quinn, Richard Briggs, 392, 395

R
railroads
Atchison, Topeka & Santa Fe, xxxii, xxxiii, 19 & n26, 21, 53, 59, 61, 196, 242, 263, 402, 408, 429, 430n9, 445
Burlington & Missouri, xxxii, 265, 349 & n122, 352, 442, 451, 457, 464 & nn80–81, 464n80
Canadian Pacific, 363
Chicago, Burlington & Quincy, 335, 349, 442, 451, 455, 464n80
Chicago, Rock Island & Pacific (CRI&P), 397
Chicago & Northwestern, 323–24 & n58
Fort Worth & Denver City, 113nn103–105, 147, 152, 155, 373, 438
Fremont, Elkhorn & Missouri Valley, 310, 316n31, 317n34, 323n53, 325, 338
Galveston, Harrisburg & San Antonio, 75
Great Northern, 362
Gulf, Colorado & Santa Fe, 99
International-Great Northern, 75
Kansas City & Southern, 438
Kansas City, Lawrence & Southern, xxxiii, 191, 196, 438
Kansas Pacific, xxxi–xxxiii, 17–18, 18, 20, 30n16, 42, 44–45, 60, 63, 178, 242–45, 247, 249, 253, 255–56, 263, 265, 270, 430n9, 447n47
Missouri, Kansas & Texas (KATY), 19
Missouri Pacific, 14, 73n13, 430n10, 468n85
Missouri River, Fort Scott & Gulf, xxxii, 10, 17
Northern Pacific, 326–27, 344, 356, 361
Rock Island, 230, 449, 451, 466–67
St. Louis & San Francisco, 19
Texas & Pacific, 107–109, 131, 141, 142, 373, 435
Texas Central, 133
Union Pacific, xxxii, 30n16, 249, 263, 279–82, 283n46n285n50, 302, 304n12, 313, 334, 336, 350, 365, 409, 431n12, 455, 457, 463–64
Union Pacific, Eastern Division. *see* Kansas Pacific
Ranch and Range in Oklahoma (Skaggs), 79
ranches. *See also* brands/branding; cattle companies; cattle-trailing outfits
1885-97 herds trailed north, 470–76
Anchor D Ranch, 390, 392, 400–401
Bar CC ranch, 237
Bar T Ranch, 322–23
Bar X Ranch, 149
Blanks and Withers Ranch, 285
Boiling Springs Ranch, 309
C. P. Ranch, 458
Circle Dot Ranch, 96, 314, 329, 331n73, 339–40, 343–46 & n113, 354–58
Cloud Ranch, 47
Cochran Ranch, 363
Cody-North Ranch, 293n70
Coffee Ranch, 337
D-Cross Ranch, 222 & n8
DHS Ranch, xxxvi
Diamond F Ranch, 237
Diamond Z Ranch, 400
Double X Bar, 309
The Elkhorn, 327
FUF Ranch, 191
H3 Ranch, 309
Hart Shoeman Ranch, 214–15 & n1
Hashknife Ranch, 138n4, 141 & n19, 321, 328, 354, 461, 464, 470, 475

Home Creek Ranch, 237
HS Ranch, 321
JA Ranch, xxxiii, 37–38, 113, 226, 234–35, 237–38, 374, 382, 388, 390, 429, 473
Jesse Hitson Ranch, 438
John Chisum Ranch, 103
King Ranch, 73–74, 141, 299–300
LE Ranch, 113–14, 236
LIT Ranch, 113–14, 374, 382, 473
LS Ranch, xxxiv, 113–14, 236, 347, 361, 374, 382, 427, 429, 432–35, 445, 458, 471, 473–75
LX Ranch, 113–14, 169, 236–37, 374, 382, 419
Maltese Cross Ranch, 327
Mill Iron Ranch, 427, 472, 474
Miller Creek Ranch, 139–40, 143
N Bar N Ranch, 308–309, 427
OX Ranch, 328, 397
Oxyoke and J, 309
Palo Duro Canyon Ranch, 110n98, 234–36
Panhandle/Frying Pan Ranch, 236–37
Point of Rocks Ranch, 403
Quarter Circle Q Ranch, 389
Quarter Circle T, 238
R2 Ranch, 145, 176
Rafter-3 Ranch, 103, 320n43
Red Fork Ranch, 192, 195
Santa Rosa Ranch, 73
Scissors Ranch, 238
Seven D Ranch, 314, 466–68, 472, 474
Seven K Ranch, 238
S-Half Circle Ranch, 389
Slash-Y Ranch, 481
Sturgis & Goddell Ranch, 323
T Anchor Ranch, 113–14, 237
TAN Ranch, 322–23
Tecumseh Ranch, 138
Three Sevens Ranch, 237
TOT Ranch, 322–23
Turkey Track Ranch, 237–38
Two Bar Ranch, 282
VVV Ranch, 323
Webb Ranch, 133, 409n53
XIT Ranch, xxxiv, xxxv, 114, 332–33, 338, 347, 359–60, 374, 382, 419, 426–27, 429, 432n14, 435–36, 440–47, 449–53, 460–61, 466–67, 469–75
Y Cross Ranch, 408
YO Ranch, 84
ranching. *See also* fencing the open range
barbed wire, 236–37
changes to cattle-trailing, 235–39, 373–78
"double wintered" cattle, 427, 442
syndicate takeover, 113–14, 323, 358, 382, 426n1
Randall County (Tex.), 237, 291
Randolph, Charles Francis, 438
Range 41W (Colo.), xxxv, 402, 411, 420–21, 427
Rapid City, S.Dak., 323n53, 325–26
Rath, Charles, 164–66, 227, 231–32
Rath, Ida Ellen, 235
Rath City (aka Reynolds City), 232
The Rath Trail (Rath), 235
Rawhide Creek, 279, 294, 301, 329–30, 333–38, 347n115, 374, 374n115, 409, 420, 425, 440, 454, 460–62, 476
Rawlins County (Kans.), 252–53, 257–58
Raymer, Colo., 455, 457
Raymer, George, 457
Reagan, John H., 417
Rector, Robert D., 145n27
Red Cloud Agency
agency relocation, 276n28, 308, 311–13, 316–17, 329
beef delivery, 58, 60, 140, 276–77, 313–18
cattle-trailing to, xxxiii, 122–23, 279

creating a route to, 93, 302–304
warehousing supplies, 281, 313
Red Cloud (Oglala chief), 312n24
Red River. *See also* Doan's Crossing; Preston's Crossing
about floods and drownings, 134
Arbuckle Trail/Chisholm Trail crossing, 47–48
Bolen's Crossing, 46
crossing into Indian Territory, 161, 168, 171–73
establishing the Texas boundary, 161–62, 238–39
Fields Crossing, 112, 429
Mobeetie Trail crossing, 164, 167
Quanah crossing, xxxiv, 153, 155–56, 186–87
Shawnee Trail crossing, 191n72
Warren Crossing, 182
Red River (movie), 46n14
Red River Station, Tex., 28n10, 49 & n28, 61 & n9, 153, 212, 354
Red River Valley (Drago), 186
Red River War, 140–41, 165, 231
Red Willow County (Neb.), 266
Redding, H. C. (Dr.), 181
Reighard, George, 222
remuda. *See* horses
Reno County (Kans.), 53
Republican River, 20, 267–69, 272, 274, 285, 380n14, 411, 449
Reynolds, A. E., 165
Reynolds, Barber Watkins, 138
Reynolds, Ben, 26n2
Reynolds, E. E., 232
Reynolds, Elizabeth ("Bettie"), 138
Reynolds, George T., 26–27, 112n100, 138, 236, 374–75, 449 & n49
Reynolds, P. G., 225n12, 229
Reynolds, William D., 26n2, 32, 375n3, 449 & n49
Reynolds City (aka Rath City), 232
Rice Springs, Tex. (aka Haskell Springs), 112, 429
Richardson, T. C., 114
Rio Grande, 3, 11, 46, 72, 284, 331n73
The Road to Medicine Lodge, Jesse Chisholm in the Indian Nations (McMurtry), vii
Robb, Seymour J., 459
Roberts, Oran M., 377
Roberts, Thomas, 25, 30
Roberts County (Tex.), 237
Robertson, Nells, 459
Robertson, Pauline and R. L., 38
Rogers, Will, x, 149
Romero, Casimiro, 236n43
Roosevelt, Theodore, 327
Ross, Bertha Doan, 149
Ross, Roy, 309
Rotary International, xxviii, 72, 150, 180
Round Rock, Tex., 46
Roundup Years (Hall), 318–19
Routt, John Long, 285
Rumans, John, 33
Runnels County (Tex.), 130–31, 133, 138, 409n53
Rust, C. H., 48, 481
Rye, Edgar, 116

S
Salina, Kans., 19n26, 44–45, 53
Saline County (Neb.), 264
Saloon Tree (aka Log Saloon), 273
San Angelo, Tex., 28, 61, 106, 119–20, 130–31, 153, 155
San Antonio, Tex., x, 61–62, 71–77, 79–86, 88–89, 93, 100, 103–104, 108–110, 115, 140, 191
San Saba River/San Saba County (Tex.), 90, 92–93, 96–99
Sanborn, H. B., 236
Sanders, John, 276
Sans Arcs Indians, 335n81
Santa Anna (Comanche Chief), 104

Santa Anna Mt./Santa Anna, Tex., 99, 102, 104–105
Santa Fe, N.Mex., 26
Saunders, Ann, xxiv
Saunders, George W.
about the career of, viii–x
death, 149
dedicating this book to, xxii
documenting WCT history, 70–71, 72n8, 479
recollections of, 75, 77, 90, 153, 373, 482–83
trail marker debate, 147–49, 174–75
Saunders, Tom B., IV, viii, xxiii–xxvi
Saville, John J. (Dr.), 312
Scholar, Wade, 332–35
Schreiner, Charles Armand, 76 & n17, 84, 91, 95
Schulyer, Neb., xxxii, 43, 263, 264, 265
Schwethelm, Ernest, 87, 89, 98
Scott, G. W., 153, 155–56
Scott, Lucien B., 236, 347
Scott, S. W., 112n100
Scranton, N.Dak., 174, 326n64, 326n65
Scribner's Magazine, 18, 47, 56, 210
Section 23, T7N, R36W (Neb.), 271
Sedalia, Mo., xxiii, xxx–xxxi, 14, 16, 25, 263–64
Sedgwick County (Kans.), 53
Sedwick, Josua T., 400
Seward County (Kans.), 227
Seward County (Neb.), 264
Seymour, Tex., 62, 142–43 & nn21–22
Shackelford County (Tex.), 31n21, 117, 121–22, 129, 131, 449n49. *See also* Albany, Tex.
Sharp, J. Peter, 309
Shaw, James, 126, 145–46, 217
Shaw, Nancy, 324
Shawnee Trail System. *See also* splinter routes
about the origins, xxi, xxiii–xxiv, xxx, 5–6, 8
a brief history, 11–12
beginnings of Texas Fever, 12
East/Old Trail, 12, 19–21, 52, 61, 263
Kansas-Missouri border issues, 14–17, 26–27
Middle Trail, 19
pre/post Civil War use, 12–14
railroad arrival in Kansas, 17–21
West Trail, xxxii, 19–21, 44, 50, 52, 264
"The Shawnee Trail" (Gard), 8
sheep/sheepherding, 3, 82, 84, 112n100, 236nn43–44, 265n6, 378n11, 455, 464–65, 467–68
Sheridan, Phillip H., 224, 313
Sheridan County (Kans.), 247
Sherrill, James, 109n93, 126n19
Shidler, Okla., 20
Shortridge, James R., 242n53
Sidney Barracks/Sidney, Neb., 279, 284, 304, 313–14, 318
Sidney-Black Hills Road, 284, 302n10, 304, 307, 314, 316–18, 322, 324, 329
Sidney (Camp Clarke) Bridge, Neb., 302–306, 314
Simpson, Bob, *433*
Simpson, John Nichols, 141, 321, 441
Simpson, William Wallace, viii
Sioux Indians, 59n1, 291, 293, 296, 308–309, 312, 319, 322, 325, 334, 361
Sitting Bull (Lakota chief), 328
Skaggs, Jimmy, 13, 16, 62, 72–73, 75n15, 77 & n21, 79, 98–99, 105, 112–13, 141, 153, 186n59, 205, 212, 387n2
Slaughter, Ben, 79n23
Slaughter, C. C., 79n23
Slaughter, George Webb (Rev.), 48, 79n23, 363
Slaughter, John B., 79n23
Slaughter, John Horton, 79–81, 89, 124, 245
Slaughter, Peter E., 79n23, 363
Slaughter, William B., x, 79n23
Slope County (N.Dak.), 327n68

Smith, Helena Huntington, xxxvi
Smith, Joseph, 263n1
Smith, L. M., 112n100
Smith, W. S., 402
Smoky Hill Cattle Pool, 255–56 & n68, 274
Smoky Hill River, 20, 247, 256, 410–11, 447n47
Smoky Hill Trail, 256, 447 & n47, 449–50
Snyder, Colo. (aka Beaver Creek Station), 452–55
Snyder, Thomas, 213
Soar, Ezra, 336, 458n69
Soldier Spring, Tex., 188 & n66
Soldiers' Grave (Ashland), Kans., 222
Solomon City, Mo., 45
Somerwell County (Tex.), 147
South Dakota. *See* Dakota Territory
South Platte River, 35, 110, 263n1, 270, 279–84, 298–99, 431n12, 441, 451–53, 455n60
Soyer, Lew, 31
Spanish American War, 327n68
Spanish fever. *See* Texas Fever
Sparrow, Joe, 418
Spearfish, S.Dak., 326, 419, 442
splinter routes, xxxix, 6. *See also* Western Cattle Trail
    about the quarantines, 173
    Caldwell Route/Trail, 104, 194–95, 200, 207, 210
    Little Missouri route to northern ranges, 352–58
    Mobeetie Trail, 164–69
    National Trail, 409–11, 419, 425, 440
    north from Sidney Bridge, 302
    to Black Hills mining camps, 322–26
    Camp Clarke and Sidney Bridge, 302–306
    Detour Route to Indian agencies, 318–22
    to the Missouri River, 326–29
    Niobrara River Route, 307–11
    White River to Indian agencies, 311–18
    north to Judith Basin, 340–46
    Northern Indian Territory, 203–207
    Ogallala, trails to/from
    heading north from, 298–301
    north to Missouri River, 287–93
    Wallace Branch, xxxiv, 251–57, 272, 274
    west to Cheyenne, 279–86, 455
    Potter-Bacon Trail (aka Potter-Bacon Cut-off), xxxiv, 110–15, 114n107, 151, 376, 392, 403–404, 407, 419–20, 427, 429–31, 437, 440, 446–48, 454
    Rawhide Creek, 329–40, 461–70
    Red Fork Ranch, 191–95
    Shawnee Trail, 12 & n7, 19–21
    Washita River to Cantonment, 195–203, 207–12
    Western Cattle Trail connections
    Canadian River, 200–203
    East/Chisholm Trail, 161
    National Trail, 389
    Wyoming Territory, 359–62
Spotted Tail (Brulé chief), 313
Springer, A. G. ("Jim"), 234
St. John, F. C. (Dr.), 149

St. John, W. R., 26
St. Joseph, Mo., 19
St. Louis Catholic Church (Castroville), 77n22
St. Louis, Mo., 11, 46, 51, 70, 137n2, 140n12, 344, 378–82, 414
St. Vrain, Ceran, 227n17
stage stations/routes, 211 & n109, 233, 237, 283n45, 304n11, 306 & n14, 311, 327 & n67, 336 & n84, 349, 355, 447. *See also* military/stage roads
    Beaver Creek Station, 453
    Buffalo Gap, D.T., 325
    Butterfield Overland Mail, 28n9, 31
    Buttermilk Station, 179
    Doan's Crossing, 164
    Fort Hat Creek, Wyo., 339–40, 346
    Horsehead Crossing, Tex., 29n13
    Horsehead Springs, D.T., 318
    Indian Territory, 203
    Lone Wells Ranche, D.T., 323
    Old Woman Creek, 339, 346
    Point of Rocks Station, 307
    Rawhide Stage Station, Wyo., 338
    Red Willow stage stop, D.T., 307
    Reynolds (aka Dugan's Road House), 225
    Running Water Ranche, D.T., 307
    Slate Springs Station, D.T., 324
    Snake Creek Station, D.T., 307
Staked Plains of Texas (aka Llano Estacado), xxxiii, xxxi & n1, 27–28, 37, 110 & n98
Standefer, W. R., 112n100
Stark County (N.Dak.), 328
Steele, Henry D., 284
Stevenson, Ed, Tom and Robert, 92
Stevenson, John D., 281
Stewart, Mac, 290–91
Stillman, Charles, xxx, 72–73 & n11
Stinnett, Tex., 165
Stoecklein, David R., xxiv
Stone, Louis, 355
Stone Calf (Cheyenne chief), 197–98
Stoneham, Colo., 455, 457
Stoneville, Mont. *See* Alzada, Mont.
Stonewall, Okla., 19
Stonewall County (Tex.), 438
The Story of a Cowboy (Hough), ix
Stroud, Okla., 19
Stuart, Bob, xxxvi
Stuart, Granville, xxxvi
Sturgis, D.T., 325–26
Sturgis, Samuel D., 119, 380
Sumner County (Kans.), 53
Sutton, E. S., 272, 274, 411–12
Swan, Alexander, 282
Sweet, Henry, 162n3
Sweetwater, Tex. *See* Mobeetie, Tex.
Sweetwater Cantonment. *See* Fort Elliott, Tex.
Sweitzer, George, 323–24
Swift, Justin and Charle, 155n47
Sykes, Godfrey ("Axolotl"), 131–33

T
Taloga, Kans., 405n47
Tascosa, Tex., 110, 113, 169, 233, 236–37, 376, 429, 438–40, 442n34
The Tascosa Pioneer, 419
Taylor, Abner, 426n1

Taylor, Creed, 89 & n41, 95
Taylor, Ethel, 185n57, 189n68
Taylor, Matthew, 87n37
Taylor, Tex., 147, 168
Taylor County (Tex.), 130–31, 138, 141 & n19
Tennant, H. S./Tennant Map, 155, 173–77, 179, 181nn41 & 44, 182, 185n56, 187–89, 206, 207, 214
Terry, Alfred H., 343
Terry's Crossing, Mont., 345
Texas
    about cattle-trailing, xxx, 4–6
    Adam-Onis Treaty of 1819, 162
    Battle of Palmito Ranch, 72 & n5
    Battle of San Jacinto, 75
    Battle of the Alamo, 74–75
    introduction of longhorn cattle, 3–4
    Red River War, 140–41, 165 & n12
    Staked Plains, xxxiii, xxxi & n1, 27–28, 37, 110
Texas County (Okla.), 388–89
The Texas Cowboys, A Photographic Portrayal (Saunders and Stoecklein), xxiv
Texas Fever (aka Spanish Fever). See *also* quarantine/quarantine laws
    1853 Missouri outbreak, 12
    cause and impact, 5–6
    control with freezing weather, 238n50, 356
    defined, xl
    herd laws. *See* Nebraska
    Kansas quarantines. *See* Kansas
Texas Geographic Magazine, 114
Texas Historical Commission, 150
Texas Panhandle. *See* No Man's Land
Texas Post Offices (Janzen), 108n91
Texas Rangers, 27
Texas Road, 11
Texas Trail. *See* Eastern/Chisholm Trail; Western Cattle Trail
Texas Trail Canyon, 274
Texas Trail Museum (Wyo.), 456, 473
Texas Trail of Fame (Fort Worth), xxiv
Texas-Montana Feeder Route. *See* feeder routes
Thatcher, J. A. and M. D., 237
Thomas, E. B., 73
Three Rivers, Tex., 73
Throckmorton County (Tex.), 26n2, 126–27, 130, 137–39, 449n49
"tick fever". *See* Texas Fever
Tienken, Henry, 288
Timms, George, 400
Timms City, Tex., 400
Tingley, Clyde, 110n95
Tittle, S. H., 146, 179, 185, 191n73, 203
Tom Green County (Tex.), 106, 130–31, 133, 138
Tongue River, 308, 342–43, 359–60
Tonkaway Indians, 121
Topeka, Kans., 19, 405n47
Torrington, Wyo., 335
Townsend, William ("Bill"), xxvi
trail system, defined, xxxix. See also Eastern/Chisholm Trail System; Goodnight Trail System; National Trail System; Shawnee Trail System; Western Cattle Trail
trail/trail branch. *See also* feeder routes; splinter routes

Abilene Trail, 43, 47, 50, 79, 154, 264–65 & n4
Atascosita Trail, xxx
Belle Fourche River Trail, 319n40
Blue Valley Trail, 264–65
Canton/Cantonment Trail, 196–97
Cherokee Trail, 240
Cloud Trail, 47
Colorado Trail, 200
Deadwood Trail, 336, 338–39, 346
Deer Trail, 430
Ellsworth Trail/Cox's Trail, 53, 270, 288n57
Fort Arbuckle Trail, xxviii–xxix, 43, 47–49, 103, 140n12, 167, 211, 448
Fort Bascom Trail, 235
Horsehead Trail/Horsehead Crossing, 29n13
Jesse Chisholm Cattle Trail, 47n18, 48–49, 212
L. B. Harris New Trail to Ellis, 60 & n2
Laredo Trail, 73n13
Mormon Trail, 335
Niobrara-Black Hills Trail, 290
Ogallala Trail, 252, 268, 274, 289
Oregon Trail, 263n1, 283, 335n81, 364
Oregon-California Trail, 20, 299, 329
Overland Trail, 283, 285n50, 431
Penrose Trail, 430
Potter-Bacon Trail, xxxiv, ???
Quanah Detour Route (aka "Ghost Trail"), xxxiv, 153–56, 164, 169, 185–87, 208
Rath Trail, 232n35
Santa Fe Trail, 20, 34n27, 37, 154, 240, 403, 430n9, 440
Smoky Hill Trail, 256, 447, 449, 450
Tascosa Trail, 233
XIT Ranch Trail, 437, 453
Trail, Okla., 203
Trail City, Colo., xxxv, xxxxiv, 385, 387n1, 402–21, 425, 429, 435, 440, 447–48, 468
The Trail Drivers of Texas (Hunter), 8, 66, 110, 117, 158, 176, 260, 384, 385, 409, 479
Trail markers and monuments
    about the history and importance, xxviii–xxix
    Albany/Shackelford County (Tex.), 108
    California Road (Leedy, Okla.), 202
    Doan's Crossing (Tex.), 148, 149, 150, 177
    Dodge City Trail (Camargo, Okla.), 204
    Elephant Rock (Vici, Okla.), 204
    Fort Dodge-Camp Supply (Bloom, Kans.), 224
    Great Western Cattle Trail
    Altus, Okla., 178
    Gage, Okla., 209
    Kerrville, Tex., 86
    Lone Wolf, Okla., 184
    Vici, Okla., 205
    No Man's Land (Gate, Okla.), 388
    Old Beef Trail (Kimble County, Tex.), 88

Old Cattle Trail (Kit Carson, Colo.), 448
    Pegleg Crossing (Menard County, Tex.), 92
    Pioneer cowboys (LaGrange, Wyo.), 459
    Rawlins County (Atwood, Kans.), 252
    Santa Anna town/mountain (Tex.), 104
    Smoky Hill Trail (Aroya, Colo.), 450
    Texas Montana Trail, 452, 453
    "Texas to Montana" Trail, xxix
    Texas Trail/Old Texas Trail
    Haigler, Neb., 272
    Hitchcock County, Neb., 268
    Lingle, Wyo., 334
    Lusk, Wyo., xxix, 338
    Madrid, Neb., 268
    Moorcroft, Wyo., 351
    Newcastle, Wyo., 348
    Pine Bluffs, Wyo., 456
    Upton, Wyo., 350
    Trail City, Colo., 406
    Trinchera Pass (Colo.), 35
    "Up the Trail" (Coleman, Tex.), 102
    Western Trail
    Baylor County (Tex.), 142
    Beaver Creek Crossing (Kans.), 252
    Brady Mountains/Cow Gap (Tex.), 100
    Friendship, Okla., 180
    Yelton Store (Okla.), 214–15
Trailing the Longhorns (Flanagan), 352
Trails South (Haywood), 235
Trego County (Kans.), 247
Trenton, N.Dak., 328
Trickham, Tex., 105
Trinidad, Colo., 33
Trinity River, 11–12, 46, 61n9
trunk lines. *See also* Western Cattle Trail
    about trails and staging areas, 6, 79
    Eastern/Chisholm Trail, 61–62
    Matamoros Feeder Route and, 71–73
    Shawnee Trail, 11, 19, 77
Tuttle, John F., 234
Twelve-mile limit (Fort Supply, I.T.), 208

U
U.S. Army. *See Fort entries*; military units
U.S. Congress, 11, 26, 138, 378–80, 413–18, 420, 425
U.S. National Park Service, xxix
Uvalde County/Uvalde, Tex., 60, 73n13, 77–78, 88, 90, 92, 100, 133, 153, 314

V
Val Marie, Can., xxviii
Valentine, Neb., 311
Vallentine, John Franklin, 213, 221, 225 & n12
Vanderslice, T. J., 225
Vernon, Tex. (aka Eagle Flat), 100, 142, 146, 149, 152, 174, 176–77, 181, 194, 418
Vici, Okla., 203–206
vigilantes, 12, 15–17, 387. *See also* outlaws
Villalobos, Gregorio de, 3n2

W
Waco, Tex., 11, 43, 46, 61–63, 75, 79

Waldrip, A. M., 99
Waldrip's Bend/Waldrip, Tex., 62, 90, 94, 99–101, 103
Walk's Camp, Colo., 451n55, 466
Ward, T. M., 92
Warren, Okla., 181–82 & n45
Washita Bend (Red River), 11
Washita Edward Rock Crossing, 195–99, 200, 214
Washita River, 47, 49, 61, 166, 172–73, 185–89
Watford City, N.Dak., 328
Watkins, Ethel E., 233n37, 235n41
We Pointed Them North, Recollections of a Cowpuncher (Huntington-Smith), xxxvi, 61
    weather
        "big die off" (1871), xxxii, 399
        blizzard of 1886-87, 70n4, 329, 399, 420
        cold controlling Texas Fever, 238n50, 356
        flooding, 48, 103, 121, 179n36, 321, 359, 362
        heat/drought, xxxv, 340, 342, 441
        lightning storms, 31, 151, 169n21, 308, 438
Weatherford, Tex., xxvi, 28, 30, 32, 34, 438, 480
Webb, Frank A., 220, 229, 235, 236n42
Webb, Walter Prescott, 61–62
Webberville, Tex., 109
Wells, John, 325
West, George, 73 & n12
West Shawnee Trail. *See* Shawnee Trail System
West Texas Historic Yearbook, 105
West Texas-Trail Museum, 473
The Western, the Greatest Texas Cattle Trail, 1874-1886 (Kraisinger and Kraisinger), xxi, xxvi, 43, 254
Western Cattle Trail. *See also* feeder routes; splinter routes
    about the origins, xxi–xxii, 58–63, 77
    blazing the trail, xxxiii, 58, 76, 85n35
    depiction in movies, 479–81
    enforcement of quarantines, 324
    feeder routes through No Man's Land, 389–92
    impact of homesteading and quarantines, 242–43
    north from Dodge City
        Hayes County (Neb.) Route 1, 266–69
        Hayes County (Neb.) Route 2, 269–71
        Hayes County (Neb.) Route 3, 271
        Hays City-Ellis Trail, 243–45, 288n57
        Kansas to Ogallala Route 1, 245–46
        Kansas to Ogallala Route 2, 246–51
        Kansas to Ogallala Route 3, 251–57
    north from Ogallala, 298–301
    to NW Territory (Canada), 362–66
    trunk lines (listed south to north)
        staging areas to Pegleg Crossing, 79–90

Pegleg Crossing to Dodge
Crossing, 93–97
to Coleman from Cow Gap,
99–103
from Coleman to Albany,
106–109
Greer County to Comanche
Springs, 173–85
Comanche Springs to Edward
Rock Crossing, 187–98
Washita Crossing to S.
Canadian River, 200–203
to/around Dodge City, 219–25,
239–42
Hayes County to Ogallala,
271–74
north to Rawhide Creek,
329–40
Montana and the northern
ranges, 346–52
Wyoming to Montana and
Canada, 359–66
Weston County Historical Society, 348,
350, 459
Westport, Mo., 16, 264
Wheatcroft, Josh, Sr., 255
Wheatcroft, Link and Josh, Jr., 255–56
Wheaton, Charles, 197–98
Wheeler, Oliver, 47–48
Wheeler County (Tex.), 166n14
Whetstone Bottom Agency, D.T., 291
Whipple, Milt, 333n76, 347, 449
Whitcomb, E. W., 322
White City, Kans., 20
Whiters, H. C., 131
Whitman, Charles W., 229n22
Whitman Road Ranch/Whitman, Kans.,
229

*Why Stop? a Guide to Texas Historical
Roadside Markers* (Aubrey and Dooley),
149
Wichita, Kans.
becoming a cattle town, xxxii–xxxiii
cattle-trailing to, 53–54, 59–60,
140n14, 191
Chisholm Trail, 49n31
quarantine closure, 213, 244, 263
railroad connections, 19, 21, 129
wagon roads and feeder routes,
196–97, 200
Wichita Falls, Tex., 146–47, 232, 285, 373
Wichita Indians, 179
Wichita Mountains, 152, 158, 163, 168,
173n32, 180, 182–85
Wichita River, 110, 143
Wiggins, Colo., 431
Wilbarger County (Tex.), 77, 119, 139,
143, 146, 161, 176
Wilburn, Kans., 230
Willard, Okla., 215
Williams, Dorothy, 187
Williams, Gladys, 455
Williams, John, 158
Williamson County (Tex.), 107, 109
Willingham, C. P. ("Cape"), 238
Williston, N.Dak., 328
Wilson, Benjamin F., 196
Wilson, J. M., 32
Wilson, Tom, 182
Wilson County (Tex.), 76–77, 115
Winona, D.T., 321
Withers, Gus, 168–69, 285, 286
Withers, Mark A., 92, 168–69, 286
Withers, Richard, 109–110, 126, 300, 346
Witter, Webster, 92
Wootton, Dick, 33–35

Worsham, William B., 145
Worsham Springs, Tex., 145 & n27
Wright, Bob, 418
Wright, D. D. ("Tex"), 105
Wright, Lyman, 82n29
Wright, Phil L., 133 & n31, 409
Wright, Robert M., 164–65, 227–28, 418
Wyoming
arrival of the railroad, 279–80
cattle-trailing to, 329, 334
Osage oil fields, 354n128
route extensions from Ogallala,
279–86
splinter route to northern ranges,
352–58
Texas-Montana feeder route, 435–42
WCT trunk lines to Canada, 359–66
Wyoming Stock Growers Association, 283

X
The XIT Ranch of Texas (Haley), 64, 371
XIT Trail, 437, 453

Y
Yates Crossing/Yates, Tex., 88
Yeakly, Arthur, 180
Yellowstone River, 191, 276, 278, 301–302,
328, 341–47, 352–53, 356–57, 360–61,
427
Yelton, Theodore A., 214
Yelton Store (Harper County, Okla.),
214–15

Z
Zavala County (Tex.), 90
Zululand Stockade, 233, 237

THE EASTERN/CHISHOLM TRAIL SYSTEM (1867 - 1889)

After the Civil War conditions on the old Shawnee Trail, that had been used prior to the war for trailing cattle, were hazardous and life threatening. The route to Sedalia, Missouri was ladened with outlaws, thieves, and bushwhackers. Of the quarter of million cattle trailed in 1866, few were able to get to market because of the outlaws and irate farmers against the Texas Fever in southeastern Kansas and southwestern Missouri. A more westerly route through eastern Kansas faced the pre-war cattle quarantine. Finally, a ray of hope was given by an innovative stockman from Illinois by the name of Joseph McCoy. He arrived in Kansas in early 1867, talked his way around the awkward cattle quarantine, negotiated with the Union Pacific, East Division (Kansas Pacific Railway), scouted out a possible location along the newly laid tracks of the railway, and settled on a small settlement named Abilene. Here the promoter built stock pens and established a destination for Texas cattle.

For the next nine seasons, thousands of Texas longhorns were trailed each year into Kansas and beyond on this Eastern route. From south Texas, the Eastern basically followed the old Shawnee Trail to north of Waco where the trail split, with the Eastern using the western fork through Fort Worth. The Trail crossed the Red River at Red River Station and picked up an old trade route on the South Canadian River in Indian Territory called Chisholm's Trail. Jesse Chisholm had established the trade route prior to the Civil War in order to trade with the Plains Indians. His well-beaten path, planned around spots where wood and water were plentiful, was a direct route to the Arkansas River near present-day Wichita. From the Arkansas River, the Trail had been marked well by McCoy to Abilene (Some drovers called the route, the "McCoy Trail"). Later on, many outfits continued north on the Eastern/Chisholm from Abilene over the Blue Valley Trail to Schuyler and Columbus Nebraska, on the Platte River.

When the Santa Fe Railway built to Newton in 1871 and to Wichita in 1872, they became the preferred cattle towns. Also in 1872, a splinter or cut-off route further west of the developing settlements in eastern Kansas, opened up to Ellsworth, Great Bend, and Hayes.

Because of the continuing threat of the Texas Fever and the advancement of settlements, the Kansas Legislature in 1875 closed the eastern part of her state to Texas cattle. Trail drivers had to find a more westerly route through Kansas. Even though the Eastern/Chisholm no longer trailed through Kansas, the Trail continued to be used through Texas and Indian Territory, utilizing the Cimarron cut-off to connect with the Western Trail. When Caldwell received rails in 1880, the Trail was somewhat revived and continued to be used to the Kansas border town until 1889.